Children Act 1975

CHAPTER 72

ARRANGEMENT OF SECTIONS

Part I

Adoption

A

PART II

CUSTODY

Custodianship orders

Custody in Scotland

PART III

CARE

Supplemental

SCHEDULES:

ELIZABETH II

Children Act 1975

1975 CHAPTER 72

An Act to make further provision for children.
[12th November 1975]

BE IT ENACTED by the Queen's most Excellent Majesty, by and with the advice and consent of the Lords Spiritual and Temporal, and Commons, in this present Parliament assembled, and by the authority of the same, as follows:—

PART I

ADOPTION

The Adoption Services

1.—(1) It is the duty of every local authority to establish and maintain within their area a service designed to meet the needs, in relation to adoption, of— 　*Establishment of Adoption Services.*

(*a*) children who have been or may be adopted,

(*b*) parents and guardians of such children, and

(*c*) persons who have adopted or may adopt a child,

and for that purpose to provide the requisite facilities, or secure that they are provided by approved adoption societies.

(2) The facilities to be provided as part of the service maintained under subsection (1) include—

(*a*) temporary board and lodging where needed by pregnant women, mothers or children ;

(*b*) arrangements for assessing children and prospective adopters, and placing children for adoption ;

(*c*) counselling for persons with problems relating to adoption.

(3) The facilities of the service maintained under subsection (1) shall be provided in conjunction with the local authority's other social services and with approved adoption societies in their area, so that help may be given in a co-ordinated manner without duplication, omission or avoidable delay.

(4) The services maintained under subsection (1) by local authorities in England and Wales may be collectively referred to as " the Adoption Service " and those maintained by local authorities in Scotland, as " the Scottish Adoption Service ", and a local authority or approved adoption society may be referred to as an adoption agency.

Local authorities' social services.

2. The social services refered to in section 1(3) are the functions of a local authority which stand referred to the authority's social services committee or, in Scotland, social work committee, including, in particular but without prejudice to the generality of the foregoing, a local authority's functions relating to—

(*a*) the promotion of the welfare of children by diminishing the need to receive children into care or keep them in care, including (in exceptional circumstances) the giving of assistance in cash ;

(*b*) the welfare of children in the care of a local authority ;

(*c*) the welfare of children who are foster children within the meaning of the Children Act 1958 ;

1958 c. 65.

(*d*) children who are subject to supervision orders made in matrimonial proceedings ;

(*e*) the provision of residential accommodation for expectant mothers and young children and of day-care facilities ;

(*f*) the regulation and inspection of nurseries and child minders ;

(*g*) care and other treatment of children through court proceedings and children's hearings.

Duty to promote welfare of child.

3. In reaching any decision relating to the adoption of a child, a court or adoption agency shall have regard to all the circumstances, first consideration being given to the need to safeguard and promote the welfare of the child throughout his childhood ; and shall so far as practicable ascertain the wishes and feelings of the child regarding the decision and give due consideration to them, having regard to his age and understanding.

4.—(1) A body desiring to act as an adoption society or, if it is already an adoption society, desiring to continue to act as such in England and Wales or in Scotland may, in the manner specified by regulations made by the Secretary of State, apply to the Secretary of State for his approval to its doing so.

(2) On an application under subsection (1), the Secretary of State shall take into account the matters relating to the applicant specified in subsections (3) to (5) and any other relevant considerations, and if, but only if, he is satisfied that the applicant is likely to make, or, if the applicant is an approved adoption society, is making, an effective contribution to the Adoption Service or, as the case may be, to the Scottish Adoption Service, he shall by notice to the applicant give his approval, which shall be operative from a date specified in the notice or, in the case of a renewal of approval, from the date of the notice.

(3) In considering the application, the Secretary of State shall have regard, in relation to the period for which approval is sought, to the following—

    (a) the applicant's adoption programme, including, in particular, its ability to make provision for children who are free for adoption,

    (b) the number and qualifications of its staff,

    (c) its financial resources, and

    (d) the organisation and control of its operations.

(4) Where it appears to the Secretary of State that the applicant is likely to operate extensively within the area of a particular local authority he shall ask the authority whether they support the application, and shall take account of any views about it put to him by the authority.

(5) Where the applicant is already an approved adoption society or, whether before or after the passing of this Act, previously acted as an adoption society, the Secretary of State, in considering the application, shall also have regard to the record and reputation of the applicant in the adoption field, and the areas within which and the scale on which it is currently operating or has operated in the past.

(6) If after considering the application the Secretary of State is not satisfied that the applicant is likely to make or, as the case may be, is making an effective contribution to the Adoption Service or, as the case may be, to the Scottish Adoption Service, the Secretary of State shall, subject to section 6(1) and (2), by notice inform the applicant that his application is refused.

PART I

(7) If not withdrawn earlier under section 5, approval given under this section shall last for a period of three years from the date on which it becomes operative, and shall then expire or, in the case of an approved adoption society whose further application for approval is pending at that time, shall expire on the date that application is granted or, as the case may be, refused.

Withdrawal of approval.

5.—(1) If, while approval of a body under section 4 is operative, it appears to the Secretary of State that the body is not making an effective contribution to the Adoption Service or, as the case may be, to the Scottish Adoption Service, he shall subject to section 6(3) and (4) by notice to the body withdraw the approval from a date specified in the notice.

(2) If an approved adoption society fails to provide the Secretary of State with information required by him for the purpose of carrying out his functions under subsection (1), or fails to verify such information in the manner required by him, he may by notice to the society withdraw the approval from a date specified in the notice.

(3) Where approval is withdrawn under subsection (1) or (2) or expires the Secretary of State may direct the body concerned to make such arrangements as to children who are in its care and other transitional matters as seem to him expedient.

Procedure on refusal to approve, or withdrawal of approval from, societies.

6.—(1) Before notifying a body which has applied for approval that the application is refused in accordance with section 4(6) the Secretary of State shall serve on the applicant a notice—

(a) setting out the reasons why he proposes to refuse the application;

(b) informing the applicant that he may make representations in writing to the Secretary of State within 28 days of the date of service of the notice.

(2) If any representations are made by the applicant in accordance with subsection (1), the Secretary of State shall give further consideration to the application taking into account those representations.

(3) The Secretary of State shall, before withdrawing approval of an adoption society in accordance with section 5(1), serve on the society a notice—

(a) setting out the reasons why he proposes to withdraw the approval; and

(b) informing the society that they may make representations in writing to the Secretary of State within 28 days of the date of service of the notice.

(4) If any representations are made by the society in accordance with subsection (3), the Secretary of State shall give further consideration to the withdrawal of approval under section 5(1) taking into account those representations.

(5) This section does not apply where the Secretary of State, after having considered any representations made by the applicant in accordance with this section, proposes to refuse approval or, as the case may be, to withdraw approval for reasons which have already been communicated to the applicant in a notice under this section.

7.—(1) If it appears to the Secretary of State that an approved adoption society, or one in relation to which approval has been withdrawn under section 5 or has expired, is inactive or defunct he may, in relation to any child who is or was in the care of the society, direct what appears to him to be the appropriate local authority to take any such action as might have been taken by the society or by the society jointly with the authority ; and if apart from this section the authority would not be entitled to take that action, or would not be entitled to take it without joining the society in the action, it shall be entitled to do so.

(2) Before giving a direction under subsection (1) the Secretary of State shall, if practicable, consult both the society and the authority.

Adoption orders

8.—(1) An adoption order is an order vesting the parental rights and duties relating to a child in the adopters, made on their application by an authorised court.

(2) The order does not affect the parental rights and duties so far as they relate to any period before the making of the order.

(3) The making of the order operates to extinguish—

    (*a*) any parental right or duty relating to the child which—

        (i) is vested in a person (not being one of the adopters) who was the parent or guardian of the child immediately before the making of the order, or

        (ii) is vested in any other person by virtue of the order of any court ; and

    (*b*) any duty arising by virtue of an agreement or the order of a court to make payments, so far as the payments are in respect of the child's maintenance for any period after the making of the order or any other matter comprised in the parental duties and relating to such a period.

(4) Subsection (3)(*b*) does not apply to a duty arising by virtue of an agreement—

(*a*) which constitutes a trust, or

(*b*) which expressly provides that the duty is not to be extinguished by the making of an adoption order.

(5) An adoption order may not be made in relation to a child who is or has been married.

(6) An adoption order shall not be made in Scotland in relation to a child who is a minor unless with the consent of the minor ; except that where the court is satisfied that the minor is incapable of giving his consent to the making of the order, it may dispense with that consent.

(7) An adoption order may contain such terms and conditions as the court thinks fit.

(8) An adoption order may be made notwithstanding that the child is an adopted child.

(9) Schedule 1 contains for England and Wales further provisions about the effect of adoption and related or comparable provisions about legitimation.

(10) Schedule 2 has effect as respects the status conferred in Scotland by adoption and related matters.

Child to live with adopters before order made.

9.—(1) Where—

(*a*) the applicant, or one of the applicants, is a parent, step-parent or relative of the child, or

(*b*) the child was placed with the applicants by an adoption agency or in pursuance of an order of the High Court,

an adoption order shall not be made unless the child is at least 19 weeks old and at all times during the preceding 13 weeks had his home with the applicants or one of them.

(2) Where subsection (1) does not apply, an adoption order shall not be made unless the child is at least twelve months old and at all times during the preceding twelve months had his home with the applicants or one of them.

(3) An adoption order shall not be made unless the court is satisfied that sufficient opportunities to see the child with the applicant or, in the case of an application by a married couple, both applicants together in the home environment have been afforded—

(*a*) where the child was placed with the applicant by an adoption agency, to that agency, or

(*b*) in any other case, to the local authority within whose area the home is.

10.—(1) Subject to sections 37(1) and 53(1), an adoption order may be made on the application of a married couple where each has attained the age of 21 but an adoption order shall not otherwise be made on the application of more than one person.

(2) An adoption order shall not be made on the application of a married couple unless—

    (*a*) at least one of them is domiciled in a part of the United Kingdom, or in the Channel Islands or the Isle of Man, or

    (*b*) the application is for a Convention adoption order and section 24 is complied with.

(3) Where the application is made to a court in England or Wales and the married couple consist of a parent and step-parent of the child, the court shall dismiss the application if it considers the matter would be better dealt with under section 42 (orders for custody etc.) of the Matrimonial Causes Act 1973.   1973 c. 18.

11.—(1) Subject to sections 37(1) and 53(1), an adoption order may be made on the application of one person where he has attained the age of 21 and—

    (*a*) is not married, or

    (*b*) is married and the court is satisfied that—

        (i) his spouse cannot be found, or

        (ii) the spouses have separated and are living apart, and the separation is likely to be permanent, or

        (iii) his spouse is by reason of ill health, whether physical or mental, incapable of making an application for an adoption order.

(2) An adoption order shall not be made on the application of one person unless—

    (*a*) he is domiciled in a part of the United Kingdom, or in the Channel Islands or the Isle of Man, or

    (*b*) the application is for a Convention adoption order and section 24 is complied with.

(3) An adoption order shall not be made on the application of the mother or father of the child alone unless the court is satisfied that—

    (*a*) the other natural parent is dead or cannot be found, or

    (*b*) there is some other reason justifying the exclusion of the other natural parent,

and where such an order is made the reason justifying the exclusion of the other natural parent shall be recorded by the court.

PART I

1973 c. 18.

(4) Where the application is made to a court in England or Wales and the applicant is a step-parent of the child the court shall dismiss the application if it considers the matter would be better dealt with under section 42 (orders for custody etc.) of the Matrimonial Causes Act 1973.

Parental agreement.

12.—(1) An adoption order shall not be made unless—

(*a*) the child is free for adoption ; or

(*b*) in the case of each parent or guardian of the child the court is satisfied that—

(i) he freely, and with full understanding of what is involved, agrees unconditionally to the making of the adoption order (whether or not he knows the identity of the applicants), or

(ii) his agreement to the making of the adoption order should be dispensed with on a ground specified in subsection (2).

(2) The grounds mentioned in subsection (1)(*b*)(ii) are that the parent or guardian—

(*a*) cannot be found or is incapable of giving agreement ;

(*b*) is withholding his agreement unreasonably ;

(*c*) has persistently failed without reasonable cause to discharge the parental duties in relation to the child ;

(*d*) has abandoned or neglected the child ;

(*e*) has persistently ill-treated the child ;

(*f*) has seriously ill-treated the child (subject to subsection (5)).

(3) Subsection (1) does not apply in any case where the child is not a United Kingdom national and the application for the adoption order is for a Convention adoption order.

(4) Agreement is ineffective for the purposes of subsection (1)(*b*)(i) if given by the mother less than six weeks after the child's birth.

(5) Subsection (2)(*f*) does not apply unless (because of the ill-treatment or for other reasons) the rehabilitation of the child within the household of the parent or guardian is unlikely.

(6) A child is free for adoption if he is the subject of an order under section 14 and the order has not been revoked under section 16.

Religious upbringing of adopted child.

13. An adoption agency shall in placing a child for adoption have regard (so far as is practicable) to any wishes of the child's parents and guardians as to the religious upbringing of the child.

14.—(1) Where, on an application by an adoption agency, an authorised court is satisfied in the case of each parent or guardian of the child that—

    (*a*) he freely, and with full understanding of what is involved, agrees generally and unconditionally to the making of an adoption order, or

    (*b*) his agreement to the making of an adoption order should be dispensed with on a ground specified in section 12(2),

the court shall, subject to subsection (5), make an order declaring the child free for adoption.

(2) No application shall be made under subsection (1) unless—

    (*a*) it is made with the consent of a parent or guardian of the child, or

    (*b*) the adoption agency is applying for dispensation under subsection (1)(*b*) of the agreement of each parent or guardian of the child, and the child is in the care of the adoption agency.

(3) No agreement required under subsection (1)(*a*) shall be dispensed with under subsection (1)(*b*) unless the child is already placed for adoption or the court is satisfied that it is likely that the child will be placed for adoption.

(4) An agreement by the mother of the child is ineffective for the purposes of this section if given less than six weeks after the child's birth.

(5) An order under this section shall not be made in Scotland in relation to a child who is a minor unless with the consent of the child ; except that where the court is satisfied that the minor is incapable of giving his consent to the making of the order, it may dispense with that consent.

(6) On the making of an order under this section, the parental rights and duties relating to the child vest in the adoption agency, and subsections (2) and (3) of section 8 apply as if the order were an adoption order and the agency were the adopters.

(7) Before making an order under this section the court shall satisfy itself that each parent or guardian who can be found has been given an opportunity of making, if he so wishes, a declaration that he prefers not to be involved in future questions concerning the adoption of the child ; and any such declaration shall be recorded by the court.

(8) Before making an order under this section in the case of an illegitimate child whose father is not its guardian, the court

PART I

1971 c. 3.
1930 c. 33.

shall satisfy itself in relation to any person claiming to be the father that either—

    (*a*) he has no intention of applying for custody of the child under section 9 of the Guardianship of Minors Act 1971 or under section 2 of the Illegitimate Children (Scotland) Act 1930, or

    (*b*) if he did apply for custody under either of those sections the application would be likely to be refused.

Progress
reports to
former
parent.

15.—(1) This section and section 16 apply to any person ("the former parent") who was required to be given an opportunity of making a declaration under section 14(7) but did not do so.

(2) Within the 14 days following the date twelve months after the making of the order under section 14, the adoption agency in which the parental rights and duties were vested on the making of the order, unless it has previously by notice to the former parent informed him that an adoption order has been made in respect of the child, shall by notice to the former parent inform him—

    (*a*) whether an adoption order has been made in respect of the child, and (if not)

    (*b*) whether the child has his home with a person with whom he has been placed for adoption.

(3) If at the time when the former parent is given notice under subsection (2) an adoption order has not been made in respect of the child, it is thereafter the duty of the adoption agency to give notice to the former parent of the making of an adoption order (if and when made), and meanwhile to give the former parent notice whenever the child is placed for adoption or ceases to have his home with a person with whom he has been placed for adoption.

(4) If at any time the former parent by notice makes a declaration to the adoption agency that he prefers not to be involved in future questions concerning the adoption of the child—

    (*a*) the agency shall secure that the declaration is recorded by the court which made the order under section 14, and

    (*b*) the agency is released from the duty of complying further with subsection (3) as respects that former parent.

Revocation of
section 14
order.

16.—(1) The former parent, at any time more than twelve months after the making of the order under section 14 when—

    (*a*) no adoption order has been made in respect of the child, and (*b*) the child does not have his home with a person with whom he has been placed for adoption,

may apply to the court which made the order for a further order revoking it on the ground that he wishes to resume the parental rights and duties.

(2) While the application is pending the adoption agency having the parental rights and duties shall not place the child for adoption without the leave of the court.

(3) Where an order freeing a child for adoption is revoked under this section—

(*a*) the parental rights and duties relating to the child are vested in the individual or, as the case may be, the individuals in whom they vested immediately before that order was made ;

(*b*) if the parental rights and duties, or any of them, vested in a local authority or voluntary organisation immediately before the order freeing the child for adoption was made, those rights and duties are vested in the individual, or as the case may be, the individuals in whom they vested immediately before they were vested in the authority or organisation ; and

(*c*) any duty extinguished by virtue of section 8(3)(*b*) is forthwith revived,

but the revocation does not affect any right or duty so far as it relates to any period before the date of the revocation.

(4) Subject to subsection (5) if the application is dismissed on the ground that to allow it would contravene the principle embodied in section 3—

(*a*) the former parent who made the application shall not be entitled to make any further application under subsection (1) in respect of the child, and

(*b*) the adoption agency is released from the duty of complying further with section 15(3) as respects that parent.

(5) Subsection (4)(*a*) shall not apply where the court which dismissed the application gives leave to the former parent to make a further application under subsection (1), but such leave shall not be given unless it appears to the court that because of a change in circumstances or for any other reason it is proper to allow the application to be made.

PART I
Care etc. of
child on
refusal of
adoption
order.

17.—(1) Where on an application for an adoption order in relation to a child under the age of 16 the court refuses to make the adoption order then—

(*a*) if it appears to the court that there are exceptional circumstances making it desirable that the child should be under the supervision of an independent person, the court may order that the child shall be under the supervision of a specified local authority or under the supervision of a probation officer ;

(*b*) if it appears to the court that there are exceptional circumstances making it impracticable or undesirable for the child to be entrusted to either of the parents or to any other individual, the court may by order commit the child to the care of a specified local authority.

(2) Where the court makes an order under subsection (1)(*b*) the order may require the payment by either parent to the local authority, while it has the care of the child, of such weekly or other periodical sum towards the maintenance of the child as the court thinks reasonable.

1973 c. 29.

(3) Sections 3 and 4 of the Guardianship Act 1973 (which contain supplementary provisions relating to children who are subject to supervision, or in the care of local authorities, by virtue of orders made under section 2 of that Act) apply in relation to an order under this section as they apply in relation to an order under section 2 of that Act.

(4) In the application of this section to Scotland—

(*a*) the words " or under the supervision of a probation officer " in subsection (1)(*a*) do not apply ;

(*b*) subsection (3) does not apply ; and

(*c*) subsections (2), (4) and (5) of section 11 of the Guardianship Act 1973 apply in relation to an order under this section as they apply in relation to an order under that section.

18.—(1) An adoption order shall not be made in respect of a child who was not placed with the applicant by an adoption agency unless the applicant has, at least three months before the date of the order, given notice to the local authority within whose area he has his home of his intention to apply for the adoption order.

(2) On receipt of such a notice the local authority shall investigate the matter and submit to the court a report of their investigation.

(3) Under subsection (2), the local authority shall in particular investigate—

(a) so far as is practicable, the suitability of the applicant, and any other matters relevant to the operation of section 3 in relation to the application ; and

(b) whether the child was placed with the applicant in contravention of section 29 of the 1958 Act.

19.—(1) Where on an application for an adoption order the Interim requirements of sections 12(1) and 18(1) are complied with the orders. court may postpone the determination of the application and make an order vesting the legal custody of the child in the applicants for a probationary period not exceeding two years upon such terms for the maintenance of the child and otherwise as the court thinks fit.

(2) Where the probationary period specified in an order under subsection (1) is less than two years, the court may by a further order extend the period to a duration not exceeding two years in all.

20.—(1) For the purpose of any application for an adoption Guardian order or an order under section 14, 16 or 25, rules shall provide ad litem and for the appointment, in such cases as are prescribed,— reporting officer.

(a) of a person to act as guardian ad litem of the child upon the hearing of the application, with the duty of safeguarding the interests of the child in the prescribed manner ;

(b) of a person to act as reporting officer for the purpose of witnessing agreements to adoption and performing such other duties as the rules may prescribe.

(2) A person who is employed—

(a) in the case of an application for an adoption order, by the adoption agency by whom the child was placed ; or

(b) in the case of an application under section 14 by the adoption agency by whom the application was made ; or

(c) in the case of an application under section 16 by the adoption agency with the parental rights and duties relating to the child,

shall not be appointed to act as guardian ad litem or reporting officer for the purposes of the application but, subject to that, the same person may if the court thinks fit be both guardian ad litem and reporting officer.

(3) Rules may provide for the reporting officer to be appointed before the application is made.

(4) In relation to Scotland, references in this section to a guardian ad litem shall be construed as references to a curator ad litem.

Hearings of applications etc. in private.

21.—(1) Proceedings in the High Court under this Part may be disposed of in chambers.

(2) All proceedings in the county court under this Part shall be heard and determined in camera.

1952 c. 55.

(3) Proceedings in the magistrates' court under this Part shall be domestic proceedings for the purposes of the Magistrates' Courts Act 1952 but section 57(2)(*d*) of that Act shall not apply in relation to any proceedings under this Part.

(4) In relation to Scotland, all proceedings before the court under this Part shall be heard and determined in camera unless the court otherwise directs.

Making of order.

22.—(1) In the case of—

    (*a*) an application for an adoption order in relation to a child who is not free for adoption ;

    (*b*) an application for an order under section 14,

rules shall require every person who can be found and whose agreement or consent to the making of the order is required to be given or dispensed with under this Act to be notified of a date and place where he may be heard on the application and of the fact that, unless he wishes or the court requires, he need not attend.

(2) In the case of an application under section 25 rules shall require every person who can be found, and whose agreement to the making of the order would be required if the application were for an adoption order (other than a Convention adoption order), to be notified as aforesaid.

(3) Where an application for an adoption order relates to a child placed by an adoption agency, the agency shall submit to the court a report on the suitability of the applicants and any other matters relevant to the operation of section 3, and shall assist the court in any manner the court may direct.

(4) The court shall not proceed to hear an application for an adoption order in relation to a child where a previous application for a British adoption order made in relation to the child by the same persons was refused by any court unless—

    (*a*) in refusing the previous application the court directed that this subsection should not apply, or

(*b*) it appears to the court that because of a change in circumstances or for any other reason it is proper to
proceed with the application.

(5) The court shall not make an adoption order in relation
to a child unless it is satisfied that the applicants have not, as
respects the child, contravened section 50 of the 1958 Act
(prohibition of certain payments in relation to adoption).

(6) In the application of this section to Scotland for the reference to hearing an application in subsection (4) there shall be
substituted a reference to determining an application.

23. On the joint application of an adoption agency in which Transfer of
the parental rights and duties relating to a child who is in parental
Great Britain are vested under section 14(6) or this section and rights and
any other adoption agency, an authorised court may if it thinks adoption
fit by order transfer the parental rights and duties to the latter agencies.
agency.

24.—(1) An adoption order shall be made as a Convention Convention
adoption order if the application is for a Convention adoption adoption
order and the following conditions are satisfied both at the orders.
time of the application and when the order is made.

(2) The child—

(*a*) must be a United Kingdom national or a national of
a Convention country, and

(*b*) must habitually reside in British territory or a Convention country, and

(*c*) must not be, or have been, married.

(3) The applicant or applicants and the child must not all be
United Kingdom nationals living in British territory.

(4) If the application is by a married couple, either—

(*a*) each must be a United Kingdom national or a national
of a Convention country, and both must habitually
reside in Great Britain, or

(*b*) both must be United Kingdom nationals, and each must
habitually reside in British territory or a Convention
country,

and if the applicants are nationals of the same Convention
country the adoption must not be prohibited by a specified
provision (as defined in subsection (8)) of the internal law of
that country.

(5) If the application is by one person, either—

    (*a*) he must be a United Kingdom national or a national of a Convention country, and must habitually reside in Great Britain, or

    (*b*) he must be a United Kingdom national, and must habitually reside in British territory or a Convention country,

and if he is a national of a Convention country the adoption must not be prohibited by a specified provision (as defined in subsection (8)) of the internal law of that country.

(6) If the child is not a United Kingdom national the order shall not be made—

    (*a*) except in accordance with the provisions, if any, relating to consents and consultations of the internal law relating to adoption of the Convention country of which the child is a national, and

    (*b*) unless the court is satisfied that each person who consents to the order in accordance with that internal law does so with full understanding of what is involved.

(7) The reference to consents and consultations in subsection (6) does not include a reference to consent by and consultation with the applicant and members of the applicant's family (including his or her spouse), and for the purposes of subsection (6) consents may be proved in the manner prescribed by rules and the court shall be treated as the authority by whom, under the law mentioned in subsection (6), consents may be dispensed with and the adoption in question may be effected ; and where the provisions there mentioned require the attendance before that authority of any person who does not reside in Great Britain, that requirement shall be treated as satisfied for the purposes of subsection (6) if—

    (*a*) that person has been given a reasonable opportunity of communicating his opinion on the adoption in question to the proper officer or clerk of the court, or to an appropriate authority of the country in question, for transmission to the court ; and

    (*b*) where he has availed himself of that opportunity, his opinion has been transmitted to the court.

(8) In subsections (4) and (5) " specified provision " means a provision specified in an order of the Secretary of State as one notified to the Government of the United Kingdom in pursuance of the provisions of the Convention which relate to prohibitions on an adoption contained in the national law of the Convention country in question.

(9) Sections 9 and 10(1) (ascertainment of nationality, and internal law of foreign country) of the Adoption Act 1968 shall apply with any necessary modifications for the purposes of this section as they apply for the purposes of that Act.

25.—(1) Where on an application made in relation to a child by a person who is not domiciled in England and Wales or Scotland an authorised court is satisfied that he intends to adopt the child under the law of or within the country in which the applicant is domiciled, the court may, subject to the following provisions of this section, make an order vesting in him the parental rights and duties relating to the child.

(2) The provisions of this Part relating to adoption orders, except sections 8(1), (9) and (10), 10(2), 11(2), 14 to 16, 19, 22(1), 23 and 24, shall apply in relation to orders under this section as they apply in relation to adoption orders subject to the modification that in section 9(1) for " 19 " and " 13 " there are substituted " 32 " and " 26 " respectively.

(3) Sections 20 to 23 and 24(4) and (5) of the 1958 Act shall apply in relation to an order under this section as they apply in relation to an adoption order except that any entry in the Registers of Births, the Register of Births or the Adopted Children Register which is required to be marked in consequence of the making of an order under this section shall, in lieu of being marked with the word " Adopted " or " Re-adopted " (with or without the addition of the word " (Scotland) " or " (England) ") be marked with the words " Proposed Foreign Adoption " or " Proposed Foreign Re-adoption ", as the case may require.

(4) References in Parts III and IV of the 1958 Act to an adoption order include references to an order under this section, and references in this Act and in the 1958 Act to the placing of children for adoption or to the making of arrangements for adoption include references to the placing of children for adoption abroad or the making of arrangements for adoption abroad.

Amendments of Adoption Act 1958

26.—(1) In section 20 of the 1958 Act, in subsection (5), after the word " except " there are inserted the words " in accordance with section 20A of this Act or ".

(2) The following section is inserted in the 1958 Act after section 20:—

20A.—(1) Subject to subsections (4) and (6) of this section the Registrar General shall on an application made in the prescribed manner by an adopted person a record of whose birth is kept by the Registrar General and who has attained the age of 18 years supply to that person on payment of the prescribed fee (if any) such information as is necessary to enable that person to obtain a certified copy of the record of his birth.

(2) On an application made in the prescribed manner by an adopted person under the age of 18 years a record of whose birth is kept by the Registrar General and who is intending to be married in England or Wales, and on payment of the prescribed fee (if any), the Registrar General shall inform the applicant whether or not it appears from information contained in the registers of live births or other records that the applicant and the person whom he intends to marry may be within the prohibited degrees of relationship for the purposes of the Marriage Act 1949.

(3) It shall be the duty of the Registrar General and each local authority and approved adoption society to provide counselling for adopted persons who apply for information under subsection (1) of this section.

(4) Before supplying any information to an applicant under subsection (1) of this section, the Registrar General shall inform the applicant that counselling services are available to him—

    (*a*) at the General Register Office ; or

    (*b*) from the local authority for the area where the applicant is at the time the application is made ; or

    (*c*) from the local authority for the area where the court sat which made the adoption order relating to the applicant ; or

    (*d*) if the applicant's adoption was arranged by an adoption society which is approved under section 4 of the Children Act 1975, from that society.

(5) If the applicant chooses to receive counselling from a local authority or an adoption society under subsection (4) the Registrar General shall send to the authority or society of the applicant's choice the information to which the applicant is entitled under subsection (1).

(6) The Registrar General shall not supply a person who was adopted before the date on which the Children Act 1975 was passed with any information

under subsection (1) of this section unless that person has attended an interview with a counsellor either at the General Register Office or in pursuance of arrangements made by the local authority or adoption society from whom the applicant is entitled to receive counselling in accordance with subsection (4).

(7) In this section " prescribed " means prescribed by regulations made by the Registrar General.".

27. In section 22 of the 1958 Act—

(*a*) the following words are added at the end of subsection (4)—

" or a local authority or an approved adoption society which is providing counselling, under subsection (4A) of this section, for that adopted person." ;

(*b*) the following subsections are inserted after subsection (4)—

" (4A) Where the Registrar General for Scotland furnishes an adopted person with information under subsection (4) of this section, he shall advise that person that counselling services are available—

(*a*) from the local authority for the area where the adopted person lives ; or

(*b*) if the adopted person's adoption was arranged by an adoption society which is approved under section 4 of the Children Act 1975, from that society,

and it shall be the duty of such local authority and approved adoption society to provide counselling for adopted persons who have been furnished with information under subsection (4) and who apply to them for counselling in respect of that information.

(4B) Where an adopted person has arranged to receive counselling under subsection (4A), the Registrar General for Scotland shall, on receipt of a request from the local authority or adoption society which is providing that counselling, and on payment of the appropriate fee, send to the authority or society an extract of the entry relating to the adopted person in the Register of Births.".

PART I

Restriction on arranging adoption and placing of children.

28. In section 29 of the 1958 Act—

(a) the following subsection is substituted for subsections (1) and (2)—

" (1) A person other than an adoption agency shall not make arrangements for the adoption of a child, or place a child for adoption, unless—

(a) the proposed adopter is a relative of the child, or

(b) he is acting in pursuance of an order of the High Court " ;

(b) the following subsections are inserted after subsection (1)—

" (2) An adoption society approved under the Children Act 1975 only as respects England and Wales shall not act as an adoption society in Scotland, except to the extent that it considers it necessary to do so in the interests of a person mentioned in section 1(1) of that Act.

(2A) An adoption society approved under the Children Act 1975 only as respects Scotland shall not act as an adoption society in England or Wales, except to the extent that it considers it necessary to do so in the interests of a person mentioned in section 1(1) of that Act." ;

(c) in subsection (3)—

(i) the following is inserted after paragraph (b)— " or

(c) receives a child placed with him in contravention of subsection (1) of this section " ;

(ii) for the words " six months " there are substituted the words " three months " and for the words " one hundred pounds " there are substituted the words " £400 " ;

(d) the following subsection is substituted for subsection (5)—

" (5) Section 17 of the Children Act 1975 shall apply where a person is convicted of a contravention of subsection (1) of this section as it applies where an application for an adoption order is refused.".

Restrictions on removal of child pending adoption.

29. The following sections are substituted for section 34 of the 1958 Act—

"Restrictions on removal where adoption agreed or application made under section 14 of Children Act 1975.

34.—(1) While an application for an adoption order is pending in a case where a parent or guardian of the child has agreed to the making of the adoption order (whether or not he knows the identity of the applicant), the parent or guardian is not entitled, against the will of the person with whom the child has his home, to remove the child from the custody of that person except with the leave of the court.

(2) While an application is pending for an order under section 14 of the Children Act 1975 and—

    (*a*) the child is in the care of the adoption agency making the application, and

    (*b*) the application was not made with the consent of each parent or guardian of the child,

no parent or guardian of the child who did not consent to the application is entitled, against the will of the person with whom the child has his home, to remove the child from the custody of that person except with the leave of the court.

(3) Any person who contravenes subsection (1) or (2) of this section commits an offence and shall be liable on summary conviction to imprisonment for a term not exceeding three months or a fine not exceeding £400 or both.

Restrictions on removal where applicant has provided home for five years.

34A.—(1) While an application for an adoption order in respect of a child made by the person with whom the child has had his home for the five years preceding the application is pending, no person is entitled, against the will of the applicant, to remove the child from the applicant's custody except with the leave of the court or under authority conferred by any enactment or on the arrest of the child.

(2) Where a person (" the prospective adopter ") gives notice in writing to the local authority within whose area he has his home that he intends to apply for an adoption order in respect of a child who for the preceding five years has had his home with the prospective adopter, no person is entitled, against the will of the prospective adopter, to remove the child from the prospective adopter's custody, except with the leave of a court or under authority conferred by any enactment or on the arrest of the child, before—

    (*a*) the prospective adopter applies for the adoption order, or

    (*b*) the period of three months from the receipt of the notice by the local authority expires,

whichever occurs first.

(3) In any case where subsection (1) or (2) of this section applies, and—

    (*a*) the child was in the care of a local authority before he began to have his home with the applicant or, as the case may be, the prospective adopter, and (*b*) the child remains in the care of the authority,

the authority shall not remove the child from the actual custody of the applicant or of the prospective adopter except in accordance with sections 35 and 36 of this Act or with the leave of the court.

(4) A local authority which receives such notice as aforesaid in respect of a child whom the authority know to be in the care of another local authority or of a voluntary organisation shall, not more than seven days after the receipt of the notice, inform that other authority or the organisation in writing that they have received the notice.

(5) Subsection (2) of this section does not apply to any further notice served by the prospective adopter on any local authority in respect of the same child during the period referred to in paragraph (*b*) of that subsection or within 28 days after its expiry.

(6) Any person who contravenes subsection (1) or (2) of this section commits an offence and shall be liable on summary conviction to imprisonment for a term not exceeding three months or a fine not exceeding £400 or both.

(7) The Secretary of State may by order made by statutory instrument a draft of which has been approved by each House of Parliament amend subsection (1) or (2) of this section to substitute a different period for the period of five years mentioned in that subsection (or the period which, by a previous order under this subsection, was substituted for that period).

(8) In relation to Scotland, subsection (3) of this section does not apply where the removal of the child is authorised, in terms of Part III of the Social Work (Scotland) Act 1968, by a justice of the peace or a children's hearing.".

Return of child taken away in breach of section 34 or 34A of 1958 Act.

30.—(1) An authorised court may on the application of a person from whose custody a child has been removed in breach of section 34 or 34A of the 1958 Act order the person who has so removed the child to return the child to the applicant.

(2) An authorised court may on the application of a person who has reasonable grounds for believing that another person is intending to remove a child from the applicant's custody in

breach of section 34 or 34A of the 1958 Act by order direct that PART I
other person not to remove the child from the applicant's custody
in breach of the said section 34 or 34A.

(3) If, in the case of an order made by the High Court under
subsection (1), the High Court or, in the case of an order made
by a county court under subsection (1), a county court is satisfied
that the child has not been returned to the applicant, the court
may make an order authorising an officer of the court to search
such premises as may be specified in the order for the child and,
if the officer finds the child, to return the child to the applicant.

(4) If a justice of the peace is satisfied by information on oath
that there are reasonable grounds for believing that a child to
whom an order under subsection (1) relates is in premises specified in the information, he may issue a search warrant authorising
a constable to search the premises for the child ; and if a constable acting in pursuance of a warrant under this section finds
the child, he shall return the child to the person on whose
application the order under subsection (1) was made.

(5) An order under subsection (3) may be enforced in like
manner as a warrant for committal.

(6) Subsections (3), (4) and (5) do not apply to Scotland.

31. In section 35 of the 1958 Act, the following subsection Return of
is inserted after subsection (5)— child on
refusal of
" (5A) Where an application for an adoption order is adoption
refused the court may, if it thinks fit, at any time before order.
the expiry of the period of seven days mentioned in subsection (3) of this section order that period to be extended
to a duration, not exceeding six weeks, specified in the
order.".

32. In section 50 (prohibition of certain payments in relation Payment of
to adoption) of the 1958 Act, the following subsections are allowances
inserted at the end— to adopters.

" (4) If an adoption agency submits to the Secretary of
State a scheme for the payment by the agency of allowances to persons who have adopted or intend to adopt a
child where arrangements for the adoption were made, or
are to be made, by that agency, and the Secretary of State
approves the scheme, this section shall not apply to any
payment made in accordance with the scheme.

(5) The Secretary of State, in the case of a scheme
approved by him under subsection (4) of this section, may at
any time—

(a) make, or approve the making by the agency of,
alterations to the scheme ;

(b) revoke the scheme.

(6) The Secretary of State shall, within seven years of the date on which section 32 of the Children Act 1975 comes into force and, thereafter, every five years, publish a report on the operation of the schemes since that date or since the publication of the last report.

(7) Subject to the following subsection, subsection (4) of this section shall expire on the seventh anniversary of the date on which it comes into force.

(8) The Secretary of State may by order made by statutory instrument at any time before the said anniversary, repeal subsection (7) of this section.

(9) An order under subsection (8) of this section shall not be made unless—

(*a*) a report has been published under subsection (6) of this section, and

(*b*) a draft of the order has been laid before Parliament and approved by resolution of each House.

(10) Notwithstanding the expiry of subsection (4) of this section or the revocation of a scheme approved under this section, subsection (1) of this section shall not apply in relation to any payment made, whether before or after the expiry of subsection (4) or the revocation of the scheme, in accordance with a scheme which was approved under this section to a person to whom such payments were made, where the scheme was not revoked, before the expiry of subsection (4) or, if the scheme was revoked, before the date of its revocation.".

Part II

Custody

Custodianship orders

Custodianship orders.

33.—(1) An authorised court may on the application of one or more persons qualified under subsection (3) make an order vesting the legal custody of a child in the applicant or, as the case may be, in one or more of the applicants if the child is in England or Wales at the time the application is made.

(2) An order under subsection (1) may be referred to as a custodianship order, and the person in whom legal custody of the child is vested under the order may be referred to as the custodian of the child.

(3) The persons qualified to apply for a custodianship order are—

   (*a*) a relative or step-parent of the child—

      (i) who applies with the consent of a person having legal custody of the child, and

      (ii) with whom the child has had his home for the three months preceding the making of the application ;

   (*b*) any person—

      (i) who applies with the consent of a person having legal custody of the child, and

      (ii) with whom the child has had his home for a period or periods before the making of the application which amount to at least twelve months and include the three months preceding the making of the application ;

   (*c*) any person with whom the child has had his home for a period or periods before the making of the application which amount to at least three years and include the three months preceding the making of the application.

(4) The mother or father of the child is not qualified under any paragraph of subsection (3).

(5) A step-parent of the child is not qualified under any paragraph of subsection (3) if in proceedings for divorce or nullity of marriage the child was named in an order made under paragraph (*b*) or (*c*) of section 41(1) (arrangements for welfare of children of family) of the Matrimonial Causes Act 1973. 1973 c. 18.

(6) If no person has legal custody of the child, or the applicant himself has legal custody or the person with legal custody cannot be found, paragraphs (*a*) and (*b*) of subsection (3) apply with the omission of sub-paragraph (i).

(7) The Secretary of State may by order a draft of which has been approved by each House of Parliament amend subsection (3)(*c*) to substitute a different period for the period of three years mentioned in that paragraph (or the period which, by a previous order under this subsection, was substituted for that period).

(8) Subsection (5) does not apply—

   (*a*) if the parent other than the one the step-parent married is dead or cannot be found, or

   (*b*) if the order referred to in subsection (5) was made under subsection (1)(*c*) of section 41 of the Matrimonial Causes Act 1973 and it has since been determined that the child was not a child of the family to whom that section applied.

(9) For the avoidance of doubt, it is hereby declared that the provisions of section 1 of the Guardianship of Minors Act 1971 apply to applications made under this Part of this Act.

(10) This section and sections 34 to 46 do not apply to Scotland.

34.—(1) An authorised court may, on making a custodianship order or while a custodianship order is in force, by order—

(*a*) on the application of the child's mother or father, make such provision as it thinks fit requiring access to the child to be given to the applicant ;

(*b*) on the application of the custodian, require the child's mother or father (or both) to make to the applicant such periodical payments towards the maintenance of the child as it thinks reasonable ;

(*c*) on the application of the child's mother or father, revoke an order requiring the applicant to contribute towards the child's maintenance made (otherwise than under this section) by any court ;

(*d*) on the application of the child's mother or father or the custodian, vary an order made (otherwise than under this section) by any court requiring the mother or father to contribute towards the child's maintenance—

·(i) by altering the amount of the contributions ;

(ii) by substituting the custodian for the person to whom the contributions were ordered to be made.

(2) References in subsection (1) to the child's mother or father include any person in relation to whom the child was treated as a child of the family (as defined in section 52(1) of the Matrimonial Causes Act 1973) but the court in deciding whether to make an order under subsection (1)(*b*) against a person who is not the child's mother or father shall have regard (among the circumstances of the case)—

(*a*) to whether that person had assumed any responsibility for the child's maintenance and, if he did, to the extent to which and the basis on which he did so, and to the length of time during which he discharged that responsibility ;

(*b*) to the liability of any other person to maintain that child.

(3) No order shall be made under subsection (1)(*b*) requiring the father of an illegitimate child to make any payments to the child's custodian.

(4) Subsections (2), (3), (4) and (6) (orders as to supervision, local authority care, maintenance etc. of children) of section 2 of the Guardianship Act 1973 and sections 3 and 4 of that Act 1973 c. **29**. (supplementary provisions) shall apply to an application for a custodianship order as they apply to an application under 1971 c. **3**. section 9 of the Guardianship of Minors Act 1971, subject to the following modifications, that is to say—

> (*a*) in section 2(2)(*b*) and (4)(*a*) of the Guardianship Act 1973 any reference to a parent of the minor to whom the order relates shall be construed as including a reference to any other individual ;
>
> (*b*) section 3(3) of that Act shall have effect as if the words " or the custodian " were inserted after the words " application of either parent ".

(5) A local authority may make contributions to a custodian towards the cost of the accommodation and maintenance of the child, except where the custodian is the husband or wife of a parent of the child.

35.—(1) An authorised court may by order revoke a Revocation custodianship order on the application of— and variation of orders.

> (*a*) the custodian, or
>
> (*b*) the mother or father, or a guardian, of the child, or
>
> (*c*) any local authority in England or Wales.

(2) The court shall not proceed to hear an application made by any person for the revocation of a custodianship order where a previous such application made by the same person was refused by that or any other court unless—

> (*a*) in refusing the previous application the court directed that this subsection should not apply, or
>
> (*b*) it appears to the court that because of a change in circumstances or for any other reason it is proper to proceed with the application.

(3) The custodian of a child may apply to an authorised court for the revocation or variation of any order made under section 34 in respect of that child.

(4) Any other person on whose application an order under section 34 was made, or who was required by such an order to contribute towards the maintenance of the child, may apply to an authorised court for the revocation or variation of that order.

B

(5) Any order made under section 34 in respect of a child who is the subject of a custodianship order shall cease to have effect on the revocation of the custodianship order.

(6) A custodianship order made in respect of a child, and any order made under section 34 in respect of the child, shall cease to have effect when the child attains the age of 18 years.

Care etc. of child on revocation of custodianship order.

36.—(1) Before revoking a custodianship order the court shall ascertain who would have legal custody of the child, if, on the revocation of the custodianship order, no further order were made under this section.

(2) If the child would not be in the legal custody of any person, the court shall, if it revokes the custodianship order, commit the care of the child to a specified local authority.

(3) If there is a person who would have legal custody of the child on the revocation of the custodianship order, the court shall consider whether it is desirable in the interests of the welfare of the child for the child to be in the legal custody of that person and—

(a) if the court is of the opinion that it would not be so desirable, it shall on revoking the custodianship order commit the care of the child to a specified local authority ;

(b) if it is of the opinion that while it is desirable for the child to be in the legal custody of that person, it is also desirable in the interests of the welfare of the child for him to be under the supervision of an independent person, the court shall, on revoking the custodianship order, order that the child shall be under the supervision of a specified local authority or of a probation officer.

(4) Before exercising its functions under this section the court shall, unless it has sufficient information before it for the purpose, request—

(a) a local authority to arrange for an officer of the authority, or

(b) a probation officer,

to make to the court a report, orally or in writing, on the desirability of the child returning to the legal custody of any individual, and it shall be the duty of the local authority or probation officer to comply with the request.

(5) Where the court makes an order under subsection (3)(a) the order may require the payment by either parent to the local authority, while it has the care of the child, of such weekly or

other periodical sum towards the maintenance of the child as PART II
the court thinks reasonable.

(6) Sections 3 and 4 of the Guardianship Act 1973 (which 1973 c. 29.
contain supplementary provisions relating to children who are
subject to supervision, or in the care of local authority, by virtue
of orders made under section 2 of that Act) apply in relation to
an order under this section as they apply in relation to an order
under section 2 of that Act.

(7) Subsections (2) to (6) of section 6 of the Guardianship
Act 1973 shall apply in relation to reports which are requested
by magistrates' courts under this section as they apply to reports
under subsection (1) of that section.

37.—(1) Where on an application for an adoption order by a Custodianship
relative of the child or by the husband or wife of the mother order on
or father of the child, whether alone or jointly with his or her application for
spouse, the requirements of section 12 or, where the application adoption or
is for a Convention adoption order, section 24(6) are satisfied, guardianship.
but the court is satisfied—

    (*a*) that the child's welfare would not be better safeguarded
        and promoted by the making of adoption order in
        favour of the applicant, than it would be by the making
        of a custodianship order in his favour, and

    (*b*) that it would be appropriate to make a custodianship
        order in the applicant's favour,

the court shall direct the application to be treated as if it had
been made by the applicant under section 33, but if the application was made jointly by the father or mother of the child
and his or her spouse, the court shall direct the application to be
treated as if made by the father's wife or the mother's husband
alone.

(2) Where on an application for an adoption order made—

    (*a*) by a person who is neither a relative of the child nor
        the husband or wife of the mother or father of the
        child ; or

    (*b*) by a married couple neither of whom falls within
        paragraph (*a*), .

the said requirements are satisfied but the court is of opinion that
it would be more appropriate to make a custodianship order in
favour of the applicant, it may direct the application to be treated
as if it had been made by the applicant under section 33.

(3) Where on an application under section 9 (orders for
custody and maintenance on application of mother or father)
of the Guardianship of Minors Act 1971 the court is of opinion 1971 c. 3.

PART II   that legal custody should be given to a person other than the mother or father, it may direct the application to be treated as if it had been made by that person under section 33.

(4) Where a direction is given under this section the applicant shall be treated (if such is not the case) as if he were qualified to apply for a custodianship order and this Part, except section 40, shall have effect accordingly.

(5) Subsection (1) does not apply to an application made by a step-parent whether alone or jointly with another person in any case where the step-parent is prevented by section 33(5) from being qualified to apply for a custodianship order in respect of the child.

(6) Subsections (1) and (2) do not apply to an application for an adoption order made by the child's mother or father alone.

Disputes
between joint
custodians.

38. If two persons have a parental right or duty vested in them jointly by a custodianship order or by virtue of section 44(2) but cannot agree on its exercise or performance, either of them may apply to an authorised court, and the court may make such order regarding the exercise of the right or performance of the duty as it thinks fit.

Reports by
local
authorities
and probation
officers.

39.—(1) A court dealing with an application made under this Part, or an application which is treated as if made under section 33, may request—

(a) a local authority to arrange for an officer of the authority, or

(b) a probation officer,

to make to the court a report, orally or in writing, with respect to any specified matter which appears to the court to be relevant to the application, and it shall be the duty of the local authority or probation officer to comply with the request.

1973 c. 29.

(2) Subsections (2) to (6) of section 6 of the Guardianship Act 1973 shall apply in relation to reports which are requested by magistrates' courts under this section as they apply to reports under subsection (1) of that section.

Notice of
application
to be given
to local
authority.

40.—(1) A custodianship order shall not be made unless the applicant has given notice of the application for the order to the local authority in whose area the child resides within the seven days following the making of the application, or such extended period as the court or local authority may allow.

(2) On receipt of a notice given by the applicant under sub-section (1) the local authority shall arrange for an officer of the authority to make a report to the court (so far as is practicable)

on the matters prescribed under subsection (3) and on any other matter which he considers to be relevant to the application.

(3) The Secretary of State shall by regulations prescribe matters which are to be included in a report under subsection (2) and, in particular, but without prejudice to the generality of the foregoing, the prescribed matters shall include—

   (*a*) the wishes and feelings of the child having regard to his age and understanding and all other matters relevant to the operation of section 1 (principle on which questions relating to custody are to be decided) of the Guardianship of Minors Act 1971 in relation to the application ;

1971 c. 3.

   (*b*) the means and suitability of the applicant ;

   (*c*) information of a kind specified in the regulations relating to members of the applicant's household ;

   (*d*) the wishes regarding the application, and the means, of the mother and father of the child.

(4) Subsections (2), (3) and (3A) of section 6 of the Guardianship Act 1973 shall apply to a report under this section which is submitted to a magistrates' court.

1973 c. 29.

41.—(1) While an application for a custodianship order in respect of a child made by the person with whom the child has at the time the application is made had his home for a period (whether continuous or not) amounting to at least three years is pending, another person is not entitled, against the will of the applicant, to remove the child from the applicant's custody except with the leave of a court or under authority conferred by any enactment or on the arrest of the child.

Restriction on removal of child where applicant has provided home for three years.

(2) In any case where subsection (1) applies, and

   (*a*) the child was in the care of a local authority before he began to have his home with the applicant, and

   (*b*) the child remains in the care of a local authority,

the authority in whose care the child is shall not remove the child from the applicant's custody except with the applicant's consent or the leave of a court.

(3) Any person who contravenes subsection (1) commits an offence and shall be liable on summary conviction to imprisonment for a term not exceeding three months or a fine not exceeding £400 or both.

(4) The Secretary of State may by order a draft of which has been approved by each House of Parliament amend subsection

(1) to substitute a different period for the period mentioned in that subsection (or the period which, by a previous order under this subsection, was substituted for that period).

Return of
child taken
away in
breach of
section 41.

42.—(1) An authorised court may on the application of a person from whose custody a child has been removed in breach of section 41 order the person who has so removed the child to return the child to the applicant.

(2) An authorised court may on the application of a person who has reasonable grounds for believing that another person is intending to remove a child from the applicant's custody in breach of section 41 by order direct that other person not to remove the child from the applicant's custody in breach of that section.

(3) If, in the case of an order made by the High Court under subsection (1), the High Court or, in the case of an order made by a county court under subsection (1), a county court is satisfied that the child has not been returned to the applicant, the court may make an order authorising an officer of the court to search such premises as may be specified in the order for the child and, if the officer finds the child, to return the child to the applicant.

(4) If a justice of the peace is satisfied by information on oath that there are reasonable grounds for believing that a child to whom an order under subsection (1) relates is in premises specified in the information, he may issue a search warrant authorising a constable to search the premises for the child ; and if a constable acting in pursuance of a warrant under this section finds the child, he shall return the child to the person on whose application the order under subsection (1) was made.

(5) An order under subsection (3) may be enforced in like manner as a warrant for committal.

Enforcement
of orders
made by
magistrates'
courts.

1952 c. 55.

43.—(1) If at a time when the custodian is entitled to actual custody of the child by virtue of a custodianship order made by a magistrates' court any other person has actual custody of him, a copy of the custodianship order may be served on that person and thereupon the order may, without prejudice to any other remedy open to the custodian, be enforced under section 54(3) of the Magistrates' Courts Act 1952 as if it were an order of a magistrates' court requiring that person to give up the child to the custodian.

(2) Any person for the time being under an obligation to make payments in pursuance of any order for the payment of money made by a magistrates' court under section 34 shall give notice of any change of address to such person (if any) as may be specified in the order ; and if he fails without reasonable excuse

to give such a notice he commits an offence and shall be liable
on summary conviction to a fine not exceeding £10.

(3) An order for the payment of money made by a magistrates' court under section 34 may be enforced in like manner as an affiliation order, and the enactments relating to affiliation orders shall apply accordingly with the necessary modifications.

44.—(1) While a custodianship order has effect in relation to   Effect of
a child the right of any person other than the custodian to legal   custodianship
custody of the child is suspended, but, subject to any further   order on
order made by any court, revives on the revocation of the   existing
custodianship order.   custody.

(2) Subsection (1) does not apply where the person already having custody is a parent of the child and the person who becomes custodian under the order is the husband or wife of the parent; and in such a case the spouses have the legal custody jointly.

45.—(1) Where a custodianship order subsists in respect of an   Affiliation
illegitimate child, and no affiliation order relating to the child   order on
has been made under the Affiliation Proceedings Act 1957, the   application by
custodian of the child may apply to a justice of the peace acting   custodian.
for the petty sessions area in which the child or the child's mother   1957 c. 55.
resides for a summons to be served under section 1 of that Act.

(2) The court shall proceed on the application as on a complaint under that section, but the person entitled to any payments under an affiliation order made on the application shall be the custodian.

(3) An application may not be made under subsection (1)—
 (*a*) if the custodian is married to the child's mother, or
 (*b*) more than three years after the custodianship order was made.

46.—(1) It is hereby declared that any jurisdiction conferred   Procedure in
on a magistrates' court by virtue of this Part is exercisable not-   magistrates'
withstanding that the proceedings are brought by or against a   courts.
person residing outside England and Wales.

(2) A magistrates' court may, subject to subsection (3), proceed on an application for an order under this Part notwithstanding that the defendant has not been served with the summons, and rules may prescribe matters as to which the court is to be satisfied before proceeding in such a case.

(3) A magistrates' court shall not—
 (*a*) make an order under this Part requiring a person to make
 .payments towards the maintenance of a child, or

B 4

PART II

(*b*) vary an order under this Part so as to increase a person's liability to make payments towards the maintenance of a child,

unless the person has been served with the summons.

(4) Rules may make provision as to the persons who are to be made defendants to a complaint for an order under this Part, and where there are two or more defendants to such a complaint

1952 c. 55.

the power of the court under section 55(1) of the Magistrates' Courts Act 1952 (power to award costs etc.) shall be deemed to include power, whatever adjudication the court makes, to order any of the parties to pay the whole or part of the costs of all or any of the parties.

(5) In this section, " rules " means rules made under section 15

1949 c. 101.

of the Justices of the Peace Act 1949.

Custody in Scotland

Granting of custody.

47.—(1) Without prejudice to any existing enactment or rule of law conferring a—

(*a*) right to apply for custody of a child ;

(*b*) power to grant custody of a child ;

any relative, step-parent or foster parent of the child is qualified to apply for, and subject to subsection (2) may be granted, such custody in the same manner as any person so qualified before the commencement of this Act.

(2) Except in the case of an application under section 2 of the

1930 c. 33.

Illegitimate Children (Scotland) Act 1930, custody of a child shall not be granted in any proceedings to a person other than a parent or guardian of the child unless that person—

(*a*) being a relative or step-parent of the child, has the consent of a parent or guardian of the child and has had care and possession of the child for the three months preceding the making of the application for custody ; or

(*b*) has the consent of a parent or guardian of the child and has had care and possession of the child for a period or periods, before such application, which amounted to at least twelve months and included the three months preceding such application ; or

(*c*) has had care and possession of the child for a period or periods before such application which amounted to at least three years and included the three months preceding such application ; or

(*d*) while not falling within paragraph (*a*), (*b*) or (*c*), can show cause, having regard to section 1 of the Guardian-

1925 c. 45.

ship of Infants Act 1925 (the principle on which

questions relating to custody, upbringing etc. of children are to be decided) why an order should be made
awarding him custody of the child.

(3) Nothing in this section shall prejudice any ancillary power
of the court in any proceedings relative to custody.

(4) The Secretary of State may by order a draft of which
has been approved by each House of Parliament amend subsection (2)(*c*) to substitute a different period for the period of
three years mentioned in that paragraph (or the period which by
a previous order under this subsection was substituted for that
period).

(5) In relation to a grant of custody to which this section
applies,

    (*a*) " guardian " has the same meaning as in the 1958 Act;

    (*b*) " foster parent " means a person who, at the commence-
        ment of the proceedings in which the grant is made,
        has had care and possession of the child for a period or
        periods amounting to at least twelve months, whether
        or not that person continues to have care and posses-
        sion of the child;

    (*c*) " relative " has the same meaning as in the 1958 Act,
        except that, where the child is illegitimate, " relative "
        does not include the father of the child.

(6) The form and manner of any consent required in terms
of subsection (2)(*a*) or (*b*) may be prescribed by act of sederunt.

48.—(1) A person making an application relating to the Miscellaneous
custody of a child shall, so far as practicable and in such manner provisions
as may be prescribed by act of sederunt, give notice of that relative to
application to each known parent of the child, and for this pur- custody.
pose the father of an illegitimate child shall be regarded as a
parent of the child.

(2) Any order made by virtue of this Part of this Act may
be varied or discharged by a subsequent order, either by the
Court *ex proprio motu* or on the application of any person
concerned.

(3) In section 11(1) of the Guardianship Act 1973, for the 1973 c. 29.
words from " Where an application " to " relates to the custody
of a child " there is substituted " Where an application relating
to the custody of a child, other than an application to which
Part II of the Matrimonial Proceedings (Children) Act 1958 1958 c. 40.
applies, is made to a court ".

(4) In section 12(2)(*a*) of the Guardianship Act 1973, for the
words from " Where an application " to " by virtue of section
11 of this Act " there is substituted " Where any application,
other than one to which Part II of the Matrimonial Proceedings

PART II

(Children) Act 1958 applies, is made to a court for custody of a child or for the variation or discharge of any order (including an order made by virtue of section 11 above) relating to the custody of a child ".

Notice to local authority of certain custody applications.

49.—(1) Where an applicant for custody of a child is a relative, step-parent or foster parent of the child, an order awarding custody to that applicant shall not except on cause shown be made unless the applicant—

> (*a*) in any case where at the time of the application he resided in Scotland, has, within the seven days following the making of the application, given notice thereof to the local authority within whose area he resided at that time ;

> (*b*) in any other case, has within such time as the court may direct given, to such local authority in Scotland as the court may specify, notice of the making of the application.

(2) On receipt of a notice under subsection (1) the local authority shall investigate and report to the court on all the circumstances of the child and on the proposed arrangements for the care and upbringing of the child.

1973 c. 29.

(3) Paragraphs (*b*) and (*c*) of subsection (2) of section 12 of the Guardianship Act 1973 shall apply in relation to an investigation and report in terms of this section as they apply in relation to an investigation and report in terms of paragraph (*a*) of subsection (2) of that section.

Payments towards maintenance of children.

50. Without prejudice to any existing powers and duties to make payments in respect of the maintenance of children, where custody of a child has been awarded to a person other than a parent of the child any local authority may make to that person payments for or towards the maintenance of the child.

Restriction on removal of child where applicant has provided home for three years.

51.—(1) Where a person has applied for custody of a child, it shall be an offence, except with the authority of a court or under authority conferred by any enactment or on the arrest of the child, to remove the child from the custody of the applicant against the will of the applicant if—

> (*a*) the child has been in the care and possession of that person for a period or periods before the making of the application which amount to at least three years ; and

> (*b*) the application is pending in any court.

(2) In any case where subsection (1) applies, and

    (*a*) the child was in the care of a local authority before he began to have his home with the applicant, and

    (*b*) the child remains in the care of a local authority,

the authority in whose care the child is shall not remove the child from the applicant's custody except—

    (i) with the applicant's consent ;

    (ii) with the leave of a court ; or

    (iii) with the authority, in terms of Part III of the Social Work (Scotland) Act 1968, of a justice of the peace or a children's hearing.

1968 c. 49.

(3) Any person who contravenes the provisions of subsection (1) commits an offence and shall be liable on summary conviction to imprisonment for a term not exceeding three months or a fine not exceeding £400 or both.

(4) The Secretary of State may by order, a draft of which has been approved by each House of Parliament, amend subsection (1) to substitute a different period for the period mentioned in that subsection (or for the period which, by a previous order under this subsection, was substituted for that period).

52. A court in which an application for custody of a child is pending may—

    (*a*) on the application of a person from whose custody the child has been removed in breach of section 51, order the person who has so removed the child to return the child to the applicant ;

    (*b*) on the application of a person who has reasonable grounds for believing that another person is intending to remove the child from the applicant's custody in breach of section 51, by order direct that other person not to remove the child from the applicant's custody in breach of that section.

Return of child taken away in breach of section 51.

53.—(1) Without prejudice to the provisions of section 19 (power to make an interim order giving custody), where on an application for an adoption order in respect of a child the applicant is a person qualified to apply for custody of the child, and the court is of opinion—

Custody order on application for adoption in Scotland.

    (*a*) in the case of an applicant who is a relative of the child or a husband or wife of the mother or father of the child (whether applying alone or jointly with his or her spouse)—

        (i) that the child's welfare would not be better safeguarded and promoted by the making of an adoption order in favour of the applicant than it would be by the making of a custody order in his favour ; and

    (ii) that it would be appropriate to make a custody order in favour of the applicant ; or

  (*b*) in any other case, that the making of a custody order in favour of the applicant would be more appropriate than the making of an adoption order in his favour,

the court shall direct that the application is to be treated as if it had been made for custody of the child ; but where such a direction is made the court shall not cease to have jurisdiction by reason only that it would not have had jurisdiction to hear an application by the applicant for custody of the child.

(2) In the application of this Part of this Act to any case where a direction under subsection (1) has been made—

  (*a*) for references in section 47(2) to the making of an application for custody there shall be substituted references to the making of an application for an adoption order ;

  (*b*) for the references in section 49 and paragraph (*a*) of subsection (1) of section 51 to the making of an application there shall be substituted references to the making of a direction in terms of subsection (1) of this section ;

  (*c*) in section 51(1) for the words " for custody of " there shall be substituted the words " for an adoption order in respect of ".

1973 c. 29.

(3) For the purposes of section 11 of the Guardianship Act 1973, any application in respect of which a direction has been made under subsection (1) of this section, is an application for custody of a child.

Jurisdiction of Scottish courts in certain applications for custody.

54.—(1) Without prejudice to any existing grounds of juris-diction, the court shall have jurisdiction in proceedings for custody of a child if at the time of application for such custody—

  (*a*) the child resides in Scotland ; and

  (*b*) the child is domiciled in England and Wales ; and

  (*c*) the person applying for custody is a person qualified, in terms of subsections (3) to (8) of section 33 of this Act, to apply in England or Wales for a custodianship order in respect of the child.

(2) For the purposes of this section, " the court " means—

  (*a*) the Court of Session ; or

  (*b*) the sheriff court of the sheriffdom within which the child resides.

55.—(1) In sections 47 to 54 " child " means a person under the age of sixteen.

(2) Sections 47 to 54 and this section apply to Scotland only.

Part II

Interpretation and extent of sections 47 to 55.

Part III

Care

Children in care of local authorities

56.—(1) In section 1 of the Children Act 1948, the following subsections are inserted after subsection (3)—

> " (3A) Except in relation to an act done—
>> (*a*) with the consent of the local authority, or
>> (*b*) by a parent or guardian of the child who has given the local authority not less than 28 days' notice of his intention to do it,
>
> subsection (8) (penalty for taking away a child in care) of section 3 of this Act shall apply to a child in the care of a local authority under this section (notwithstanding that no resolution is in force under section 2 of this Act with respect to the child) if he has been in the care of that local authority throughout the preceding six months ; and for the purposes of the application of paragraph (*b*) of that subsection in such a case a parent or guardian of the child shall not be taken to have lawful authority to take him away.
>
> (3B) The Secretary of State may by order a draft of which has been approved by each House of Parliament amend subsection (3A) of this section by substituting a different period for the period of 28 days or of six months mentioned in that subsection (or the period which, by a previous order under this subsection, was substituted for that period)."

(2) The following section is inserted after section 33 of the Children Act 1948—

Restriction on removal of child from care.

1948 c. 43.

> 33A.—(1) Section 3(8) of this Act shall apply in relation to children who are not in the care of local authorities under section 1 of this Act but who are in voluntary homes or are boarded out, as it applies by virtue of subsection (3A) of the said section 1 to children in the care of the local authority, except that in the case of a child who is not in the care of a local authority the references in subsection (3A) to a local authority shall be construed as references

" Restriction on removal of child from care of voluntary organisation.

to the voluntary organisation in whose care the child is.

(2) For the purposes of this section—

(*a*) a child is boarded out if he is boarded out, by the voluntary organisation in whose care he is, with foster parents to live in their home as a member of their family ;

(*b*) " voluntary home " includes a controlled community home and an assisted community home.".

Substitution of s. 2 of Children Act 1948.

1948 c. 43.

57. The following section is substituted for section 2 of the Children Act 1948.

" Assumption by local authority of parental rights and duties.

2.—(1) Subject to the provisions of this Part of this Act, if it appears to a local authority in relation to any child who is in their care under the foregoing section—

(*a*) that his parents are dead and he has no guardian or custodian ; or

(*b*) that a parent of his—

(i) has abandoned him, or

(ii) suffers from some permanent disability rendering him incapable of caring for the child, or

1959 c. 72.

(iii) while not falling within sub-paragraph (ii) of this paragraph, suffers from a mental disorder (within the meaning of the Mental Health Act 1959), which renders him unfit to have the care of the child, or

(iv) is of such habits or mode of life as to be unfit to have the care of the child, or

(v) has so consistently failed without reasonable cause to discharge the obligations of a parent as to be unfit to have the care of the child ; or

(*c*) that a resolution under paragraph (*b*) of this subsection is in force in relation to one parent of the child who is, or is likely to become, a member of the household comprising the child and his other parent ; or

(*d*) that throughout the three years preceding the passing of the resolution the child has

been in the care of a local authority under
the foregoing section, or partly in the care
of a local authority and partly in the care
of a voluntary organisation,

the local authority may resolve that there shall vest
in them the parental rights and duties with respect
to that child, and, if the rights and duties were vested
in the parent on whose account the resolution was
passed jointly with another person, they shall also
be vested in the local authority jointly with that
other person.

(2) In the case of a resolution passed under paragraph (*b*), (*c*) or (*d*) of subsection (1) of this section,
unless the person whose parental rights and duties
have under the resolution vested in the local authority
has consented in writing to the passing of the resolution, the local authority, if that person's whereabouts
are known to them, shall forthwith after the passing
of the resolution serve on him notice in writing of
the passing thereof.

(3) Every notice served by a local authority under
subsection (2) of this section shall inform the person
on whom the notice is served of his right to object to
the resolution and the effect of any objection made
by him.

(4) If, not later than one month after notice is
served on a person under subsection (2) of this
section, he serves a counter-notice in writing on the
local authority objecting to the resolution, the resolution shall, subject to the provisions of subsection (5)
of this section, lapse on the expiry of fourteen days
from the service of the counter-notice.

(5) Where a counter-notice has been served on a
local authority under subsection (4) of this section,
the authority may not later than fourteen days after
the receipt by them of the counter-notice complain
to a juvenile court having jurisdiction in the area of
the authority, and in that event the resolution shall
not lapse until the determination of the complaint;
and the court may on the hearing of the complaint
order that the resolution shall not lapse by reason
of the service of the counter-notice:

Provided that the court shall not so order unless
satisfied—

(*a*) that the grounds mentioned in subsection (1)
of this section on which the local authority

purported to pass the resolution were made out, and

(*b*) that at the time of the hearing there continued to be grounds on which a resolution under subsection (1) of this section could be founded, and

(*c*) that it is in the interests of the child to do so.

(6) While a resolution passed under subsection (1)(*b*), (*c*) or (*d*) of this section is in force with respect to a child, section 1(3) of this Act shall not apply in relation to the person who, but for the resolution, would have the parental rights and duties in relation to the child.

(7) Any notice under this section (including a counter-notice) may be served by post, so however that a notice served by a local authority under subsection (2) of this section shall not be duly served by post unless it is sent by registered post or recorded delivery service.

(8) A resolution under this section shall cease to have effect if—

(*a*) the child is adopted ;

(*b*) an order in respect of the child is made under section 14 or 25 of the Children Act 1975 ; or

(*c*) a guardian of the child is appointed under section 5 of the Guardianship of Minors Act 1971.

1971 c. 3.

(9) Where, after a child has been received into the care of a local authority under the foregoing section, the whereabouts of any parent of his have remained unknown for twelve months, then, for the purposes of this section, the parent shall be deemed to have abandoned the child.

(10) The Secretary of State may by order a draft of which has been approved by each House of Parliament amend subsection (1)(*d*) of this section to substitute a different period for the period mentioned in that paragraph (or the period which, by a previous order under this subsection, was substituted for that period).

(11) In this section—

" parent ", except in subsection (1)(*a*), includes a guardian or custodian ;

PART III

" parental rights and duties ", in relation to a particular child, means all rights and duties which by law the mother and father have in relation to a legitimate child and his property except the right to consent or refuse to consent to the making of an application under section 14 of the Children Act 1975 and the right to agree or refuse to agree to the making of an adoption order or an order under section 25 of that Act.".

58. In the Children Act 1948, the following sections are inserted after section 4—

"Appeal to High Court.

4A. An appeal shall lie to the High Court from the making by a juvenile court of an order under section 2(5) or section 4(3) of this Act (orders confirming or terminating local authority resolutions under section 2(1) of this Act), or from the refusal by a juvenile court to make such an order.

Guardians ad litem and reports in care proceedings.

4B.—(1) In any proceedings under section 2(5) or 4(3) or 4A of this Act, a juvenile court or the High Court may, where it considers it necessary in order to safeguard the interests of the child to whom the proceedings relate, by order make the child a party to the proceedings and appoint, subject to rules of court, a guardian ad litem of the child for the purposes of the proceedings.

(2) A guardian ad litem appointed in pursuance of this section shall be under a duty to safeguard the interests of the child in the manner prescribed by rules of court.

(3) Section 6 of the Guardianship Act 1973 shall apply in relation to complaints under section 2(5) or 4(3) of this Act as it applies in relation to applications under section 3(3) of the said Act of 1973.".

Supplementary provisions relating to care proceedings.

1948 c. 43.

1973 c. 29.

59. In section 12 of the Children Act 1948, the following subsections are substituted for subsection (1)—

" (1) In reaching any decision relating to a child in their care, a local authority shall give first consideration to the need to safeguard and promote the welfare of the child throughout his childhood ; and shall so far as practicable ascertain the wishes and feelings of the child regarding the decision and give due consideration to them, having regard to his age and understanding.

General duty of local authority in care cases.

(1A) If it appears to the local authority that it is necessary, for the purpose of protecting members of the public, to exercise their powers in relation to a particular child in their care in a manner which may not be consistent with their duty under the foregoing subsection, the authority may, notwithstanding that duty, act in that manner.".

Children in care of voluntary organisations in England and Wales

60.—(1) Where it appears to a local authority as respects a child in the care of a voluntary organisation which is an incorporated body—

(a) that the child is not in the care of any local authority ; and

(b) that a condition specified in section 2(1) of the Children Act 1948 is satisfied ; and

(c) that it is necessary in the interests of the welfare of the child for the parental rights and duties to be vested in the organisation,

the authority may, subject to subsections (5) and (6), resolve that there shall vest in the organisation the parental rights and duties with respect to that child.

(2) While a resolution under this section is in force the parental rights and duties shall vest in the organisation in whose care the child is when the resolution is passed.

(3) If, immediately before the resolution is passed, the parental rights and duties are vested in the parent in relation to whom the resolution is passed jointly with any other person, then on the passing of the resolution the parental rights and duties shall vest jointly in that other person and the organisation in whose care the child is.

(4) In determining, for the purposes of subsection (1) of this section, whether the condition specified in section 2(1)(b)(i) of the Children Act 1948 is satisfied, if the whereabouts of any parent of the child have remained unknown for twelve months, that parent shall be deemed to have abandoned the child.

(5) A resolution under subsection (1) may not be passed by a local authority in respect of any child unless—

(a) the child is living in the area of the authority either in a voluntary home or with foster parents with whom he has been boarded by the organisation in whose care he is ; and

(b) that organisation has requested the authority to pass the resolution.

(6) The parental rights and duties which may vest in an organisation by virtue of this section do not include the right to consent or refuse to consent to the making of an application under section 14 and the right to agree or refuse to agree to the making of an adoption order or an order under section 25 ; and regulations made under section 33(1) of the Children Act 1948 shall apply to the emigration of a child notwithstanding that the parental rights and duties relating to the child are vested in the voluntary organisation.

(7) Subsection (8) of section 2 of the Children Act 1948 shall apply in relation to a resolution under subsection (1) as if it were a resolution under the said section 2.

61.—(1) If it appears to a local authority, having regard to the interests of the welfare of a child living within their area, the parental rights and duties with respect to whom are by virtue of a resolution under section 60 vested in a voluntary organisa- tion, that it is necessary that the parental rights and duties should <br> no longer be vested in the organisation, the local authority shall resolve that there shall vest in them the parental rights and duties relating to the child.

(2) The local authority shall within seven days of passing a resolution under subsection (1) by notice in writing inform the organisation and each parent, guardian or custodian of the child whose whereabouts are known to them that the resolution has been passed.

62.—(1) A resolution under subsection (1) of section 60 shall cease to have effect on the passing of a resolution under sub- section (1) of section 61.

(2) Section 6 of the Children Act 1948 shall have effect in relation to a resolution under subsection (1) of section 60 as it has effect in relation to a resolution under section 2 of that Act.

(3) A resolution under subsection (1) of section 61 shall be deemed to be a resolution under section 2 of the Children Act 1948 except that sections 2(2) to (7) and 4(3) of that Act shall not apply.

63.—(1) Subsections (2) to (5) and (7) of section 2 of the Children Act 1948 shall apply to a resolution under section 60 as they apply to a resolution under the said section 2, with the substitution for the reference in subsection (2) to the vesting of parental rights and duties in the local authority of a reference to the vesting of parental rights and duties in the voluntary organisation.

(2) An appeal may be made—

(*a*) where the complaint relates to a resolution under section 60, by a person deprived of parental rights and duties by the resolution, or

(*b*) where the complaint relates to a resolution under section 61, by a person who but for that resolution and an earlier resolution under section 60 would have parental rights and duties,

to a juvenile court having jurisdiction in the area of the authority which passed the resolution, on the ground that—

(i) there was no ground for the making of the resolution, or

(ii) that the resolution should in the interests of the child be determined.

(3) An appeal shall lie to the High Court against the decision of a juvenile court under this section.

1948 c. 43.   (4) Section 4B of the Children Act 1948 shall apply in relation to proceedings under this section.

Conflict of interest between parent and child

Addition of new sections to Children and Young Persons Act 1969.

1969 c. 54.

64. The following heading and sections are inserted after section 32 of the Children and Young Persons Act 1969—

" *Conflict of interest between parent and child or young person*

Conflict of interest between parent and child or young person.

32A.—(1) If before or in the course of proceedings in respect of a child or young person—

(*a*) in pursuance of section 1 of this Act, or

(*b*) on an application under section 15(1) of this Act for the discharge of a relevant supervision order or a supervision order made under section 21(2) of this Act on the discharge of a relevant care order ; or

(*c*) on an application under section 21(2) of this Act for the discharge of a relevant care order or a care order made under section 15(1) of this Act on the discharge of a relevant supervision order ; or

(*d*) on an appeal to the Crown Court under section 2(12) of this Act, or

(*e*) on an appeal to the Crown Court under section 16(8) of this Act against the dismissal of an application for the discharge of a relevant supervision order or against a care order made under section 15(1) on the discharge of—

(i) a relevant supervision order ; or

(ii) a supervision order made under section 21(2) on the discharge of a relevant care order ; or

(f) on an appeal to the Crown Court under section 21(4) of this Act against the dismissal of an application for the discharge of a relevant care order or against a supervision order made under section 21(2) on the discharge of—

(i) a relevant care order ; or

(ii) a care order made under section 15(1) on the discharge of a relevant supervision order,

it appears to the court that there is or may be a conflict, on any matter relevant to the proceedings, between the interests of the child or young person and those of his parent or guardian, the court may order that in relation to the proceedings the parent or guardian is not to be treated as representing the child or young person or as otherwise authorised to act on his behalf.

(2) If an application such as is referred to in subsection (1)(*b*) or (*c*) of this section is unopposed, the court, unless satisfied that to do so is not necessary for safeguarding the interests of the child or young person, shall order that in relation to proceedings on the application no parent or guardian of his shall be treated as representing him or as otherwise authorised to act on his behalf; but where the application was made by a parent or guardian on his behalf the order shall not invalidate the application.

(3) Where an order is made under subsection (1) or (2) of this section for the purposes of proceedings on an application within subsection (1)(*a*), (*b*) or (*c*) of this section, that order shall also have effect for the purposes of any appeal to the Crown Court arising out of those proceedings.

(4) The power of the court to make orders for the purposes of an application within subsection (1)(*a*), (*b*) or (*c*) of this section shall also be exercis-

able, before the hearing of the application, by a single justice.

(5) In this section—

" relevant care order " means a care order made under section 1 of this Act ;

" relevant supervision order " means a supervision order made under section 1 of this Act.

Safeguarding of interests of child or young person where section 32A order made.   32B.—(1) Where the court makes an order under section 32A(2) of this Act the court, unless satisfied that to do so is not necessary for safeguarding the interests of the child or young person, shall in accordance with rules of court appoint a guardian ad litem of the child or young person for the purposes of the proceedings.

In this subsection " court " includes a single justice.

(2) Rules of court shall provide for the appointment of a guardian ad litem of the child or young person for the purposes of any proceedings to which an order under section 32A(1) of this Act relates.

(3) A guardian ad litem appointed in pursuance of this section shall be under a duty to safeguard the interests of the child or young person in the manner prescribed by rules of court.".

Legal aid for parents where order made under new s. 32A of 1969 Act.

1974 c. 4.   **65.** In section 28 (power to order legal aid to be given) of the Legal Aid Act 1974—

(*a*) in subsection (1), for " subsections (3) and (6) " there is substituted " subsections (3), (6) and (6A) ", and

(*b*) the following subsection is inserted after subsection (6)—

" (6A) Where a court makes an order under section 32A of the Children and Young Persons Act 1969 affecting the parent or guardian of a person in relation to any proceedings, it may order that the parent or guardian shall be given legal aid for the purpose of taking such part in the proceedings as may be allowed by rules of court.

In this subsection " guardian " has the same meaning as in the Children and Young Persons Act 1933.".

66. In the Social Work (Scotland) Act 1968 the following section is inserted after section 34—

PART II
Safeguarding
of interests of
children before
children's
hearings etc.
in Scotland.
1968 c. 49.

"Safeguarding
of interests
of children
before
children's
hearings
etc.

34A.—(1) In any proceedings—

(*a*) before a children's hearing ;

(*b*) before the sheriff on an application under section 42(2)(*c*) of this Act ;

(*c*) before the sheriff on an appeal under section 49 or 51 of this Act,

the chairman (in the case of proceedings referred to in paragraph (*a*) above) or the sheriff (in any other case)—

(i) shall consider whether it is necessary for the purpose of safeguarding the interests of the child in the proceedings, because there is or may be a conflict, on any matter relevant to the proceedings, between the interests of the child and those of his parent, to appoint a person to act for that purpose ; and

(ii) without prejudice to any existing power to appoint a person to represent the interests of the child, may, if he thinks fit, appoint a person to act for the purpose specified in paragraph (i) above.

(2) The power to make rules under—

(*a*) section 35(4) of this Act,

(*b*) section 32 of the Sheriff Courts (Scotland) Act 1971,

shall include power to make rules providing for—

(i) the procedure in relation to the disposal of matters arising under this section ;

(ii) appointment under subsection (1) of this section, the functions of a person so appointed and any right of such a person to information relating to the proceedings in question.

(3) The expenses of a person appointed under subsection (1) of this section shall—

(*a*) in so far as reasonably incurred by him in safeguarding the interests of the child in the proceedings, and

(b) except in so far as otherwise defrayed in terms of regulations made under section 103(2) of the Children Act 1975,

be borne by the local authority for whose area the children's panel from which the relevant children's hearing has been constituted is formed.

(4) For the purposes of subsection (3) of this section, "relevant children's hearing" means—

(a) in the case of proceedings referred to in subsection (1)(a) of this section, the children's hearing;

(b) in the case of proceedings referred to in subsection (1)(b) of this section, the children's hearing who have directed the application;

(c) in the case of proceedings referred to in subsection (1)(c) of this section, the children's hearing whose decision is being appealed against.".

Absence from care and children in need of secure accommodation

Recovery of children in care of local authorities.

1948 c. 43.

1963 c. 37.

67.—(1) This section applies to a child—

(a) who is in the care of a local authority under section 1 of the Children Act 1948; and

(b) with respect to whom there is in force a resolution under section 2 of that Act; and

(c) who—

(i) has run away from accommodation provided for him by the local authority under Part II of the said Act; or

(ii) has been taken away from such accommodation contrary to section 3(8) of the said Act; or

(iii) has not been returned to the local authority as required by a notice served under section 49 of the Children and Young Persons Act 1963 on a person under whose charge and control the child was, in accordance with section 13(2) of the said Act of 1948, allowed to be.

(2) If a justice of the peace is satisfied by information on oath that there are reasonable grounds for believing that a person specified in the information can produce the child to whom this section applies, he may issue a summons directed to the person so specified and requiring him to attend and produce the child

PART III

(2) The conditions subject to which grants are made under subsection (1) of this section may include conditions for securing the repayment in whole or in part of such grants.

(3) In this section " secure accommodation " means accommodation provided for the purpose of restricting the liberty of children.".

Further amendments of Social Work (Scotland) Act 1968

Amendment of s. 15 of Social Work (Scotland) Act 1968.

1968 c. 49.

73. In section 15 of the Social Work (Scotland) Act 1968 the following subsections are inserted after subsection (3)—

" (3A) Subsection (8) (penalty for taking away a child in care etc.) of section 17 of this Act shall apply to a child in the care of a local authority under this section, notwithstanding that no resolution is in force under section 16 of this Act with respect to the child, if he has been in the care of that local authority throughout the preceding six months ; and for the purposes of the application of paragraph (b) of that subsection in such a case a parent or guardian of the child shall not be taken to have lawful authority to take him away :

Provided that that subsection shall not by virtue of this subsection apply in relation to an act done—

(a) with the consent of the local authority, or

(b) by a parent or guardian of the child who has given the local authority not less than 28 days' notice of his intention to do it.

(3B) The Secretary of State may by order, a draft of which has been approved by each House of Parliament, amend subsection (3A) of this section by substituting a different period for the period of 28 days or of six months mentioned in that subsection (or for the period which by a previous order under this subsection, was substituted for that period).".

Substitution of s. 16 of Social Work (Scotland) Act 1968.

74. The following section is substituted for section 16 of the Social Work (Scotland) Act 1968—

" Resolution by local authority in respect of assumption and vesting of parental rights and powers.

16.—(1) Subject to the provisions of this Part of this Act, a local authority may resolve—

(a) that there shall vest in them the relevant parental rights and powers with respect to any child who is in their care under section 15 of this Act ; or

(b) that there shall vest in a voluntary organisation which is an incorporated body, or a

before a magistrates' court acting for the same petty sessions area as the justice.

PART III

(3) Without prejudice to the powers under subsection (2) above, if a justice of the peace is satisfied by information on oath that there are reasonable grounds for believing that a child to whom this section applies is in premises specified in the information, he may issue a search warrant authorising a person named in the warrant, being an officer of the local authority in whose care the child is, to search the premises for the child ; and if the child is found, he shall be placed in such accommodation as the local authority may provide for him under Part II of the Children Act 1948.

1948 c. 43.

(4) A person who, without reasonable excuse, fails to comply with a summons under subsection (2) shall, without prejudice to any liability apart from this subsection, be guilty of an offence and liable on summary conviction to a fine not exceeding £100.

Extension of powers under section 32 of the Children and Young Persons Act 1969.

1969 c. 54.

68.—(1) Section 32 of the Children and Young Persons Act 1969 (detention of absentees) shall have effect subject to the following provisions of this section.

(2) In subsection (1) of the said section 32, paragraph (b) shall cease to have effect.

(3) After subsection (1) of the said section 32, there is inserted the following subsection :—

" (1A) If a child or young person is absent from a place of safety to which he has been taken in pursuance of section 2(5), 16(3) or 28 of this Act without the consent of—

(a) the person who made the arrangements for his detention in the place of safety in pursuance of the said section 2(5) or 16(3), or

(b) the person on whose application an authorisation relating to the child or young person has been issued under the said section 28,

he may be arrested by a constable anywhere in the United Kingdom or the Channel Islands without a warrant, and shall, if so arrested, be conducted to the place of safety at the expense of the person referred to in paragraph (a) or (b) (as the case may be) of this subsection.".

(4) In subsection (2) of the said section 32, after the words " subsection (1) " there are inserted the words " or (1A) ", and for the words " twenty pounds " there is substituted the word " £100 ".

PART III

(5) After the said subsection (2), the following subsections are inserted—

"(2A) Without prejudice to its powers under subsection (2) of this section, a magistrates' court (within the meaning of that subsection) may, if it is satisfied by information on oath that there are reasonable grounds for believing that a person who is absent as mentioned in subsection (1) or (1A) of this section is in premises specified in the information, issue a search warrant authorising a constable to search the premises for that person.

(2B) A court shall not issue a summons or search warrant under subsection (2) or (2A) of this section in any case where the person who is absent is a person to whom subsection (1A) of this section applies, unless the information referred to in the said subsection (2) or (2A) is given by the person referred to in subsection (1A)(*a*) or (*b*) (as the case may be) of this section.".

(6) In subsection (3) of the said section 32, for the words "one hundred pounds" there is substituted the word "£400".

(7) In subsection (4) of the said section 32, for the words "subsection (1)" there are substituted the words "subsections (1), (1A) and (2A)", and for the words "that subsection" there are substituted the words "subsection (1).".

Certificates of unruly character. 1969 c. 54.

69. The court shall not certify under section 22(5) or section 23(2) or (3) of the Children and Young Persons Act 1969 (committals to remand centres or prison) that a child is of so unruly a character that he cannot safely be committed to the care of a local authority unless the conditions prescribed by order made by the Secretary of State are satisfied in relation to that child.

In this section, "court" includes a justice.

Children of unruly character in Scotland. 1975 c. 21.

70. The following provisions of the Criminal Procedure (Scotland) Act 1975 (which relate to children of unruly character) shall be amended in the manner specified in paragraphs (*a*) to (*c*) below—

(*a*) in sections 23(1)(*b*), 24(1), 297(1) and 329(1)(*b*) of the said Act of 1975 the following words are added at the end—

"; but the court shall not so certify a child unless such conditions as the Secretary of State may by order made by statutory instrument prescribe are satisfied in relation to the child.";

(*b*) in sections 23(3) and 329(3) of the said Act of 1975 the following words are added at the end—

"; but a commitment shall not be so revoked unless such conditions as the Secretary of State may

by order made by statutory instrument prescribe are satisfied in relation to the said person.";

(*c*) in sections 24(2) and 297(2) of the said Act of 1975 the following words are added at the end—

"; but a commitment shall not be so revoked unless such conditions as the Secretary of State may by order made by statutory instrument prescribe are satisfied in relation to the child.".

Grants in respect of secure accommodation for children in England and Wales. 1969 c. 54.

71. The following section is inserted after section 64 of the Children and Young Persons Act 1969—

"Grants in respect of secure accommodation.

64A.—(1) The Secretary of State may make to local authorities out of moneys provided by Parliament grants of such amount and subject to such conditions as he may with the consent of the Treasury determine in respect of expenditure incurred by the authorities in providing secure accommodation in community homes other than assisted community homes.

(2) The Secretary of State may with the consent of the Treasury require the local authority to repay the grant, in whole or in part, if the secure accommodation in respect of which the grant was made (including such accommodation in a controlled community home) ceases to be used as such.

(3) In this section "secure accommodation" means accommodation provided for the purposes of restricting the liberty of children in a community home.".

Grants in respect of secure accommodation for children in Scotland. 1968 c. 4

72. The following section is inserted after section 59 of the Social Work (Scotland) Act 1968—

"Grants in respect of secure accommodation for children.

59A.—(1) The Secretary of State may make to a local authority grants of such amount and subject to such conditions as he may with the consent of the Treasury determine in respect of expenditure incurred by the authority in—

(*a*) providing;

(*b*) joining with another local authority in providing; or

(*c*) contributing by way of grant under section 10(3) of this Act to the provision by a voluntary organisation of,

secure accommodation in residential establishments.

trust within the meaning of section 2(*a*) of the Trusts (Scotland) Act 1921, the relevant parental rights and powers with respect to any child who is in the care of that organisation,

if it appears to the local authority—

(i) that the parents of the child are dead and that he has no guardian ; or

(ii) that there exists in respect of a parent or guardian of the child (the said parent or guardian being hereafter in this Part of this Act referred to as the person on whose account the resolution was passed) any of the circumstances specified in subsection (2) of this section ; or

(iii) that a resolution under this subsection is in force in terms of sub-paragraph (ii) above in relation to one parent of the child and that parent is, or is likely to become, a member of the household comprising the child and his other parent ; or

(iv) that throughout the three years preceding the passing of the resolution the child has been in the care of a local authority under section 15 of this Act, or in the care of a voluntary organisation or partly the one and partly the other.

(2) The circumstances referred to in sub-paragraph (ii) of subsection (1) of this section are that the person on whose account the resolution was passed—

(*a*) has abandoned the child ; or

(*b*) suffers from some permanent disability rendering him incapable of caring for the child ; or

(*c*) while not falling within paragraph (*b*) of this subsection, suffers from a mental disorder (within the meaning of the Mental Health (Scotland) Act 1960) which renders him unfit to have the care of the child ; or

(*d*) is of such habits or mode of life as to be unfit to have the care of the child ; or

(*e*) has so persistently failed without reasonable cause to discharge the obligations of a parent or guardian as to be unfit to have the care of the child.

(3) In this section " the relevant parental rights and powers " means all the rights and powers in relation to the child (other than the right to consent or refuse to consent to the making of an application under section 14 or 25 of the Children Act 1975 and the right to agree or refuse to agree to the making of an adoption order)—

> (*a*) where the resolution was passed by virtue of circumstances specified in sub-paragraph (i) of subsection (1) of this section, which the deceased parents would have if they were still living ;
>
> (*b*) where the resolution was passed by virtue of circumstances specified in sub-paragraph (ii) of that subsection, of the person on whose account the resolution was passed ;
>
> (*c*) where the resolution was passed by virtue of circumstances specified in sub-paragraph (iii) of that subsection, of the parent other than the one on whose account the previous resolution was passed ;
>
> (*d*) where the resolution was passed by virtue of circumstances specified in sub-paragraph (iv) of that subsection, of the parents or guardian of the child.

(4) A local authority shall not pass a resolution under paragraph (*b*) of subsection (1) of this section unless—

> (*a*) it is satisfied that the child is not in the care of any local authority under any enactment ; and
>
> (*b*) it is satisfied that it is necessary in the interests of the welfare of the child for the parental rights and powers to be vested in the voluntary organisation ; and
>
> (*c*) the child is living in the area of the local authority either in a residential establishment or with foster parents with whom he has been boarded out by the voluntary organisation in whose care he is ; and
>
> (*d*) that organisation has requested the local authority to pass the resolution.

(5) In the case of a resolution passed under subsection (1) of this section by virtue of circumstances specified in sub-paragraph (ii), (iii) or (iv) thereof, unless the person whose parental rights and powers

have under the resolution vested in the local autho- rity or in the voluntary organisation as the case may be, has consented in writing to the passing of the resolution, the local authority, if that person's where- abouts are known to them, shall forthwith after the passing of the resolution serve on him notice in writ- ing of the passing thereof.

(6) Every notice served by a local authority under subsection (5) of this section shall inform the person on whom the notice is served of his right to object to the resolution and of the effect of any objection made by him.

(7) If, not later than one month after notice is served on a person under subsection (5) of this section, he serves a counter-notice in writing on the local authority objecting to the resolution, the reso- lution shall, subject to the provisions of subsection (8) of this section, lapse on the expiry of fourteen days from the service of the counter-notice.

(8) Where a counter-notice has been served on a local authority under subsection (7) of this section, the authority may, not later than fourteen days after the receipt by them of the counter-notice, make a summary application in respect thereto to the sheriff having jurisdiction in the area of the autho- rity, and in that event the resolution shall not lapse until the determination of the application ; and the sheriff may, on the hearing of the application, order that the resolution shall not lapse by reason of the service of the counter-notice:

Provided that the sheriff shall not so order unless satisfied—

(a) that it is in the interests of the child to do so ; and

(b) that the grounds mentioned in subsection (1) of this section on which the local authority purported to pass the resolution were made out ; and

(c) that at the time of the hearing there continued to be grounds on which a resolution under subsection (1) of this section could be founded.

(9) While a resolution passed under subsection (1) of this section by virtue of circumstances specified in sub-paragraph (ii), (iii) or (iv) thereof is in force with respect to a child, that part of subsection (3) of

section 15 of this Act from the words " and nothing in this section shall authorise " onwards shall not apply in relation to the person who, but for the resolution, would have the relevant parental rights and powers in relation to the child.

(10) Any notice under this section (including a counter-notice) may be served by post, but a notice served by a local authority under subsection (5) of this section shall not be duly served by post unless it is sent by registered post or recorded delivery service.

(11) A resolution under this section shall cease to have effect if—

    (*a*) the child becomes the subject of an adoption order within the meaning of Schedule 2 to the Children Act 1975 ; or

    (*b*) an order in respect of the child is made under section 14 or section 25 of the Children Act 1975 ; or

    (*c*) a person is appointed, under section 4(2A) of the Guardianship of Infants Act 1925, to be the guardian of the child ; or

    (*d*) it is a resolution under paragraph (*b*) of subsection (1) of this section and a resolution is passed under subsection (1) of section 16A of this Act in respect of the child.

(12) If the whereabouts of any parent or guardian of a child have remained unknown for twelve months, and throughout that period the child has been in the care of a local authority under section 15 of this Act, or in the care of a voluntary organisation, or partly the one and partly the other, then for the purposes of this section that parent or guardian shall be deemed to have abandoned the child.

(13) The Secretary of State may by order, a draft of which has been approved by each House of Parliament, amend sub-paragraph (iv) of subsection (1) of this section to substitute a different period for the period of three years mentioned in that sub-paragraph (or for the period which, by a previous order under this subsection, was substituted for that period).".

75. The following section is inserted after section 16 of the Social Work (Scotland) Act 1968—

PART III
Duty of local authority in Scotland to assume parental rights and powers vested in a voluntary organisation.
1968 c. 49.

" Duty of local authority to assume parental rights and powers vested in a voluntary organisation.

16A.—(1) If it appears to a local authority, having regard to the interests of the welfare of a child living within their area, the parental rights and powers in respect of whom are by virtue of a resolution under section 16(1)(*b*) of this Act (hereafter in this section referred to as " the earlier resolution ") vested in a voluntary organisation, that it is necessary that the said parental rights and powers should no longer be vested in the organisation, the local authority shall resolve that the said parental rights and powers shall vest in them ; and the said parental rights and powers shall so vest from the date of the resolution under this subsection.

(2) The local authority shall, within seven days of passing a resolution under subsection (1) of this section, by notice in writing inform—

(*a*) the organisation who but for that resolution ; and

(*b*) any person, in so far as that person's whereabouts are known to them, who, but for that resolution and the earlier resolution,

would have the parental rights and powers in respect of the child, of the passing thereof.

(3) On a summary application being made for the determining of a resolution under subsection (1) of this section by a person who but for that resolution and the earlier resolution would have the parental rights and powers in respect of the child, the sheriff having jurisdiction where the applicant resides may order that—

(*a*) the resolution under subsection (1) of this section shall continue to have effect ; or

(*b*) the resolution under subsection (1) of this section shall cease to have effect and that the earlier resolution shall again take effect ; or

(*c*) the resolution under subsection (1) of this section shall cease to have effect and that the parental rights and powers in respect of the child shall again vest in the applicant ; or

(*d*) the resolution under subsection (1) of this section shall continue to have effect, but

C

that either for a fixed period or until the sheriff, or if the order so provides, the local authority, otherwise directs, the local authority shall allow the care of the child to be taken over by, and the child to be under the control of, the applicant.

(4) In hearing an application under subsection (3) of this section the sheriff may consider whether there was any ground for the making of the earlier resolution, and if he is satisfied that there was no ground for the making of that earlier resolution he shall make an order under subsection (3)(*c*) of this section.

(5) In this section "the parental rights and powers" means all the rights and powers in relation to the child which in accordance with the earlier resolution were vested in the voluntary organisation.

(6) While a resolution under subsection (1) of this section is in force with respect to a child, the child shall be deemed to have been received into and to be in the care of the local authority by virtue of section 15 of this Act, and subsections (2) to (5) of that section shall apply accordingly ; except that where the earlier resolution was passed by virtue of circumstances specified in sub-paragraph (ii), (iii) or (iv) of subsection (1) of section 16 of this Act, that part of subsection (3) of section 15 of this Act from the words " and nothing in this section shall authorise " onwards shall not apply in relation to the person who but for the earlier resolution and the resolution under subsection (1) of this section, would have the parental rights and powers in relation to the child.

(7) Subsection (11)(*a*), (*b*) and (*c*) of section 16, subsections (3) and (4) to (9) of section 17 and subsections (1), (2), (4) and (4A) of section 18 of this Act shall apply to a resolution under this section as they apply to a resolution under section 16(1)(*a*) of this Act.

(8) A notice served by a local authority under subsection (2) of this section shall not be duly served by post unless it is sent by registered post or recorded delivery service.".

76. In section 17 of the Social Work (Scotland) Act 1968 (effect of assumption of parental rights) the following subsection is inserted after subsection (9)—

> " (10) Where an offence under subsection (8) or (9) of this section has been or is believed to have been committed, a constable, or any person authorised by any court or by any justice of the peace, may take and return the child to the local authority or voluntary organisation in whom are vested the parental rights and powers relating to the child.".

PART III

Return of children taken away in breach of section 17(8) or (9) of Social Work (Scotland) Act 1968.

1968 c. 49.

77. In section 18 of the Social Work (Scotland) Act 1968 the following subsection is inserted after subsection (4)—

> " (4A) A court may entertain an application under—
>
> > (*a*) section 8 of the Children Act 1975 for an adoption order in respect of a child ;
> >
> > (*b*) section 14 of the Children Act 1975 for an order declaring a child free for adoption ;
> >
> > (*c*) section 25 of the Children Act 1975 for an order vesting the parental rights and duties relating to a child ;
>
> notwithstanding that, by virtue of a resolution under section 16 of this Act, a local authority or a voluntary organisation have parental rights with respect to him.".

78. In the Social Work (Scotland) Act 1968 the following section is inserted after section 18—

> " Safeguard-
> ing of
> interests of
> children in
> proceedings
> relating to
> the assump-
> tion of
> parental
> rights.
>
> 18A.—(1) In any proceedings under section 16(8), 16A(3) or 18(3) of this Act, the sheriff—
>
> > (*a*) shall consider whether it is necessary to appoint a person for the purpose of safe-guarding the interests of the child in the proceedings ; and
> >
> > (*b*) without prejudice to any existing power to appoint a person to represent the interests of the child, may, if he thinks fit, appoint a person to act for the purpose specified in paragraph (*a*) above.
>
> (2) The power to make rules under section 32 of the Sheriff Courts (Scotland) Act 1971 shall include power to make rules providing for—
>
> > (*a*) the procedure in relation to the disposal of matters arising under this section ;
> >
> > (*b*) appointment under subsection (1) of this section, the functions of a person so appointed

Safeguarding of interests of children in proceedings in Scotland relating to the assumption of parental rights.

1971 c. 58.

and any right of such a person to information relating to the proceedings in question.".

Amendment of section 20 of Social Work (Scotland) Act. 1968 c. 49.

79. The following subsection is substituted for subsection (1) of section 20 of the Social Work (Scotland) Act 1968—

" (1) Where a child is in the care of a local authority under any enactment, the local authority shall, in reaching any decision relating to the child, give first consideration to the need to safeguard and promote the welfare of the child throughout his childhood ; and shall so far as practicable ascertain the wishes and feelings of the child regarding the decision and give due consideration to them, having regard to his age and understanding.".

Review of case of child in care in Scotland.

80. In the Social Work (Scotland) Act 1968 the following section is inserted after section 20—

" Review of case of child in care.

20A.—(1) Without prejudice to their general duty under section 20(1) of this Act, it shall be the duty of a local authority who have at any time had a child in their care throughout the preceding six months and have not during that period held a review of his case, to review his case as soon as is practicable after the expiration of that period and, if a supervision requirement is in force with respect to him, the local authority shall consider in the course of the review whether to refer his case to their reporter for review of that requirement by a children's hearing.

(2) The Secretary of State may by regulations—

　(*a*) amend subsection (1) of this section by—

　　　(i) substituting a different period for the period of six months mentioned in that subsection (or for any period which, by previous regulations under this subsection, was substituted for that period) ;

　　　(ii) specifying different periods in respect of the first review under that subsection occurring after a child has been taken into care, and in respect of subsequent such reviews ;

　(*b*) make provision as to the manner in which cases are to be reviewed under this section ;

　(*c*) make provision as to the considerations to which the local authority are to have regard in reviewing cases under this section.".

81. The following section is inserted after section 25 of the Social Work (Scotland) Act 1968—

"*Restriction on removal of child from care of voluntary organisation.*" 25A.—(1) Section 17(8) of this Act shall apply in relation to a child who is not in the care of a local authority under section 15 of this Act but who is in the care of a voluntary organisation, as it applies by virtue of subsection (3A) of the said section 15 to a child in the care of a local authority except that, in the case of a child who is not in the care of a local authority, references in subsection (3A) to a local authority shall be construed as references to the voluntary organisation in whose care the child is.

(2) For the purposes of this section, a child is in the care of a voluntary organisation if the voluntary organisation is providing accommodation for the child in a residential establishment or has boarded out the child.".

PART III
Restriction on removal of child from care of voluntary organisation.
1968 c. 49.

82. The following section is inserted after section 36 of the Social Work (Scotland) Act 1968—

"*Power of reporters to conduct proceedings before a sheriff.*" 36A. The Secretary of State and the Lord Advocate may, by regulations—

(*a*) empower officers or any officer or class of officers appointed under section 36 of this Act, whether or not they are advocates or solicitors, to conduct before a sheriff—

(i) any proceedings which, under this Act are heard by the sheriff in chambers;

(ii) any application under section 37 or 40 of this Act in relation to a warrant;

(*b*) prescribe such requirements as they think fit as to qualifications, training or experience necessary for any officer to be so empowered.".

Power of reporters to conduct proceedings under the Social Work (Scotland) Act 1968.

83. In section 37 of the Social Work (Scotland) Act 1968—

(*a*) the following subsection is inserted after subsection (1)—

" (1A) Where a local authority receive information suggesting that a child may be in need of compulsory measures of care, they shall—

(*a*) cause enquiries to be made into the case unless they are satisfied that such enquiries are unnecessary; and

Amendment of section 37 of Social Work (Scotland) Act 1968.

C 3

    (*b*) if it appears to them that the child may be in need of compulsory measures of care, give to the reporter such information about the child as they may have been able to discover.";

(*b*) for subsection (2) there is substituted—

    " (2) A constable or any person authorised by any court or by any justice of the peace may take to a place of safety any child—

    (*a*) in respect of whom any of the offences mentioned in Schedule 1 to the Criminal Procedure (Scotland) Act 1975 has been or is believed to have been committed ; or

    (*b*) who is a member of the same household as a child in respect of whom such an offence has been or is believed to have been committed ; or

    (*c*) who is, or is likely to become, a member of the same household as a person who has committed or is believed to have committed such an offence ; or

    (*d*) in respect of whom an offence under section 21(1) of the Children and Young Persons (Scotland) Act 1937 has been or is believed to have been committed ; or

    (*e*) who is likely to be caused unnecessary suffering or serious impairment of health because there is, or is believed to be, in respect of the child a lack of parental care,

and any child so taken to a place of safety or any child who has taken refuge in a place of safety may be detained there until arrangements can be made for him to be brought before a children's hearing under the following provisions of this Part of this Act ; and, where a child is so detained, the constable or the person authorised as aforesaid or the occupier of the place of safety shall forthwith inform the reporter of the case." ;

(*c*) in subsection (5), after " renewed " there is inserted " by a children's hearing " ;

(d) the following subsections are inserted after subsection
(5)—

" (5A) Where a warrant has been renewed under subsection (5) of this section but it appears to the reporter—

(a) that the children's hearing will not be able to dispose of the child's case before the expiry of the period of detention required by the warrant as renewed ; and

(b) that further detention of the child is necessary in the child's own interest,

the reporter may apply to the sheriff for a warrant requiring the child to be detained in a place of safety for such a period not exceeding twenty-one days as may be necessary and the sheriff may issue such a warrant if he is satisfied that such detention is necessary in the child's own interest.

(5B) On cause shown a warrant authorising detention under subsection (5A) of this section may be renewed by the sheriff on one occasion only, for the period mentioned in that subsection on the application of the reporter.".

84. In section 40 of the Social Work (Scotland) Act 1968—
    (a) for subsection (7) there is substituted—
      " (7) Where a children's hearing before whom a child is brought are unable to dispose of his case and—

Amendment of section 40 of Social Work (Scotland) Act 1968.
1968 c. 49.

(a) have reason to believe that the child may not attend at any hearing of his case, or at any proceedings arising from the case or may fail to comply with a requirement under section 43(4) of this Act ; or

(b) are satisfied that detention of the child is necessary in his own interest,

they may issue a warrant requiring the child to be detained in a place of safety for such a period not exceeding twenty-one days as may be necessary." ;

    (b) for subsection (8) there is substituted—
      " (8) On cause shown a warrant authorising detention under subsection (7) of this section may be renewed by a children's hearing on one occasion only, for the

period mentioned in that subsection, on the application of the reporter." ;

(*c*) the following subsections are inserted after subsection (8)—

" (8A) Where a warrant has been renewed under subsection (8) of this section but it appears to the reporter—

(*a*) that the children's hearing will not be able to dispose of the child's case before the expiry of the period of detention required by the warrant as renewed ; and

(*b*) that further detention of the child is necessary in the child's own interest,

the reporter may apply to the sheriff for a warrant requiring the child to be detained in a place of safety for such a period not exceeding twenty-one days as may be necessary, and the sheriff may issue such a warrant if he is satisfied that such detention is necessary in the child's own interest.

(8B) On cause shown, a warrant authorising detention under subsection (8A) of this section may be renewed by the sheriff on one occasion only, for the period mentioned in that subsection, on the application of the reporter.".

PART IV

FURTHER AMENDMENTS
OF LAW OF ENGLAND AND WALES

Explanation of concepts

Parental rights and duties.

85.—(1) In this Act, unless the context otherwise requires, " the parental rights and duties " means as respects a particular child (whether legitimate or not), all the rights and duties which by law the mother and father have in relation to a legitimate child and his property ; and references to a parental right or duty shall be construed accordingly and shall include a right of access and any other element included in a right or duty.

1973 c. 29.

(2) Subject to section 1(2) of the Guardianship Act 1973 (which relates to separation agreements between husband and wife), a person cannot surrender or transfer to another any parental right or duty he has as respects a child.

(3) Where two or more persons have a parental right or duty jointly, any one of them may exercise or perform it in any manner without the other or others if the other or, as the case may be, one or more of the others have not signified disapproval of its exercise or performance in that manner.

(4) From the death of a person who has a parental right or duty jointly with one other person, or jointly with two or more other persons, that other person has the right or duty exclusively or, as the case may be, those other persons have it jointly.

(5) Where subsection (4) does not apply on the death of a person who has a parental right or duty, that right or duty lapses, but without prejudice to its acquisition by another person at any time under any enactment.

(6) Subsections (4) and (5) apply in relation to the dissolution of a body corporate as they apply in relation to the death of an individual.

(7) Except as otherwise provided by or under any enactment, while the mother of an illegitimate child is living she has the parental rights and duties exclusively.

86. In this Act, unless the context otherwise requires, " legal custody " means, as respects a child, so much of the parental rights and duties as relate to the person of the child (including the place and manner in which his time is spent) ; but a person shall not by virtue of having legal custody of a child be entitled to effect or arrange for his emigration from the United Kingdom unless he is a parent or guardian of the child.

Legal custody.

87.—(1) A person has actual custody of a child if he has actual possession of his person, whether or not that possession is shared with one or more other persons.

Actual custody.

(2) While a person not having legal custody of a child has actual custody of the child he has the like duties in relation to the child as a custodian would have by virtue of his legal custody.

(3) In this Act, unless the context otherwise requires, references to the person with whom a child has his home refer to the person who, disregarding absence of the child at a hospital or boarding school and any other temporary absence, has actual custody of the child.

88. A child is in the care of a voluntary organisation if—
    (*a*) the organisation has actual custody of him, or
    (*b*) having had actual custody of him, the organisation has transferred that custody to an individual who does not have legal custody of him.

Child in care of voluntary organisation.

PART IV
Amendment of
Interpretation
Act 1889.
1889 c. 63.

"Meaning of
expressions
relating to
children.

89.—(1) In the Interpretation Act 1889 after section 19 there is inserted the following section—

19A.—(1) In any Act passed after the Children Act 1975, unless the contrary intention appears—

> (a) the expression "the parental rights and duties",
>
> (b) the expression "legal custody" (as respects a child), and
>
> (c) references to the person with whom a child has his home,

shall be construed in accordance with Part IV of the Children Act 1975.

(2) This section does not extend to Scotland or Northern Ireland."

Reports in guardianship and matrimonial proceedings

Procedure in
guardianship
proceedings.
1973 c. 29.

90.—(1) The following subsections are substituted for subsections (2) and (3) of section 6 of the Guardianship Act 1973:—

> "(2) A report made in pursuance of subsection (1) above to a magistrates' court shall be made to the court at a hearing of the application unless it is in writing in which case—
>
> > (a) a copy of the report shall be given to each party to the proceedings or to his counsel or solicitor either before or during a hearing of the application; and
> >
> > (b) if the court thinks fit, the report, or such part of the report as the court requires, shall be read aloud at a hearing of the application.
>
> (3) A magistrates' court may and, if requested to do so at the hearing by a party to the proceedings or his counsel or solicitor, shall, require the officer by whom the report was made to give evidence of or with respect to the matters referred to in the report and if the officer gives such evidence, any party to the proceedings may give or call evidence with respect to any such matter or any matter referred to in the officer's evidence.
>
> (3A) A magistrates' court may take account of—
>
> > (a) any statement contained in a report made at a hearing of the application or of which copies have been given to the parties or their representatives in accordance with subsection (2)(a) above; and

(*b*) any evidence given by the officer under PART IV
subsection (3) above,

in so far as the statement or evidence is, in the
opinion of the court, relevant to the application, notwithstanding any enactment or rule of law to the
contrary.".

(2) The following subsection is added after subsection (5) of
the said section 6—

" (6) A single justice may request a report under
subsection (1) of this section before the hearing of
the application, but in such a case the report shall
be made to the court which hears the application, and
the foregoing provisions of this section shall apply
accordingly.".

91.—(1) The following subsections are substituted for sub- Procedure in
sections (3) and (4) of section 4 of the Matrimonial Proceedings matrimonial
(Magistrates' Courts) Act 1960— proceedings.

1960 c. 48.

" (3) A report made in pursuance of subsection
(2) of this section shall be made to the court at a
hearing of the complaint unless it is in writing in
which case—

(*a*) a copy of the report shall be given to each
party to the proceedings or to his counsel
or solicitor either before or during a hearing
of the complaint ; and

(*b*) if the court thinks fit, the report, or such
parts of the report as the court requires,
shall be read aloud at a hearing of the
complaint.

(4) The court may and, if requested to do so at the
hearing by a party to the proceedings or his counsel
or solicitor, shall, require the officer by whom the
report was made to give evidence on or with respect
to the matters referred to in the report and if the
officer gives such evidence, any party to the proceedings may give or call evidence on or with respect
to any such matter or any matter referred to in the
officer's evidence.

(4A) Subject to the next following subsection, the
court may take account of—

(*a*) any statement contained in a report made at
a hearing of the complaint or of which
copies have been given to the parties or
their representatives in accordance with
subsection (3)(*a*) of this section ; and

(*b*) any evidence given by the officer under sub-section (4) of this section,

in so far as the statement or evidence relates to the matters specified by the court under subsection (2) of this section, notwithstanding any enactment or rule of law to the contrary.".

(2) In subsection (5) of the said section 4, for " subsection (4) " there is substituted " subsections (4) and (4A) ".

Registration of births

Registration
of births of
abandoned
children.

1953 c. 20.

92. The following section is inserted after section 3 of the Births and Deaths Registration Act 1953—

" Registra-
tion of
births of
abandoned
children.

3A.—(1) Where the place and date of birth of a child who was abandoned are unknown to, and cannot be ascertained by, the person who has charge of the child, that person may apply to the Registrar General for the child's birth to be registered under this section.

(2) On an application under this section the Registrar General shall enter in a register maintained at the General Register Office—

(*a*) as the child's place of birth, if the child was found by the applicant or by any person from whom (directly or indirectly) the applicant took charge of the child, the registration district and sub-district where the child was found, or, in any other case, where the child was abandoned ;

(*b*) as the child's date of birth, the date which, having regard to such evidence as is pro-duced to him, appears to him to be the most likely date of birth of the child, and

(*c*) such other particulars as may be prescribed.

(3) The Registrar General shall not register a child's birth under this section if—

(*a*) he is satisfied that the child was not born in England or Wales ; or

· (*b*) the child has been adopted in pursuance of a court order made in the United Kingdom, the Isle of Man or the Channel Islands ; or

(*c*) subject to subsection (5) below, the child's birth is known to have been previously registered under this Act.

(4) If no entry can be traced in any register of births relating to a person who has attained the age

of 18 and has not been adopted as aforesaid, that person may apply to the Registrar General for his birth to be registered under this section.

(5) On the application of—

>(a) a person having the charge of a child whose birth had been registered under this Act by virtue of the proviso to section 1 of this Act (as originally enacted), or

>(b) any such child who has attained the age of 18 years,

the Registrar General shall re-register the birth of the child under this section, and shall direct the officer having custody of the register of births in which the entry relating to the child was previously made to enter in the margin of the register a reference to the re-registration of the birth."

93.—(1) At the end of paragraph (b) of section 10 of the Births and Deaths Registration Act of 1953 (which makes provision for the registration of fathers of illegitimate children) there is added " or

>Registration of father of illegitimate child.
>1953 c. 20.

>(c) at the request of the mother (which shall be made in writing) on production of—

>>(i) a certified copy of an order made under section 4 of the Affiliation Proceedings Act 1957 naming that person as the putative father of the child, and

>1957 c. 55.

>>(ii) if the child has attained the age of 16 years, the written consent of the child to the registration of that person as his father."

(2) After the said section 10 there is inserted the following section—

>" Re-registration of births of illegitimate children.

10A.—(1) Where the birth of an illegitimate child has been registered under this Act but no person has been registered as the child's father, the registrar shall re-register the birth so as to show a person as the father—

>(a) at the joint request of the mother and of that person ; or

>(b) at the request of the mother on production of—

>>(i) a declaration in the prescribed form made by the mother stating that that person is the father of the child ; and

(ii) a statutory declaration made by that person acknowledging himself to be the father of the child ; or

(c) at the request of the mother (which shall be made in writing) on production of—

(i) a certified copy of an order made under section 4 of the Affiliation Proceedings Act 1957 naming that person as the putative father of that child, and

(ii) if the child has attained the age of 16 years, the written consent of the child to the registration of that person as his father ;

but no birth shall be re-registered under this section except in the prescribed manner and with the authority of the Registrar General.

(2) On the re-registration of a birth under this section—

(a) the registrar and the mother shall sign the register ;

(b) in the case of a request under paragraph (a) of subsection (1) of this section, the other person making the request shall also sign the register ; and

(c) if the re-registration takes place more than three months after the birth, the superintendent registrar shall also sign the register.".

(3) In section 9 of the said Act of 1953 (which enables information required to be given to the registrar to be given to other persons) after subsection (3) there are added the following subsections—

" (4) A request made under section 10 of this Act may be included in a declaration under subsection (1) of this section, and, if the request is made under paragraph (b) or (c) of that section, the documents required by that paragraph to be produced shall be produced to the officer in whose presence the declaration is made and sent by him with the declaration to the registrar.

(5) A request made under section 10A of this Act instead of being made to the registrar may be made by making and signing in the presence of and delivering to a prescribed officer a statement in the prescribed form and producing to the officer any documents required to be produced by that section, and—

(a) the officer shall send the request together with those documents, if any, to the

registrar who shall with the authority of the
Registrar General re-register the birth as
if the request had been made to him ; and

(*b*) the person or persons who sign the statement shall be deemed to have signed the
register as required by subsection (2) of that
section.".

Extent of Part IV

94. This Part does not extend to Scotland.

PART V

MISCELLANEOUS AND SUPPLEMENTAL

Foster children

95.—(1) In section 1 of the Children Act 1958 (visiting of
foster children), the words " so far as appears to the authority
to be appropriate " shall cease to have effect, and for the words
" from time to time " there are substituted the words " in accordance with regulations made under section 2A of this Act ".

(2) In section 1A of the Children Act 1958 (visiting of foster
children in Scotland) the words " where the local authority consider such a course to be necessary or expedient for the purposes
of this section," shall cease to have effect, and for the words
" from time to time " there are substituted the words " in
accordance with regulations made under section 2A of this
Act.".

(3) The following section is inserted in the said Act after
section 2—

  2A.—(1) The Secretary of State may make regulations requiring foster children in a local authority's
area to be visited by an officer of the local authority
on specified occasions or within specified periods of
time.

(2) Every person who is maintaining a foster child
within the area of a local authority on the date on
which regulations made under subsection (1) of this
section come into operation, and who before that date
has not given notice in respect of the child to the
local authority under section 3(1) of this Act, shall
within eight weeks of that date give written notice
that he is maintaining the child to the local authority.

(3) Regulations under this section shall be made by statutory instrument which shall be subject to annulment in pursuance of a resolution of either House of Parliament.".

(4) In section 3 of the said Act, as it applies to England and Wales, (duty of persons maintaining foster children to notify local authority)—

(*a*) in subsection (5A), for the words " one or more foster children " there are substituted the words " a foster child ", and for the words " foster children " and " any foster children " there are substituted the words " that foster child " ;

(*b*) in subsection (5B) for the words " foster children " there are substituted the words " a foster child ", and for the words " any of them as a " there is substituted the word " that " ; and

(*c*) the following subsection is added at the end—

" (8) Subsection (2A) of this section shall cease to have effect on the date regulations made under section 2A of this Act come into operation.".

Notification by parents.
1958 c. 65.

96.—(1) The following section is inserted in the Children Act 1958 after section 3—

" Notification by parents.

3A.—(1) The Secretary of State may by regulations made by statutory instrument make provision for requiring parents whose children are or are going to be maintained as foster children to give to the local authority for the area where the children are, or are going to be, living as foster children, such information about the fostering as may be specified in the regulations.

(2) Regulations under this section—

(*a*) may include such incidental and supplementary provisions as the Secretary of State thinks fit ;

(*b*) shall be subject to annulment in pursuance of a resolution of either House of Parliament.".

(2) In section 14 of the said Act (offences), in subsection (1)(*a*), after the words " this Part of this Act " there are inserted the words " or under regulations made under section 3A of this Act ".

97.—(1) In section 37 of the Children Act 1958 the following subsections are inserted after subsection (1)—

PART V

Advertisements relating to foster children.

1958 c. 65.

" (1A) The Secretary of State may by regulations prohibit the parent or guardian of any child from publishing or causing to be published an advertisement indicating that foster parents are sought for the child.

(1B) The Secretary of State may by regulations prohibit—

(*a*) a member of a class of persons specified in the regulations, or

(*b*) a person other than a person, or other than a member of a class of persons, specified in the regulations,

from publishing or causing to be published any advertisement indicating that he is willing to undertake, or to arrange for, the care and maintenance of a child.

(1C) Regulations made under this section—

(*a*) may make different provision for different cases or classes of cases, and

(*b*) may exclude certain cases or classes of cases,

and shall be made by statutory instrument subject to annulment in pursuance of a resolution of either House of Parliament.".

(2) In subsection (2) of the said section 37, after the words " this section " there are inserted the words " or of regulations made under this section ".

Inquiries

98.—(1) The Secretary of State may cause an inquiry to be held into any matter relating to—

Inquiries in England and Wales.

(*a*) the functions of the social services committee of a local authority, in so far as those functions relate to children ;

(*b*) the functions of an adoption agency ;

(*c*) the functions of a voluntary organisation in so far as those functions relate to voluntary homes ;

(*d*) a home maintained by the Secretary of State for the accommodation of children who are in the care of local authorities and are in need of the particular facilities and services provided in the home ;

(*e*) the detention of a child under section 53 of the Children and Young Persons Act 1933.

1933 c. 12.

PART V

(2) The Secretary of State may, before an inquiry is commenced, direct that it shall be held in private, but where no such direction has been given, the person holding the inquiry may if he thinks fit hold it or any part of it in private.

1972 c. 70.

(3) Subsections (2) to (5) of section 250 of the Local Government Act 1972 (powers in relation to local inquiries) shall apply in relation to an inquiry under this section as they apply in relation to a local inquiry under that section.

(4) In this section—

" functions " includes powers and duties which a person has otherwise than by virtue of any enactment ;

" voluntary home " means a home or other institution for the boarding, care and maintenance of poor children which is supported wholly or partly by voluntary contributions, but does not include a mental nursing home or residential home for mentally disordered persons within the meaning of Part III of the Mental Health Act 1959.

1959 c. 72.

(5) This section does not apply to Scotland.

Inquiries in Scotland.

99.—(1) In Scotland the Secretary of State may cause an inquiry to be held into any matter relating to—

1968 c. 49.

(*a*) the functions of a local authority under the Social Work (Scotland) Act 1968 in so far as the matter relates to children ;

(*b*) the functions of a local authority under the enactments specified in paragraph (*a*) of section 1(4) and paragraphs (*b*) to (*e*) and (*h*) of section 2(2) of the Social Work (Scotland) Act 1968 ;

(*c*) the functions of an adoption society ;

(*d*) the functions of a voluntary organisation in so far as those functions relate to establishments to which sections 61 to 68 of the Social Work (Scotland) Act 1968 apply and in so far as the matter relates to children ; or

(*e*) the detention of a child under—

1937 c. 37.

(i) section 57 or 58A of the Children and Young Persons (Scotland) Act 1937 ; or

1975 c. 21.

(ii) section 206 or 413 of the Criminal Procedure (Scotland) Act 1975.

(2) The Secretary of State may, before an inquiry is commenced, direct that it shall be held in private, but where no such direction has been given, the person holding the inquiry may if he thinks fit hold it or any part of it in private.

(3) Subsections (2) to (8) of section 210 of the Local Government (Scotland) Act 1973 (powers in relation to local inquiries)
shall apply in relation to an inquiry under this section as they
apply in relation to a local inquiry under that section.

(4) In this section " functions " includes powers and duties
exercisable otherwise than by virtue of any enactment.

Supplemental

100.—(1) In this Act " authorised court ", as respects an
application for an order relating to a child, shall be construed
as follows.

(2) If the child is in England or Wales when the application
is made, the following are authorised courts—

    (*a*) the High Court ;

    (*b*) the county court within whose district the child is and,
in the case of an application under section 14, any
county court within whose district a parent or guardian
of the child is ;

    (*c*) any other county court prescribed by rules made under
section 102 of the County Courts Act 1959 ;

    (*d*) a magistrates' court within whose area the child is
and, in the case of an application under section 14,
a magistrates' court within whose area a parent or
guardian of the child is.

(3) If the child is in Scotland when the application is made,
the following are authorised courts—

    (*a*) the Court of Session ;

    (*b*) the sheriff court of the sheriffdom within which the child
is.

(4) If, in the case of an application for an adoption order
or an order under section 14, the child is not in Great Britain
when the application is made, the following are authorised
courts—

    (*a*) the High Court ;

    (*b*) the Court of Session.

(5) In the case of a Convention adoption order paragraphs
(*b*), (*c*) and (*d*) of subsection (2) or, as the case may be, paragraph (*b*) of subsection (3) do not apply.

(6) In the case of an order under section 25, paragraph (*d*)
of subsection (2) does not apply.

(7) Subsection (2) applies in the case of an application for
an order under section 34, 35 or 38 relating to a child who is

subject to a custodianship order whether or not the child is in England or Wales and for the purposes of such an application the following are also authorised courts—

> (*a*) the court which made the custodianship order and, where that court is a magistrates' court, any other magistrates' court acting for the same petty session area ;
>
> (*b*) the county court within whose district the applicant is ;
>
> (*c*) a magistrates' court within whose area the applicant is ;
>
> (*d*) where the application is made under section 35 and the child's mother or father or custodian is the petitioner or respondent in proceedings for a decree of divorce, nullity or judicial separation which are pending in a court in England or Wales, that court.

(8) Subsection (2) does not apply in the case of an application under section 30 or 42 but for the purposes of such an application the following are authorised courts—

> (*a*) if there is pending in respect of the child an application for an adoption order or an order under section 14 or a custodianship order, the court in which that application is pending ;
>
> (*b*) in any other case, the High Court, the county court within whose district the applicant lives and the magistrates' court within whose area the applicant lives.

(9) Subsections (3) and (8) do not apply in the case of an application under section 30 in Scotland but for the purposes of such an application the following are authorised courts—

> (*a*) if there is pending in respect of the child an application for—
>
>> (i) an adoption order ; or
>>
>> (ii) an order under section 14,
>
> the court in which that application is pending ;
>
> (*b*) in any other case—
>
>> (i) the Court of Session ;
>>
>> (ii) the sheriff court of the sheriffdom within which the applicant resides.

Appeals etc.   **101.**—(1) Where any application has been made under this Act to a county court, the High Court may, at the instance of any party to the application, order the application to be removed to the High Court and there proceeded with on such terms as to costs as it thinks proper.

(2) Subject to subsection (3), where on an application to a magistrates' court under this Act the court makes or refuses to make an order, an appeal shall lie to the High Court.

(3) Where an application is made to a magistrates' court under this Act, and the court considers that the matter is one which would more conveniently be dealt with by the High Court, the magistrates' court shall refuse to make an order, and in that case no appeal shall lie to the High Court.

102.—(1) Any agreement or consent which is required by Evidence of Part I, except section 24(6), or Part II to be given to the making agreement of any order or application for an order may be given in writing, and consent. and, if the document signifying the agreement or consent is—

> (*a*) in the case of an adoption order or an application for an order under section 14, witnessed in accordance with rules, or
>
> (*b*) in the case of an application made under Part II, witnessed in accordance with rules of court,

it shall be admissible in evidence without further proof of the signature of the person by whom it was executed.

(2) A document signifying such agreement or consent which purports to be witnessed in accordance with rules or, as the case may be, with rules of court shall be presumed to be so witnessed, and to have been executed and witnessed on the date and at the place specified in the document, unless the contrary is proved.

(3) In the application of this section to Scotland—

> (*a*) for " made under Part II " there is substituted " to which Part II applies " ;
>
> (*b*) for " admissible in evidence " there is substituted " sufficient evidence " ; and
>
> (*c*) for " rules of court " there is substituted " act of sederunt ".

103.—(1) The Secretary of State may by regulations make Panel for provision for the establishment of a panel of persons from guardians ad whom— litem and reporting

> (*a*) guardians ad litem and reporting officers may in officers. accordance with rules or rules of court be appointed for the purposes of—
>
>> (i) section 20 of this Act ;
>>
>> (ii) section 32B of the Children and Young 1969 c. 54. Persons Act 1969 ;
>>
>> (iii) section 4B of the Children Act 1948 ;   1948 c. 43.
>
> (*b*) persons may be appointed for the purposes of section 18A or 34A of the Social Work (Scotland) Act 1968.   1968 c. 49.

PART V

(2) Regulations under subsection (1) may provide for the expenses incurred by members of the panel to be defrayed by local authorities.

(3) In relation to Scotland, the reference in subsection (1) to guardians ad litem shall be construed as a reference to curators ad litem.

Saving for powers of High Court.

104. Nothing in this Act shall restrict or affect the jurisdiction of the High Court to appoint or remove guardians, or otherwise in respect of children.

Periodic review of Act.

105. The Secretary of State shall, within three years of the first of the dates appointed by order by the Secretary of State under section 108(2) and, thereafter, every five years lay before Parliament a report on the operation of those sections of the Act which are in force at that time ; and the Secretary of State shall institute such research as is necessary to provide the information for these reports.

Regulations and orders.

106.—(1) Where a power to make regulations or orders is exercisable by the Secretary of State by virtue of this Act, regulations or orders made in the exercise of that power shall be made by statutory instrument and may—

(a) make different provision in relation to different cases or classes of case, and

(b) exclude certain cases or classes of case.

(2) A statutory instrument containing regulations made by the Secretary of State under section 103 shall be subject to annulment in pursuance of a resolution of either House of Parliament.

(3) Any power conferred on the Secretary of State by this Act to make orders includes a power to vary or revoke an order so made.

Interpretation.

107.—(1) In this Act, unless the context otherwise requires—

" adoption order " means an order under section 8(1) ;

" adoption society " has the same meaning as in the 1958 Act ;

" approved adoption society " means an adoption society approved under Part I ;

" area ", in relation to a magistrates' court, means the commission area (within the meaning of section 1 of the Administration of Justice Act 1973) for which the court is appointed ;

1973 c. 15.

" authorised court " shall be construed in accordance with
section 100 ;

" British adoption order " means an adoption order, or
any provision for the adoption of a child effected
under the law of Northern Ireland or any British
territory outside the United Kingdom ;

" British territory " means, for the purposes of any provision
of this Act, any of the following countries, that is to
say, the United Kingdom, the Channel Islands, the
Isle of Man and a colony, being a country designated
for the purposes of that provision by order of the
Secretary of State or, if no country is so designated,
any of those countries ;

" child ", except where used to express a relationship,
means a person who has not attained the age of 18 ;

" the Convention " means the Convention relating to the
adoption of children concluded at The Hague on 15th
November 1965 and signed on behalf of the United
Kingdom on that date ;

" Convention adoption order " means an adoption order
made as mentioned in section 24(1) ;

" Convention country " means any country outside British
territory, being a country for the time being designated
by an order of the Secretary of State as a country in
which, in his opinion, the Convention is in force ;

" guardian " means—

(a) a person appointed by deed or will in accordance with the provisions of the Guardianship of
Infants Acts 1886 and 1925 or the Guardianship 1971 c. 3.
of Minors Act 1971 or by a court of competent
jurisdiction to be the guardian of the child, and

(b) in relation to the adoption of an illegitimate
child, includes the father where he has custody of
the child by virtue of an order under section 9 of
the Guardianship of Minors Act 1971, or under
section 2 of the Illegitimate Children (Scotland) Act 1930 c. 33.
1930 ;

" home " shall be construed in accordance with section
87(3) ;

" local authority " means in relation to England and Wales
the council of a county (other than a metropolitan
county), a metropolitan district, a London borough or
the Common Council of the City of London ;

" notice " means a notice in writing ;

PART V

1949 c. 101.

1958 c. 5
(7 & 8 Eliz. 2).

" relative " has the same meaning as in the 1958 Act ;

" rules " means, in England and Wales, rules made under section 9(3) of the 1958 Act or made by virtue of section 9(4) of the 1958 Act under section 15 of the Justices of the Peace Act 1949 ;

" the 1958 Act " means the Adoption Act 1958 ;

" United Kingdom national " means, for the purposes of any provision of this Act, a citizen of the United Kingdom and Colonies satisfying such conditions, if any, as the Secretary of State may by order specify for the purposes of that provision ;

" voluntary organisation " means a body, other than a public or local authority, the activities of which are not carried on for profit.

(2) In this Act, in relation to Scotland, unless the context otherwise requires—

" actual custody " means care and possession ;

" legal custody " means custody ;

" local authority " means a regional or islands council ; and

" rules " means rules made by act of sederunt.

(3) Except so far as the context otherwise requires, any reference in this Act to an enactment shall be construed as a reference to that enactment as amended by or under any other enactment, including this Act.

(4) In this Act, except where otherwise indicated—

(a) a reference to a numbered Part, section or Schedule is a reference to the Part or section of, or the Schedule to, this Act so numbered, and

(b) a reference in a section to a numbered subsection is a reference to the subsection of that section so numbered, and

(c) a reference in a section, subsection or Schedule to a numbered paragraph is a reference to the paragraph of that section, subsection or Schedule so numbered.

Amendments, repeals, commencement and transitory provisions.

108.—(1) Subject to the following provisions of this section—

(a) the enactments specified in Schedule 3 shall have effect subject to the amendments specified in that Schedule (being minor amendments or amendments consequential on the preceding provisions of this Act), and

(b) the enactments specified in Schedule 4 are repealed to the extent shown in column 3 of that Schedule.

(2) This Act, except the provisions specified in subsections (3) and (4), shall come into force on such date as the Secretary of State may by order appoint and different dates may be appointed for, or for different purposes of, different provisions.

(3) Sections 71, 72 and 82, this section, section 109 and paragraph 57 of Schedule 3 shall come into force on the passing of this Act.

(4) The following provisions of this Act shall come into force on 1st January 1976—

    (*a*) sections 3, 8(9) and (10), 13, 59, 83 to 91, 94, 98, 99, 100 and 103 to 107 ;

    (*b*) Schedules 1 and 2 ;

    (*c*) in Schedule 3, paragraphs 1, 2, 3, 4, 6, 8, 9, 13(6) 15, 17, 18, 19, 20, 21(1) (2) and (4), 22 to 25, 27(*b*), 29, 33, 34 (*b*), 35, 36 (*b*), 38, 39 (*c*) (*d*) and (*e*), 40, 43, 48, 49, 51 (*a*), 52 (*f*) (ii) and (*g*) (ii), 54, 55, 58 to 63, 65 to 70, 75 (3), 77, 78, 81 and 83 ;

    (*d*) Parts I, II and III of Schedule 4.

(5) Until the date appointed under subsection (2) for sections 4 to 7, in this Act and in the 1958 Act " adoption agency " means a local authority or a registered adoption society within the meaning of the 1958 Act.

(6) Until the date so appointed for section 12, section 5(1) of the 1958 Act shall, in relation to an application made after 31st December 1975 for an adoption order, have effect with the addition at the end of paragraph (*b*) of the following words " or

    (*c*) has seriously ill-treated the child and that (whether because of the ill-treatment or for other reasons) the rehabilitation of the child within the household of that person is unlikely."

(7) Until the date so appointed for section 18, section 21A of the Children and Young Persons Act 1969 shall have effect as 1969 c. 54. if for references to section 25 there were substituted references to section 53 of the 1958 Act.

(8) An order under subsection (2) may make such transitional provision as appears to the Secretary of State to be necessary or expedient in connection with the provisions thereby brought into force, including such adaptations of those provisions or any provision of this Act then in force or any provision of the 1958 Act as appear to him to be necessary or expedient in consequence of the partial operation of this Act.

109.—(1) This Act may be cited as the Children Act 1975.

(2) This Act, except—

    (*a*) section 68 ;

    (*b*) paragraphs 10, 11 and 63 of Schedule 3 ; and

    (*c*) Schedule 4 in so far as it repeals—

1968 c. 53.

        (i) the words " or adoption " in section 9(5) of the Adoption Act 1968, and

1958 c. 5
(7 & 8 Eliz. 2).

        (ii) the references in that Act to section 19 of the Adoption Act 1958,

does not extend to Northern Ireland.

(3) Subsection (1) of section 68 extends to the Channel Islands.

SCHEDULES

SCHEDULE 1

Section 8.

STATUS CONFERRED BY ADOPTION OR LEGITIMATION IN ENGLAND AND WALES

PART I

INTERPRETATION

1.—(1) This Part applies for the construction of this Schedule, except where the context otherwise requires.

(2) " Adoption " means adoption—

    (*a*) by an adoption order as defined in section 107,

    (*b*) by an adoption order made under the 1958 Act or the Adoption Act 1950 or any enactment repealed by the 1950 c. 26. Adoption Act 1950,

    (*c*) by an order made in Northern Ireland, the Isle of Man or in any of the Channel Islands,

    (*d*) which is an overseas adoption as defined by section 4(3) of the Adoption Act 1968, or   1968 c. 53.

    (*e*) which is an adoption recognised by the law of England and Wales, and effected under the law of any other country,

and cognate expressions shall be construed accordingly.

(3) " Legitimation " means—

    (*a*) legitimation under section 1 of the Legitimacy Act 1926,   1926 c. 60.

    (*b*) legitimation within section 8 of that Act (legitimation by extraneous law), or

    (*c*) legitimation (whether or not by virtue of subsequent marriage of the parents) recognised by the law of England and Wales, and effected under the law of any other country,

and cognate expressions shall be construed accordingly.

(4) These definitions of adoption and legitimation include, where the context admits, those effected before the passing of this Act, and the date of an adoption effected by an order is the date of the making of the order.

(5) " Existing ", in relation to any enactment or other instrument, means one passed or made before 1st January 1976 (and whether or not before the passing of this Act).

(6) The death of the testator is the date at which a will or codicil is to be regarded as made.

Dispositions of property

2.—(1) In this Schedule—

" disposition " includes the conferring of a power of appointment and any other disposition of an interest in or right over property ;

" power of appointment " includes any discretionary power to transfer a beneficial interest in property without the furnishing of valuable consideration.

(2) This Schedule applies to an oral disposition of property as if contained in an instrument made when the disposition was made.

PART II

ADOPTION ORDERS

Status conferred by adoption

3.—(1) An adopted child shall be treated in law—

(a) where the adopters are a married couple, as if he had been born as a child of the marriage (whether or not he was in fact born after the marriage was solemnized) ;

(b) in any other case, as if he had been born to the adopter in wedlock (but not as a child of any actual marriage of the adopter).

(2) An adopted child shall be treated in law as if he were not the child of any person other than the adopters or adopter.

(3) It is hereby declared that this paragraph prevents an adopted child from being illegitimate.

(4) This paragraph has effect—

(a) in the case of an adoption before 1st January 1976, from that date, and

(b) in the case of any other adoption, from the date of the adoption.

(5) Subject to the provisions of this Part, this paragraph applies for the construction of enactments or instruments passed or made before the adoption or later, and so applies subject to any contrary indication.

(6) Subject to the provisions of this Part, this paragraph has effect as respects things done, or events occurring, after the adoption, or after 31st December 1975, whichever is the later.

Vocabulary

4. A relationship existing by virtue of paragraph 3 may be referred to as an adoptive relationship, and—

(a) a male adopter may be referred to as the adoptive father ;

(b) a female adopter may be referred to as the adoptive mother ;

(*c*) any other relative of any degree under an adoptive relationship may be referred to as an adoptive relative of that
degree,

but this paragraph does not prevent the term " parent ", or any
other term not qualified by the word " adoptive ", being treated as
including an adoptive relative.

Instruments and enactments concerning property

5.—(1) Paragraph 3—

(*a*) does not apply to an existing instrument or enactment so
far as it contains a disposition of property, and

(*b*) does not apply to any public general Act in its application
to any disposition of property in an existing instrument
or enactment.

(2) The repeal by this Act of sections 16 and 17 of the 1958 Act,
and of provisions containing references to those sections, does not
affect their application in relation to a disposition of property
effected by an existing instrument.

(3) For the purposes of this paragraph, and of paragraph 6,
provisions of the law of intestate succession applicable to the estate
of a deceased person shall be treated as if contained in an instrument
executed by him (while of full capacity) immediately before his
death.

6.—(1) Subject to any contrary indication, the rules of construction contained in this paragraph apply to any instrument,
other than an existing instrument, so far as it contains a disposition
of property.

(2) In applying paragraph 3(1) to a disposition which depends on
the date of birth of a child or children of the adoptive parent or
parents, the disposition shall be construed as if—

(*a*) the adopted child had been born on the date of adoption,

(*b*) two or more children adopted on the same date had been
born on that date in the order of their actual births,

but this does not affect any reference to the age of a child.

(3) Examples of phrases in wills on which sub-paragraph (2) can
operate are—

1. Children of A " living at my death or born afterwards ".

2. Children of A " living at my death or born afterwards
before any one of such children for the time being in
existence attains a vested interest, and who attain the age
of 21 years ".

3. As in example 1 or 2, but referring to grandchildren of A,
instead of children of A.

4. A for life " until he has a child ", and then to his child or
children.

Note. Sub-paragraph (2) will not affect the reference to the age
of 21 years in example 2.

SCH. 1

(4) Paragraph 3(2) does not prejudice any interest vested in possession in the adopted child before the adoption, or any interest expectant (whether immediately or not) upon an interest so vested.

(5) Where it is necessary to determine for the purposes of a disposition of property effected by an instrument whether a woman can have a child, it shall be presumed that once a woman has attained the age of fifty-five she will not adopt a child after execution of the instrument, and notwithstanding paragraph 3 if she does so the child shall not be treated as her child or as the child of her spouse (if any) for the purposes of the instrument.

(6) In this paragraph " instrument " includes a private Act settling property, but not any other enactment.

(7) Paragraph 3(6) has effect subject to this paragraph.

Other enactments and instruments

1949 c. 76.
1956 c. 69.

7.—(1) Paragraph 3 does not apply for the purposes of the table of kindred and affinity in Schedule 1 to the Marriage Act 1949 or sections 10 and 11 (incest) of the Sexual Offences Act 1956.

(2) Paragraph 3 does not apply for the purposes of any provision of—

(*a*) the British Nationality Acts 1948 to 1965,

1971 c. 77.

(*b*) the Immigration Act 1971,

(*c*) any instrument having effect under an enactment within paragraph (*a*) or (*b*), or

(*d*) any other provision of the law for the time being in force which determines citizenship of the United Kingdom and Colonies.

1975 c. 14.

(3) Paragraph 3 shall not prevent a person being treated as a near relative of a deceased person for the purposes of section 32 of the Social Security Act 1975 (payment of death grant), if apart from paragraph 3 he would be so treated.

(4) Paragraph 3 does not apply for the purposes of section 70(3)(*b*) or section 73(2) of the Social Security Act 1975 (payment of industrial death benefit to or in respect of an illegitimate child of the deceased and the child's mother).

(5) Subject to regulations made under section 72 of the Social Security Act 1975 (entitlement of certain relatives of deceased to industrial death benefit), paragraph 3 shall not affect the entitlement to an industrial death benefit of a person who would, apart from paragraph 3, be treated as a relative of a deceased person for the purposes of the said section 72.

Pensions

8. Paragraph 3(2) does not affect entitlement to a pension which is payable to or for the benefit of a child and is in payment at the time of his adoption.

Adoption of child by natural parents

9. In the case of a child adopted by one of its natural parents as sole adoptive parent, paragraph 3(2) has no effect as respects entitlement to property depending on relationship to that parent, or as respects anything else depending on that relationship.

Peerages, etc.

10. An adoption does not affect the descent of any peerage or dignity or title of honour.

Insurance

11. Where a child is adopted whose natural parent has effected an insurance with a friendly society or a collecting society or an industrial insurance company for the payment on the death of the child of money for funeral expenses, the rights and liabilities under the policy shall by virtue of the adoption be transferred to the adoptive parents who shall for the purposes of the enactments relating to such societies and companies be treated as the person who took out the policy.

PART III

LEGITIMATION

Instruments concerning property

12.—(1) Subject to any contrary indication, the rules of construction contained in this paragraph apply to any instrument, other than an existing instrument, so far as the instrument contains a disposition of property.

(2) For the purposes of this paragraph, provisions of the law of intestate succession applicable to the estate of a deceased person shall be treated as if contained in an instrument executed by him (while of full capacity) immediately before his death.

(3) A legitimated person, and any other person, shall be entitled to take any interest as if the legitimated person had been born legitimate.

(4) A disposition which depends on the date of birth of a child or children of the parent or parents shall be construed as if—

    (*a*) a legitimated child had been born on the date of legitimation,

    (*b*) two or more children legitimated on the same date had been born on that date in the order of their actual births,

but this does not affect any reference to the age of a child.

(5) Examples of phrases in wills on which sub-paragraph (4) can operate are set out in paragraph 6(3).

(6) If an illegitimate person, or a person adopted by one of his natural parents, dies (before the passing of this Act or later) and—

(*a*) his parents subsequently marry, and

(*b*) the deceased would, if living at the time of the marriage, have become a legitimated person,

section 1(1) of the Legitimacy Act 1926 and this paragraph shall apply for the construction of the instrument so far as it relates to the taking of interests by, or in succession to, his spouse, children and remoter issue as if he was legitimated at the date of the marriage.

(7) In this paragraph " instrument " includes a private Act settling property, but not any other enactment.

(8) Section 1(1) of the Legitimacy Act 1926 has effect subject to the provisions of this paragraph.

(9) Part II of Schedule 4, which repeals enactments superseded by this paragraph, has effect as respects any instrument, other than an existing instrument.

Legitimation of adopted child

13.—(1) Paragraph 3 does not prevent an adopted child being legitimated under the Legitimacy Act 1926 if either natural parent is the sole adoptive parent.

(2) Where an adopted child (with a sole adoptive parent) is legitimated—

(*a*) paragraph 3(2) shall not apply after the legitimation to the natural relationship with the other natural parent, and

(*b*) revocation of the adoption order in consequence of the legitimation shall not affect Part II as it applies to any instrument made before the date of legitimation.

Part IV

Supplemental

Dispositions depending on date of birth

14.—(1) Where a disposition depends on the date of birth of a child who was born illegitimate and who—

(*a*) is adopted by one of the natural parents as sole adoptive parent, or

(*b*) is legitimated (or, if deceased, is treated as legitimated),

paragraph 6(2) and paragraph 12(4) do not affect entitlement under Part II of the Family Law Reform Act 1969 (illegitimate children).

(2) Where a disposition depends on the date of birth of an adopted child who is legitimated (or, if deceased, is treated as

legitimated), paragraph 12(4) does not affect entitlement by virtue of paragraph 6(2).

(3) This paragraph applies for example where—

(*a*) a testator dies in 1976 bequeathing a legacy to his eldest grandchild living at a specified time,

(*b*) his daughter has an illegitimate child in 1977 who is the first grandchild,

(*c*) his married son has a child in 1978,

(*d*) subsequently the illegitimate child is adopted by the mother as sole adoptive parent or is legitimated,

and in all those cases the daughter's child remains the eldest grandchild of the testator throughout.

Protection of trustees and personal representatives

15.—(1) A trustee or personal representative is not under a duty, by virtue of the law relating to trusts or the administration of estates, to enquire, before conveying or distributing any property, whether—

(*a*) any adoption has been effected or revoked, or

(*b*) any person is illegitimate, or is adopted by one of his natural parents, and could be legitimated (or if deceased be treated as legitimated),

if that fact could affect entitlement to the property.

(2) A trustee or personal representative shall not be liable to any person by reason of a conveyance or distribution of the property made without regard to any such fact if he has not received notice of the fact before the conveyance or distribution.

(3) This paragraph does not prejudice the right of a person to follow the property, or any property representing it, into the hands of another person, other than a purchaser, who has received it.

Property devolving with peerages, etc.

16.—(1) This Schedule shall not affect the devolution of any property limited (expressly or not) to devolve (as nearly as the law permits) along with any peerage or dignity or title of honour.

(2) This paragraph applies only if and so far as a contrary intention is not expressed in the instrument, and shall have effect subject to the terms of the instrument.

Entails

17. It is hereby declared that references in this Schedule to dispositions of property include references to a disposition by the creation of an entailed interest.

D

PART V

EXTENT

18. This Schedule does not apply to Scotland.

SCHEDULE 2

STATUS CONFERRED IN SCOTLAND BY ADOPTION

General

1.—(1) In Scotland, a child who is the subject of an adoption order shall, subject to the provisions of this Schedule, be treated in law—

    (a) where the adopters are a married couple, as if he had been born as a legitimate child of the marriage (whether or not he was in fact born after the marriage was constituted) ;

    (b) in any other case, as if he had been born as a legitimate child of the adopter (but not as a child of any actual marriage of the adopter),

and as if he were not the child of any person other than the adopters or adopter.

(2) Where an illegitimate child has been adopted by one of his natural parents as sole adoptive parent and the adopter thereafter marries the other natural parent, sub-paragraph (1) shall not affect any enactment or rule of law whereby, by virtue of the marriage, the child is rendered the legitimate child of both natural parents.

(3) Sub-paragraph (1) does not apply in determining the prohibited degrees of consanguinity and affinity in respect of the law relating to marriage or in respect of the crime of incest, except that, on the making of an adoption order, the adopter and the child shall be deemed, for all time coming, to be within the said prohibited degrees in respect of the law relating to marriage.

(4) Sub-paragraph (1) does not apply for the purposes of any provision of—

    (a) the British Nationality Acts 1948 to 1965,

    (b) the Immigration Act 1971,

    (c) any instrument having effect under an enactment within paragraph (a) or (b), or

    (d) any other law for the time being in force which determines citizenship of the United Kingdom and Colonies.

(5) This paragraph has effect—

    (a) in the case of an adoption before 1st January 1976, from that date, and

    (b) in the case of any other adoption, from the date of the adoption.

(6) Subject to the provisions of this Schedule, this paragraph applies for the construction of any enactments or instruments passed or made before or after the commencement of this Act so far as the context admits.

(7) Subject to the provisions of this Schedule, this paragraph does not affect things done or events occurring before the adoption or, where the adoption took place before 1st January 1976, before that date.

Pensions

2. The provision in paragraph 1(1) whereby a child who is the subject of an adoption order is to be treated in law as if he were not the child of any person other than the adopters or adopter shall not affect entitlement to a pension which is payable to, or for the benefit of, the child and is in payment at the time of his adoption.

Insurance

3. Where a child is adopted whose natural parent has effected an insurance with a friendly society or a collecting society or an industrial insurance company for the payment on the death of the child of money for funeral expenses, the rights and liabilities under the policy shall by virtue of the adoption be transferred to the adoptive parents who shall for the purposes of the enactments relating to such societies and companies be treated as the person who took out the policy.

Social Security

4.—(1) Paragraph 1 shall not prevent a person being treated as a near relative of a deceased person for the purposes of section 32 of the Social Security Act 1975 (payment of death grant), if apart 1975 c. 14. from paragraph 1 he would be so treated.

(2) Paragraph 1 does not apply for the purposes of section 70(3)(*b*) or section 73(2) of the Social Security Act 1975 (payment of industrial death benefit to or in respect of an illegitimate child of the deceased and the child's mother).

(3) Subject to regulations made under section 72 of the Social Security Act 1975 (entitlement of certain relatives of deceased to industrial death benefit), paragraph 1 shall not affect the entitlement to an industrial death benefit of a person who would, apart from paragraph 1, be treated as a relative of a deceased person for the purposes of the said section 72.

Succession and Property

5.—(1) Paragraph 1 does not affect the existing law relating to adopted persons in respect of—

(*a*) the succession to a deceased person (whether testate or intestate), and

(*b*) the disposal of property by virtue of any inter vivos deed.

(2) In section 23 of the Succession (Scotland) Act 1964 (adopted 1964 c. 41. person to be treated for purposes of succession, etc., as child of adopter)—

(*a*) in subsection (3) (property devolving along with a title or honour, etc.), after "this section" there is inserted "or in the Children Act 1975";

(*b*) in subsection (5) (meaning of " adoption order "), for the words from " an order " to " Northern Ireland " there are substituted the words—

" (*a*) an adoption order under the Children Act 1975 ;

(*b*) an adoption order under the Adoption Act 1958 or the Adoption Act 1950 or any enactment repealed by the Adoption Act 1950 ;

(*c*) an order effecting an adoption made in Northern Ireland, the Isle of Man or any of the Channel Islands ;

(*d*) an " overseas adoption " as defined in section 4(3) of the Adoption Act 1968 ; or

(*e*) any other adoption recognised by the law of Scotland ;

(whether the order took effect before or after the commencement of this Act) ; ".

(3) In section 24 of the said Act of 1964 (provisions supplementary to section 23), after subsection (1) there is inserted the following subsection—

" (1A) Where, in relation to any purpose specified in section 23(1) of this Act, any right is conferred or any obligation is imposed, whether by operation of law or under any deed coming into operation after the commencement of the Children Act 1975, by reference to the relative seniority of the members of a class of persons, then, without prejudice to any entitlement under Part I of the Law Reform (Miscellaneous Provisions) (Scotland) Act 1968 of an illegitimate child who is adopted by one of his parents,

(*a*) any member of that class who is an adopted person shall rank as if he had been born on the date of his adoption, and

(*b*) if two or more members of the class are adopted persons whose dates of adoption are the same, they shall rank as between themselves in accordance with their respective times of birth.".

(4) In section 37(1) of the said Act of 1964 (exclusion from Act of matters relating to titles, etc.), after " nothing in this Act " there is inserted " or (as respects paragraph (*a*) of this subsection) in the Children Act 1975 ".

Adoption and Legitimation

6.—(1) In section 26 of the Adoption Act 1958, after subsection (1) there is inserted the following subsection—

" (1A) Subsection (1) above does not apply to Scotland, and where the natural parents of an illegitimate child, one of whom has adopted him in Scotland, have subsequently married each other, the court by which the adoption order was made may, on the application of any of the parties concerned, revoke that order.".

(2) Section 1 of the Legitimation (Scotland) Act 1968, (requirements Sch. 2 and effects of legitimation) is renumbered subsection (1) and at the 1968 c. 22. end there is added the following subsection—

" (2) Subsection (1) above shall apply in relation to an illegitimate person who has been adopted by one of his natural parents as sole adoptive parent, where the adopter thereafter marries the other natural parent, as it applies in relation to any illegitimate person, to the effect of rendering that person the legitimate child of both natural parents; and in this Act "illegitimate", "legitimated" and cognate expressions shall be construed accordingly.".

(3) In section 6(2) of the said Act of 1968, for the words from " of an adoption order " to " 1958 " there are substituted the words " (under this section or otherwise) of any adoption order within the meaning of Schedule 2 to the Children Act 1975, in consequence of the marriage of the parents of the adopted person to each other ".

Interpretation

7. In this Schedule, " adoption order " means—

(*a*) an adoption order as defined in section 107 ;

(*b*) an adoption order under the 1958 Act or the Adoption Act 1950 or any enactment repealed by the Adoption Act 1950 ; 1950 c. 26.

(*c*) an order effecting an adoption made in Northern Ireland, the Isle of Man or any of the Channel Islands ;

(*d*) an " overseas adoption " as defined in section 4(3) of the Adoption Act 1968 ; or 1968 c. 53.

(*e*) any other adoption recognised by the law of Scotland ;

(whether the order took effect before or after the commencement of this Act) ; and cognate expressions shall be construed accordingly.

SCHEDULE 3 Section 108.

MINOR AND CONSEQUENTIAL AMENDMENTS

Children and Young Persons Act 1933 (23 *and* 24 *Geo.* 5 *c.* 12)

1. In section 1(1)(*b*), for the words " one hundred pounds " there are substituted the words " £400 ".

Children and Young Persons (Scotland) Act 1937 (*c.* 37)

2. In section 12(1)(*b*) for the words " twenty-five pounds " there is substituted " £400 ".

Education Act 1944 (*c.* 31)

3. In section 106, the following subsection is substituted for subsection (4)—

" (4) In this section ' guardian ' means the person having legal custody of the child or young person, as defined by section 86 of the Children Act 1975."

D 3

Children Act 1948 (*c.* 43)

4. In section 3(8) for the words " twenty pounds " and " two months " there are substituted respectively the words " £400 " and " three months ".

5. In section 4—

(*a*) in subsection (3)(*a*) after the words " parent or guardian " there are inserted the words " or custodian " ;

(*b*) for subsection (3)(*b*) there is substituted—

" (*b*) in the case of a resolution passed by virtue of paragraph (*b*), (*c*) or (*d*) of subsection (1) of the said section 2, by the person who, but for the resolution, would have the parental rights and duties in relation to the child, ".

6. In section 43(1), for the words " and the Adoption Act 1968 " there are substituted the words " the Adoption Act 1968 and the Children Act 1975 ".

Marriage Act 1949 (*c.* 76)

7. In section 3(1), after the words " shall be required " there are inserted the words " unless the infant is subject to a custodianship order, when the consent of the custodian and, where the custodian is the husband or wife of a parent of the infant, of that parent shall be required ".

8. In Part I of Schedule 1—

(*a*) after " Mother " there is inserted " Adoptive mother or former adoptive mother " ;

(*b*) after " Daughter " there is inserted " Adoptive daughter or former. adoptive daughter " ;

(*c*) after " Father " there is inserted " Adoptive father or former adoptive father " ;

(*d*) after " Son " there is inserted " Adoptive son or former adoptive son ".

9. In Schedule 2 in paragraph 2(*b*) after the words " deceased parent " there are inserted the words " or by the court under section 3 of the Guardianship of Minors Act 1971 ".

Maintenance Orders Act 1950 (*c.* 37)

10. In section 15, after the words " Maintenance Orders (Reciprocal Enforcement) Act 1972 " there are inserted the words " or sections 33 to 45 of the Children Act 1975 ".

11. In section 16(2)(*a*), after sub-paragraph (v) there are inserted the following sub-paragraphs—

" (vi) section 4 of the Affiliation Proceedings Act 1957 on an application made under section 45 of the Children Act 1975 ;

(vii) section 34(1)(*b*) of the Children Act 1975 ; ".

Magistrates' Courts Act 1952 (*c.* 55)

12. In section 56(1) (meaning of "domestic proceedings"), the following paragraph is inserted after paragraph (*e*)—

> "(*f*) under the Adoption Act 1958 or Part I or II of the Children Act 1975 ",

and there are added at the end the following words " or proceedings on an information ".

Births and Deaths Registration Act 1953 (*c.* 20)

13.—(1) For " living new-born child " in each place where it occurs, except sections 6, 7, 8, 34(3) and 36, there is substituted " still-born child ".

(2) In section 1(2) after paragraph (*d*) there is added—

> "(*e*) in the case of a still-born child found exposed, the person who found the child."

(3) In section 14(1)(*a*) after " section 10 " there is inserted " or 10A ".

(4) In section 30 after subsection (1) there is inserted the following subsection—

> "(1A) The Registrar General shall cause an index to be made and kept in the General Register Office of the entries in the register kept by him under section 3A of this Act."

(5) In section 34—

> (*a*) in subsection (2) after paragraph (*c*) there is added the following paragraph—
>
> > "(*d*) in relation to the re-registration of a birth under section 9(5) of this Act " ;
>
> (*b*) in subsection (3) after " new-born child " there is inserted " or still-born child ".

(6) In section 41—

> (*a*) after the definition of " disposal " there is inserted the following definition—
>
> > "' father ', in relation to an adopted child, means the child's natural father ; " ;
>
> (*b*) after the definition of " the Minister " there is inserted the following definition—
>
> > "' mother ', in relation to an adopted child, means the child's natural mother ; ".

Affiliation Proceedings Act 1957 (*c.* 55)

14. In section 5(2) there is inserted at the end the following paragraph—

> "(*e*) section 45 of the Children Act 1975 (which enables the custodian of a child to apply for an affiliation order under this Act within three years after the making of the custodianship order).".

Housing Act 1957 (c. 56)

15. In Schedule 2, in paragraph 4(7) for the words " any illegitimate son or daughter, and any adopted son or daughter " there are substituted the words " and any illegitimate son or daughter ".

Children Act 1958 (6 & 7 *Eliz.* 2 *c.* 65)

16. In section 2, as it applies in England and Wales,—

    (*a*) in subsection (1), after the word " guardian " there is inserted the word " custodian " ;

    (*b*) in subsection (4A),—

        (i) for the words " registered adoption society as is referred to in Part II of the Adoption Act 1958 " there are substituted the words " adoption society approved under Part I of the Children Act 1975 ", and

        (ii) for the words " that Act " there are substituted the words " the Adoption Act 1958 ".

17. In section 2 as it applies to Scotland, after subsection (4) there is inserted the following subsection—

    " (4A) A child is not a foster child for the purposes of this Part of this Act while he is placed in the care and possession of a person who proposes to adopt him under arrangements made by such an adoption agency as is referred to in Part I of the Children Act 1975 or while he is a protected child within the meaning of Part IV of the Adoption Act 1958."

18. In section 6 for the words " obtained their consent " there are substituted the words " obtained their written consent ".

19. In section 14(2), for the words " one hundred pounds " there are substituted the words " £400 ".

20. In section 37(2), for the words " one hundred pounds " there are substituted the words " £400 ".

Adoption Act 1958 (7 & 8 *Eliz.* 2. *c.* 5)

21.—(1) For " Adoption Rules " in each place where it occurs there is substituted " rules ".

(2) For "infant " and " infants " in each place where they occur there are respectively substituted " child " and " children ".

(3) For " registered adoption society " in each place where it occurs there is substituted " approved adoption society ".

(4) For " care and possession " in each place where it occurs there is substituted " actual custody ".

22. In section 9(3), for " this Part of this Act " in each place where it occurs there is substituted " the relevant provisions ", and at the end there is inserted—

    " In this subsection ' the relevant provisions ' means this Part, Part III and Part V of this Act and Part I of the Children Act 1975."

23. In section 11(2), for " this Part of this Act " in each place where it occurs there is substituted " the relevant provisions ", and at the end there is inserted—

" In this subsection ' the relevant provisions ' means this Part and Parts III and V of this Act and Part I of the Children Act 1975.".

24. In section 21(1) for the words from " the form " to the end there is substituted " such form as the Registrar General may by regulations specify ".

25. In section 23(1) for the words from " the form " to the end there is substituted " such form as the Registrar General for Scotland may by regulations specify ".

26. In section 26(2) after the words " adoption order " there are inserted the words " other than a Convention adoption order ".

27. In section 32—

(a) the following subsections are substituted for subsection (1)—

" (1) The Secretary of State may by regulations prohibit unincorporated bodies from applying for approval under section 4 of the Children Act 1975 (Approval of adoption societies) ; and he shall not approve any unincorporated body whose application is contrary to regulations made under this subsection.

(1A) The Secretary of State may make regulations for any purpose relating to the exercise of its functions by an approved adoption society." ;

(b) in subsection (2), for " (1) " there is substituted " (2) " and for the words from " twenty-five pounds " to the end of the subsection there is substituted the word " £400 " ;

(c) the following subsection is added after subsection (3)—

" (4) Regulations under this section may make different provisions in relation to different cases or classes of cases and may exclude certain cases or classes of cases."

28. In section 33—

(a) in subsection (1)—

(i) for " registered by the authority under this Part of this Act " there is substituted " approved under Part I of the Children Act 1975 " ;

(ii) for " the exercise of " to the end there is substituted " its own information or that of the Secretary of State " ;

(b) in subsection (2), for " by statutory declaration " there is substituted " in a manner specified in the notice ".

29. In section 35(6) for the word " six " there is substituted the word " three " and for the words " one hundred pounds " there are substituted the words " £400 ".

30. In section 36—

(*a*) in subsection (1) for the words " subsection (2) of section 3 of this Act " there are substituted the words " section 18(1) of the Children Act 1975 " ; and

(*b*) for subsection (3), there is substituted the following—

" (3) A local authority which receives such notice as aforesaid in respect of a child whom the authority know to be in the care of another local authority shall, not more than seven days after the receipt of the notice, inform that other authority in writing that they have received the notice."

31. In section 37—

(*a*) in subsection (1) for the words " subsection (2) of section 3 of this Act " there are substituted the words " section 18(1) of the Children Act 1975 " ;

(*b*) the following subsections are substituted for subsection (4)—

" (4) A protected child ceases to be a protected child—

(*a*) on the appointment of a guardian for him under the Guardianship of Minors Act 1971 ;

(*b*) on the notification to the local authority for the area where the child has his home that the application for an adoption order has been withdrawn ;

(*c*) on the making of any of the following orders in respect of the child—

(i) an adoption order ;

(ii) an order under section 17 of the Children Act 1975 ;

(iii) a custodianship order ;

(iv) an order under section 42, 43 or 44 of the Matrimonial Causes Act 1973 ; or

(*d*) on his attaining the age of 18,

whichever first occurs.

(4A) In relation to Scotland—

(*a*) subsection (4) does not apply ; and

(*b*) a protected child ceases to be a protected child when—

(i) the application for an adoption order lapses or is withdrawn ;

(ii) the application for an adoption order is granted or otherwise determined :

(iii) an order is made awarding custody of the child ;

(iv) an order is made appointing a guardian of the child ; or

(v) the child attains the age of 18.".

32. In section 40(6) for the words from the beginning to " that is to say " there are substituted the following words " The particulars referred to in subsection (4) of this section are ".

33. In section 44(2), for the word " six " there is substituted the word " three " and for the words " one hundred pounds " there are substituted the words " £400 ".

34. In section 50—

(a) in subsection (1), in paragraph (b), for " any consent " there is substituted " any agreement or consent " ;

(b) in subsection (2), for the word " six " there is substituted the word " three " and for the words " one hundred pounds " there are substituted the words " £400 " ;

(c) in subsection (3), for " adoption society " there is substituted " approved adoption society ".

35. In section 51(2), for the words " fifty pounds " there is substituted the word " £400 ".

36. In section 52(1)—

(a) for the words " fifty-three of this Act " there are substituted the words " twenty-five of the Children Act 1975 " ; and

(b) for the word " six " there is substituted the word " three " and for the words " one hundred pounds " there are substituted the words " £400 ".

37. In section 55, after the words " this Act " there are inserted the words " or Part I of the Children Act 1975 ".

38. For section 56 there is substituted the following section—

" Rules and regulations.

56.—(1) Any power to make rules or regulations conferred by this Act on the Lord Chancellor, the Secretary of State, the Registrar General or the Registrar General for Scotland shall be exercisable by statutory instrument which shall be subject to annulment in pursuance of a resolution of either House of Parliament.

(2) The Registrar General shall not make regulations under section 20A or 21 of this Act except with the approval of the Secretary of State.

(3) The Registrar General for Scotland shall not make regulations under section 23 of this Act except with the approval of the Secretary of State.

(4) The Statutory Instruments Act 1946 shall apply to a statutory instrument containing regulations made for the purposes of this Act by the Registrar General for Scotland as if the regulations had been made by a Minister of the Crown."

39. In section 57(1)—

(a) for the definition of " adoption order " there is substituted " ' adoption order ' means an order under section 1 of this Act or section 8(1) of the Children Act 1975 ; ",

(b) there are inserted after the definition of " adoption society " the words " ' approved adoption society ' means an adoption society approved under Part I of the Children Act 1975 ; ",

(c) after the definition of " body of persons " there are inserted the following definitions—

" " child ", except where used to express a relationship, means a person who has not attained the age of 18 ;

" Convention adoption order " has the same meaning as in the Children Act 1975 ; ",

(d) for the definition of " guardian " there is substituted " ' guardian ' means—

(a) a person appointed by deed or will in accordance with the provisions of the Guardianship of Infants Acts 1886 and 1925 or the Guardianship of Minors Act 1971 or by a court of competent jurisdiction to be the guardian of the child, and

(b) in the case of an illegitimate child, includes the father where he has custody of the child by virtue of an order under section 9 of the Guardianship of Minors Act 1971, or under section 2 of the Illegitimate Children (Scotland) Act 1930 ; ",

(e) after the definition of " relative " there is inserted the following definition—

" " voluntary organisation " means a body other than a public or local authority the activities of which are not carried on for profit."

40. After section 57(1) there is inserted—

" (1A) In this Act, in relation to Scotland, unless the context otherwise requires " actual custody " means care and possession.".

County Courts Act 1959 (c. 22)

41. In section 109(2) the following paragraph is inserted after paragraph (g)—

" (h) any proceedings under the Guardianship of Minors Acts 1971 and 1973 or the Children Act 1975."

Children and Young Persons Act 1963 (c. 37)

42. In section 49(1), for the words " twenty pounds " there are substituted the words " £100 ".

Perpetuities and Accumulations Act 1964 (c. 55)

43. In section 4, the following subsection is inserted at the end—

" (7) For the avoidance of doubt it is hereby declared that a question arising under section 3 of this Act or subsection (1)(a) above of whether a disposition would be void apart from this section is to be determined as if subsection (6) above had been a separate section of this Act."

Adoption Act 1964 (*c.* 57)

44. In section 1, the following subsection is substituted for sub-section (5)—

"(5) Section 8(3) and (4) of, and paragraph 11 of Schedule 1 and paragraph 3 of Schedule 2 to, the Children Act 1975 apply in relation to a child who is the subject of an order which is similar to an order under section 25 of that Act and is made (whether before or after this subsection has effect) in Northern Ireland, the Isle of Man or any of the Channel Islands, as they apply in relation to a child who is the subject of an adoption order."

45. In section 3(3)—

(*a*) for the words " section 53 of the said Act of 1958 " there are substituted the words " section 25 of the Children Act 1975 " ;

(*b*) for the words from " the word ' Provisionally ' " to the end of the subsection there are substituted the words " the words ' Proposed Foreign Adoption ' or, as the case may require, ' Proposed Foreign Re-adoption ' followed by the name, in brackets, of the country in which the order was made."

Health Services and Public Health Act 1968 (*c.* 46)

46. For section 64(3)(*a*) there is substituted—

"(*a*) ' the relevant enactments ' means—

(i) Parts III and IV of the Children and Young Persons Act 1933,

(ii) the National Health Service Act 1946,

(iii) Part III of the National Assistance Act 1948,

(iv) the Children Act 1948,

(v) the Adoption Act 1958,

(vi) the Children Act 1958,

(vii) section 9 of the Mental Health Act 1959,

(viii) section 10 of the Mental Health Act 1959, so far as it relates to cases mentioned in paragraph (*a*) of that section,

(ix) section 2(1)(*f*) of the Matrimonial Proceedings (Magistrates' Courts) Act 1960,

(x) the Children and Young Persons Act 1963, except Part II and section 56,

(xi) this Act,

(xii) the Adoption Act 1968,

(xiii) section 7(4) of the Family Law Reform Act 1969,

(xiv) the Children and Young Persons Act 1969, except so far as it relates to any voluntary home designated as mentioned in section 39(1) of that Act as a controlled or assisted community home,

(xv) section 43 of the Matrimonial Causes Act 1973,

(xvi) the National Health Service Reorganisation Act 1973,

(xvii) the Children Act 1975."

47. For section 65(3)(*b*) there is substituted—

" (*b*) ' the relevant enactments ' means—

(i) Parts III and IV of the Children and Young Persons Act 1933,

(ii) Part III of the National Health Service Act 1946,

(iii) Part III of the National Assistance Act 1948,

(iv) the Children Act 1948,

(v) the Adoption Act 1958,

(vi) section 3 of the Disabled Persons (Employment) Act 1958,

(vii) the Children Act 1958,

(viii) section 9 of the Mental Health Act 1959,

(ix) section 10 of the Mental Health Act 1959, so far as it relates to cases mentioned in paragraph (*a*) of that section,

(x) section 2(1)(*f*) of the Matrimonial Proceedings (Magistrates' Courts) Act 1960,

(xi) the Children and Young Persons Act 1963, except Part II and section 56,

(xii) this Act,

(xiii) the Adoption Act 1968,

(xiv) section 7(4) of the Family Law Reform Act 1969,

(xv) the Children and Young Persons Act 1969,

(xvi) section 43 of the Matrimonial Causes Act 1973,

(xvii) the National Health Service Reorganisation Act 1973,

(xviii) the Children Act 1975."

Social Work (*Scotland*) *Act* 1968 (*c.* 49)

48. In section 2(2) (functions of the social work committee), the following paragraph is inserted after paragraph (*g*)—

" (*h*) the Children Act 1975,".

49. For section 5(2) there is substituted—

" (2) The Secretary of State may make regulations in relation to—

(*a*) the performance of the functions assigned to local authorities by this Act ;

(*b*) the activities of voluntary organisations in so far as those activities are concerned with the like purposes ;

(*c*) the performance of the functions referred to social work committees under section 2(2)(*b*) to (*e*) and (*h*) of this Act ;

(*d*) the performance of the functions transferred to local authorities by section 1(4)(*a*) of this Act.".

50. In section 6(1)(*b*), after sub-paragraph (ii) there is inserted the following sub-paragraph—

" (iii) a child who has been placed for adoption by an adoption agency (within the meaning of section 1 of the Children Act 1975) ; ".

51. In section 10—

(*a*) in subsection (1), for the words from " with his functions " to the end there is substituted " with—

(*a*) his functions ;

(*b*) the functions of local authorities,

under this Act or under the enactments specified in paragraph (*a*) of section 1(4) and paragraphs (*b*) to (*e*) and (*h*) of section 2(2) of this Act, in circumstances where it appears to the Secretary of State that such grants or loans should be made." ;

(*b*) after subsection (3) there is inserted—

" (3A) In subsection (3) above, " voluntary organisation the sole or primary object of which is to promote social welfare " includes an adoption society approved under Part I of the Children Act 1975.".

52. In section 17—

(*a*) in subsection (3), for " section 16 " there is substituted " section 16(1)(*a*) " and after " local authority " there is inserted " , in whom are vested in accordance with the resolution the parental rights and powers in respect of a child," ;

(*b*) the following subsection is inserted after subsection (3)—

" (3A) A resolution under section 16(1)(*b*) of this Act shall not prevent the voluntary organisation, in whom are vested in accordance with the resolution the parental rights and powers in respect of a child, from allowing, either for a fixed period or until the voluntary organisation otherwise determine, the care of the child to be taken over by, and the child to be under the control of, a parent, guardian, relative or friend in any case where it appears to the voluntary organisation to be for the benefit of the child." ;

(*c*) in subsection (4), for " section 16 " there is substituted " section 16(1)(*a*) " ;

(*d*) in subsection (6), for the words " the said section 16 " there is substituted " section 16 of this Act " ;

(*e*) in subsection (7), after the words " local authority " there are inserted the words " or a voluntary organisation " ;

(*f*) in subsection (8)—

(i) for the words " to whom this section applies " there is substituted ", in respect of whom a resolution under section 16 of this Act is in effect," ; and

(ii) for the words " fifty pounds " there is substituted " £400 " ;

(*g*) in subsection (9)—

(i) for the words " where a local authority have, in accordance with subsection (3) of this section, allowed " there is substituted—

" Where—

(*a*) a local authority have, in accordance with subsection (3) of this section ; or

(*b*) a voluntary organisation have, in accordance with subsection (3A) of this section,
allowed " ;

(ii) for the words " fifty pounds " there is substituted " £400 ".

53. In section 18—

(*a*) in subsection (2), for " section 16 " there is substituted " section 16(1)(*a*) " ;

(*b*) in subsection (3)—

(i) in paragraph (*a*), for " paragraph (*a*) " there is substituted " sub-paragraph (i) " ;

(ii) for paragraph (*b*) there is substituted " (*b*) in the case of a resolution passed by virtue of circumstances specified in sub-paragraph (ii), (iii), or (iv) of subsection (1) of the said section 16, by the person who, but for the resolution, would have the parental rights and powers in relation to the child," ;

(iii) after the words " otherwise direct, the local authority " there are inserted the words ", and any voluntary organisation having parental rights and powers with respect to the child," ;

(*c*) in subsection (4), after the words " local authority " there are inserted the words " or voluntary organisation ".

54. In section 32(2)—

(*a*) for paragraphs (*b*) and (*c*) there is substituted—

" (*b*) he is falling into bad associations or is exposed to moral danger ; or

(*c*) lack of parental care is likely to cause him unnecessary suffering or seriously to impair his health or development ; or " ;

(*b*) in paragraph (*d*), for the words " Children and Young Persons (Scotland) Act 1937 " there is substituted " Criminal Procedure (Scotland) Act 1975 " ;

(c) after paragraph (d) there is inserted—
> " (dd) the child is, or is likely to become, a member of the same household as a person who has committed any of the offences mentioned in Schedule 1 to the Criminal Procedure (Scotland) Act 1975 ; or ".

55. In section 35(5)(a) at the end there is inserted " and to such other persons as may be prescribed ; ".

56. In section 44(5), after " 20 ", there is inserted " 20A.".

57. In section 49(3) for the words " The sheriff may examine the reporter and " there is substituted—
> " The reporter, whether or not he is conducting the proceedings before the sheriff, may be examined by the sheriff ; and the sheriff may examine ".

58. In section 69—

> (a) in subsection (1), at the end there are added the following words—
>> " ; and a court, if satisfied that there are reasonable grounds for believing that the child is within any premises, may grant a search warrant authorising a constable to search those premises for the child.".

> (b) for subsection (5) there is substituted—

" (5) In this and the next following section any reference—

> (a) to a child absconding includes a reference to his being unlawfully taken away ;

> (b) to a child absconding from a place or from the control of a person includes a reference to his absconding while being taken to, or awaiting being taken to, that place or that person as the case may be.".

59. In section 70, at the end there are added the following words—
> " ; and a court, if satisfied that there are reasonable grounds for believing that the child is within any premises, may grant a search warrant authorising a constable to search those premises for the child.".

60. In section 71, for the words " one hundred pounds " there is substituted " £400 ".

Adoption Act 1968 (c. 53)

61. In section 8(2)—

> (a) for the words " form set out in Schedule 1 to the Act of 1958, as modified by this subsection " there are substituted the words " form specified for the purposes of this subsection in regulations made by the Registrar General under section 21 of the Act of 1958 "; and

> (b) the words from " and for the purposes " to the end are repealed.

62. In section 8(5)—

(*a*) for paragraph (*b*) there is substituted—

" (*b*) for the references to section 21 of the Act of 1958 there shall be substituted references to section 23 of that Act ; " ;

(*b*) paragraph (*c*) is repealed ;

(*c*) for paragraph (*d*) there is substituted—

" (*c*) in subsection (4), for the reference to section 14 of the Births and Deaths Registration Act 1953 there shall be substituted a reference to section 20(1) of the Registration of Births, Deaths and Marriages (Scotland) Act 1965 (which provides for re-registration of births in certain cases)."

63. In section 9(5), for the words " a specified order or an overseas adoption " there are substituted the words " or a specified order ".

64. In section 11(1)—

(*a*) for the definition of " adoption order " there is substituted the following definition—

" " adoption order " means an order made under section 8 of the Children Act 1975 as a Convention adoption order ;" ;

(*b*) in the definition of " specified order " for the words " section 1 of this Act " there are substituted the words " sections 8(1) and 24 of the Children Act 1975 ".

65. In section 12(2), for the words from " made by virtue of " to " any of those provisions) " there are substituted the words " containing rules made by the Lord Chancellor under subsection (1) of this section ".

Housing Act 1969 (*c.* 33)

66. In section 86(2) for the words " any illegitimate son or daughter and any adopted son or daughter " there are substituted the words " and any illegitimate son or daughter ".

Children and Young Persons Act 1969 (*c.* 54)

67. In section 1(2) the following paragraph is inserted after paragraph (*b*)—

" (*bb*) it is probable that the conditions set out in paragraph (*a*) of this subsection will be satisfied in his case, having regard to the fact that a person who has been convicted of an offence mentioned in Schedule 1 to the Act of 1933 is, or may become, a member of the same household as the child ; ".

68. The following section is inserted after section 11—

" Local authority functions under certain supervision orders. 11A. The Secretary of State may make regulations with respect to the exercise by a local authority of their functions in a case where a person has been placed under their supervision by an order made under section 1(3)(*b*) or 21(2) of this Act."

69. In section 21—

(*a*) the following subsection is inserted after subsection (2)—

" (2A) A juvenile court shall not make an order under subsection (2) of this section in the case of a person who has not attained the age of 18 and appears to the court to be in need of care or control unless the court is satisfied that, whether through the making of a supervision order or otherwise, he will receive that care or control. " ;

(*b*) in subsection (3) for " the preceding subsection " there is substituted " subsection (2) of this section ".

70. The following section is inserted after section 21—

"Termination of care order on adoption, etc. 21A. A care order relating to a child shall cease to have effect—

(*a*) on the adoption of the child ;

(*b*) if an order under section 14 or section 25 of the Children Act 1975 is made in relation to the child ;

(*c*) if an order similar to an order under section 25 of the Children Act 1975 is made in Northern Ireland, the Isle of Man or any of the Channel Islands in relation to the child."

71. In section 27—

(*a*) in subsection (3), for the words " their general duty aforesaid " there are substituted the words " their general duty under section 12(1) of the Children Act 1948 " ;

(*b*) the following subsections are substituted for subsection (4)—

" (4) Without prejudice to their general duty under the said section 12, it shall be the duty of a local authority to review the case of each child in their care in accordance with regulations made under the following subsection.

(5) The Secretary of State may by regulations make provision as to—

(*a*) the manner in which cases are to be reviewed under this section ;

(*b*) the considerations to which the local authority are to have regard in reviewing cases under this section ; and

(*c*) the time when a child's case is first to be reviewed and the frequency of subsequent reviews under this section."

72. In section 58(1), the following paragraph is inserted after paragraph (*b*)—

"(*bb*) premises in which a child is living with a person other than his parent, guardian, relative or custodian, with whom he has been placed by an adoption agency (within the meaning of section 1 of the Children Act 1975) ; ".

Administration of Justice Act 1970 (*c.* 31)

73.—(1) In Schedule 1—

(*a*) after "*Appellate Business*" there is inserted the following paragraph—

"Proceedings on appeal under section 4A of the Children Act 1948 ; " ;

(*b*) at the end there is inserted the following paragraph—

"Proceedings on appeal under the Children Act 1975 ".

(2) In Schedule 8—

(*a*) in paragraph 5, after the words " Social Security Act 1966 " there are inserted the words " or section 45 of the Children Act 1975 " ;

(*b*) after paragraph 11, there is inserted the following paragraph—

" 12. An order under section 34(1)(*b*) of the Children Act 1975 (payments of maintenance in respect of a child to his custodian).".

Local Authority Social Services Act 1970 (*c.* 42)

74. In Schedule 1—

(*a*) at the end of the entry relating to the Adoption Act 1958 there are added the following words " Counselling services for adopted persons " ;

(*b*) the following is inserted at the end—

" Children Act 1975 (c. 72)

Part I	...	Maintenance of Adoption Service ; functions of local authority as adoption agency ; applications for orders freeing children for adoption ; inquiries carried out by local authorities in adoption cases.
Part II	...	Application by local authority for revocation of custodianship order ; inquiries carried out by local authority in custodianship cases.".

Guardianship of Minors Act 1971 (*c.* 3)

75.—(1) In section 9—

(*a*) in subsection (2) for " any person (whether or not one of the parents) " there is substituted " one of the parents ' and the words " or either of the parents " are repealed ;

(*b*) in subsection (3), the proviso is repealed ;

(*c*) in subsection (4), the words from " or (before or after the death of either parent) " to the end are repealed ;

SCH. 3

(*d*) the following subsections are inserted after subsection (4)—

" (5) An order shall not be made under subsection (1) of this section giving custody to a person other than the mother or father.

(6) An order shall not be made under subsection (1) of this section at any time when the minor is free for adoption (within the meaning of section 12(6) of the Children Act 1975) ".

(2) In section 13(2), after the words " order for the payment of money " there are inserted the words " made by a magistrates' court ".

(3) In section 16—

(*a*) in subsection (1) for " the High Court shall " there is substituted " the High Court may " ;

(*b*) in subsection (4) for " the magistrates' court may " there is substituted " the magistrates' court shall " ;

(*c*) in subsection (5), for the words from " section 9 " to " so given " there are substituted the words " section 3(3) or 4(3A) of the Guardianship Act 1973 for the discharge or variation of a supervision order or, as the case may be, an order giving the care of a minor to a local authority or an order requiring payments to be made to an authority to whom care of a minor is so given ".

Attachment of Earnings Act 1971 (c. 32)

76. In Schedule 1—

(*a*) in paragraph 6, after the words " Social Security Act 1966 " there are inserted the words " or section 45 of the Children Act 1975 " ;

(*b*) after paragraph 11, there is inserted the following paragraph—

" 12. An order under section 34(1)(*b*) of the Children Act 1975 (payments of maintenance in respect of a child to his custodian)."

Parliamentary and Other Pensions Act 1972 (c. 48)

77. In section 15(6), for the words " a stepchild or adopted child " there are substituted the words " or a stepchild ".

Matrimonial Causes Act 1973 (c. 18)

78. In section 44(1), for the words " custody of any person " there are substituted the words " care of any person ".

79. In section 50(1), at the end of paragraph (*e*) there are inserted the following words—

" or

(*f*) proceedings to which section 100(7)(*d*) of the Children Act 1975 applies (certain applications for revocation and variation of custodianship etc. orders) ; ".

Guardianship Act 1973 (*c.* 29)

80.—(1) In section 4(3) for the words from " the following provisions " to the end there are substituted the following words " sections 12(2) and 13 of the Guardianship of Minors Act 1971 shall apply as if the order made under section 2 of this Act were an order under section 9 of the Guardianship of Minors Act 1971."

(2) After section 4(3) there is inserted the following subsection—

" (3A) An order under section 2(2)(*b*) or (3) above relating to a minor may be varied or discharged by a subsequent order made on the application of either parent or after the death of either parent on the application of any guardian under the Guardianship of Minors Act 1971 or on the application of the local authority to whose care the minor was committed by the order under section 2(2)(*b*)."

81. In section 6(1), for " section 9 of the Guardianship of Minors Act 1971 or section " there is substituted " section 5 or 9 of the Guardianship of Minors Act 1971 or section 1(3) or ".

Legal Aid Act 1974 (*c.* 4)

82. In Schedule 1—

(*a*) for paragraph 3(*d*), there is substituted—

" (*d*) proceedings in which the making of an order under Part I of the Children Act 1975 is opposed by any party to the proceedings ; " ;

(*b*) the following paragraphs are inserted after paragraph 3(*e*)—

" (*f*) proceedings under Part II of the Children Act 1975 ;

(*g*) proceedings under section 63(2) of the Children Act 1975 ".

Housing Act 1974 (*c.* 44)

83. In section 129(4), for the words " any illegitimate son or daughter and any adopted son or daughter " there are substituted the words " and any illegitimate son or daughter ".

SCHEDULE 4

FURTHER REPEALS

PART I

STATUS OF ADOPTED CHILD

Chapter	Short Title	Extent of Repeal
16 & 17 Geo. 5. c. 29.	Adoption of Children Act 1926.	The whole Act so far as un-repealed.
3 & 4 Geo. 6. c. 42.	Law Reform (Miscellane-ous Provisions) (Scot-land) Act 1940.	Section 2(1) and (3).
11 & 12 Geo. 6. c. 43.	Children Act 1948.	In section 59(1), in the definition of " parent ", paragraph (a).
11 & 12 Geo. 6. c. 53.	Nurseries and Child-Minders Regulation Act 1948.	In section 13(2), in the defini-tion of " relative " (as in-serted by section 13 of the Adoption of Children Act 1949), paragraph (a).
12 & 13 Geo. 6. c. 76.	Marriage Act 1949.	In section 68(3), the words from " includes " to " but ".
12, 13 & 14 Geo. 6. c. 98.	Adoption of Children Act 1949.	Section 13(1)(a).
14 & 15 Geo. 6. c. 11.	Administration of Justice (Pensions) Act 1950.	Section 26(2).
1 & 2 Eliz. 2. c. 20.	Births and Deaths Regi-stration Act 1953.	In section 41, in the definition of " relative " the words from " and in relation to " to the end.
3 & 4 Eliz. 2. c. 18.	Army Act 1955.	In section 150(5), in the para-graph relating to a child of a person, the words " or adopted " and the words from " and in this paragraph " to the end of the paragraph.
3 & 4 Eliz. 2. c. 19.	Air Force Act 1955.	In section 15(5), in the para-graph relating to a child of a person, the words " or adopted " and the words from " and in this paragraph " to the end of the paragraph.
4 & 5 Eliz. 2. c. 69.	Sexual Offences Act 1956.	In section 28(4), in paragraph (a) the words from " has been adopted " to " a girl who " and the words " (and has not been so adopted) ".
4 & 5 Eliz. 2. c. 70.	Marriage (Scotland) Act 1956.	In section 1(5), paragraph (a) and the words " or adoptive parent " in paragraph (b).
6 & 7 Eliz. 2. c. 65.	Children Act 1958.	In section 17, the definition of " parent ".
6 & 7 Eliz. 2. c. 40.	Matrimonial Proceedings (Children) Act 1958.	In section 7(1)(b), the words " or an adopted ". Section 7(3).
7 & 8 Eliz. 2. c. 5.	Adoption Act 1958.	Sections 13 and 14. Section 15(1), (2) and (3). Sections 16 and 17. Section 18(1). Section 25.

Chapter	Short Title	Extent of Repeal
7 & 8 Eliz. 2. c. 5.—*cont.*	Adoption Act 1958.—*cont.*	In section 52(1) the words " (whether in law or in fact) ". In section 57(1), in the definition of " relative " paragraph (*a*). Section 58(2) and (3). In Schedule 5, paragraphs 1 to 4.
7 & 8 Eliz. 2. c. 65.	Fatal Accidents Act 1959.	In section 1, subsection (2)(*a*) and subsection (3).
7 & 8 Eliz. 2. c. 72.	Mental Health Act 1959.	In section 49, in subsection (2) the words from " an adopted person " to " as aforesaid ", and subsection (5).
8 & 9 Eliz. 2. c. 48.	Matrimonial Proceedings (Magistrates Courts) Act 1960.	In section 16(1), the words " or adopted " and " but does not include a child adopted by some other person or persons ", and the words from " and ' adopted ' " to the end.
8 & 9 Eliz. 2. c. 59.	Adoption Act 1960.	Section 1(2).
8 & 9 Eliz. 2. c. 61.	Mental Health (Scotland) Act 1960.	In section 45, in subsection (2) the words from " adopted person " to " person; and "; and subsection (5).
1964 c. 57.	Adoption Act 1964.	Section 1(1), (2) and (4).
1965 c. 49.	Registration of Births, Deaths and Marriages (Scotland) Act 1965.	In section 56(1), in the definition of " relative " the words from " and in relation to " to the end.
1965 c. 53.	Family Allowances Act 1965.	Section 17(4).
1967 c. 29.	Housing Subsidies Act 1967.	In section 24(3)(*c*), the word " adopted ".
1967 c. 81.	Companies Act 1967.	In section 30(2), the words "and adopted son " and " and adopted daughter ". In section 31(5), the words "and adopted son " and " and adopted daughter ".
1967 c. 88.	Leasehold Reform Act 1967.	In section 7(7), the words " and any adopted son or daughter". In section 18(3), the words "and any adopted son or daughter".
1968 c. 49.	Social Work (Scotland) Act 1968.	In section 94(1), in the definition of " parent ", paragraph (*a*).
1968 c. 53.	Adoption Act 1968.	Section 4(1) and (2). Section 10(2) and (3).
1968 c. 71.	Race Relations Act 1968.	In section 7(4) the words " and any adopted son or daughter".
1971 c. 56.	Pensions (Increase) Act 1971.	In section 3(7), the words from " and includes " to the end.
1973 c. 16.	Education Act 1973.	In section 3(5), the words from " and a child " to the end.

Chapter	Short Title	Extent of Repeal
1973 c. 18.	Matrimonial Causes Act 1973.	In section 52(1), the definition of " adopted " and, in the definition of " child ", the words " or adopted ".
1973 c. 45.	Domicile and Matrimonial Proceedings Act 1973.	In section 4(5), the words from " and in its application " to the end.
1975 c. 14.	Social Security Act 1975.	In section 32(3)(*c*), the words " the same relationship by adoption and to include also ". In section 71(6), the words "and a parent by adoption ". In section 161(2), the words " a son or daughter by adoption and ". In Schedule 20, in the definition of " relative " the words " or adoption ".
1975 c. 61.	Child Benefit Act 1975.	Section 24(3)(*c*).

The repeals of sections 16 and 17 of the 1958 Act, and of provisions containing references to those sections, have effect subject to paragraph 5(2) of Schedule 1, and the other repeals in this Part have effect as respect things done, or events occurring, after 31st December 1975.

PART II

LEGITIMATION

Chapter	Short Title	Extent of Repeal
17 Geo. 5 60.	Legitimacy Act 1926.	Section 1(3). Sections 3 to 5. In section 8(2), the words from " and to the taking " to " of a legitimated person ". In section 11, the definitions of " disposition ", " intestate " and " entailed interest ".
1969 c. 46.	Family Law Reform Act 1969.	Section 14(8). Section 15(4) and (6).

These repeals have effect subject to paragraph 12(9) of Schedule 1.

PART III

MISCELLANEOUS

Chapter	Short Title	Extent of Repeal
23 & 24 Geo. 5 c. 12.	Children and Young Persons Act 1933.	In section 1, in subsection (1) (*a*), the words " not exceeding one hundred pounds ", and in subsection (5), the words from " the maximum " to " pounds, and ".
1937 c. 37.	Children and Young Persons (Scotland) Act 1937.	In section 12, in subsection (1)(*a*), the words " not exceeding one hundred pounds ", and in subsection (5)(*a*) the words from " the maximum " to " pounds, and ".
7 & 8 Eliz. 2. c. 5.	Adoption Act 1958.	In section 4(2), the words from " (either " to " brought up) ". Section 7(1)(*b*) and (2). Section 21(3). In section 20(4), the words from " pursuant to " to " in force ". Section 49. In section 57(1) the definition of " infant ". Schedules 1 and 2.
1963 c. 37.	Children and Young Persons Act 1963.	Section 54.
1965 c. 49.	Registration of Births, Deaths and Marriages (Scotland) Act 1965.	Section 54(1)(*d*).
1968 c. 22.	Legitimation (Scotland) Act 1968.	In section 6(3), the words " or to subsection (1) of that section ".
1968 c. 53.	Adoption Act 1968.	Sections 1 to 3. In section 9(5), the words " of adoption ". In section 11(1), the definition of " qualified infant " " qualified person " and " qualified spouses ". In section 12(1), the words " or under Part I of the Act 1958 in its application adoption orders and prop adoption orders ", the wo " or the said Part I " in bo places where they occur and the words from " and the rules " to the end. In section 14(3), the words from " except the " to " 1958 and ".
1969 c. 54.	Children and Young Persons Act 1969.	Section 27(2).
1973 c. 29.	Guardianship Act 1973.	Section 3(5).

These repeals take effect on 1st January 1976.

PART VIII

Adoption: Evidence of Agreement & Guardians Ad Litem

Chapter	Short Title	Extent of Repeal
7 & 8 Eliz. 2. c. 5.	Adoption Act 1958.	Section 6. Section 9(7) and (8). Section 11(4) and (5).

These repeals take effect on the date section 20 comes into force.

PART IX

Inquiries etc. by Adoption Agencies

Chapter	Short Title	Extent of Repeal
7 & 8 Eliz. 2. c. 5.	Adoption Act 1958.	Section 3. Section 8. Section 53. In section 57(1), the definition of " Compulsory School age ".

These repeals take effect on the date section 18 comes into force.

PART X

Grants etc. for Voluntary Organisations

Chapter	Short Title	Extent of Repeal
10 & 11 Geo. 6 c. 43.	Children Act 1948.	Section 45(2). Section 46.
1969 c. 54.	Children and Young Persons Act 1969.	Section 65(2).

These repeals take effect on the date paragraphs 46 and 47 of Schedule 3 come into force.

SCH. 4

PART XI

PROTECTED CHILDREN

Chapter	Short Title	Extent of Repeal
7 & 8 Eliz. 2. c. 5.	Adoption Act 1958.	In section 37(1), paragraph (*a*), the words " of the person first mentioned in paragraph (*a*) of this subsection or, as the case may be," and the words " but is not a foster child within the meaning of Part I of the Children Act 1958 ". Section 37(2) and (5). Section 40(1), (2) and (3). Sections 41 and 42. In section 43(1), the words from " or in contravention " to " of this Act ".

These repeals take effect on the date paragraph 31 of Schedule 3 comes into force.

PART XII

CUSTODIANSHIP

Chapter	Short Title	Extent of Repeal
1973 c. 29.	Guardianship Act 1973.	In section 2, in subsection (2) (*b*), the words " or to any other individual " and in subsection (4)(*a*) the words " or to any person given the custody of the minor ". In section 3(3), the words from " or (before " to " section 9(1) of that Act " and the words from " and section 16(5) " to the end.

These repeals take effect on the date section 33 comes into force.

PRODUCED IN ENGLAND BY COMMERCIAL COLOUR PRESS LONDON
FOR HAROLD GLOVER
Controller of Her Majesty's Stationery Office and Queens' Printer of Acts of Parliament

Dd.294329 K16 1/77 CCP

ROBERT IRWIN

For Lust of Knowing
The Orientalists and their Enemies

PENGUIN BOOKS

PENGUIN BOOKS

Published by the Penguin Group
Penguin Books Ltd, 80 Strand, London WC2R ORL, England
Penguin Group (USA) Inc., 375 Hudson Street, New York, New York 10014, USA
Penguin Group (Canada), 90 Eglinton Avenue East, Suite 700, Toronto, Ontario, Canada M4P 2Y3
(a division of Pearson Penguin Canada Inc.)
Penguin Ireland, 25 St Stephen's Green, Dublin 2, Ireland
(a division of Penguin Books Ltd)
Penguin Group (Australia), 250 Camberwell Road, Camberwell, Victoria 3124, Australia
(a division of Pearson Australia Group Pty Ltd)
Penguin Books India Pvt Ltd, 11 Community Centre, Panchsheel Park, New Delhi – 110 017, India
Penguin Group (NZ), 67 Apollo Drive, Mairangi Bay, Auckland 1310, New Zealand
(a division of Pearson New Zealand Ltd)
Penguin Books (South Africa) (Pty) Ltd, 24 Sturdee Avenue, Rosebank, Johannesburg 2196, South Africa

Penguin Books Ltd, Registered Offices: 80 Strand, London WC2R ORL, England

www.penguin.com

First published by Allen Lane 2006
Published in Penguin Books 2007
1

Copyright © Robert Irwin, 2006
All rights reserved

The moral right of the author has been asserted

Typeset by Rowland Phototypesetting Ltd, Bury St Edmunds, Suffolk
Printed in England by Clays Ltd, St Ives plc

ISBN: 978–0–140–28923–7

Contents

Introduction

'Are you an Orientalist?' asked the underling.

I winced inwardly. It was a word with undertones, dark ones; an Orientalist went around in native dress, carried a pocket theodolite and worked for the ultimate and total dominance of the West.

Tim Mackintosh-Smith, *Travels with a Tangerine: A Journey in the Footsteps of Ibn Battutah* (2002)

A man lives not only his own personal life as an individual, but also, consciously or unconsciously, the life of his epoch and his contemporaries.

Thomas Mann, *The Magic Mountain* (1924)

I sometimes think of myself as a living fossil, for I was taught in a school where daily chapel services and the study of Latin were compulsory for everyone (though Greek was only for the clever boys). The teaching of Latin relied heavily on the rote learning of declensions and the elements of parsing and scansion. Our textbooks dated back to the beginning of the twentieth century or even earlier. The classics masters lingered lovingly on such weighty matters as whether the Roman 'V' should be pronounced as a 'W' or not. I used to play the alphabet game during the sermons and there were lengthy sermons at least once a week. Classical and biblical figures were presented to us as models for behaviour – King David, Simon Maccabeus, Gaius Mucius Scaevola, or Scipio Africanus. The system of education I endured was certainly much closer to that practised in the seventeenth and eighteenth centuries than to the system which prevails in the twenty-first century. Today, education no longer places such a heavy stress on the achievements of individual heroes and, in most schools, Christian indoctrination has been replaced by something vaguer, kinder and more multicultural. Rote learning of anything has fallen out of favour. Even so, I now find that my early immersion in both the Bible and in Latin texts proves to be useful in understanding the origins and formation of Orientalism, for, as we shall see, Orientalism developed in the shade of the much grander discourses of the Bible and of the classics.

I have done my best to make this book interesting, so that it can be read for pleasure, as well as for information. However, this has created problems for me, in that a leading theme of my book is that its subject is neither very important nor very glamorous – still less actually sinister. The older way of acquiring learning was a bit boring. Serious scholarship often is. Most of what Orientalists do will seem quite dull to non-Orientalists. There is nothing so very exciting about pedants busily engaged in making philological comparisons between Arabic and Hebrew, or cataloguing the coins of Fatimid Egypt, or establishing the basic chronology of Harun al-Rashid's military campaigns against Byzantium. Scholarship used to place little emphasis on accessibility or on contemporary socio-political relevance. The key early Orientalist texts were written in learned Latin and therefore could only be read by an educated elite. Also there were then fewer pressures to publish and many translations and academic essays remained in manuscript. Pious bishops, worthy patrons, timid antiquarians, museum curators with time on their hands, bewigged and gowned dons pursued their recondite enquiries in dusty tomes. They managed to find excitement in long-forgotten controversies regarding the decrees of the Council of Chalcedon or the correct manner of pronouncing Attic Greek. In their minds, they walked and talked with dead men. Many of the Orientalists I shall be discussing regarded their scholarly research as a form of prayer, and, Catholic or Protestant, they went to their graves convinced that, once their last breath was drawn, they would face eternal salvation or damnation. It is difficult for most of us now imaginatively to enter this past.

Orientalism was and is a subset of Western scholarship in general;

the history of academic Orientalism is therefore a special case study of the role of academics in cultural life. Who taught whom and how does academic transmission work? How does one achieve recognition as a scholar? In any century what resources were necessary and available in order to pursue a proper study of another culture? Was the study of Arabic and Islam really important within the broader framework of Western intellectual life? These are simple questions that have not yet been answered. Then there are murkier issues raised by Orientalism's critics, such as to what extent have academics working in this area been witting or unwitting collaborators with imperialism and Zionism? Are certain dictionaries and encyclopedias indictable as agents of cultural expropriation? Come to that, are all of Orientalism's critics writing in good faith, or does some of the polemic have an agenda which is related to internal academic politics, anti-Semitism or fundamentalist Islam?

This book would not have been written but for Edward Said's earlier book *Orientalism*, which was first published in 1978. Said added an afterword to a reissue in 1995, but none of the errors of fact and interpretation in the first edition were corrected in the expanded version. What does his book say? In a nutshell, it is this: Orientalism, the hegemonic discourse of imperialism, is a discourse that constrains everything that can be written and thought in the West about the Orient and more particularly about Islam and the Arabs. It has legitimized Western penetration of the Arab lands and their appropriation and it underwrites the Zionist project. Though Said is not consistent about the beginnings of Orientalism, on the whole he argued that it originated in the work of French and British scholars in the late eighteenth century. However, the discursive formation was not restricted to scholars, as imperialist administrators, explorers and novelists also participated in, or were victims of, this discourse. The West possesses a monopoly over how the Orient may be represented. Representations of the Orient invariably carry implications about Western superiority, or even, quite often, flat statements of that superiority. Note that it is only possible to talk of representations of the Orient, as the Orient has no objective reality, being merely a construct of Orientalism. Characteristically Orientalism is essentialist, racialist, patronizing and ideologically motivated.

Although some admirers of Said's book have conceded that it contains many errors and often misrepresents the achievements of the Orientalists it discusses, they sometimes go on to argue that it deserves praise and attention because of the subsequent debate and research it has provoked. I am not so sure about this. Most of the subsequent debate has taken place within the parameters set out by Edward Said. Much that is certainly central to the history of Orientalism has been quietly excluded by him, while all sorts of extraneous material have been called upon to support an indictment of the integrity and worth of certain scholars. One finds oneself having to discuss not what actually happened in the past, but what Said and his partisans think ought to have happened. Once one has entered the labyrinth of false turns, *trompe-l'œil* perspectives and cul-de-sacs, it is quite difficult to think one's way out again and reflect rationally and dispassionately about the subject. The distortion of the subject matter of *Orientalism* is so fundamental that to accept its broad framework as something to work with and then correct would be merely to waste one's time. I have therefore corralled most of my disagreements with Said within a single chapter. This has left me more space to discuss the principal works produced by major Orientalists that were so oddly ignored or disparaged in *Orientalism*. To set my cards out on the table at this early stage, that book seems to me to be a work of malignant charlatanry in which it is hard to distinguish honest mistakes from wilful misrepresentations. This may seem to my readers to depart from the normal restraint and courtesies of academic debate, but I am afraid that *Orientalism* led the way in these respects. Said, who died in 2003, was a well-respected figure. In attacking his most important book, I fear that I shall alienate some of my friends: on the other hand I shall certainly also infuriate old enemies and I shall take great pleasure in that. I really am attacking the book rather than the man. I have no significant disagreements with what Said has written about Palestine, Israel, Kipling's *Kim*, or Glenn Gould's piano playing.

Orientalism has been a bestseller – whether it deserved to have been is another matter. *For Lust of Knowing* will cover much of the same ground in what I hope is a more coherent and accessible fashion. The 'ground' in question is vast, for though the Orientalists were always few in number and rarely famous figures, the work they did was heavily influenced by work done in biblical exegesis, literary criticism, historiography and other grander disciplines, and sometimes, on the other hand, the research done by Orientalists had implications for the way the Bible or Homer was read, or it shed some light on how languages in general evolved. Therefore issues presented in this book have implications for those working in literary, historical, theological and cultural studies – as well, of course, for those working in Oriental studies. Critical books on Orientalism by Anouar Abdel-Malek, Edward Said, Alain Grosrichard and others have also raised profound and difficult questions about the nature of discourse, 'the Other', 'the Gaze' and a wide range of related epistemological issues. To engage with these and other critical accounts, it is necessary to consider the potential relevance for the study of Orientalism of concepts formulated by Antonio Gramsci, Michel Foucault and others. The conclusions reached after a study of the true history of Orientalism (or at least a truer one) may have relevance for controversies in loosely related fields. (I am thinking, for example, of Martin Bernal's *Black Athena: The Afroasiatic Roots of Classical Civilization* (1987) and of Edith Hall's *Inventing the Barbarian: Greek Self-Definition through Tragedy* (1989).)

At this early stage, only a few words are necessary concerning the meaning of 'Orientalism', as it is used in Said's book and in my book. In the eighteenth century the French word 'Orientaliste' described someone who was preoccupied with Levantine matters (not Chinese or Indian). In Britain, 'Orientalist', as used in the late eighteenth century, referred at first to a style rather than to a scholarly discipline. 'Dragons are a sure mark of orientalism' according to Thomas Warton's *History of English Poetry* (1774–81). Only in the early nineteenth century did it come to refer to the study of any and all Asian languages and cultures. There was a period in the 1830s when 'Orientalist' acquired a quite specific meaning in the context of British India. The 'Orientalists' there were administrators and scholars who advocated working with the traditional Muslim and Hindu institutions and customs as much as possible and of studying, teaching and researching the Indian cultural legacy. Such men were opposed and ultimately defeated by Anglicists like Macaulay and Bentinck, who, broadly speaking, preferred to impose British institutions and culture on the subcontinent.

Subsequently 'Orientalist' has tended to be used of those who have made a special study of Asian (and North African) languages and cultures. Since the 1960s at least Orientalism has been under attack from Islamicists, Marxists and others, and the word 'Orientalist' has acquired pejorative overtones. Nevertheless if anyone wants to call me an 'Orientalist', I shall be flattered, rather than offended.

When A. J. Arberry published his little book *British Orientalists* in 1943, he wrote about scholars who travelled in or wrote about Arabia, Persia, India, Indonesia and the Far East. In 1978 Said came to use the word 'Orientalism' in a newly restrictive sense, as referring to those who travelled, studied or wrote about the Arab world and even here he excluded consideration of North Africa west of Egypt. I cannot guess why he excluded North Africa, but, that omission apart, in this particular instance I am happy to accept his somewhat arbitrary delimitation of the subject matter, for it is the history of Western studies of Islam, Arabic and Arab history and culture that interests me the most. However, it is often necessary to cast a sideways glance at what was happening in contemporary Persian and Turkish studies – particularly Turkish, for it would be arbitrary to detach study of the pre-modern Arab world totally from Ottoman studies. Developments in Sinology and Egyptology are also sometimes relevant and, of course, any study of Orientalism that fails to engage with the overwhelming importance of biblical and Hebrew studies and of religion in general for the way Islam and the Arabs were studied and written about would be preposterous and thoroughly anachronistic.

Some writers have thought that the origins of Orientalism are to be found in ancient Greece. Others have suggested a much later start with the decrees of the Council of Vienne in 1311–12. Others again believe that there was no Orientalism worthy of the name prior to Bonaparte's invasion of Egypt in 1798. From the latter point of view, the rise of Orientalism begins at about the same time as the great age of European imperialism. My own view, which I shall be setting out in more detail in the course of this book, is that there was nobody one could consider to be a serious Orientalist prior to Guillaume Postel (*c.* 1510–81), and that Orientalism either begins in the sixteenth century with him or, if not quite so early as that, then no later than the mid-seventeenth century, when Jacob Golius (1596–1667) and

Edward Pococke (1604–91), as well as other not quite so learned or industrious figures, published their ground-breaking researches. However, I shall briefly discuss what might be mistakenly interpreted as evidence of early Orientalism in antiquity and the Middle Ages, before rushing on to the seventeenth and later centuries.

Until the late nineteenth century, Orientalism had little in the way of institutional structures and the heyday of institutional Orientalism only arrived in the second half of the twentieth century. The research institutes, the banks of reference books, the specialist conferences and professional associations came then. Therefore, *For Lust of Knowing* is mostly a story of individual scholars, often lonely and eccentric men. Intellectual eminences such as Postel, Erpenius and Silvestre de Sacy scoured Europe for similarly learned correspondents who might have some inkling of the nature of the recondite problems that they worked upon. Since there was no overarching and constraining discourse of Orientalism, there were many competing agendas and styles of thought. Therefore this book contains many sketches of individual Orientalists – dabblers, obsessives, evangelists, freethinkers, madmen, charlatans, pedants, romantics. (Even so, perhaps still not enough of them.) There can be no single chronicle of Orientalism that can be set within clearly defined limits.

Edward Pococke was probably the best Arabist of his day and, much later, Antoine Isaac Silvestre de Sacy was the most distinguished scholar of classical Arabic in the early nineteenth century. Nevertheless, I can produce better translations from Arabic than either of those impressive figures. This is not because I am cleverer or more industrious than they were, but I have been instructed by careful teachers, whereas Pococke and Silvestre de Sacy had effectively to teach themselves. Moreover, I have access to much better dictionaries and grammars and other reference tools, such as the excellent *Encyclopaedia of Islam*. A recurring theme of this book is the way in which each generation of Arabists found the previous generation's work unsatisfactory. It was more or less inevitable that this should be so. By today's standards, nobody's Arabic in the seventeenth and eighteenth centuries was that good. The early Orientalists were often ruthless in denouncing each other's translations and editing decisions. Rivalry and rancour have been powerful driving forces in the story of Orientalism.

7

For Lust of Knowing contains no discussion of Flaubert's letters from Egypt, Disraeli's novels, Delacroix's painting of *The Death of Sardanapalus*, or Verdi's *Aida*. I am hostile to the notion that Orientalism can be viewed primarily as a canon of literary and other artistic masterpieces, mostly composed by dead, white males. The products of mainstream Orientalism were less colourful and less fluent than that. Orientalism in its most important aspect was founded upon academic drudgery and close attention to philological detail. I do not believe that the novelist Flaubert and the Arabist and Islamicist Sir Hamilton Gibb were really contributing to essentially the same discourse or were the victims of it. However, the distinction between academic and artistic production is, of course, not hard-edged. For example, William Beckford's novel *Vathek* has academic-looking footnotes and, on the other hand, Gibb's understanding of Saladin's career was greatly influenced by his enthusiasm for Walter Scott's novel *The Talisman*. There is a significant overlap between Orientalist scholarship and artistic works of an Oriental inspiration, but it is, I believe, only an overlap and not evidence of a single cohesive discourse. Nevertheless the way Islam and the Arabs have been presented by Western writers and artists is clearly important, as well as interesting in its own right, and I shall be discussing it in a second volume, entitled *The Arts of Orientalism*.

In the course of writing this book I have benefited from conversations with Helen Irwin, Mary Beard, Tom Holland, Charles Burnett, Roz Kaveney and Professor Hugh Kennedy. I am grateful to my editor, Stefan McGrath, for his enthusiasm. I have also benefited from the editing of Jane Robertson. They are not responsible for any errors in this book – I only wish they were. I have slated some critics of Orientalism for their factual errors, yet I am acutely conscious that in covering such a vast field as the history of Orientalism, I am bound to have made quite a few errors of my own. At least I tried to get things right.

Since publication of the hardback, various friends and critics (and they overlap to a surprising extent) have pointed out a number of errors. Since I believe in getting facts right, I have corrected the errors. I am particularly grateful to Sir James Craig, Ted Gorton, Alastair Hamilton, Malcolm Jack, David Morgan, Basim Musallam and Amir Taheri.

I

The Clash of Ancient Civilizations

But how did it all begin? If it is history we want, then it is a history of conflict. And the conflict begins with the abduction of a girl, or with the sacrifice of a girl. And the one is continually becoming the other. It was the 'merchant wolves', arriving by ship from Phoenicia, who carried off the tauropárthenos from Argos. Tauropárthenos means 'the virgin dedicated to the bull'. Her name was Io. Like a beacon signalling from mountain to mountain, this rape lit the bonfire of hatred between the two continents. From that moment on, Europe and Asia never stopped fighting each other, blow answering blow. Thus the Cretans, 'the boars of Ida', carried off Europa from Asia . . .

Roberto Calasso, *The Marriage of Cadmus and Harmony* (1993)

TROY, AN ORIENTALIST BATTLEFIELD?

Is Orientalism an eternal given? Or was it a discourse that was formed in, say, the early fourteenth century, when the establishment of chairs of Arabic was decreed by the Council of Vienne? Or, say, in the late eighteenth century, when Bonaparte invaded Egypt and his team of savants catalogued the antiquarian and ethnographic details of the land? Or was this perhaps a clash of cultures that went back to pre-Islamic and even pre-Christian times? In *Crusade, Commerce and*

Culture, the Arab historian Aziz Atiya argued that the Crusades had to be seen in the context of a much older and enduring conflict between East and West: 'These relations go far back into antiquity beyond the confines of the medieval world. The bone of contention was the undefined frontier of Europe, otherwise described as the spiritual frontiers of the West vis-à-vis Asia.'[1] According to Atiya, the Greek mind created the frontier between Europe and Asia – the earliest version of the 'Eastern Question'. For this Greek mind, the Hellenistic legacy 'aimed at encompassing the whole world'. Edward Said developed a similar argument: 'Consider the first demarcation between Orient and West. It already seems bold by the time of the *Iliad*.'[2]

'Barbarian' (or in Greek *barbaros*) was originally a linguistic concept and it applied to all non-Greek-speaking peoples. As such, it applied to both civilized and uncivilized peoples. Thus the Greeks considered the Persians to be 'barbarians', but hardly uncouth or uncultured. Greeks were impressed by the Phoenician alphabet, Lydian coinage and Egyptian sculpture. (Martin Bernal in *Black Athena: The Afroasiatic Roots of Classical Civilization* (1987), has argued controversially that the Greek culture in its essentials was derived from that of the Egyptians.) In general, the Greeks admired Orientals, while despising the Thracians and Scythians on their northern frontiers. 'Barbarians' were just as likely to be Westerners as Orientals. Greeks envied the wealth of Gyges and Croesus, rulers of Lydia in Asia Minor.[3] As Calasso notes: 'Right from the beginning, Greek elegance is opposed to Asiatic sumptuousness with its prodigal mix of solemnity and abundance.'[4] In fact the demarcation between Greek and Oriental is not so very clear in Homer. Nowhere in the *Iliad* (which was probably produced in the eighth century BC) are the Trojans called barbarians, nor are they treated as such. Only the Carians, from South West Asia Minor, are characterized as 'barbarians' by Homer. One thing that militated against a hypothetical contraposition of 'Greek' and 'barbarian' in this early period is that there was no word for 'Greek' in ancient Greece. 'Graeci' (meaning Greeks) is a later Roman coinage. However, the concept of the Hellene and Hellenic culture was in circulation by the time of Herodotus.

The Orientalist Bernard Lewis, in a discussion of 'insider' and 'outsider' in the world of antiquity, has suggested that the tendency to make such distinctions is common to all times and all places. However, the distinctions were not necessarily fixed and irrevocable. Though the Jews distinguished between Jew and Gentile, they were prepared to accept converts. Similarly, the Greeks distinguished between Greek and barbarian, but they allowed that it was possible to cease to be a barbarian by adopting Greek language and culture. Lewis continues: 'There is another respect in which Greeks and Jews were unique in the ancient world – in their compassion for an enemy. There is nothing elsewhere to compare with the sympathetic portrayal by the Greek dramatist Aeschylus – himself a veteran of the Persian wars – of the sufferings of the vanquished Persians . . .'[5] Edward Said has taken a rather different point of view of the same play, *The Persians*. According to him, Aeschylus dumps on to Asia 'the feelings of emptiness, loss and disaster . . . also the lament that in some glorious past Asia fared better, was itself victorious over Europe'.[6]

THE PERSIANS

If the Persians needed to make play with the notion of an 'Other' or to construct an archive of racial stereotypes or to put on plays and write histories in order to justify their conquests, those activities have gone unrecorded. They just seem to have set about trying to conquer their neighbours. In the sixth century BC the Persian empire expanded westwards to include Lydia and the Greek cities of Asia Minor. Then Darius made careful preparations for the conquest of Athens (490 BC). After a prolonged standoff, the Persians were heavily defeated at Marathon and, after an abortive attempt to capture Athens, the First Persian War came to an ignominious end. Darius died in 485 BC and it was left to his son, Xerxes, to plan a renewed campaign of conquest. In 480 BC an enormous Persian army crossed over into Europe. This army (which, by the way, included large numbers of Greeks) was defeated at Thermopylae and at Plataea and their fleet was defeated at Salamis. That was the end of Persian attempts to conquer Greece. It is possible that these attempts to conquer Greece encouraged the Greeks to think more of themselves as a distinctive race. (The Persians certainly thought of themselves as a distinctive race and they referred to all foreigners as *anarya*, non-Aryan. The stone reliefs of the Persian citadel of Persepolis depicted the subject races in their various costumes bringing tribute to their Persian overlords.)

The Persians by Aeschylus was first staged in 472 BC, seven years after the withdrawal of the Persian army from mainland Greece. Both the author and his audience were veterans of that war. Aeschylus's brother was killed in the aftermath of Marathon. His hand was cut off as he was hanging on to a Persian ship. Aeschylus's play commemorates the triumph of Greek arms against vastly superior forces. However, as Lewis has indicated, it seeks to do this from the Persian point of view. The play, which is set in Persia, opens with a chorus of Persians anxiously speculating about the fate of Xerxes's expedition. Atossa, the emperor's mother, has had ominous dreams. Then a messenger arrives with a detailed report of the disaster of Salamis. (In Greek terms, this was a *peripeteia*, a surprising turn of events.) The chorus summons up the ghost of Xerxes's father, Darius, and the ghost declares the disaster to have been brought about through the hubris of Xerxes and predicts the defeat at Plataea. Darius is presented as a capable and heroic figure. With the arrival of Xerxes himself, lamentations are redoubled at the court. It is important to bear in mind that the play really is a tragedy, even though the Greeks are not its victims.[7]

THE FATHER OF HISTORY

Voltaire thought that history began with Herodotus's history of the Graeco-Persian war. Much of the *History* written by Herodotus of Halicarnassus (*c.* 490–425 BC) was based on first-hand experience, for the author had travelled widely in Asia Minor, Scythia, Egypt, Babylon and elsewhere. Moreover, so far as his information on Persia was concerned, much of this is likely to have come from Greek mercenaries who had served in the Persian armies. Greek-speaking Persians may also have served as Herodotus's informants. It has been suggested that the Persian wars served as the original stimulus for the writing of the book and that Herodotus's account of those wars was written first, with the other parts on Egypt and elsewhere being written later.

The *History* opens with a preface on the legendary origins of the hostility between the Europeans and the Asiatics. Thus Herodotus narrates the stories of the rapes of Io, Europa and Medea, before proceeding on to the Trojan War. Although he stresses the antiquity of the quarrel between the East and the West, there is absolutely no hint in his *History* that the Trojans are in any sense inferior to the Greeks. Real history in Herodotus's book begins not with the legends that make up the story of the Trojan War but with the career of the last king of Lydia, Croesus, and his defeat by the Persians and their conquest of the Lydians. More generally, Herodotus was especially interested in the victims of Persian imperialism: Lydians, Egyptians, Scythians and Libyans.

Herodotus seems to have been singularly free of racial prejudice and because of his open-minded interest in other cultures he was known as the 'barbarophile'. He wrote an admiring account of the achievements of the Egyptian pharaohs and he harped on the grandeur of Egypt and Lydia before those lands fell to the Persians. As for the Persians, Herodotus tended to focus on the ways in which the Persians differed from the Greeks – in their tradition of despotic rule, their practice of polygamy, in their birthday celebrations and other matters. However, these were specific differences and there is no sense in Herodotus of some overarching Otherness. Incidentally, one thing that struck him about the Persians was their racism: 'After their own nation they hold their nearest neighbours most in honour, then the nearest but one – and so on, their respect decreasing as the distance grows, and the most remote being the most despised. Themselves they consider in every way superior to everyone else in the world, and allow other nations a share of good qualities decreasing according to distance, the furthest off being in their view the worst.'[8] He consistently stressed the importance of *nomoi*, or traditional behavioural norms, forming social customs. He thought that long-established custom could make anything seem normal and the strange ways of the Persians merely furnished proofs of Herodotus's way of thinking. Moreover, though he enumerated the ways in which foreign cultures differed from Greek culture, this did not imply the superiority of Greek culture, and Herodotus repeatedly acknowledged Greece's various debts to other cultures, particularly those of Egypt and Phoenicia.

Indeed, he believed that Greece had been originally colonized from the East and that the Spartans were the descendants of the Egyptians. Certainly the Persians were far less alien in his eyes than the Scythians. According to Said, Herodotus conquered the Orient by visiting it and writing about it.[9] Perhaps, but if so, his was an entirely metaphorical conquest.

OCCIDENTAL FRENZY

The dramatist Euripides (c. 484–406 BC) was the best known of the great Greek tragedians. His play, *The Bacchae*, was probably produced posthumously in Athens in 405 BC and is widely regarded as his masterpiece. It deals with the coming of the god Dionysius to Thebes. The Theban women become his orgiastic devotees, or Bacchantes, but the city's king Pentheus refuses to acknowledge the divinity of Dionysius – this despite such clear manifestations of Dionysius' power as the destruction of Pentheus' palace. Then Dionysius, disguised as one of his cultists, persuades Pentheus to disguise himself as a woman in order to witness the Dionysian mysteries. However, Pentheus is unmasked and torn to pieces by the Bacchantes.[10]

According to Said, in *The Bacchae* Euripides links Dionysius with threatening Oriental mysteries. The play, which was produced at a time when Oriental cults were spreading, presented the lure of the Orient as an insinuating danger: 'Dionysius is explicitly connected with his Asiatic origin.'[11] But what 'Asiatic origin'? Dionysius was the son of Zeus and Semele, the Theban daughter of Cadmus, who in turn was grandfather of Pentheus. It follows that Dionysius is no more Asiatic than Pentheus. The only grounds for possibly thinking of him as an Asiatic was that he had conquered a large part of Asia (but, on those grounds, one would also have to regard Warren Hastings and General Allenby as Asiatics). It would be sad if a dyspeptic reading put people off reading the play as it is not a polemical tract attacking the introduction of new Oriental ideologies into Greece. *The Bacchae* is a work of imagination that has nothing to do with agitprop. In the play, Euripides presents the rational and the irrational as being found within the individual, rather than distributed between the two continents. As E. R. Dodds pointed out in *The Greeks and the Irrational*, the play was not intended as an attack on Dionysiac cults, for to 'resist Dionysius is to repress the elemental in one's own nature'.[12] The legitimacy of Dionysius' divine status is emphatically affirmed.

Instead, the play commemorates the obstinacy and folly of Pentheus. His grandfather Cadmus, the seer Teiresias and the Chorus all warn him against opposing the Dionysiac rites. Their warnings are seen by Said as presaging Orientalism: 'hereafter Oriental mysteries will be taken seriously, not least because they challenge the rational Western mind to new exercises of its enduring ambition and power'.[13] But by the time Euripides wrote this play, the Dionysiac cult was an accepted part of the spiritual landscape of Athens and there is no evidence that Euripides or any of his contemporaries thought of Dionysius as an irrational Oriental. The play refers to his 'white skin' and, according to legend, he first entered Greece from Thrace (so from the north, not the east). The actual cult was probably Mycenaean in origin. In the twentieth century the theme of the Dionysiac strain within Greek culture and Western culture more generally was taken up and studied by the great German cultural historian and iconographer, Aby Warburg. Sir Ernst Gombrich (who later became director of London University's Warburg Institute) summarized Warburg's approach: 'In its myth we find enshrined the extremes of emotion and self-abandon from which modern man must shrink in awe but which, as preserved in the symbols of art, contains those very moulds of emotion which alone make artistic expression possible. Without the primeval passion which was discharged in maenadic dances and Bacchantic frenzy, Greek art would never have been able to create those "superlatives" of gesture with which the greatest of Renaissance artists expressed the deepest human values.'[14] Far from being Asian monopolies, the Dionysiac, the frenzied and the irrational lie at the roots of Western culture.

LOVING AND HATING THE PERSIANS

Xenophon (c. 430–354 BC) was a disciple of Socrates and a historian. An aristocrat, he was out of sympathy with the Athenian republic of his time and therefore he took service for a while in the army of the Persian prince Cyrus, son of King Darius II. Xenophon's *Cyropaedia* ('Education of Cyrus') presented an idealized portrait of the Persian king in order to serve as a vehicle for Xenophon's meditations on statecraft and related matters. He rather idealized the achievements of the founder of the dynasty Cyrus the Great (539–529 BC), so that the *Cyropaedia* reads as a mixture of political treatise and historical novel.[15] In Xenophon's book, the Greeks would do well to emulate the achievements of Cyrus, the perfect ruler and general. Xenophon's account of the admirable Persian constitution was really his own invention. However, by the time he wrote, it was clear that the Persian empire was in difficulties and the work ends up condemning Persian luxury and chronicling the disorder into which Persia had fallen after the death of Cyrus. It should also be noted that in his *Anabasis*, his account of the long march home of a band of 10,000 Greek soldiers after Cyrus had been defeated in his attempt to take the throne from his brother Artaxerxes II, Xenophon presented the Persians as soft and treacherous. Even so the *Anabasis* is more concerned with Greek politics and the rhetoric of leadership than it is with the Persians and, as the Italian novelist and critic Italo Calvino remarked of Xenophon, in this book he consistently showed respect for the hostile lands they travelled through: 'If he often displays an aloofness or aversion towards "barbarian" customs, it must also be said that "colonialist" hypocrisy is completely foreign to him. He is aware of being at the head of a horde of foreign parasites . . .'[16]

Although Aeschylus, Euripides and Herodotus cannot fairly be presented as unambiguous prototypes of the Orientalist accomplices of imperialism, this is not to say that racial and anti-Oriental stereotyping cannot be found in Greek writings. It would be astonishing if all Greeks were entirely free of such prejudices. The famous philosopher Aristotle (384–322 BC) was understandably prejudiced in favour of what he knew best, which was the city state, and in his treatise, *The*

Politics, he presented an unflattering portrait of Oriental despotism. He claimed that Persia was typical of tyrannies that forbade private associations and exercised close surveillance of their citizens. But tyranny was not a specifically Oriental institution and Aristotle discussed Persian tyranny in the same breath as that of Periander of Corinth.[17] Similarly he ranked Persia with Sparta and Crete as being among the martial races. On the other hand, Aristotle did believe that tyranny was more acceptable to non-Greek races: 'and it is because barbarians are by natural character more slavish than Greeks (and Asiatics than Europeans) that they tolerate despotic rule without resentment'.[18] Towards the end of *The Politics* he speculated on the effects that climate had on the people of Europe, making them full of spirit, whereas 'the Asiatic races have both brains and skill, but are lacking in courage and will-power; so they have remained enslaved and subject'.[19] However, it is important to bear in mind that Aristotle was not really very interested in Asia or its problems. He was writing about Greece and its city states, even though such states had been doomed by the rise of Alexander's Macedonian empire and both Greek and Persian territories had been incorporated within its borders. The physician Hippocrates (d. *c.* 400 BC), like Aristotle, believed that climate and region had a role in shaping people.[20] In *On Airs, Waters and Places*, he compared geophysical conditions in Asia and Europe and argued that Asian temperament was different from that of the European because the climate was different. (Earlier Herodotus had made his quasi-fictional Cyrus remark that 'a soft country makes soft men'.) This sort of thinking would resurface in the seventeenth century in the writing of Montesquieu.

ARABIAN ROME

In the Roman period, Rome fought a series of wars against the Parthian and Sasanian rulers of Persia. However, fighting on the empire's eastern front does not seem to have been accompanied by any distinctive racist propaganda about sinister Orientals. Long before the rise of Islam in the seventh century, there were large numbers of Arabs settled in Rome's eastern provinces and some Arabs were prominent in Roman society. The Emperor Philip (AD 244–49) was an Arab. The Emperor Severus married an Arab and hence the Severan line (AD 193–235) was half Arab. The famous Neoplatonist philosopher, Iamblichus, was an Arab. But the word Arab was more commonly used to describe a nomadic or semi-nomadic way of life than it was used as a racial designation. The full contribution of Arabs (and of Persians, Berbers and others) to Roman culture and society has been masked by the tendency of the Arabs of the cities to assume Roman or Greek names. The satirical poet Juvenal complained about the prevalence of Oriental cultural influence in Rome: 'the Orontes [a river in Syria] has flowed into the Tiber'. In his *Satires* he associated the Greek and Syrian inhabitants of Rome with decadence and soft living. Most of the inhabitants of the eastern provinces of the Roman empire were Arabs or Aramaic speakers. Rome maintained on its eastern frontier a series of client kingdoms – Emesa, Nabataea, Palmyra and Edessa – which were Arab. Palmyra and Petra were great cities of commerce and high culture. Strabo and Diodorus Siculus wrote with admiration of the Nabataean Arabs of the region. Arab auxiliaries fought in Roman armies against the Persians. Not only had Arabs been settling throughout the eastern provinces of the empire centuries before the Islamic conquests, but there were also communities of Arabs in some of the ports of the western Mediterranean. Some Arab communities even settled in Roman Britain.[21] Arabs participated in a Mediterranean-centred classical culture and in the medieval centuries that followed, Islam was to become one of the chief legatees of that culture.

Some have argued that in the centuries that followed the writings of Aeschylus, Euripides and Herodotus, the Greeks and Romans continued to develop a taxonomic lore about the Orient and this was passed on to Christian Europe. At first sight, this may seem plausible, but there is a big gap in continuity and until the fifteenth century very few scholars in Western Europe were able to read Greek. As we shall see when we come to consider the writings of such medieval figures as Peter the Venerable and Ricoldo da Monte Croce, they do not seem to owe anything at all to any taxonomic lore adumbrated by Greek playwrights and historians. They had their own fresh medieval Christian prejudices.

2

An Ancient Heresy or a
New Paganism

*And at that time Sir Palamides, the Saracen, was in that
country, and well cherished with the king and queen. And
every day Sir Palamides drew unto La Beale Isoud and prof-
fered her many gifts, for he loved her passingly well. All that
espied Tramtrist, and full well knew he Sir Palamides for a
noble knight and a mighty man.*

Sir Thomas Malory, *Morte d'Arthur*, Book VIII, ch. 9

THE COMING OF ISLAM

'Of the Middle East in about AD 600 one thing can be said for certain:
its chances of being conquered by Arab tribesmen in the name of a
new religion were so remote that nobody had even speculated that
it might happen. Islam came upon the world as a totally unexpected development . . .'[1] Nevertheless, by 632, the year of the Prophet
Muhammad's death, most of the Arabian peninsula had submitted
to Islam. In the next few years, not only Syria was taken from
the Byzantines, but the Sasanian Persians had also been defeated and
their capital, Ctesiphon, occupied. The Arabs conquered Egypt in
642. Thereafter Arab armies pressed on eastwards through Iran and
Khurasan, ultimately reaching the frontiers of China, while other
Arab and Berber forces moved westwards across North Africa and
crossed into Spain in 711. For a while, it even seemed that areas of
the south of France and Switzerland might be included within the
frontier of the Arab caliphate. For reasons that remain mysterious,

the new conquerors were referred to in the earliest Latin sources either as 'Hagarenes' or as 'Saracens'. Though the Muslim Arabs made little attempt to convert their newly conquered subjects, nevertheless there were political, social and, above all, fiscal advantages in converting to Islam. Consequently Christendom was faced with not just a military threat, but an ideological one as well.

It was natural for Christian thinkers to interpret the unfamiliar and unexpected phenomenon of Islam in terms of what was familiar to them already. Therefore they tended to present Islam to themselves not as a new religion, but rather as the variant of an old heresy. As Richard Southern has observed: 'There was only one way in which this chaos (as it must have appeared) of truth and falsehood could be treated by a twelfth-century thinker if it were to be brought within the range of his equipment: it must be treated as a heresy, more mysterious in its operation than other heresies which had appeared in the course of Christian history, but like them a more or less deliberate perversion of the true faith, which required refutation by the ordinary rules of argument.'[2] Usually Christian thinkers characterized Islam as a variant of Arianism. Arius (c. 250–c. 336) had taught that God the Son was inferior to God the Father and, unlike God the Father, Jesus was born of a woman, endured mortal tribulations and ultimately death. This doctrine was rejected by the Council of Nicaea in 325. The contention that Islam was a Christian heresy was bolstered by the dissemination of the legend of Muhammad's early encounter with a heretical monk. The twelve-year-old Muhammad's meeting with a Christian monk called Bahira (or, in some versions, Sergius) in the Syrian desert is attested by Ibn Hisham's ninth-century life of the Prophet. In the Muslim version, the monk recognized the seal of prophethood between Muhammad's shoulders and foretold his future importance. Christian polemicists, however, invented tales about how a monk (in some versions actually a renegade cardinal) instructed Muhammad in the elements of a pernicious Christian heresy.[3]

During the Middle Ages, Christians came under attack from Muslim polemicists. Muslims rejected the idea that a God could be born from a woman's flesh. They denied that Jesus had died on the cross. They claimed that the Christians were not true monotheists, for they really worshipped three gods.[4] Christians were also alleged to have tampered with the texts of the Old and New Testaments. The Christians for their part characterized Islam as a sensual cult – and hence its sanctioning of polygamy. Pointing to the number of women taken as wives by the Prophet, they accused him of being motivated by sensuality. Islam was a violent religion that owed its success to force of arms. Christian polemicists derided the earthy, sexual nature of paradise as described in the Qur'an. They mocked the failure of Muhammad to perform miracles. But of course, the most fundamental issue was the Muslims' refusal to acknowledge the divinity of Christ.[5]

There was a tendency among those writing in Greek and Latin to explain the Muslims' capture of Jerusalem and the other Muslim successes in terms of punishment for Christian lack of unity and other failings. (This sort of explanation would remain popular well into the eighteenth century.) There were also some pious thinkers who interpreted the triumph of Islam as a presage of the Last Days. The Muslims were surely one of the horns of the fourth beast, foretold by Daniel in the Old Testament, whose coming immediately preceded the enthronement of the Ancient of Days: 'After this I saw in the night visions, and behold a fourth beast, dreadful and terrible, and strong exceedingly; and it had great iron teeth; it devoured and brake in pieces, and stamped the residue with the feet of it: and it was diverse from all the beasts that were before it; and it had ten horns.'[6]

But though a handful of churchmen composed libellous polemics or prophecies directed against Islam, the essential fact was that most Christians had no interest at all in the new religion. Bishop Arculf went on pilgrimage to Jerusalem around the year 700. Since he was possessed by the desire to walk and worship in the place where Christ had once walked, the Muslims (who had been in occupation of Jerusalem since 637) were all but invisible to him. He merely noted that in the Temple area, 'the Saracens have now erected a square house of prayer, in a rough manner, by raising planks and beams upon some remains of old ruins, and it is said that it will hold about three thousand men', before he went on to write about the Christian holy places.[7] Similarly, the Venerable Bede in his *History* mentioned the attacks of Saracen pirates on the British Isles, without troubling to enquire as to their religion.

THE EASTERN CHRISTIAN RESPONSE

St John of Damascus, also known as Yuhanna ibn Mansur (d. *c.* 749), was probably the first to engage with Muslim theology in some detail. John of Damascus seems to have been of Arab parentage. He certainly knew Arabic, though he was also literate and indeed fluent in Greek. In Damascus, he had been a schoolfriend of Yazid, son of the Umayyad Caliph Muawiya I. When the Byzantines still ruled Syria, John's father had worked for the Emperor Heraclius as a financial official. John did the same for the Umayyad caliphs, even though John apparently regarded himself as formally a subject of the Byzantine emperor. In 724 he left public life, as it had become impossible for Christians to continue to hold high office under the caliphs in Syria. The former public servant retired to the monastery of St Sabas in Palestine, where he studied theology and philosophy.

'The last Father of the Byzantine Church', as Peter Brown has characterized John, wrote extensively upon theological matters. Islam, as such, was not a major issue in his eyes. Arab rule in Syria was viewed as a temporary vexation. He was far more concerned with the iconoclast movement within the Orthodox Church and his priority was to combat those who denied the validity of prayer before holy images and who sought to destroy the icons of the Church. Most of what he wrote about Islam was written within the context of a much wider survey of the schisms that threatened the Church. His orthodox summa, *The Fount of Knowledge*, written in Greek some time after 742, was concerned primarily with Christological problems and it became the basic text of Byzantine orthodoxy on such matters. The work is in three parts, the second of which is devoted to heresies. Over a hundred heresies are discussed, but they divide into four basic types: Barbarism, Scythism, Hellenism and Judaism. For most of the section on heresy, John drew on earlier knowledge, but the sections covering iconoclasm and Islam seem to be original with him. Islam is covered in a chapter on 'The Heresy of the Ishmaelites' (though John also called the Muslims Hagarenes). Naturally he concentrated on the Islamic doctrine concerning Christ, which he denounced because Muslims denied Christ's special redemptive mission. John transmitted the polemical legend that Muhammad had been instructed by an Arian monk. The reason that John judged Muhammad to be an Arian heretic was that Muhammad, like the Arians, denied co-eternity of the Son with the Father. John also argued that much of the alleged Prophetic revelation was lifted from Old and New Testaments. John evidently knew the Qur'an fairly well and adduced what he thought were textual parallelisms between the revelation received by Muhammad and the earlier scriptures. He denounced the sanctioning of polygamy as immoral. He also made polemical use of the episode when Zayd ibn Haritha, Muhammad's adopted son, having married the beautiful Zaynab, was induced to divorce her so that the Prophet could marry her. There was a Qur'anic revelation to sanction this.[8] In John's eyes, this was further evidence of the sensuality of Islam. (Today it is widely accepted among scholars that the Prophet's marriages were chiefly contracted for political rather than sexual purposes.)

The hostility that pervades John's account of Islam should be understood within the context of the time. Christians living under Islamic rule were tolerated, but there were strict limits to that tolerance. Under the Umayyad Caliph 'Abd al-Malik (r. 685–705) Arabic replaced Greek as the administrative language. Under Yazid II (r. 720–24) Christians were actively persecuted and Christian images and crosses were destroyed throughout the caliphate. The Church of St John in Damascus was demolished to make way for the Umayyad Mosque. The Monastery of St Sabas, where St John pursued his studies and composed his polemics, is situated ten miles to the south of Jerusalem. The cellar of its chapel contains the skulls of monks massacred in Bedouin raids. John was a stylish and learned writer, but since he wrote in Greek his impact was at first limited until *The Fount of Knowledge* was translated into Latin in the twelfth century and then became known to Aquinas, who read a few pages every day. John also wrote specifically against iconoclasm in *Three Orations Against the Calumniators of the Holy Icons* and he produced a short *Disputation* (between a Muslim and Christian). He was more concerned with propping up the fate of wavering Christians than with mounting a direct assault on Islam itself.[9]

It was more or less inevitable that the earliest attacks on Islam should have been drafted in the Near East by Christians who felt their faith was under threat. 'Abd al-Masih ibn Ishaq al-Kindi (though this was probably not his real name) was a Christian Arab who compiled an attack on Islam some time in the ninth or tenth centuries. His *Risala*, or 'Letter', was presented as an epistolary exchange between a Christian and a Muslim. The letter, allegedly drafted by a Muslim, put forward a not very persuasive case for conversion to Islam. The much longer Christian reply included a hostile version of the life of the Prophet, which denounced him for, among other things, an excessive recourse to violence and the repeated practice of taking many beautiful women as his wives. It also inevitably included the story of the Prophet's instruction by the heretical monk and drew attention to his fifteen wives. Al-Kindi defended the doctrine of the Trinity against Muslim claims that it was only faintly disguised polytheism. He drew attention to the violent means used to spread Islam. He pointed to areas where the Qur'an appeared to contradict itself and he queried the Muslim doctrine of abrogation, by which certain parts of the Qur'an are held to cancel out others. He argued against the Arabic of the Qur'an being the language of God, for, if this was the case, why were there so many loan words in it? Al-Kindi's Arabic was translated into Latin in the twelfth century in Toledo under the patronage of Peter of Cluny (see below). Versions of the *Risala* were frequently included in later compilations of anti-Muslim material, and for centuries in Western Europe al-Kindi's rather inventive treatise was regarded as the major source on the life of the Prophet. Al-Kindi's treatise offered the appearance of balance, as it mingled praise and blame of the Prophet (though much more blame than praise), and there was very little other material available in Latin against which it was possible to check the *Risala*'s fabrications and misunderstandings.[10]

THE SPANISH RESPONSE

Serious Christian attempts to understand Islam as opposed to mere abuse began in Spain, though naturally the clerics who sought to understand Islam better only did so in order to have more material with which to refute its errors. Even so, there were some who disapproved of any study of Islam or Arabic for whatever reason. In the ninth century Paul Alvarus denounced those Christians who were engaged in 'building up great libraries of them [Arabic writings] at enormous cost ... hardly one can write a passable Latin letter to a friend, but innumerable are those who can express themselves in Arabic and can compose poetry in that language better than the Arabs themselves'. Christians in Spain pursued the study of Arabic philosophy, theology, science and so forth while neglecting their Latin and indeed their own faith.[11] Alvarus assigned Islam a maleficent apocalyptic role, for it prepared the way for the coming of the Antichrist, as prophesied in the Book of Daniel. He denounced Islam as a combination of several heresies and a cunningly deliberate mingling of truth and error. Much of the appeal of the false faith was the sensual self-indulgence that it allowed its adherents. Alvarus, having consulted the stars on the matter, was confident that Islam was doomed. Under his influence, several Spanish Christians sought and found martyrdom at the hands of the Muslims. Those who abused Islam or who sought to convert Muslims to Christianity faced the death penalty. Alvarus's friend, the learned cleric Eulogius, was arrested for hiding a convert from Islam to Christianity and he was subsequently beheaded. He was one of the last of a number of fanatical Christians who, by publicly denouncing Islam and its Prophet, courted and found martyrdom in Cordova in the 850s.[12]

Nevertheless, in general, the caliphate of Cordova was a remarkably tolerant regime under which Christians and Jews, as well as Muslims, were able to prosper, though, as in Umayyad Syria, there were limits to that tolerance and the Christians and Jews were discriminated against in all sorts of ways.[13] The caliphate of Cordova fell apart in the early decades of the eleventh century and towards the end of the same century Spain was occupied by the Almoravids, Moroccan Berbers who espoused a much more bigoted form of Islam. Both Christians and Jews were intermittently persecuted by the new masters of al-Andalus (Muslim Spain). In 1066 there was a massacre of Jews in Granada.[14] A number of Christian churches were demolished and many Christians and Jews were deported to North Africa. The old *convivencia*, or tolerant mode of co-existence, was under strain.

It was not only Christians, like Alvarus, who worried about their co-religionaries immersing themselves in Arabic books. Muslims were suspicious too. Ibn 'Abdun, a market inspector in Seville writing around the year 1100, warned his fellow Muslims against the selling of Arabic books to Jews and Christians, because, he claimed, they translated those books and then claimed their authorship as their own.[15] In the twelfth century Toledo became the chief centre for Christian translations and studies of Arabic materials. In 1085 this important Muslim city had fallen to the army of Alfonso VI of Castile. One of the important consequences of this was that large numbers of Arabic manuscripts came into Christian hands. Raimundo, Archbishop of Toledo (1125–51), encouraged scholars to come to Toledo and work on the Arabic texts.[16] Raimundo's project received powerful encouragement from one of the most influential churchmen in Europe, Peter the Venerable, the Abbot of Cluny. Having visited Cluniac houses in northern Spain in 1142, Peter was distressed that the Cluniac monks were making so little effort to combat the ideological threat posed by Islam: 'I was indignant that the Latins did not know the cause of such perdition and, by that ignorance could not be moved to put up any resistance.'[17]

THE TRANSLATION MOVEMENT

At Peter's behest the Qur'an was translated into Latin for the first time in 1143 by an Englishman, Robert of Ketton. (It should be noted that, according to Islamic doctrine, the Qur'an, the Word of God, is strictly untranslatable; only approximations are possible.) A Muslim, a certain Muhammad, was also hired to ensure the accuracy of the translation. Robert of Ketton's rendering, though soon forgotten, was rediscovered in the sixteenth century and it then held the field until the seventeenth-century translations of Du Ryer and Marracci appeared in French and Latin respectively. Of course, Peter had only commissioned the translation of the Qur'an the better to refute it and, at around the same time, Robert of Ketton and his scholarly colleague Hermann of Carinthia were also commissioned to translate other works for polemical purposes. Al-Kindi's debate between a Christian and a Muslim was a natural choice to be translated and the Latin version was given the title *Epistola Saraceni*. *Fabulae Saracenorum*, put together by Robert, was a collection of Islamic traditions on a wide range of topics. Hermann of Carinthia produced *Liber Generationis Mahumet*, a translation of a treatise on the Prophet's genealogy. He also translated *The Questions of Abdallah ibn Salam* as *Doctrina Mahumet*, a rather curious didactic dialogue, in which 'Abdallah the Jew questioned the Prophet Muhammad about cosmology, numerology, the Afterlife and sundry other matters' (and throwing in a few riddles as well). At the end of the interrogation, the Jew is so satisfied with the answers he has received that he converts to Islam.[18]

Apart from the Qur'an, the materials that the Toledo group chose to translate were rather folkloric in nature. They made no attempt to come to grips with the strong scholastic tradition of Islamic theology and philosophy. In correspondence with the great Cistercian, Bernard of Clairvaux, Peter confided that he was still undecided whether the Muslims were heretics or pagans. Bernard (and he probably represented majority opinion in this respect) was hostile to Peter's interest in Islamic lore. Bernard seems to have thought that the best way of dealing with Islamic doctrine was to ignore it altogether.[19] In the centuries to come there would be many Christians who argued that those who studied and translated the books of the Muslims ran the risk of being infected by them.

Peter also wrote a refutation of Islam, *The Abominable Heresy or Sect of the Saracens*, in which he addressed the Muslims as follows: 'I approach you not with arms but with words; not with force but with reason; not in hatred but in love.'[20] (In fact it is clear from letters written to other Christians that Peter was keen on using force of arms to deal with the threat of Islam and he supported the *Reconquista* and the Crusade.) Peter's treatise, which was formally addressed to the Muslims, was in any case a fairly pointless exercise, for it was drafted in Latin and was never translated into Arabic. It is important to bear in mind that in an age of manuscripts it was one thing to write a treatise, but another to get it circulated. Christians outside the Spanish peninsula had little interest in Islam and therefore manuscripts dealing with the subject tended to languish in single copies. As for Robert of Ketton's translation of the Qur'an, few medieval scholars even knew of its existence and in 1209 or 1210, Mark of Toledo, unaware that the work had already been done, translated the Qur'an all over again (and his version attracted even fewer readers).[21] Robert of Ketton's translation only achieved a wider readership when it was printed in Zurich in 1543, some four hundred years after its original draft.

Though Peter had hired his translators to provide materials with which to combat Islamic doctrine, Robert of Ketton and Hermann of Carinthia seem to have been primarily interested in scientific, mathematical and divinatory works. Robert was to translate works on alchemy, algebra and the astrolabe. Hermann translated various works on astronomy. A great deal has been written about the impetus that translations from the Arabic gave to Western mathematics, science and philosophy from the twelfth century onwards, and this is correct.[22] Translations of Arabic treatises on mathematics were especially important. Arabic texts were the main channel for introducing Euclid's mathematics to the West and this was to be of crucial importance for the later development of Western science. Moreover, there were also Arabic mathematicians who were of importance in their own right. The ninth-century mathematician Muhammad ibn Musa al-Khwarizmi's treatise on algebra, *Hisab al-Jabr wa al-muqabala*, was the first Arab mathematical work to be translated into Latin and was of fundamental influence for the development of mathematics in the West. In particular, the celebrated Pisan mathematician Lionardo Fibonacci drew heavily on al-Khwarizmi and other Arab mathematicians in his own work. Al-Khwarizmi also wrote *On Indian Calculation* (the Latin title was *Algoritmi de numero indorum*), which introduced readers of the Latin version to the use of what today we call 'Arabic numerals', though, as the title of the treatise indicates, such numerals actually originated in India. 'Arabic numerals', including the crucial zero, allowed much more sophisticated calculations than had been possible for the greatest mathematical minds of previous centuries. Yet, despite the obvious advantages it offered, there were widespread prejudices against the new-fangled notation and it was centuries before it replaced the cumbrous Roman numeral system in most European countries. Finally al-Khwarizmi produced the *Zij*, a set of astronomical tables that was much studied in the West. Ibn al-Haytham (*c.* 965–1039), who was known in the West as Alhazen, produced a major work on optics and the application of mathematics to such optical problems as refraction. Ibn al-Haytham demonstrated that light travels from the object to the eye, whereas previously Ptolemy and Euclid had argued that the eye perceived things by sending rays out to the objects. Al-Khwarizmi and Ibn al-Haytham were studied and commentated on in the West, but there were other even more sophisticated mathematicians in the medieval Islamic world whose work remained unknown in Europe until modern times.[23]

The medieval Arab contribution to the development of European philosophy was no less significant. Scholars in Paris, Oxford, Bologna and elsewhere became acquainted with the works of Aristotle mostly via translations from the Arabic. Gerald of Cremona (c. 1114–87), who worked in Toledo and who was perhaps the most important translator of scientific works, also translated several of the most important works of Aristotle from Arabic. Arabic commentaries on Aristotle were hardly less important in their impact on the teaching of philosophy and theology in Paris and Oxford. The eleventh-century philosopher Ibn Sina, or Avicenna as he was known to the Latinists, was far and away the most important of the commentators on Aristotle. As Bertrand Russell observed, Avicenna 'spent his life in the sort of places that one used to think exist only in poetry', as he grew up and studied in Bokhara, Khiva, Khorasan and Tehran.[24] In his copious writings Ibn Sina sought to reconcile Greek philosophy with Islamic theology in a way that was to have a massive impact on the development of European scholasticism, as Christian thinkers used variations of Avicenna's arguments to reconcile Aristotelian philosophy with Christian doctrine.

The works of Avicenna started to be translated in Toledo in the late twelfth century. At first Western scholastics had some difficulty in distinguishing his ideas from those of Aristotle. Furthermore, when they came to translate the Sufi mystic al-Ghazali's polemical attack on Avicenna, they misinterpreted it as merely a synopsis of Avicenna's philosophy. Despite these difficulties, as well as those inherent in translating complex philosophical terms, Avicenna's way of reasoning about the universe and ultimate things seemed to open up exciting perspectives. It dominated thirteenth-century philosophizing. It provided both material for scholastic disputations and an armoury of debating strategies. 'The importance of Avicenna's thought for the

West cannot be overestimated' as Gordon Leff put it. However, Leff went on to suggest that there were negative as well as positive aspects to this. In particular, Christian thinkers had difficulties with Avicenna's determinism, for, since he taught that everything was both necessary and determined, this appeared to deny God free will.[25]

It would be easy to adduce other examples of sensible, worthwhile and even brilliant examples of Arabic scholarship that had a crucial influence on the evolution of culture and technology in medieval Christendom. However, it is worth pausing to consider whether much of what was translated was of any value at all. The trouble with Islamic science was that much of it was not particularly scientific, even though enthusiastic translators in Spain evidently thought that it was. They translated works on astrology, alchemy, numerology, scapulimancy (divination from the cracks on scorched sheep's bones), geomancy (divination from marks in the sand), haruspication (divination from entrails), and similar recondite practices. The earliest translations in Spain from Arabic all dealt with divination or with those parts of mathematics that would be necessary to practise divination.[26] In the long run, some Western thinkers would use mathematics for architecture, engineering and ballistics, while others would develop it as a purely speculative system of thought. In the shorter term, however, sophisticated mathematical operations were mostly used as the handmaidens of astrology, in order to determine by astrological means the fates of dynasties, love affairs and harvests.

Only a few examples will be given here of Arab occult works that were translated into Latin, but they are all important ones. Jabir ibn Hayyan can be charitably described as the 'father of modern chemistry'. However, 'Jabir' was not really a single person, but rather a corpus of effectively anonymous literature and, moreover, that literature mostly dealt with such occult matters as the making of talismans and recipes for poisons that could allegedly kill at a distance.[27] The *Ghayat al-Hakim*, translated into Latin in the thirteenth century as *Picatrix* and spuriously attributed to a famous Spanish Arab mathematician, al-Majriti, was even more sinister in its intentions. It is a collection of rather malevolent spells using disgusting ingredients.[28] The ninth-century polymath Abu Yusuf Yaqub ibn Ishaq al-Kindi studied and wrote in Baghdad and Basra. (This al-Kindi is not to be confused with the much less impressive Christian polemicist discussed earlier.) According to Fritz Zimmerman, al-Kindi 'wrote on questions of mathematics, logic, metaphysics and ethics, but also on perfumes, drugs, foods, precious stones, musical instruments, swords, bees and pigeons' – and much else besides. Al-Kindi used astrology to determine the duration of the Arab caliphate and, in general, his writings were pervaded by occult beliefs and practices. In *De Radiis* ('On Rays'), a treatise that has survived only in its twelfth-century Latin translation, al-Kindi expounded an essentially magical view of the universe, in which occult radiation from the stars influenced human affairs. Each star exercised an influence on a special group of objects. Although stellar rays were most important, everything in the universe emitted rays. Also, according to *De Radiis*, words possessed magical powers, particularly if uttered under particularly favourable stellar conjunctions and combined with the use of talismanic images and the magical sacrifice of animals. Despite al-Kindi's attempt to present his material in a way that looked logical and scientific, it was still only scientific in the broadest and woolliest sense. Other works by al-Kindi that were translated dealt with the predictive power of dreams and with astrology.[29]

The early translators were keen to translate Aristotle, for he enjoyed enormous prestige, as he was known to have been Alexander the Great's tutor. However, they were poorly equipped to judge what had actually been written by Aristotle and what had not. A great deal of what they translated was not by Aristotle but was drafted by other, crazier hands. Among the many pseudepigrapha that were claimed to be by Aristotle were a Neoplatonist *Theology*, an alchemical treatise, *On the Twelve Waters of the Secret River*, an astrological *Book on the Properties of the Elements and of the Planets*, and above all the *Secreta Secretorum* ('Secret of Secrets'), which, before being translated into Latin, had circulated widely in the Arab world under the title *Sirr al-Asrar*. In Europe too it became a popular and influential work and more than two hundred manuscripts of the Latin version have survived. The *Secreta Secretorum*, which originally was put together in Syriac in the eighth century, is an encyclopedic treatise that deals with politics, ethics and medicine, but it also put forward astrological notions, and a belief in the occult virtues of plants and stones pervades its treatment of many subjects. The book is full of quaint stories, including that of the legend of the poison maiden. The poison maiden was a carefully dosed-up young woman who was sent to Alexander by a hostile potentate and her toxic embrace would certainly have killed Alexander had not the cunning plan been detected by the watchful Aristotle.[30]

AVICENNA IN THE WEST

There were also problems with regard to Aristotle's commentator, Avicenna, and the reverence with which he was treated. Avicenna wrote about two hundred books and many of them dealt with occult matters. Avicenna argued in *Liber de anima* ('The Book of the Spirit') that the imagination could work on a body at a distance, and hence real powers could be ascribed to the evil eye.[31] This theme was to be taken up by Christian occultists. Given the quantity of occult material being translated and studied in Toledo, it is not surprising that the city acquired a reputation for magic and the black arts. According to Charles Homer Haskins, 'Spain became the scene of visions and prophecies, of mystifications like Virgil of Cordova, of legends like the university of demonology at Toledo.'[32]

Avicenna was as famous as a medical authority as he was as a philosopher and student of the unseen. His *al-Qanun fi al-Tibb* ('The Canon of Medicine'), which was translated by Gerald of Cremona in the twelfth century, became a standard textbook on medicine in medieval Europe. With the advent of printing in the fifteenth century, there were sixteen editions in that century alone. Much of what Avicenna recycled in the *Qanun* derived from the Greek physicians Hippocrates (*c.* 460–*c.* 370 BC) and Galen (AD 129–99). Nothing written by Hippocrates survives, but his medical doctrines were known through the summaries provided by Galen. The latter was a Greek surgeon who had operated on gladiators before becoming Marcus Aurelius's physician. Galen, in his various treatises, compiled the observations and theories of his predecessors and his medical views were shaped as much by philosophy as they were by clinical observation. Galenic medicine was based on the theory of the four humours (blood, phlegm, black bile, yellow bile) and diseases caused by an imbalance between those humours. The health of the body depended upon maintaining the correct balance between hotness, coldness, dryness and wetness. Consequently medicines were divided into four basic types: warmers, coolers, purges and sudorifics (substances that cause the body to sweat). Galen viewed the heart as a furnace (rather than a pump, which would be a more accurate analogy). Galen's version of how the body worked was fundamentally mistaken and Galenic medicine did not actually help anyone to get better.[33] It was a systematic way of misunderstanding the world and, in general, a sick person was probably better off going to a wise woman than consulting a learned physician who had immersed himself in Galen.

Avicenna's *Qanun* was an unoriginal compilation which drew heavily upon Galenic medical misapprehensions. 'No personal experiences of the author and no new ideas are found in it,' according to Manfred Ullman. Avicenna does not seem to have carried out any dissections and, in fact, Islamic law bans the dissection of human bodies. The *Qanun*'s chief value lay in the way it laid out older materials in a systematic fashion. But much of the material so presented was both bizarre and useless. For example, Avicenna, following his predecessors, declared that madness was caused by an imbalance in the biles. In particular, a predominance of black bile was the cause of melancholia (though Avicenna accepted that jinn (demons) could also cause melancholia). Excessive hairiness was one of the symptoms of this sad affliction. Lycanthropia, or werewolfism, was another possible version of melancholia. It is unlikely that Avicenna ever had to treat a werewolf; rather he was unthinkingly transmitting a piece of ancient Greek folklore that had found its way into the medical textbooks. According to Galen and to Avicenna following him, bleeding was a cure for all sorts of diseases (and one wonders if, in an age before sterilization became the norm, more people did not die of the cure than the complaint). Cauterization was another painful but trusted standby in this sort of medicine. The activities of the jinn apart, Avicenna denied that there were magical causes and cures and he also wrote a refutation of astrology. However, though he sought to adopt rationalist positions, his great medical work was really an antiquarian and bookish reworking of Greek learning that had little practical relevance to the real health problems of the medieval Near East – or those of Europe.[34]

A loosely analogous problem arose regarding the transmission of Greek astronomical learning via the Arabs to the West. It was essentially the Ptolemaic system that was being transmitted, studied and elaborated upon and the problem with this picture of the universe was that it was predicated upon the assumption that the earth was at the centre of the universe, so that the sun and the rest of the planets circled around it, with the sphere of the fixed stars serving as the universe's outer shell. This system was set out in the immensely influential *Almagest* of Claudius Ptolemy (*c.* AD 100–178). The Ptolemaic system had the advantage of providing a framework for observations and calculations, even if the system was over-elaborate and based on a false premise. The *Almagest* (which was translated from Arabic by the tireless Gerald of Cremona) was an extremely complex work. Although it did allow one to predict the position of stars from year to year, in fact most medieval students of astronomy (including Dante) preferred to use abridged or simplified versions of Ptolemy's work written by other hands. Not until the sixteenth century did figures like Galileo, Kepler and Copernicus succeed in thinking their way out of the increasingly unwieldy Ptolemaic model. In the Middle Ages Ptolemy's astronomy tended to be bundled in with his astrology.[35] Like the writings of Galen and Avicenna, the Ptolemaic treatises gave aspiring scholars something to exercise their minds on, but, at the end of all the mental exercising, not so very much was likely to have been achieved. Translations of scientific works from Arabic, which had begun in the twelfth century, petered out in the early thirteenth century. After the fourteenth century, there were no more such translations. Greek learning, mediated by Arab scholarship, had provided stimulus and misinformation in equal measure.

AVERROES AND THE
LATIN AVERROISTS

To return to philosophy, the impact of Averroes on Western scholastic philosophy was in some respects even greater than that of Avicenna. Averroes (the name is a Latinate distortion of the actual Arab name Ibn Rushd) was born in 1126 in Cordova and died in 1198 in Marrakesh. Like Avicenna, Averroes, who was known as the 'Commentator', was chiefly valued in the West for his expositions of Aristotle's philosophy. What was distinctive in his thinking was that he held (or at least was thought to hold) that there was no necessary harmony between faith and reason. He taught that the existence of God could be proved by reason and that the world had always existed and he rejected the immortality of the personal soul. Averroes was translated into Latin in the early thirteenth century by Michael Scot and, from the 1230s onwards, Averroism was an important and somewhat contentious issue first in Paris and then in Oxford. Averroist Christian philosophers, like Siger of Brabant, believed that Averroes had demonstrated the unity of the intellect shared by all humanity. Also Siger and his partisans argued that, though the Averroist interpretation of the world might not be correct, it was the correct reading of Aristotle. Although Aquinas fiercely opposed Siger's interpretation of Averroes, Dante decided retrospectively to smooth over their differences and placed them side by side in the Heaven of the Sun in *Paradiso*, where Aquinas is made to praise Siger's logic. Averroes's writings attracted careless readers and partisans on both sides and, for a while, anybody suspected of any kind of freethinking was likely to be labelled an Averroist. Curiously, despite the denunciations and attempts to ban the teaching of Averroism in the universities, his views were actually more widely known and discussed in Christian Europe than they were in the Islamic world.[36]

Despite Averroism's association with suspect and vaguely atheistic ideas, nevertheless the Arab philosopher was studied with great attention and respect by perfectly orthodox figures like St Thomas Aquinas and Dante. In his massive theological treatise, *Summa contra Gentiles*, Aquinas proposed to use reason rather than scripture to convert the unbelieving and Averroes was cited 503 times in the course of the *Summa*'s arguments. (Impressive although this was, it is doubtful whether a single infidel has ever been converted by wading through Aquinas's Latin.) In the *Summa*, chapter 6 of book 5 dealt with Islam. Predictably Aquinas presented Muhammad as the founder of a heresy who cunningly made use of both truth and falsity. Muhammad delivered his message first to 'men not learned in divine method . . . but bestial people living in deserts'.[37] Although Averroism was for a while the rage among high-flying scholastics, from the mid-fourteenth century onwards it was on the wane and, more generally, there was a steep decline in Arabic studies. In the fifteenth century, as we shall see, several leading humanist thinkers went out of their way to express doubts about the reliability or value of studying Greek philosophy via what were usually inelegant and inaccurate Arabic translations. A great deal of Aristotle and his Arab commentators had been badly translated into barbarous Latin of a sort that made the fastidious Latin stylists of the fifteenth and sixteenth centuries wince. After Averroes had been rendered into Latin, there were no important translations from Arabic until the seventeenth century.

THE CRUSADERS AND THEIR NEIGHBOURS

Most of the translation work was done in Spain and, to a lesser extent, in Sicily. It might have been thought that the establishment of the Crusader principalities in the eastern Mediterranean in the twelfth century might have served as a channel of cultural influence that would have allowed Franks or Westerners to become more familiar with Arabic and Islamic high culture. However, scholars tended not to go on Crusades or settle in the East and a Paris-trained intellectual, like William Archbishop of Tyre, was a rarity. The twelfth-century scientific translator Adelard of Bath also seems to have visited Crusader Syria, though there is no evidence about what he did there. It was also the case that, unless the Franks had chosen to interest themselves in the study of the Qur'an and the orally transmitted traditions concerning the Prophet Muhammad and his contemporaries, there was probably not so very much they could have learned from their Muslim subjects and neighbours in the twelfth century. The places that the Crusaders had conquered in Syria and Palestine were small towns that traded in soap, leather and glass. These places were intellectual backwaters and a long way from the great Islamic cultural centres of Baghdad or Isfahan. The last great age of cultural efflorescence in Syria had taken place under the Hamdanid princes in Aleppo in the tenth century. The famous poets al-Mutanabbi and Abu Tammam, the philosopher al-Farabi, the preacher Ibn Nubata and many others had flourished under the benign patronage of this great Arab dynasty. By the 1090s, Syria and Palestine boasted no philosophers, scientists, poets or historians of any real eminence or originality. Doubtless the cultural decline was exacerbated by the coming of the Crusaders, as the latter killed scholars and either destroyed libraries or redistributed their contents. (We know that they ransomed the Arabic books looted in Jerusalem to the Fatimid garrison in Ascalon.)

Proximity to the Muslims in Palestine and Syria did not at first encourage any understanding of Islam. In his early twelfth-century chronicle of the First Crusade, *Gesta Dei per Francos*, Guibert of Nogent, when he came to write about the career of Muhammad, observed that 'it is safe to speak evil of one whose malignity exceeds whatever ill can be spoken'. In other words, when faced with something so bad, it was not necessary to check one's facts and Guibert seems to have relied on misinformation brought back by pilgrims from the Holy Land. However, Guibert was at pains to correct one popular misconception, as he pointed out that it was not true that Muslims regarded Muhammad as God.[38]

In the thirteenth century, prominent thinkers such as Roger Bacon and Ramon Lull came to advocate preaching and conversion as the way for Christianity to triumph over Islam. Also, the preaching orders of the Franciscans and Dominicans sent out preachers to the Middle East and other infidel regions. It was inevitable that those preachers had to acquire some knowledge of Islam and Arabs in order to inform their preaching. Though James of Vitry (c. 1160–1240) was not a friar, he was primarily a preacher and he had travelled up and down the coast of the Crusader principalities, preaching especially to the Muslims before he was appointed Bishop of Acre in 1219. He claimed to have converted a few and he suggested that more would have come over but for the contrast Muslims saw between the earthly delights offered by their religion and the stringent demands made by Christian morality. Presumably James of Vitry preached to the Muslims in Arabic, though this is not clear. Although he had some knowledge of Muslim beliefs, this was not due to systematic study. Rather he relied on scraps of oral information, not all of which were accurate. For example, he claimed that Muslims secretly worshipped an idol of Muhammad that was kept inside the Dome of the Rock in Jerusalem.[39]

William of Tripoli, a missionary based in the Dominican convent in the Crusader city of Acre, certainly knew Arabic very well. His *Tractatus de Statu Saracenorum* (1273) was a guide to Islamic beliefs and customs. He had read the Qur'an and he was particularly interested in the account the Qur'an gave of Jesus. However, he also accepted such familiar anti-Muslim libels as the story that the heretical monk Bahira taught Muhammad heresy, as well as the story that Muhammad only banned alcohol after getting disgracefully drunk himself. William claimed to have baptized more than a thousand Muslims (which seems wildly improbable) and he did not think that most Muslims were far from salvation, for he saw that Islam had a great deal in common with Christianity. Moreover, he thought that Islam was close to collapse and then the Muslims were bound to convert to the true faith. He had heard that this had been foretold by Muslim astrologers. Therefore there was no need for another crusade. William's view of the way things were shaping up in the East was unusually sanguine. Less than twenty years later, in 1291, Muslim armies under the command of the Mamluk Sultan al-Ashraf Khalil overran Acre and the rest of the Crusader cities and castles on the Syro-Palestinian littoral.[40]

Ricoldo da Monte Croce, a Dominican missionary, was in Iraq at the time of the fall of Acre. He saw the Christian captives being brought into Baghdad to be sold as slaves and he speculated about the fate of any nuns who might have been captured. (According to the folk-lore of the period, nuns were especially sought by the masters of harems because they were reputed to breed exceptionally fine warriors.) Ricoldo was baffled at the success and wealth of the Muslims. Why had God granted them all these things? All the same, he was exceptional in the depth and detail of his knowledge of Islam and also in his favourable estimation of Muslim manners and customs. In his *Itinerarius*, or 'Journey', he had much praise for the Arabs: 'We therefore report certain Muslim works of perfection thus briefly, rather to shame the Christians than to praise the Muslims. For who will not be astonished if he carefully considers how great among these same Muslims is the attention to study, the devotion in prayer, pity for the poor, reverence for the name of God and the prophets and the holy places, their serious ways, their kindness to strangers, and their concord and love towards each other.' *Gravitas* was a leading feature of Muslim life.

Ricoldo was also particularly impressed by their *madrasas*, or religious colleges, and he correctly identified the two main ones as the Nizamiyya and the Mustansariyya. Ricoldo's homiletic contrast of virtuous Saracens with sinful Christians was to be taken up by other Christian writers, including John de Mandeville. Though the Saracens' devotion was admired, it was still, as far as Ricoldo was concerned, a devotion to a false faith and he excoriated their holy law as confused, obscure, lying, irrational and violent. (He had been attacked by Muslim Mongols when he left Baghdad. They beat him, tried to force him to convert to Islam and made him work as a camel driver. These things may have prejudiced him against the religion.) Later, in 1310, he also wrote a refutation of the Qur'an entitled *Improbatio alchorani*. Writing of his experience as a missionary, he observed that it was very difficult to convey a correct idea of the Trinity to a Muslim audience and that it was easier to attack Islam than to defend Christianity.[41]

THE WICKED CHRISTIANS

Ricoldo (and John de Mandeville after him) only praised Muslim manners and customs in order to make his fellow Christians feel ashamed of their shortcomings and, in general, it must be evident from much of the above that Christian polemicists made only perfunctory attempts to understand their Muslim adversaries. The Muslims reciprocated and wrote their own inaccurate and libellous polemics about Christians and Christendom and, if Christians accused Muslims of worshipping idols, it was also the case that Muslims accused Christians of polytheism. The Andalusian jurist and belletrist Ibn Hazm (994–1064) wrote a delightful treatise on courtly love called *Ring of the Dove*. But he also wrote the lengthy and rancorous *Kitab al-Fisal fi-al-Milal wa-al-Ahwa' wa-al-Nihal*, or 'Book of Distinction in the Religions, Heresies, Sects', in which he sought to demonstrate the superiority of Sunni Islam to all other faiths and sects. The *Kitab al-Fisal* included a long and fierce attack on Judaism and Christianity. According to Ibn Hazm, Christians had tampered with the New Testament and removed prophecies concerning the coming of Muhammad. They corrupted the Gospels with lies. 'All this shows the Christian community is altogether vile.'[42]

The rigorous Muslim jurist and theologian Ibn Taymiyya (1263–1328) similarly considered the Christian scriptures to have been carelessly corrupted.[43] It was a commonplace of Muslim polemic to denounce Christian sexual freedom and lack of sexual jealousy. According to Ibrahim ibn Yaqub, writing in Islamic Spain, Slavic men divorced their women if they discovered them to be virgins. The same source denounced the Christians of Galicia in northern Spain as men who washed at most only twice a year. (Of course, he may well have been right about the second point.) The Persian al-Qazwini's thirteenth-century *Cosmography* made the same claim about Franks in general. (Qazwini died in 1283.)[44] The anonymous *Sea of Virtues*, written in twelfth-century Syria, mocked the Christians for worshipping someone who was incapable of saving himself from execution. Moreover 'anyone who believes that his God came out of a woman's privates is quite mad'. According to the anonymous author, unmarried women are allowed to fornicate with whomever they like, but sleeping with priests in churches was regarded as especially meritorious.[45] Ibn 'Abdun, inspector of markets and morals in early twelfth-century Seville, after decreeing that Christians and Jews were not allowed to employ Muslim servants, continued: 'Muslim women shall be prevented from entering their abominable churches, for the priests are evil-doers, fornicators and sodomites. Frankish women must be forbidden to enter the church except on days of religious services or festivals, for it is their habit to eat and drink and fornicate with the priests, among whom there is not one who has not two or more women with whom he sleeps.'[46]

At a more popular and entertaining level, Arabic folk epics about legendary and quasi-legendary heroes such as Antar, Sayyid Battal and Baybars presented the Franks as vainglorious and cowardly warriors and portrayed Europe as a region of sorcerers, poisoners and pirates.[47] Western epics tended to present a reversed mirror image of this, in which the Christians were paladins and the Saracens were the bad guys. It is important to remember that for much of the Middle Ages Christendom was on the defensive and, for example, the *Chanson de Roland* commemorates defeat, not victory. In the *Chanson*, which was written perhaps towards the end of the eleventh century, the heroic knight Roland and his small army is lured by an evil and treacherous counsellor, Ganelon, into a Saracen ambush in the Pyrenees. Subsequently Roland's liege lord the Emperor Charlemagne takes vengeance on the Saracens. Their commander, King Marsilion, is treacherous, but the Saracens are shown to be brave warriors and appreciated as such:

> From Balaguet there cometh an Emir,
> His form is noble, his eyes are bold and clear,
> When on his horse he's mounted in career
> He bears him bravely in his battle-gear,
> And for his courage he's famous far and near;
> Were he but Christian, right knightly he'd appear.[48]

Whoever composed the *Chanson* was not in the least interested in the realities of Islam. Just as the Christians worship the Holy Trinity, so the Saracen paynim, or pagans, worship their own dark trinity of idols: Mahound (a corruption of Muhammad), Termagant and Apollyon. Since the Christians have the Bible, it is (rightly) assumed that the Muslims too have a holy book. Saracen society appears to be feudal and chivalric, just like that of France under Charlemagne. There is no significant sense of the 'Other'. The *Chanson de Roland* and other similar heroic poems of medieval France dealt in fantasy and those who composed those fantasies felt no need to consult any Latin translation of the Qur'an or Cluniac polemic in order to find out what Islam was really like. The Saracens were stock fantasy villains and, as such, the precursors of the Red Indians and the Daleks.[49]

THE MUSLIM IN MEDIEVAL
WESTERN LITERATURE

A similar lack of curiosity about Islam and the Arab way of life is also characteristic of more serious literature in the medieval period. For example, the first thing to be said about Dante's attitude to Islam is that he was almost totally uninterested in it, one way or the other. He was very interested in the struggle between Papacy and Empire and between their Guelf and Ghibelline partisans. He was even more interested in the fate of his adored Beatrice in the afterlife and, above all, he meditated upon the divine 'love that moves the stars'. But he seems scarcely aware of the world that existed beyond the frontiers of Christendom. In his *Divine Comedy* (which he probably began to compose in 1307), five Muslims are mentioned, all briefly. Muhammad and his cousin 'Ali were not treated as founders of a new and false religion, but rather as sowers of dissension.[50] Since Dante seems to have erroneously believed that Muhammad had started out as a Christian, he therefore did not regard him as some totally alien 'Other'. However, since Muhammad and his followers had given the true Christian Church a lot of trouble, it was inevitable that he should have been damned in Dante's eyes. But then Dante put quite a lot of Christian Italians, including one of his own relatives, in yet lower circles of Hell. In so far as Dante was interested in anything Arabic, it was primarily the Averroist philosophy taught by the scholastic Siger of Brabant that engaged his favourable interest. The only other Muslims to feature in the Divine Comedy – 'great Saladin, aloof and alone', Avicenna and Averroes – are in Limbo with other heroic and virtuous pagans.[51] They are there because, despite their virtues, they did not and could not choose Christ. (Virgil, who acted as Dante's guide through Hell, was similarly a denizen of Limbo.) However, at the risk of repetition, Dante's lack of interest in Islam is conspicuous.[52]

Muslims feature in some of the stories of the *Decameron* by Giovanni Boccaccio (*c.* 1313–75). The third story in the first day of storytelling presents a favourable portrait of Saladin as a generous and courageous ruler. This is the story of the three rings. In it Saladin asks a wise Jew which is the best religion. The Jew tells the story of a man close to death who had three sons. The sons were led to believe that whoever received the father's ring would be his true heir. However, they did not realize that the father had had two more rings made that were identical in every way, so that it was impossible to tell who had the exclusive claim to his inheritance. From this tale, the Jew drew a moral: 'My lord, I say it is the same with the three Laws given by God our Father to three peoples, concerning which you have questioned me. Each of them thinks it has the inheritance, the true Law, and carries out His Commandments; but which does have it is a question as far from being settled as that of the rings.' (Boccaccio also presented a highly favourable portrait of Saladin in the ninth story of the tenth day.)

Boccaccio seems to have been familiar with some of the stories that appeared in *The Thousand and One Nights* and he presented reworkings of several famous Oriental stories, such as the tale of the generosity of Hatim Tai in his *Decameron*.[53] Ramon Lull, the Catalan polymath, was similarly familiar with Arabic story lore. Lull (*c.* 1232–1315) was born to a wealthy Catalan family in Majorca and spent his life as a young rip. Then he experienced a religious crisis. According to one story, he was pursuing someone else's beautiful young wife. She was virtuous and resisted his suit, but he was persistent. 'After asking permission of her husband to employ a drastic remedy, she summoned her admirer to attend her in some secluded place – perhaps her own chamber – when, instead of yielding, as no doubt he expected, to his demands, she uncovered her bosom, and displayed a breast that was being slowly consumed by a loathly cancer. "See Ramon," she cried, "the foulness of this body that has won thy affection! How much better hadst thou done to have set thy love on Jesus Christ, of whom thou mayest have a prize that is eternal!"'

Lull's decision to abandon the pursuit of worldly things and leave his family for the service of Christ took place in 1263. Before his conversion, he had composed troubadour love poetry, but afterwards he wrote laments about his past enslavement to lust for women. He particularly dedicated himself to working for the conversion of Muslims and Jews: 'to give up his life and soul for the sake of His love and honour; and to accomplish this by carrying out the task of converting to His worship and service the Saracens who in such

43

numbers surrounded the Christians on all sides.' It was obvious to Lull that anyone who proposed to do missionary work amongst the Muslims would need to master Arabic, but studying that language was not a straightforward matter in the Middle Ages, for there were no university courses on the language, nor any Arabic grammars. Lull therefore purchased a Moorish slave, intending that the slave should teach him Arabic. One day Lull received a report that the Moor had been blaspheming against Christ and he therefore struck the Moor several times. The Moor, accustomed as he was in his role as a teacher of Arabic to be treated as a master, became very angry. After biding his time for a few days, he went for Lull with a knife, crying, 'Now you shall die!' He succeeded in wounding Lull, before Lull wrested the knife from him. The Moor committed suicide in prison.

Lull spent nine years studying Arabic and Islam in Majorca. There was some urgency in his studies, for he feared that the Mongols, who at that time had conquered most of Asia, including Iran and Iraq, would convert to Islam unless Christian missionaries reached them first. His earliest works were all written in Arabic: *The Compendium of the Logic of al-Ghazali*, *The Book of Contemplation* and *The Book of the Gentile and the Three Wise Men*. He also translated al-Ghazali's logic into rhymed Catalan verse. Since Lull had encountered the writings of the Sufi mystical thinker al-Ghazali (*c.* 1033–1111) and examined his logic early on in his studies, Sufism exercised a strong influence on Lull's subsequent writings. Lull was a staggeringly prolific writer and it has been calculated that he wrote approximately two hundred and fifty books. Only a few of these works will be discussed here. *The Book of the Gentile and the Three Wise Men* features a debate between a Christian, a Saracen and a Jew in front of a neutral Gentile. The Saracen's prayer is accurately described, as are the main points of Islamic doctrine. Lull claimed that he relied for his information on the Qur'an, *Hadith* (reported sayings and deeds of the Prophet Muhammad) and on commentaries on both. Lull's Christian spokesman stressed the materialistic nature of the Muslim notion of paradise, but the Saracen replied that there is also a spiritual glory in paradise and this consists of the vision and contemplation of God. The Saracen tried and failed with the argument that, since Muhammad is so widely revered, God must have approved this reverence and therefore Muhammad is indeed a Prophet. The Saracen was the last to speak in the disputation, but the Gentile departed without pronouncing a verdict. The three resolved to continue to debate until they should be all of one mind. It is possible that *The Book of the Gentile* was modelled on an unidentified Arabic source.[54]

Besides writing many treatises on theology and philosophy, Lull also wrote a novel. *Blanquerna* is a missionary romance, in which the eponymous hero decides as a young man to become a hermit. His dismayed parents try to use the daughter of a friend to lure him away from this austere path, but their encounter only results in his converting her to a religious vocation. She becomes a nun, while Blanquerna wanders through many strange lands looking for the right place to build his hermitage. Like Bunyan's pilgrim, he faces all sorts of trials and has many encounters with allegorical personages. Eventually he elects instead for the monastic life and he rises to become first abbot of his monastery and then a bishop and finally pope. After years of presiding over the Church as a reforming pope, he resigns the Papacy and returns to his original goal and becomes a hermit. In retirement, he writes two books, *The Book of the Lover and the Beloved* and *The Art of Contemplation*. The book ends abruptly with the appearance of the emperor who is looking for Blanquerna and is guided to his hermitage.[55]

Blanquerna's rambling narrative is studded with fables and short stories most of which seem to derive from Arabic originals. The boxing of tales within tales was characteristic of medieval Arabic literature and is found in such well-known story collections as *Kalila wa-Dimna* and *The Thousand and One Nights*. *The Book of the Lover and the Beloved*, which is boxed within *Blanquerna*, and which deals with the approach of the mystic to God who is the 'Beloved', was, according to Lull, made 'according to the manner of the Sufis' and, as is the case with *The Book of the Gentile*, it is possible that it was modelled on a lost Arabic book. Certainly the book is pervaded by Arab themes and in it Lull makes explicit his admiration for Sufism: Blanquerna remembered that 'a Saracen related to him that the Saracens have certain religious men, and that among others are certain men called Sufis, who are most prized amongst them, and these men have words of love and brief examples which give to men great devotion'. Lull seems to have absorbed the Sufi practice of meditating on the names of God and turned it into a Christian devotional practice. At the time that he wrote *Blanquerna*, Lull believed that missionary work and disputations were Christendom's best hope of defeating the Islamic menace and he was hostile to the idea of further Crusades. In *The Art of Contemplation* Lull argued, among other things, that going on crusade was a bad idea, for if God had approved of the Crusades they would have been more successful in the past. Elsewhere in *Blanquerna*, the Sultan of Egypt expresses sarcastic surprise that Christian Crusaders should seek to imitate the violent ways of Muhammad, rather than the peaceful preaching of Christ and his Apostles.

There is no space here to outline the contents of the rest of Lull's two hundred-odd writings, though many of them shed light on his various opinions about Arabs and his proposals for dealing with the menace of Islam. With the possible exception of Ricoldo da Monte Croce, no medieval European thinker appears to have been more familiar with Arabic literature and thought. Lull found much to admire in it. Apart from his passion for Sufism, he praised the beauty of the Qur'an and he claimed that Muslims lived longer than Christians because their diet and clothing were more sensible. Even so, he was adamant that the Muslim religion was false and its followers damned. Averroism was a particularly reprehensible Muslim doctrine and during his final stay in Paris Lull penned several attacks against Averroism and the Averroist interpretation of Aristotle. He seems to have regarded Averroism as the heart of Islam's evil and the Averroist idea of the two truths as being particularly damnable. It is likely that Lull's special hostility owed a lot to his early reading of al-Ghazali, the leading critic of Averroes in the Islamic world.

Though Lull had first put his faith in missionary endeavour, after the fall of what was left of the Kingdom of Jerusalem to the Muslim Mamluks in 1291, he came round to the view that force was also necessary and a new crusade was indeed desirable. (However, Lull maintained that a knowledge of Arabic would be just as necessary for the Crusader as it was for the missionary.) In a late work, *The Disputation with Hamar the Saracen*, Lull expressed anxiety that Christendom was facing the double menace of Islam and the Mongols. A third of the Mongols had already converted to Islam. Moreover, the Mamluk Sultan of Egypt was successful in recruiting Christian renegades and a third of his army consisted of such men. This treatise was written in prison in Bougie, Algeria. In 1295 Lull had become a Franciscan tertiary (that is to say, he became attached to the preaching order, while still remaining a layman). Thereafter, he went three times on preaching missions to North Africa, courting martyrdom in doing so, for anyone who sought to convert Muslims from their faith was liable to the death penalty. On his third visit he achieved his ambition and he was stoned to death by a mob in 1315 or 1316.

The prolific and diversely talented Lull is perhaps best known for his *Ars Magna*, a treatise that describes a kind of medieval hand-operated computer. It consisted of a revolving wheel with letters on it signifying abstract principles. The rotation of its circles could be made to demonstrate the existence of God and the truths of Christian dogma and Lull seems to have hoped that a Muslim would only have to see it in operation in order to become converted. He was a genius whose writings are full of fantasies, quirks and prejudices – exemplified, for instance, in his tireless campaign against female cosmetics. In the medievalist Richard Southern's excellent pioneering work, *Western Views of Islam in the Middle Ages* (1962), Southern wrote that, though Lull was 'one of the most commanding figures in the study of Islam', he would not say much about him, because he had 'a streak of madness to which I cannot do justice'. On the other hand, the famous twentieth-century Orientalist Louis Massignon praised Lull for the depth of his sympathy for Islam and for his recognition of how close to Christianity it was.[56] However, this may be a case of like calling to like, for, as we shall see, there was a streak of madness in Massignon also.

The campaigning of Lull and others, including the famous philosopher and scientist Roger Bacon, persuaded the Church Council of Vienne (1311–12) to decree that chairs of Greek, Hebrew, Aramaic and Arabic should be established at the universities of Avignon, Paris, Oxford, Bologna and Salamanca. The proponents of the measure urged that the teaching of Oriental languages should serve the twofold purpose of assisting in the conversion of the infidel and advancing biblical exegesis. The chairs of Greek and Hebrew fluttered in and out of existence at some of the universities, but no chair in Arabic was established anywhere. The teaching of Arabic was supposed to be funded by extra ecclesiastical funding and it never happened. The Council of Basel (1341) attempted to revive the decree, but to no purpose at all. Edward Said has stated that the Council of Vienne marked the beginning of Orientalism's formal existence.[57] In fact, as far as the study and teaching of Arabic was concerned, its decree was a dead letter. Rather, as Southern noted, it was 'the last salute to a dying ideal'.[58] Crusade projects continued to be put together in the fourteenth and fifteenth centuries, but few expeditions were mounted and fewer still actually achieved anything. There was a parallel (though temporary) decline in interest in sending missionaries out to convert the Muslims. As Southern, again, has pointed out, Christendom in the fourteenth century knew less about Islam than it had done in the twelfth century.[59] The failure of papal missions sent out to convert the Mongols was particularly demoralizing as grand hopes had been entertained of forming an alliance with Mongols who might be brought over to Christianity and used against the Muslims in the Near East.

THE WICKEDNESS OF ISLAM
AND THE PAPACY

Those who did wish to study Islam faced considerable difficulties. Outside Spain, it was difficult to find complete copies of the Qur'an anywhere in Europe. When John of Segovia (c. 1400–1458) decided to learn Arabic and translate the Qur'an as an aid to disputations with Muslims, he looked for an Arab or a scholar of Arabic to teach him the language. Having failed in this, he had to teach himself. Having accomplished this and gone on to translate the Qur'an (the translation has since been lost) and written a refutation of it, he was promptly attacked by Jean Germain, Bishop of Nevers and Chalon and Chancellor of the Order of the Golden Fleece, for having given publicity to the doctrines of an abominable heresy.[60] For centuries to come, those who attempted to translate Arabic or to study Islam ran the risk of being accused of being crypto-Muslim sympathizers.

It was also the case that for centuries to come those who wrote about Islam tended to do so not because they were interested in Islam per se, but because they wished to use discussion of its rituals and practices as a stick with which to beat the Papacy, or alternatively, as a stick with which to beat those who urged reform of the Catholic Church. The English scholastic, John Wyclif (c. 1324–84), campaigned for reform of the Papacy and for the translation of the Bible into vernacular languages. As Wyclif made plain in various of his writings, though the Muslims were misguided, they were no more so than most Catholics. Islam, as he understood it, was just like the Catholic Church he knew – violent, corrupt and greedy. The rise of Islam had been caused by the pride and greed of the Church. Power and wealth were the inappropriate characteristics of both the Papacy and Islam. Indeed, in Wyclif's eyes, the Catholic Church was, in a sense, a Muslim institution.[61] This kind of accusation, a tarring by association, was to become a familiar motif and, as we shall see, Martin Luther was to make similar polemical points about the resemblances between the Papacy and Islam.

The poet William Langland (c. 1332–c. 1400) also used a distorted version of Islam in order to make polemical points against the established Church. In his great poem, *Piers Plowman*, he argued against the priesthood's monopoly of the keys of salvation and he suggested that Muslims and Jews might also be saved independently of the sacraments of the Church. He went on to present a familiar polemical portrait of the origins of Islam in which Muhammad, a renegade priest, thwarted in his ambition to become Pope, set up a new religion. The Prophet cunningly trained a dove to sit on his shoulder and peck grains of corn from his ear, so that the people he preached to would believe that the dove was a messenger from heaven whispering into his ear. Although Langland's story is both fanciful and hostile, it is important to note that he was not really interested in the origins of Islam as such, for he immediately went on to reproach the Christian priesthood of his own time for feeding a dove called Avarice and of behaving as dishonestly as Muhammad.[62]

THE ROMANCE OF THE ORIENT

Romancers and geographers liked to linger on the territory of Islam and the lands of the East more generally as a place of wonders, where treasures, marvels and strange tribes and beasts abounded. As Robert Bartlett has noted, 'Asia had the reputation of being vast, rich, and full of marvels. The wealth and fertility of India was fabulous. William of Newburgh, discussing the situation of the Holy Land, mentioned that the Bible asserts the special place of Palestine, but considers that this cannot mean that it is the richest and most fertile part of the world "unless what is recorded about India be false" ... The East was also where nature was most playful, producing wonders and oddities of all kinds.'[63] The marvels of the East included the coffin of the Prophet Muhammad, which allegedly floated in the air sustained by concealed magnets; the Ka'ba at Mecca, which was reported to be a shrine full of idols that killed any birds which alighted upon them; the vegetable lamb of Tartary, which grew up as a plant and only became detached when mature; the Valley of Diamonds, whose precious stones were collected by prospectors using giant birds; and the empire of the fabulously wealthy and ancient Christian king, Prester John. Modern science fiction locates its wonders in distant galaxies; medieval marvel-mongers set their wonders in remote parts of the East. Apart from being the home of wondrous monsters and great treasures, the East was also a place of wisdom – most notably the wisdom of the Indian gymnosophists and the Chinese sages.

The most popular account of the marvels of Asia was provided in 1356 or 1357 by an author who called himself Sir John Mandeville. Mandeville presented his work as a reliable guide to pilgrims going to the Holy Land and claimed that he wrote it to satisfy the intellectual curiosity of those who wished to go on pilgrimage, but who could not because of a papal ban then in force. In fact, his book ranges much more widely throughout the lands of Asia and is largely a compilation of entertaining marvels including the vegetable lamb, the fountain of youth and anthills of gold dust. Whether there really was an English knight called Sir John Mandeville is debatable and, indeed, the issue is still being debated. (M. C. Seymour conjectured that the book may have been written by a French clergyman.) The important thing about the author, whoever he was, is that he had many readers over a long period of time and approximately three hundred manuscripts of his work in various languages survive from the medieval period.[64]

Although his account of the marvels of the East is full of the most amazing nonsense, there is no reason to believe that his readership was seriously misled by his fabrications. Mandeville wrote to entertain and his audience read to be entertained. This was an age when travel writers were not required to stick rigorously to the facts. Other travel writers, such as Marco Polo and Ludovico Varthema, produced travel narratives that, though they were less richly fantastical than Mandeville's, still had plenty of fantasy in them. Indeed, Mandeville, who probably never set foot in Asia and who drew instead on the libraries of Europe, was merely recycling older travellers' tales. He claimed in his prologue to have fought for the Mamluk Sultan of Egypt in his wars against the Bedouins and he claimed to have enjoyed a high status with the Sultan. Although this was not the case and although much of Mandeville was wild fantasy, the information on the Middle East was relatively accurate.

He described an audience that he pretended to have had with the Sultan. The Sultan spoke first: 'He asked how Christians governed themselves in our countries. And I said, "Lord, well enough – thanks be to God." And he answered and said, "Truly no. It is not so. For your priests do not serve God properly by righteous living, as they should do. For they ought to give less learned men an example of how to live well and they do the opposite, giving examples of all manner of wickedness. And as a result, on holy days, when people should go to church to serve God, they go to the tavern and spend all the day – and perhaps all the night – in drinking and gluttony, like beasts without reason which do not know when they have had enough. And afterwards through drunkenness they fall to proud speeches, fighting and quarrelling, till someone kills somebody. Christian men commonly deceive one another, and swear the most important oaths falsely . . ." '[65] More follows in the same vein, as Mandeville uses the Sultan as his homiletic mouthpiece to denounce Christian pride, extravagant dressing, lechery, covetousness and so forth.

By contrast, the Muslims are described by Mandeville as 'very devout and honest in their law, keeping well the commandments of the Koran, which God sent them by his messenger Muhammad, to whom, so they say, the angel Gabriel spoke often, telling him the will of God'. Mandeville subscribed to the old idea that the Christians had lost their lands in the East to the Muslims as a punishment for sin. Mandeville's praise of Muslim virtues in order to instil a sense of shame in his Christian readers followed earlier exercises in the same vein by Ricoldo da Monte Croce and others. More specifically, Mandeville's dialogue seems to have been modelled on a similar reported conversation that was alleged to have taken place between Canon William of Utrecht and a Saracen nobleman, after Saladin's capture of Jerusalem, as reported in the thirteenth-century *Dialogus Miraculorum* of Caesarius of Heisterbach.[66] For his account of Muslim doctrine and practice, Mandeville again drew heavily on William of Tripoli's *Tractatus de Statu Saracenorum* (*c.* 1273) and Vincent of Beauvais's thirteenth-century encyclopedia, the *Speculum Historiale*.[67] Like William of Tripoli, Mandeville stressed how much Islam had in common with Christianity and he professed optimism that the Muslims might be converted to Christianity. Even so, it is important to note that Mandeville was not exclusively concerned with Muslim matters and, if anything, he was even more interested in the doctrines and affairs of the Eastern Christians.

Although Mandeville presented a fairly favourable account of the Muslims of his own time, his account of the origins of Islam was marred by the customary nonsense about Muhammad's dealings with hermits and his fits of epilepsy passed off as visits from Gabriel. He also presented an array of what purported to be Arabic letters, as well as a specimen Arabic vocabulary, though it is clear that Mandeville knew no Arabic and the supposed Arabic letters are no such thing. On the other hand his account of the Holy Land is fairly reliable, if only because it plagiarized earlier, more sober narratives of pilgrimage, in particular the *Itinerarium* of Wilhelm von Bodensele (*c.* 1336). Mandeville followed the convention of pilgrim literature by calling for holy war, but he suggested that it had to be fought by holy men.

For reasons that are not clear, Ziauddin Sardar has referred to Mandeville as 'the doyen and model of all travel writers, patron and archetype of all Orientalists'.[68] But this would be to confer on Mandeville a serious, academic status that the writer did not aspire to. As we have seen, he neither travelled, nor did he know any Arabic. Samuel Johnson more appropriately praised Mandeville for 'force of thought and beauty of expression' and Mary B. Campbell has argued that one should regard him as the first serious writer of prose fiction since Petronius.[69] In the long run, as we shall see, Mandeville's celebratory enthusiasm for Asia's marvels would find its echo in the writings of Europe's first great Orientalist, Guillaume Postel (a scholar who did travel and who knew Arabic very well). Moreover, Mandeville's enthusiastic cataloguing of exotic marvels would find a further echo in another mode, in the seventeenth- and eighteenth-century cabinets of curiosities, in those collections of rare artefacts, antiquities and taxidermically faked monsters.

This has been a chapter about medieval European studies of Islam and polemics against it and, therefore, Islam and all sorts of Muslim matters have been at the centre of it. However, more generally, Islam did not feature largely in medieval European thought. It played, at best, a minor role in forming the self-image of Christendom. Moreover, we find no sense in medieval European writing that the Middle East was technologically, economically or militarily backward and there were some, like Adelard of Bath, who recognized that Arab culture was in some respects more advanced. The Arabs and Turks were not regarded as barbarians, nor were they consciously regarded as non-European, for there was little or no sense of any kind of European identity in this period. Clearly, a great deal of misinformation about Islam circulated throughout medieval Christendom. Equally obviously, this was because those who touched on Islamic matters did not trouble to get their facts right and polemical fantasy better answered their needs. Getting things right was what the Orientalists did from the sixteenth century onwards.

3

Renaissance Orientalism

THE FLIGHT FROM ARAB LEARNING

The word 'Renaissance' is likely to conjure up associations with new inventions, explorations of uncharted territories, freethinking, breaking away from old artistic conventions, freshness, cultural springtime and so on. But the European Renaissance of the fifteenth and sixteenth centuries was above all inspired and driven by the close textual study of old manuscripts, for the Renaissance, or 'rebirth', was essentially a rediscovery of the literature of antiquity and its humanist culture. In the context of the Renaissance, humanism meant the return to classical sources and the application of techniques of textual criticism to those sources, as well as the adoption of classical models for behaviour. As humanist scholars sought to recover the original texts of such writers as Thucydides, Herodotus, Cicero and Juvenal and to model their own style upon classical masters, there was a corresponding decline in interest in Arabic. The Arabs were now often denounced for having perverted the sense or style of the classical texts they transmitted and, indeed, additional problems had frequently arisen because the Arabic translations themselves had then been badly translated into Latin.[1] Already, in the thirteenth century, the Franciscan philosopher Roger Bacon had expressed his contempt for the hacks who translated from Arabic into Latin, but who 'understand neither the subject matter, nor the languages – not even Latin'.[2] Moreover, as more scholars acquired direct access to Greek texts, it was coming to be realized how misleading the Arabic versions of Greek originals could be. The style-conscious humanist despised the painfully conscientious medieval word-for-word crib translations and the former enthusiasm for Arabic (in, admittedly, restricted scholarly circles) now often shaded into outright hostility.

The Italian poet and humanist scholar Francesco Petrarch (1304–74) was an early and articulate critic of Arabic texts and culture. He loathed Arab science. In a letter to a medical friend, he faintly praised but mostly damned Arab medicine and literature: 'Nobody has such winning ways; nobody also is more tender and more lacking in vigour, and, to use the right words, meaner and more perverted. The minds of men are inclined to act differently; but as you used to say, every man radiates his own peculiar mental discipline. To sum up: I will not be persuaded that any good can come from Arabia . . .'[3] Petrarch strove to write flawless Ciceronian Latin and, steeped in Latinity and Latin canons of what constituted good verse, he was confident in his condemnation of the literature of the Arabs and especially their poetry (though there is no evidence that he had actually bothered to read any). Petrarch, a stern Christian moralist who had made a close study of the writings of St Augustine, was also hostile to Averroism, for, among other pernicious notions, the Averroist idea of the double truth and the doctrine of the eternity of the world seemed to threaten the Christian faith. He cherished his Latinate culture as a shield against sin. In a letter to Boccaccio, he described being visited by an Averroist, who 'belonged to that sect of men who practise philosophy after the modern fashion and think they are not efficient enough if they do not bark at Christ and His heavenly doctrine'.[4] The visitor infuriated Petrarch by proclaiming the superiority of the writings of Averroes to those of St Paul and St Augustine. Petrarch went on to urge another friend, Luigi Marsili, to write 'contra canem illum rabidum Averroim' (against that rabid dog Averroes).[5]

Averroes was not the only target of Petrarch and those who thought like him. They were more generally hostile to late medieval scholasticism and its heavy, uncritical dependence on Aristotle. Petrarch declared that Aristotle's 'brilliance has stunned many bleary and weak eyes and made many a man fall into the ditches of error'.[6] In the previous century, the Oxford philosopher Roger Bacon, shocked by the appalling quality of the Latin translations of Aristotle's works, declared that, if he could, he would have had them all burned.[7] The great Italian humanist Lorenzo Valla (1405–57) attacked Avicenna and Averroes for their blind reverence towards Aristotle.[8] 'Arabism' became a pejorative term, as Arabic became associated fairly narrowly with Averroism and outmoded scholastic ways of thought.

Petrarch, having failed to learn Greek, exalted Latin writers against Greek ones. However, those who did know Greek very well were just as likely to be hostile to reliance on Arabic translations and commentaries. For a while, 'Arabist' came to mean someone who was not familiar with the original Greek, but who relied on a Latin translation of Arabic. Renaissance humanists, no longer content to rely on clumsily written and inaccurately translated Arabic versions of Greek texts, instead hunted for manuscripts of the Greek originals in monastic libraries and elsewhere. Some humanist scholars set out for the Near East to look for manuscripts, copy inscriptions and make records of the classical ruins. The Arabs who lived in the shadows of those ruins were more or less invisible to these scholars. Cyriac of Ancona (1391–1456) travelled through Turkey, Greece and Egypt noting down inscriptions and collecting antiquities. He proclaimed that the goal of archaeology was to 'wake the dead', in other words to revive the glorious culture of classical antiquity.[9] Bernardo Michelozzi and Bonsignore Bonsignori, who toured the Levant in 1497–8, were primarily looking for Greek and Latin manuscripts, rather than Arabic ones, and Byzantine scholars provided much of what they were looking for.[10] Several fifteenth-century manuscript prospectors went off on a doomed quest for the lost books of Livy's history, preferably in the original Latin, but, failing that, in some Arabic rendering. In truth, there was not so very much classical learning that was preserved only in Arabic and which still awaited translation. Books five, six and seven of Apollonius's *Conics* were discovered in an Arabic version in the early seventeenth century and these three supplemented the first four books that had survived in the original Greek. (The *Conics*, by one of the greatest of Greek mathematicians, Apollonius of Perga, in the third century BC, dealt with the properties of conic sections: circle, ellipse, parabola and hyperbola. The poet and mathematician Umar Khayyam had been familiar with the *Conics* and elaborated on some of its propositions.)[11] But the rediscovery of parts of Apollonius's work in Arabic was an exceptional case and manuscript hunters quested in vain for such chimeras as an Arabic version of the lost books of Livy.

Despite the widespread reaction against Arab learning, Averroism still had its champions and the University of Padua, in particular, remained a centre of Averroist studies and of Aristotelian scholarship more generally. The German Nicholas of Cusa (1401–64), who studied at Padua and who was influenced by Paduan Averroism, was a man of broad interests, including research into squaring the circle – an enterprise in which he believed he had succeeded. (Not until 1882 was it proved to be impossible.) He also developed a heliocentric model of the planetary system and he calculated that the end of the world was due in 1734. In 1448 he became a cardinal and he played an important part in the negotiations to bring the Greek Orthodox Church into union with Rome. None of this concerns us here. In 1460 Nicholas of Cusa wrote *Cribratio Alcoran* ('The Sieving of the Qur'an') in which he took a critical approach to the text of the Qur'an (or rather the inadequate Latin version that was available to him). He concluded that the Qur'an showed clear signs of having been influenced by Nestorian Christianity. Nestorians hold that the divinity and humanity of Christ were not united in a single self-conscious personality. However, the Jewish role in shaping the Qur'an was even more obvious to him. This influence came in two ways. First, Muhammad was guided by a hypothetical Jewish adviser and, secondly, after Muhammad's death, other Jews inserted anti-Christian polemic into the text of the Qur'an. Nicholas of Cusa's thesis can be considered as an early example of the application of critical techniques to the text of the Qur'an, albeit in a primitive and bungled fashion. His speculations about Christian and Jewish influence on the Qur'an would be picked up again in the nineteenth century. He had fastened on what he perceived to be the Christian elements in Islam, not in order to belittle the latter faith, but rather to demonstrate its compatibility with Christianity. If he could succeed in this, then he thought he might persuade the Ottoman Sultan Mehmed II to convert to Christianity. Though his views found favour with his friend, Pope Pius II, they found no favour whatsoever with the Ottoman Sultan.[12]

HERMETIC WISDOM

The mystically minded and conciliatory Nicholas of Cusa sought to expound a common spiritual ground on which the Catholics, Greek Orthodox and Hussites could agree with one another and with the Muslims: 'Religion and the worship of God, in all men endowed with the spirit, are fundamentally, in all the diversity of rites, one and the same.' The Italian nobleman Pico della Mirandola (1463–94), called 'the phoenix of his age', was a more combative character. Pico studied first Hebrew and then Aramaic and Arabic. He was taught by Flavius Mithridates, a Jewish convert to Christianity, and by Elias de Medigo, another Jew, who also introduced Pico to Averroist thought. (Many of the Jews in fifteenth-century Italy had arrived there fleeing from Spanish persecution.) In the last quarter of the fifteenth century Christian cabalism, the Christian reinterpretation of certain esoteric rabbinic texts, started to become fashionable in intellectual circles in Italy and elsewhere. Pico, one of the founders of this movement, took up the study of Hebrew in order to master cabalism and then use the Cabala to demonstrate the truths of the Christian version of the Bible. He studied the text of the Bible for the hidden meanings that he thought it contained. 'There is no knowledge which makes us more certain of the divinity of Christ than magic and Cabala.' He believed in the application of gematria (a cabalistic method of interpreting the Hebrew Scriptures by interchanging words whose letters have the same numerical value when added) in order to tease out the hidden meaning of the biblical text. As the primal language, the one spoken by Adam and Eve in the Garden of Eden, the Hebrew language contained magical properties found in none of its successor languages.

Though enthusiastic about ancient Hebrew wisdom, Pico's attitude to Arabic learning was ambivalent and, despite his studies in Oriental languages, he was hostile to the Arab philosophers: 'Leave to us in Heaven's name Pythagoras, Plato and Aristotle, and keep your Omar, your Alchibitius, your Abenzoar, your Abenragel.' He also denounced Arabic poetry (though, like Petrarch, he seems to have avoided reading any). Yet, for all Pico's professed contempt for Arab learning, he opened his famous *Oration on the Dignity of Man* (c. 1486) by referring to his reading of 'the records of the Arabians' and quoting a certain 'Abdala the Saracen' who, when asked what was the most wonderful thing in the world, replied: 'There is nothing to be seen more wonderful than man.' Although the declamation that followed was mostly supported by quotations from classical Latin authors and appeals to the authority of the ancient Hebrews and the Zoroastrians, Pico also had words of praise for the Arab thinkers: Averroes, Avempace (more correctly, Ibn Bajja), al-Farabi, Avicenna and al-Kindi. Similarly, in his hardly less well-known treatise against astrology, he cited Avicenna and Averroes. (Even if one despised Arabic learning, it was still desirable to appeal to its authority.) Incidentally, it is worth noting that Pico did not attack astrology from the point of view of a modern rationalist but rather as a defender of another branch of occultism, known as natural magic. Pico died young and in the long run his preoccupations and style of thinking influenced only a handful of eccentric intellectuals. In his own lifetime, several of his cabalistic theses were condemned as heretical by the Church and many of the Hermetic texts whose antiquity Pico had placed his faith in, were subsequently shown to be forgeries of late antiquity.[13]

Pico and his contemporaries were fascinated by what little they knew about ancient Egypt. In the fifteenth century Egypt was thought of as the source of most of what later came to be identified as Greek culture – a theory that has been quite recently revived and vigorously and controversially argued by Martin Bernal.[14] Renaissance Platonists, such as Marsilio Ficino, believed that Egyptian hieroglyphs represented Platonic ideas about the universe and divine things. The Egyptian priesthood used the esoteric hieroglyphs to conceal divine mysteries from the profane.[15] It was Ficino who in 1471 translated the *Corpus Hermeticum* from Greek into Latin. This was a body of Platonist and occult writings attributed to an ancient and semi-divine sage Hermes Trismegistus, who in some of his aspects can be considered as a classicized version of the Egyptian god, Thoth. Pico naively believed in the literal existence of this figure and in what seemed to be cryptic prophecies of the coming of Christ by Hermes Trismegistus.[16] As we shall see, early in the next century Isaac Casaubon was to demonstrate that Pico's faith in the authenticity and antiquity of the Hermetic writings was misplaced. In the seventeenth century, that fascinating thinker Athanasius Kircher (on whom, see the next chapter) would make a more determined assault on the mysteries of the hieroglyphs. However, primitive Egyptology, based on false premises and fuelling wild hopes of rediscovering lost ancient wisdom, made even less progress in the centuries that immediately followed than Arabic studies did. Study of the language and culture of the ancient Egyptians became the intellectually marginalized province of dabblers in cabalism, Rosicrucianism and Freemasonry.

THE STRUGGLE FOR GLOBAL SUPREMACY

The fifteenth and sixteenth centuries were the great age of the Muslim empires: Mughal India, Safavid Persia, Mamluk Egypt and Syria, and Ottoman Turkey. Several European observers warned that Christendom was a shrinking island surrounded by the rising tide of Islam. The fall of Constantinople to the Ottoman Sultan Mehmed II in 1453 seemed to threaten Christendom's very survival. Its capture by the Turks was not only a political and military disaster, but also a cultural disaster for humanist Europe. As Aeneas Sylvius (later Pope Pius II) wrote, it was 'the second death of Homer and Plato'. The conquest of Constantinople was followed by further Turkish conquests of Greek islands and Balkan territories. In 1521 Suleiman the Magnificent captured Belgrade and then destroyed the Hungarian army at the Battle of Mohacs in 1526 and the Turks besieged Hapsburg Vienna for the first time in 1529. A little to the east, the Turks were pushing on into what is nowadays Romania. In the Mediterranean they occupied Rhodes in 1522, Cyprus in 1571 and Crete in 1669. Elsewhere in the world, particularly in South East Asia and sub-Saharan Africa, Islam continued to make converts and expand its territory. A significant number of those who fought for the Ottomans and who commanded or crewed the ships of the Barbary corsairs were European renegades who had converted from Christianity to Islam. Such cases were widely publicized and denounced from pulpits across Europe.[17] Christendom was under siege.

Only in the West had Christian armies made significant gains from

Islam. In 1492 what was left of the Nasrid kingdom of Granada surrendered to the Spanish Catholic monarchs, Ferdinand and Isabella. That same year Columbus set out on his voyage of exploration across the Atlantic. His venture had been inspired by the ideology of the Crusades. He hoped to gain independent trading access to the wealth of the Indies and to outflank the Islamic empires of the Ottomans, Mamluks and Safavids. He believed that he lived very close to the Last Days and he was inspired by knowledge that astrologers had predicted the imminent collapse of Muhammad's sect and the coming of the Antichrist. Columbus set out his aims in a document addressed to Ferdinand and Isabella: 'Your Highnesses, as good Christian and Catholic princes, devout and propagators of the Christian faith, as well as enemies of the sect of Mahomet and of all idolatries and heresies, conceived the plan of sending me, Christopher Columbus, to this country of the Indies, there to see the princes, the peoples, the territory, their disposition and all things else, and the way in which one might convert these regions to our holy faith.'[18] When Columbus set sail across the Atlantic, he was careful to include in the ship's complement an Arabic-speaking Jew, for his expectation was that they would reach the East Indies, where there were known to be many Arabic-speaking Muslim traders in the ports of China, Malaysia and India. It must have been somewhat disappointing to discover when he first touched land that the Caribs were quite ignorant of Arabic.

There was at first a reluctance to acknowledge that America really was a new and different continent. Benito Arias Montano, Spanish organizer of the Antwerp Polyglot Bible project, was so convinced that America must have been known to authors of the Bible that he added to the texts of the Antwerp edition a list of the Hebrew forms of American place names that he thought he had discovered in the Bible.[19] The Fleming Ogier Ghiselin de Busbecq, the Hapsburg ambassador to Ottoman Istanbul from 1554 to 1562, believed that the Christian powers were wasting their time and resources in America, while Christianity's very survival was threatened by Ottoman advances in Europe and he denounced those who wasted resources in 'seeking the Indies and the Antipodes across vast fields of ocean, in search of gold'. Some Turkish observers, however, were more perceptive.[20]

Around 1580 an Ottoman geographer, the author of *Tarikh al-Hind al-Garbi* ('History of the India of the West'), warned that the European settlements on the coasts of the Americas posed long-term economic dangers to the prosperity and survival of the sultanate.[21] True to the crusading spirit of Columbus, when the Spaniards did set about colonizing the Americas, they conducted themselves as if they were fighting a new holy war. The literature of the period frequently compared the barbarous, pagan American Indians to the Muslims and both were regularly accused by Christian writers of idolatry, sodomy and indolence.[22]

THE RISE OF TRAVEL LITERATURE

The discovery of America also fostered a renewed enthusiasm for travel literature. Curiously, however, people were far more interested in reading about the Islamic lands and the lands yet further east than they were in reading about the New World. Giambattista Ramusio published an extremely popular collection of travel narratives, *Racolta de Navigazioni et viaggi* (Venice, 1550–59), and it was chiefly through Ramusio's collection that Marco Polo's account of his journey to the Great Khan became better known. In the 1580s and 1590s Richard Hakluyt published a series of narratives of exploration, mostly concerning voyages to the Americas. Then, in 1613, Samuel Purchas published an English equivalent to Ramusio's anthology, *Purchas his Pilgrimage, or Relations of the World and the Religions observed in all the Ages*, and in 1625 he followed this up with two further books which collected together travellers' accounts of all parts of the then known world. Purchas was a fervent partisan for Mandeville's travel writings. The account given by Purchas of Xanadu was to inspire Coleridge's famous poem. As the title of Purchas's collection suggests, he conceived of travelling as a kind of act of piety.[23]

Pilgrimage to the Holy Land was still very popular in the last decades of the fifteenth century and a copious and repetitive literature of pilgrimage was produced in that period. Thereafter the fashion for actually going on pilgrimage to Jerusalem, as opposed to reading about it, declined steeply. Even so, those who travelled in the East often modelled their narratives on the precedents provided by literary pilgrims, as did, for example, Jean Thenaud who accompanied the French ambassador to the Mamluk Sultan of Egypt, Qansuh al-Ghuri, in 1512.[24] Pierre Belon was another literary traveller who went out in the entourage of a French ambassador, though he went to Istanbul in the 1540s. Belon was a naturalist who investigated the zoology and botany of Turkey, Egypt and Syria and the results of those researches appeared in *Les observations de plusieurs singularitez et choses memorables trouvées en Grece, Asie, Iudée, Égypte Arabie et autres pays estranges* (1554). Belon, who was also responsible for introducing hitherto unknown Middle Eastern plants to France, was murdered in 1564, possibly by a Huguenot.[25] Ogier Ghiselin de Busbecq (1522–92), the Hapsburg ambassador in Constantinople who feared that the Turks were making gains in Europe while the Christian powers squandered their resources in America, has already been mentioned. Like many diplomats in the early modern period, Busbecq also pursued a wide range of scholarly interests, as a linguist, antiquarian, zoologist and botanist. When he returned to Europe he brought with him 264 Greek manuscripts, as well as a considerable collection of Greek and Roman coins and six female camels. His letters from Turkey to a friend, initially published in Latin as the *Itinera Constantinopolitanum et Amasium. Eiusdem ... de acie contra Turcam instruenda consilium* (1581), gave a portrait of Turkish life that is infused with a classicist's sensibility and quotations from Pliny, Polybius, Galen and Plautus.[26]

Though Nicolas de Nicolay (1517–83) can be variously described as a soldier, spy or cartographer, he was effectively a professional travel writer who travelled throughout Europe, North Africa and Turkey and then wrote about his experiences, most notably in *Les quatre premiers livres des navigations et peregrinations orientales* (1567). Nicolay's book was illustrated with the exotic costumes of the East and was presumably much consulted by European painters of Eastern themes as well as by people who had been invited to fancy-dress parties.[27] However, the number of travellers who went out to the Near East and then wrote about their experience in the sixteenth century was a mere trickle compared to what it would become in the seventeenth century. As merchants, pilgrims and scholar adventurers brought exotic objects of all kinds back to Europe – American Indian drums, unusual seashells, Persian ceramics, hitherto unknown herbs, stuffed mermen, Chinese ivories, Indian money, narwhal horns and so on – private collectors set up cabinets of curiosity that were unsystematic collections of the rare and the marvellous. The cabinet of curiosity, a primitive and often fanciful attempt to organize the flood of new knowledge coming from exotic parts, besides being the ancestor of the museum, was also one of the institutional precursors of serious Orientalism.[28]

Apart from travellers' narratives of the exotic parts, European scholars also learned a great deal from native informants. Leo Africanus was easily the most important of these informants in the sixteenth century. Leo, whose original name was Hasan ibn Muhammad al-Wazzan, was an Arab, born in Granada in 1493 or 1494. His family migrated to Fez in Morocco when he was young. Hasan received a good education and as a young man he served on various North African diplomatic missions, so that he came to know parts of Africa, including Egypt, quite well. In 1518 he was captured by corsairs close to Jerba, an island off the Tunisian coast, and brought to Rome. There he learned Italian. The Medici Pope Leo X became his patron and therefore, when Hasan converted in 1520, he took Leo as his Christian name. Leo Africanus studied the Latin historians. He wrote a great deal, most of which has not survived, and, among other things, he provided biographies of famous learned Arabs for use by European scholars. Leo also had links with the Christian cabalists and he introduced Guillaume Postel to the *za'irja*, a strange kind of North African divination machine, consisting of concentric rotating wheels inscribed with letters, which could be made to answer questions about unseen things. He also provided crucial information about which Arabic works were important and this was to guide generations of future manuscript hunters in their search for Arabic works. It was from Leo, for example, that the West learned about the importance of al-Hariri's twelfth-century classic literary *jeu d'esprit*, the *Maqamat*, as well as the philosopher-historian Ibn Khaldun's theoretical prolegomena to the study of history, the *Muqaddima*. However, Leo's chief work was *The History and Description of Africa and the Notable Things Therein Contained*. He wrote this in (poor) Italian and finished the manuscript in 1526. The *Description* is mostly about Africa north of the Sahara and the section on Leo's home town, Fez, is especially detailed. Leo drew heavily on his own observations as a travelling ambassador, but he also took a great deal from the poet Ibn al-Raqiq al-Qayrawani's lost history of North Africa and he cited classic works by authors like al-Mas'udi, al-Idrisi and Ibn Khaldun. Ramusio published the *Description* in 1550 and it was later translated into Latin, French and English (the last by John Pory). Some time before 1550 Leo slipped away back to North Africa and, home once more, he presumably resumed his Muslim identity.[29]

In general, Christian attempts to evangelize among the Muslims of the Near East and North Africa had no success and in the sixteenth century it was more a matter of writing treatises for the hypothetical use of missionaries than of sending preachers out into the infidel fields. Moreover, some of those who wrote books about Islam or Oriental languages, though they suggested that such studies might be useful in the furtherance of missionary activities, seem to have been using that claim as a pretext to justify their more purely intellectual interest in the exotic. The declaration in the preface to a treatise on, say, the Arabic language, that it had some exalted Christian purpose, might well be successful in securing patronage and a financial subsidy from some senior ecclesiastical dignitary. It is also useful to remember that Catholic and Protestant missions were not necessarily directed towards the Muslims. Quite often the proposed aim was to bring the Eastern Christian Arabs, Greeks and Copts into the Catholic or Protestant fold. In particular, Catholics and Lutherans competed with each other to reach an ecumenical understanding with the Greek Orthodox Christians who were now subjects of the Ottoman Sultan. The only Eastern Church that was in communion with Rome was the Maronite Church. Lebanese Maronites in Italy, under the patronage of the Pope and the Republic of Venice, were instrumental in fostering the study of Syriac, and Maronites also provided the Vatican library with Arabic manuscripts.[30] In addition to attempts to correct the ways of the Eastern Christians (as missionary-minded folk in the West saw the matter), for centuries to come other Christian missionaries worked on the conversion of the Jews, for many believed that the total conversion of the Jews was a necessary precondition for the end of the world.

(This was a period when the pious actually looked forward to the end of the world with some enthusiasm.)

THE CRAZY FATHER OF
ORIENTALISM: GUILLAUME POSTEL

Though Guillaume Postel was in some senses a wholly exceptional figure, in many ways he was entirely a product of his times. Like Thenaud, Busbecq and Belon, Postel took scholarly advantage of French diplomatic missions in the Near East; he was a writer who produced both scholarly treatises for those who were versed in Latin and Hebrew, as well as accounts of Turkish and Muslim manners and customs that were written in the vernacular and aimed at a wider French readership; the intellectual heir of Pico's Christian cabalism and of Nicholas of Cusa's strivings for concord between the world's great faiths; and an advocate of preaching missions to the Muslims.

That Guillaume Postel – the first true Orientalist – was also a complete lunatic may be taken as an ominous presage for the future history of an intellectual discipline. Born in 1510, he was an orphan and child prodigy, who first supported himself by working as a servant in a school at Beaucé, where he allegedly taught himself Hebrew. He subsequently found inspiration in his reading of Pico della Mirandola on the cabalistic version of Christianity and he followed Pico in believing that the occult doctrines of the Cabala could be used to demonstrate the truths of Christianity and therefore the study of Hebrew and mastery of the Cabala could be of great use to missionaries, as they could use this occult lore to demonstrate the irrefutable truths of Christianity. However, Postel's mastery of the Jewish sources was far greater than Pico's. Postel translated a large part of the cabalistic text, the *Zohar*, into Latin. He was also one of the grand figures in research on the primordial language, the *Ursprache*. In his *De originibus seu de Hebraicae linguae et gentis antiquitate* (1538), he argued that Hebrew was the primordial language and from it descended, not only Arabic and Chaldaean but also Hindi and Greek – and all other tongues. His belief in the primacy of Hebrew was not in his time particularly controversial. What was a little eccentric was his idea that in order to achieve world peace and a utopian manner of life it was necessary for everyone to return to speaking Hebrew, for it was the *via veritas perdita*, 'the lost way of truth'. Moreover, he held that the very structure of the Hebrew language, divinely ordained as it was, would confirm the Christian revelation. Given the extraordinary status he assigned to Hebrew studies, his interest in other languages was inevitably subsidiary to those studies. However, his knowledge of Greek was also excellent and he wrote a pioneering study of Athenian institutions.

In 1535–7 Postel accompanied the French ambassador sent by François I to Suleiman the Magnificent in Constantinople, where Postel's commission was to collect Oriental manuscripts for the French king. At the same time, Postel studied Arabic and Turkish. In Istanbul he learnt Arabic so fast that his teacher thought that he might be a demon. He also managed to pick up colloquial Greek, and Armenian. (He later boasted that he would be able to travel as far as the frontier of China without experiencing any language problems.) He studied Arabic primarily in order to improve his knowledge of Hebrew, for the two Semitic languages had many grammatical features and items of vocabulary in common. But Arabic was also useful for study of the doctrines of the Eastern Christians. In 1539 he became holder of the first chair of Arabic in Paris – at the Collège de France. (The Collège de France was a humanist institute of higher learning founded by François I in 1530.) Around 1538–43 Postel, drawing heavily on medieval Arab grammars, wrote and published *Grammatica Arabica*, the first ever grammar of classical Arabic in Europe. Although it was not a particularly accurate one, it would remain the basic textbook until Erpenius, drawing on and improving Postel's work, published his Arabic grammar in 1613. After Postel undertook another eastern trip, this time to the Holy Land in 1549, a slightly puzzling story circulated that his beard had been grey when he set out for the East and black when he returned. There were also rumours that this amazingly learned and mysterious figure possessed the elixir of life. As a result of his trips to the Near East, he was able to publish *De la république des Turcs, et là ou l'occasion s'offera, des meurs et loys de tous Muhamedistes* (1559), which was followed by two companion volumes with even more verbose titles. These books introduced French readers to the life of the Prophet, the history of Islam, the Arabic langauge, as well as the religion, laws, customs of the Ottoman Turks.

In his lifetime he was the foremost expert on Arabic and Islam in Europe, but he was also quite barmy. In Venice in 1547 he had met up with a woman called Johanna, whom he confidently identified with the Shekinah (divine presence) of the Cabala, the Angelic Pope, the Mater Mundi, the New Eve, and the consummation of eternity, among other things. Johanna (like Superman) had X-ray vision, so that she could see Satan sitting at the centre of the earth. Postel, impressed, became her disciple. By the time he returned from his second trip to the Middle East, the Mater Mundi was dead. However, this was only a temporary setback, as in 1551 she returned to this world and possessed Postel's body, so that he became the Mater Mundi, the New Eve and so on. (He does not say if he got the X-ray vision.) As prophet of the New Age, he then produced a succession of strange books and pamphlets, which got him into trouble with the Inquisition in Venice. However, the Inquisition, in an unusually benign frame of mind, decreed that he was not a heretic, merely insane. An official of the Holy Office, who had examined Postel's writings for heresy in 1555, reported that, though his ideas were definitely heretical, 'no one, fortunately, could possibly understand them except the author'. Postel was imprisoned in Italy from 1555 until 1559 and then again detained as a lunatic in St Martin des Champs in Paris from 1563. The latter term of incarceration was more in the way of a comfortable and honourable medical house arrest, as his erudition, as well as his amiable personality, continued to command enormous respect until his death in 1581.

Postel's erudition drew heavily on the Cabala and Neoplatonism, but also on what he could discover of the doctrines of such Muslim groups as the Druze and the Isma'ilis. In particular, his notion of the successive incarnation of the Divine in men (and he considered himself an outstanding example) may have ultimately been derived from his reading of Druze literature. He was especially enthusiastic about the Druze because he had determined that they were of French origin and that their name derived from 'Druid'. The alleged Frenchness of the Druze was particularly important, as Postel was a fervent patriot who believed that the French were the chosen people of the Last Days and that the King of France had the rightful claim to be king of the world by virtue of his direct descent from Noah (though one would have thought that there were many in Postel's time who could have made a similar claim).

Doubtless there were many sixteenth-century Frenchmen who believed that they belonged to the chosen race. But Postel had plenty of other more unusual ideas – such as his belief in the superiority of women. And to stick with Oriental issues, he argued that Muhammad was a genuine Prophet and that Muslims should be considered as half Christians. Furthermore, his *De la république des Turcs et là ou 'l'occasion s'offera, des meurs et loys de tous Muhamedistes* offered an unusually favourable account of Muslim manners and customs. While not wholly uncritical of the way of life of the Turks, he thought that they were better than Christians in the way that they arranged marriages and divorces, in their charity, in their provision for education and in the decorous quiet of their prayers. He admired and praised the Ottoman sultan's palace-harem, the Seraglio (and he was by no means the only European visitor to Istanbul to do so). He maintained that almost everything in Asia was superior to almost everything in Christendom: 'All things that we hold in the West as of extraordinary artifice are like mere shadows of oriental excellencies.' The East as a whole was superior to the West, because the earthly paradise had been located there. He cited supporting evidence for Eastern excellence, such as borametz, an oriental bush which bore lambs as its fruit, or another oriental tree which produced bread, wine, silk, vinegar and oil. (Pico della Mirandola had entertained vaguely similar notions about the Orient, for he believed that the sun was stronger in the eastern part of the world, where it produced gems, perfumes, lions, tigers and elephants.) Another proof provided by Postel for the superiority of the East was that the Three Wise Men came from there. As late as the eighteenth century, leading thinkers in the European Enlightenment looked for stimulus to Oriental sages – not just to Buddha and Confucius, but also to Near Eastern figures such as the ancient Arabian sage Luqman, the Aesop of the Arabs.

Postel also held the East to be superior in its arts and manufactures. While few of his contemporaries would have gone along with Postel on the superiority of women, still less the X-ray vision of the incarnation of the Shekinah living in Venice, nevertheless his views of the Orient were quite widely shared in the sixteenth and seventeenth centuries. The French jeweller Jean Chardin (1643–1713) conducted a careful survey of Safavid Persia's various crafts and industries, at the end of which he concluded that in a majority, though by no means all, Persia was more advanced than Western Europe. Others feared Ottoman military superiority, for it was only towards the end of the seventeenth century that the military tide could be seen to have turned.

Postel found much to admire in both Ottoman and Arabic culture, but his study of Islam was essentially driven by fear. Until late in the seventeenth century, Ottoman Turkish advances in the Balkans seemed to threaten the very survival of Christendom. He fearfully perceived that Islam already prevailed in ten twelfths of the known world. At the same time the rise of Protestantism presented a corresponding danger within Christendom's frontiers. He was convinced that Islam and Protestantism were dangerously alike and he wrote a treatise on the equivalence of these threats, *Alcorani seu legis Mahometi et Evangelistum concordiae liber* (Paris, 1543). Protestant reformers were, like Muhammad before them, sowers of schism. 'The spiritual sons of Luther are the little bastards of Mahom', as he put it. Postel also held the common view that Islam had been sent as a scourge of the Oriental Christians because of their divisions and contumaciousness. He wanted to find and publish the texts of Eastern Christians in order to expose their errors. Having come across a bogus Hadith, or saying, attributed to the Prophet Muhammad (in this case falsely), to the effect that the translation of the Qur'an into other languages would be the doom of the Muslims, Postel had no hesitation in translating large chunks of it into Latin in *De Orbis Concordia Libri Quatuor* (1544). As well as a translation of parts of the Qur'an, Postel's book also gave an account of the life of the Prophet, as well as attacks on both the Qur'an and the Prophet. Yet, despite his hostility to the Prophet's revelation, he did not write of him as an impostor. Moreover, as its title suggests, *De Orbis Concordia* was not so much a work of polemic as the setting out of a programme for universal harmony and the search for a common ground for all faiths, that common ground being a rationally and philosophically explained

Catholicism. In the turbulent context of the religious wars of the sixteenth century, his ideas in this area were almost as mad as his notions about the Mater Mundi and the Shekinah.[31]

Postel died in 1581. Despite his apparently marginal position as the crazy Cabalist with impractical plans for world peace, he maintained contacts with all the leading Orientalists and Oriental projects. Postel's pupils included Raphelengius and Joseph Justus Scaliger (on both of whom more shortly). The manuscripts he collected in the East were also important for future scholarly researches. In particular, a manuscript of the fourteenth-century Syrian prince Abu al-Fida's geography was to be much studied, as it provided a lot of vital information for cartographers about eastern lands.

THE PRINTED QUR'AN

Postel had also advised Theodor Bibliander in his work on a printed Latin version of the Qur'an. It is one of the striking paradoxes in the history of Western culture that the invention of printing had at first an archaicizing effect, as neglected medieval texts were given a much wider circulation than they had achieved when they were first written. (The first books that Caxton printed did not deal with new technology or the latest literary fashions, but were mostly medieval chivalric treatises.) Prior to the sixteenth century, very few scholars had had access to the manuscript of Robert of Ketton's twelfth-century translation of the Qur'an into Latin. However, in 1543 Theodor Bibliander, a Protestant scholar of Jewish exegetical writings, produced an edition of Robert of Ketton's work, under the title *Machumetis Saracenorum principis, eiusque successorum vitae, ac doctrina, ipseque Alcoran, Quo velut authentico legum diuinarum codice Agareni & Turcae ...* (and so on and so on). Bibliander's version of the text was to be printed in three further editions in Basel and Zurich in the years that followed. The printed version of Robert of Ketton's translation was accompanied by medieval attacks on the Prophet and Muslims by Peter the Venerable and others. Despite the anti-Islamic polemical baggage, the man who first printed this version of the Qur'an, Johann Herbst, was imprisoned by the city council of Basel for disseminating pro-Muslim propaganda. It was feared that even the most virtuous or sophisticated reader might be seduced by the heresies of the damnable book.[32] As several later printers would discover, anyone who printed the Qur'an ran the risk of being accused of being a crypto-Muslim and therefore sentenced to a term in prison. On the other hand, there was so much interest among the reading public in a book that had such a wicked reputation, that printing a translation of the Qur'an was quite a profitable enterprise.

Herbst's imprisonment had been of short duration, for the leader of the Reformation in Germany, Martin Luther (1483–1546), sprang to the defence of Bibliander and his printer. One of the manuscripts Bibliander had used for his edition had been provided by Luther, who also wrote the preface to Bibliander's second edition which was published in Basle in 1550. When he was younger, Luther had preached that the Turks should not be resisted, as their coming was a punishment for sin. Later, when a Turkish army besieged Vienna in 1529, he changed his mind.[33] Even so, he does not seem to have been particularly conscious of the ideological threat posed by Islam, until, late in life, he stumbled across Ricoldo da Monte Croce's *Im probatio al chorani*, which so impressed him that he translated it into German in 1542. Although Luther interested himself in the medieval polemics against Islam (and he also wrote a preface to Nicholas of Cusa's *Cribratio Alcoran*), he did not in fact believe that it was possible to convert the Muslims, for he held that they had hardened their heart against Christianity and were beyond redemption. On the other hand, a new Crusade against Islam would be useless as long as Christendom was divided and given over to sin. It was even possible that the Turks would triumph over the Christians and, to some extent, he wrote to prepare his readership for that eventuality. But for all Luther's horrified fascination with Islam, he still regarded the Pope as the real Antichrist, for Luther found the doctrines of Islam to be gross and preposterous by comparison with the sophisticated corruption of Roman Catholicism. Just as the Catholic Postel had conceived of true Christianity as being under assault from the two-pronged menace of Islam and Protestantism, so Luther thought that the menace came from Islam and the Catholic Church. Despite the advances that the Turks were making in the Balkans, Luther was certain that the corruption of the Catholic Church was the greater menace to the true faith. The Antichrist's head was the Pope, while his body was Islam. This was a period when, if a person thought of defining himself in terms of an 'Other', then, if that person was a Protestant, the 'Other' was likely to be a Catholic, and vice versa. According to Luther, 'Turca et Papa in formis religionis nihil different aut variant, nisi in ceremoniis' (The Turk and the Pope do not differ in the form of their religion, unless it be in the rituals).[34]

POLYGLOTS

There is a certain sort of triumphalist history of European culture that presents the progress of the arts and sciences in terms of smooth, incremental gains. In this progress every grand intellectual endeavour inevitably brings results that benefit the world. But such a selective version of intellectual history neglects the past importance of grand projects, supported by the best minds and often by copious funding that still went nowhere. Cultural history is (or at least should be) full of cul-de-sacs, such as the labours of Joseph Justus Scaliger, James Ussher, Count Jean Potocki and others to establish a universal chronology that would confirm the apparent time-frame set out by the Bible, or the attempts to square the circle, by Nicholas of Cusa and others. The production in the sixteenth and seventeenth centuries of the polyglot Bibles was another great scholarly enterprise that today has been more or less forgotten.

A polyglot Bible is one in which the text is printed in various languages in parallel columns. The purpose of this was to allow a more accurate reading of the original text and to correct what were possibly misleading renderings in the Latin Vulgate scriptures.[35] The earliest polyglot Bibles were essentially Catholic enterprises. The Complutensian Polyglot Bible of 1514–17 was produced in Spain and included texts in Hebrew, Greek and Latin. The Antwerp Polyglot of 1569–72, though it built upon the readings established by the Complutensian Bible, was a more ambitious production and it was more widely distributed. Apart from anything else, the Antwerp Bible was a set-piece display of the state of the printer's art. Christophe

Plantin, a merchant prince of the world of printing and publishing, was also famous for printing in 1570 Abraham Ortelius's *Theatrum orbis terrarum*, a universal atlas whose publication pushed contemporary printing technology to its limits. The polyglot Bible was hardly less of a technical tour de force. The Vulgate Latin text was laid out in parallel with Greek, Hebrew, Aramaic and Syriac versions and the exotic typefaces were deployed in a range of sizes. Furthermore, a team of Europe's leading biblical scholars also provided a vast scholarly apparatus. Although no Arabic text of the Bible was printed, Arabic expertise was required in order to shed light on some of the problems posed by the texts in the other Semitic languages: Hebrew, Aramaic and Syriac.[36] The scholar who supervised the Antwerp Polyglot Bible project, Benito Arias Montano, was a biblical scholar who had mastered Arabic as well as Hebrew.[37] (Arias Montano was the man who thought that America featured in the Old Testament.) It was also inevitable that Postel should be called upon to advise. As has already been mentioned, Postel had also taught Franciscus Raphelengius (1539–97). Nevertheless, the latter, a Paris-educated Fleming who became a proof-reader at the Plantin printing-house, seems to have picked up most of his Arabic by teaching himself as he worked on the polyglot Bible. He is a striking, but by no means untypical, example of a man who acquired a mastery of Arabic outside of any academic institution. He later became Professor of Hebrew in Leiden and his distinguished career as a scholar of Hebrew and Arabic, as well as of Latin, Chaldaean, Syriac, Persian and Ethiopian, will be discussed in the next chapter.[38]

The Antwerp Polyglot Bible, under the patronage of Philip II of Spain, was a Catholic enterprise (though there were many Catholics who doubted the wisdom of challenging the reliability of St Jerome's Vulgate), and in the sixteenth century the study of Arabic and Islam was still dominated by Catholic scholarship. For a long time Italian cities, and in particular Rome and Venice, were the leading centres for the study of Islam. The Vatican library was founded in 1475. By 1488 it had twenty-two Arabic manuscripts. In the longer run, this library was the recipient of more manuscripts donated by Oriental Christians. However, until at least the end of the seventeenth century, the study of Arabic outside the great libraries was severely hampered by the sheer difficulty and expense of acquiring Arabic manuscripts, and of getting Arabic manuscripts, with their strangely shaped letters, printed.

The Papacy sponsored the earliest experiments in printing in Arabic and in 1514 Pope Julius II sponsored Gregorio de' Gregori's printing of *Kitab salat al-sawa'i*, a book of hours with an Arabic typeface, designed to be used by Eastern Christians. It was the first book ever to be printed in Arabic lettering. This was followed by the Genoese Dominican Agostino Giustiniani's printing of a polyglot Psalter in 1516, in which the Psalms appeared in Latin, Greek, Hebrew, Aramaic and Arabic. Then a Venetian printer, Paganino de Paganini, produced a Qur'an for the use of missionaries in 1537–8. These early printed texts had a limited distribution and an experimental character. The typefaces did not follow the cursive Arabic script closely enough and hence must have seemed unattractive to Arab readers. Things changed with the establishment of the Medici Oriental Press. This was set up in Rome in 1584 under the direction of Giovan Battista Raimondi and the patronage of Pope Gregory XIII. It was the first printing press in Europe dedicated to printing books in an Arabic typeface and the typeface it used was strikingly elegant. The primary aim in printing books in Arabic was not to assist the academic study of the Arab world nor even to publish polemical works against Islam, but rather to produce Arabic books that could be used in preaching missions to the Oriental Christians (the Copts, Maronites, Nestorians and others), seeking to convert those lost sheep to Catholicism. One of its most important publications was a version of the Gospels in Arabic in 1591. However, the Medici Press also published that standard medical textbook, the *Canon* of Avicenna, as well as a selection of grammars and works of learning, for European consumption, including al-Idrisi's twelfth-century geography of the world. It found few takers for what it printed and consequently ran at a substantial loss. After the printing of only seven Arabic texts, the project was abandoned in 1595.[39]

Raimondi and his patrons had hoped that the press might do good business in the Near East, since there were no Muslim printing presses employing Arabic typefaces. Though Greeks, Jews and Armenians in the Ottoman empire were eventually allowed to print books in their own languages, Muslim theologians argued that to set up the holy language of the Qur'an in print would be a kind of desecration. (Apart from the religious objection to printing, the vested interests of the professional scribes and copyists also had some weight.) Only in the late eighteenth century was Ibrahim Muteferrika allowed to set up a printing press using an Arabic typeface in Istanbul.[40] Several Western writers in the sixteenth and seventeenth centuries suggested that the invention and use of printing in the West demonstrated Christendom's superiority to Islam, though the theme of the West's technological superiority to the rest of the world was not yet fully articulated.

THE LATINITY OF SIXTEENTH-CENTURY ORIENTALISM

Enough has been said here about the subordination of Arabic to Hebrew studies. The study of Arabic was also dominated by the preoccupations of classicists, though the boundaries between the scholarly disciplines were not sharp, for the greatest classicists of the age had usually also mastered Hebrew as a matter of course. Classical scholars only occasionally troubled to pick up a smattering of Arabic. Nevertheless, they often took a friendly interest in the language and the embryonic Orientalism of the sixteenth and seventeenth centuries only managed to limp along because of the interest of such famous classical scholars as Scaliger, Isaac Casaubon, Lancelot Andrewes and Henry Saville. Joseph Justus Scaliger (1540–1609) was a polymath and by common consent the greatest scholar of his age, 'the prince of scholars'. His family was of Italian origin and came from Geneva. He was the son of the no less famous controversialist, grammarian and philosopher Julius Caesar Scaliger (1484–1558). His father, a harsh taskmaster, demanded that the child Joseph Justus make a short speech in Latin every day. However, the father forbade his son the study of Greek, which Joseph Justus took up only after his father's death, having decided that 'those who do not know Greek know nothing at all'. At sixteen, he wrote a tragedy in Latin. Later he would write poetry in the same language. Forced to be a genius by his father's educational programme, Joseph Justus Scaliger seems to have been a tormented figure. All his life he suffered from strange dreams and chronic constipation. He slept little and often forgot to eat. He also related that once, when riding by a marsh, he encountered the Devil in the guise of a black man who sought to lure him into the quagmire.[41]

Having grown up in France as a Catholic, Scaliger converted to Calvinism in 1562. In the same year Postel, shortly before he was arrested for heresy, got Scaliger interested in Oriental languages – in the first instance, in Hebrew. Thereafter, Scaliger revered Postel, though with reservations: 'Postellus excellens philosophus, cosmographus, mathematicus, historicus stultus, linguarum non ignarus, sed nullius ad unguem peritus. Invideo illi Arabicam linguam.' (Postel an excellent philosopher, cosmographer and mathematician, a foolish historian, he knows many languages, but is not expert in any single one. I envy him his Arabic.) Scaliger was chiefly famous as a classicist and philologist and he edited a series of important Latin and Greek texts. His edition of the notoriously corrupt and difficult *Astronomica* by Manilius, a first-century AD didactic treatise on astrology, was particularly esteemed. (Later classicists of the first rank, including Richard Bentley and A. E. Housman, would also crack their skulls on the same text.) Scaliger was quite messianic about the importance of language: 'Our theological disputes arise from ignorance of grammar.' He also studied Syriac, Coptic, Arabic and Persian and he published *Proverbia Arabica*, a short collection of Arab proverbs.

Nevertheless, his knowledge of Arabic and the other Oriental languages was slight and he was mainly interested in Arabic sources for the light they could shed on the chronology of the world. In the sixteenth and seventeenth centuries, the chronology of the world was an exciting and controversial subject, or, as Anthony Grafton has put it, 'a legendarily rebarbative subject'. James Ussher's *Annales Veteris et Novi Testamenti* (1650–54) fixed the Creation of the world as taking place on 23 October 4004 BC and the Flood was confidently dated by him at 1,656 years after the Creation. But Ussher only relied on the Bible, supplemented by Greek and Latin sources. Scaliger, in his great work on chronology, *Opus de emendatione temporum* (1583), cast his net more widely and used a range of exotic sources, including Arabic ones. Scaliger and others attempted to collate data from the Bible and classical historians with what scholars thought they knew about the chronology of Egyptian history, as well as Chinese chronology and the Aztec calendar, in order to produce a unified timeline of world history that would confirm the chronology of the Bible. The growing problems of the chronologists were one of the minor consequences of the expansion of European power throughout the world and the resultant influx of exotic and inconsistent data, almost none of which seemed to support what could be deduced from the Scriptures. Some of Europe's best minds, including Leibniz and Newton, as well as Scaliger, struggled with chronological issues. (Postel, by the way, had argued that Romulus had invented a faulty calendar in order to extirpate the memory of Noah.) Scaliger did his best, even if he was obliged to conclude that anyone who thought that they had fully worked out the chronology of the Kings of Israel would have to be mad.

Scaliger had studied with Postel and admired him, but he did not share the latter's faith in missionary work and future world harmony and believed that Arabic-speaking missionaries would have little chance of success. He suggested that Postel's Arabic was not actually that good and he also thought that Postel's emphasis on learning Arabic through the study of translations of the Gospels into that language was mistaken. It was much better to study Arabic by working on the Qur'an and indigenous works of Arabic literature. 'You can no more master Arabic without the Qur'an than Hebrew without the Bible,' as he remarked to Casaubon.[42] (One great advantage of learning Arabic from the Qur'an was and is the fact that it is the only text that is normally vowelled. Arabic manuscripts of other works not only omitted the vowels, but were often slapdash about adding the diacritical marks that distinguished some consonants from others.) Scaliger identified the paucity of Arabic manuscripts in European libraries as being the major problem of the time. He was also hostile to the notions that knowing Hebrew was a big help in learning Arabic and that the main purpose of studying Arabic was to further Hebrew studies. He suggested that the study of Turkish and the use of Turkish guides, grammars and dictionaries of Arabic, might be of more use to European Arabists.

Perhaps because the struggle for intellectual ascendancy and the quest for patronage were so acute in this period, scholarly rivalry and rancour were common. Scaliger was dismissive of all his fellow scholars, except for Raphelengius, to whom he condescended to lend manuscripts and whom he helped on his primitive Latin dictionary, *Thesaurus linguae arabicae*. (As we shall see, Erpenius and other Arabists who came later habitually disparaged the work of their predecessors and contemporaries.) In 1592 Scaliger was invited to the University of Leiden, where he stayed until he died in 1609. He hated lecturing. However, he was an influential figure behind the scenes and it was almost certainly at his urging that a Chair of Arabic was established at Leiden in 1599. His ideas regarding the need to assemble more Arabic manuscripts, to detach Arabic from Hebrew studies and to have recourse to Turkish aids certainly exercised a massive influence on the first significant incumbent of that chair, Thomas Erpenius.

Isaac Casaubon (1559–1614), a friend and rival of Scaliger's, also encouraged Erpenius's work on Arabic grammar and literature. Like Scaliger, Casaubon was a Protestant refugee from France and as such another example of the intellectual diaspora that occurred as a result of religious persecution there. Subsequently spiritual head-hunters in Paris tried very hard to win him over to the Catholic faith, though without success. Like Scaliger, Casaubon was a classicist and philologist and, with Scaliger, he was probably the most famous intellectual in sixteenth-century Europe. Indeed Scaliger called him 'the most learned man in Europe'. Greek and Hebrew were not regarded by sixteenth-century Protestants as marginal subjects, primarily fit for drilling the unformed minds of public schoolboys. Rather, close study of the languages of the Bible was one of the keys to eternal salvation. Casaubon produced critical editions and commentaries on a range of Greek texts. (George Eliot borrowed Casaubon's name for the pedantic and over-ambitious scholar to whom Dorothea is unhappily married in the novel *Middlemarch*.) His translations of some of the Greek texts into Latin were also welcomed by scholars of fewer attainments. His main claim to fame was his demonstration, in *De rebus sacris et ecclesiasticis exercitationes XVI ad Baronii annales*, that the Hermetic writings had not been written in Egyptian by an ancient sage called Hermes Trismegistus, that those writings were not nearly as old as had been supposed and that, since they did not predate the life of Christ, they could not be read as prophesying His coming or, more generally, as confirming the truths of Christianity (as Pico della Mirandola had supposed). Instead, the Hermetic writings could be shown to have borrowed from both the Bible and Plato. Although Casaubon eventually settled in England in 1610, he was shocked by the limited range of intellectual interests in England: 'The only reading which flourishes here is theology; no books but theological books, and those of English authors are published here. The educated men in this part of the world condemn everything which does not bear upon theology.' Although he was not really an Arabist himself, he collected Arabic books and manuscripts and a copy survives of the Medici Press's edition of an Arab grammar, the *Ajurrumiyya*, annotated in Casaubon's hand. He was more generally a key figure in advancing Arabic studies in Europe and, like Scaliger, a sponsor of Erpenius, the first great seventeenth-century Orientalist. Casaubon was fervently pious and he dreamed of the formation of an ecumenical alliance between Protestantism and the Eastern Churches. It is clear from the work diary that he kept, and which was posthumously published, that he regarded scholarly research as a form of prayer.[43]

Postel apart, most of those who interested themselves in Arabic in the sixteenth century were, like Casaubon, amateurs. These amateurs did useful work in the way of collecting manuscripts and sponsoring and funding the next generation of more dedicated academic Orientalists. In the seventeenth century Casaubon's benign interest in Arabic would be sustained by English churchmen, classicists and scholars with philological or scientific interests. In the next century, with the notable exception of Marracci, Protestants dominated the study of Islam and Arabs. The proto-Orientalism of the sixteenth century was mostly a Catholic affair. Postel was a Catholic, though an eccentric one. The Papacy welcomed Maronite Arabs to Rome and made a start in acquiring manuscripts for the Vatican library. As we have seen, the Medici Press in Rome was established under papal patronage. Plantin's press in Antwerp published a huge amount of literature for the furtherance of Catholic worship and study and the pious Catholic, Philip II of Spain, had been the ultimate patron of the Antwerp Polyglot Bible. In the century that followed, Antwerp's status as a commercial and intellectual centre declined steeply. The next great polyglot Bible would be produced in London, while Antwerp's intellectual role would be usurped by Leiden in the Dutch Republic. Although the Medici Press's hope of substantial sales in the Near East had not been realized, enlightened printers like Raimondi and Plantin had had a spearheading role in the sixteenth-century in fostering Oriental studies. In the seventeenth century, that role would be taken over by a handful of university professors, above all by Erpenius and Golius at Leiden and Pococke at Oxford.

4

The Holiness of Oriental Studies

Thus it is not without wonder, how those learned Arabicks *so tamely delivered up their belief unto the absurdities of the* Alcoran. *How the noble* Geber, Avicenna *and* Almanzor, *should rest satisfied in the causes of Earthquakes, delivered from the doctrine of their* Prophet; *that is, from the motion of a great Bull, upon whose horns all the earth is poised. How their faiths could decline so low, as to concede their generations in Heaven, to be made by the smell of a* Citron, *or that the felicity of their Paradise should consist of a Jubile of copulation, that is, a coition of one act prolonged unto fifty years. Thus it is almost beyond wonder, how the belief of reasonable creatures, should ever submit unto Idolatry . . .*

Sir Thomas Browne, *Pseudodoxia Epidemica*,
The First book, Chap V

THE LANGUAGE OF SCHOLARSHIP

This chapter, like its predecessors, is devoted to those who interested themselves in Islam, Arabic and the Arabs. Yet one still needs to remind oneself that not many people were so interested. Those who were tended to be somewhat detached from worldly affairs and their approach to Islam and the Arabs was usually scholarly and anti-quarian rather than utilitarian. In this respect, the studies of the Orientalists reflected seventeenth- and eighteenth-century scholarship more broadly. The Orientalists tended to model their study of Oriental languages on the way Latin and Greek were studied by their contemporaries. The paradox here is that, though living languages such as Arabic, Persian and Chinese were studied as if they were dead languages, this was not really the case with Latin and Greek. Latin was a living language in the seventeenth and eighteenth centuries. Not only was it the normal language of scholarly discourse, but poets and playwrights composed in it and children might use it in their playground games. Philosophy and science required the precision of Latin and, as Bill Bryson has pointed out, such epoch-making, forward-looking works by Englishmen as Francis Bacon's *Novum Organum* (1620), William Harvey's *De motu cordis* (1628), Isaac Newton's *Philosophiae naturalis principia mathematica* (1687) were composed in that language. English was not considered to be a suitable vehicle for the discussion of serious scholarly matters. Even grammars and dictionaries of English were routinely produced in Latin and their authors struggled to make English grammar fit the straitjacket of Latin grammar, as for example in Thomas Smith's *De Recta et Emendata Linguae Anglicae Scriptione Dialogus* (1568), Alexander Gil's *Logonomia Anglica* (1619) and John Wallis's *Grammatica Linguae Anglicanae* (1653). It was inevitable that those major works that were written in the vernacular, such as Bunyan's *Pilgrim's Progress* or Cervantes's *Don Quixote*, should then be translated into Latin, so that they could achieve a wider, international readership.[1]

Latin was a prerequisite for the study of Arabic, for the dictionaries and grammars of Arabic were in Latin, as was almost all the supporting scholarly literature. The men (yes, all men) who took to the study of Arabic had first studied Latin and Greek (and almost always Hebrew too and quite often Syriac as well). As scholars became acquainted with the treasures of Arabic literature, they tended to compare that literature to Greek and Latin classics. When, in the late eighteenth century, William Jones (see the next chapter) translated Arabic and Persian works in order to introduce them to an English public, it was inevitable that he should attempt to fit the Oriental verses into classical genres and so he enthused about Persian 'pastorals', 'eclogues' and so forth. Even in the twentieth century, R. A. Nicholson, who had been trained as a classicist, found it most natural to compare the pre-Islamic poetry he presented in his *A Literary*

History of the Arabs to Greek and Roman exemplars. On the other hand, those who were bored by the great works of antiquity, and who thought the arts and learning of the ancient Greeks and Romans had been overrated (and they were a vociferous minority), seized on Oriental literature as providing a treasury of new images, modes of expression and heroes which might provide some escape from the constraints of classical precedents. The heroes included the pre-Islamic warrior-poet 'Antar, the Abbasid Caliph Harun al-Rashid and the chivalrous Sultan Saladin. Aesop now faced competition from newly discovered ancient Arabian sages, including Luqman and 'Ali (the Prophet's cousin and the alleged source of a collection of improving *Sentences*, on which see below). D'Herbelot's *Bibliothèque orientale*, an early version of the *Encyclopaedia of Islam*, published at the end of the seventeenth century, would have a Plutarchan cast, as anecdotes and snatches of poetry were used to cast light on the lives and moral character of the Oriental great. Not only did the dictionaries of Arabic compiled by Europeans give their meanings in Latin, but the earliest grammars of Arabic were closely – too closely – modelled on grammars of the Latin language. The great Dutch Orientalists of the seventeenth century who worked on those dictionaries and grammars – Raphelengius, Erpenius and Golius – adopted Latinate names, rather than write under their barbarous-sounding original Dutch names. This was, of course, also a period in which Dutch – and Hungarian, Polish, Russian and Danish – scholars found it relatively easy to have direct access to an international readership as they could publish in Latin.

Though there were certainly fewer individuals who were fluent in Greek, still it was not unknown for scholars to converse in that language (and of course Greek was esteemed as an essential tool for New Testament studies). Besides Latin, Hebrew was also more or less essential for Orientalists because most printers lacked an Arabic font so that scholars who wanted to publish in the field were often reduced to transliterating Arabic words into Hebrew, so that the Arabic *Aliph* became a Hebrew *Aleph*, the Arabic *Ba* a Hebrew *Beth*, and so forth.

STUDY AS DEVOTION

In modern times, Arabic studies have flourished (in so far as they have flourished at all) in university departments. But seventeenth-century universities gave only limited remuneration and support to those who studied Oriental subjects. Therefore the role of the individual patron was much more important. Happily the great and the good took their responsibilities seriously. Such grand and wealthy figures as Archbishop William Laud, Sir Thomas Bodley, Bishop Lancelot Andrewes and Sir Henry Savile may have known only a little Arabic, or in some cases none at all, but Arabic studies in the seventeenth century could not have survived and prospered without their benevolent interest. Since few books published on the Middle East could hope to recoup their costs in sales to the public, a subvention from a patron was usually a necessity. As the historian David C. Douglas has written of the slightly later period: 'It is very easy to ridicule the circumstances that attended the private patronage of letters in the early years of the eighteenth century, and the fulsome compliments of contemporary dedications have nourished the self-satisfaction of an age which prefers the flattery of a large public to the delectation of a patron. But hasty writing designed to extract money as rapidly as possible from the largest number of pockets is not necessarily a better means of producing good books than the effort to please the exigent taste of a cultured and wealthy class.'[2] As we shall see, in many cases the patron was actually the initiator of a scholarly project and not just a person to whom application might be made for funding. Laud, Andrewes and others had a clear vision of the direction that they wished scholarship to take.

Most of the patrons who had the resources and interest to sponsor Orientalist research were churchmen. Most of those who actually did the research were similarly churchmen. Salvation – the salvation of one's own soul and the salvation of others – was the central issue of the age. Scholars came to Arabic only after studying the Bible and probably Hebrew and Syriac. The study of all three Semitic languages was effectively regarded as part of theology. Very few people, if any, studied Islam for its own sake. Instead, polemical Christians elaborated the outlines of a life of Muhammad and of the rise of Islam that were often intended to be used in intraconfessional polemic. For example, Catholic scholars made use of an exposition of the 'horrible heresies and perversions' of Islam in order to attack what they claimed were essentially similar Protestant deviations from the true faith. Was not Protestant denial of the efficacy of intercession by saints and the Protestant adherence to predestination essentially the same as the Muslim position on those matters? The Protestants, for their part, attacked the Pope as a latterday Muhammad and found all sorts of sinister similarities between Islam and Roman Catholicism. The real nature of Islam was not an issue. Protestant scholars also energetically researched the Arabic literature of the Eastern Christian Churches in order to discover in it arguments and precedents to set against such things as the Bishop of Rome's claim to primacy or the Catholic doctrines of transubstantiation and purgatory. As the Arabist William Bedwell put it: 'The writings of the [Christian] Arabs say nothing about purgatory, about the impious sacrifice of the mass, about the primacy of Peter and his apostles, about meritorious justification, and there is not a word about those other figments of the imagination.'[3] Protestants also had to fight polemical battles on a second front, against other sectarians. The Socinian sect, which taught that Jesus was not God but only a prophet of God, was obviously vulnerable to the accusation that its doctrine was a form of crypto-Islam. Unitarians, who also rejected the divinity of Christ, could be tarred with the same brush. Followers of Deism, or 'natural religion', who denied the supernatural and Christian miracles, were often polemically portrayed as Islam's fellow travellers.

As has been indicated in the previous chapter, missions to the East tended to concentrate on trying to win over Oriental Christians rather than to convert Muslims. Incidentally, a leading theme of the histories of the rise of Islam written at this time was that it was a punishment meted out by God to the Eastern Christians for their divisions and decadence. The medieval legend of the sinister Nestorian monk who set Muhammad on the heresiarch's path remained popular in the early modern period. A few, but only a few, Orientalists thought that it might be possible to win converts among the Muslims. As far as missionaries were concerned what was at stake in winning the argument was the rescue of the souls of the benighted from the flames of Hell. The Muslims, of course, regarded Christian missions in a much less benign light. From the seventeenth-century Christian perspective, Muslims were inferior, not because of their race or culture, but because they professed a faith that was not true and thereby they faced damnation. Even so, there were many who thought it dangerous to engage in debate with the Muslims at all, for there were definite risks inherent in studying Muslim doctrine. In quite a few countries, including England under Cromwell, the printing of the Qur'an continued to be banned.[4]

THE FIRST GOLDEN AGE OF BRITISH ORIENTALISM

The seventeenth century, and in particular the decades prior to the outbreak of the Civil War in 1642, was the heyday of Arabic and Islamic studies in England. In this period England (together with Holland) achieved a pre-eminence in Islamic studies that it would not regain until the second half of the twentieth century. However, the life and writings of William Bedwell (1563–1632) got English Orientalism off to an unpromising start. Bedwell was the first Englishman to study Arabic since the Middle Ages. Sadly, although he was enthusiastic, he does not seem to have been particularly bright and Erpenius, who studied with him, thought that he was lazy. He started out as rector of St Ethelburga in Bishopsgate. From 1604 onwards he was employed on the translation of the Bible – the King James Version – under the supervision of Lancelot Andrewes, who was then Bishop of Ely. Andrewes paid for Bedwell to go over to Leiden to study Arabic and then found him preferment as a vicar of Tottenham High Cross. For the rest of his life Bedwell would pursue the study of Arabic. (His other lifelong object of study was the measuring techniques of craftsmen.) He is perhaps best known as the author of *Mahomet Unmasked. Or a Discoverie of the manifold Forgeries, Falsehoods, and Impieties of the Blasphemous Seducer Mahomet. With a demonstration of the Insufficiencie of his Law, contained in the cursed Alcoran. Written long since in Arabicke and now done into English*

... as the first half of the title runs, yet it cannot be said that he is well known.

Bedwell knew little about Arabs and he hated Islam. He saw it as his Christian task to produce an edition of various of the *Epistles* in Arabic and Latin and he was one of those clergymen who hoped to find support for the status and doctrines of the Church of England in the Arabic writings of Eastern Christian Churches. He also had grander plans and he worked on a dictionary that was going to be vaster than that of the Dutchman Raphelengius, but he never finished it. (It was arranged according to the Hebrew alphabetic order, which would probably have suited a potential readership composed almost entirely of learned clergymen.) He made not particularly convincing efforts to persuade his limited readership that knowledge of Arabic was actually useful, as, he claimed, it was the language of diplomacy from the Fortunate Islands to the China Seas. However, though in this period diplomatic contacts with Morocco were commonly conducted in Arabic, elsewhere in the Middle East, Persian or Turkish was the more common language of diplomacy. Bedwell briefly taught Pococke and Erpenius, but, as we shall see, both these scholars were to surpass him. Bedwell achieved little, but he effectively worked alone, with only sporadic contacts with like-minded scholars, most of whom were on the Continent. Although Alastair Hamilton, the author of a fine biography of the man, has written that Bedwell's life 'is not just the story of failure, of frustrated plans and unprinted books', nevertheless that is the impression that persists.[5] The English public was not particularly interested in Arabic studies and Bedwell only made as much progress as he did because of the support and encouragement of his patron, Lancelot Andrewes, who seems to have employed him to pursue the researches that he himself did not have time to undertake in detail. It is to Andrewes that we now turn.

Lancelot Andrewes (1555–1626), successively Bishop of Ely, Chichester and Winchester, was one of the intellectual stars of the age. Described as 'an angel in the pulpit', he was particularly famous for the stylish prose of his sermons, whose meditations were cast in metaphysical mode, relying as they did on erudite speculation, incongruity and far-fetched paradoxes. His sermons drew heavily on his Latin and Greek learning and used textual criticism for homiletic purposes. According to John Aubrey's *Brief Lives*, King James I, who favoured the bishop because of his preaching, asked a Scottish lord what he thought of the sermons. The lord replied that the bishop 'was learned, but he did play with his text as a Jack-an-apes does, who takes up a thing and tosses and playes with it, and then takes up another, and plays a little with it. Here's a pretty thing, and there's a pretty thing.' However, according to a more recent critic, Andrewes's sermons 'rank with the finest prose of their time'. That critic was the poet T. S. Eliot, who recycled some of Andrewes's eloquent phrase-making in both the *Four Quartets* and *Journey of the Magi* (and in the seventeenth century Andrewes's sermons had already provided the poet John Donne with literary inspiration).[6]

Andrewes believed that the Christian faith could be revived through learning. He pursued his scholarly researches in the morning and 'he was afraid he was no true scholar who came to see him before noon'. His hours of scholarship were invariably preceded by prayer and sometimes he prayed in Hebrew. His early education had been chiefly in the classics and a Jesuit critic accused him of having acquired his bishopric through reading Terence and Plautus. Andrewes, who was one of the divines who presided over the Authorized Version of the Bible, made himself a master of patristic theology and, allegedly, of fifteen languages. According to Thomas Fuller, author of *The History of the Worthies of England*, he could 'almost have served as an interpreter-general at the confusion of tongues' (that is, after the fall of the Tower of Babel). He had an international reputation and kept up an international correspondence. He was a friend of the scholars Casaubon and Erpenius and it was perhaps under their influence that he acquired a smattering of Arabic. According to Bedwell, Andrewes began work on a dictionary of Arabic but nothing came of it. He owned one of the only two copies of Raphelengius's Arabic *Lexicon* in England.[7] At one stage, he tried to get the great Dutch Orientalist Erpenius to come to England and, having failed, he seems to have tried to make Bedwell into the English equivalent of Erpenius.

ARABIC COMES TO OXFORD

James I was arguably the only learned king ever to sit on England's throne, apart from Alfred, and it was natural that learned clerics were preferred by him. William Laud, Archbishop of Canterbury from 1633 until his beheading in 1645, was pre-eminent among those learned clerics. He had been a pupil of Andrewes and was strongly influenced by his style of Christian scholarship, as well as his commitment to Oriental learning. Laud collected Oriental manuscripts, which were eventually acquired by Oxford's Bodleian Library.[8] In 1630 Laud, who at that time was still Bishop of London, had become Chancellor of Oxford University and, horrified by the somnolent complacency of the place (nothing changes, some would say), he decided to try to raise its scholarship to continental standards. When the seventeenth century opened, Oxford enjoyed an international reputation as a centre for intellectual torpor. Laud was determined to make the place a centre for international learning. The presence of a first-class library in Oxford was one of the necessary preconditions for this intellectual renewal and the formation of the Bodleian Library took place in this century under the patronage of Sir Thomas Bodley, John Selden and Laud himself. Laud also attached great importance to the teaching of Oriental languages. A Hebrew professorship had existed at Oxford from the 1530s. Laud believed that close study of the original Hebrew of the Old Testament would provide vital support for the Church of England in its doctrinal struggle with the Roman Catholics. It already served as a cornerstone for biblical criticism. Arabic was of some use in elucidating some points in Hebrew vocabulary and grammar (though it was really much less useful than partisans for the Arabic language claimed).

There had already been some abortive attempts to establish the teaching of Arabic at Oxford on a regular basis. In 1610 Abudacnus had arrived in Oxford. 'Abudacnus' was a Latinate rendering of the latter part of the name of Yusuf ibn Abu Dhaqan. 'Joseph, Father of the Beard', therefore also known as Joseph Barbatus, was a Coptic Christian from Egypt who had travelled around Europe giving lessons in Arabic – to Erpenius among others. Although Abudacnus stayed in

Oxford until 1613, he does not seem to have been an inspiring teacher and his sojourn had little lasting impact. One problem was that he spoke the Egyptian colloquial form of the language and could not read classical Arabic properly, whereas those European scholars he had contact with were familiar only with classical Arabic. (Western scholars had little or no sense of the evolution of the Arabic language and its spawning of various colloquial forms.) In 1613 Abudacnus crossed back over to the Continent and resumed the life of a peripatetic scholar *manqué*.[9]

Matthias Pasor (1599–1658), who arrived in Oxford over a decade later, was a more substantial scholar. A former teacher of mathematics and theology at Heidelberg and a refugee from the Thirty Years War, Pasor had arrived in Oxford in 1624, having previously and briefly studied Arabic at Leiden. He taught (though preached might be the better word) that through Arabic one could acquire a better understanding of the Scriptures and, based on that better understanding, the manifold errors of Catholicism could be more easily confuted. Pasor's *Oratio pro linguae Arabicae professione*, a speech he delivered in 1626, drew on Erpenius's earlier oration in Leiden (see below) and Pasor's speech was in turn to be extensively plagiarized and was plundered by later professors of Arabic as a source for their inaugural lectures. However, Pasor taught Arabic only for a year before moving on to Hebrew, Syriac and Aramaic. Moreover, his studies in Arabic had been hasty rather than profound. Arabic was one subject among many that had briefly engaged his interest.[10]

The teachings of Abudacnus and Pasor had provided a fitful inspiration for those at Oxford who had considered studying Arabic. In the early seventeenth century, a real or pretended knowledge of Arabic became a blazon of erudition (as Mordechai Feingold has put it).[11] There was a growing belief in the 1620s and 1630s that scientific information of value to astronomers, geographers and mathematicians lay buried in as yet unread Arabic manuscripts. The wealthy and flamboyant Warden of Merton College, Oxford, Sir Henry Savile (1549–1622), took the lead in promoting this sort of research. Like so many of the leading patrons of Arabic studies, he was himself a classicist. Savile entertained vainglorious dreams of rivalling Europe's most learned scholar, the mighty Scaliger. Savile translated Tacitus's history and edited St John Chrysostom. He was also an expert on the text of the Authorized Version of the Bible and on the history of medieval English monasteries and he collected manuscripts. Moreover his classical and antiquarian studies ran in tandem with mathematical and scientific interests. He worked hard but fruitlessly at attempts to square the circle (an intellectual activity that, like the compiling of polyglot Bibles or world chronologies, subsequently went out of fashion). He studied Ptolemy's treatise on astronomy, the *Almagest*, and in 1619 he founded the Savilian Chairs of Geometry and Astronomy.[12]

In 1643 John Greaves became the Savilian Professor of Astronomy. Greaves (1602–52), a fellow of Merton, was a mathematician and, like the man who endowed his chair, he was convinced that there was still a great deal of worthwhile scientific material to be found in classical and Oriental manuscripts. He was particularly interested in Arabic and Persian writers on astronomy and in 1638–9, encouraged by Laud, Greaves (who at that time was Professor of Geometry at Gresham College, London) travelled to Italy, Istanbul and Egypt on a hunt for scientific manuscripts. In Istanbul, he suborned an Ottoman soldier to steal a beautiful copy of Ptolemy's *Almagest* from the Sultan's library and in Egypt he made careful measurements of the Great Pyramid. Back in England in 1646 Greaves published *Pyramidagraphia or a Discourse on the Pyramids of Egypt*. His main interest was in metrology – the units of measurement used by the ancient Egyptians, Romans and others – as well as the measurement of the size of the earth. In 1648 he was disgraced as a Royalist and lost his professorship. (It is curious how closely an interest in Arabic was associated in the seventeenth century with Royalist sympathies.) In enforced retirement he published a number of treatises, including the noteworthy *Of the Manner of Hatching Eggs at Cairo* (a remarkably early study of battery farming). In 1649 he published *Elementa Linguae Persicae*, a Persian grammar. His interest in Persian was unusual as Persian was even more of a Cinderella subject than Arabic. Above all, Greaves worked on the *Zij*, astronomical tables compiled in Persian at the behest of Ulugh Beg, the Timurid ruler of Transoxiana and Khurasan in the fifteenth century. Greaves also studied the fourteenth-century Arab Syrian prince Abu al-Fida's *Geography* (but he was dismayed by the numerous errors in that text, including getting the Red Sea quite wrong). Despite Greaves's hopes for the future of this kind of research, he was one of the last scholars to try to extract useful scientific data from medieval Arabic and Persian manuscripts. Eventually Greaves himself concluded that there was not really any useful geographic information in Abu al-Fida's work. Greaves, who was keen on getting things printed in Arabic, had a private income, which was just as well, as setting texts up in an Arabic typeface was an expensive pastime.[13]

EDWARD POCOCKE

Greaves had been a protégé of Laud and he became a friend and ally of the man who was perhaps the greatest Orientalist of the seventeenth century, Edward Pococke (1604–91).[14] Laud was consistently sympathetic to the cause of Oriental scholarship, and the Laudian Professorship of Arabic was established in 1636 in the first instance to give Pococke suitable employment. Though Laud had never met Pococke, but only corresponded with him about exotic coins, he relied on the emphatic recommendation of Vossius, a Dutch mathematician who was convinced of the value of medieval Arab mathematical manuscripts. Pococke had studied Latin, Greek and Hebrew at Oxford and attended Pasor's lectures in 1626–7. He went on to learn what he could from Bedwell. However, Pococke was to owe his excellent knowledge of Arabic to his prolonged sojourn in Aleppo from 1630 to 1636 as chaplain to the Levant Company. The Levant Company had been chartered in 1581 to trade in the lands of the Ottoman Sultan. An embassy was then established at Istanbul and consulates in Smyrna and Aleppo. The latter was the Levant Company's main trading centre or 'factory' in Syria and it dealt primarily in cotton, much of which was grown in Syria and Palestine, as well as in silks imported by caravans coming from points further east. The chaplaincy at Aleppo in effect served as a studentship in Arabic and Islamic studies and several other distinguished scholars were to hold this post subsequently, among them Robert Huntington, who used his sojourn there in 1671–8 to collect Oriental manuscripts which he eventually bequeathed to Oxford's Bodleian Library. However, Pococke was the intellectual star in this learned sequence of Levant Company chaplains.

On his return to England in 1636, he was given the Chair that Laud had founded. Pococke was Professor not just of Arabic, but also of Hebrew and, although his interest in Arabic was intense and he had a good mastery of the language, nevertheless Arabic took second place to his study of Hebrew and of the Old Testament in Hebrew. He emphasized the value of commentaries on religious matters written by Jews who wrote in Arabic, for example the twelfth-century rabbi, philosopher and physician Maimonides, and one of his major works was an edition of Maimonides's *Porta Mosis*, a set of discourses on the Mishna, which Maimonides had written in Arabic but using Hebrew letters. Although today Pococke is chiefly famous (in so far as he is famous at all) as an Arabist, he was a Hebraist of first rank and one of the greatest scholars to work in that field. Like most Orientalists in the early modern period, Pococke studied Arabic in order to understand the Bible better and, like Bedwell, he had a strong interest in the Oriental Christians. Although Pococke's interest in Islam was entirely hostile, his was a kind of hostility that was conducive to sound scholarship, as he was particularly concerned to discredit Western folklore and crude polemical lies about the Prophet and Muslim doctrine in order that Islam's real errors could be exposed. It was, Pococke thought, better to study the Qur'an and its commentaries critically than to waste time fabricating incredible nonsense about great magnets holding Muhammad's tomb up in the air and similar medieval legends.

In 1637 Pococke took time off from his teaching and went to Istanbul to hunt for manuscripts. He did not return until 1641, by which time Laud was imprisoned in the Tower (where Pococke visited him) and the Long Parliament was in session. The years that followed were difficult ones, as Pococke was known to be a fervent Royalist. Under the Commonwealth the Laudian Professor of Arabic received no stipend and Pococke struggled to survive by teaching Hebrew. Though his position was precarious, he was protected to some extent by his international reputation as a scholar, as well as by a few influential friends on the Parliamentary side, most notably the jurist, historian, antiquarian and respected Parliamentarian John Selden (1584–1654). Selden's interests ranged rather widely and he wrote on matters such as the history of trial by combat and of tithes in medieval England. But he was also interested in Oriental religions, especially those of ancient Syria. His treatise, *De Diis Syriis* (1617), made him famous as an Orientalist. His Hebrew was good and he had a smattering of Arabic and he collected manuscripts in both languages (and they also ended up in the Bodleian Library). Although Selden's main Oriental interest was in rabbinical law, he had translated from Arabic a fragment of the *Nazm al-Jawhar* ('String of Pearls'), a Christian history of the world from the Creation onwards, written by the Melkite Patriarch of Alexandria, Said ib Bitriq Eutychius (876–940). Selden recruited Pococke to assist him in editing a small section of this chronicle in order to make contemporary polemical points against those who maintained the primacy of bishops. Later in 1652 Pococke would produce an edition and translation into Latin of the whole of Eutychius. Erpenius was the only other person hitherto to have translated an Arabic chronicle into Latin.

Eutychius and what Eutychius had to say about such matters as the fifth-century Council of Chalcedon was Selden's ruling passion, but, as far as Pococke himself was concerned, the work he did on Bar Hebraeus was much closer to his own interests and of far greater significance for the development of Orientalism in general. Bar Hebraeus, also known as Abu al-Faraj, was a thirteenth-century Christian Arab chronicler who drew heavily on Muslim chronicles to compile his own history from the Creation to his own time. In 1650 Pococke published the *Specimen historiae Arabum* (1650), in which a long extract translated into Latin from Bar Hebraeus's work served as a vehicle for the copious annotations that were based on Pococke's much more general knowledge of Middle Eastern history and culture. For a long time this work was to be among the first ports of call for anyone studying the history of Islam.

During the hard times of the Commonwealth, Pococke, like several other Royalist scholars who were out of favour, also found refuge of a kind in working on a new polyglot Bible. Just as several of the sixteenth century's leading Orientalists had come together to work on the Antwerp Polyglot Bible, so in 1655–7 a team of English scholars with Oriental interests came together to work on the London Polyglot Bible. Besides Pococke himself, they included Abraham Wheelocke (the Cambridge Professor of Arabic), Edmund Castell (later Professor of Arabic), Thomas Hyde (a Persianist) and Thomas Greaves (like his brother John, an Arabist). The London Polyglot was even grander and more scholarly than the predecessor produced in Antwerp and it included Syriac and Arabic versions of parts of the text. By the seventeenth century, however, most Catholics had come round to the view that the Latin Vulgate sufficed for faith, whereas Protestants were more committed to close philological study of the biblical text. Pococke advised on the Arabic text of the Pentateuch. Wheelocke described the enterprise as 'the vindicating of the Gospel opposed by ranting enthusiasts in these dayes'.[15] The publication of the London Polyglot Bible was not particularly well received. One critic denounced it for 'affording a foundation for Mohammedanism; as a chief and principal prop of Popery; as the root of much hidden Atheism in the world'.[16] The fashion for such grandiose philological projects came to an end with this expensive publication and there were to be no further polyglots.

Apart from his work on the polyglot, Pococke produced a complete translation of Bar Hebraeus and he appended to it a history of the Arabs composed by himself. Produced in his later years, this was a major work in the field of Arabic studies. But though Bar Hebraeus, *Historia compendiosa dynastiarum* was published in 1663, it received so little attention that Pococke, depressed, spent less time on Arab and Islamic matters and turned instead to a study of minor Hebrew prophets, which was more likely to lead on to fame and fortune (though in fact it did not do so). Despite his increasing concentration in later years on biblical matters, Pococke was prodigiously energetic and in the course of his career he produced a remarkable body of Orientalist scholarship, some of it in published form and some as lecture notes. The publications included an edition and Latin translation with annotations of the *Lamiyyat* of al-Tughrai (1061–1120), a lengthy *qasida*, or ode, in which al-Tughrai lamented the corrupt times that he lived in and complained that he was neglected in his old age while other younger men were preferred. Since the ode was famous, or notorious, for its obscure language, Pococke's edition, *Carmen Tograi*, was a tour de force. He worked on various other

Arabic texts, dealing with literature, proverbs and history. Pococke's scholarly exploration of texts by among others al-Maydani, al-Hariri, 'Abd al-Latif al-Baghdadi and Ibn 'Arabshah formed the core of what was still being studied by Arabists right up to the early nineteenth century.

Pococke's best-known Arabic translation was a translation of Ibn Tufayl's twelfth-century Arabic philosophical fable, *Hayy ibn Yaqzan* as *Philosophus Autodidactus*, published in 1671. This story about a foundling, reared by a gazelle on a desert island, who learns first to fend for himself and then to explore the way the universe works and ultimately to discover God, may possibly have had some influence on Daniel Defoe's *Robinson Crusoe*. Ibn Tufayl's fantasy may also have had a role in shaping English empirical philosophy as it was developed by John Locke and others. Like *Hayy ibn Yaqzan*, Locke's *An Essay Concerning Human Understanding* (1690) is an enquiry into what sorts of things God has fitted humans to know.

Among Pococke's minor works was his translation of an extremely brief anonymous treatise in Arabic on coffee-drinking, *The Nature of the drink Kauhi, or Coffe, and the Berry of which it is made. Described by an Arabian Philistian* (1659). Coffee-drinking originated in Yemen some time around the thirteenth century and spread throughout the Ottoman empire in the sixteenth century. Pococke is said to have been the first man in England to drink coffee. Those who were suspicious of the new drink claimed that it brought on his palsy. (The Arab author, for his part, warned that drinking coffee with milk might bring on leprosy.) For a long time coffee-drinking was to be regarded with great suspicion in some circles, as it was tainted with Mahometanism.[17] Pococke ranked together with Golius as the greatest scholar of Arabic in the seventeenth century, but he left no disciples who were capable of matching his erudition and acuity.

ARABIC COMES TO CAMBRIDGE

The Laudian Professorship that was established in Oxford in 1636 had been preceded by the foundation at Cambridge in 1632 of the Thomas Adams Chair of Arabic. Thomas Adams was a wealthy draper and Lord Mayor of London, who hoped that he might, through his benefaction, be instrumental in converting the Muslims. The teaching of Arabic, he felt, should serve the purpose of 'the enlarging of the borders of the Church, and propagation of Christian religion to them who now sitt in darkness'.[18] Abraham Wheelocke (c. 1593–1653), the first scholar to hold the Thomas Adams Chair of Arabic at Cambridge, was fervent against Islam: 'Set aside some grosse idolatories of the church of Roome, & their Tyrannicall goernment, the onli pressure on the bodie of the Church of Christ is Mahomets Alcoran, I desire to breath out my last breth in this cause, and to my poore skil, I would endeavour to write Notes against the Alcoran in the Language of the Alcoran, which is the Arabick.'[19] However, he had a rather curious attitude to the 'Arabick' that he was supposed to teach. He pointed out that it was a difficult language, not particularly useful and besides there were not very many books in that language available in Britain. Consequently he regarded it as part of his academic duty to discourage students from taking up the subject. He was quite successful in this and on one occasion, finding that no pupils had turned up for his lectures, he posted the notice to the effect that 'Tomorrow the professor of Arabic will go into the wilderness'. He published practically nothing in or on Arabic, though he planned to write a refutation of the Qur'an. Wheelocke was also Reader in Anglo-Saxon and he was much keener on that subject than he was on Oriental matters. In so far as he was interested in the Eastern Churches, it was their possible importance as sources for Anglo-Saxon Christianity that engaged his attention. He also enjoyed composing occasional poetry in Latin. Despite his two professorships, his financial circumstances were always precarious, though not as precarious as those of his successor in the Chair.

The Reverend Edmund Castell (1606–86), the second holder of the Thomas Adams Professorship, from 1667 until 1685, was in some respects a more considerable figure. Like so many of his colleagues, Castell was not in the slightest interested in Islam. Rather, his chief enthusiasm was for trying to establish links with the Eastern Christian Churches. However, he also hoped that Arabic might be useful in identifying obscure plants mentioned in the Bible. He had worked on the London Polyglot Bible and his own work on the *Lexicon*

Heptaglotton (1669), a comparative dictionary of seven languages (Hebrew, Aramaic, Syriac, Samaritan, Ethiopian, Arabic and Persian), evolved out of that project. Essentially it was a dictionary of Semitic languages and Persian was included only because it had not yet been demonstrated that Persian was not a Semitic language. (In fact, Persian is an Indo-Aryan language.) If for not much else, the *Lexicon* might be useful for reading the polyglot Bible. It ran to 4,007 pages and included descriptions of the grammars of the various languages.

Castell regarded himself as being on some kind of holiday if he worked less than sixteen hours a day. But he was always miserable and full of complaint and by the time he had finished his polyglot dictionary, people had lost their enthusiasm for studying the polyglot Bible. Castell ruined himself in his typographically extravagant enterprise. Five hundred copies remained unsold at the time of his death and rats ate much of what was left. Yet more copies perished in the Great Fire of London. Not only did he lose a small fortune but he plunged so deep into the study of Oriental languages that he allegedly had forgotten his own. He ended up a half-blind pauper.[20] (Later, as we shall see, Simon Ockley and George Sale were similarly ruined by their Orientalist enthusiasms.)

Although Wheelocke left an unimpressive legacy as an Arabist, he had mastered Persian and he taught this language to Thomas Hyde (1636–1703). Hyde subsequently moved to Oxford. A corpulent and abstracted polymathic scholar, he worked on the Arabic, Persian and Syriac texts of the polyglot Bible. Eventually he combined the post of Librarian of the Bodleian with the Laudian Professorship of Arabic (1691) and the Regius Professorship of Hebrew (1697). Hyde was also alleged to know Turkish, Malay, Armenian and Chinese and he acted as a translator for Charles II. He supervised the printing of the Gospels into Malay. His wide interests also included Oriental games, sea monsters and mermaids. He worked on the star tables of Ulugh Beg that John Greaves had previously made a start on. Like Greaves, he was interested in Abu al-Fida's *Geography* and planned to edit it, but nothing came of this. Hyde regarded the *Historia religionis veterum Persarum* (1700) as his major work, but his account of the pre-Islamic religions of Persia, especially Zoroastrianism, relied so heavily on much later Persian sources from the Islamic era that this study was of limited value. Certainly it brought him little reward and John Cleland (who did achieve success with his pornographic novel, *Fanny Hill*) remembers Hyde using unsold copies of his study of the religions of Persia to boil his kettle. Hyde had a downbeat view of the value of giving lectures on Arabic, 'hearers being scarce and practicers more scarce'.[21]

According to Humphrey Prideaux (1648–1724), Hyde 'doth not understand common sense in his own language, and therefore I cannot conceive how he can make sense of anything that is writ in another'. However, Prideaux's own book on Muhammad was to be criticized by a bookseller to whom he offered it for publication, who said he 'could wish there were a little more humour in it'. This book was *The True Nature of Imposture fully display'd in the Life of Mahomet*, published in 1697.[22] It certainly was short on humour, as its author used the pretext of a history of the life of the Prophet as a vehicle for denunciations of the Deists and all sorts of religious extremists: 'Have we not Reason to fear, that God may in the same Manner raise up some *Mahomet* against us for our utter Confusion . . . And by what the *Socinian*, the *Quaker*, and the *Deist* begin to advance in this Land, we may have reason to fear, that Wrath hath some Time since gone forth from the Lord for the Punishment of these our Iniquities and Gainsayings, and that the Plague is already among us.'[23] Prideaux, whose life of Muhammad was part of a planned 'History of the ruin of the Eastern Church', considered the rise of Islam to be a punishment for the Eastern Christians' divisions and heresies. Although he complained about the desperate shortage of books in Arabic, his knowledge of Arabic was either slight or non-existent. (His claim that the Arabic language was very like English raises considerable doubts in my mind.) He drew so heavily on the works of earlier writers that the 'real nature of the imposture' was Prideaux's pretence to be an Arabist. His book was full of errors, as George Sale in the following century enthusiastically pointed out. Prideaux's *Connection* (1716–18), a historical and theological treatise about the period between the end of the Old and the beginning of the New Testament, was a more substantial and scholarly work. After Pococke's death, Prideaux had been offered the Laudian Professorship, but, fortunately perhaps, he turned it down and Hyde, who was more truly committed to Orientalism, took it up. However, Hyde's successor as Laudian Professor of Arabic, John Wallis (1703–38), was an unproductive academic nonentity, more fond of good company than learned books, and, as we shall see in the next chapter, the prestige and achievements of English Orientalism declined steeply in the eighteenth century.

THE GOLDEN AGE OF DUTCH ORIENTALISM

During the seventeenth century, English Orientalists corresponded regularly with their fellow Protestant Orientalists in Holland. The University of Leiden, founded in 1575 in the immediate aftermath of the Dutch Revolt against Spain, was the centre of Dutch Orientalism and of academic life more generally. Indeed, it was the leading Protestant university in Europe and the place swarmed with British, German and French Huguenot students. In its early years the university drew heavily on French scholarship and Joseph Scaliger was only the grandest of various French scholars whom it recruited. Despite Leiden's vital intellectual life and numerous bookshops, the crusty Scaliger described the place as 'a swamp within a swamp'. Leiden's Chair of Arabic was established in 1600 and for two centuries thereafter Leiden was to dominate Oriental studies. The groundwork for Leiden's ascendancy in this area was laid by Scaliger and Franciscus Raphelengius, both of whom had studied Arabic with Postel before introducing it to Leiden. (Raphelengius's work on the Antwerp Polyglot Bible for the Plantin Press has been mentioned in the previous chapter.)

Raphelengius moved from Antwerp to Leiden in 1585 and eventually became Professor of Hebrew. He was responsible for setting up the first Arabic press in Holland and was also the first to compile for publication an Arabic–Latin dictionary, the *Lexicon Arabico–Latinum* (posthumously published in 1613, after his death in 1597). In this work, Raphelengius had drawn heavily on a Mozarabic Latin–Arabic glossary, which had been compiled by Arab-speaking Christians living under Moorish rule in twelfth-century Toledo, to assist them in the study of Latin. Clearly this was an awkward source to draw on for a dictionary intended to guide scholars already fluent in Latin in their study of the unfamiliar Arabic tongue. Postel had acquired the manuscript, but it ended up in Leiden. Raphelengius's dictionary was not a very well ordered or accurate compilation, and the chief market was among biblical scholars, interested in Hebrew and Aramaic.[24]

After Raphelengius's death in 1597, the scholar Erpenius (Thomas van Erpe) (1584–1625) saw Raphelengius's dictionary through the press and provided additions and corrections of his own. (Erpenius, in working on the dictionary, followed Scaliger's earlier counsel that Orientalists should make use of Turkish translations of the great medieval dictionaries.) If the Catholic Postel was the first true Orientalist, Erpenius was certainly the first great Protestant Orientalist. Erpenius was a pupil and client of Scaliger and he had also studied with Bedwell, though he failed to learn very much from the latter. In 1613 Erpenius was appointed Professor of Oriental Languages (1613–24). His inaugural oration on the *sapientia* (wisdom) of the Arabs was to be much plagiarized by later professors of Arabic. He had been so quick to learn Arabic that he was accused of using magic to do so (just like Postel before him). Erpenius claimed that Arabic was not a difficult language to learn. (I have to confess that this has not been my experience.) He also debunked the notion that Arabic was useful for studying Hebrew, even though that was why he had himself started to study Arabic and indeed his chief intellectual interest was in the vowelling of Hebrew. He recommended studying Turkish in order to understand Arabic better, in large part because of the usefulness of Turkish–Arabic dictionaries, which enabled him to make many emendations to Raphelengius's dictionary. (It should be noted that in the seventeenth century almost no one thought that Turkish was worth studying in its own right. Whereas the Arabs were respected for their culture and science, Europeans tended to regard the Turks as the barbarous descendants of the Scythians.)

Erpenius was an industrious scholar and produced editions of many classic works of Arabic literature, to serve as a basis for teaching. Among his discoveries was the *Geography* of Abu al-Fida that was later to be worked on by Greaves. Erpenius was able to make use of the Arabic manuscripts assembled by Postel (some of which were in Leiden and others in Heidelberg) in order to produce the *Historia Saracenica* of 1625. This history relied heavily on a chronicle by a thirteenth-century Coptic Christian, al-Makin. Although al-Makin was a Christian, his chronicle was mostly compiled from earlier Muslim sources, so Erpenius made what was in effect a Muslim version of Muslim history available in Europe for the first time. However, Erpenius's *magnum opus* was his *Grammatica Arabica*, published in Leiden in 1613. In this, the first proper grammar of Arabic in a European language, he struggled to impose an unsuitable Latinate grammatical structure on the usages of classical Arabic. Erpenius's grammar was reworked by Silvestre de Sacy in the early nineteenth century, then revised by the Norwegian Karl Caspari in 1848, and Caspari was revised in 1859 by William Wright as *A Grammar of the Arabic Language*, which remains a standard work to this day. Orientalism in the seventeenth century was a rancorous and competitive field, rife with backbiting and plagiarism, in which Erpenius was entirely at home. He was outspokenly dismissive of the work of others.[25]

After Erpenius's untimely death of the plague, his star pupil Golius (Jacob Gool) (1596–1667) succeeded him as Professor. Golius had a background in philosophy and theology and he had studied mathematics and astronomy before switching to Orientalism. He held the Chair of Mathematics and, like Greaves, he believed that Western mathematicians still had much to learn from the Arabs. He travelled widely in North Africa and the Middle East where he hunted for manuscripts. In Morocco he had served the Dutch embassy as an engineer. He spent time in Morocco and it was there that he located a copy of Ibn Khallikan's thirteenth-century biographical dictionary and other works identified by Leo Africanus as key sources for understanding Arab thought and literature. In 1636 Golius published the Arabic text of Ibn 'Arabshah's life of Tamerlane, the *'Aja'ib al-Maqdur*. (This was to become a standard text for teaching Arabic throughout Europe and many students must have cursed Golius, for Ibn 'Arabshah wrote in a monstrously florid and opaque style.) Whereas Raphelengius's dictionary was not much more than a glorified word list, Golius's Arabic–Latin dictionary, the *Lexicon Arabico–Latinum* (1653), became obsolete only in the nineteenth century.

Golius followed Erpenius in basing his dictionary upon the great medieval Arab dictionaries, supplemented by Turkish–Arabic dictionaries. (Even so, as Pococke noted, there were still serious gaps in Golius's dictionary.)

Golius disliked the subordination of the study of Arabic to that of Hebrew and Syriac and preferred to study Turkish and Persian. He also studied other languages, including Chinese. Golius was a genius and he revelled in it. He quarrelled with his rivals, disparaged their scholarship and obstructed their access to key manuscripts. He acknowledged only Pococke as an intellectual equal. Like the great Scaliger before him, Golius considered teaching to be beneath his dignity. It was perhaps partly because of this that when he died in 1677 the sequence of great Leiden Orientalists came to a temporary halt.[26] The fortunes of Orientalism in Leiden would revive briefly with the appointment of Albert Schultens to a professorship in 1729.

CATHOLIC ORIENTALISM

Catholic Orientalism, such as it was, owed little to the advances being made by Orientalists in the Protestant north. In Rome and other Catholic centres there seems to have been less interest in making use of Arabic manuscripts for scientific purposes. However, Catholics were just as interested in making contact with Eastern Christians – especially the Maronites, Lebanese Christians in communion with Rome, for whom a college had been founded by Pope Gregory XIII in Rome in 1584. Maronite scholars, native speakers in Arabic and Syriac, assisted in the publication of a handful of books printed in Arabic by the Medici Press.[27] However, new translations of the Qur'an were produced by Catholics with the aim of assisting missionaries to the Muslim lands, or alternatively fuelling anti-Muslim polemic. The translation of the Qur'an into French in 1647 by André du Ryer, the former French vice-consul in Alexandria, had an introduction that declared that the translation had been produced for the use of missionaries, so that they might have material for their missions of conversion. This was a traditional excuse used by those who wished to avoid censorship and ecclesiastical disapproval of any translation of the

Qur'an. The risks involved in publishing any such translation were considerable, but so were the profits, as the Qur'an was widely regarded as a kind of black book, or Satanic text, and there were always readers eager for such novelties.

In Du Ryer's case, it seems that his real aim was to produce a readable translation that would make the French public aware of one of the glories of Arabic literature. Like Galland who translated *The Thousand and One Nights* half a century later, Du Ryer set upon improving the barbarousness of the Arabic by turning it into a stately and courtly French. 'I have made the Prophet speak French,' he declared. Du Ryer's was the first complete translation of the Qur'an since the Middle Ages and the first translation ever into a vernacular. He made extensive use of Muslim *tafsir* literature to elucidate the difficulties in the text of the Qur'an. However, he had to work without a decent Arabic dictionary or grammar. His translation was inevitably rather inaccurate and those who produced later translations were careful to rubbish the work of their predecessor. Marracci claimed that Du Ryer had depended on unreliable advisers. There were 'mistakes in every page' according to George Sale. As Alastair Hamilton and Francis Richard put it in their study of the life and works of Du Ryer: 'European Arabists, like most scholars, have seldom distinguished themselves by their charitable treatment of their colleagues, and Du Ryer was the victim of their malice.'[28] Despite Du Ryer's declaration of pious Christian intentions, the publication gave rise to a great deal of protest as people accused him of furthering the interests of Islam by publicizing its false doctrines. Even so his scandalous translation sold very well and was itself translated into English, Dutch, German and Russian.

Similar accusations were made of the next translation, this time into Latin, though this was in every respect a superior work of scholarship. Ludovico Marracci (1612–1700) was a member of the Regular Clergy of the Mother of God and Pope Innocent XI's confessor. Marracci taught himself Greek, Hebrew, Syriac, Chaldaean and Arabic. He was one of those who had worked on the *Biblia Sacra Arabica* (1671), a translation of the Bible into Arabic, before going on to produce a four-volume attack on the Qur'an, the *Prodromus ad refutationem Alcorani* (1691), as a prelude to the publication in 1698 of *Alcorani textus universus*, a volume which included the Arabic text and

Marracci's translation into Latin. The Latin text, a literal translation, was accompanied by lengthy and hostile annotations. Islam 'totally excludes those mysteries of our faith'. Islam was destined to flourish because the world was full of fools and people naturally inclined to evil. In that respect it did not differ greatly from Protestantism, which Marracci viewed as essentially a variant form of Islam.

Although he was savage in his denunciation of Muslim doctrines, the hostility was not founded upon ignorance. He had spent forty years studying what he regarded as a damned text and his annotations drew heavily upon the works of Muslim commentators. Despite his ferociously hostile commentary, the Pope at first forbade him to publish the text. In the seventeenth century it was thought dangerous to study Islam. Yet no such prejudice applied to studying the pagan doctrines and rituals of ancient Greece and Rome. Marracci's translation was to be much drawn upon by George Sale in the next century, and it is notable that Sale's citation of Muslim commentators seems to be restricted to those already cited by Marracci. Apart from Islamic matters, Marracci's other speciality was biographies of saintly nuns.[29]

It must be stressed that only a tiny handful of scholars had any interest in Arabic at all. In this period the learned world at large was much more interested in Hebrew and, to a lesser extent, in the mysteries of Egyptian hieroglyphics. Prior to the sixteenth century, it had been widely believed that civilization and language was Egyptian in origin. Thereafter the focus shifted to ancient Greece as the source of European civilization, while most scholars accepted that Hebrew was the primal language, from which all other languages, including ancient Egyptian, were descended.

In the seventeenth century the torch of mad linguistics passed from Guillaume Postel to Athanasius Kircher (1601–80), the omnivorously studious and bizarre Jesuit thinker, who was described by one of his critics as 'the most learned of all madmen'.[30] Kircher taught Oriental languages in Würzburg before settling at the Jesuit College in Rome in 1635. There he was bullied by Nicolas-Claude Fabri de Peresc, an aristocratic antiquarian who collected mummies and who had acquired some Egyptian papyri, into doing researches into Pharaonic Egyptian and Coptic (the language of the descendants of the ancient Egyptians). Seventeenth-century Rome had more than a dozen obelisks that provided material for him to work on. His *Oedipus Aegyptiacus* (1652–5) was an attempt, backed up by a knowledge of Coptic, to interpret Pharaonic hieroglyphs as a Hermetic language that embodied mystical and philosophical truths. By 'Hermetic' Kircher meant that the language had literally been devised by Hermes Trismegistus and was organized in such a way that its ideograms represented the fundamental metaphysical forces operative in the real world. (Kircher obstinately regarded Hermes as a historical figure of great antiquity, despite Isaac Casaubon's earlier demonstration that the Hermetic literature had been forged in late antiquity.) Kircher's 'decipherment' of the hieroglyphs allowed him to present an exciting picture of ancient Egyptian culture that was both quite mystical and utterly false. However, at least he had guessed the hieroglyphs to be a form of writing; some of his predecessors had regarded them as merely decorative.[31] He presented the ancient Egyptian Hermetic revelation as a prefiguration of the Christian revelation.

Another of his wonderfully strange books, the *Turris Babel* (1679), was a study of the history of the world, the architecture of the ill-fated Tower of Babel and the curse of the confusion of tongues. When Adam named each beast with its real Hebrew name, this was not an arbitrary act, but a cabalistic operation that disclosed the names of the beasts by permuting the Hebrew letters so as to define their real natures. All the world's surviving languages were degenerate renditions of the original Hermetic mysteries as revealed in Hebrew. Kircher held that Chinese ideograms, with their precise and fairly easily discoverable meanings, were inferior to the Egyptian hieroglyphs from which they derived. As for the Egyptian hieroglyphs, he mistakenly believed that they were pictographs illustrating higher theological mysteries. Kircher, like Postel, believed in linguistic unification as a prerequisite for world peace. He wrote also on a diverse range of subjects, including codes and code-breaking, music, Atlantis, birdsong, Noah's Ark, magic lanterns, volcanoes, China, mathematics and pyramidology. Forty-four of his books and some two thousand letters survive. He devised a vomiting machine and eavesdropping statues, as well as a kind of piano powered by screeching cats. He also helped Bernini erect the obelisk in the Piazza Navona and he taught the principles of perspective to Poussin. Kircher's famous cabinet of curiosities, the Museo Kircheriano in the Roman College of the Vatican, reflected his diverse interests: Egyptological curios, stuffed animals, odd stones, sunspots, automata, microscopes, rhinoceros horns and medical anomalies. (The remains of this collection can be found today in Rome's Museo Preistorico ed Etnografico L. Pigorini.) Kircher was one of the last scholars to aspire to know everything. The philosopher Leibniz (1646–1716) was probably the last.

Kircher's overweening fascination with the esoteric, bizarre and monstrous meant that his publications, though they touched on almost all fields of research, were usually marginal to mainstream scholarship on those areas and that was certainly true of his contribution to the study of Arabic and Islam. Pietro della Vale, the Roman traveller in the Arab lands, Iran and India, provided Kircher with the manuscript of a Coptic–Arabic dictionary, and since knowledge of Arabic was a necessary precondition for the study of Coptic, Kircher acquired some rudiments of that language. His daft views on the history of the pyramids and how they were built by Hermes Trismegistus were probably based on Arabic sources. Kircher seems to have produced a (now lost) translation from Arabic and Hebrew of a work by Avicenna on medicinal herbs. Even so Kircher did not find Arabic to be particularly interesting. Also, though he was tolerant, even appreciative, of most religions, he detested Islam and what he believed to be its promises of sensual bliss in the afterlife. More generally, much of Kircher's Oriental expertise and research materials had been provided by Jesuit missions in distant parts, especially in China, but the Jesuits had failed to establish themselves in the Arab lands. Kircher was primarily a Sinologist and Egyptologist. In the twentieth century one particular aspect of his arcane thinking has been revived by Martin Bernal in *Black Athena* (1987), in which Kircher's belief in the Egyptian sources of Greek wisdom has been resurrected and updated by Bernal in a highly controversial form.[32]

Pococke, Erpenius, Golius and Marracci would have few intellectual heirs. Kircher's fascination with Chinese culture and Egyptian hieroglyphs more accurately presaged future developments in the eighteenth century when, on the whole, the intelligentsia were more interested in Chinese sages than they were in Arabian prophets and warriors.

5

Enlightenment of a Sort

Dons admirable! Dons of might!
Uprising on my inward sight
Compact of ancient tales, and port,
And sleep – and learning of a sort.

Hilaire Belloc, 'Lines to a Don'

Clergymen in Oxbridge colleges and rural rectories who interested themselves in Arabic texts for scholarly and theological reasons were not at all interested in real live Arabs, but only wanted to know more about the manner of life of Abraham and Moses, to identify the flora and fauna of the Bible and map out the topography of ancient Palestine. Princes, diplomats, soldiers and merchants, however, had a more immediate interest in the Turks and the Ottoman Turkish empire. Until the late seventeenth century the West's interest in the Turks was mostly driven by fear. The Ottomans in the seventeenth century ruled over almost the whole of the Balkans. Only the tiny mountain principality of Montenegro preserved a nominal independence. The Turks had twice besieged Vienna, in 1529 and 1683. The Ottoman navy dominated the eastern Mediterranean. Richard Knolles in his *General History of the Turks* (1603) had described the Turks as 'the present terror of the world'.[1] Christian thinkers in the West anxiously asked themselves why it was that God seemed to favour that great Muslim empire and there were some who feared that the Muslims were destined to conquer the whole of Christendom. In the sixteenth century Ogier Ghiselin de Busbecq, the imperial ambassador in Constantinople, had argued that this was the most likely outcome: 'On [the Turks' side] are the resources of a mighty empire, strength unimpaired, habituation to victory, endurance of toil, unity, discipline, frugality and watchfulness. On our side is public poverty, private luxury, impaired strength, broken spirit, lack of endurance and training; the soldiers are insubordinate, the officers are avaricious; there is contempt for discipline; license, recklessness, drunkenness and debauch are rife; and worst of all, the enemy is accustomed to victory, and we to defeat. Can we doubt what the result will be?' Busbecq thought that the Christians were squandering their resources in exploring and colonizing the Americas.[2]

In the late seventeenth century, the French traveller Jean de Thévenot, in *Relation d'un Voyage fait au Levant* (3 volumes, 1665, 1674, 1678), was perhaps the first to diagnose a sickness in what was superficially still a great power in the East, for he judged that the Ottoman empire was in rapid decline: 'All these peoples have nothing more to boast about than their ruins and their rags.'[3] Thévenot's analysis proved to be an accurate one and a few decades later, in 1699, by the Treaty of Carlowitz, the Turks had to accept humiliating defeat and cede Hungary, Transylvania and Podolia to an alliance of Christian powers. Western fears of the triumph of Islam and the Turk abated.

Neither ancient fears nor a new predatory interest in the Near East had translated into any substantial interest in the language or culture of the Turks. Knolles, the author of a *General History of the Turks*, quoted at the start of this chapter, knew no Turkish. There was no chair in Turkish studies in any European university in the sixteenth and seventeenth centuries, nor was there any interest in translating Turkish literature. There was nothing that could be called a tradition of Turkish studies in Britain or France until the twentieth century.[4] Although eighteenth-century diplomats, merchants, soldiers and manuscript hunters travelled extensively in the Ottoman empire, they tended to rely on local Christians and Jews to act as interpreters of the alien language and culture. Phanariot Greeks, Maronites and Armenians served as agents of the various European powers.

Those who acted as intermediaries and interpreters were known as *tarjumans* or dragomans (from the Arabic *tarjama*, 'to translate'). There were schools for such translators in Paris, Venice and Pera (the suburb of Constantinople on the north side of the Golden Horn).[5] We shall discuss the careers of two such dragomans, Jean-Joseph Marcel and Freiherr von Hammer-Purgstall, subsequently. The training such men received was in contemporary Arabic or Turkish and it was very different from the sort of thing taught at universities by the intellectual heirs of Pococke or Erpenius. The great Orientalist Sir William Jones (on whom see below) was to comment disparagingly on the scholarly attainments of the dragomans: 'It has generally happened that persons who have resided among the TURKS, and who from their skill in EASTERN dialects, have best been qualified to present us with an exact account of that nation, were either confined to a low sphere of life, or were engaged in views of interest, and but little addicted to polite letters or philosophy; while they, who, from their exalted stations and refined taste for literature, have had both the opportunity and inclination of penetrating into the secrets of TURKISH policy, were totally ignorant of the language used at Constantinople, and consequently were destitute of the sole means by which they might learn, with any degree of certainty, the sentiments and prejudices of so singular a people . . . As to the generality of interpreters, we cannot expect from men of their condition any depth of reasoning, or acuteness of observation; if mere words are all they profess, mere words must be all they can pretend to know.' Jones's animadversions notwithstanding, the institution was to have a long history and Sir Andrew Ryan in his autobiography, *The Last of the Dragomans*, describes attending such a school for interpreters in Constantinople in 1899.

Conditions of trade within the Ottoman sultanate were regulated by commercial treaties known as the Capitulations. The French were granted Capitulations in the Ottoman empire as early as 1535. In the second half of the seventeenth century Jean-Baptiste Colbert, the chief minister of Louis XIV, was particularly interested in promoting France's commercial interests in the Levant. (He also sponsored hunts for Oriental manuscripts and antiquities.) A Levant Company was founded at Marseilles in 1671. The French were particularly involved in the purchase of cotton from Palestinian and Lebanese ports. There was also a strong French commercial presence in Alexandria and in the course of the eighteenth century the merchants of Marseilles and their political allies began to contemplate the desirability of a French occupation of Egypt. As the sultanate declined, the ambassadors of France, Britain and the other powers were successful in getting ever more extravagant concessions and privileges. Their merchants acquired a status not far short of diplomatic immunity. Moreover their servants and interpreters, many of them native Christians and Jews, were often covered by the same privileges.

France's Levant Company competed with the British Levant Company. Britain's main commercial base in the Near East was the British Levant Company's 'factory' in Aleppo, a city that was a major staging post for the silk trade.[6] (In those days 'factory' referred to a trading settlement in another country.) By the early eighteenth century the British Levant Company was in steep decline, while the fortunes of the British East India Company, by contrast, prospered. Britain's rivalry with France spanned the continents. This was to come to a head in the Seven Years War (1756–63) in which European and global territorial ambitions were thoroughly muddled. As Macaulay put it in a famous essay on Frederick the Great: 'In order that he might rob a neighbour whom he had promised to defend, black men fought on the coast of Coramandel, and red men scalped each other by the Great Lakes of North America.' If the British did define their own identity by distinguishing it from some notional 'Other' that was corrupt, despotic and licentious, then France was certainly that Other. William Hogarth's painting, *The Gate of Calais* (1749), with its depiction of scrawny priest-ridden Frenchmen slavering enviously over beef destined for the British, graphically illustrated British contempt for the French.

The ultimate triumph of the British over the French in India in the late eighteenth century was the crucial step towards establishing the greatest empire the world has ever seen. Though the British Levant Company still retained its 'factories' in Aleppo and elsewhere in the Middle East, Britain's commercial ambitions were increasingly focused on India. From the 1740s onwards the British and French, represented by their respective India Companies, fought over the remains of the Mughal empire in India. In 1761, in the late stages of the Seven Years War, the French were decisively defeated and the British East India Company became the major power in the subcontinent. The Company had an interest in training its employees in the relevant languages and eventually it set up exams in Arabic and offered small financial bonuses for those who passed the exams. The Company also sponsored John Richardson's *A Grammar of the Arabick Language* (1776).[7] Nevertheless, Persian and Turkish were really far more important for the imperialist project. Persian was the language of the Indian courts, but somehow even this failed to lead to any corresponding growth in interest in Persian studies in England until William Jones took up the language as a schoolboy craze. As for Sanskrit studies, as we shall see, this was pioneered by a Frenchman, Anquetil-Duperron, and then, from the late eighteenth century onwards, the field was more or less monopolized by German academics and writers.

While the French were increasingly dominating the commerce of the eastern Mediterranean and the British were establishing their Raj in India, the Dutch were setting about the colonization of Java and Sumatra and other islands and the Russians were expanding in Central Asia, as well as continuing to make territorial gains at the expense of Ottoman Turkey. Yet only perhaps in Russia was there a correlation between the numbers of Muslims conquered by the imperialist power and a growth in Orientalist studies. On the whole British and French diplomats, soldiers and merchants in the Levant and Muslim India worked with native interpreters and informants. It was a rare individual who took the trouble to acquaint himself with the Qur'an and Arabic and Persian literature. In the early eighteenth century there was as yet little crossover between the worlds of imperialism and Orientalism.

THE FIRST ENCYCLOPEDIA OF ISLAM

Although Latin continued to be the chief language of scholarship, the various vernaculars gained in academic respectability from the end of the seventeenth century onwards. France was the territory where there was the greatest chance of finding serious books published in the vernacular rather than in Latin. (German scholars tended obstinately to stick with Latin.) As far as Orientalism was concerned, the publication in French of d'Herbelot's encyclopedic *Bibliothèque orientale* was a landmark, as the broader reading public in France only really became aware of the literature and history of the Arabs, Persians and Turks when that work appeared. Galland's subsequent publication of a translation of *The Thousand and One Nights* into French further increased general awareness of and interest in Oriental culture.

Barthélémy d'Herbelot (1625–95) was a fervent Catholic who, after first studying the classics and philosophy, took up the study of Hebrew in order to understand the Old Testament better. He went on to become Professor of Syriac at the Collège de France. D'Herbelot was one of a number of antiquarians and Orientalists whose studies were sponsored by Colbert. Although the *Bibliothèque* can be seen as a forerunner of the twentieth-century *Encyclopaedia of Islam* and was indeed used as a work of reference, nevertheless d'Herbelot's compilation had a rather belle-lettristic flavour, as anecdotes and occasional verses padded out the entries. Plutarch's *Lives* furnished a literary model, as d'Herbelot was as interested in drawing out morals as chronicling events. He had never travelled in the Middle East and naturally he had no interest in its contemporary politics or commerce. Like the encyclopedias that succeeded it, the *Bibliothèque*'s entries were arranged in alphabetical order. He was vaguely apologetic about it, claiming that it 'does not produce as much confusion as one might imagine'.[8] Gibbon in the footnotes to *The Decline and Fall of the Roman Empire* patronized it as 'an agreeable miscellany' and claimed that he never could 'digest the alphabetical order'. Gibbon also noted that d'Herbelot seemed to be stronger on Persian than on Arabic history, though he could hardly have written the later volumes of his history without frequent recourse to the *Bibliothèque orientale*.[9]

The *Bibliothèque* concentrated on Arabic, Persian and Turkish culture, though an appendix devoted to Chinese culture was added in a later edition. In his researches, d'Herbelot relied on the Arabic manuscripts that had been assembled under the patronage of Colbert and others and placed in the royal library. D'Herbelot, who had no notion of source criticism, made exceptionally heavy use of late Persian compilations, but his task was made easier by one particular manuscript that had been acquired by Colbert's agent, Antoine Galland, in Istanbul. This was the *Kashf al-Zunun* by Hajji Khalifa, also known as Katib Celebi. Hajji Khalifa was a seventeenth-century

Turkish historian and bibliographer of manuscripts and his *Kashf al-Zunun* listed and briefly described 14,500 works in Arabic, Persian and Turkish. This was the great discovery and reference resource of seventeenth-century Orientalism and it was translated into Latin much later by Gustav Flugel (in 1853–8). The *Kashf al-Zunun* decisively shaped Orientalists' image of Islamic culture.[10] Among other things, Hajji Khalifa's alphabetical organization may have influenced d'Herbelot's decision to organize his material in the same way. D'Herbelot also drew heavily on al-Zamakhshari (1075–1144), a Qur'anic commentator who also wrote on grammar and lexicography. When dealing with Arab history, it was natural that d'Herbelot, a devout Catholic, should rely where possible on Christian Arab chroniclers and, following his medieval and Renaissance precursors, he fiercely denounced Muhammad as an impostor. D'Herbelot argued that a great deal of the Islamic revelation derived from the Old Testament and Jewish lore. For d'Herbelot, who was steeped in the Greek and Latin classics, the Orient was an unexplored antiquity and, though he was not particularly interested in pre-Islamic Arabia, he was passionately interested in pre-Islamic Persia and Egypt.

D'Herbelot died before his *Bibliothèque orientale* could be printed, but it was published in 1697 by his friend and associate, Antoine Galland. Galland also wrote an introduction to the work in which, among other things, he suggested that a study of the Arabic sources might shed additional light on the history of the Crusades. Galland, like d'Herbelot, had been thoroughly educated in the classics and early on in his career his chief area of expertise had been in numismatics. From 1670 to 1675 he was attached to the French embassy in Constantinople where, assisted by the embassy's Greek dragomans, he learnt Turkish. Having mastered Turkish, he studied Arabic and Persian with Turks in Constantinople. He had a second spell in the Orient from 1679 to 1688. One of his main missions was to hunt out rare coins, medals, curios and manuscripts for Louis XV. His other important task was to research the opinions of the various prelates of the Eastern Churches regarding the real presence of Christ in the eucharist and transubstantiation. It was hoped that their opinions might be used by Jansenist polemicists against Protestants. There is a Rochefoucauldian flavour to Galland's *Pensées morales des Arabes*, which he published in 1682 and, in general, this was an age when Arab culture was given a courtly and sententious gloss by its European translators and popularizers. Later, Galland held the Chair of Arabic at the Collège Royale from 1709 onwards.

From 1704, Galland commenced the publication of his translation of the work that would make him famous, *The Thousand and One Nights*. The final volumes of *Les Mille et une nuits* came out in 1717. He intended his translation of the medieval story collection to be not merely a literary entertainment, but also a work of instruction that would inform its readership about the way of life of Oriental peoples, and to that end he inserted numerous explanatory glosses in his translation. In the introduction to the first volume, he wrote that part of the pleasure of reading these stories was in learning about 'the customs and manners of Orientals, and the ceremonies, both pagan and Mohammedan, for these things are better described in these tales than in the accounts of writers and travellers'.

D'Herbelot and Galland were the first Orientalists to take a serious interest in the secular literature of the Middle East. Galland's translation of the *Nights* swiftly became a raging bestseller (as did the translations of his French into English, German and other languages).[11] The *Bibliothèque orientale*, on the other hand, was an expensive book and it never sold well in France. With the death of Galland, serious research in France into Islam and Arab culture more or less ceased for a while.

Although future editions of the *Bibliothèque* would appear with corrections and additions, those corrections and additions were based on the researches of scholars who were not Frenchmen, such as Schultens and Reiske (on both of whom see below). Prominent French writers who wrote about Islam later in the eighteenth century usually knew no Arabic or any other Oriental language. For example, Henri, Comte de Boulainvilliers's posthumously published *Vie de Mahomet* (1730) was really an exercise in church- and establishment-bashing.[12] Boulainvilliers relied heavily on the writings of Edward Pococke, though Pococke, a Royalist churchman, would have been horrified by the use made of his researches. The *Vie de Mahomet* set out to shock by denying that the Prophet Muhammad was an impostor and instead praising him as a great statesman and orator. Islam was presented as a pastoral Arab anticipation of eighteenth-century Deism. Boulain-villiers, who knew no Arabic, was one of a number of writers who adopted the device of pretending to write about Arabian matters when their real targets were the Catholic Church and the French monarchy.

Libertine and Enlightenment authors were particularly fond of this sort of literary disguise. Voltaire wrote by turns in dispraise and praise of the Prophet, depending on what local political point he wished to make. His play, *Le Fanatisme, ou Mahomet le Prophète*, presented Muhammad as an impostor and tyrant. On the other hand, in the *Essai sur l'histoire générale*, Voltaire praised the Prophet as a great, cunning and bold leader. (Quite a few French Enlightenment thinkers took to praising Islam as a way of attacking Christianity, the Pope or the Bourbon monarchy.) Even so Voltaire still took it for granted that the Prophet was an impostor, and though he might have appeared to vacillate about the merits of Islam and the Prophet, he was, like most eighteenth-century thinkers, quite unambiguous in his attitude to the medieval Crusades. He maintained that the only thing that Europeans gained from the Crusades was leprosy.[13]

SLEEPY DONS AND IMPOVERISHED ORIENTALISTS

The stagnation of French Orientalism throughout most of the eigh-teenth century was mirrored in England. In general, this was not a good time for English universities. Oxford and Cambridge were intellectually stagnant. Only theological controversies continued to rouse much passion. In a letter of 1734, the poet Thomas Gray wrote to Horace Walpole about Cambridge as follows: 'The Masters of Colledges [*sic*] are twelve gray-hair'd Gentlefolks, who are all mad with Pride; the Fellows are sleepy, drunken, dull, illiterate Things; the Fellows-Com: are imitators of the Fellows, or else Beaux, or else nothing.' Horace Walpole thought no better of Oxford and described it as 'the nursery of nonsense and bigotry'.[14] Edward Gibbon, look-ing back on his time at Oxford, wrote as follows: 'To the University of Oxford I acknowledge no obligation; and she will as cheerfully renounce me for a son, as I am willing to disclaim her for a mother.

I spent fourteen months at Magdalen College: they proved the fourteen months most idle and unprofitable of my life.' Gibbon had vaguely thought of studying Arabic at Oxford, but was discouraged by his tutor from doing so.[15] Much later, in the 1790s, Chateaubriand, an émigré exile in England, gloomily celebrated the decay of that country's seats of learning: 'Already the nurseries of knowledge, Oxford and Cambridge, are assuming a deserted aspect: their colleges and Gothic chapels, half-abandoned, distress the eye: in their cloisters, near the sepulchral stones of the middle ages, lie, forgotten, the marble annals of the ancient peoples of Greece: ruins guarding ruins.' Sluggards and dullards occupied the university chairs. When lectures on Oriental matters were given, which was rarely, they were poorly attended. In the course of his study of the nineteenth-century biographer of Scaliger and university reformer Mark Pattison, John Sparrow had occasion to record that it 'is often said that Oxford did not emerge from the eighteenth century until half way through the nineteenth'.[16]

On the whole academics were no longer so very interested in the precise text of the Bible and after the Restoration there was a decline in interest in the polyglot Bible project. Nevertheless, as a young man in France Jean Gagnier (1670?–1740) had become interested in Hebrew and Arabic after being shown a copy of a polyglot Bible. He later moved to England and, having converted to Anglicanism, became an English clergyman. In 1723 he published the Arabic text of the section of Abu al-Fida's fourteenth-century chronicle that dealt with the life of Muhammad, together with a Latin translation. He became Lord Almoner's Professor of Arabic in Cambridge in 1724. Gagnier was a real scholar and he swiftly detected how much of Boulainvilliers's biography of the Prophet was sheer fantasy, so he produced his own *Vie de Mahomet* (1732) to refute the errors of the earlier book and to denounce the alleged rationality of Islam (a theme that was sometimes taken up French Deists and rationalists). However, Gagnier's book had little impact, at least initially.[17]

Although d'Herbelot and Galland had covered quite wide areas of history and literature, it was two Englishmen, Simon Ockley and George Sale, who pioneered the serious presentation of Islam in a vernacular tongue. Simon Ockley (1678–1720) studied Hebrew at Cambridge and around 1701 started to teach himself Arabic.[18] (There was, of course, no one in Cambridge capable of teaching it.) He became a vicar in 1705 and in 1708 he published a translation of Ibn Tufayl's desert island fable, *Hayy ibn Yaqzan*, under the title *The Improvement of Human Reason, exhibited in the Life of Hai ebn Yoqdhan*. Ockley's English translation had been preceded by Pococke's Latin one, the *Philosophus Autodidactus* (1671). It is more likely that Daniel Defoe read Ockley's English than Pocoke's Latin before going on to write *Robinson Crusoe* (1719).

In 1711 Ockley became the fifth person to occupy the Thomas Adams Chair of Arabic at Cambridge. Ockley, an enthusiast for Oriental culture, did not think so very highly of his own: 'So far as fear of God is concerned, the control of the appetites, prudence and sobriety in conduct of life, decency and moderation in all circumstances – in regard to all these things (and after all, they yield to none in importance) I declare that if the West has added one single *iota* to the accumulated wisdom of the East, my powers of perception have been strangely in abeyance.' His major work was *The History of the Saracens* (2 volumes, 1708–18). This covered the early history of the Arabs from the death of Muhammad in 632 (the life of Muhammad having already been covered by Prideaux until the death of the Caliph 'Abd al-Malik in 705). Like several of his predecessors, Ockley was at first primarily interested in the history of the Eastern Church. Nevertheless, as he wrote and researched, he became interested in the history of the Arabs for their own sake and, while he routinely referred to Muhammad as an impostor, he nevertheless portrayed the Muslim Arab warriors as heroes. Ockley presented the history of a people remarkable both for arms and for learning. Although he was based in Cambridge, he commuted regularly to Oxford because the Bodleian had a much better collection of Arabic manuscripts. In his history he relied heavily on d'Herbelot's *Bibliothèque*, but since he knew Arabic he also made use of a chronicler whom he believed to be al-Waqidi (d. 823), but whom modern Orientalists prefer to call pseudo-Waqidi, as the chronicle ascribed to Waqidi is a pseudonymous later work containing many legendary elements.

Ockley's attempts to learn Persian were 'frustrated by malignant and envious stars'. He noted that his treatment was very different from the generous patronage that Pétis de la Croix received from

Colbert. It was still not possible to pursue Oriental studies without the sustained support of a wealthy patron and Ockley was not successful in securing one. His uncouthness and rumours that he was a heavy drinker may have had something to do with this, though it was also the case that the study of Arabic was no longer as fashionable as it had been in the age of Laud and Andrewes. Ockley's professorship brought him almost no money and his chief but inadequate income came from the vicarage of Swavesey. The second volume of the *History of the Saracens* was completed in prison in Cambridge Castle, as he was arrested for debt in 1717. At least his jail turned out to be a more peaceful place to do research in than his miserable vicarage. He died in prison, leaving a wife and six children in extreme poverty. He features prominently in Isaac Disraeli's *Calamities of Authors* (1813), where he was described as 'perhaps the first who exhibited to us other heroes than those of Greece and Rome; sages more contemplative, and a people more magnificent than the iron masters of the world'. It was Ockley's *History of the Saracens* that got Gibbon interested in Islam and inspired him with the wish to study Arabic at Oxford. Gibbon called him 'spirited and learned', adding that his work did 'not deserve the petulant animadversions of Reiske'.[19]

Gibbon's account of the rise of empire of the Arabs, when it eventually came to be incorporated in *The Decline and Fall of the Roman Empire*, relied heavily not only on Ockley and d'Herbelot, but also on the work of George Sale (1697?–1736). Part of Sale's attraction for Gibbon may have been the stylish and stately cadences favoured by the writer. As P. M. Holt has pointed out, Sale 'was the first notable English Arabist who was not in holy orders'. Moreover he was neither an academic nor a traveller. He was a London solicitor, outside the university system, and he learned Arabic from two Syrian Christians in London. Even so, there was a Christian background to Sale's Orientalism, as he first worked for the Society for the Promotion of Christian Knowledge, checking its translation of the New Testament into Arabic before, in 1734, producing a translation of the Qur'an into English. (Sale also believed that God had reserved the future glory of the overthrow of Islam to the Protestants.) Sale's translation relied quite heavily on Marracci's Latin version and, like Marracci's version, it was more than just a translation, for it contained a lot of prefatory explanatory matter on the history and culture of Muslims. This 'Preliminary Discourse' was translated in France where it attracted Voltaire's enthusiasm. In the cautionary opening address to the reader, Sale suggested that he did not need to justify publishing his translation of the Qur'an, as Christian faith could not possibly be threatened by 'so manifest a forgery'. He regarded the Arabs as the scourge of God visited on the Christians for their errors and schisms. He also took the opportunity to denounce 'the writers of the Romish communion' for the inadequacies of their refutations of Islam. As he saw it, the Catholic missionaries to Muslim lands were crippled by their worship of images and doctrine of transubstantiation. No sensible Muslim was likely to be won over by such a superstition-ridden religion. 'The Protestants alone are able to attack the Koran with success.'

In order to clear space for his translation, he disparaged those of his predecessors, including Robert of Ketton's Latin translation and Du Ryer's French one. Marracci's translation was exact and literal and, though Sale did not like Marracci's lengthy refutations of Islamic doctrines, he still acknowledged the use he had made of the Latin translation. Although Sale made it perfectly clear that he considered Muhammad to be an impostor, 'how criminal soever Muhammad may have been in imposing a false religion on mankind, the praises due to his real virtues ought not to be denied him'. Despite this damnably faint praise, many of his readers thought his portrait of the Prophet and the rise of Islam much too favourable and Gibbon called Sale 'half a Musulman'.[20]

Those merchants who were not particularly interested in history or Christian polemics, but who wished to learn about the contemporary Middle East, were best served by Alexander Russell's *The Natural History of Aleppo, containing a Description of the City, and the Principal Natural Productions in its Neighbourhood, together with an Account of the Climate, Inhabitants and Diseases; Particularly of the Plague, with the Methods used by the Europeans for their Preservation* (1756, revised edition 1794, by his half-brother Patrick). Alexander Russell was from 1745 to 1753 resident physician to the merchant community of the English Levant Company at Aleppo. He was a particular expert on the plague. Indeed, the original intent was to give an account of the plague and a means of countering it. However, the extremely lengthy second chapter covered such matters as population, language, dress, consumption of coffee and tobacco, eating habits, religious ceremonies, family life, entertainments and funerary rites.[21] Russell's book was in its time the classic and authoritative source on everyday life in a Muslim country and was the acknowledged inspiration in the following century of Lane's *Manners and Customs of the Modern Egyptians*. Lane in his preface was to praise the 'excellent and learned work' of the Russell brothers.[22] Like his half-brother, Patrick had strong scientific interests and was a particular expert on botany and on earthquakes. Patrick considerably added to *The Natural History of Aleppo* and gave it a more human dimension. In his account of Arabic culture he drew upon the researches of Sir William Jones into Arabic literature and it is to him that we now turn.

'ORIENTAL JONES'

According to the twentieth-century Turcologist Harold Bowen, Sir William Jones (1746–94), also known as 'Oriental Jones', mastered thirteen languages and dabbled in twenty-eight.[23] As a schoolboy he started off with Hebrew but, finding that language too easy to be interesting, he then moved on to Arabic. He translated bits of the English version of *The Arabian Nights* back into Arabic for his amusement. (One took one's amusements where one could find them in those days.) While a student at Oxford, he retained Mirza, a Syrian from Aleppo, to teach him the language. (As in Cambridge fifty years earlier, there was no academic fellow capable of doing the job.) After Arabic, Jones moved on to Persian and Turkish. He translated a life of the Persian ruler Nadir Shah for Christian VII of Denmark and this was published in 1770. Jones's *Grammar of the Persian Language*, published only a year later, was really of more use to poets than to imperial administrators, as Jones's grasp of Persian was somewhat erratic and secondly he was more interested in introducing Persian poets to a European audience than he was in producing a crib for merchants and administrators working in exotic parts. The *Grammar* is full of extracts from the famous medieval Persian poets. Jones's explorations of Persian poetry had persuaded him that European literature was stale and needed liberating from classical models: 'Asiaticks excel the inhabitants of colder regions in the liveliness of their fancy, and the richness of their invention.'[24]

On the other hand, though Jones had discovered something fresh and different in Persian poetry, he also thought of it in another sense as perfectly familiar. His sense of the sheer Otherness of Persian poetry being imperfect, he described Firdawsi's eleventh-century epic, the *Shahnama*, as being written in 'the spirit of our Dryden and the sweetness of Pope'. (The justice of this comparison is not obvious to a modern reader.) He also compared Firdawsi to Homer and Hafiz of Shiraz to Petrarch. Jones was keen that gentlemen of leisure should take up the study of Persian: 'I may confidently affirm that few odes of the Greeks or Romans upon similar subjects are more finely polished than the songs of these Persian poets.' As with the study of Latin and Greek literature, study of Persian was character-building: 'There is scarce a lesson of morality or a tender sentiment in any European language to which a parallel may not be brought from the poets of Asia.'[25]

Though he devoted less time to Arabic literature, he produced a number of important, though error-strewn, translations from Arabic poetry. In 1782 he published the *Moallakat* (more correctly *Mu'allaqat*). This collection of seven pre-Islamic Arabian odes by diverse hands was treated by him as a series of essays in the pastoral. The Arab poets then became so many Oriental versions of Theocritus on camel-back – herdsmen in lush landscapes singing of their love for some nymph or other. Part of the trouble was that the term 'Arabia Felix' ('Happy Arabia') had given Jones a quite fanciful notion that a verdant, rather English-looking countryside prevailed in South West Arabia. Though he knew as little about the people as he did about the countryside, he judged the noble and fierce Arabs to be superior to the softer Persians and Hindus. (Such generalizations were common in pre-modern times and not just in Western culture.)

It was impossible to make a living as an Orientalist and, in the introduction to the Persian *Grammar*, he had complained of the diffi-culty of finding patronage for Oriental studies. At an early stage in his life Jones's father had considered attaching him to a chambers to get a legal education, but Jones had resisted this on the understandable grounds that the quality of the Latin used in English law books was so very bad. However, in the end he had to knuckle down to legal studies and he was called to the Bar in 1774. There were various false turns in his career. For instance, he had hoped to become an MP, but his liberalism, his hostility to slavery and support of American independence counted against him. Nevertheless, in 1783 he was appointed Judge of the High Court in Calcutta and a knighthood came with the appointment. He was happy to sail out to India as, among other things, he hoped to find evidence in India for the Flood of Genesis.

When he set out for Calcutta, he had had no intention of studying Sanskrit. Having once succumbed to that erudite temptation, he was soon declaring that Sanskrit was 'more perfect than Greek, more copious than Latin, and more exquisitely refined than either' and thereafter he switched to the study of Sanskrit and comparative philology. In 1786 Jones was the first to make the link between Sanskrit and Greek and Latin and declare that the three languages must have descended from a common ancestor. The establishment of an Indo-Aryan family of languages by European philologists is something that has been resented by Edward Said and he appears to doubt the validity of their findings, though he does not explain why.[26] Though Jones's linkage of Sanskrit to a large group of European languages was sound enough, his ethnology was somewhat archaic and confused, as he held that Greeks, Indians, Chinese, Japanese, Mexicans and Peruvians all descended from Noah's son, Ham. Ethnologists who came after him tended to make Ham the father of just the black peoples.

In 1784 Jones founded the Asiatick Society of Bengal, the prototype and inspiration for the later learned associations of Orientalists, the Société Asiatique and the Royal Asiatic Society.[27] Jones was also the first Orientalist to engage seriously, though briefly, with Turkish literature and, besides that and his other Oriental interests, he was an amateur astronomer, botanist, musician, historian of chess and an expert on pangolins. His explorations of Arabic and Persian poetry were as much or more an event in English literature as they were in Oriental studies. Byron, Southey and Moore all read him. Tennyson's

'Locksley Hall' owes a great deal to Jones's *Mu'allaqat*. Jones's researches were also important for German literature. Goethe (1749–1832) and Friedrich Rückert (1788–1866) were both inspired by his translations to explore Oriental themes in their poetry – but all that is really the subject of another book.

Although Jones was the great pioneer of Indian studies, his chief heirs in this field were French and German, and Indological and Sanskrit studies were dominated by such scholars as Jean Pierre Abel Rémusat, August Wilhelm Schlegel, Eugène Burnouf and Max Müller. It was the French who set up the first university chair in Sanskrit.[28] Many British East India Company officials and soldiers took up Persian or one or more of the Indian languages, but it was rare for such people to acquire more than a colloquial smattering. In *La Renaissance orientale* (1950) Raymond Schwab argued that the true beginnings of Orientalism are to be found in the late eighteenth century. Although he produced a great deal of evidence for this contention, he was chiefly interested in India and his conclusion is true, at best, only for Indian studies. As we have seen, Arabic studies began as early as the seventeenth century with Postel, Pococke, Erpenius, Golius and Marracci. There were no comparably grand figures in their field in the eighteenth century. Nevertheless, it does seem to be true that Indian studies took off in the late eighteenth century.

The great French Indologist, Abraham Hyacinthe Anquetil-Duperron, lived in Mughal India from 1755 to 1761. He published an edition of the Zoroastrian *Zend-Avesta*, as well as a narrative of his travels. He was hostile to the stereotypical portrait of Oriental despotism presented by *L'Esprit des lois* (1748), in which Montesquieu argued that despotism, conditioned by material and climatic factors, was pervasive throughout Asia and was savagely arbitrary, demanded blind obedience and was centred around the mysteries of the harem. As far as Anquetil-Duperron was concerned, such a portrait of Asian politics and society could only serve as an instrument of oppression over the peoples of Asia. In *Législation orientale* (1778), he used his close knowledge of Indian matters to refute Montesquieu's contentions that Oriental despots were not bound by the law and that there was no private property under the Moghuls.

Like so many Orientalists who came after him, Anquetil-Duperron was fiercely anti-imperialist. In the introduction to another work, *Le Despotisme considéré dans les trois états où il passe pour être, la Turquie, la Perse et l'Hindoustan*, he expressed his fear that the concept of Oriental despotism had been summoned up by certain Western thinkers in order to justify the oppressive rule of Europeans over Asia.[29] In many respects, Anquetil-Duperron antipated the main tenets of Said's *Orientalism*, though Said, who discusses him, chooses not to mention this. Samuel Johnson was, like Anquetil-Duperron, suspicious of Montesquieu's manner of argument and he remarked to Boswell that Montesquieu was always able to find some obscure Oriental example to back up anything that he wanted to say.[30]

ALL'S QUIET IN HOLLAND

Sale, Russell and Jones made important contributions to Islamic studies, but they did so outside the universities. Leiden was no less moribund than Oxford and Cambridge. After Golius, Oriental studies in Leiden went into a steep decline.[31] The most distinguished figure in the opening decades of the eighteenth century, Adrian Reeland (1676–1718), was to become Professor of Oriental Languages at Utrecht, not Leiden.[32] By the age of fourteen this prodigy knew some Hebrew, Syriac, Aramaic and Arabic. Arabic was exactly the sort of subject any young genius in this period should aspire to know, thanks to its reputation as a recondite and difficult language. Reeland was a polymath with interests in and knowledge of most things, as well as being a poet. Like Postel and Kircher before him, he speculated crazily about the nature of the *Ursprache*, or primal language, and the descent of all modern languages from it. In *De religione Mohammedica* (1705) and other works he combated misrepresentations of Islam. However, he was utterly typical in his approach to Arabic studies in that he considered that Arabic's chief importance was as a handmaiden to Hebrew and biblical studies and hence his heavy emphasis on a philological approach.

Later in the century, Albert Schultens (1686–1750), a professor first at Amsterdam and then at Leiden, took essentially the same approach.[33]

He was primarily a Hebraist and his *Dissertatio theologico-philologica de utilitate linguae arabicae in interpretanda sacra lingua* ('Theologico-Philological Dissertation on the Utility of the Arabic Language for the Interpretation of Holy Scripture'), published in 1706, took it for granted that study of Arabic should be subordinated to that of Hebrew and actually took issue with those academics who argued that, since Hebrew was the divine language, study of any other was quite pointless. Nevertheless, though Schultens was eloquent in making the case for comparative Semitic philology (embracing Hebrew, Arabic, Syriac and Chaldaean), he was not actually very good at it.

The soundness of Schultens's philology was criticized by Johann Jacob Reiske (1716–74), the greatest Greek and Arabic scholar of the eighteenth century.[34] Reiske had been Schultens's student but became his opponent. Reiske, the foremost German Orientalist of first rank, was primarily a classicist. He was born in poverty, brought up in an orphanage, and died in poverty. Having taught himself Greek, his first important published work was on the Attic orators. He produced editions of their speeches and then an edition of Theocritus. He was prone to intense depressions and his wife was driven to learn Latin and Greek to keep him happy. Perhaps because of his classical formation, Reiske took a more literary approach to Arabic and was hostile to Schultens's stress on Hebrew, a language that Reiske refused to learn. In 1738 he moved to Leiden. It was a mistake: 'This served me an ill turn. Dearly, too dearly have I had to pay for my folly! I became a martyr for Arabic literature. Oh if my burning thirst of those days for this literature, which only made me unhappy coming as it did too early, at a time when nobody needed it and still less appreciated it enough to reward or encourage it, oh if it could find its way into a soul which could some day bring life to happier times! If that day ever comes (though there is hardly room for hope) then Arabic literature will be better appreciated and studied with greater application than it is now.'[35] Reiske never succeeded in obtaining a chair in Leiden or anywhere else. He was suspected of being a free thinker as he did not attend church on Sundays, but the real reason for this was that he was too poor to afford a coat to go to church in. Coming from a humble background, he had no private income and, despite being the best

Arabist and one of the best classicists of the century, he was forced to do hack work in order to survive.

Nevertheless, he did important work in Arabic literature and he campaigned vigorously for it to be studied as a subject in its own right. He translated histories by Abu al-Fida and Ibn 'Arabshah into Latin. It is noteworthy how in the seventeenth, eighteenth and nineteenth centuries the same authors got translated again and again. Pococke, Greaves and Gagnier had already worked on Abu al-Fida and, after Reiske, many were to work on Ibn 'Arabshah, most notably Silvestre de Sacy. Other works or authors that were recurrently chosen for editions or translations included the *Proverbs* of 'Ali, the *Proverbs* of Luqman, the chronicle of al-Makin, the Ramlah *Maqamat* of al-Hariri and the al-Tughrai poem known as the *Lamiyyat*. In part, this phenomenon may indicate how few worthwhile Arabic manuscripts had been acquired by European libraries. Even complete manuscripts of the Qur'an were hard to get hold of. One may also suspect that scholars in this period were not so keen to venture into virgin territory and some of them at least preferred to crib covertly from their predecessors. Reiske also translated the tenth-century poet Mutanabbi into German. (In this period it was still most unusual to translate Arabic into a vernacular language.)

Despite France's predatory ambitions in the Middle East and Egypt, there were no major Arabists in France until the appearance of Silvestre de Sacy (on whom, see the next chapter). The decline of Orientalism in the eighteenth century was fairly pervasive throughout Europe. Not only did few patrons take an interest in this recondite branch of learning, but the public at large was somewhat suspicious of the study of Arabic and Islam, suspecting those who undertook such studies to be crypto-Muslims. Moreover hopes had faded since the seventeenth century of finding much of any scientific value in Arabic books (though exceptionally there was interest in Ulugh Beg's astronomical tables in Persian). Although Avicenna's Galenic medical treatise, the *Canon*, was still being taught in some places, elsewhere it was coming to be realized that most of this body of 'knowledge' would have to be discarded if medicine was to make any progress. By 1700 the great age of hunting for Arabic manuscripts had come to an end. Though some enthusiastic scholars had tried to present the knowledge of Arabic as vital for international commerce, this was not really true and European traders got along fine without recourse to Oriental scholarship. At the same time missionaries had achieved very little indeed in the idle East and those few converts they did succeed in making tended to be from some form of Eastern Christianity rather than from Islam. The short-lived craze for Arabic was succeeded by an equally transient fashion for Chinese studies and Chinoiserie. The eccentric Jesuit Athanasius Kircher had done much to awaken interest in China by producing his *China Monumentis* (1667) with its surreally fantastic illustrations. In general, Europe was dependent on Jesuit missionaries for much of its information on China. A literary cult of the Chinese sage developed, English landowners had their gardens landscaped in the Chinese manner, French *philosophes* brooded on the supposed merits of Chinese imperial despotism, and the German philosopher Leibniz studied the *I Ching*.[36]

RUSSIA IN ASIA

If Oriental studies stagnated in most of Europe, in Russia they were barely beginning and, if one wishes to make close connections between Orientalism and imperialism, then it is surely to Russia that one should first turn. The origins of Russian Orientalism are most curious – indeed they begin with the cabinet of curiosities assembled by Peter the Great (1672–1725). As is well known, Peter was determined to modernize his empire and put an end to the medieval attitudes and customs that were an obstacle to commercial and military progress. (It is interesting to note that Peter's sponsorship of teaching and publishing in Latin was part of the great modernizing project.) In the years 1697–8 Peter undertook his 'Great Embassy' to Western Europe, where he studied shipbuilding, mining techniques and much else. Among other things he was struck by the role in the West of cabinets of curiosity in organizing knowledge and stimulating research. Having visited several Dutch collections of curiosities and works of art, he began collecting himself when he returned to Russia. His agents scoured Europe, buying up not just individual curiosities but whole collections of such things. Peter the Great's Cabinet of Curiosities

(Kabinet Redkostei) was open to the public, or at least to those members of the public who could pass as gentlemen or ladies. The gentlefolk could inspect a live dwarf, a live hermaphrodite, teeth from Alexander's elephants, manuscripts in exotic languages, stuffed monsters and a magnificent hoard of Scythian gold. In this manner Peter hoped to instruct his barbarous Russian subjects. From 1724 onwards the collection was administered by the St Petersburg Academy of Sciences and in the long run the Cabinet of Curiosities would become a fully fledged Museum of the Academy of Science.[37] Much of its contents were transferred to the Asiatic Museum which opened in 1818 and the Asiatic Museum would in turn become the kernel of the Institute of Oriental Studies.

At the same time as Peter was educating his subjects, he was seeking to add to their number. In Central Asia and the Caucasus, Russia was acquiring an empire inhabited mostly by Muslims and it was obviously desirable to understand Islam better in order to govern those Muslims more effectively. In 1702 a special school for the study of Oriental languages was established. In 1716 Peter had the Qur'an translated from the French version of Du Ryer. Peter also commissioned Dmitri Kantemir's *The System or Condition of the Muhamedan Religion* (1722). He sent five scholars to Persia to study Oriental languages. As Russia expanded into the Islamic lands it acquired more materials to fuel Oriental studies and, for example, the capture of Derbent in the Caucasus (1722) led to an influx of Oriental manuscripts into Petersburg.[38]

DENMARK IN THE ORIENT

Reiske apart, Germany produced no Arabists of real note for most of the eighteenth century. However, the Hebrew scholar and Professor of Philosophy at the Hanoverian University of Göttingen, Johann-David Michaelis (1717–91), was one of the age's great intellectual patrons of Islamic and Arabic studies.[39] Michaelis's own knowledge of Arabic seems to have been slight, though he translated Erpenius's grammar from Latin into German. Michaelis was best known for his *Einleitung in die göttlichen Schriften des Neuen Bundes* (1750), in which he sought to distinguish on textual and philological grounds those books that had actually been written by the Apostles from those which had not. He was sceptical about the idea that Hebrew was the primal language and similarly sceptical about the received account of the descent of the world's great racial groups from the sons of Noah. But he had no doubt that the study of Arabic and the contemporary Middle East should be subordinated to the study of Hebrew and the Bible and it was he who was the mastermind behind the Danish expedition to Egypt and the Arabian peninsula in the years 1761 to 1767, a scholarly venture that can be considered as the paradigmatic Orientalist penetration of the Islamic lands.

The commissioning from William Jones by Christian VII of Denmark of a translation from the Persian of a life of Nadir Shah has already been noted. There was a significant tradition of Oriental studies in Denmark in this period. In the early seventeenth century Adam Olearius had travelled to Persia in order to investigate the prospects for Danish trade in the lands of the Safavid Shah and subsequently Olearius wrote up his travels.[40] In 1737 Christian VI had sent an expedition including Frederick Ludvig Norden on a mission to establish trade links with Ethiopia. Though the exhibition never did get that far, Norden subsequently published maps and sketches of the journey up the Nile.[41]

The Danish King Frederick V (1746–66) was an enlightened patron of the arts and sciences. It was therefore to him that Michaelis turned for sponsorship of an expedition that was intended to be an exercise in biblical research. Though the Danish king agreed to fund the project, it was effectively organized by Michaelis and the University of Göttingen. Michaelis was a believer in Arabic in the service of Hebrew studies and he proposed an expedition to Arabia Felix (effectively the modern Yemen), as the South Arabian dialect was distinct from the Arabic spoken elsewhere in the peninsula and 'knowing that it is this form of Arabic, which we learned, that has been the most important tool to date in understanding the Hebrew language, what illumination can we not expect to be cast over the Bible, the most important book of ancient times, by learning the Eastern Arabian dialects, as well as we know the Western?' In addition to the study of this particular branch of the Arabic language, the expedition was to seek out manuscripts (especially of the Bible), survey the topography, enquire into the effects of polygamy on population growth, and record the vegetation and wildlife. Michaelis was particularly keen to receive data that would help in identifying the flora and fauna of the Bible. He also thought that the contemporary Arabs had a way of life similar to that of the ancient Hebrews. To these ends Michaelis produced a detailed questionnaire that the members of the expedition were supposed to fill in as they proceeded.

Acting on Frederick V's behalf, the University of Copenhagen also produced a lengthy and detailed set of articles for the guidance of the expedition. According to Article X: 'All members of the company shall show the greatest courtesy to the inhabitants of Arabia. They are not to raise any objections to their religion, more than that, they shall give no indication – not even indirectly – that they despise it; they shall refrain from that which is the abomination of the inhabitants of Arabia. And also, as necessary in the course of their tasks, they should proceed in such a manner as to draw the least attention as possible, shrouding anything which might arouse the suspicion among the ignorant Muhamedans that they were searching for treasure, practising sorcery, or spying with the intention of harming the country . . .'

The ill-fated expedition that was sent out in 1761 included a naturalist, a philologist, a physician, an artist, a cartographer and an orderly. Of these six, only the cartographer Carsten Niebuhr was to survive the rigours of the expedition and return to Denmark alive. But he was a remarkable and determined man and, even before reaching Arabia, he had made a systematic survey of the manners and customs of Cairo and the details of its material life, including costumes, implements, craft techniques and so forth. Having travelled out from Constantinople and Cairo to Yemen and from there to Bombay, he returned via Oman, Persia, Iraq and Syria. He returned to Denmark with important transcriptions of hieroglyphics and of cuneiform, as well as excellent maps of the Nile Delta and parts of Arabia and the Red Sea. Niebuhr was very fond of the Arabs and had little but good to report of them (though he was not so fond of the Turks). He wrote up his discoveries and adventures in German in three volumes published in 1772–8.[42]

THE ARRIVAL OF THE SAVANTS
IN EGYPT

Though Michaelis's enquiries and Niebuhr's discoveries epitomized Orientalist interest in the Middle East in this period, at the same time French politicians, merchants and soldiers had developed a more predatory interest in that region. There were plenty of French theorists ready to argue that Ottoman Turkey, a typical Oriental despotism, was in full decay, because, as the statesman and economist Anne-Robert-Jacques Turgot argued, despotism conduced inevitably to slavery, polygamy and softness.[43] Others held that it was Turkey's espousal of a satanic religion that had doomed it. Others again attributed it to the Ottoman lands' failure to keep up with Western commercial and industrial developments. In the 1770s François, Baron de Tott, had been sent by the French Foreign Office on a mission, ostensibly to inspect French consular posts in the eastern Mediterranean, but actually to spy out Ottoman strengths and weaknesses. In 1779 he produced a memorandum which put the case for a French invasion of Egypt. He thought the decayed state of the government there meant that there would be little resistance and he suggested that the French invaders should present themselves as on a mission from the Ottoman sultan to liberate the Egyptian people from the corrupt Mamluk beys.[44]

> 'My name is Ozymandias, king of kings:
> Look on my works, ye Mighty, and despair!'
> Nothing beside remains. Round the decay
> Of that colossal wreck, boundless and bare
> The lone and level sands stretch far away.

Shelley's poem, in which the above lines appear, was allegedly inspired by the arrival in the British Museum of the head of Rameses II which had been brought out of a ruined temple in Thebes.[45] As mentioned earlier, the celebrated seventeenth-century traveller in the Middle East, Jean Thévenot, considered that the Middle East was rich only in ruins. Ancient ruins set in an arid wilderness was the topos, or stock theme, that fuelled the French project to conquer Egypt.

Constantin-François de Chasseboeuf, comte de Volney, made Oriental ruins his peculiar speciality. His interest in the Middle East had initially been inspired by a reading of Herodotus. He studied Erpenius's grammar and the questionnaire compiled by Michaelis and had then tried to learn Arabic at the Collège de France, but he found the teaching there totally unsatisfactory, for the teachers worked from classical texts and had no interest in the contemporary spoken language. As Abbé Barthélémy put it, 'One does not learn these languages to speak them . . .' So Volney decided to make a fresh start at learning Arabic as it was spoken in Egypt.

In 1783 he arrived in Alexandria and then spent two years and four months travelling in the Middle East. He was struck by the poverty, backwardness, depopulation, corruption and slavery that prevailed throughout the region. Like many Western observers of the time, he thought that Turkish despotism, together with the fatalistic attitudes fostered by Islam, were the causes of the miserable condition of the Arabs. He believed that there was something in Islam that actually colluded with political tyranny. Volney was opposed to Islam – but then he was opposed to all religions, especially Christianity. In stressing the determining and negative roles of religion and politics, he was setting himself against Montesquieu, who had argued that climate had a determining role in shaping societies and that Asiatics were naturally indolent. Volney believed that the Ottoman empire was doomed to fall apart: 'I swear by the ruin of so many empires destroyed: the empire of the Crescent shall suffer the fate of the states whose scheme of government it copied.'

Though he was sure that the Arabs, Kurds and other subject races were longing to be liberated from the Turk, nevertheless he was opposed to European intervention in the region. Indeed, it seems plausible that Volney's journey and subsequent book were sponsored by influential French figures who were similarly opposed. Volney's chief aim seems to have been to dispute this and he argued that, in the end, 'we would only have conquered Egypt to devastate it'. He was then the leading spokesman for those who opposed de Tott's project for the invasion of Egypt. Volney published his observations in *Voyage en Egypte et en Syrie* in 1787. It was widely read and one of its readers was Bonaparte.

Volney's even more famous work, *Les Ruines, ou méditations sur les révolutions des empires* (1791), opened with a meditation on the ruins of Palmyra in eastern Syria: 'Je vous salue, ruines solitaires, tombeaux saints, murs silencieux! C'est vous que j'invoque; c'est à vous que j'adresse ma prière.' (I salute you, solitary ruins, holy tombs, silent walls. It is you that I invoke. It is to you that I address my prayer.) Everybody read this book. It was a bestseller and the talk of the salons, spas and gaming rooms. Even Frankenstein's monster read it. (Arguably, recent Frankenstein films have seriously traduced the monster by undervaluing its engagement with cultural studies – but that is to digress.) Be that as it may, no one reads *Les Ruines* nowadays. It is quite hard going. After the sonorous opening invocation, Volney presented himself as sitting amidst the ruins of Palmyra, musing on the grandeur of the place as it once was and on the causes of the passing of its greatness. All of a sudden, there appears beside him a spectral genius, or genie, who takes the author aloft and gives him an airborne lecture on the causes of the rise and fall of empires and lots of other things besides. The key question was why the East was so impoverished and backward compared with the West. The prevalence of despotism in the East was a large part of the answer. Volney, steeped in the classics, found it natural to compare the Mamluks and Pashas to the tyrants of Syracuse and other oppressive despots of classical antiquity. So there was nothing inherently exotic, or Other, about despotism. Soon, though, the Sultans and Pashas would go the way of the French king, for Volney was confident in the ultimate triumph of Liberty, Equality and Fraternity throughout the world – and more specifically he believed in the future revolt of the Arab nation. Volney was an Arab nationalist before most Arabs were.[46]

From 1802 onwards Volney campaigned to get a chair in colloquial Arabic established in France, so that this useful language could be taught to diplomats and merchants. However, this came to pass only in 1830, as he was fiercely opposed by the grand French Orientalist, Silvestre de Sacy. The latter seemed to take pride in the fact that he had not learned Arabic from any Shaykh, but only from books. He could not speak Arabic, still less teach spoken Arabic to others. Since there was no great literature in modern Arabic, he interested himself only in the medieval classics.[47] (His approach to Arabic still had its heirs and supporters in British universities as late as the 1960s.) There were others in the field who thought as Silvestre de Sacy did and, according to Volney, there was not a single professor in Paris who could speak Arabic properly.

In 1798 a French fleet carrying a French army under the command of General Bonaparte arrived on the coast of Egypt. The French went on swiftly to occupy the Delta ports and then Cairo, before invading Palestine.[48] It is tempting to read Volney's *Voyage en Egypte et en Syrie* as a blueprint for that disastrous imperialist adventure and that is a temptation to which Said succumbed. As if what Volney had been saying in that book was '*Allez la France!* Now here is a golden opportunity for some ambitious young Frenchman, or perhaps a Corsican, to carve out a French empire in this backward part of the world.' But that is to get Volney exactly wrong. The subtext of *Voyage* and of a later tract, *Considérations sur la guerre actuelle des Turcs* (1788) (which Said has muddled with *Voyage*) is that one should forget about Egypt as a territory that is ripe to be colonized. Volney was not saying that in order to conquer Egypt the French ought first to fight the Turks, then the English and finally deal with the Muslims. Rather he was arguing that first the French would have to fight the Turks, then they would have a battle on their hands with the English and then, finally, they would still have to fight the Muslims. Volney thought that, faced with such opposition, the occupation of Egypt was not feasible and that Muslim resistance to French rule would be particularly intractable.[49] How right he was. The 1798 French expedition to Egypt was a military disaster to be compared with the Gallipoli landings, the Arnhem parachute drop and Dien Bien Phu. The most astonishing thing about the debacle is that its commander, Bonaparte, went on to have quite a successful military career.

A powerful lobby of Marseilles merchants had been pressing for a French invasion of Egypt in order to secure a market for French products. The French were conscious of having lost out in America and India. The occupation of Egypt would threaten British possessions in India. Bonaparte, who had studied the campaigns of Alexander the Great, seems to have dreamed of using Egypt as a base for the conquest both of Constantinople and of India. Moreover, while one may well be sceptical about motives for the French expedition, it will not do to be totally cynical. It is likely that some of those who sponsored or accompanied the expedition were genuinely committed to a mission of liberation and civilization and they thought of themselves as going to wage war on the chateaux of the Mamluk beys in order to liberate the oppressed fellahin. Theirs was a *mission civilisatrice* enforced at the point of a gun. The expedition took with it a printing press that had an Arabic typeface. After his forces had landed in Egypt, Bonaparte issued a proclamation in Arabic that sought to win the support of the Egyptian people against their Mamluk Caucasian Turkish masters and declared among other things: 'For too many years that gang of slaves, purchased in Georgia and the Caucasus, has tyrannized over the most beautiful region of the world. But almighty God, who rules the universe, has decreed that their reign shall come to an end.'[50] The French sought to present themselves as liberators rather than crusaders in the tradition of Louis IX, but though some of Bonaparte's officers denounced Christianity and declared themselves to be atheists, the puzzled or sceptical Muslims took atheism to be merely another version of Christianity.

Said says many of Bonaparte's Arabic interpreters had been students of the great Orientalist Silvestre de Sacy, but this does not seem very likely. De Sacy began teaching only in 1796 and, as has been indicated, he was perfectly incapable of teaching the Egyptian colloquial. Certainly Said provides no evidence at all for the involvement of France's leading Orientalist in the Egyptian project. The Orientalist Louis Mathieu Langlès (1763–1824), a student of Arabic and Persian, was asked to go, but he timidly refused, as he felt more comfortable in a library than he would have done in Egypt. However Langlès (whom Maxime Rodinson has described as 'an Orientalist of questionable merit') had played a leading part in the foundation of the Ecole spéciale des langues orientales vivantes, an institution that was unusual in teaching spoken languages – in theory at least – and, as we shall see, two of Bonaparte's interpreters had previously studied there.

Bonaparte took an impressive team of scientists, scholars and artists with him on the expedition to Egypt. A large number of Bonaparte's team of savants were experts in civil engineering. The Institute of Egypt, as it was eventually set up in Cairo, was divided into four sections: Mathematics, Physics, Political Economy and, finally,

Literature and Art. In this last section there was just one Arabist, Jean-Michel Venture de Paradis. This man, who was Bonaparte's chief interpreter, was aged sixty in 1798 and therefore the doyen of the expedition. Venture de Paradis had not studied Arabic in academic circles. Rather, he was the son of a dragoman and he had worked as a dragoman himself in Istanbul, Sidon, Cairo and Tunis before becoming Professor of Turkish at the Ecole spéciale des langues orientales vivantes. In the 1780s he had supported de Tott's interventionist policies regarding the Middle East. At around the same time he worked on a translation of a late medieval Egyptian administration manual by Khalil al-Zahiri, the *Zubda Kashf al-Asrar*, which he never got round to publishing. (He translated this text not because he had an antiquarian interest in what life was like in fifteenth-century Egypt, but rather because he thought that Khalil al-Zahiri's data might still be largely valid for contemporary Egypt.) In 1790 he published a memoir on the need to study Oriental languages in order to promote commercial and political relations. He stated that in France professors gave lectures that no one attended and manuscripts languished in the libraries unread. France was lagging behind Germany and Britain in this respect. In Egypt he played a crucial role because of his previous knowledge of the land and his personal contacts and he was in effect Bonaparte's first minister for all Oriental matters. The Egyptian scholar and historian al-Jabarti met him and praised him as an eloquent and likeable man. Venture de Paradis died of dysentery in 1799 at Nazareth and was buried under the walls of Acre.[51] After Nelson's destruction of the French fleet at Aboukir Bay, the death of Venture de Paradis was one of the greatest of the many disasters that befell the French expeditionary force.

The death of Venture de Paradis left Bonaparte without any real expert guidance on Arab politics, religion and society. He seems to have brought only a couple of other Arabic interpreters from France out with him and they were less grand and less experienced. The first of these, Jean-Joseph Marcel (1776–1854), took up Hebrew and Arabic at fifteen and as a student at the Ecole spéciale des langues orientales vivantes, he had studied under Langlès, but he had then pursued an early career in mining and the manufacture of saltpetre. He went into hiding during the Terror. In Egypt with the French expedition he supervised the operations of the printing press in Alexandria that produced documents in French, Arabic and Greek. He was industrious and, besides acting as interpreter, he put together an Arabic grammar and studied Arabic poetry.[52] Less seems to be known about Amadée Jaubert, who also studied at the Ecole and who became Bonaparte's personal interpreter after the death of Venture de Paradis. He later taught Turkish at the Ecole and wrote four memoirs for the *Description de l'Egypte*.[53]

As has been noted, Bonaparte had brought with him a team of savants. Some of the Egyptian Institute's tasks were purely practical, such as improving army baking ovens, trying to brew beer without hops, introducing new crops and investigating the practicability of digging a canal across the Suez peninsula. But there was a more scholarly component to the Institute. Al-Jabarti, who visited it, was impressed by the dedication of the scholars: 'Some of the French were studying Arabic and learning verses from the Qur'an by heart; in a word they were great scholars and they loved the sciences, especially mathematics and philology. Day and night they applied themselves to learning Arabic . . .'[54] The French research brief was modelled on a famous address given by Sir William Jones at the inaugural meeting of the Asiatick Society of Bengal in 1784, 'A Discourse on the Institution of a Society for Inquiry into the History, Civil and Natural, the Antiquities, Arts, Sciences and Literature of Asia'. In that *Discourse*, Jones had set out a programme for his fellow scholars that would take an interdisciplinary approach to the history and culture of India. It was a thoroughly idealistic project, inspired by a vision of Asia that Jones had had as the ship he was on sailed between Persia and India: 'Asia, which has ever been esteemed the nurse of sciences, the inventress of delightful and of useful arts, the scene of glorious actions, fertile in the productions of human genius, abounding in natural wonders, and infinitely diversified in the forms of religion and government, in the laws, manners, customs and languages, as well as in the features and complexions of men.'[55] Jones had wanted his fellow Orientalists to learn from Asian institutions, crafts and sciences.

Jones considered the mastery of Oriental languages to be not so much a part of scholarship in its own right, but rather a means towards more practical goals, and the French followed him in this. The results of the French researches, the *Description de l'Egypte*, was commissioned in 1802 and started to appear in 1809, though its twenty-third volume only appeared in 1828. The high price of the extravagantly printed volumes militated against widespread sales. Bonaparte had hoped that its publication would retrospectively turn a military and political disaster into a cultural and scientific triumph. The *Description* seems in part to have been modelled on the work of the Russells on Aleppo. Though the French savants covered the manners and customs of the Egyptian people, their trades, industries, costumes, musical instruments and so forth, it is evident from the briefest acquaintance with the *Description* that what they were chiefly interested in was Egypt's Pharaonic legacy. Egypt's Islamic heritage was much less significant.[56] Therefore, though the scholarly invasion of Egypt was a milestone in the history of Egyptology, effectively its founding document, it had little or no influence on the way Arabic and Islamic studies developed in the following century.

6

Oriental Studies in the Age of
Steam and Cant

*To give an accurate and exhaustive account of that period
would need a far less brilliant pen than mine.*

Max Beerbohm, *1880*

THE FOUNDER OF MODERN
ORIENTALISM

The Ecole spéciale des langues orientales vivantes was founded in
1795 and was headed first by Louis Mathieu Langlès and then by
Silvestre de Sacy. However, not too much weight should be placed on
the term 'vivantes', for, as we have seen, the second of these professors
had no interest at all in the living spoken languages of the Orient.
Antoine Isaac Silvestre de Sacy (1758–1838) was the son of a notary
and came from a Jansenist background. (The Jansenists were Catholic
rigorists who held that good works are only possible with God's
grace and that only a minority of individuals are predestined to
God's salvation. There was a strong intellectual tradition centred
around the Abbey of Port Royal and Jansenist thinkers had done
important work on French grammar and logic and would extend their
approach to Oriental languages.) A man of stern piety, de Sacy first
studied Hebrew for religious reasons. Subsequently, he was encouraged by conversations with Dom Berthereau to take up the study
of Arabic. Berthereau, an unsystematically scholarly monk in the
Benedictine Maurist order, had been asked by his superiors to learn
Arabic so as to research more thoroughly the history of the Crusades

and France's part in them. He had taught himself Arabic but, though he made a large number of fragmentary translations of Arabic materials that bore on the Crusades, there were no direct results of his researches in his lifetime. On the other hand, the engagement of de Sacy in Arabic and other Eastern languages was a watershed in the history of Orientalism.

Like Berthereau, de Sacy had some difficulty in learning Arabic. There was no one in the universities who was capable of teaching him. He got some help from a dragoman called Etienne le Grand and he may also have had lessons from a learned Jew in Paris, though this is obscure. There were almost no texts to study and only one worthwhile grammar, that of Golius, but de Sacy toiled away, teaching himself by memorizing key texts from classical Arabic literature. Eventually de Sacy was to master Arabic, Syriac, Ethiopian, Persian and Turkish, as well as Hebrew, Aramaic and Mandaean and the usual number of European languages that any self-respecting nineteenth-century academic would expect to be at home in. His first employment was at the Royal Court of Moneys (the mint) where he worked from 1781 onwards. A fervent royalist, he viewed the French Revolution with dismay and in 1792 retired from public service for a while, before re-emerging after the overthrow of Robespierre.

In 1795 de Sacy became a professor in the Ecole spéciale des langues orientales vivantes. Not only had he no time for living languages, but also, unlike many of his learned contemporaries, he had no interest in the comparative study of languages. He also had no interest in visiting exotic parts (unless one counts Genoa, which he visited to do research in its archives). He was a sombre, severe and polemical figure. Judged by modern standards, his teaching was quite dreadful. His students were expected to learn by rote and memorize sections of the grammars and selected texts, but, as will soon become apparent, he must even so have been an inspiring figure. Together with Champollion, the decipherer of the Rosetta Stone, he was one of the co-founders of the Société Asiatique in 1821 and its first president. Bonaparte made him a baron in 1814 and in 1832 under the monarchy he became a peer of France.[1]

A chrestomathy is an anthology of literary passages, usually for the use of students learning a foreign language, and this was exactly what de Sacy's *Chrestomathie arabe* was. He published this collection of extracts compiled from manuscripts in 1806, intending it to be used by students of the Ecole spéciale des langues orientales vivantes. In his introduction, he listed the few Arabic printed texts that it was possible to come by in Paris at the beginning of the nineteenth century: the proverbs of the pre-Islamic sage Luqman, the Qur'an, Ibn al-Muqaffa's *Kalila wa-Dimna* (a mirror for princes cast in the form of a collection of beast fables) and Ibn Arabshah's floridly overwritten life of Tamerlane. In the previous century, Reiske had argued that Arab poetry should be studied for its literary merits. De Sacy's emphasis was different, for he upheld the study of ancient Arabic poetry as useful source material on the early history of the Arabs and Arabic philology. (Like Reiske, de Sacy had to defend Arabic poetry from those who declared that there was no point at all in studying it.) Despite his unromantic approach to Arab poetry, de Sacy seems to have been the first European scholar to understand how Arab metre actually worked. He had strong views on Arabic prose. He disapproved of the disordered imagination and sloppy colloquialisms of *The Thousand and One Nights*. He also had a poor opinion of al-Hariri's *Maqamat* as fiction. The *Maqamat*, composed in the twelfth century, is a picaresquely episodic celebration of the erudite eloquence of a wily rogue and scrounger called Abu Zayd. Even educated Arabs resort to a commentary in order to understand what Abu Zayd is saying. However, the sheer difficulty of the grammar and vocabulary of al-Hariri's picaresque display of linguistic fireworks made it an eminently suitable text to inflict upon students and so de Sacy published the Arabic text together with a commentary in 1822.

In many ways his driest and most difficult work is also the most interesting. In his *Grammaire arabe* (1810, second edition 1831), he aimed, first, to set out the grammar of the Arabic language in what he judged to be the logical way and then in the way that the Arab grammarians used it. The two were, of course, quite different. The logic of his grammar was strongly influenced by the logic and grammar of Port Royal. The monastery of Port Royal, near Paris, produced two massively influential works, the *Grammaire générale et raisonnée de Port Royal* (1660) and *La Logique; ou, L'Art de penser* (1662). The Jansenist grammarians of Port Royal upheld the Cartesian view that the general features of grammatical structures are common to all languages – also a view that in modern times has been taken up by Noam Chomsky, in particular, in his *Cartesian Linguistics: A Chapter in the History of Rationalist Thought* (1966). The Port Royal grammarians believed in the isomorphism of language, thought and reality – that is to say that language mirrored thought and thought in turn mirrored reality. (I am reminded of a certain French general who is alleged to have remarked that 'It seems to me that French is the most perfect of all languages because its grammar exactly reflects the way I think.')

Logic apart, de Sacy was also obsessed with irregularities and rarities. In this he had much in common with the medieval Arab grammarians and lexicographers whom he studied with so much enthusiasm. In particular, the grammarians of ninth-century Kufa in Iraq interested themselves in irregularities and anomalies, in contradistinction to the grammarians of nearby Basra who preferred to stress the normative and regular features of the language. Medieval Arabic grammars were backward-looking texts, as their compilers did not seek to register the way Arabic was actually spoken or written in their own lifetimes, but rather they sought to deduce from linguistic lore how Arabic had been spoken at the time of the revelation of the Qur'an to the Prophet.[2] There was thus a striking parallel between the *nahw*, or 'way', of Arabic grammar and the *Sunna* or custom of the Prophet, that is to say the orally transmitted corpus of reports about his sayings and doings and those of his immediate companions. De Sacy intended that his grammar should replace Erpenius's *Grammatica Arabica* and in particular that the new grammar should break free from the Latinate structure that Erpenius had imposed upon Arabic grammar. To some extent de Sacy was successful and he was a pioneer in introducing Arabic technical terms into his grammar. Though the Göttingen Orientalist Heinrich Ewald later criticized the grammar for following Arab models too closely, a modern student of that grammar (if it is possible to envisage such a person) would probably be more struck by its Latinate approach. Besides his researches based on Arabic texts, de Sacy also published on the pre-Islamic antiquities of Persia, Persian grammar, the writings attributed to the Persian poet al-Attar, the decipherment of Egyptian hieroglyphics, a history of the kings of Mauritania and Samaritan texts. This was an age when the Orientalist was expected to spread himself rather widely.

Since de Sacy was a fervent Christian, it was more or less inevitable that he should regard Muhammad as a skilled impostor. However, de Sacy was less interested in mainstream Islam than he was in its various schismatic, secretive and sometimes subversive movements. Having lived through the horrors of the Jacobin terror, he projected his horror of revolutionary conspiracy backwards into the early history of Islam and presented the Druzes, the Isma'ilis and Nusayris as forerunners of such sinister modern movements as the Freemasons, Carbonari and Jacobins. In the introduction to his *Exposé de la religion des Druzes* (1838), he declared that he had been impelled to write this book by 'the desire that this portrait of one of the most notorious follies of the human spirit may serve to teach men who take pride in the superiority of their enlightenment what aberrations human reason is capable of when it is left to itself'. De Sacy's Druzes were atheistic revolutionaries who drew upon Shi'ite political fanaticism and a mixture of Greek and Persian philosophy. He found plenty in polemical Sunni Muslim sources to support his prejudices. He spent his whole career working on and off on the Druzes. (His views on Oriental secretive quasi-masonic fanatics were pretty similar to those of von Hammer-Purgstall (on whom see below).

De Sacy had strong views on other matters too. In the previous century Montesquieu had argued, on the basis of a fairly superficial knowledge of Oriental history and society, that in Oriental despotisms all the land belonged to the prince and there were no civil laws regarding property, or succession, or commerce, or rights of women. (As we have already seen, Dr Johnson had grumbled that Montesquieu was always able to dredge up the practices of some obscure and exotic culture in order to support whatever argument he wished to make.) Drawing upon the *Description de l'Egypte*, as well as the fifteenth-century Egyptian historian al-Maqrizi's topographical *Khitat*, Silvestre de Sacy produced a lengthy treatise on Egyptian land tenure specifically in order to refute Montesquieu. To take another issue, de Sacy's brief career in the Royal Court of Moneys had given him strong views on sound money. Here again he found support for his views in al-Maqrizi who, in his view, was a much sounder man than most financial theorists in contemporary Europe. De Sacy was pleased to discover that the Fatimid Egyptian caliphs, unlike some foolish modern governments, realized that the ratio of gold to silver must be variable. 'Doubtless one will note with pleasure that Maqrizi had ideas about true monetary principles which are more correct than many writers in our own century.'[3]

THE INTELLECTUAL LEGACY OF
SILVESTRE DE SACY

After the deaths of Schultens and Reiske, there were no Orientalists of first rank until the appearance of de Sacy, and by the time he died most of the remaining Orientalists of first rank had been trained by him. As Daniel Reig has remarked, with Silvestre de Sacy 'Orientalism . . . entered the libraries and at times even shut itself up in them'. But Reig also notes that Orientalism did not totally abandon the salons.[4] Indeed, despite de Sacy's ferocious scholarship and personal austerity, he did in fact frequent the salons, where he met Prosper Mérimée, Stendhal and Sainte-Beuve among others. De Sacy was a thoroughly political animal and hence his success in establishing chairs in Oriental studies and setting up learned panels, societies and journals. A large part of his achievement was in establishing Orientalist institutions that would survive him. Although he was hardly the first Orientalist (think of Postel, Pococke and Erpenius), it was de Sacy more than any other who created Orientalism as a sustained discipline with a regular flow of teachers, students, rituals of intellectual initiation and academic standards.

As has been noted, de Sacy was one of the founders of the Société Asiatique in 1821 and this was followed in 1823 by the first issue of the Société's *Journal Asiatique*. Substantially earlier, in 1784 William Jones had set up the Asiatick Society of Bengal and its attendant learned journal, *Asiatick Researches*. Britain's Royal Asiatic Society (1823) and its *Journal* drew its inspiration from Jones's institution. The American Oriental Society was founded in 1842 and the Deutsche Morgenländische Gesellschaft was established in 1845 (with its *Zeitschrift* starting to appear four years later). In the long run, these societies and periodicals would provide important support for institutional Orientalism.[5]

However, this was in the long run and the present chapter deals chiefly with individuals and the motives, passions and rivalries of those individuals. For a long time there was no cohesion in the world of the Orientalist. Their first Congress took place in Paris only in 1873. Moreover, in the nineteenth century the learned societies of Orientalists were not yet what they have since become, the adjuncts of academic Orientalism. They were largely the province of enthusiastic amateurs, often leisured aristocrats or clergymen. Throughout the nineteenth century the presidency of the Royal Asiatic Society was monopolized by earls, knights and right honourables. A fair number of maharajas and other Indian princes were also members.[6] The articles that appeared in the Orientalist journals were not systematically refereed (as is the rule nowadays). The bulk of the articles consisted of Oriental texts and sometimes their attempted decipherment or translation. There was little in the way of analysis or synthesis. The Orientalist societies, like most nineteenth-century societies, were male institutions; female Orientalists did not make their mark until the twentieth century.

At first relatively little space was devoted to Arab matters in the heavyweight Orientalist periodicals. The *Journal Asiatique*'s coverage was somewhat weighted towards the Far East. There were a lot of articles in the *Journal of the Royal Asiatic Society* about ancient cultures and such controversial matters as the decipherment of cuneiform. Also, since many of the contributors had served in India as administrators or soldiers, there were many articles about Sanskrit studies, Pali texts, early Indian Buddhism and so forth. If there was a connection between nineteenth-century imperialism and Orientalism, it was chiefly this – that imperial servants, lonely and bored in remote outposts, took up the study of exotic languages and histories as their hobby. William Muir, who wrote about the history of the caliphs, and Charles Lyall, who published marvellous editions and translations of pre-Islamic poetry, are only two of the most prominent examples of amateur scholars who first took up the study of early Arab culture while serving in India.[7]

The coverage of the *Zeitschrift der Deutschen Morgenländischen Gesellschaft* was also heavily weighted towards Indian matters. Although the Germans had no empire in India, they were fascinated by their Aryan origins, which they traced back to ancient India. Moreover, the heavy stress on philological studies in German universities fostered the study of Sanskrit and its links with other Indo-Aryan languages. The Indian Brahmans distinguished between Aryan and non-Aryan, equating this with civilized and non-civilized, and this theme was taken up in the first place by German Orientalists.[8] It is one of the threads that feeds into modern European racism. On the other hand, the study of India's ancient cultures by German and other Orientalists is part of the background to the 'Bengal renaissance' and, beyond that, to the rise of Indian nationalism, as ancient India's past was explored and lost classics of Sanskrit literature were rediscovered.[9]

It was inevitable that French Orientalism in the first half of the nineteenth century should be dominated by de Sacy's students. The most prominent of these was Etienne-Marc Quatremère (1782–1857). Like de Sacy, Quatremère was a Jansenist and like de Sacy he loathed the French Revolution. He had had an exciting, that is to say horrible, childhood, as after his father was executed by a revolutionary tribunal he and his mother had to go into hiding with peasants in the countryside. Like de Sacy, he was educated in the classics and largely self-taught in Hebrew. He fell under the master's spell at the Ecole spéciale des langues orientales vivantes and learned Arabic with him. He worked for a while in the Bibliothèque Impériale, before becoming Professor of Hebrew, Chaldaic and Syriac at the Collège de France in 1819. He was a hard worker with wide interests and, among other things, he worked on Phoenician, Pharaonic inscriptions, and Persian and Mamluk Egyptian history. As far as Mamluk history is concerned, he edited and translated part of al-Maqrizi's chronicle, the *Kitab al-Suluk*, under the title *Histoire des sultans mamlouks*, de l'Égypte, not because he had all that much interest in the history of Mamluk Egypt, but rather because he was fascinated by the vocabulary of fifteenth-century Arabic and particularly in those lexicographic nuggets that had not been defined in the standard Arabic dictionaries. As a consequence, his lexical footnotes ran on for page after page, often reducing the text they were supposed to be commenting on to two or three lines at the top of the page.

Like his teacher, Quatremère was a passionate philologist in an age when philology was thought of as one of the cutting-edge sciences. Nietzsche described philology as 'slow reading'. Nineteenth-century philologists believed that by correct application of their techniques they could not only discover lost languages but also reconstitute the ancient societies that had used those languages. Quatremère believed in close attention to philological detail and he did not allow himself to speculate or generalize about the materials that he studied. However, he sometimes found himself at odds with German philologists, when he perceived that their researches on the language of the Old Testament were leading to conclusions that threatened his fervently held Christian belief. The German Arabist Freytag accused him of wanting to reserve the whole field of Arabic studies to himself.[10]

One other publication of his is worth pausing on. That is his edition of the *Muqaddimah, Prolégomènes d'Ebn Khaldun: texte arabe* (1859). De Sacy had first discovered Ibn Khaldun and included extracts in his *Chrestomathie*. Subsequently, another of de Sacy's students, the Irish expatriate William MacGuckin, Baron de Slane (1801–78), translated the *Muqaddimah* into French. Among other things, de Slane used his translation to mount an onslaught on the scholarship of Quatremère. The Dutch Orientalist Reinhart Dozy suggested that the edition was the product of senility.[11] Franz Rosenthal, a twentieth-century Orientalist, who translated the *Muqaddimah* into (rather awkward) English, described Quatremère as 'a scholar of great merits but also, it seems, one who was at odds with his colleagues and with the world in general'.[12] He was erudite, austere, reclusive and, in general, the epitome of what most people then thought an Orientalist should be. As for the *Muqaddimah* itself, in this great work, the North African philosopher and historian Ibn Khaldun (1332–1406) set forth a philosophy of history based upon the cyclical rise and fall of dynasties. A new dynasty was brought to power by tribal armies held together by *'asabiyya* (roughly 'social solidarity'), but within a few generations that same dynasty, enfeebled by sedentarization and luxury, would be brought down by an invasion by fresh bands of vigorous nomads. Arnold Toynbee, in his *A Study of History*, described the *Muqaddimah* as 'undoubtedly the greatest work of its kind that has ever been created by any mind in any time or place' and there is more to Ibn Khaldun's encyclopedic philosophy of history than can even be hinted at here. What is important for our purposes is that, in the long run, Ibn Khaldun's ideas were to be immensely influential on the way Western Orientalists thought about North African history and about Islamic history more generally.[13] Aloys Sprenger, Alfred von Kremer, Carl Heinrich Becker, David Ayalon, Albert Hourani and Marshall Hodgson were strongly affected by him and Ibn Khaldun was not just read by historians. The philosopher and sociologist Ernest Gellner was also strongly influenced by Ibn Khaldun (too strongly, I would say).[14] Whether Ibn Khaldun's impact on Western thought was entirely benign is debatable.

THE GERMANS ARE COMING

In addition to the students mentioned above, de Sacy taught quite a number of other distinguished French scholars, including Champollion, Rémusat, Burnouf, Reinaud and Garcin de Tassy (another Jansenist). Even so, though de Sacy exercised an enormous influence on French Orientalism, his influence on parallel developments in Germany and Russia is even more striking, but before considering the achievements and publications of his German disciples, it is necessary first to turn to a contemporary Orientalist whose approach to Eastern texts was quite different. The Austrian Joseph Freiherr von Hammer-Purgstall (1774–1856) started out as a dragoman and interpreter in the Levant. He mastered, with varying degrees of competence, Turkish, Persian and Arabic. On his return to Europe he was employed by the Austrian Chancery and ennobled as a baron. From 1807 onwards, he settled in Vienna and produced a series of books, articles and translations on Oriental topics.[15] Though Hammer-Purgstall and de Sacy corresponded and co-operated on, among other things, the periodical known as both *Mines de l'Orient* and *Fundgruben des Orients* (Vienna, 1809–18), Hammer-Purgstall, unlike his French colleague, was a prolific and careless writer. He had no academic training and he was full of ideas and insights, many of which were not only wrong but also slightly mad. His main work was the ten-volume history of the Ottoman empire, *Geschichte des Osmanisches Reiches* (1827–35), which is not much more than an uncritical compilation of Turkish and Greek source material gutted and ordered approximately according to chronology, but such is the slow progress of Oriental studies that it still features in bibliographies today. He also wrote a history of Persian literature, *Geschichte der schönen Redekünste Persiens* (1818). His translations in that history as well as in numerous articles on Persian poets such as Hafiz of Shiraz and Jalal al-Din Rumi inspired both Goethe and Ralph Waldo Emerson – which is surprising, as Hammer-Purgstall's translations are clumsy and ugly. His Arabic seems to have been worse than his Persian and the twentieth-century Arabist, R. A. Nicholson, remarked of Hammer-Purgstall's rendering of a mystical poem by Ibn al-Farid that ' "translation" of a literary work usually implies that some attempt has been made to understand it, I prefer to say that Hammer rendered the poem into German rhymed verse by a method peculiar to himself, which appears to have consisted in picking out two or three words in each couplet and filling the void with any ideas which might strike his fancy'.[16] Hammer-Purgstall's enthusiasm for Oriental poetry and romance was limitless, but rather woolly.

Like Silvestre de Sacy, Hammer-Purgstall interested himself in Oriental sects and, like de Sacy, he was extremely conservative and nervous also about secret revolutionary conspiracies. Doubtless the paranoia of his master Metternich about international conspiracies also influenced him. Hammer-Purgstall went further than de Sacy in suggesting that sinister Western groups like the Illuminists, the Freemasons and the Rosicrucians had Oriental origins. In *The Mysteries of Baphomet Revealed* (1818), Hammer-Purgstall brought his Orientalist expertise to bear on the history of the Knights Templar and the trial and condemnation of the order at the beginning of the fourteenth century. On the basis of the records of trial proceedings, which had been rigged to bring in the verdict desired by the Templars' enemy, Philip IV of France, plus some rather dubious (i.e. fake) archaeological artefacts, Hammer-Purgstall concluded that the Knights Templar were indeed guilty as charged of heresy and blasphemy. They were apostates from Christianity who worshipped the demon

Baphomet. If this was not enough, they also worshipped the Grail, which was a Gnostic object of adoration. A skewed reading of Wolfram von Eschenbach's medieval epic poem, *Parzival*, provided evidence of this.[17]

In the same year that he sought to unmask the horrid heresy of the Templars, he also published *Geschichte der Assassinen* on the Assassins, or Hashishin sect, whom he presented as proto-Masons intent on conspiracy to subvert the world. His history of this sect was intended as a warning against 'the pernicious influence of secret societies . . . and . . . the dreadful prostitution of religion to the horrors of unbridled ambition'. The Assassins of Syria and Iran were the ancestors of Europe's subversives, the Illuminati: 'To believe nothing and to dare all was, in two words, the sum of this system, which annihilated every principle of religion and morality, and had no other object than to execute ambitious designs with suitable ministers, who daring all and knowing nothing, since they consider everything a cheat and nothing forbidden, are the best tools of an infernal policy. A system which, with no other aim than the gratification of an insatiable lust for domination, instead of seeking the highest of human objects, precipitates itself into the abyss, and mangling itself, is buried amidst the ruins of thrones and altars, the wreck of national happiness, and the universal execration of mankind.'[18]

Hammer-Purgstall's enthusiasm for Persian mystical poetry and his fantasies about sinister Oriental sects were both alike part of a Romantic reaction to the Enlightenment values of the late eighteenth century. Reason and science were at a discount among those who sought wisdom in the East and who dreamt of finding a lost wholeness situated in an ideal Oriental past. Hammer-Purgstall's researches greatly influenced Friedrich Rückert (1788–1866), the Romantic poet and professor whose extremely free translations of Arabic poetry and of the wisdom of the Brahmins are really part of the history of German literature rather than of the serious study of the Orient.[19]

Heinrich Leberecht Fleischer (1801–88) was not a Romantic. After studying theology in Leipzig, he went to Paris in 1824 to study with de Sacy. Fleischer was in Dresden and then Leipzig from 1835 to 1888 where he taught Arabic, Persian and Turkish. He edited two of the great medieval commentators on the Qur'an, al-Zamakhshari and al-Baydawi. (These sorts of scholarly undertakings may seem dull to the modern eye, but such critical editions of key works were the necessary basis for a more profound understanding of Islam.) He was also the leading figure behind the founding of the Deutsche Morgen-ländische Gesellschaft. De Sacy taught quite a number of other German Orientalists, including Freytag, Ahlwardt, Habicht, Gustav Weil, Kosegarten, Gustav Flügel, Franz Bopp, Eichhorn and Mohl, but Fleischer was his most important pupil, becoming, after de Sacy, the teacher of the next generation of Orientalists, including Caspari, Dietrici, Goldziher, Hartmann, Sachau, Rosen and others. Both the content and the style of Fleischer's teaching were modelled on that of de Sacy, as Fleischer was a grammatical positivist with a narrow philological approach.[20]

The dominance of Germans in Orientalism in the nineteenth and early twentieth centuries was due in part to the large number of universities in Germany. In the opening decades of the nineteenth century every German prince seems to have felt the need to have a university and those who decided to have an Oriental chair usually sent their candidates to de Sacy to be trained. (Heinrich Ewald was the only important Arabist of his generation not trained by de Sacy and Ewald was primarily a Hebraist.) The Lutheran University of Göttingen (founded in 1734) enjoyed a particular prestige and it was there that members of the Protestant nobility tended to study. (Some of those Protestants were English, Dutch and Scandinavian.) Göttingen's approach to the classics was particularly important in shaping the intellectual map of Europe in this century. Hitherto Latin and Greek authors had been studied in order to imitate their style alone. Rote-learning played an important part in this process. However, classicists at Göttingen now began to concentrate on the content and the under-lying philosophy of the texts they studied.[21]

Biblical studies and classical studies were the dominant intellectual discourses of the nineteenth century and there was a considerable overlap between the two. As has been noted, the great theologian and biblical expert, Michaelis, had presided at Göttingen in the late eighteenth century and it was his enquiries that had inspired the Danish expedition to the Middle East. He was also the teacher of

Johann Gottfried Eichhorn (1752–1827) and Friedrich August Wolf (1759–1824). From 1788 onwards Eichhorn held the Chair of Oriental Studies at Göttingen and did important work on, among other things, the pre-Islamic Arabian kingdoms of Ghassan and Hira. However, his main work was in biblical studies and his *Einleitung im Alte Testament* ('Introduction to the Old Testament') was one of the most important documents of the age. Samuel Taylor Coleridge, who plagiarized so many German thinkers without acknowledgement, pillaged Eichhorn. Eichhorn had speculated about a primitive Oriental mentality and suggested that, though the Book of Genesis was not literally true, it mythologized events that had actually happened.[22] The classicist Friedrich August Wolf, who taught at Halle and then Berlin, was in turn inspired by Eichhorn's *Einleitung*, whose methodology he applied to Greek texts. In *Prolegomena ad Homerum* (1795) Wolf demonstrated that the textual unity of both the *Iliad* and the *Odyssey* was illusory and he set out a methodology for detecting the various strata of their composition by various hands over the centuries. Wolf was perhaps the leading figure in a generation of classicists who sought to place the texts they studied in a wider historical and cultural context.[23] Although Göttingen was the pre-eminent centre for state-of-the-art research in nineteenth-century Europe, Tübingen, with its vast theological faculty, was hardly less important and it was there that David Friedrich Strauss (1808–74) did the research that led on to his scandalous *Das Leben Jesu* (1835), a biography that was based on a destructively critical analysis of the Gospels. Of course, such investigations by Eichhorn, Wolf and others had no direct relevance to the study of the Qur'an and the early history of Islam, but in the long run it was inevitable that scholars who had cut their teeth on source-critical techniques, as applied to the Bible or Greek and Latin texts, should think of applying those same techniques to early Arabic materials.

A key feature of the century was the emancipation of the Jews in Germany, Britain and elsewhere and their consequent entry into the universities. Already by the 1840s a striking number of professors in Germany were Jewish, as Disraeli had noted in his novel, *Coningsby*. Jewish scholars played an important role in pioneering critical approaches to Islam and the Qur'an – approaches that surely owed something to the rabbinic and Talmudic education that so many of them had received. Abraham Geiger (1810–74) had had a Talmudic education before studying in Bonn with Wilhem Freytag (one of de Sacy's disciples). In 1833, while still a young man, Geiger had published a prize-winning essay, *Was hat Muhammed aus dem Judentum aufgenommen?* ('What did Muhammad adopt from Judaism?'), in which Geiger sought to identify those elements in the Qur'an that he thought the Prophet had deliberately borrowed from the Jews. Though the essay was enormously influential for later critical approaches to Islam, Geiger was not so very interested in Arabic sources and after doing some work on Muslim Spain, he returned to his main interest, Jewish studies.[24]

Gustav Weil (1808–89) started out in rabbinic studies, before studying Arabic in Heidelberg and then going on to Paris in 1830 to study with de Sacy. Weil also travelled in Egypt and Istanbul. This industrious, if somewhat dull, scholar wrote the standard life of the Prophet, as well as a history of the caliphate in five volumes (1846–62). Weil seems to have been innocent of the advanced critical techniques being used by scholars in parallel fields. His historiographical technique hardly amounted to more than translating or condensing extracts from medieval Arab chronicles and sticking them together in chronological order with little, if anything, in the way of interpretation or analysis. In particular, he relied heavily on manuscripts of al-Tabari, a tenth-century chronicler who is one of the standard sources on the early history of Islam and the caliphate. Inevitably, Weil found much to criticize in Hammer-Purgstall's romantic fantasies.[25]

If al-Tabari was his source, Leopold von Ranke's *Die römische Päpste im 16. und 17. Jahrhundert* (1834–6) was the model for Weil's fact-driven, dry-as-dust mode of proceeding. Ranke (1795–1886), who taught in Berlin, sought to present history 'as it really happened'. (These days such an ambition seems remarkably naive.) His approach was anti-Romantic and based on research on primary sources, backed up by footnotes. He used philological expertise to expose forged documents. Although Ranke, a staggeringly prolific scholar whose collected works consist of fifty-four volumes, presented himself as an objective scholar just seeking to understand what it was that his sources had to tell him, nevertheless he had an overall vision of history that amounted to a shaping agenda. History had a mysterious divine purpose and it was the task of the historian to uncover that purpose. God made use of races and civilizations as his instruments and then discarded them. During the Middle Ages, Islamic civilization had served the divine will but, having been defeated by the Latin and Roman peoples, that civilization became a dead thing and was to be studied as such. Islam had served its purpose. It had preserved monotheism, it had transmitted the classical heritage to Europe, and finally it was the entity against which Europe had defined itself. (It would seem Ranke was the first to think of Islam as the 'Other' in this way.) However, having fulfilled these useful functions, Islamic culture was unable to break free from the bonds of the Middle Ages. World history was for Ranke and many who came after him the story of the triumph of the West.[26]

Elsewhere in Germany other industrious Germans did the dull but necessary groundwork of editing and publishing the Arabic sources. For example, Gustav Leberecht Flugel edited Hajji Khalifa's great catalogue of some 14,500 Arabic, Persian and Turkish writings, as well as Ibn al-Nadim's tenth-century listing of works in Arabic, the *Fihrist*.[27] As has been noted, it was also the Germans rather than the British who dominated Indian and Sanskrit studies and these Germans tended to argue for the superiority of Indo-Aryan cultures over those of the Semites. Friedrich von Schlegel's *Über die Sprache und Weisheit der Indien* (1808) argued for the superiority of Sanskrit-based languages over Arabic. His brother August Wilhelm von Schlegel was similarly keen on Indian and Sanskrit: 'Everything, yes, everything without exception has its origin in India.'[28] Accordingly, August Wilhelm argued that *The Arabian Nights* had their ultimate origin in India. (De Sacy had erroneously believed the origin of these stories was purely Arab.) The first Sanskrit grammars were compiled by German and Austrian missionaries and Germany's first chair of Sanskrit was established in 1818 (for August Wilhelm von Schlegel at Bonn), whereas Britain acquired one only in 1833. The engagement of the Schlegel brothers with Indian culture was in large part romantic, but de Sacy's student, Franz Bopp, put things on a more scientific basis with his comparative grammar of the Indo-Germanic languages, the *Vergleichende Grammatik des Sanskrit, Zend Griechischen,*

Lateinischen, Litthausischen Gothischen und Deutschen (1833). In it he made a systematic comparison of the conjugational systems used in those languages. Prior to the nineteenth century, philology had been a branch of rhetoric, but Bopp established the principles for the historical study of languages.[29] The idea that Sanskrit culture might be older than Hebrew culture was a shocking and exciting one.

Continental scholars also led the way in Chinese studies and the great collection of Chinese texts was in Paris's Bibliothèque Nationale, but increasingly Germans competed with French scholars in this field. Though the British had many commercial interests in China – the sale of opium among them – this did not lead to any corresponding explosion of interest in Chinese studies in Britain. When Thomas Wade was appointed to a Chair of Chinese in Cambridge in 1888, he declared that 'I assume that my pupils, should I have any, will be intending missionaries or interpreters . . . My advice to applicants in either category is that they should make their way to China with all speed.'[30] When, in the following century, Arthur Waley, self-taught in Chinese and a great translator of its poetry, was offered the Cambridge Chair, his response was 'I would rather be dead'.[31]

RUSSIA, OR ASIA IN EUROPE

Outside Germany, de Sacy's chief intellectual legacy was in Russia. Here he regularly advised the Russian Tsar about whom to appoint to Orientalist teaching posts. The first Oriental Institute in Russia was set up by de Sacy's students in St Petersburg. His students also found employment in the Ministry of External Affairs. Many of de Sacy's intellectual missionaries were German and perhaps the most important of these was the Persianist Bernhard Dorn, who taught Afghan and Caucasian studies, Islamic numismatics and other subjects. Dorn also catalogued the manuscripts of Mount Sinai.[32] In 1804 Tsar Alexander I issued a directive calling for the teaching of the languages of the Bible and the Orient. In 1807 a professorship of Asiatic studies was established in Kazan, which became the main centre for Oriental studies in the empire. In 1818 an Asiatic Museum opened in St Petersburg under the supervision of the German

Orientalist, Christian Martin Frähn (1782–1851), the real founder of Middle East scholarship in Russia, who had started teaching in Kazan and then moved to St Petersburg. He was assisted at the Asiatic Museum by two French students of de Sacy. He pioneered the study of Arabic sources on the history of medieval Russia.[33] Interest in Oriental and Islamic subject-matter increased as the Russians expanded in the Black Sea and the Caucasus regions at the expense of Turkey and Persia. In the late 1820s the Muslim tribesmen of Chechnya and Daghestan launched a holy war against the Russian empire – a war that found various echoes in the literature of the period.

The dominance of German scholarship in Russian universities caused some resentment in Orthodox, anti-rational and Europhobe circles. However, it would be a mistake to think of nineteenth-century Orientalism as being monopolized by Western scholars. In Russia in particular this was not the case. Quite a number of Persians, Afghans, Turks and others taught at the University of Kazan and elsewhere in the Russian empire. For example, Mirza Kazem-Beg taught Arabic and Persian and Islamic history at the University of Kazan before becoming Professor of Persian in St Petersburg. Shaykh Muhammad 'Ayyad al-Tantawi (1810–61) was headhunted from his teaching post at Cairo's al-Azhar, where he had already taught Weil, Edward William Lane and other Westerners who wanted to learn Arabic. He arrived in Russia in 1840 and became Professor of Arabic at St Petersburg. He used traditional Azhari teaching techniques, which relied heavily on rote-learning and on the transmission of the opinions of earlier generations of scholars, something that many of his students found hard-going.[34] In the next generation, Baron Viktor Romanovich Rosen (1849–1908), the son of a Baltic aristocrat from Tallinn and a student of the philologically meticulous Fleischer, dominated the study of Arab culture in Russia pioneering modern techniques of textual analysis. He was an enthusiast for and expert on the eleventh-century poet al-Ma'arri. He studied early Arabic accounts of Russia. He denounced Eurocentric ways of looking at world history. Kratchkovsky (on whom much more later) was his pupil and described him as 'always lively'.[35]

THE BRITISH EMPIRE: MANY MUSLIM SUBJECTS, BUT FEW ORIENTALISTS

De Sacy had students who went on to distinguished careers elsewhere in Europe, among them the Spaniard Pascual de Gayangos and the Swede Johann Tornberg. The Irish Arabist de Slane apart (and de Slane settled in Paris), de Sacy had no British students of note. British university life, in so far as there was a university life at all, was dominated by biblical studies and the classics. Classical studies, in particular, thrived. From the late eighteenth century onwards there was a revival of interest in Greek and Roman culture, fostered in part by the Romantic enthusiasm for the Greek revolt against the Turks, by the Romantic cult of ruins and the mid-eighteenth-century discovery of the ruins of Pompeii, and, above all, by the growing importance of the public schools (in American terms, expensive private schools) and the stress that those schools placed upon study of the classics as character-building. As Richard Jenkyns has pointed out, authors such as Cardinal Newman (*Apologia pro Vita Sua*), Thomas Hughes (*Tom Brown's Schooldays*) and Thomas Hardy (*Jude the Obscure*) could use Greek type in their texts in the confident expectation that their readers, mostly public-school-educated, would be able to read it.[36] Greek and Latin trained the mind and made good citizens and a detailed knowledge of the history of the Roman empire shaped the thoughts of the rulers of the British Raj.

In the late eighteenth and early nineteenth centuries the prevailing ethos of government in British India was quite different from what it later became. In *White Mughals: Love and Betrayal in Eighteenth-Century India*, William Dalrymple has noted that the British then 'inhabited a world that was far more hybrid, and with far less clearly defined ethnic, national and religious borders, than we have been conditioned to expect . . . It was as if this early promiscuous mingling of races and ideas, modes of dress and ways of living, was something that was on no one's agenda and suited nobody's version of events.'[37] The word 'Orientalist', in the sense of one versed in Oriental languages and literatures, entered the English language as early as 1779. (The French equivalent appeared twenty years later.) In the eighteenth and nineteenth centuries 'the Orient' tended to refer to the Near East and Ottoman North Africa, rather than Asia more generally. In India, however, 'Orientalist' had, for a while, quite a specialized sense, as it referred to a Briton who not only studied Indian culture, but also advocated governing in India in accordance with local laws and customs.[38] Warren Hastings, the first governor-general of India and the patron of the Asiatick Society of Bengal, was the grandest proponent of such an approach. Hastings hired Brahmin pundits to codify Hindu law and he encouraged his subordinates to study Islamic law. From 1772 until approximately 1830, 'Orientalists' dominated the government of India. The founding in 1800 of the College of Fort William in Calcutta was one fruit of their policies. The College not only taught Greek and Latin, but also Arabic, Persian, Sanskrit, Urdu, Hindi and Bengali. Most of the teaching was done by *munshis* (native language teachers).[39] Fort William also published some texts in Arabic, including in 1814–18 an important edition of *The Thousand and One Nights* (known to specialists in the field as Calcutta I). Later, after Fort William had closed, Sir William Hay Macnaghten, the greatest linguist ever produced by the College, published a second edition. Both editions, with their colourful stories of magic, adultery and treasure hunting, had been produced as texts to be studied by administrators seeking to improve their Arabic.[40] However, the College was more interested in Persian and the Indian languages (and Persian was Macnaghten's real speciality). Persian was the language of the princely courts and administration, but Arabic was necessary for the study of Persian. Many of the key texts in Islamic law were also in Arabic, but even so not many people studied it.

More generally, the enthusiasm of British officers and administrators was part of the background to the Bengal renaissance and to the increased interest of Hindus in finding out about their own past. Fort William ceased teaching in 1830. Its closure was part of a fairly widespread reaction against British Indian 'Orientalism'. This reaction was spearheaded by an alliance of Evangelicals and Utilitarians in the home country. 'Orientalists' had opposed and resisted missionary activity in India and this was resented by the Evangelicals. In 1817 the Utilitarian thinker James Mill published a three-volume *History of British India*, in which he comprehensively disparaged Oriental culture. That culture was, he believed, the product of despotism, superstition and poverty and there was no point in pretending that Europe could learn anything from it.[41] The same sort of point was made with misconceived eloquence by the statesman and man of letters, Lord Macaulay. In a minute on education in India, written in 1835, he claimed to have talked to Orientalists, but 'I have never found one among them who could deny that a single shelf of a good European library was worth the whole native literature of India and Arabia'. Or, as he also put it, 'all the historical information which has been collected in the Sanskrit language is less valuable than what may be found in the paltry abridgements used at preparatory schools in England'.[42] Mill had never been out to India and neither he nor Macaulay had actually troubled to learn Sanskrit. Both were convinced that the Indians' only hope was to learn modern, Western ways. In this new environment, Fort William's teaching programme was obviously an unnecessary expense. Macaulay powerfully urged that Greek and Latin should be at the heart of the East India Company exams. The content of the classics as such was less important than the well mapped-out techniques of intellectual training that were part of the classical formation: 'If, instead of learning Greek, we learned the Cherokee, the man who understood the Cherokee best ... would generally be a superior man to him who was destitute of these accomplishments.'[43]

Macaulay and his allies had their way and, later in the century, Sir Richard Burton was to complain, in the introduction to his translation of *The Arabian Nights*, that 'England has forgotten, apparently, that she is at present the greatest Mohammedan empire in the world, and in her Civil Service examinations she insists on a smattering of Greek and Latin, rather than a knowledge of Arabic.' In 1850, the distinguished scholar of Sanskrit and Persian, Edward Byles Cowell (1826–1903), made a similar point: 'England, in spite of her vast opportunities, has done least for Oriental literature of the learned nations of Europe; France and Germany have in every department (except Lexicography, where Wilson stands unrivalled) left her far behind; and this reflection is truly humiliating when one visits the Library of East India House and sees the stores of Oriental lore, which lie on their shelves, unread and almost unknown. German scholars come over to London and study the MSS., to correct their own editions; but hardly a solitary English scholar can be found to avail himself of the treasures which his countrymen have brought from the East almost to his very door.' (The Wilson in question, Horace Hayman Wilson, compiled a Sanskrit–English dictionary.)[44] Cowell, who as a fifteen-year-old had discovered Sir William Jones's *Poesae Asiaticae Commentarii*, a commentary on Persian and Arabic poetry, then sought tuition in Persian from a retired Indian Army officer and later taught himself and his wife Sanskrit. (He wanted to have something to talk to her about over the breakfast table.) In 1867 he became the first to occupy Cambridge's newly established Chair of Sanskrit. Despite his status as a Sanskritologist, he kept a watching brief over Persian studies and he was the friend of the eminent Persianists, including Palmer and Browne and Edward Fitz-Gerald.[45] It was a manuscript of Cowell's that furnished the source for FitzGerald's fine, if very free, version of *The Rubáiyát of Omar Khayyám*.

Sir William Muir (1819–1905) was one of the few prominent Arabists or Islamicists that British India produced. (Sir Charles Lyall, the other great example, will be discussed in the next chapter.) Muir had had a distinguished career in the Indian administration where he played a leading role in the struggle against female infanticide and rose to become Lieutenant Governor of the North-West Frontier Province, before turning to academic matters and becoming Principal of Edinburgh University. Although he spent much of his life studying Islam, he hated the subject. In part, his horror of Islam may have been influenced by his experience of the Indian Mutiny. Despite his fervent Christianity, *The Caliphate, its rise, decline and fall* (1891) may also have been influenced by Gibbon's account of the decline and fall of the Roman empire. The caliphate was in the end brought low by barbarism and superstition, though in Muir's book both the barbarism and the superstition were Muslim. Muir denounced the Prophet as both a servant of the Devil and an epileptic. Any Hadiths that showed the Prophet in a bad light were bound to be true: those that portrayed him more favourably were dubious. Although Muir listed some of the key Arabic sources for the medieval period, it is not clear how many of these he cited directly from the Arabic. He was comfortable in

German, and he relied heavily on Weil's earlier history of the caliphate. This meant that, when Muir was not engaged in anti-Islamic polemical rant, his history was pretty dull. He also translated the medieval Christian al-Kindi's anti-Islamic polemic, the *Apology*, and in 1887 the Religious Tract Society published his fervently Christian *The Rise and Decline of Islam*.[46] Missionaries in India were still having recourse to these works in the twentieth century.

LANE'S ETHNOGRAPHY OF EGYPT

Muir acquired his expertise in Arabic and knowledge of Islam outside the universities. The same was true of Edward William Lane (1801–76), who trained as a metal-engraver. Early on in life, however, he developed a passion for ancient Egypt, possibly inspired by seeing a presentation by Giovanni Battista Belzoni, the fairground strong man turned Egyptologist. He was twenty-four when he first caught sight of the Alexandrian monument known as Pompey's Pillar: 'It seemed as if it rose from the sea; for neither the city nor the hills in its neighbourhood could yet be discerned. Soon afterwards we saw the tops of two lofty hills of rubbish, each crowned with a fort; and next we distinguished the vessels in the Old Harbour, intercepting almost entirely the view of the town, which lies upon a low flat site.'[47]

Lane had of course seen the great French *Description de l'Egypte* and admired it, though with increasing reservations, as he travelled throughout Egypt and began to reckon up the vast number of errors and misrepresentations. As far as the essay on contemporary Egyptian customs was concerned, he thought it was based on too much philosophy and not enough observation. His first ambition was to publish a survey of Egypt that concentrated on the antiquities and which would establish his reputation as an Egyptologist.

He believed that he had an undertaking from a famous London publisher, John Murray, to publish this mighty project. However Murray, who had also taken on a survey of Egyptian antiquities by John Gardner Wilkinson, delayed and prevaricated and as part of the strategy of delay suggested that Lane turn one of his chapters that was devoted to contemporary Egypt into a whole book. As a consequence Wilkinson, the author of *Topography of Thebes, and General View of Egypt* (1835) and *Manners and Customs of the Ancient Egyptians* (1837), faced no challenge from Lane, who went on to produce further studies of the Arabs and Arabic.

Thus Lane's *Manners and Customs of the Modern Egyptians* (1836) was a by-blow of his original ambition to make a visual and literary record of what remained of ancient Egypt. *Manners and Customs* dealt with strictly contemporary matters and Lane took as his model Alexander Russell's *The Natural History of Aleppo* and, in particular, the second chapter where Russell had discussed such matters as population, language, dress, consumption of coffee and tobacco, eating habits, religious ceremonies, family life, story-telling, entertainments and funerary rites. Lane thought that Russell had devoted too much space to the manners and customs of the ruling Turkish elite and not enough to those of the Arabs. (Lane levelled a similar criticism against the French survey.) He became well acquainted with the Arabs and their manner of life in Cairo. He lived near the Bab al-Hadid in old Cairo and dressed as a Turk – that is, as a member of Egypt's ruling caste. Outside Cairo and Alexandria foreigners who travelled about in Western clothes were liable to attract ridicule and even stoning. He studied Arabic with, among others, al-Tantawi, the shaykh who eventually went off to teach in Russia. Lane's book, which was written for a general readership, was published by the Society for the Diffusion of Useful Knowledge, an organization which aimed its publications 'to all classes of the community, particularly to such as are unable to avail themselves of experienced teachers, or may prefer learning by themselves'. Lane's book sold well and was often reprinted. British academics (and as we shall see there were hardly any of these in Arabic studies) were not interested in modern Egypt. Only in the twentieth century did academics turn to Lane's book as an important source on 'modern Egyptians'.

Since *Manners and Customs* had sold well, Lane was encouraged to go on to produce his translation of *The Thousand and One Nights, commonly called the Arabian Nights' Entertainments* (1838–41). He thought of this as an educational project. In his preface to *Manners and Customs*, he had already remarked of *The Arabian Nights* that it 'presents most admirable pictures of the manners and customs of the Arabs and particularly those of the Egyptians' and that 'if the English reader had possessed a close translation of it with sufficient illustrative notes, I might almost have spared myself the present undertaking'. This then was what Lane now set out to do. While his Victorian readers read eagerly of enchanted caliphs, princesses, jinns, sorcerers and mysteriously abandoned cities, he was busy in efforts to distract them with barrages of annotations on Muslim ablutions, circumcision rituals, the use of henna, the etymology of obscure Arabic words and so forth.[48] The Bulaq Press, established in 1822, was the Arab world's first printing press and in 1835 it had published one of the earliest printed versions of the *Nights*.[49] It was more or less inevitable that this should be the version that Lane translated, as he regularly frequented the Press and had become a friend of Ibrahim al-Dasuqi, who taught in that part of Cairo. Additionally, he relied heavily on advice from 'the first philologist of the first Arab college of the present day [al-Azhar]', al-Tantawi. In the nineteenth century, it was common for Orientalists to work in close collaboration with Arab, Turkish and Persian scholars. Similarly, when Burton produced his later translation of the *Nights*, he relied heavily on the advice of his friend, Yacoub Artin Pasha.

From 1842 onwards, Lane was engaged on his grandest project yet, as he started to compile his *Arabic–English Lexicon*.[50] His chief, but by no means only, source was the vast eighteenth-century dictionary of classical Arabic, the *Taj al-'Arus* ('Crown of the Bride'), but he supplemented its information with that from other equally vast medieval dictionaries and read widely in the literature, in order to furnish the lexical entries with illustrations of usage. Al-Dasuqi was employed to find the necessary manuscripts on which the dictionary was to be based. Lane became so engrossed in this monumental task that the only recreation he took was to spend half an hour walking on his roof at sunset. In 1848 ill-health obliged him to return to England, but he continued to work on the dictionary and he used to complain that he had become so used to the cursive calligraphy of his Arabic manuscripts that he found Western print a great strain on his eyes. By 1876, the year of his death, Lane had reached *fa*, the twentieth letter of the twenty-eight-letter alphabet. Although Lane had received an honorary degree from Leiden in the previous year, he had spent his life researching and publishing outside the university system. To this day his great dictionary remains incomplete. There were no other British Arabists or Islamists of note in the early to mid-nineteenth century. Things started to change only later in the century with the appointment of William Wright and David Samuel Margoliouth to professorships in Cambridge and Oxford respectively.

TWO OF SAID'S ORIENTALIST ARCHVILLAINS

Ernest Renan (1823–92) is the central figure, the paradigmatic Orientalist and racist in Edward Said's book, and as such he has more pages devoted to him than de Sacy, Louis Massignon or Bernard Lewis.[51] Renan studied for the priesthood at the Seminary of Saint-Sulpice, but in 1845 he experienced a philologically based crisis of faith and renounced Catholicism. In 1843 he had started to study Hebrew and he later widened his range to include Syriac and Arabic. Renan's teacher of Arabic at Saint-Sulpice was the biblical scholar, M. Le Hir, and Renan was later to explain that his own grasp of Arabic was so bad because his teacher's had been similarly bad. Later Renan studied various subjects with students of Silvestre de Sacy and (perhaps because of this?) he came to loathe all that de Sacy stood for. Renan judged him to be 'the typical orthodox scholar ... but if one looks further, one sees the strange spectacle of a man, who, though he possesses one of the vastest eruditions of modern times, has never had an important critical insight'. More generally he had a disparaging opinion of earlier French Orientalists, especially by comparison with the learned Germans: 'quelles misères et songez à ce qui se passait alors en Allemagne'. Moreover Renan's temperament was more romantic, speculative and slapdash than that of de Sacy.

If Renan is going to be considered as a serious Arabist, then we must turn to his second published thesis. Having first in 1852 written a thesis in Latin, *De Philosophia Peripatetico apud Syros* ('On the Peripatetic Philosophy Among the Syrians'), he went on in that same year to defend a thesis on *Averroès et l'averroïsme* and to publish it in edited form in 1861. This was a study of the famous twelfth-century philosopher Ibn Rushd or Averroes and the impact of his ideas about the immortality of the soul and the double truth on medieval Western scholastics. The most striking feature of the published version is that, almost without exception, Renan preferred inaccurate translations of Ibn Rushd into Latin to using original Arabic texts. The suspicion must be that Renan's Arabic was not up to it. His book is less a serious study of Islamic philosophy and more a fable about the rise of rationalism in the West. Arabists who later worked on Averroes found Renan's view that the Muslim philosopher was a secret atheist to be unfounded. Goldziher was swift to point out that Renan had failed to use two absolutely essential sources: al-Ghazali's pietistic attack on the philosophy of Avicenna and Averroes's response to al-Ghazali.[52]

By contrast, Renan's Hebrew was quite good. Renan had been impressed by work being done on Sanskrit and on the Indo-Aryan family of languages and, in particular, the German Sanskritologist Franz Bopp's comparative grammar of the Indo-Germanic or Indo-Aryan languages, the *Vergleichende Grammatik des Sanskrit, Zend Griechischen, Lateinischen, Litthausischen Gothischen und Deutschen* (1833). Renan considered the possible influence of language on the Semitic character in *Nouvelles Considérations sur le caractère général des peuples sémitiques* (1859). The *Histoire générale et système comparé des langues sémitiques* (1863) was Renan's attempt to do for the Semitic languages what Bopp had done for the Indo-Aryan ones. However, Renan had wide interests and in the years to come he wrote about the future of research, the decadence of democracy, the Apostles, Breton folklore, Marcus Aurelius, contemporary morality, the origins of Christianity, Greece, Berbers, the history of Israel, the morale of the French nation after the Franco-Prussian War and childhood memories. He was above all a recycler of *idées reçues*. He also wrote low-grade novels. He was much in demand as a stylish journalist and general pundit. He became a familiar of the salons, though not necessarily a particularly stylish familiar. The Goncourt brothers described him as 'short and podgy, badly built with a calf's head covered with the callosities of a monkey's rump'.[53]

In 1861 he was promoted to the Chair of Hebrew at the Collège de

France, but he was suspended after his inaugural lecture in which he controversially referred to Jesus as 'un homme incomparable' (the implication being that he was indeed a man and not God). He went on to confirm his status as a dangerous atheistic thinker by publishing *Vie de Jésus* (1863), a scandalous bestseller that stripped away all that was supernatural in the traditional story of Jesus. Renan suggested that Jesus's success in propagating his teaching was largely due to the fact that it was well adapted to the religious feelings of the Semites. Renan held that philology and specifically the philological study of the Indo-Aryan and Semitic languages had established the common origins of whites, but not that of Chinese or blacks. The Semites, like the Aryans, had played a role in the great project of civilization, though their time was now past. Renan's racism merely put a pompous pseudo-scientific gloss on ideas that already circulated in the street. People did not need to have Orientalists invent racism for them.

He believed that, unlike the other great world religions, 'Islam was born in the full light of history'. (As we shall see, this belief was to be seriously challenged in the second half of the twentieth century.) He took a fairly favourable view of the Prophet: 'On the whole, Muhammad seems to us like a gentleman, sensitive, faithful, free from rancour and hatred. His affections were sincere: his character was inclined to kindness.'[54] Renan believed that Islam had since become an intellectual and spiritual prison and he thought it would not survive the twentieth century, as it was doomed to wither away in the face of scientific progress. This was in accord with his Comtean belief that humanity was destined to advance from superstition to metaphysics and then ultimately to positive scientific knowledge. The Semites had played their part in world history by introducing monotheism, but with that their task was over and the rest of the story would consist of the triumph of science and rationalism, which was also the triumph of the West. At first he had taken a tolerably favourable view of Islam and it was only after a couple of visits to the Middle East in 1860 and 1865 that he adopted the position that Islam was acting as a brake on progress in the region: 'The Muslims are the first victims of Islam.' In *L'Islamisme et la Science* he put forward the view that Islam and science were intrinsically inimical (and, though he obviously did not spell it out, Catholicism and science were incompatible too). This thesis was attacked, though in moderate terms, by a leading Muslim thinker and political agitator, Jamal al-Din al-Afghani. Al-Afghani believed that the Middle East had to catch up but that it would. The Islamic world had yet to experience its Reformation.[55]

Renan's other critics were Orientalists. Ignaz Goldziher, the commanding figure in Arabic and Islamic scholarship in the late nineteenth and early twentieth centuries, was particularly savage in his criticism of Renan.[56] In his 'Mahomet et les origines de l'Islam' (*Revue des Deux Mondes*, 15 December 1851) Renan had generalized madly and ignorantly about the absolute lack of the supernatural in the teachings of the 'philosopher' Muhammad. The Semitic soul was, Renan thought, inherently monotheist and hostile to all kinds of mythology: 'The desert itself is monotheist.' Though Goldziher, who had done serious research on the mythology of the early Semites, demonstrated that this was nonsense, Renan refused to answer those criticisms or even to acknowledge his existence. However other Orientalists, including Heinrich Ewald, William Robertson Smith and Max Müller, criticized him on this issue. Henri Lammens attacked the quality of his Arabic and Michael Jan de Goeje ripped into Renan in an important speech at the 1883 Leiden Conference of Orientalists.

Renan's original teacher, Le Hir, had been steeped in specifically German biblical textual techniques. Throughout Renan's career, he would revere German scholarship: 'I studied Germany and believed myself to have entered a temple.' It was after all among the Germans that the major advances were being made in the study of Sanskrit and related languages. In 1870, the year of the Franco-Prussian War, he told the Goncourt brothers that it was not surprising that the Germans had won the war: 'Yes, gentlemen, the Germans are a superior race.'[57] His enthusiasm for German scholarship and Germans in general, as well as his perceptions of the limitations of the Semitic mentality, were shared by his friend, Gobineau.

Count Joseph-Arthur de Gobineau (1816–82) developed Renan's ideas about the distinction between Semites and Aryans and shared Renan's view that the Germans were superior to the French. Some of the influence ran the other way, as Gobineau's ideas had some influence on Renan, though many of Gobineau's ideas were far too bizarre for Renan to swallow. Gobineau had pursued a military and then a diplomatic career, in tandem with that of a novelist. In 1849 he became the *chef du cabinet* of the Foreign Minister, Alexis de Tocqueville (also famous as a political theorist). From 1855 to 1858 and from 1861 to 1863 he was in Tehran successively as First Secretary, Chargé d'affaires and Minister. Drawing on the sojourns in Persia, he produced *Mémoire sur l'état social de la Perse actuelle* (1856), *Trois Ans en Asie* (1859), *Les Religions et les Philosophies dans l'Asie Centrale* (1865) and the *Histoire des Perses* (1869).[58]

In so far as Gobineau is studied today, it is as a racial theorist and as an influence on the racial thinking of Houston Chamberlain, Alfred Rosenberg and Adolf Hitler. Gobineau's *Essai sur l'inégalité des races humaines* (2 volumes, 1853–5) is much cited, especially by those who have not read it. However, though the Nazi theorists presented a triumphalist version of history in which the superior Aryan was predestined to dominate inferior races, Gobineau's own view was different. He believed that the Aryans were doomed by centuries of miscegenation and that 'Humanity's best days are already behind us.' Though Gobineau and Renan were both racists, they were at opposite poles of a racist spectrum, for, while Renan thought that racial admixture was not a bad thing, Gobineau thought it to be the source of all evil. Unlike the proto-Nazis and Nazis, Gobineau actually admired the Jews for, among other things, their racial exclusiveness. Furthermore, unlike most racists, including British and French racists, he was anticolonialist, as he regarded colonialism as just another symptom of racial and cultural decay. 'Asia is a very appetizing dish, but one which poisons those who consume it.' Strong races were doomed to be corrupted by the weaker races that they had conquered. He held that it was very difficult to transport civilization from one region to another and he was confident that India would become independent from the British one day.

In *Orientalism*, Edward Said implied that Gobineau was a key figure in 'the official genealogy of Orientalism', whatever that may be, but there is no sign that he had actually read Gobineau (and it does not look as though Schwab, on whom Said relies here, had read Gobineau either). Gobineau was not a trained Orientalist and though he had developed a passion for Oriental languages when a teenager in Switzerland, neither his Persian nor his Arabic ever amounted to much. His venture into serious academic territory in the form of an attempted decipherment of the various cuneiform scripts was, as we shall see, a disastrous exercise in self-deception. His observations on Persia were those of a diplomat and man of letters, albeit one with some extremely odd ideas. He loved Persia and was to look back on his time at the Tehran posting as his golden years, but that did not stop him from judging the Persians to be the decadent products of racial intermingling. (If any Persian readers are affronted by this, it may be some consolation for them to know that he had an even lower opinion of the United States in that respect.) He thought the Persian society and economy were crippled by a pervasive quietism and he judged Sufism in its higher manifestations to be a disguised form of atheism. He was probably also the only visitor to Persia under the Qajars in the mid-nineteenth century to find the place to be too democratic.[59] He thought that, in general, the Asians were strong on intuition but short on logic. For this reason, he enlisted the help of a Persian Jewish rabbi and, with his help, he translated Descartes' *Discours de la méthode* into Persian.

Gobineau's views on the horrors of democracy and revolution had been shaped by his experience of 1848, 'the Year of Revolutions' in France and elsewhere. His views on Asia's cultures and languages had similarly already been formed before he arrived in Persia, where he saw what he was expecting to see. 'Everything we think, and all the ways we think, have their origin in Asia' is the opening sentence of *Les Religions et les Philosophies dans l'Asie Centrale*. In Gobineau's vision of history, the Aryans started out on Central Asian plateaux and different branches of the super-race migrated from there to India, Persia and Europe. He found what he was expecting to see in Persia, which was that degenerate Aryans had become contaminated by their contacts with Semitic peoples. He constructed his early history of Persia from very few sources – mainly the Bible and Herodotus. Unlike ordinary, workaday Orientalists, Gobineau believed that the Sasanians (who ruled in Persia from AD 226 to 642) were Semites. As the centralizing conquerors of the older Aryan feudal Persia, they corrupted and destroyed its glorious Aryan vigour and therefore

Gobineau thought it best to bring his history of Persia to an end with the coming of the Sasanians.

As for the Arabs who replaced the Sasanians as rulers of Persia from the seventh century onwards, he thought that they had become corrupted by intermarriage with black people. His reading of the pre-Islamic odes that comprise the *Mu'allaqat* persuaded him that the early Arabs were barbarous. The coming of Muhammad and the propagation of the Qur'an had civilized them somewhat. Like Renan, he considered Islam to be an expression of the Semitic spirit. Semitic peoples were by their nature servile before God. However it was quietism rather than Islam as such that was the bane of Asia. He argued that Shi'ism, as it developed from the eighth century onwards, was a kind of revolt of the Aryan Persians against Semitic Islam. (This racial approach to the development of Islamic doctrine was to be attacked by the great Orientalist, Julius Wellhausen.) Like de Sacy and Hammer-Purgstall, Gobineau was most interested in sectarian breakaways from mainstream Islam and he was particularly interested in the messianic movement of the Babis which arose in Persia in the 1840s and which was subjected to savage repression by the Qajars in the following decades. His interest in this persecuted minority (whom he bizarrely regarded as the spiritual heirs of Chaldaeanism and other cults of antiquity) inspired Edward Granville Browne to go out to Persia. (Browne was a grander figure and a serious Orientalist, on whom see next chapter.)

Gobineau's later, superficially imposing, work on the decipherment of cuneiform was actually nonsense, merely the speculative work of a crank. He published two worthless works of linguistic scholarship, *Lectures des textes cunéiformes* (1858) and *Traité des écritures cunéiformes* (2 volumes, Paris, 1864). These volumes mingled obscure chimerical fantasies about the adventures of the Aryan race with speculation about his own genealogy (he thought he was descended from the Vikings). He took the Bible as his main source, but drew also on a range of cabalistic and other occult material. He took it for granted that the linguistic stability of the Middle East was such that cuneiform could not possibly represent a dead language, but had to be read as either Arabic or a mixture of Arabic and Persian which he called Huzarwesh. However, what he published demonstrated not only that he had fantastically daft ideas about cuneiform, but also that his ideas about how the Arabic language worked were hardly less erroneous. His comprehensive misreading of all sorts of cuneiform inscriptions was further fuelled by his rejection of what had by the mid-nineteenth century become the conventional scholarly view that the Indo-Aryan languages had originated in the Indian subcontinent. He produced repetitive, magical talismanic readings of all the inscriptions. By the time he published his proposed decryptions of cuneiform, a large part had already been successfully deciphered by other scholars, including Grotefeld, Henry Rawlinson and others. But Gobineau mocked their labours and sneered at 'the glass world' inhabited by the Orientalists. Some Orientalists responded by savagely demolishing Gobineau's proposed decipherments; others, the majority, simply ignored what he had written.[60] His work in the field of ancient languages had the sort of importance for Oriental studies that attempts to patent perpetual motion machines have had for the history of science. Far from being part of an Orientalist genealogy, he was both the first and the last to pursue his peculiar lines of enquiry. However, as a romancer he has some merit and his collection of short stories, *Nouvelles Asiatiques* (1876), is worth reading.

Renan and Gobineau were in their different ways racists. The banality of Renan's racism has already been remarked upon. Robertson Smith (on whom see below) was another kind of racist; he thought that the Arabs were a superior race, though the Negroes were inferior. Racism was pervasive in nineteenth-century Europe. However, having said that, one has not said very much, as there were so many different types of racism and racist stereotyping had yet to assume the form it eventually took in the early Fascist decades of the twentieth century. The tendency to generalize about racial characteristics was not something invented by nineteenth-century Orientalists, nor was it confined to white Europeans. One only has to look at medieval Arab guides to the purchase of slaves of different races or to consider the traditional Chinese attitude to foreigners (whom they divided into 'cooked barbarians' and 'uncooked barbarians') to see that this was so. In part, racist attitudes in any period or region are the product of the natural tendency to think in generalities. In nineteenth-century Europe, in the absence of any serious prior research, it seemed possible that there might be a scientific basis to racial differences. There was no reason to rule this out a priori. Some of nineteenth-century racism's agendas would seem quite strange to later generations of racists. In part, those agendas were linked to an increasing preoccupation with the nation and nationalism. Victorian authors speculated at enormous length about the respective contributions made to the English by the Anglo-Saxon and then the Norman invaders, while Frenchmen, like Gobineau, made under-researched claims about the Germanic origins of their aristocracy. (But Gobineau's claim to be a count was another of his fictions.)

Renan's own view, however, was that what made the French nation, or any nation, was not race, but shared historical memories. More-over, as we have seen, he thought that language rather than bloodlines defined a race. Unlike the Fascist racists of the twentieth century, the nineteenth-century racists were not necessarily triumphalist. The pessimistic Gobineau was not alone here and, for example, Fabre d'Olivet, an eccentric scholar who wrote about Hebrew and linguistic matters more generally, believed that in the long run the blacks, who were stronger, were destined to enslave the whites.[61]

BACK TO SERIOUS ORIENTALISTS

As the numbers of Orientalists increased, so did their disagreements and feuds, and the Dutchman Reinhart P. Dozy (1820–83) contrib-uted more than his fair share to these.[62] In the early nineteenth century, Dutch Orientalism had experienced a modest revival under the slightly dull scholar, Théodore-Guillaume-Jean Juynboll (1802–61), who moved over from theology to Arabic and produced useful work on medieval Arab geography. Dozy was not dull and he came to Arabic studies via romantic literature. He had been entranced by accounts of old Moorish Spain in such works as Chateaubriand's *Aventures du dernier des Abencerrages* (1826) and Washington Irving's *Tales of the Alhambra* (1832). He took up Arabic in the first instance 'in order to bathe himself in waves of poetry'. His rather dry and pedantic teacher Hendrik Weijers pushed him towards history. Dozy thereupon read Quatremère's *Histoire des sultans mamlouks* and was enraptured by the philological riches he discovered therein. His first major work was

Recherches sur l'histoire politique et littéraire de l'Espagne pendant le moyen âge (1849), a study of Spanish Muslim history up to 1110 that was also a savagely polemical attack on his predecessors among the Spanish historians, José Antonio Conde and Pascual de Gayangos. Conde had died in 1820, but Dozy's brutality cost him the friendship of Gayangos. Renan was terrified at the severity of the judgement on Conde's inadequate Arabic (as well he might be) and Dozy's student, de Goeje, described it as a 'death sentence' on Conde. Spanish historians were enraged by Dozy's debunking of Spain's national hero, al-Cid, who, he argued, was merely a treacherous mercenary and 'more Muslim than Catholic'. Dozy's critics suggested that he placed too much reliance on Arabic sources on this topic.

Dozy went on to publish his *Histoire des Musulmans d'Espagne* (1861). At the time he was criticized for having written such a work of scholarship in French rather than Latin. However, he had been strongly influenced by the contemporary vivid and romantic French style of writing history. As a consequence Dozy's narrative has some of the feel of a novel of passion, as he invented dialogue and conjured up the look of things in order to give his readers the feeling that they were there in the medieval Moorish past. Dozy hated German pedantry and he clashed with Fleischer on editorial details. Dozy was a merciless controversialist and his history overflowed with strongly felt prejudices. He was liberal and anti-clerical and it was perhaps because of this that he took strongly against the Almoravids, the fiercely religious and puritanical Berber tribesmen who had occupied much of Muslim Spain in the twelfth century. He had strong views on racial matters and his vision of history was coloured by his belief that though the Arabs were capable of conquering an empire, they were incapable of holding it. The progress of the Arabs was held back by the prescriptions of the Qur'an and the backward-looking nature of Islamic law. Dozy disliked what he read about Muhammad and he shared the view (widespread among European scholars of the time) that the Prophet was epileptic. The romantic in Dozy much preferred pre-Islamic Arabia with its camel rustlers and warrior poets.

Finally, Dozy's early work as a research student on the medieval Arabic terminology of costume bore fruit in a wider-ranging work, the *Supplément aux dictionnaires arabes* (2 volumes, 1881). His study of the vocabulary of costume as well as his reading of Quatremère and then of the Spanish Arabic sources had made him aware of the vast number of words that had been circulating in the Arabic-speaking world without being admitted into the famous dictionaries of classical Arabic. As we have seen, Lane had relied on those dictionaries. The other standard dictionary that circulated in the nineteenth century was Georg Wilhelm Freytag's *Lexicon Arabico–Latinum* (1830–37), but this was not much more than a revamping of Golius's seventeenth-century compilation that had in turn been based on the great classical Arabic dictionaries. Dozy's dictionary was based on words found in texts rather than in other dictionaries, and in many cases he had to guess their meaning from context. His dictionary was the product of wide and discriminating reading and it is regularly consulted by scholars to this day.

A BELATED REVIVAL OF ORIENTAL
STUDIES IN BRITAIN

For much of the century Oriental studies were even more stagnant in Britain than they had been in Holland. Dozy was not impressed by Oxford and Cambridge and he judged that these places were held back by ecclesiastical shackles. It is not possible to understand what was happening in British universities in this period without coming to terms with the intense religiosity of the age. G. M. Young, the superbly eloquent historian of Victorian Britain, characterized that period as 'an age of flashing eyes and curling lips, more easily touched, more easily shocked, more ready to spurn, to flaunt, to admire and, above all, to preach'.[63] Intellectual life in Britain throughout the nineteenth century was dominated by theological controversies. Most of the new critical techniques that were now being applied to the study of the Bible had been pioneered by German scholars. Young, having remarked on the challenge posed by the researches of Sir Charles Lyell and other geologists to the traditional chronology laid down by the Bible, went on to observe that a 'far more serious onslaught was preparing ... English divinity was not equipped to meet – for its comfort, it was hardly capable of understanding – the new critical methods of the Germans: it is a singular fact that England could not, before Lightfoot, show one scholar in the field of Biblical learning able and willing to match the scholars of Germany ... The flock was left undefended against the ravages of David Strauss.'[64] David Strauss's *Das Leben Jesu, kritisch bearbeitet* (2 volumes, 1835–6) daringly suggested that the miraculous and supernatural events associated with Jesus had been foisted on to his life prior to the composition of the Gospels. The Gospels were then, at least in part, the records of myths. In 1846 Marian Evans (better known as the novelist George Eliot) published a widely read English translation of Strauss's work. If the life of the Christian Son of God was to be treated in this manner, it was hardly likely that in the long run Muhammad's biography would escape similar treatment.

In the short term, however, there was little interest in Britain in doing serious research into Islam and the Arabic language. Richard Burton, in his famous (or notorious) translation of *The Arabian Nights* (1885–8), had pointed out that Britain now ruled over the greatest empire of Muslims ever seen and he thought that this ought to have led to a much greater interest in Muslim languages and cultures.[65] This indeed was what might have been expected. Yet Major C. M. Watson, a member of the Imperial Institute, put the paradox plainly in a letter to Sir Frederick Abel in 1887: 'Although England has greater interests in the East than any other European country, yet for some unexplained reason, she is the most behindhand in encouraging the study of modern oriental languages.' Like Gibbon, Burton had wanted to study Arabic at Oxford but had been unable to find anyone who was prepared to teach him. When he went up in 1840, it was to study Greek and Latin, but, since this was boring, he set to teaching himself from Erpenius's *Grammatica Arabica* (1613). The then Laudian Professor of Arabic at Oxford refused to teach individual students, claiming that he was only paid to teach classes and, since he discouraged those individual students who might have formed such classes, he never had to do any teaching. Burton's efforts to teach himself were seriously impeded by his failure to realize that Arabic was written from right to left and it was only when he encountered de Sacy's distinguished Spanish student Pascual de Gayangos in Oxford that this fundamental misapprehension was corrected.[66] Later in life, Burton acquired a reputation as a brilliant linguist that seems to have been somewhat inflated.

Like many of his lively-minded contemporaries, Burton hated and despised Oxford. In part, the decay of Oriental studies in Oxford reflected the broader stagnation of British universities in the early nineteenth century. It is a big mistake to project the intellectual power and industriousness of a modern university like, say, Columbia in New York back to nineteenth-century Oxbridge (though Edward Said seems to be assuming this). Besides allowing the sons of peers and similar folk to grow a little older in pleasant and idle surroundings, the wealthy Oxbridge colleges were, as much as anything else, training places for Anglican clergymen. But this was to change.

Mark Pattison, a fellow of Lincoln College, Oxford, and an expert on the lives of Casaubon and Scaliger, put forward proposals for university reform in the 1850s and 1860s that were based on his travels around German universities.[67] Oxford in Pattison's day had only twenty professors to Leipzig's more than a hundred. There were also far more university students in Germany. A tiny proportion of the population went to university in England. Pattison was particularly impressed by the German scholars in classical studies and their use of philological techniques, as well as their emphasis on institutions and social factors in the history of antiquity. Part of the trouble was that Oxbridge faced little competition within Britain. In the course of the 1820s and 1830s the University of London (consisting at first of University College and King's College) came into being. The University of Durham was founded in 1832, but it remained tiny until the second half of the twentieth century. The Scottish universities, including Edinburgh and St Andrews, had longer histories, but they did not teach Arabic or Islamic studies.

Serious university reform got under way in the 1870s with a series of parliamentary acts and royal commissions. Fortuitously 1870 was the date at which William Wright was appointed to the Thomas Adams Chair of Arabic in Cambridge.[68] With this appointment Cambridge acquired an Orientalist of the first rank, something it had not possessed since the seventeenth century: the prestige of Cambridge Orientalism was established. (Oxford, meanwhile, had to wait until 1889 and the appointment of David Samuel Margoliouth to the

Laudian professorship. On Margoliouth, see the next chapter.) Wright was born on the frontier of Nepal, the son of a captain in the service of the East India Company. He did a first degree at the University of St Andrews, and went on to the German university of Halle where he studied first Syriac and then Arabic. He also picked up Persian, Turkish and Sanskrit at about the same time. His schooling in German philological techniques was at least as important as the languages he had mastered. He then went on to Leiden, where the redoubtable Dozy was his doctoral supervisor. His research consisted of editing the unique Leiden manuscript of Ibn Jubayr's *Travels*. (The Spanish Muslim, Ibn Jubayr, went on haj to Mecca in the late twelfth century and produced a remarkably lively account not just of the Muslim lands he travelled through, but also of the Crusader Kingdom of Jerusalem and Norman Sicily.)

Wright was appointed to a chair of Arabic at University College, London, and then to one at Trinity College, Dublin, where he also taught Hindustani. While in Dublin, he produced *A Grammar of the Arabic Language* (1859–62). This was effectively a translation and expansion of an Arabic grammar published in Latin in 1848 by a Norwegian student of Fleischer's, Karl Paul Caspari. Wright received help from Fleischer, who had made many corrections to de Sacy's earlier grammar and, in the preface to the second edition of his *Grammar* (1874), Wright wrote: 'Professor Fleischer will, I trust, look upon the dedication as a mark of respect for the Oriental scholarship of Germany, whereof he is one of the worthiest representatives.'[69] Wright's *Grammar* is still in use today, which is a little surprising, as it is rather difficult to use and those wishing to get full value from it should first acquaint themselves with the elements of Latin, Hebrew, Ethiopic and Syriac.

In 1861 he resigned his academic post in order to catalogue the Syriac manuscripts at the British Museum. His edition of al-Mubarrad's literary anthology, *al-Kamil* (a ninth-century collection of grammatical and literary studies), was published by the Deutsche Morgenländische Gesellschaft. (His kind of scholarship had a bigger audience in Germany than in Britain.) In 1870 Wright was appointed Thomas Adams Professor at Cambridge, a post he retained until his death. However, despite his intimidatingly deep knowledge of the

Arabic language, he really seems to have been much more interested in Syriac Christian literature. Like most nineteenth-century Orientalists, he was far more interested in the Bible than the Qur'an and he also worked on the New Testament Apocrypha and was a member of the Old Testament Revision Committee. He died in 1889 and his *Lectures on the Comparative Grammar of the Semitic Languages* were published posthumously a year later. Although it is difficult to present this pious and scholarly professor in such a way as to make him seem exciting to a modern readership, nevertheless Wright had effectively made England a major centre for Arabic studies, something it had not been since the days of Pococke, and his achievement was to be consolidated by his near contemporaries Edward Palmer and William Robertson Smith.

Most nineteenth-century Orientalists were, like Wright, creatures of libraries and college committees. But one at least of Wright's students, Edward Palmer, polyglot, spy and poet, was different.[70] Palmer, whose life was the stuff of doomed romance, was born in 1840. He had an undistinguished school career, though it was as a schoolboy that he learnt Romany by frequenting gypsy campsites. He went on to work as a junior clerk with a wine merchant in the City (and it was during this fairly idle period that he mastered mesmerism and mind-reading as well as attending spiritualist seances). He was apt to study eighteen hours a day, a habit that may have exacerbated his always frail health. This phase of his life came to an end when he fell victim to consumption in 1859. During his convalescence in Cambridge, he tried to improve his schoolboy Greek and Latin and then, after meeting an Indian teacher, he took up the study first of Urdu and Persian and then of Arabic and Hebrew. In 1863, as a relatively mature student, Palmer was awarded a scholarship to read classical studies at Cambridge. He achieved only a third-class degree. However Edward Byles Cowell, the Professor of Sanskrit at Cambridge and a leading authority on Persian, having tested Palmer's Persian, succeeded in getting him made a fellow of St John's College, Cambridge. Palmer supplemented his scant income by writing newspaper articles in Persian and Urdu for an Indian newspaper. In 1869 the Palestine Exploration Fund provided funds for Palmer to begin a topographical survey of the Sinai peninsula. The main point of this and subsequent surveys of the region was to establish the veracity of the narrative of Exodus and to underpin the detail of the biblical narrative more generally by interviewing Bedouin about the place names of the peninsula. Palmer returned there in 1870 to continue with this work. Not only did these desert ventures improve his Arabic, but the desert air was thought to be good for his weak lungs. As a result of his work for the Palestine Exploration Fund, he became friendly with its secretary, Walter Besant, the novelist and later founder of the Royal Society of Literature. The two men shared an enthusiasm for Rabelais, French poetry and Freemasonry and together they wrote *Jerusalem, a Short History of the City of Herod and of Saladin*, which was published in 1871.

That same year Palmer was appointed to the Lord Almoner's Chair in Arabic at Cambridge. Unfortunately this professorship was less well endowed than the Thomas Adams Chair and Palmer was paid only £40 a year as professor. However, he did so much lecturing that his salary was eventually increased by £250. In his short life he wrote copiously. Among other things he published *The Desert of the Exodus* (based on his travels in the Sinai Desert), a short Arabic dictionary, a short Persian dictionary, an edition and translation of the complete poems of the thirteenth-century Egyptian Baha' al-Din Zuhayr, a not very accurate translation of the Qur'an, and a translation of the New Testament into Persian. He also contributed to a translation of Romany songs and he wrote the article on legerdemain for the *Encyclopaedia Britannica*. His interests were bemusingly wide-ranging and his catchphrase was 'I wonder what will happen next'. Given his wild, gypsyish temperament, it is not surprising that he became a close friend of the explorer and adventurer, Sir Richard Burton.

Palmer was not happy in Cambridge. His friend Besant thought the university environment very dull, believing that this was in part because of the penchant of English scholars for grammar and in part because of 'the very recent and still partial emancipation of scholarship from the Church'. Palmer's approach to the subjects he studied was habitually brilliant but unsystematic. He did not care much for the rules of grammar, preferring to listen to how native speakers used their language. It always rankled with Palmer that he did not get the Thomas Adams chair to which Wright had been appointed. Also despite or because of the amount of teaching he did, he hated teaching: 'I am tired of residence and of giving elementary lectures, which after all are no part of a Professor's duty.' He thought that there must be something better than 'teaching boys the Persian alphabet'. Besides, the money was dreadful. In 1881 Palmer left Cambridge and became a leader writer on the *Standard*. As a journalist he wrote articles on an amazing range of subjects.

Meanwhile, in Egypt, the nationalist politician Arabi Pasha took over as Prime Minister and Minister of War in 1882. There were anti-European riots in Alexandria and this led to British and French fears that they might lose control of the Suez Canal. In June 1882 Palmer was sent out on a secret mission to negotiate with, and if necessary bribe, the Bedouin tribesmen close to the Suez Canal and make sure that they did not attack British forces there. The British fleet bombarded Alexandria and in September the British army under Sir Garnet Wolseley defeated Arabi's forces at Tel el-Kebir. But by then Palmer, aged only forty-two, was dead. He and a couple of British army officers were murdered by Bedouin tribesmen for the gold they were carrying. Palmer is said to have cursed his captors in eloquent Arabic before being shot and hurled over a cliff. Prior to Palmer's body being discovered and his death confirmed, his friend Richard Burton had been officially commissioned to look for him.

Palmer had picked up subjects as casually as he dropped them. Very few British scholars in the nineteenth century had the proper philological training to participate fully in the advances in Orientalism being pioneered on the Continent. Wright was one exception. William Robertson Smith (1846–94) was another.[71] Born and educated in Aberdeenshire, his early education relied heavily on the memorizing of Greek and Latin texts – a pedagogic technique characterized by his biographers as 'an excellent practice, now unfortunately much disused'. Having taken up Hebrew studies at the Free Church College in Edinburgh, he made repeated visits to Germany from 1867 onwards in order to further those studies. He loved Germany and loved the Germans – except for one thing, which was 'their laxity in observing the Sabbath'. In 1870 he became Professor of Oriental Languages and Old Testament Exegesis at the Free Church College. After a visit to Göttingen in 1872, he developed an interest in Arabic and as his biographers observe, 'it was not unnatural that he looked to Germany for instruction and assistance' in this subject. In 1878–9 he toured Egypt and other Arab lands in order to improve his Arabic. Back in Britain, Smith became a close friend of William Wright. He also became a favoured protégé of Palmer, though the two men could hardly have been more different. Palmer was a literary aesthete, whereas Smith's scholarship was powered and underpinned by a stern Christian piety. It was his approach to Christian doctrine that turned him into one of the most controversial figures in Victorian Britain. In 1881 he was dismissed by the General Assembly of the Free Church of Scotland from the Chair of Old Testament Studies of the Free College in Aberdeen. He was dismissed because of the tenor of various articles that he had written on the Bible for the ninth edition of the *Encyclopaedia Britannica*, in which, and in publications elsewhere, he made use of German source-critical techniques and treated the Bible as a group of historical documents rather than as the unchallengeable word of God.

Deprived of his Aberdeen professorship, he found work writing more articles for the *Encyclopaedia Britannica*, of which he eventually became editor. He was one of the few people, perhaps the only one, to have read through the whole of the *Encyclopaedia* in its ninth edition. His duties as editor gained him the acquaintanceship of most of the British intellectual and cultural elite of the late nineteenth century, including Charles Darwin, Thomas Henry Huxley and Edward Burne-Jones. Although he had previously published studies of problems in the Old Testament, he now became increasingly interested in the study of primitive rituals, kinship and marriage more generally. He had already published a seminal article on 'Animal Worship and Animal Tribes among the Arabs and in the Old Testament' in the *Journal of Philology* in 1880.

After Palmer's murder, Smith succeeded him in the Lord Almoner's professorship. As has been noted, this was not well endowed and Smith received £50 a year for delivering one lecture in the course of the year. He moved on to become university librarian before eventually, after his friend Wright's death in 1889, occupying the rather grander Thomas Adams Chair of Arabic. Although Smith's chair was in Arabic, he continued to be preoccupied with problems concerning the Bible and the ancient Hebrews. In particular, he worked on the chronology of the production of the various books of the Bible.

In 1885 he also published *Kinship and Marriage in Early Arabia*, which drew upon both pre-Islamic poetry and contemporary accounts of Bedouin practice in order to argue that early Arab society was matriarchal and matrilocal (that is to say that the husband joined the wife's clan upon marriage). *Mutterrecht* or the power of women in primitive Arab society was presented by Smith as a product of Arab sensuality. Over the centuries, however, matriarchy was replaced by patriarchy, and female infanticide and polygamy consolidated male dominance. What was true for the Arabs went for the ancient Hebrews too, for he seems to have regarded the early Jews as camel-rearing Bedouin. For both early Arabs and Hebrews, 'religious life involved clans living in close fellowship with their clan god'. On the other hand, the perceived natural conservatism of the Bedouin that Muhammad had found so hard to combat, meant that their present manner of life was an excellent guide to the way things were done in biblical times. The scorching hot desert of Arabia was a kind of refrigerator in which ancient Semitic practices were preserved.

In 1889 Smith published his *Lectures on the Religion of the Semites*, which dealt with the rituals of sacrifice, communion and atonement as practised by early Hebrew and Arab tribesmen. He argued that rituals arise before the mythologies or creeds that are constructed around them and that all primitive religions pass through a totemistic stage. True religion originates in magic and superstition but outgrows them. Prophets tailored their messages to the societies and circumstances they spoke to and, if this applied to Samuel and Ezekiel, it also applied to Muhammad. Smith's study of the Hadiths, the body of traditions associated with the Prophet, persuaded him that these had been invented and compiled over a long period in much the same way as Pentateuchal law had been. Smith might have done more but for poor health, and the book does not quite have a finished feel. Although twentieth-century anthropologists like James Frazer and Claude Lévi-Strauss continued to explore the themes that Smith raised, his ideas on totemism and primitive matriarchy are no longer accepted. On the other hand, his argument that tribal genealogies are social constructs, rather than literal records, commands widespread assent among anthropologists today. He was a fiery, energetic character who regarded slack scholarship as a form of immorality. Every Christmas, but only at Christmas, he read a novel, out of some sort of reluctant sense of cultural duty. As he lay on his deathbed in 1894 he was planning the *Encyclopaedia Biblica*. This great reference work, together with the *Encyclopaedia Britannica*, must be regarded as the key model for the later, fundamental document of modern Orientalism, the *Encyclopaedia of Islam*.

GERMANS STILL LEAD THE FIELD

Smith's views on the slow evolution of both early Jewish law and the Hadith corpus were similar to those of his German friend, Julius Wellhausen (1844–1918).[72] Albert Hourani, a leading twentieth-century historian of the Arabs and Islam, argued that Wellhausen and Goldziher were the first people to study Islam seriously.[73] (The slightly younger and more long-lived Goldziher will be discussed at length in the next chapter.) Wellhausen came from a Lutheran background. He had become interested in biblical history after hearing Heinrich Ewald's lectures in Göttingen. Although Ewald was a considerable Arabist and had produced a two-volume *Grammatica critica linguae Arabicae* (1831–3), he was only interested in using Arabic in the furtherance of the study of ancient Israel. This was Wellhausen's prejudice too and his fame today, such as it is, rests chiefly upon his Old Testament researches. In 1878 he produced *Prolegomena zur Geschichte Israels*, in which he sought to discover through close source-criticism the real history of the early Hebrew folk, before it was written up and distorted by the post-exilic priesthood. In 1892 Wellhausen became Professor in Göttingen, where he worked closely with Nöldeke, another former student of Ewald's.

Although Wellhausen was to become a friend and intellectual ally of Robertson Smith, he was very different in temperament, being large, convivial and keen on his beer. He was also a stylish and witty writer. Though the application of source-critical techniques to biblical texts would strike many as a dry and dusty activity, there was nothing dry about Wellhausen and he felt passionately about the history of the early Israelites. He loved the early Hebrews with their ancient and wild pagan rituals. He hated the later priests of Israel with their joy-destroying codes of ritual and law. The end of ancient Hebrew polytheism was a kind of *Götterdämmerung*, or twilight of the gods. At least that was how he viewed the process. He preferred his ancient Hebrews to be wild and hard-drinking. He took the view that ancient Semitic religion was ancestor worship. In this he was probably influenced by the French historian Fustel du Coulanges, who had put forward a similar argument regarding the ancient Greeks and Romans. But obviously Wellhausen's ideas were also rather similar to those of Robertson Smith.

Because of the problems he discovered in his Hebrew material, he believed that the lore of the pre-Islamic Arabs provided the best evidence for the way of life of the early Hebrews. Eventually he moved on from close scrutiny of the Old Testament and became interested in the romantic and colourful world of the Arabs: 'I have made the transition from the Old Testament to the Arabs with the intention of getting to know the wild vine upon which priests and prophets grafted the Torah of Yahweh. For I have no doubt that some idea of the original characteristics with which the Hebrews entered history may most easily be won by means of a comparison with Arab antiquity.'[74] In this field too he was a great lover and hater. He loved the Umayyad caliphs, who presided over the Arab heartlands from 661 till 750. He hated the Abbasid caliphs who came after them. 'To hell with the Abbasids! They might as well already be there.' A fervent patriot, he thought that the Abbasids were not fit to hold a candle to the German Kaisers. Wellhausen much preferred what he saw as the earlier Umayyads' penchant for politicking and high living. He was also a keen if decidedly belated supporter of the seventh-century Kharijites who rebelled against the caliphate and whom he admired for their passion and activism. More generally, he applauded historical signs of schism within Islam as indicators of social dynamism.

From 1879 onwards, edited volumes of the tenth-century historian al-Tabari started to appear. This enabled Wellhausen and others to adopt a more analytic approach to the early history of the Arab caliphate. Instead of translating and then pasting together snippets from Arabic chronicles, which was pretty much what William Muir had done in his history of the caliphate, Wellhausen tried to sift the surviving texts and to deduce what lost original sources those texts were based on and how the historical narrative was distorted over the centuries. This, of course, was exactly what contemporary biblical scholars were doing. Wellhausen himself had already demonstrated, to his own satisfaction at least, that the Pentateuch was composed by four different writers (and not by Moses, as previous generations used to believe). Wellhausen now attempted to carry out the same kind of operation on the earliest Arabic sources concerning the early history of Islam. In doing so, he conjured up what have since been shown to be imaginary Medinese and Iraqi schools of transmission of historical information. His conclusions were demolished by Albrecht Noth in the twentieth century. Thus Wellhausen's sophisticated techniques of textual analysis do not in the end seem to have brought him any closer to the historical truth than did Muir's methodological naivety. Even so, his *Das arabische Reich und sein Sturz* (1902) was for a long time the major work of Islamic history. Having dealt with Umayyad history, he seems to have become bored with the subject and switched his attention to New Testament studies.

Wellhausen had introduced historical method to Islamic history. Methodical Germans and Austrians dominated the writing of Islamic history in the nineteenth and twentieth centuries. Apart from Well-hausen, Aloys Sprenger (1813–93) and Alfred von Kremer (1828–89) were the key figures. Both were inspired by their reading of the fourteenth-century philosopher-historian Ibn Khaldun to take a broader and less tediously fact-driven approach to Islamic history. Sprenger in *Das Leben und die Lehre des Mohammed* ('The Life and Teachings of Muhammad', 1861–5) treated the rise of Islam as a product of its times. He also stressed the impact of Islamic culture on Western civilization.[75] Von Kremer was an Austrian diplomat who took up the study of Islamic cultural history.[76] He was not interested in political detail, preferring to write about the broad sweep of things. In the *Geschichte der herrschenden Ideen des Islams, Gottesbegriff, Prophetie und Staatsidee* (1868) he put forward an idealist vision of the whole of Islamic history and argued that civilization progressed when there was a clash of ideas and decayed when there was no such clash. His *Kulturgeschichte des Orients unter den Chalifen* (1875–7), which concentrated on the heyday of the Abbasid caliphs, was the first major study of Islamic cultural life. The Orient was pillaged by German historians and religious thinkers for material that they could use in more general debates about the future of civilization, the nature of culture and the primacy of ideas in historical evolution. Leopold von Ranke's grandiose vision of world history cast a long shadow and the Cinderella subject of Islamic history was mostly conducted under that shadow. In the twentieth century, German historicism would give way to theories and methodologies pioneered by British and American historians and sociologists, and Orientalists would take their lead from them. Finally, it is noteworthy that the Americans had yet to make a significant contribution to the field.

7

A House Divided Against Itself

*His preoccupation was with the words themselves and what
they meant; the slightest hitch in the text and he was absorbed,
with all his imagination and powers in play. He was intent on
knowing precisely what the words of that liturgy meant, to
the priests who translated it, to the scribe who copied it somewhere in a Central Asian town in the sixth century . . . Outside
the text his imagination, so active upon the words themselves,
so lively in his everyday life, seemed not to be engaged. He
gave only a passing thought to the societies where this religion
grew or to the people in the congregations which used this
liturgy. There was something in such speculations which
offended his taste – 'romantic' he called them as a term of
abuse.*

A portrait of Roy Calvert, compiler of a dictionary of
Soghdian in C. P. Snow's novel, *The Light and the Dark* (1947)

The *Encyclopaedia of Islam* is the most important document in the
history of twentieth-century Orientalism. William Robertson Smith,
the editor of the ninth edition of the *Encyclopaedia Britannica* and a
key figure in the team of the *Encyclopaedia Biblica*, had proposed
that a major reference work should be devoted to Islam, roughly along
the lines of the two great enterprises he had worked upon. (The
Encyclopaedia Biblica, devoted to biblical and Hebrew matters, had
been planned by Smith but was published posthumously in the years
1899–1903.) At various conferences held in the last decades of the

nineteenth century, two leading Orientalists of the next generation, the Dutchman Michael Jan de Goeje (1836–1909) and the Hungarian Ignaz Goldziher (1850–1921), continued to agitate on behalf of Smith's scheme. Although, as we shall see, Goldziher was easily the grandest Orientalist of his generation, he was inconveniently distant from Leiden, which was the Dutch base where the articles for the *Encyclopaedia* were to be edited and printed. (Leiden was the pre-eminent centre for Islamic studies in the late nineteenth and early twentieth centuries.) Therefore his place as editor was taken over by two Dutchmen, Martin Theodor Houtsma, a scholar who specialized in Seljuk Turkish history, and Arent Jan Wensinck, a specialist in the early history of Islam. At the beginning of the twentieth century, the English language had not yet become the language of international scholarship. So the *Encyclopaedia of Islam* was printed in three languages – English, French and German. For this and other reasons, the project was complex and expensive. Scholars started to research their articles around 1908 and the first complete volume appeared in 1913. The *Encyclopaedia*, four fat volumes of approximately 1,200 double-columned pages plus a supplementary volume of afterthoughts, was completed in 1938.

Although the production of the *Encyclopaedia* took place in Holland and Dutch scholars provided a remarkably large number of contributions, the Germans (Becker, Brockelmann, Plessner and Schacht among them) also made a considerable contribution and indeed scholars from all over Europe collaborated on the vast enterprise.[1] Such an international project was made possible by the increasingly frequent international gatherings of Orientalists, the first of which, the International Congress of Orientalists, had taken place in 1873.

Fuad Köprülü (1890–1966) a distinguished Turkish historian, was a leading contributor, but otherwise relatively few Turks, Arabs or Persians were invited to contribute (and it seems that many who were invited to contribute failed to do so on time). The historian of medieval Islam, R. Stephen Humphreys, has observed that the first edition of the *Encyclopaedia* represents 'a specifically European interpretation of Islamic civilization. The point is not that this interpretation is "wrong", but that the questions addressed in these volumes often differ sharply from those which Muslims have traditionally asked about themselves.'[2] (As we shall see in the chapter on 'Enemies of Orientalism', the *Encyclopaedia* has had plenty of enemies in the Middle East.) On the other hand, the *Encyclopaedia* can be criticized for overstressing the importance of the Islamic religion in the history of what is commonly known as Islamic culture. It was also overwhelmingly an encyclopedia of medieval Islam.

De Goeje, one of the founding figures of the *Encyclopaedia*, had been a student of Reinhart Dozy and he became perhaps the greatest Arabist in his lifetime. His strengths lay in his skills as a philologist and editor. He was industrious and prolific. His edition of al-Tabari, the chronicler of the Abbasid caliphs, was of particular importance for the study of the early history of Islam. His care for accuracy and serious scholarship meant that he hated everything that Ernest Renan had stood for.[3] De Goeje's contempt for Renan was something that he shared with the other key figure in the launch of the *Encyclopaedia*, Ignaz Goldziher.

THE GREATEST OF THE ORIENTALISTS

Ignaz Goldziher was a Hungarian Jew and his early studies were in the Talmud. He went on to study in Budapest at its Gymnasium (a superior secondary school specializing in classical studies). He also sat in on the lectures of the university's 'Professor' of Oriental Languages, Arminius Vámbéry. Although Vámbéry (1832–1913) made no significant contribution to Arabic studies, he is such a curious figure that he is worth pausing on briefly here. Like Goldziher, he was a Hungarian Jew and had studied Hebrew and the Talmud as a child. In 1857 he set out for Istanbul where he earned a living as a teacher and mastered Turkish. In the years 1863–4, he travelled through Armenia, Persia and Turkestan disguised as a dervish. His chief aim was to seek evidence of the original Magyar homeland in Central Asia. On his return to Europe he went to London where he was lionized, before proceeding on to Vienna. After an interview with the Emperor Franz Josef, he was given a job teaching Turkish, Arabic and Persian at the University of Pest. Although he was not a professor, he pretended that he was. He supplemented his earnings by writing about his adventures and producing pieces of polemical journalism.

In particular, he campaigned tirelessly against the spread of the Russian empire in Muslim Central Asia. He believed in the future of a free, democratic and modernizing Muslim world: 'We alone, we think, have the right to be mighty and free, and the rest of humanity to be subject to us and never taste the golden fruits of liberty.' According to Vámbéry, Europeans 'tend to forget that constitutional government is by no means a new thing in Islam, for anything more democratic than the doctrine of the Arabian Prophet it would be difficult to find in any other religion'.[4] Though Vámbéry lacked professional skills, he was successful in demonstrating that Turkish and Magyar belonged to the same linguistic family. He was very pro-British and spent a lot of his time in London. (It was after a dinner at which Vámbéry had talked about Balkan superstitions that Bram Stoker went home and had the nightmare that inspired his novel *Dracula*.)[5]

'My wanderings have left powerful impressions on my mind. Is it surprising if I stand sometimes bewildered, like a child in Regent Street, or in the salons of British nobles, thinking of the deserts of Central Asia, and of the tents of the Kirghiz and Turkomans?' Vámbéry, known to his contemporaries as 'the dervish', was an adventurous and resourceful figure, but he was no true scholar. Indeed, he was something of a charlatan and Goldziher despised him for this. Vámbéry was not a great teacher and, according to some of the few students he pretended to teach, his teaching method consisted of sending them away to teach themselves. But Goldziher also disapproved of his teacher's abandonment of the Jewish faith in order to advance his career, as well as his ideas about forcing Muslims to accommodate themselves to modernity.

In 1868 Goldziher left Hungary for the more scholarly environment of Germany, where he studied with various Orientalists and philologists, including the Hebraist, Abraham Geiger. Above all, he studied at Leipzig with the philologically sound and meticulous Fleischer. (No one would have dreamed of calling Fleischer 'dervish'.) Goldziher's work with Fleischer put him just one link down the scholarly chain of transmission from Silvestre de Sacy. In 1871 Goldziher visited

Holland and conferred with Dozy and de Goeje. The years 1873 to 1874 were his formative *Wanderjahre*, as it was then that he travelled in the Middle East and studied with the Muslim scholars of the al-Azhar in Cairo. He recorded the encounters and revelations of his year in the lands of Islam in a diary. It was while he was in Damascus that he decided that Islam was better than Judaism or Christianity. He also came to identify with progressive forces in the region. In particular, he formed a friendship with the writer and activist Jamal al-Din al-Afghani, who at that time was in Egypt campaigning for the country's independence.

From 1872 onwards Goldziher taught Hebrew in Budapest and published in that field. Then in 1876 he secured a not particularly remunerative job as the secretary of the Israelite Community (the liberal Jewish community) in Budapest. He occupied this rather humble job for thirty years, even though he was offered the Cambridge professorship after the death of William Robertson Smith, as well as various professorships in Germany. For most of his life, Goldziher's status in the world of Orientalism depended not on a formal academic rank, but on his sheer brilliance and industry. Anti-Semitism in Hungary made it almost impossible for Jews to get university posts. Only in 1905 did he move on from his secretaryship to become Professor of Semitic Philology at Budapest. He died in 1921.

Goldziher's mind was formed by the overlapping worlds of the German and Jewish Enlightenment. He spent much of his life battling with an obscurantist rabbinate and opposing the narrow ritualism of Orthodox Judaism. In 1876 he published *Der Mythos bei den Hebrä-ern und seine geschichtliche Entwicklung* ('Hebrew Myths and their Historical Evolution'). This study was written under the influence of Friedrich Max Müller, the Sanskrit expert and comparative philologist, who had put forward ideas about the nature of primitive mythology and argued that early myths derived ultimately from people's perception of such basic natural phenomena as day and night, earth, sky, stars and sea – and, above all, the sun. The theories that Max Müller had developed in relation to Indo-Aryan mythology were reapplied by Goldziher to the early beliefs of the Hebrews and their advance from polytheism to monotheism. Obviously this put him in conflict with Renan, who had previously generalized grandly on the intrinsic monotheism of the Semitic spirit and the incapacity of the Jews and Arabs to generate any kind of mythology. Goldziher considered all that to be racist nonsense: 'There is no such thing as a psychology particular to a given race.'[6] His first interest was in Hebrew mythology, but when he turned to the early beliefs of the Arabs, he pointed out that they only reluctantly abandoned polytheism under pressure from Muhammad and his supporters. Eventually, in a famous speech delivered in Budapest in 1893, entitled 'Renan as Orientalist', he attacked both the notion of an intuitive monotheism of the Semites and the supposed scholarship of Renan.

Only in 1881 did Goldziher start to publish in Islamic and Arabic studies. He wrote on a wide range of topics: he outlined the evidence for foreign influences on the Qur'an; he stressed the magical and ritual aspects of poetry; he explored the Shu'ubiyya (the anti-Arabic movement of the eighth and ninth centuries); he demonstrated that the culture of Muslim Andalusia generally lagged behind that of the Middle East and took its lead from the latter. However, his most far-reaching (and, in the eyes of many Muslims, most destructive) contribution was in the area of Hadith studies, especially his essay, 'On the Development of Hadith'. Here his thinking, like that of Wellhausen, was strongly influenced by the work of Abraham Geiger on the evolution of Old Testament stories. This interest in the evolution specifically of early narratives was transferred by Goldziher to Islamic studies, where he studied how stories about the Prophet and his contemporaries evolved over the centuries. Here he was successful in demonstrating that, notwithstanding their long chain of authorities that seemed to authenticate the oral transmission of Hadiths (I was told by Abu Hamza, who had it from Ismail ibn Abi Bakr that he heard Faisal al-Isfahani say, etc. . . .), most Hadiths could not be traced back to the Prophet, but were fabricated in later centuries.

This was not the purely destructive exercise that it seems at first sight. Having discounted them as evidence for what went on in the early seventh century, it then became possible to use Hadiths as a different kind of source – to shed light on the evolving preoccupations and debates within the Islamic community, as they were formulated in order to answer particular problems regarding law, ritual and everyday living in particular communities at particular times during the late eighth and early ninth centuries. The context of this sort of material was, if anything, even more interesting than its content. Hadiths were now seen to be interesting and important for they illustrated evolving trends in law, theology and so forth. A lot of traditions concerning the Prophet and his companions could be seen to have been invented in order to support or oppose the Umayyad caliphs. A lot of early Muslim law that ostensibly referred back to the practices of the Prophet and his companions could be seen to derive from Roman law or pre-existing provincial law. Goldziher's crucial essay, 'On the Development of the Hadith', was reprinted in *Muhammedanische Studien* (2 volumes, 1889–90), a collection that includes most of his important essays. The other key book, *Vorlesungen über den Islam* (1910) was translated in 1982 as *Introduction to Islamic Theology and Law*, though this general survey ranged more widely than that.

The German Arabist and cultural historian Alfred von Kremer (1828–89) had pioneered the study of the spiritual evolution of Islam.[7] Wellhausen and Goldziher followed him in this and they in turn would be followed by Louis Massignon and Bernard Lewis who similarly focused on the way Islam was not something fixed by the decree of the Prophet in the seventh century, but evolved and adapted over the centuries. Goldziher was particularly interested in the part played by schismatic religious and political groupings in Islamic history (among them the Kharijites, Carmathians and Isma'ilis), as he saw schism and dissension as indicators of the vitality and continuing evolution of the Islamic faith. Prior to Goldziher, historians of early Islam had mostly focused on the life of the Prophet, whereas Goldziher was more concerned with the revivalist movements that arose in later centuries. This concern carried over into his perception of the Muslim world in the twentieth century. He believed in the future of Islam and its ability to revive itself from within. As has been noted, he was hostile to colonialism and the Westernization of the Near East. He had supported the Egyptian nationalist revolt of Arabi Pasha (in 1881–2). In 1920 he wrote a letter to a Christian Arab friend in Mosul: 'I have lived for your nation and for my own. If you return to your homeland, tell this to your brothers.' A year later Goldziher was dead.[8]

Despite the relatively humble posts that Goldziher occupied for

most of his career, he was perfectly well aware how clever and important he was. He was an arrogant and passionate scholar. According
to Lawrence Conrad, a leading historian of early Islam and an expert
on the life and works of Goldziher, 'The formulations of Goldziher
remain to this day the basic underpinnings of the field.'[9] According
to Albert Hourani, the author of *A History of the Arab Peoples*,
'Goldziher shaped our view of what Islam is more than anyone else.'[10]
The famous Orientalist Louis Massignon declared that Goldziher was
'the uncontested master of Islamic studies in the eyes of Western
Orientalists' and that he had exercised a 'vast and complex personal
influence on our studies'.[11] Massignon's student, Bernard Lewis, the
author of *The Origins of Modern Turkey* and *The Arabs in History*
among much else, echoed this verdict: 'Probably the greatest of all
was Ignaz Goldziher ... a pious Hungarian Jew whose magnificent
series of studies on Muslim theology, law and culture rank him, by
common consent, as one of the founders and masters of modern
Islamic studies.'[12] Kratchkovsky, perhaps the greatest of twentieth-
century Russian Orientalists, declared that 'Islamic studies took definite shape as long ago as the end of the nineteenth century, thanks to
the work of the Dutchman Snouck Hurgronje and the Hungarian I.
Goldziher.'[13] According to Jacques Waardenburg (who, like Conrad,
has made a special study of Goldziher's work), 'It is no exaggeration,
in our opinion, to say that Goldziher had created Islamology in the
full sense of the term; if one thinks moreover that he inspired
the production of the *Encyclopaedia of Islam*, the foundation of the
review *Der Islam* and the numerous researches of colleagues ...'[14] In
other words, a book on Middle Eastern and Islamic studies that gave
no account of Goldziher's work in the field would not be worth the
paper it was printed on.

Apart from publishing copiously, Goldziher was keen on correspondence. Much of his impact on Islamic studies was due to the contacts
he made and the ideas he exchanged with other Orientalists. Apart
from his writings, Goldziher was a fervent attendee of Orientalist
conferences and he believed that giving lectures at such events was
just as important as publishing articles. As the example of the *Encyclopaedia of Islam* suggests, Orientalism in the early twentieth century
was to a considerable extent a collaborative European enterprise.

However, though the Orientalists corresponded and co-operated, it will become apparent that otherwise they had little in common: there was hardly an Orientalist type or a common Orientalist discourse. In this chapter I shall be discussing a range of approaches, among them Nöldeke's Prussian jingoism, Hurgronje's colonialist approach to Islam, Lammens's polemical Christian agenda and Margoliouth's crossword-solving approach to Arab texts.

THE CENTRALITY OF GERMAN ORIENTALISM

Theodor Nöldeke (1836–1930) was a rationalist positivist. His doctorate was entitled *De origine et compositione Surarum qoranicarum ipsiusque Qorani* ('Concerning the origin of the Qur'an and the composition of its suras') and this was later expanded into a more mature study, published in 1860 as *Geschichte des Korans*. He was the first to use historical method in an attempt to work out the chronological ordering of the revelation of various suras, or chapters of the Qur'an. Broadly speaking he dated the more mystical suras to the early years of the Prophet's preaching in Mecca, while assigning the longer suras with their detail on legal and social matters to the Prophet's later sojourn in Medina. Although Nöldeke's conclusions are now widely queried by specialists in Qur'anic studies, they were for a long time highly influential and without them, for example, the biographies of Muhammad by William Montgomery Watt in 1953 and 1956 and by Maxime Rodinson in 1961 could not have been written. In the long run, however, Nöldeke became disillusioned with Qur'anic studies: 'It is my ultimate wish not to be harassed by Muhammad and the Koran. When I was young I was preoccupied with these subjects for some reason or other. I must confess that they seem to be more mysterious now than ever before . . . I am too modern a European to see clearly into that world of dreams.'[15]

This disillusion carried over into his study of Arabic literature. 'Whether the aesthetic pleasure to be drawn from Arabic poetry is worth the effort in order to reach an approximate understanding is questionable. But the study is necessary as an important means to penetrate deeply the essence of the Arab people.'[16] Goldziher was an enthusiast for Arabic literature and wrote a short history of it, but Nöldeke thought that Arabic literature was of negligible aesthetic value. It seems that Nöldeke, the positivist, was reacting against the wild and woolly enthusiasms of Germans of an earlier generation, including the Schlegels, Herder and Rückert, for all things Oriental. Goldziher was a fervent admirer of Islam, even though he remained attached to his own Jewish faith. Nöldeke, on the other hand, condemned Islam, just as he condemned all religions. He was also at odds with William Robertson Smith, as he disapproved of his way of bolstering his arguments by calling on all sorts of comparative material mostly from primitive cultures. Smith treated the Arabs of the desert as fascinating barbarians, but Nöldeke did not think that they were as barbarous as all that. He was a fierce Prussian nationalist and racial bigot. In these respects he was an outsider in the community of Orientalists. In at least one respect, however, he belonged to the grand tradition of de Sacy and Fleischer: he had never been to the Middle East and he could not actually speak Arabic.

As we shall see, the political opinions of Carl Heinrich Becker (1876–1933) were at the opposite pole from those of Nöldeke. The continuity of German Orientalism is well illustrated by the fact that Becker had studied with various students of Fleischer, who had been the student of de Sacy. Becker started out as a Semiticist and Assyriologist, before specializing in the history of Islam. However, unlike purist disciples of de Sacy and Fleischer, Becker thought as a historian rather than as a philologist. Like Von Kremer before him, he regarded Islam as a late version of Hellenism and in *Der Islam im Rahmen einer allgemeinen Kulturgeschichte* (1922) and *Das Erbe der Antike im Orient und Okzident* (1931), he presented Muslim civilization as one of the chief heirs of the cultural legacy of antiquity. 'Without Alexander the Great there would be no Islamic civilization.'[17] The religion of Islam was not some Asiatic, alien 'Other', but was rather a Christian heresy and something that was very much a product of the Mediterranean world. As for Islamic philosophy, this was just late antique Greek philosophy under another name. Culture and society took precedence over religious revelation in Becker's thought and Islam was shaped by society rather than the reverse. As a young man, Becker had known Max Weber and he tended to think in Weberian sociological terms. He was perhaps also the first to study the economic history of the Islamic world.

As Becker saw it, although Islam, like Christendom, was the heir of antiquity, it had failed to assimilate all to which it was potentially an heir. From a European point of view, Islamic society was defective, as it failed to develop or acquire autonomous urban institutions, an ecclesiastical organization, feudalism, humanism, citizenship, individualism and capitalism. The European point of view was the only point of view Becker believed he could take, as he thought that it was impossible to cross cultural frontiers and understand a culture from the inside. In 1907 he was appointed to a post at Hamburg's Colonial Institute, a place for training administrators to serve in Germany's colonies. (Before the First World War, Germany had a substantial empire in Africa and the South Seas.) He was keen on using *Islamwissenschaft* (the scientific study of Islam) to further German colonial interests. Like Goldziher and the British Arabist Hamilton Gibb he took it for granted that Islamic society was dynamic and evolving and consequently took a keen interest in contemporary Middle Eastern issues. Despite the commitment to German imperialism in his early years, he was in most respects a progressive, liberal figure and in the 1920s he became Minister of Sciences, Arts and Public Instruction in the Weimar government. As a Weimarist, he viewed the rise of Hitler as a disaster. He died in the year the Nazis came to power.

AN IMPERIALIST ORIENTALIST

Just as Nöldeke's Prussian nationalism made him stand out among his fellow Orientalists, so the practical involvement of Christian Snouck Hurgronje (1857–1936) with imperialist projects was unusual. The son of a Dutch Calvinist pastor, he studied biblical history and criticism at the University of Leiden. But in 1887 he abandoned his original ambition to become a Calvinist pastor and instead took up the study of Arabic with de Goeje. Hurgronje did early research on the pre-Islamic origins of the haj to Mecca. In this research and later work he was much influenced by Goldziher with whom he corresponded and it was Goldziher who pushed him towards the study of *fiqh* (Muslim jurisprudence). Hurgronje also studied with Nöldeke in Strasburg. In 1885 he set off for the Middle East where he planned to improve his Arabic and do original research. Disguised as a Muslim, he spent several months in Mecca taking copious notes and numerous photographs. The result was a book that he published in German, *Mekka* (1888–9). This consisted of two volumes, as well as an atlas of photographs. From the first he was slightly unusual among his Orientalist peers in the interest he took in contemporary Islam. *Mekka* was a careful record of the manners and customs of the local inhabitants as well as the visiting pilgrims, detailing their beliefs, rituals and everyday life.

After his adventures in the Hejaz, Hurgronje became more interested in the Dutch East Indies. In 1889 he entered the service of the Ministry of the Colonies and left for Batavia, the Dutch centre of administration in Java. There he held a research post in the Dutch colonial administration and advised its officials on how to deal with Muslims and, more specifically, he gave guidance on points of Islamic law. He observed Islamic law as it was in contemporary practice, rather than just reading what was prescribed in the old law books. He was also interested in the survival of pagan beliefs and practices in the South East Asian version of Islam as well as the latitudinarianism of the local versions of Sufism. He produced a major report on customs and beliefs in the region of Atjeh in north-west Sumatra. He was a firm believer in the benefits of Dutch colonialism for the inhabitants of the Indies and he had no doubts about the virtues of Westernization for the Indonesians, nor about the benefits to Holland of assimilating Indonesians into Dutch society (and hence later he consistently encouraged Indonesians to come and study at Leiden University). In the meantime Indonesians needed defending from the full rigours of both colonialism and fundamentalist Islam. He feared the reactionary force of Pan-Islam. This kind of politico-religious paranoia was quite widespread at the time and in Britain it found expression in editorials in *The Times* as well as in novels by Talbot Mundy and John Buchan.

In 1906 Hurgronje returned to Holland and was appointed to the Chair of Arabic at Leiden University, but he continued to advise the government and colonial officials. Although he was for a long time a supporter of what he saw as ethical imperialism and he had believed in educating the Indonesians to make them the partners of the Dutch, he eventually became disillusioned and turned against Dutch colonial policy. Though he had participated in shaping that policy, he was more or less unique among Dutch Orientalists in doing so. His career as an imperialist scholar-administrator has been worth dwelling on, if only for its rarity, but, though his intellectual collusion with imperialism was unusual, it was not unique.[18] The case of Becker has already been mentioned and, as we shall see, Massignon worked hard to further French colonial interests in North Africa and Syria.

Unlike most of his academic colleagues, Hurgronje had first-hand experience of Muslim societies, both in the heartlands and at the margins. Like Goldziher, he did not regard Islam as something fixed or as a body of ritual and belief with a past but no future. It was precisely Islam's power to expand, tolerate and assimilate that fascinated him. His industry and his expertise, particularly in the areas of Islamic law and Hadiths, as well as his post at Leiden, made it inevitable that he should be closely involved in the *Encyclopaedia of Islam*. In the early twentieth century Dutch and German scholars dominated Orientalism and de Goeje, Goldziher, Nöldeke and Snouck Hurgronje were the giants of their age. German Orientalists were famous for their productivity and the Syrian intellectual Kurd 'Ali, who attended the 1928 Oxford Congress of Orientalists, noted how all the Germans who attended had stooped backs from overwork.[19]

A CHRISTIAN ORIENTALIST

On the whole German Orientalists had been successful in emancipating themselves from the old tradition of confessional polemic. However, even in the twentieth century there were some scholars who attacked the history of Islam from a hostile Christian point of view, though the Belgian Jesuit Henri Lammens (1862–1937) was unusual in the depth of his hostility. Lammens, who taught at the Roman Catholic University of St Joseph in Beirut, wrote copiously about the origins of Islam.[20] Although he took a critical view of the sources on the subject, his criticisms owed more to confessional hostility than they did to methodological sophistication. His rule of thumb was that any early source material that was critical of the Prophet was unlikely to have been invented and was therefore true. On the other hand, he scrutinized material favourable to the Prophet and his contemporaries in order to discredit it if possible. Reading the relevant Arabic sources was for him like 'travelling in a region of mirages'. Lammens's hyper-critical approach to the sources on early Islam led Goldziher to ask: 'What would remain of the Gospels if he applied to them the same methods he applies to the Qur'an?' Nöldeke similarly expressed reservations about Lammens's methodology.

Lammens regarded the Prophet as a lascivious impostor, echoing here the theme of medieval Christian polemics. He attempted to give the rise of Islam a political and economic context that had been previously lacking and in *La République marchande de la Mecque vers l'an 600 de notre ère* (1910) he suggested that the aristocrats of the Quraysh tribe in Mecca had grown wealthy from spice caravans that travelled through the seventh-century Hejaz. Though there was no direct evidence for any of this, his presentation (or invention) of the socio-economic background was enormously influential and later biographers of Muhammad, such as Montgomery Watt and Maxime Rodinson, relied heavily on the model furnished by Lammens. Only in 1987 was this model systematically analysed and demolished by Patricia Crone in her *Meccan Trade and the Rise of Islam*. Crone described Lammens as 'a notoriously unreliable scholar whose name is rarely mentioned in the secondary literature without some ex-pression of caution or disapproval'.[21] Lammens, who gloried in his 'holy contempt for Islam', admired the Umayyad caliphs, who, he believed, had refused to allow themselves to be dominated by Islam. The seventh-century Umayyad Caliph Mu'awiya was his particular hero, for Lammens claimed that he was the founder of the Syrian nation. On the other hand, he was not so keen on the priestcraft of the Abbasids. (In these particular prejudices he followed in the footsteps of Wellhausen.) Lammens, who loved Syria, regarded the Arab Muslim conquest as the greatest disaster that had ever befallen that region.

THE PRINCE AMONG SCHOLARS

When one contemplates the career of Leone Caetani, Prince of Teano and Duke of Sermoneta (1869–1935), it is hard not to think of the fictional career of Don Fabrizio Corbera, Prince of Salina, as conjured up in Tomasi di Lampedusa's marvellous novel, *Il Gattopardo* (1958, translated as *The Leopard*). Like Fabrizio, Caetani was a scholar aristocrat, but whereas Fabrizio devoted himself to astronomy, Caetani studied the early centuries of Islam. He taught himself Oriental languages and then set about compiling vast annals of the early history of Islam, constructed from lengthy translations selected from the earliest Arabic sources together with analytical commentaries. He was a positivistic disciple of Auguste Comte and had a fiercely critical approach towards those sources. Also in keeping with his positivism, he tended to minimize the role of the spiritual in history, preferring to stress economic and political factors as more important. Conflicts that were apparently religious were usually political or economic in origin. He believed that the increasing desiccation of the Arabian peninsula was a major underlying cause of the Islamic conquests, as the Arab tribes were obliged to leave their former territories and look for better pasturage elsewhere. According to Goldziher, 'Caetani clearly demonstrates in various parts of his work on Islam, the Arabs' drive to conquest sprang chiefly from material want and cupidity . . .' They pushed out from the arid peninsula in a hunt for lusher territories to dominate. Although Caetani was not a Marxist, his writings gave them plenty to draw upon.

Whereas Becker had presented Islamic culture as one of the heirs of Hellenistic culture, Caetani took the opposite point of view, regarding the Islamic religion as the revolt of the East against European domination and the rejection of Greek civilization. His analytical chronicle, the *Annali dell'Islam*, was published in ten volumes in the years 1905–26. Although he had planned to take it up to 1517, the year of the Ottoman conquest of Egypt, he never completed the full annals for the seventh century. He also worked on another vast enterprise, the *Onomasticon Arabicum* (an encyclopedia of Arab place names), but this never got beyond the letter A.[22]

BROWNE AND LIBERTY

The anti-colonialist Caetani was nicknamed 'the Turk' for his fierce opposition to his own country's occupation of Libya. There has been a marked tendency for Orientalists to be anti-imperialists, as their enthusiasm for Arab or Persian or Turkish culture often went hand in hand with a dislike of seeing those people defeated and dominated by the Italians, Russians, British or French. This was certainly the case with Edward Granville Browne (1862–1926).[23] He first became emotionally involved in Near Eastern matters while still a schoolboy, because of his passionate support for the Turks in their war against the Russians (1877–8). Later in life, as an internationally renowned Cambridge professor, he campaigned for Persian freedom and democracy. The young Browne had wanted to enlist in the Turkish army, but the war with the Russians concluded while he was still struggling to teach himself the Turkish language. Instead, he went to read medicine at Cambridge. Then he took up Oriental languages as well and studied Arabic with the mesmerizingly brilliant Edward Palmer. Browne arranged tuition in Persian from a Hindu gentleman in 1880 and later studied with an eccentric Persian, who had invented his own religion and resided in Limehouse.

In 1884 Browne secured a first-class degree in the Indian Languages tripos (Turkish, Arabic, Persian and Hindustani). However, he was told by the Thomas Adams Professor of Arabic, William Wright, that one really needed private means to pursue Oriental studies, as there were almost no jobs in the field: 'And from the Government you must look for nothing, for it has long shown, and still continues to show, an increasing indisposition to offer the slightest encouragement to the study of Eastern languages.' Browne, who later in his memoir *A Year Amongst the Persians* recorded Wright's words, added, 'Often I reflect in bitterness that England, though more directly interested in the East than any other country save Russia, offers less encouragement to her sons to engage in the study of Oriental languages than any other great European nation.'[24] Having been so discouraged by Wright, Browne went to London in 1884 and, in accordance with his father's wishes, carried on with medicine at St Bartholomew's. Though work as a medical student was arduous and distressing, he found comfort in reading the Sufis, 'whose mystical idealism, which had long since cast its spell over my mind, now supplied me with a powerful antidote against the pessimistic tendencies evoked by the daily contemplation of misery and pain ... Never before or since have I realized so clearly the immortality, greatness, and the virtue of the spirit of man, or the misery of its earthly environment: it seemed to me like a prince in rags ...'[25]

In 1887 Browne's destiny changed. He was elected a fellow at Pembroke College , Cambridge, with some prospect that he might be asked to teach the Persian language. He thereupon resolved to go out to Persia in order to improve his mastery of the language. The shaping role of the *Wanderjahre* is a recurrent feature in the history of Orientalism. Many of Goldziher's and Wright's insights were first formulated as a result of their early travels in the East. Browne wrote a classic of travel literature that is also a chronicle of intellectual exploration. *A Year Amongst the Persians* details his travels through Persia in 1887–8 and his picaresque encounters with Persian noblemen, mystics, philosophers, Zoroastrian priests, magicians, 'and social gatherings where wine and music, dance and song, beguiled away the soft spring days, or the moonlit nights'. Having read Gobineau, Browne had become particularly interested in the messianic Babi movement, but by the time he reached Persia, most of the Babis had deserted that movement and joined the breakaway Baha'i faith. The Baha'is were savagely persecuted by the Persian government and the Shi'ite religious authorities. The courage of the Baha'is in withstanding persecution led Browne to compare them to the early Christians. While in Kerman, he received a telegram from Cambridge informing him that a lectureship in Persian had just been created and offering him the post. He thereupon returned to England.

A Year Amongst the Persians was published in 1893, and Browne never returned to the land he loved so much. Indeed he hardly ever left Cambridge, even for London. In Cambridge he became a celebrated academic personality – one of the sights of the place. Laurence Graffety-Smith, a student and future member of the Levant Consular Service, described him as follows: 'Physically considered, he epitomized the processes of evolution: he was short and broad in the shoulder, with a stoop, and grotesquely long arms dangled in his shambling walk. His finely chiselled face was a radiance of intellect and of love for his fellow man.' Graffety-Smith added that his lectures had the confusion of 'a pack of hounds' in full cry'.[26] Reader Bullard, another student and future diplomat agreed: 'As a teacher in the narrow sense he was a joke ... but Browne had to be taken for what he was: a meteor, not a locomotive.'[27] Browne was impatient with dull-witted students. He was also prodigiously garrulous and spoke at a torrential speed and hardly listened to anything he was told. However, his speech was always entertaining and he was famously convivial. Denison Ross, the future director of the School of Oriental Studies, recalled engaging in table-turning in Browne's rooms in Pembroke and on another occasion taking Persian hashish there.[28]

Browne's mastery of Persian, Arabic and Turkish seems to have been perfect and he was alleged to dream in Persian. However, Cambridge had no professorship of Persian, so in 1902 he became the Thomas Adams Professor of Arabic and lectured on Arabic, and in 1921 he published *Arabian Medicine*. But his chief publications were in Persian studies, especially the fundamental *A Literary History of Persia* (4 volumes, 1902–24). He was Britain's first truly eminent Persianist since Thomas Hyde in the seventeenth century and Sir William Jones in the mid to late eighteenth century. Though Browne was a great expert on medieval Persian poetry, he was even more interested in contemporary Persia, in the Constitutional Movement, in the precariously free Persian press and in Persian resistance to the encroachments of Russian imperialism. According to another of his students who went on to have a distinguished diplomatic career, Sir Andrew Ryan, 'the last of the dragomans', Browne 'valued living oriental languages, not merely because they were still spoken, but because they were spoken by people whose aspirations enlisted his warmest sympathies'.[29] In the second volume of *The Literary History of Persia*, he had written: 'Year by year almost, the number of independent Muslim states grows less and less, while such as remain – Persia, Turkey, Arabia, Morocco and a few others – are ever more overshadowed by the menace of European interference.'[30]

Browne chronicled Russian atrocities in Tabriz and elsewhere. Not only did he campaign vigorously against the Russians and the complaisant British Foreign Office, he also agitated in favour of the Boers and for Irish Home Rule and he denounced Anglo-Indian officialdom. As noted, Browne was a specialist in Persian who mostly published in that area. I have lingered over his career partly because he is so interesting, but also because Browne was a superb Arabist. It is not possible to be a first-rate Persianist without a good command of Arabic. As Ann Lambton has pointed out in her *Persian Grammar*: 'There is a very large Arabic element in Persian. This element is an indispensable part of the spoken and written word.'[31] It is not just a matter of the entry of Arabic loan words into the Persian language, but also of whole phrases and constructions. Moreover, and most important for our purposes, Browne was an important and influential teacher of Arabic. Most of the important British Arabists of the next generation, including Reynold Alleyne Nicholson (1868–1945), the future author of *A Literary History of the Arabs*, were taught by Browne.

After undergraduate studies in Cambridge, followed by a year with Browne, Nicholson had studied in Leiden and Strasbourg with de Goeje and Nöldeke. Nicholson did important work editing and translating Arabic and Persian texts, especially Sufi ones.[32] Some of these had previously been translated by Hammer-Purgstall, but since the latter usually translated them into gibberish, Nicholson did valuable work here. His most important and accessible work was his *Literary History of the Arabs* (1907). This was intended as a companion volume to Browne's *Literary History of Persia*. In this book Nicholson, a classicist to his fingertips, devoted less than three pages to literary developments in the Arab world after 1798 and, as far as he was concerned, the main literary development in the modern world was the translation of European works into Arabic. The Arabs' own literary achievements were all firmly in the past, which 'affords an ample and splendid field of study'. He had read the classics at Cambridge and won the Porson Prize for verses in Greek and he only switched to Arabic and Persian for Part Two of the Cambridge exams. It is not surprising then that his history of Arabic literature is replete with comparisons and allusions to Greek and Roman authors. Pre-Islamic odes were compared to the *Odyssey* and the *Iliad*. Thus al-Ma'arri is compared to Lucian and Ibn Khaldun to Gibbon. Mas'udi is referred to as the 'Herodotus of the Arabs' as well as their 'Sueton-ius'. Abu Muslim's advance west against the Umayyads is compared to Caesar's crossing of the Rubicon. The Battle of Badr, fought between the followers of Muhammad and the pagan Quraysh, was compared to that of Marathon, fought between the ancient Greeks and Persians. *Laus duplex*, the Roman rhetorical figure, appears in Arabic also. The Abbasid historians' maligning of the Umayyads was compared by Nicholson to Tacitus's misrepresentation of Tiberius. Nicholson took for granted that all of his readers would be familiar with this sort of stuff. He never travelled out to the Middle East. What would have been the point? Indeed, although he taught both classical Arabic and Persian, he was unable to speak either of these languages.

The other striking feature of *A Literary History of the Arabs* is its heavy debt to continental scholarship. As Nicholson put it in the introduction: 'the reader will see for himself how much is derived from Von Kremer, Goldziher, Nöldeke, and Wellhausen, to mention only a few of the leading authorities'.[33] Although Nicholson knew a huge amount about Arabic literature, he did not like it very much and he found Arabic poetry much more alien than Persian. He judged the Qur'an to be 'obscure, tiresome, uninteresting: a farrago of long-winded narratives and prosaic exhortations'.[34] He preferred Persian mystical poetry and translated an enormous amount of the verses of the remarkable thirteenth-century Sufi, Jalal al-Din Rumi, but even Rumi was described by him as 'rambling, tedious and often obscure'. Nicholson's Edwardian style of translation has not worn well. As Franklin D. Lewis notes, 'Nicholson's verse translations, which reflect a Victorian sensibility, were already in his own day rather out of touch with the revolution of literary modernism and today sound quite dated and sentimental.'[35] Faced with the occasional obscenity in Rumi he translated it into a Latin that was modelled on the erotic Latin verses of Juvenal and Persius. However, for all his limitations, he was a learned, accurate, diligent scholar who did a huge amount to introduce the Western world to the classics of Arabic and Persian literature. His work on Sufism was particularly valuable as he was one of the first to present Muslim mystical experiences as valid rather than drug-induced hallucinations or disguised atheism. Although his protégé and successor as professor, A. J. Arberry, called him 'the dervish', there was nothing very wild or exotic about Nicholson. A round of golf was as much excitement as he ever encountered.

Arabic and Persian were taught as dead classical languages by Nicholson and his academic contemporaries. At first sight this sort of approach was not useful for Britain's proconsuls, diplomats and adventurers in the Middle East. But then consider that the proconsular mentality was formed by a deep familiarity with Greek and Latin. Lord Curzon, Sir Ronald Storrs, T. E. Lawrence and most of the rest of them were steeped in the Greek and Rome classics. Readings of Thucydides, Herodotus and Tacitus guided those who governed the British empire. Lord Cromer, the proconsul in Egypt, was obsessed with the Roman empire and its decline and fall. Sir Ronald Storrs used to read the *Odyssey* before breakfast. T. E. Lawrence read the Greek poets during his time as an archaeologist at Carcemish and later translated the *Odyssey*. Colonial administrators were much more likely to be familiar with the campaigns of Caesar than those of Muhammad and the Quraysh.

THE BELATED REVIVAL OF OXFORD ORIENTALISM

The appointment of William Robertson Smith to the Thomas Adams Professorship in 1870 had established a great intellectual tradition in Arabic studies at Cambridge that would include Edward Palmer and then the twentieth-century professors, Browne, Nicholson, A. J. Arberry and Malcolm Lyons. But the first intellectually commanding figure to hold the Laudian Chair of Arabic in Oxford since the seventeenth century, Margoliouth, was appointed only in 1889.[36] David Samuel Margoliouth (1858–1940), the son of a Jewish rabbi who had converted to Christianity, was born in Bethnal Green. He won a scholarship to Winchester and later read classics at Oxford and was awarded a first. Although he was to make a name for himself as an Arabist, he was first a classicist and he taught Latin and Greek to, among others, the future Regius Professor of Greek Gilbert Murray and the historian H. A. L. Fisher. Murray thought that Margoliouth lectured on Pindar not because he particularly liked the Greek poet's works, but because they raised difficult textual problems. Margoliouth was an eccentric genius in several languages, including Persian, Hebrew and Sanskrit. He was also striking in appearance. An Italian maid exclaimed on seeing him, 'Questo bel animale feroce!'

Having tutored the classics for most of the 1880s and published some fairly dry stuff about scholia (classical commentaries), he took up Arabic and was appointed Laudian Professor at the age of thirty – a post which he held until his retirement in 1937. He became ordained and gained a reputation as a great preacher. During the First World War he lectured in India. After the war, he spent a lot of time in Baghdad. The travel writer and influential political figure Gertrude Bell, who was in Baghdad in 1918, wrote home to England about Margoliouth's appearance there and how he lectured for fifty minutes by the clock on the ancient splendours of Baghdad in classical Arabic and without a note. 'It is the talk of the town. It's generally admitted that he knows more of Arabic language and history than any Arab here.' But in another letter she noted that at a later lecture given by Margoliouth, a brave member of the audience asked, 'How do you say in Arabic – Do you drive a motor car?', which angered the classically erudite professor.[37] According to *The Times*'s obituary of Margoliouth, he 'spoke the vernacular with scholarly precision; but the accent and intonation were not very much like any Arab', and the general consensus seems to have been that he spoke an Arabic that was so pure that ordinary Arabs could not understand it.

In the year he became professor he published *Analecta Orientalia ad Poeticam Aristoteleam* (1887), a collection of translations of Arabic and Syriac texts that might be used for textual criticism of the Greek text of Aristotle's *Poetics*. Margoliouth, who was brilliant at crosswords and anagrams, had the kind of beautiful mind that could see patterns where none existed. Among other things he conducted eccentric investigations into possible anagrams and chronograms in the *Iliad* and *Odyssey*. He believed that Homer had signed his epics, but disguised his signature in anagrams. In *The Homer of Aristotle* (1924) he argued that the Homeric epics were full of chronograms (words or phrases where the letters form a date). This kind of approach made little impression on more orthodox classical scholars.

His ideas about the Bible were similarly eccentric, as he entertained the strange belief that the Book of Daniel was written when it purported to be (sixth century BC) and therefore that its prophecies were genuine. Margoliouth's taste for making things difficult even extended to domestic matters and instead of telling his dog to 'Sit!' he used to order it to 'Assume the recumbent position!'

In the field of Arabic studies, he did solid work translating or editing such important medieval writers as al-Tanukhi, Miskawayh, al-Ma'arri, al-Baydawi, al-Yaqut and Ibn al-Jawzi. He did important work on Arabic papyrology. However, he also published several works that were accessible to a wider public and somewhat offensive to Muslims. He wrote *Mohammed and the Rise of Islam* (1906) for the popular 'Heroes of the Nations' series. In this book, Margoliouth's Gibbonian scepticism, oddly combined with Christian fervour, led him to present a thoroughly hostile portrait of Muhammad. He argued, like many before him, that Muhammad was an epileptic who had fits. However, where medieval polemicists had argued that the Prophet had married so many wives because of his excessive sensuality, Margoliouth argued that the marriages were mostly made in order to seal political pacts. He also suggested analogies between the founder of Islam and Brigham Young, the founder of the Mormon faith. As H. A. R. Gibb, his successor in the Laudian Chair of Arabic, wrote in his obituary of Margoliouth, 'the ironical tone which informed his observations disturbed many of his European and sometimes infuriated his Muslim readers'.[38] Among other things, he had suggested that there was no evidence that the Islamic faith improved the morality of those pagan Arabs who converted to it – rather the contrary. As for Muhammad, he was 'a robber chief'.

He went on in 1911 to write a book aimed at a broad audience, entitled *Mohammedanism*, in which potted history and other forms of elementary explication alternated with expressions of sheer prejudice. In this book he suggested that 'literary and scientific ability has usually been the result of the entry into Islam of Indo-Germanic elements'. In 1925 he published an extremely important article in the *Journal of the Royal Asiatic Society* in which he denied the authenticity of pre-Islamic poetry. Just a year later the distinguished Egyptian critic, novelist and historian Taha Husayn published a book *Fi al-Shi'r al-Jahili* ('On Pre-Islamic Poetry') in which he made essentially the same case. The arguments advanced by Margoliouth and Taha Husayn were highly controversial, as the discrediting of pre-Islamic poetry led on inevitably to doubts about the dating and composition of the Qur'an. Margoliouth was the first academic Orientalist to become president of the Royal Asiatic Society in 1937. Hitherto peers and gentlemen scholars had dominated that institution. Gladstone thought him one of the two most impressive men in Oxford. Denison Ross (on whom see below) thought him the most learned man he had ever met.

OUTSIDE OXBRIDGE

Like Nöldeke, Margoliouth did not think much of Arabic literature. Writing in the *Encyclopaedia of Islam* on al-Hariri's *Maqamat*, he commented that the 'reasons for this extraordinary success . . . are somewhat difficult to fathom and must be accounted for by the decline of literary taste'. And in his *Mohammedanism*, he observed that the failure of Arabic poetry to match that of Europe was 'in the main due to the unsuitability of the Heat-Belt for continuous intellectual effort'.

Sir Charles James Lyall (1845–1920), who devoted most of his leisure hours to the study and translation of early Arabic poetry, seems to have had similar reservations: 'To us much in these poems seems tedious and even repellent. The narrow range of the Kasida [ode], with its conventional framework, tends to produce monotony, and it is not easy to come into close touch with the life that is so realistically described.'[39] Lyall had studied Hebrew and then Arabic at Oxford, before entering the Bengal Civil Service. While employed in the service of the Raj he took up the translation of Arabic and especially pre-Islamic poetry as a recreation. Consideration of Lyall's career as an administrator and first-rate scholar prompts the reflection that the commonest link between Orientalism and empire was that the former was often the hobby of the masters of the latter. While on leave in Europe, Lyall studied with Nöldeke, to whom he dedicated his two collections of Arabic poetry and whom he called 'the acknowledged master of all European scholars in this field of study'. Lyall was a brilliant translator and his translations are still worth reading today. Despite his expressed reservations about the *qasidas*, he rendered them into vivid, poetic English. The original inspiration for his metrical translations of Arabic poetry came from his reading of the lyrical translations of Oriental poetry by Friedrich Rückert. But Lyall was also a meticulous philological editor and he followed the example of the Germans (again), as well as the Dutch and William Wright in that field.[40]

In Britain, there had been a long tradition of disparaging the Crusaders as barbaric and bigoted warmongers and of praising the Saracens as paladins of chivalry. Indeed, it was widely believed that chivalry originated in the Muslim East. The most perfect exemplar of Muslim chivalry was, of course, the twelfth-century Ayyubid Sultan Saladin. He was praised by Gibbon and became the hero of novels by Sir Walter Scott, G. A. Henty and Rider Haggard among many others. *Saladin and the Fall of the Kingdom of Jerusalem* (1898) by Stanley Lane-Poole (1854–1931) gave academic legitimacy to Saladin's heroic status, as Lane-Poole's was the first biography to be based on Arabic sources. His book appeared in a series devoted to 'Heroes of the Nations', though it was never clear exactly which nation the Kurdish Saladin belonged to. The story that Lane-Poole told was highly romanticized and absurdly biased against Saladin's Muslim and Christian enemies. Lane-Poole was a great-nephew of Edward William Lane and he republished several of his uncle's books and struggled (and failed) to complete Lane's great dictionary, as well as producing several popular narratives of Islamic history. He worked on cataloguing Muslim coins in the British Museum before becoming Professor of Arabic at Trinity College, Dublin.[41]

There is little to say about American Orientalism in the nineteenth or early twentieth centuries. Though there were, of course, distinguished individuals in the United States who interested themselves in Arabic and Islamic studies, they were few and there was no sustained academic tradition in these areas. Also it is perfectly clear that American Orientalists looked to Germany for inspiration and guidance. America's first Arabist of note, Edward Eldbridge Salisbury (1814–1901), after early studies in theology and Hebrew, travelled to Europe in 1837 and studied Arabic with de Sacy, before moving on to study philology and Sanskrit with Bopp in Berlin. In 1841 Salisbury was appointed Professor of Arabic and Sanskrit at Yale. This was the first Orientalist teaching post in the United States. However Salisbury, who spread his academic interests quite widely, seems to have been more interested in Sanskrit matters than Arabic ones.[42]

Charles Cutler Torrey (1863–1956) was another American Orientalist with broad interests, though in his case only in the area of Semitic studies and languages. Torrey, who was initially schooled in New England biblical scholarship, later went to Strasburg to study with the intimidating Nöldecke (who was described by Torrey as 'nobody's spring chicken').[43] One reason for crossing the Atlantic was to learn German – a vital language for any aspiring Semiticist. Although Torrey went on to publish numerous editions and specialized studies, he was not a pathfinder like his German teacher.

Duncan Black MacDonald (1863–1943), born in Glasgow and trained in Berlin before moving to Hartford in Connecticut, is the first US-based Orientalist worth lingering on. He did important work on Arab magic and superstition and on the manuscripts of *The Thousand and One Nights*. He also wrote copiously about Muslim–Christian relations and was involved in sending out Protestant missions to the Middle East.[44] In general, however, Americans were to contribute little to Orientalist scholarship until the second half of the twentieth century. There were few academic posts in the field and, for a long time, there were very few texts and manuscripts available to the students. The American Oriental Society, founded in 1842, was at first an association for interested amateurs. In the longer run, as we shall see, American Orientalism was put on firmer foundations by recruiting intellectual stars from across the Atlantic.

AFTER THE GREAT WAR

It was more or less inevitable that during the First World War and the years that immediately followed tensions should arise between German Orientalists and the rest. The internationalist spirit of academic Orientalism was strained to breaking point. As late as 1918 Torrey was still worrying about American Orientalism's over-dependence on German studies. But after the war German scholarship became suspect in some quarters and the prejudice even extended to philology in general, as this was the German speciality par excellence. As J. R. R. Tolkien, an expert on medieval literature and language as well as a novelist, noted: '"Philology" is in some quarters treated as though it were one of the things the late war was fought to end.'[45] Although the fascicules of the *Encyclopaedia of Islam* had originally been published in English, French and German, after the war the German version was dropped.

The break-up of the Ottoman empire was another important result of the war and one that also had consequences for the development of Orientalism. Until the war Germans and Swiss had led the way in the exploration of the monuments and archaeological sites of the Middle East. They included Alois Musil, who discovered the frescoes at Qusayr Amra in Jordan, Max van Berchem, who compiled the *Corpus Inscriptionum Arabicarum* and Friedrich Sarre who, together with Ernst Herzfeld, made a detailed archaeological survey of Mesopotamia.[46] After the war, Syria and Lebanon were placed under a French mandate, while Britain took over in Iraq, Jordan and Palestine. As a result, French and British scholars gained easier access to archaeological sites and monuments. The French led the way in urban and rural history. In particular, they mounted massive surveys of Islamic cities, both in the Levant and in North Africa. Roger le Tourneau produced several important books on Fez. Dominique Sourdel and Janine Sourdel-Thoumine worked on the architecture and topography of Damascus. Georges Marçais surveyed North African architecture. They and others in the field began to elaborate theories about the distinctive nature of the Islamic city.[47]

Jean Sauvaget (1901–50), a literary archaeologist who never excavated, made effective use of literary sources for urban history and architecture and published important studies of Aleppo and Damascus. In Egypt, Gaston Wiet (1887–1971), the director of the Museum of Arab Art in Cairo, was one of the foremost experts on the history of Cairo. For a long time Wiet's catalogues of the contents of that museum were among the very few substantial guides to Islamic art objects. The Egyptian King Fuad, resentful of the British occupation of Egypt, tended to favour French scholars over British ones. The

French in Egypt were the particular object of detestation of the intimidating Professor of Muslim Art and Architecture at the Fuad I University, Keppel Archibald Cameron Cresswell (1879–1974). He sternly advised the art historian Oleg Grabar to 'Beware of Sauvaget!' But it is perhaps worth noting that he detested Jews and Arabs almost as much as he did the French. He used always to have a stick with him when he walked through the streets of Cairo, so that if he saw a man maltreating a horse or a donkey, he could give that man a beating.[48] As for Sauvaget, the trouble with him was not just that he was French, but also that he had ideas (always a bad sign to Cresswell's way of thinking).

The classic theory of the 'Islamic city' had first been developed by the French in Algeria, and then exported to Syria – where Sauvaget was its main exponent. He was obsessed with the *Nachleben* (or afterlife) of antiquity. He wanted to find Rome in Damascus, Latakia and elsewhere. Therefore, the main focus of his interest was naturally Umayyad Syria, but he was more generally interested in the notion of the Islamic city. In his work on 'the silent web of Islamic history', he treated buildings as texts (and really only as texts for, like Cresswell, he had a healthy dislike for art historians). When dealing with manuscripts, Sauvaget (and Claude Cahen after him) placed great stress on understanding the sources of one's sources, or, to put it another way, it was not enough to parrot the information of late compilers like Ibn al-Athir or al-Maqrizi. Sauvaget also made effective use of local chroniclers. Cresswell, by contrast, did not trouble with theories about antiquity or the nature of pre-modern urban life. He concentrated narrowly on the chronology of the great Islamic monuments of Egypt and Syria and, despite his cantankerous prejudices, he did valuable work in this field, particularly as he worked at a time when people in the field were having difficulty in distinguishing Islamic monuments from Byzantine ones.[49]

THE ORIGINS OF SOAS

During the First World War British troops had defended Egypt and invaded Palestine, Syria and Iraq. They had also attempted a disastrous landing at Gallipoli. In the Hejaz T. E. Lawrence, according to his own account in *The Seven Pillars of Wisdom*, played a leading role in igniting the Arab Revolt. 'Britain's Moment in the Middle East' had come. The country's direct wartime stake in the Middle East gave ammunition to those who had been campaigning for the establishment in London of a specialist institution for the teaching of Oriental languages and cultures. In the previous century Max Müller, Lyall and others had campaigned for such an institution and the Royal Asiatic Society had also lobbied for it. The peers Curzon and Cromer, who had strong political interests in the East, viewed the Orientalists' campaign with favour. In 1917 the School of Oriental Studies in Finsbury Circus was opened in the presence of Lord Curzon and the War Cabinet. Though it was established by the government, it was not well funded and successive directors struggled to make ends meet and keep the institute afloat.[50]

The first director of the School of Oriental Studies was the flamboyant and vainglorious Sir Edward Denison Ross (1871–1940). Ross, who was linguistically gifted, went to Paris to study Hebrew with Renan and Persian with Charles Schefer. Renan 'made biblical criticism as entertaining as a detective story'. Schefer, the wealthy Persianist, lived in a chateau with his collection of Islamic art. Denison Ross also did research on Persian history in Strasburg with Nöldeke, whom he described as 'one of the most brilliant Orientalists the world has ever seen'. In the same year he attended lectures by Baron Viktor Rosen in St Petersburg. Denison Ross was like a bee flitting from one flower to another, but never staying long. In 1895 he became Professor of Persian at University College London and in the years that followed he got to know Edward Granville Browne and fell under his spell. In 1896 he produced a thesis on Isma'il, the first of the Persian Safavid Shahs. In 1897 he enjoyed a *Wanderjahr* that took him from London to St Petersburg and then on to Bukhara and Samarkand. Later he worked for the Indian Education Service in Calcutta.

Ross was Director of the School of Oriental Studies and Professor of Persian until his retirement in 1937. He dabbled in all sorts of subjects. For a while he took up Chinese and Uighur, but then lost interest. He was a brilliant dilettante, who used to declare that 'half the charm of oriental studies lies in their obscurity'. He was also a bon viveur, social climber, name dropper and enfant terrible. He used to go about wearing a black velour hat and carrying a Malacca cane. Cyril Philips, who later became Director, hated him. But Freya Stark, who studied Arabic at the School of Oriental Studies, before setting out on the travels through the Middle East that were to make her famous, found him enchanting: 'As we sat at our work, Sir Denison would trot in and out like a full moon dancing on the tips of its toes.'[51]

In the early years of the School Thomas Arnold (1864–1930) was Professor of Arabic and Islamic Studies and he was assisted by Hamilton Gibb. They taught tiny classes of half a dozen or so students. Arnold had read classics at Cambridge, but became interested in Islam and studied with Robertson Smith and Wellhausen. He went out to teach philosophy in the Muslim Anglo-Oriental College of Aligarh in India. In 1896 he published *The Preaching of Islam* (1896), an early major study of the spread of the Muslim message. He worked for a while at the India Office before moving to the School of Oriental Studies in 1917. There he turned to the study of Islamic art and was indeed one of the first scholars seriously to engage with this subject.[52] His *Painting in Islam* (1928) was a pioneering work in English. But this field, like so many others, was dominated by German scholarship and consequently it was from Germany and Austria that America was to recruit its leading historians of Islamic art, including Ernst Herzfeld at Chicago and Richard Ettinghausen at New York's Metropolitan Museum. Arnold died just a year too early to witness the great Persian Exhibition held in Burlington House, London, in 1931. Ross had a leading part in organizing this exhibition, which was a major event and was to inspire many who went on to do valuable work in Persian studies and Islamic art. (A previous exhibition of Islamic art in Munich in 1910 was similarly important.)

In 1937 the much less flamboyant Ralph Turner, a specialist in Indian studies, followed Denison Ross as Director of the School (which a year later became the School of Oriental and African Studies).

Ross and then Turner presided over an institution that was infested by eccentrics. Quite a few of its eminent professors regarded teaching as beneath their dignity. Sir Reginald Johnston, the Professor of Chinese from 1931 to 1937, used to turn up at the School once a year. Otherwise he lived as a recluse in Argyll. (The story is that when the School in despair advertised for someone who would actually do the teaching, Johnston was one of those who applied.) David Marshall Lang, the Professor of Caucasian Studies, did his best to discourage students from taking up his subject. The Arabist J. Heyworth-Dunne, who was wealthy and lived in a house furnished in the Islamic style, cultivated an air of sinister mystery. The linguistic genius Harold Bailey, who became lecturer in Iranian studies in 1929, was reputed to know fifty languages, including Sanskrit, Khotanese, Avestan, Ossetic, Pali, Prakrit, Chechen, Abkhaz, Circassian, Ubykh and even Welsh, but he possessed no small talk at all in any language.[53] Bailey, who studied Manichaeanism, must have been one of the sources for C. P. Snow's fictional Orientalist Roy Calvert in *The Light and the Dark*.

Orientalists had sold to the government the idea of the School as an imperial training centre, but most of those appointed seem to have been academics who despised the idea of vocational training. Cyril Philips, who taught at the School during Denison Ross's directorship and later became Director of the School of Oriental and African Studies himself, did not get on with Denison Ross and disapproved of the way the place was run: 'The study of Oriental subjects in Britain owed much to the German philological tradition of teaching and scholarship in which each professor and head of department arrogated, and was awarded excessive deference by his chosen circle of *dozenten*. A tradition of unrelenting, unpleasant, and often personal controversy had also carried over . . .'[54] As noted, there was not much money available. The young Financial Secretary to the Treasury, Stanley Baldwin, observed to Ross in the opening years of the School's existence, 'The opportunity of earning an income from the teaching of Oriental languages must be so limited that it does not appear to me that you ought to have any difficulty in retaining your existing lecturers or acquiring new ones on existing terms.'[55]

THE HOLY MADMAN – MASSIGNON

It must already be clear that, from Postel onwards, the ranks of the Orientalists have included more than their fair share of eccentrics. Few, however, can match Louis Massignon (1883–1962) for sheer strangeness.[56] His father was a painter, sculptor and medallist and a friend of the Orientalist painter Jan-Baptist Huysmans (1826–1906). Jan-Baptist was the father of the famous novelist Joris-Karl Huysmans (1848–1907). Though the latter's early novels, *A Rebours* and *Là-Bas* had dealt with decadent and Satanist subjects, he moved on to write novels with Catholic themes, in particular redemptory suffering and martyrdom. Incongruously, Huysmans's meditations on the Christian meaning of redemptive suffering seem to have been first inspired by the teaching of Abbé Boullan, a defrocked priest and Satanist. Huysmans believed that it was possible through conscious acceptance of one's own physical and spiritual sufferings to take some of the burden of sin and suffering from others. In his death agonies Huysmans was to pray for Massignon's soul.

Earlier in the nineteenth century similar belief in redemptive suffering had pervaded the writings of the arch-royalist and reactionary Joseph de Maistre (1755–1821). De Maistre held that the monstrous French Revolution was a blood sacrifice that had been necessary for national regeneration. The shedding of blood was a purifying act and the public executioner was consequently the guarantor of the community. According to his bizarre masterpiece of reactionary political theory, the *Soirées de Saint-Petersbourg*, the 'whole earth, continually steeped in blood, is nothing but an immense altar on which every living thing must be sacrificed without end, without restraint, without respite until the consummation of the world, the extinction of evil, the death of death'.[57] For Massignon, as for de Maistre, humanity was redeemed by blood sacrifice. The theme of mystical substitution – of atonement for the sins of others by offering up one's sufferings on their behalf – was to pervade his life and works. It is also possible that Massignon acquired a lifelong interest in secretive and esoteric groups from a reading of de Maistre (an Illuminist and Freemason).

While still at school Massignon became friends with Henri

Maspero, the future Sinologist and son of the famous Egyptologist and archaeologist, Gaston Maspero, and it was through the Masperos that Massignon first became interested in Oriental matters. He studied Islam and Arabic in Paris and Morocco and produced a philologically oriented thesis on Leo Africanus (the sixteenth-century Moroccan who converted to Catholicism in Rome and produced an important and lengthy description of Africa). In 1904 he went out to Morocco where he met Marshal Lyautey, the protectorate's military administrator, and became his friend and protégé. In the next few decades Massignon would receive several commissions to do research and advise on conditions in French colonial Morocco and Syria. In 1905 he met Goldziher at an Orientalist conference in Algiers. This meeting and a subsequent encounter with Goldziher in Copenhagen exercised a crucial influence on Massignon's direction as an Orientalist and there seems to have been a sense in which Massignon regarded himself as Goldziher's intellectual son and was so regarded by Goldziher. In particular, Goldziher's advocacy of *Verinnerlichung*, or interiorizing what one observes, strongly appealed to Massignon. Moreover, when in 1906 Massignon went to study at the al-Azhar in Cairo, he may have been following Goldziher's example.

But weirder, less straightforwardly academic contacts also shaped Massignon's mind. In 1906 on the boat out from Marseilles to Alexandria, he had encountered an aristocratic young Spanish homosexual, Luis de Cuadra, for whom he conceived a great passion. De Cuadra was a convert to Islam and during their time together in Alexandria and Cairo he sought to introduce Massignon to the interior life of Islam. Despite his religious conversion, de Cuadra led a wild life. In 1913 he fell seriously ill from typhus, whereupon Massignon prayed for his recovery, for his return to Christianity and the adoption of a less hedonistic life. Though de Cuadra recovered from the typhus, he did not otherwise improve. In 1921 Luis committed suicide in prison in Spain and his suicide was swiftly followed by that of his father. This tragedy was to mark Massignon for the rest of his life.

De Cuadra had introduced Massignon to the life and teachings of al-Hallaj, a controversial Sufi who had been hanged and then beheaded for heresy in Baghdad in 922. It was in pursuance of research on al-Hallaj that Massignon went to Iraq. Since he lived as an Arab he fell under suspicion of being a spy and was briefly imprisoned by the Turkish police and threatened with death (according to his own uncorroborated account). However, he escaped and it was during his flight that on 8 May 1908, before the ruins of Taq, the palace of Sasanian Emperor Khusrau, he experienced a mystical epiphany when he seemed to hear the doves above him call out 'Haqq, haqq'. (*Haqq* is the Arabic for truth and one of the heretical statements that al-Hallaj had been accused of making was '*Ana al-Haqq*', meaning 'I am the Truth', a statement that seemed to imply the mystic's identity with God.) In 1909 Massignon formally converted to Catholicism. Emaciated, always sombrely dressed and burning with a spiritual fervour, he looked like a latter-day Savonarola. The Catholic novelist François Mauriac, who encountered him at this time, recorded that he 'ascends to the highest levels of mysticism, and like many saints talks only about himself and offers himself endlessly as an example. He decked me out in Persian fabrics: he himself was dressed up like an Egyptian student. He talks about his disordered life when he brushed up against God in the slums of Cairo.'[58]

During the First World War, he worked for the Ministry of Foreign Affairs, then fought with distinction in the Dardanelles and Macedonia before ending up in the Middle East as the French High Commissioner Georges Picot's assistant political officer. It was Picot who, together with the British representative, Mark Sykes, drew up the agreement that divided the Arab lands that had formerly been part of the Ottoman empire into French and British spheres of control. Massignon was on the Anglo-French committee that drafted the Sykes–Picot agreement. In the closing stages of the war he was part of the French team that worked to prevent the Hashemite prince, Faisal, establishing an independent Arab monarchy in Syria.[59] In 1919 he got a post at the Collège de France, teaching the sociology of Islam, where he remained for most of the rest of his life. (The Collège was an elite institution with a distinguished history. Postel had taught there in the sixteenth century.)

The book that came out of the research in Egypt and Cairo, *La Passion d'al-Hallaj martyr mystique de l'Islam*, published in four volumes in 1925, is a weird book by a weird man about another weird man. In this book, Massignon not only presented a life of the much travelled and wonder-working Sufi, but furnished a rich and detailed portrait of the Baghdadi milieu in which he preached and studied his spiritual legacy. It is a seductive book but a highly problematic one. An American historian of the Middle East, R. Stephen Humphreys, recently described the book as 'an astonishing tour de force which cannot be – and perhaps should not be – duplicated'.[60] A reviewer of the English translation of Massignon's book (which appeared in 1983) noted that it 'combines extraordinary erudition with extremely incisive thought in a considerable variety of disciplines. The main thesis would, however, appear to be wrong.'[61] There are in fact very few reliable primary sources on al-Hallaj's life and teachings. Massignon made use of this deficiency, as he cast his net widely to present a Christian Catholic version of the Muslim Sufi's life. Al-Hallaj's execution in 922 was a kind of re-enactment of the Crucifixion, as al-Hallaj offered up his life for the Muslim community in an act of mystical substitution. Not only was he a Muslim Christ figure, he was also in a sense a precursor of Joan of Arc and Charles de Foucauld, the hermit martyred in the Algerian desert in 1916. (As we shall see, Massignon was a fervent French nationalist.) Though al-Hallaj was the obsession of a lifetime, Massignon was to declare that 'I do not pretend that the study of his life has yielded to me the secret of his heart, but rather it is he who has fathomed mine and who fathoms it still.'

Though the book is indeed brilliant, its fragmentary, digressive text reads oddly. It is more like a building site than a finished work of scholarship. Its footnoting is shoddy and inadequate, as the eventual American publishers of the English translation found to their cost. The notion of redemption through self-sacrifice that Massignon imposed on the story is quite alien to the Islamic mystical tradition. Nor does Islam recognize saints in the Catholic sense. As far as Massignon was concerned, al-Hallaj's performance of miracles was proof of his sainthood. (This sort of argument does not go down well with more conventional Orientalists.) Massignon's cult of al-Hallaj as a central figure in the Islamic tradition led him to disparage later, more influential Sufis such as the thirteenth-century Andalusian Ibn al-'Arabi. However, many Muslims in medieval times and, for that matter, today regard al-Hallaj as a heterodox and marginal figure.

Massignon disliked Shi'a Islam in large part because he believed that the Shi'as were responsible for his hero's death. He seems to have thought of Shi'ism as an early version of conspiratorial proto-Freemasonry or communism. Ironically his hostility to Shi'ism led him to underestimate the actual influence of this version of Islam on al-Hallaj's thinking. (Incidentally, Massignon's lifelong prejudice against Shi'ism was quite widely shared by Orientalists in the first three quarters of the twentieth century. Such grand figures as Goldziher and Hamilton Gibb presented Islamic history from a point of view that was unthinkingly Sunni in its perspective. Shi'ism was seen as a peculiarly backward and superstitious form of Islam that had no future. The Iranian revolution of 1979 was to change perceptions.)

Massignon's work on al-Hallaj was presented and successfully defended as a thesis in 1922. At the same time he presented a comple-mentary thesis. This was also published, under the title *Essai sur les origines du lexique technique de la mystique musulmane.* Here Massignon took a philological approach to selected Sufi texts, his aim being to demonstrate the Qur'anic origins of Sufism. In this he was running against the broad Orientalist orthodoxy of the time, which was to emphasize (and almost certainly overemphasize) unIslamic sources for Sufism, such as Christianity, Gnosticism, Buddhism and Hinduism. Massignon's grounding in German philological techniques and his probing for deep meanings in lexical items was to pervade most of his future researches on Islam and the Arabs. His philology was wedded to mysticism, as he believed that God was immanent in the structure of the Arabic language. That language was ideal for describing the shattering effect of the transcendent Deity entering this world. The speaking of Persian by many Muslims, especially Shi'is, was one of the things that had contributed to the degeneracy of Islam. Echoing Renan, Massignon suggested that the apparent sterility of Semitic languages arises from the fact that they are designed for interior contemplation. Although he was at first quite strongly influ-enced by Renan and Renan's presentation of German-style philology, it was more or less inevitable that he should eventually turn against the lapsed Catholic atheist and denounce Renan for his lack of sym-pathy for the cultures he wrote about. However, Massignon's own 'sympathy' for Islam was decidedly ambivalent and in a letter to the Catholic poet and dramatist Paul Claudel (another disciple of

Huysmans's doctrine of vicarious suffering), Massignon described his project as being to study the language of the Qur'an and thereby demolish it.[62]

As a teacher at the Collège de France from 1925, Massignon's charismatic and anguished lectures on the meaning of Islam and the mysteries of the Arabic language won him numerous disciples (and since his death these disciples have published numerous memoirs that amount to a hagiography of their master). However, not all his students were totally enchanted. Maxime Rodinson (on whom see below) thought that the amount of time Massignon devoted in his lectures to talking about sex, especially homosexual sex, was bizarre.[63] The Sura of Joseph in the Qur'an was a particularly favoured topic, as the beauty of the young Joseph in Egypt was celebrated in this sura. Massignon was also an unsystematic racist. Though he had many Jewish students, he seems to have been prejudiced against them and the young British Jew Bernard Lewis, who studied with him later, recalled that he was never sure whether he was regarded with suspicion by him because he belonged to the race that crucified Christ or because he belonged to the race that burnt Joan of Arc at the stake. Belgians were not much better. Massignon told the Arabist André Miquel that the Belgians avoided thought, 'for, as we know, thinking involves suffering'.[64] His other eccentricities included a fondness for lying on tombs. De Cuadra had introduced Massignon to the Qarafa cemetery in Cairo and ever since then he had cultivated a morbid obsession with tombs and cemeteries, one result of which was the publication in 1958 of an important article, 'La cité des morts au Caire', which dealt with topography, funerary rites and the very Massignonian theme of prayers of intercession.

For all his oddities he was very much a man of his times, and his agenda as an Orientalist should be seen in the context of the Catholic revival that took place in France in the first half of the twentieth century. Massignon's thinking should be related to that of other contemporaries such as Charles de Foucauld, Paul Claudel, Charles Péguy, Léon Bloy, Georges Bernanos and Jacques Maritain. Péguy was a leading figure behind the cult of Joan of Arc and the campaign that led to her canonization in 1920. Bloy, like Massignon, meditated on redemptory suffering. Bernanos's hostility to materialism and science probably influenced Massignon's attitude to those modern evils. Massignon's own Catholic engagement with Islam almost certainly influenced the deliberations of Vatican II and the Council's declaration that 'Throughout history even to the present day, there is found among different peoples a certain awareness of a hidden power, which lies behind the course of nature and the events of human life. At times there is present even a recognition of a supreme being, or still more of a Father . . . The Catholic Church rejects nothing of what is true and holy in these religions.'[65]

History, as Massignon conceived it, was the work of God. History was ultimately the history of holiness and was based on archetypes that manifested themselves in dreams. (Massignon was always particularly interested in dreams and his interest in them and in archetypes eventually brought him into close contact with Jung.) His methodology, if that is the word for it, was based on compassion, introspection, the quest for originality and globality. As Said put it in his essay, 'Islam, Philology and French Culture', for Massignon 'History . . . is made up of chains of individual witnesses scattered throughout Europe and the Orient, interceding with and substituting for one another.'[66] Jesus, al-Hallaj, Joan of Arc and de Foucauld were among those witnesses and Massignon strove throughout his life to join that holy chain. Philology was one of the means to that end, for it was 'the science of compassion'. Evidently his notion of philology was somewhat different from that of, say, Fleischer or Quatremère.

Abraham, Isaac and Ishmael were among the archetypal figures that featured prominently in Massignon's personal mythology. He took the figure of Abraham as it features in Islamic tradition and presented him as an archetype of the holy figure who offers hospitality and compassion and who offers himself as a substitute for the sins of others. Ishmael, the son of Abraham, and ancestor of the Arab race, had transmitted this cult of Abrahamic hospitality to his descendants. His brother Isaac, the ancestor of the Jews, had been chosen by Abraham as his successor over Ishmael the wanderer, who, as the disinherited son, prefigured the disinherited Muslims of modern times. The whole history of the Middle East could be read as the struggle between the two brothers. The great mission of the twentieth century, as Massignon saw it, was to bring Ishmael back within the fold of the true faith.

Massignon was a fervent patriot. His cult of Joan of Arc has already been mentioned and he was similarly devoted to the crusading king and saint, Louis IX. His belief in France's sacred destiny went hand in hand with an aversion to the British and their empire. He accused Britain of fostering hatred between Hindu and Muslim and he founded a group known as Les Amis du Gandhi. At first, Massignon felt rather differently about France's empire and *mission civilisatrice* in the Middle East and North Africa. He deluded himself into believing that the Arabs had accepted French colonialism in the spirit of sacred hospitality.

Ever since his first visit to Morocco in 1904 Massignon had been a friend and protégé of Marshal Lyautey. In the early 1920s he worked for Lyautey's colonial administration, researching craft guilds in Morocco. In general, French Orientalists tended to do research in Arab cities under French control, such as Fez, Casablanca, Tunis, Damascus and Beirut, and this encouraged them to present Islam as, above all, a religion of the cities. Moreover, Massignon and his colleagues took the view that there was such a thing as the distinctive Islamic city, centred around the mosque and the souq. Massignon came to believe that craft guilds played a central role in the life of the Islamic city and that Isma'ili Shi'ism was the dominant ideology in those guilds. Subsequently scholars have challenged Massignon's ideas of Isma'ilism, demonstrating that there were no such things as guilds in medieval Islam and querying the essentialist notion of the 'Islamic city'. His belief in esoterically motivated medieval craft guilds was of a piece with the twentieth-century French obsession with secret societies and sinister heterodoxies (Cathars, Templars, Illuminists, Freemasons and so on). As for the 'Islamic city', this had been conjured up by French historians and archaeologists on the basis of their knowledge of cities in French-controlled North Africa, but with little reference to cities further east in the Persian- and Turkish-speaking lands.

Though Massignon was for a long time a believer in the French imperial project, he thought that the French colonial authorities should work with the Arab Muslims rather than play off the religious and racial minorities (Christian, Jewish, Berber, Kabyle, Druze and so on) against them. In the longer term he came to think of imperialism in the region as an abuse of the hospitality that he imagined had been on offer and he became a prominent opponent of French colonialist policies in North Africa. From 1953 onwards he campaigned for the return of the Sultan of Morocco from his enforced exile in Madagascar. Later on, he protested against French policies in Algeria and, together with François Mauriac and Jean-Paul Sartre, he agitated for Algerian independence. (In general it is striking how many twentieth-century French Orientalists were anti-imperialist – among them Jacques Berque, Vincent Monteil, Charles André Julien, Régis Blachère, Claude Cahen and Maxime Rodinson.) Massignon became increasingly hostile to the Catholic Church in his own time as well as to 'the rich, developed, arrogant West' and he argued that a revived Islam should take the lead against the oppression of superior technology, science and banking produced by a godless Europe.

He was a consistent anti-Zionist and a partisan for Palestinian rights. In part this was because of his identification with Arab and Muslim culture, but in part it seems to have been because he did not like Jews very much. There were a lot of Jews teaching at the Collège de France – until, that is, the Second World War and the purges instituted by the Vichy regime. During the 1920s Massignon, like many Catholic thinkers, had been close to the extreme right-wing organization, Action Française. He viewed with dismay the influx into France of Jews fleeing Nazism. In 1938 he had argued that French Jews were leading France to destruction. He believed that the war, when it came, was largely the result of the scheming of British (and Jewish) financiers. On the other hand, he did remain friendly with individual Jewish scholars and he despised the Vichy regime. After the war, he came to fear that Israel, once established, would be in effect an Anglo-American colony and he prayed that Palestinians and Jews would combine against Anglo-American hegemony. He hated the technocracy and atheism of the leading Zionists. In 1945 he intervened to prevent Hajj Amin al-Hussaini, the Mufti of Jerusalem, from being extradited from France. During the war al-Hussaini, in the hope of seeing a Palestine cleansed of Jews, had put himself in the service of the Nazis.

When Massignon died in 1962 many of those who knew him regarded him as a saint. He believed that Christians had a great deal to learn from Muslims about true monotheism, the nature of prayer and much else. He prayed for the salvation of Muslims and for their coming over to the true faith. His own deep religious convictions led him to empathize with Muslims and at the same time to patronize them. His history of Islam was permeated by esoteric and Christological themes that only he and his disciples found in that history.

ORIENTALISM IN THE SERVICE OF THE BOLSHEVIK EMPIRE

Massignon had been involved in the French colonial enterprise in North Africa. Snouck Hurgronje spent much of his life in the service of Dutch colonialism. However, if one wants to give full and proper consideration to the relationship between Orientalism and imperialism, then one should turn to Russia with its vast empire of Muslim subjects in the Caucasus and Central Asia. No history of Orientalism can be regarded as serious if it has totally neglected the contribution of the Russians. The opening year of the twentieth century saw the establishment of the Imperial Oriental Institute in St Petersburg. Viktor Rosen was at that time the dominating figure and the teacher of Barthold and Kratchkovsky, the two greatest Russian Orientalists of the early twentieth century and the guardians of a pre-communist tradition of scholarship.

According to *The Great Soviet Encyclopedia*, Vasili Vladimirovich Bartold (1869–1930) had a bourgeois upbringing and consequently embraced an idealist conception of historical processes.[67] Although he paid a lot of attention to the class struggle, he was no communist. He remained an idealist who tended to place emphasis on ideological factors rather than material ones. He was primarily a Turcologist, who tended to present a positive picture of pre-modern Turco-Mongol culture, and consequently he was attacked by the orthodox communist Orientalist Petrushevsky for his 'racialist-nationalist idealization of the Turco-Tatar nomads'. Moreover, his views on the economic consequences of the Mongol invasions 'cannot be accepted by Soviet historiography'. (Bartold had argued that accounts of Mongol destruction and savagery in the thirteenth century were exaggerated and that in some respects the Mongol occupation of medieval Russia had had beneficial results.[68]) *The Great Soviet Encyclopedia* echoed Petrushevsky and decreed that not enough 'consideration is given to the fact that the Mongol conquest led to the destruction of productive forces and the protracted enslavement of subjugated peoples'. The communist Orientalist Belyaev pronounced Bartold's *The World of Islam* to be a valuable work of vulgarization, 'despite being written from the standpoint of European bourgeois Orientalism'. Smirnov, another communist academic hack, denounced Bartold for not regarding Islam as an ideology and for failing to detect the class-based nature of Islam and 'the fact that it always and everywhere serves as an instrument of exploitation and coercion of the toiling masses'. Bartold's books were banned by the Soviet authorities for a while, but then reprinted in the 1960s with corrective annotations. Though Bartold's main work was on Turkish materials, he was also an Arabist and, for example, in an article on 'The Koran and the Sea', he argued that the maritime references in the Qur'an could not have come from Jewish sources.

Bartold's old-fashioned scholarly respect for facts and his bourgeois idealism attracted an enormous amount of criticism from more craven or ideologically deluded colleagues. Nevertheless, his international reputation saved him from losing his teaching post or worse. The same was true of his contemporary Ignatius Kratchkovsky (1883–1951).[69] As a schoolboy, the book-mad Kratchkovsky had tried to learn Arabic from de Sacy's grammar, before learning the language properly with Viktor Rosen. In the relatively free and easy last days of the old Russian empire Kratchkovsky travelled out to Lebanon and Egypt where he made many friends among the Arab intelligentsia. Things became much harder once the Bolshevik Revolution got under way and he recorded that the director of the library that he was working in had died of malnutrition. Although Kratchkovsky was frequently attacked by his younger colleagues because of the old-fashioned nature of his scholarship and his highly suspicious contacts with Orientalists abroad, he survived – but only just. He suffered from the 'bourgeois' defect of paying too much attention to foreign scholarship and therefore minimizing the glorious achievements of Russians in the field. He held that an Arabist must be familiar with English, French and German, 'but also with Italian because since the second half of this century works in this language on Arabic subjects have taken their place in the forefront of learned literature'. Spanish was also desirable, if one was going to study the Arabs in Spain.[70] In 1930 he invited Massignon to Russia on a visit of academic goodwill and, as a consequence, was jailed for nine months, as the Soviet authorities decided that Massignon was really a spy. Kratchkovsky, who was frequently prone to depression, tended to take refuge in obscure Oriental books and manuscripts. He was in charge of the Leningrad Academy during the bitter siege of that city in 1941 and 1942, during which he immersed himself in a manuscript of al-Maqqari's *Nafh al-Tib* (a sixteenth-century account of the past glories of Muslim Spain).

'My heart is saddened. The shades of the teachers do not hide from us the shades of our pupils who passed away before us. Many of these do I see: a life full of hardships and two devastating wars cut down the young shoots before their prime and it was not given to all to attain full blossom. But they all had entered the realm of learning and had felt its fascination. To them, as to me, the manuscripts had spoken in the tongue of the living, and they had come to me with the treasures which they had unearthed.'[71] These melancholy reflections came at the end of his memoir of a life in Orientalism. Few Orientalists have produced autobiographies (but notable exceptions are Denison Ross, André Miquel and Maxime Rodinson). As Kratchkovsky observed, 'scholars seldom speak about themselves, their development, the emotions which accompanied their work and the circumstances in which they made their discoveries'. Kratchkovsky's *Among Arabic Manuscripts* (1945, English translation 1953), despite its frequent reference to hardship and depression, is easily the most delightful example of the genre.

Kratchkovsky was fabulously prolific and moved from topic to topic. Like Hamilton Gibb, he was extremely interested in modernist and reformist movements in the Middle East and in the modern Arabic novel. However, his major work was a comprehensive work on the medieval Arab geographers, published in Russian but subsequently translated into Arabic, and still of use today.[72] He also produced a Russian translation of the Qur'an from the Arabic. (All but one of the previous Russian 'translations' had actually been made from

European languages.) As noted, he enjoyed an international reputation. However, it is time to turn to some of his less estimable and sometimes rather bizarre colleagues and successors.

Soviet Orientalists were at the service of an empire with a vast population of Muslims. In 1917 the Bolshevik regime issued a decree guaranteeing freedom of conscience for Muslims. According to a proclamation of the Scientific Association of Russian Orientalists in 1921, 'Moscow is the new Mecca; it is the Medina of all repressed peoples.' Yet, despite the fair-seeming promises, Islam was pilloried in the Soviet museums of atheism and Soviet Orientalists were enlisted to combat Islamic superstition. There was also a fierce campaign against the use of the Arabic script. It was described as the script of the reactionary mullahs and Sufis and as not being particularly well adapted to rendering the Turkic languages. Possession of books in the Arabic script could lead to the death sentence: Islamic culture and social structures were things that the Muslim peoples had to be weaned away from. Broadly speaking, the Soviet orthodoxy was that Islamic society had to pass through five stages: primitive society, slave-holding, feudal, capitalist and Marxist socialist.[73]

The life of the Prophet and the first century of Islam were subjected to particularly fierce scrutiny by Soviet Orientalists. Some scholars were content to do not much more than present the rise of Islam within a determining economic context. E. A. Belyaev, for example, accepted that the Prophet was a historical figure. His *Arabs, Islam and the Arab Caliphate in the Early Middle Ages* placed heavy emphasis on the role of the physical environment in the rise of Islam. More specifically, Islam was a religion that arose to serve the interests of the slave-owning mercantile bourgeoisie of Mecca and Medina. The Qur'an was not revealed by the Prophet, but concocted after the latter's death. Early Islamic society made the transition from a slave-owning patriarchal society to a more advanced feudalism. Belyaev stressed the importance of heterodox and revolutionary movements in the early Islamic period, such as the Mazdakites and the Kharijites, and he was a keen, if belated, supporter of the aspirations of the working masses of the early medieval Middle East, which he thought these movements represented. He also emphasized the destructive nature of the early Arab conquests.[74] (The denunciation of the nomad invasions, whether Arab, Turkish or Mongol, was a routine duty for Soviet scholars.) Although Belyaev tried to make a point of ignoring both European and Arab scholarship in his field as such scholarship was inevitably ideologically tainted, he was still denounced by some of his colleagues for paying too much attention to such material.

Some Soviet Orientalists took a much more destructive approach to Islamic history. Klimovich wrote an article entitled 'Did Muhammad exist?' in which the answer to the question so posed was no. All the sources on the Prophet's life were late and dubious. In *The Contents of the Koran* (1928), Klimovich sought to lay bare its internal contradictions. It was, he maintained, a document drafted on behalf of the exploiters – the mercantile bourgeoisie of Mecca and Medina – that promised the exploited masses a paradise in the never-never that was the main force behind Islam.[75] The Prophet was a back-formation – a figure retrospectively invented in order to give the religion a founder. N. A. Morozov went further yet and argued in *Christ* (1930) that, until the shock of the Crusades, Islam and Judaism were indistinguishable from one another. There were indications in the Qur'an that it was composed as late as the eleventh century. Islam could not possibly have originated in the Arabian peninsula, as it was too far from the main centres of civilization to give birth to a new religion. Muhammad and the early caliphs were merely mythical figures. Inconsistently, Morozov, having suggested that early Islam did not differ from Judaism, also suggested that early Islam was merely a version of the Christian Arian heresy.[76] (Arians denied that Christ was fully divine or consubstantial with God the Father.) Needless to say, no Soviet scholars took the traditional Muslim view of the origins of Islam. The only substantial debate was over the question whether the rise of that religion represented a triumph of the bourgeoisie or if it reflected an earlier phase in historical evolution, the transition from a slave-owning society to a feudal one.

NAZI ORIENTALISM

The German and Nazi agenda in Middle Eastern studies was less obvious and less pervasive than the Soviet Russian one. In so far as they took any interest in Oriental matters at all, Nazi ideologues were more interested in Indian and Tibetan matters, and a motley band of scholars and eccentrics under the patronage of Heinrich Himmler and Alfred Rosenberg quested for the origins of the Teutonic master race somewhere in Asia.[77] Walther Wüst, a keen Nazi, a specialist in the Veda (the ancient holy books of the Hindus) and an Orientalist in the broad sense, was the key figure in this quasi-scientific research into the Asian origins of the Aryans. The Veda, as presented by him, were blessedly free of any Semitic taint and fully in accord with Hitler's *Mein Kampf*. By contrast, the Nazis took little interest in Arab or Islamic studies, despite widespread hopes in the Arab world that the Nazis would liberate them from British and French colonialism. In *Mein Kampf*, Hitler had expressed his contempt for Arab nationalists.[78] He considered that Arabs deserved to be colonized. Several institutes of Oriental studies were closed during the Nazi period.

In the introduction to a supplementary volume of his *Geschichte der Arabische Literatur* ('A History of Arabic Literature'), Carl Brockelmann (1868–1956) described the Arabist and Weimar Minister, Carl Heinrich Becker, as 'the minister against German culture'.[79] Brockelmann, an extreme right-winger, had had a traditional German university education, in the course of which he had acquired the duelling scar that was de rigueur among right-wing student fraternities. However, he had also studied with the mighty Goldziher whom he revered as the master of Islamic studies. Brockelmann's *Geschichte der Arabischen Literatur* (1898–1902 and supplementary volumes 1937–42) comes second only to the *Encyclopaedia of Islam* among the important Orientalist publications of the twentieth century. It is not, as its title might suggest, a narrative history of Arabic literature. It is rather a vast annotated catalogue of all the Arabic manuscripts and printed books that were known to Brockelmann. As such it is an indispensable work of reference. Yet he compiled the book only in order to persuade his publisher to take his real enthusiasm, his edition of Ibn Qutayba's *Uyun al-Akhbar* (a ninth-century anthology of Arabic prose and poetry).[80]

Brockelmann's work on Arabic manuscripts was very much in the German philological tradition as pioneered by Fleischer. Hans Heinrich Schaeder (1896–1957), on the other hand, was the scholarly heir to a more romantic approach to Islam that can be traced back to von Hammer-Purgstall, Goethe and Rückert. At school he had studied Latin, Greek, English, French and Hebrew. During the First World War he pursued a self-taught course of European literature and Oriental grammar and he came to adopt a conservative, Junker position. When, in the aftermath of the war, Oswald Spengler published his *Der Untergang des Abendlandes* ('Decline of the West'), Schaeder was influenced by that. He also read T. S. Eliot's essays on culture and tradition and Hugo von Hofmannsthal's melancholy *fin de siècle* fantasies. As an Arabist, Schaeder studied with Carl Heinrich Becker and he shared the latter's overwhelming enthusiasm for the Graeco-Latin heritage. Schaeder's early work was on the eighth-century Arab Sufi, Hasan of Basra, and the fourteenth-century Persian poet, Hafiz of Shiraz (who may or may not also have been a Sufi). Having read Massignon's book on the martyrdom of al-Hallaj, he fell under the mesmerizing spell of the book's author and concentrated his researches on religious and, more specifically, Sufi terminology. Like Massignon, Schaeder was a convert to Catholicism and he relied more on inspiration than solidly referenced research. Apart from Massignon, Goethe was the other *maître à penser* who influenced his interpretation of Sufism. He wrote a study on Goethe's *Erlebnis des Ostens* ('Experience of the East'). Goethe's poetry was a kind of private Bible and Schaeder regarded Goethe's collection of Oriental pastiches, the *West–östlicher Divan*, as the foundation document of Orientalism. This enthusiasm for Goethe was something that he passed on to his student Annemarie Schimmel (later to become famous as a saintly and learned interpreter of Sufism).

From 1931 until 1944 Schaeder was Professor of Oriental Philology and Religious History at Berlin and a leading spokesman of Nazi Orientalism. He wrote a history of Orientalism, which excluded all mention of the contribution of Jewish scholars. Schaeder's racism pervaded his thinking on Middle Eastern culture too. One German

Orientalist remembered Schaeder exclaiming to him, 'Aha, you work on Islamic philosophy! But there were no Muslim philosophers. They were all infidels.' Schaeder's view was that the Semitic Arabs were incapable of that kind of abstract and speculative thought, so that Islamic philosophy was really the creation of Persian and other races. Although the Arabs had translated a lot of Greek materials, they chose only utilitarian subjects to translate and therefore they had failed to inherit the Graeco-Latin humanism that was the special heritage of Western Europe. In the long run, Islamic culture, like all other non-European forms of culture, was doomed to disappear. History was the story of the triumph of the West. After the Second World War Schaeder taught at Göttingen (1946–57), where his ideas were shaped by his literary romanticism and his racism.[81] But at the risk of labouring the obvious, this does not mean that all he published on Sufism and Manichaeanism was worthless. On the contrary, his work on Sufism was fundamental and is of lasting value and, as Annemarie Schimmel has pointed out, two of the leading Jewish scholars who fled to the United States – Gustav von Grunebaum and Franz Rosenthal – revered Schaeder.[82]

With the coming to power of the Nazis, Germany suffered a haemorrhage of scholarship as Jewish professors and others fled to France, Britain, the United States and elsewhere. The great tradition of German Orientalism that had begun with Fleischer and Hammer-Purgstall effectively came to an end. On the other hand, the diaspora of scholars in this field effectively re-established Orientalism on a new and more profound basis in Israel, Britain and the United States – and that will be one of the leading themes of the next chapter.

8

The All Too Brief Heyday
of Orientalism

Mostly he inclined to the ancient Chinese. He commanded them to step out of the volume and shelf to which they belonged, beckoned to them, offered them chairs, greeted them, threatened them, and according to his taste put his own words into their mouths and defended his own opinions against them until at length he had silenced them.

Elias Canetti, *Auto-da-Fé* (1946)

THE WAR AND ITS OUTCOME

The Second World War was the making of academic Orientalism in Britain. Hitherto the study and teaching of Arabic and Islamic studies had depended on a handful of often grand, but rather eccentric figures. In the wake of the war, additional departments were established and enough scholars entered the field for proper scholarly discourse to take place. Historians replaced philologists as the authors of works on Islamic history. Anthropologists, sociologists and geographers also began to make a contribution. Moreover, there was growing emphasis on teaching the modern and spoken versions of Oriental languages. During the Second World War a number of Orientalists had worked in intelligence. Charles Beckingham, the future translator of the fourteenth-century North African globetrotter Ibn Battuta, was at Bletchley Park. Freddie Beeston (on whom see below) was in military intelligence. Bernard Lewis was posted to Istanbul, where he also seems to have worked for intelligence. Others found their linguistic expertise being employed in less glamorous spheres, such as broadcasting and postal censorship. Margoliouth, Hamilton Gibb, Lewis and R. B. Serjeant were among the academic Arabists who made broadcasts for the BBC Arabic Service during the war. Large numbers of troops were posted in Egypt and fought in North Africa and Syria. Never before had there been such a demand for people with a good knowledge of contemporary spoken Arabic. Towards the end of the war, Britain directly or indirectly controlled most of the Middle East from Iran to Morocco. One minor consequence of this was that in London the School of Oriental and African Studies (SOAS) was crowded with servicemen, diplomats and administrators taking language and culture courses before setting out for the Far East, India and Sudan. At the same time, MECAS (the Middle East Centre for Arab Studies), which at that time was based in Jerusalem, was also providing British personnel with crash courses in Arabic.[1]

The wartime perception by ministers and civil servants of the usefulness of Arabic (something that had no real precedent) carried over into the immediate post-war period. In 1944, dismayed by Britain's earlier reverses in the Far East, the then Secretary of State for Foreign Affairs, Anthony Eden, set up a committee under the chairmanship of Lord Scarborough (a former governor of Bombay) 'to examine the facilities offered by universities and other educational institutions in Great Britain for the study of Oriental, Slavonic, East European and African languages and cultures, to consider what advantage is being taken of these facilities and to formulate recommendations for their improvement'. (Eden, incidentally, was an Arabist and a former student of Margoliouth.) The committee brought out its report in 1946. It found that British Orientalism lagged behind that on the Continent to a disturbing degree and it recommended vastly expanded funding for African, Asian, East European and Slavonic studies and that this expansion should take place irrespective of student demand. (Those were the days.) The Cambridge Arabist Arberry called it 'the Charter of Modern Orientalism'.[2] In practice, London University's SOAS and the School of East European and Slavonic Studies got most of what money was immediately available, though Durham and Manchester also benefited. Durham was unusual in paying as much attention as it did to modern Arabic. James Craig, who was a lecturer in Durham in the 1940s and 1950s before going on eventually to become Ambassador to Saudi Arabia, remarked that, 'In those days Arabic in England was taught exactly like Latin and Greek and at the end of my studies, though I had read a great deal of pre-Islamic poetry and knew all about the jussive mood, I was quite unable to say "good morning" in Arabic.' Prior to the publication of an English version of Hans Wehr's *Arabisches Wörterbuch* in 1960, English students were still using Freytag's *Lexicon Arabico–Latinum*. Professor Hamilton Gibb warned Craig against spending time in the Middle East, as 'it will corrupt your classical'.[3]

We also learn from Craig that by 1949 Gibb believed that the role of the Orientalist was coming to an end. After all, he argued, the Arabs had the language advantage when it came to the study of their own literature. All that the upcoming generation of Arab teachers and students needed to do was to master the methodology of their chosen fields. But on the whole, and with certain exceptions, Gibb's expectations have not been fulfilled. Books published by academics in Arab universities still tend to be somewhat old-fashioned in their methodology and presentation. What is published in the Arab world is often out of date and, as it were, superseded in advance by research published in the West. Stephan Conermann, a professor at the German University of Kiel, after briefly surveying work published by Arabs on Mamluk history in the 1990s and the reception of that work by specialist reviewers in the West, wrote as follows:

It seems to me that we find ourselves in an Orientalist predicament. On the one hand, considering the postmodern reappraisal of the colonial past, generally it is politically incorrect to make derogatory remarks about the scholarly works of Arab historians. As a product of Western socialization, one is not only suspected of judging the 'natives' as foolish and incompetent but also of reducing them to the rank of mere objects to be studied. On the other hand, in the age of ongoing globalization the Western scientific approach carries the day. If science stands for a special kind of communication that has been (at least temporarily) established by scholars who dominate this discourse, it can be taken for granted that everyone who wants to be part of the game has to follow its rules. This is of course – in spite of the overall calling for authenticity – the endeavour of the majority of Arab scholars.[4]

Conermann went on to identify the causes of the perceived problem as being, first, the old-fashioned hierarchical structure of Arab universities which obliged the students to defer to their professors with their dated scholastic agendas, and secondly, the restricted access Arab scholars had to recent Western publications, and consequently and thirdly, their failure to keep up with the methodological debates of recent decades. There is still no Arabic equivalent of the *Encyclopaedia of Islam*. In this respect, among others, there is a contrast to be made with Turkish scholarship. Turkish academics used the European *Encyclopaedia* as the basis for their own *Islam Ansiklopedisi* (1940–), the latter offering of course increased coverage of the Turkish heritage. Von Grunebaum, who had a rather downbeat view of the degree to which Arab academics had adapted to modern methodologies, observed that 'only the Turks among Muslims have successfully adapted to Western historiography'. Albert Hourani argued that part of the problem was that the Arab scholars who were any good went and got jobs in the West.[5] Indeed, a striking number of Arabs occupy teaching posts in the United States.

In order to improve British opportunities and problems in the postwar era, SOAS and other institutions were being given money to promote the teaching of exotic languages with the utilitarian aim of furthering Britain's military, diplomatic and commercial presence in the world. However, the academic mindset being what it has always been, in practice the subventions from the Foreign Office were often used to fund the study of such recondite matters as the study of pre-Islamic poetry, the origins of Taoist philosophy, the philology of various dead languages of the Caucasus and so forth. Ralph Turner, who had succeeded Denison Ross as Director of SOAS in 1938, was determined that the place should remain 'a repository of learning'. The reluctance of university Arabists to move away from traditional preoccupations deriving from classical studies, biblical studies and philology meant that the army and the colonial service had to fund its own Arabic institution in the Middle East. Driven out by the growing turbulence in Palestine, MECAS moved from Jerusalem to Shemlan in the Lebanon. There it gained a reputation, which may not have been entirely undeserved, for being a 'nest of spies'. However, its main aim was certainly to teach language skills to administrators, businessmen and officers who worked publicly and uncontroversially in the Arabic-speaking world. After only a few years, both the universities and MECAS suffered from post-war retrenchment and financial austerity.[6] There were simply not enough funds to supply anachronistic imperial dreams and soon what has been called Britain's 'moment in the Middle East' would be coming to an end. In the event, full-blown academic Orientalism was, just like subaltern studies (studies of history from the point of view of inferior groups, in particular studies of colonial rule from the perspective of the colonized), a product of the post-colonial era. From 1954 onwards the massive labour of substantially revising and expanding the *Encyclopaedia of Islam* got under way. In the early stages Hamilton Gibb, Evariste Lévi-Provençal and Joseph Schacht were its editors. (Lévi-Provençal was a French expert on medieval Spain.) This time around, more Muslim scholars were invited to contribute to the *Encyclopaedia*, though arguably still not enough.

GIBB AND ARBERRY

Although Oxford and Cambridge no longer exercised the sort of monopoly over Arabic and Islamic studies they once had, it was still the case that, until his departure for the United States in 1955, the most influential Arabist in Britain was the Laudian Professor of Arabic at Oxford, Sir Hamilton Alexander Rosskeen Gibb (1895–1971).[7] Gibb, who was born in Alexandria, studied Semitic languages at Edinburgh University. An early reading of Sir Walter Scott's romantic novel, *The Talisman*, shaped his future portrait of Saladin, the leader of the Muslim counter-crusade. A committed Christian, Gibb identified strongly with Saladin's well-advertised piety. In 1937, after previously teaching at SOAS, Gibb was appointed to the professorship at Oxford. Like most Orientalists who thought seriously about Islamic history, Gibb was strongly influenced by Goldziher. However, the influence of the fourteenth-century North African philosopher-historian Ibn Khaldun was at least as strong. Ideas derived from both sources came together in Gibb's brilliant and highly influential (though perhaps misleading) essay of grand synthesis, 'An Interpretation of Islamic History' (first published in 1953). Among other things, Ibn Khaldun had argued that regimes that failed to observe the Shar'ia or holy law were doomed to follow a recurrent cycle of rise and decline. Gibb, like Ibn Khaldun, believed in historical laws. According to one obituary of Gibb, history was for him 'the search for patterns on the web of human life'.[8]

As we have seen, Goldziher had placed heavy emphasis on the ways in which Islamic societies were not static, but evolved over the centuries. However, Goldziher tended to see evolution as a more or less exclusively Sunni phenomenon. In the shadow of Goldziher, Gibb formulated an overarching vision of Islamic history as the long march extending over many generations of the Sunni Muslim community and its repeated successes in warding off threats from Shi'ism, antinomian Sufism and philosophy as well as from external enemies like the Crusaders and Mongols. For Gibb Shi'ism was an adversarial cult rather than a (or even the) legitimate Islamic tradition. Gibb, like most historians of his generation and the next, took it for granted that the golden age of Islamic civilization was under the Abbasid caliphs (c. 750–945). Thereafter, the story of Islam was one of decline. Gibb's Saladin was austere, frugal and pious as befitted an honorary Scotsman. He was an exceptional figure who rose above the conventional politicking of the age, and sought to reunite the Islamic community. Saladin recaptured Jerusalem from the Crusaders. But, though Saladin was a hero, he was a hero *manqué*. In the late twelfth century he had struggled to recreate the golden moment of the Abbasids and he had failed. In Gibb's line of thinking, one can detect half-echoes of Ibn Khaldun, who had argued that Saladin was an exceptional figure who had used the jihad to revive the *'isaba*, or social solidarity, of the Muslim community.

When Gibb came to write a history of Arabic literature, he brought the story to an end in the mid-thirteenth century – despite the fact that he took an unusually serious interest in contemporary Arabic literature. As a Christian moralist, he was inclined to blame Islam's decline on carnality, greed and mysticism. On the other hand, he did not regard that decline as irreversible. Indeed, he had great faith in the future of Arabic nationalism and democracy, and, as we have seen, he was waiting for Arab scholars to take over from the Orientalists.

It may be that the interest that Gibb took in modern Arabic literature, thought and politics was something that had been forced upon him by the Second World War. Although he was in many ways an old-fashioned Christian gentleman with romantic ideas about the heroes of the medieval past, he was also keen on an interdisciplinary approach to Islamic studies, including, for example, making use of insights from anthropology. That sort of thing was not popular in the Oxford of the 1950s and it must have been one of the factors that led him to abandon Oxford and go to Harvard where he was given the mission of establishing a Middle East Centre. Because of his unyielding vision as well as his immense prestige, he was successful in the short term, but in the long term the Centre was not a success, as it depended entirely upon his personality and reputation. He was an autocratic figure, who did not suffer contradiction easily (as we shall see when we come to his confrontation with Kedourie). In 1964 he suffered a severe stroke and returned to England to live in retirement outside Oxford. His interests covered almost all aspects of Islamic history and culture, including pre-Islamic poetry, the Islamization of Central Asia, Saladin's campaigns against the Crusaders, the administrative structure of the Ottoman empire, modern Arab reform movements and contemporary Arabic literature. This breadth of interests was occasioned by demand. There were still so very few Orientalists in Britain that they were called upon to pronounce on a very wide range of issues.

The corresponding figure to Gibb at Cambridge, the holder of the Thomas Adams Chair in Arabic, was a very different character. Arthur John Arberry, who was born in 1905, won a classics scholarship to Cambridge and in an autobiographical essay he remarks of himself that before 'going up to Pembroke College at Michaelmas 1924 I had read everything worth reading in Greek and Latin'.[9] He studied classical textual criticism with the famous poet and don A. E. Housman and secured a first in both parts of the Cambridge examinations. In 1926 a meeting with Reynold Nicholson got him interested in Arabic and Persian. In effect, Arberry became Nicholson's disciple. His switch from classics to Arabic was paradigmatic of Oxbridge Orientalism whose ranks were largely filled by brilliant young classicists who decided to move from the overcrowded field of Greek and Latin studies to the wider pastures of Arabic studies. It was more or less inevitable that such scholars should wish to treat Arabic as a dead classical language. In the 1930s Arberry became head of the classics department at Cairo University and taught Greek and Latin to the Egyptians. Back in England he worked in the India Office Library. His earliest research was conducted on the strange, almost Surrealist, tenth-century Arab Sufi poet, al-Niffari. As a child, Arberry had lost his faith in Christianity, but he regained it through reading the Sufis. Thereafter, he became a leading translator of the Arabic and Persian literature of the Sufis and an interpreter of their doctrines.

During the war he was employed as a postal censor. Then, from 1944 onwards, he taught at SOAS, before in 1947 becoming Thomas Adams Professor in Cambridge. Arberry seems not to have been a great teacher. One of his students recalled how his teaching technique consisted of taking them at a swift canter through an obscure medieval Arabic text and then vanishing with a cry of 'Good luck in your exams!' to be seen no more that year. Another who was taught by him in the 1960s recalls that Arberry was by then known as 'the living fossil'. On the other hand, he was a fabulously prolific author, translator and editor. In the long run his industriousness sapped his health and he seems to have suffered some kind of breakdown. His translations vary wildly in quality and while, for example, his translation, *The Koran Interpreted* (1955), is an outstanding achievement, his translation of selections from *The Thousand and One Nights* can most charitably described as hackwork. He was not a modest man and he revelled publicly in his prolific output. Late in life, however, he became embittered at the lack of public recognition and he lived in expectation of a knighthood that never came his way. He was a Fellow of the British Academy and, after his death in 1969, in an obituary in the *Proceedings of the British Academy*, his career was subjected to one of the most brutal and sustained hatchet jobs in academic history. According to the obituarist G. M. Wickens (whom I guess to have been a disgruntled colleague), Arberry 'wrote and spoke primarily to fulfil his own needs and aspirations rather than to communicate with a clearly envisioned audience'. He was vain, vague, reclusive, embittered, childish, administratively incompetent, facile, arch, out of date. He was also quite ignorant of modern scholarly techniques. In addition he had written as a 'man of letters' for 'a mid-Victorian, middle-class public'. One gathers from Wickens's account that one of Arberry's few redeeming qualities was that he loved to spend hours watching television.[10]

THE BELATED BEGINNINGS OF AMERICAN ORIENTALISM

Gibb's passage across the Atlantic heralded the shape of things to come. From the 1930s onwards the United States was acquiring extensive interests in the oil-rich kingdom of Saudi Arabia and from the 1940s on, with ambitions to supplant Britain as the leading power in the Middle East, the US was expanding its provision of teaching of Islam, Arabic, Persian and Turkish. In order to set up the new institutes and departments, it relied heavily on recruiting established Orientalists from Britain and the rest of Europe.[11] Even before Gibb's arrival at Harvard, a number of scholarly refugees from Nazi Europe had found academic posts in the United States, including Grunebaum, Ettinghausen, Franz Rosenthal at Yale and S. D. Goitein at Princeton. In 1958 the National Defense Act provided funds for area and language studies in America. Gibb's passage from Britain to the United States was to be followed by Bernard Lewis (to Princeton), Roger Owen (to Harvard) and Joseph Schacht (to Columbia). The brain drain from Britain has continued to the present day. Relatively recent migrants include Michael Cook, Patricia Crone, Peter Sluglett and David Morgan.

But not all the recruits have been from Europe. One of the striking features of modern American Orientalism has been the number of prominent Arabs in the field, among them the Syrian Philip Hitti (the author of a once standard general survey, *A History of the Arabs* (1946)), Aziz Suriyal Atiya (an Egyptian at Utah and author of an important book, *The Crusades in the Late Middle Ages*), Nabia Abbott (a leading papyrologist), Majid Khadduri, an expert on Islamic law, Muhsin Mahdi (an authority on Arabic philosophy as well as on *The Thousand and One Nights*), and also Fuad Ajami and Bassam Tibi (both experts on modern Arab society and politics).

Even so, it remains the case that, for most of the twentieth century, American Orientalism was dominated by intellectual eminences imported from Europe. Gustave E. von Grunebaum (1909–72) is one of the most important examples of this phenomenon, as he was in his way as grand a figure as Gibb.[12] Born in Vienna, Grunebaum emigrated to the United States in 1938. He taught at Chicago and then, from 1957 onwards, he presided over the Near Eastern Center at the University of California, Los Angeles. As a student in Vienna, he had moved from biblical to classical and humanist studies and he brought European techniques and preoccupations with him. In going on to study Islam he was really studying the West: 'And there may be no better guide to our own soul than the civilization which a great French scholar has called "The Occident of the East", the world of Islam.' Previously Nöldeke, who taught in Vienna, had lectured and written on the pre-Islamic poets, arguing for their importance as a source on the early history of the Arabs, but denying their literary merit. Grunebaum reacted against his teacher and in a series of specialized studies he upheld the aesthetic merits of pre-Islamic poetry.

In Chicago Grunebaum moved on to much grander surveys of Islamic civilization. He took a Hegelian view of what he saw as Islamic decadence. Islamic civilization, having transmitted Greek wisdom from the West, had performed its historic task and had no future role in history. The comparison of Islamic civilization to the classical civilization that had preceded it, almost always to Islam's disadvantage, was a constant theme in his writings. Islam was a mimetic civilization, compounded of borrowings from other cultures and incapable of independent innovation. Its copycat civilization reached its peak under the Abbasids in the ninth century, but thereafter it was doomed to stagnate, as Muslims were constrained by the intransigence of the Qur'anic revelation and doomed by their religion's fatalism. 'Classical Islam' was conceived of by him as 'a model whose reconstitution was both an obligation and an impossibility'. (The theme of the 'unfulfilled promise' of Islamic civilization was also taken up in Bernard Lewis's *The Arabs in History*, first published in 1950.) Grunebaum considered that Muslims were incapable of grasping the value of knowledge that was not utilitarian and it was because of this, for example, that treatises on mathematics and mechanics were translated from Greek into Arabic, but the tragedies of Aeschylus were not. He maintained that Arabic poetry lacked the notion of an 'I' and of individuality. In general, he envisaged Islamic civilization as being defined by prohibitions, omissions and absences – 'no pork, no figurative art, no drama, no objective studying of other cultures and so forth and so on'.

Although Grunebaum's view of Arab culture was overwhelmingly shaped by his early immersion in classical studies, he was open to more modern ideas and in particular he tried to make use of the insights of social anthropologists. He was particularly influenced by the ideas of the anthropologist Alfred Kroeber (who worked on Californian Indians) and Kroeber's idea that the individual is subordinate to culture. Kroeber's *The Nature of Culture* (1952) was also the source of the idea of Islamic civilization as a system of exclusions. Von Grunebaum was a vastly well-read, charming and erudite polyglot, but he seems to have been incapable of guiding his students up to the intellectual heights that he inhabited. He seems neither to have had disciples nor wished for them. Muhsin Mahdi, a later professor of Arabic at Harvard, remembers Gibb listening to Grunebaum talking in a committee and then saying something along the lines of 'You know, this is like a steel ball, what you said. There is no way to get inside at all. There is no way to open it and see its internal structure. And if you let it fall, it will hurt your feet. So you have to handle it with care.' Grunebaum was a sociable academic who was active in setting up conferences and founding MESA (Middle East Studies Association), but he left no school of disciples.

The study of Islamic art in the United States was spearheaded by Europeans trained in the German tradition. Richard Ettinghausen (1906–79) had studied with Carl Heinrich Becker and worked as a museum assistant in Berlin before the rise of the Nazis forced him to cross the Atlantic in 1934.[13] He taught in Washington and New York and supervised the Islamic collections of the Freer Gallery and the Metropolitan Museum of Art in New York. Although he wrote general books on Arab painting and Islamic art, he specialized in focusing closely on selected objects and making use of literary sources in Arabic, Persian and Turkish to interpret their imagery. He shared the preoccupation with iconography that was the *raison d'être* of London

University's Warburg Institute. He led the way in exploring the visual vocabulary of Islamic culture – the seasons, the signs of the zodiac, the princely cycle, the repertoire of mythological beasts and so forth.

Born in Strasbourg in France in 1929, Oleg Grabar studied at Harvard and started teaching in the United States in the 1950s.[14] In 1980 he became Aga Khan Professor of Islamic Art at Harvard and later was a professor at the Princeton Institute of Advanced Studies. In his early years he took part in various archaeological digs in the Middle East. His most important publications were first on early Islamic architecture, the typology of palaces and on illustrated manuscripts. Later he moved on to the study of the meaning of Islamic ornament. Grabar's approach has been more theoretical and less closely tied to the objects than that of Ettinghausen. But, important though his publications have been, Grabar's influence has been at least as much through the Islamic art historians that he trained. Ernst Herzfeld, another leading expert on Islamic art and archaeology, similarly moved from America to the Princeton Institute of Advanced Studies.

Shlomo Dov Goitein (1900–1985) published on religious aspects of Islamic life, but eventually became one of the most important historians of the Near Eastern medieval economy.[15] He was born in Bavaria into a family of Hungarian rabbis and studied at Frankfurt. He left Germany in the 1920s and taught at the Hebrew University of Jerusalem, before moving to the United States in the 1950s. He ended up at the Institute of Advanced Studies in Princeton. In the five-volume *A Mediterranean Society: The Jewish Communities of the Arab World as Portrayed in the Documents of the Cairo Geniza* (1967–88), he used a massive archive of records of medieval Jewish life in the Middle East to produce a remarkably detailed survey of all aspects of everyday life, but especially of commercial practice.

Franz Rosenthal (1914–2003) studied with Schaeder and Paul Kraus in Germany and acquired the traditional Orientalist grounding in philology, but he left Germany in 1938 after Kristallnacht and eventually became a professor in Yale. An excellent classicist who knew Homer and Hesiod by heart, he was a specialist in Graeco-Arabic studies and was the author of *Der Fortleben der Antike im Islam* ('The Classical Heritage in Islam', 1965). He was also a specialist in historiography and the translator into English of Ibn Khaldun's historico-philosophical *magnum opus*, the *Muqaddimah*. He produced specialized studies of hashish and gambling in medieval Islam that make fascinating reading.[16]

Walter Cook, a senior figure at Princeton, remarked, apropos of the influx of brilliant Jews into American academic life, that 'Hitler is my best friend; he shakes the tree and I collect the apples.'[17] One consequence of the migration of Jewish scholars to the United States was that English came to replace German as the leading language of Orientalism. Not all those who left Nazi Germany were Jews, however. Joseph Schacht (1902–69), born in Upper Silesia, came from a Catholic family.[18] Having studied Hebrew in a Gymnasium (a top-grade secondary school), he then studied Oriental languages and philological method more generally. He left Germany in 1936 in protest against the Nazi accession to power and taught at the University of Cairo for a while, before coming to America where he became a professor at the University of Columbia in New York. He followed up Goldziher's work on Hadiths and investigated the *isnads*, or chains of transmission that were supposed to authenticate traditions concerning what the Prophet was supposed to have said and done.

Muhammad ibn Idris al-Shafi'i (767–820) was the leading jurist of his age and founded a major school of Islamic law that still survives today. Understanding of the evolution of Shafi'ite law is fundamental to the study of Sunni Muslim institutions and society. Goldziher had not been able to study al-Shafi'i properly as a critical edition of the man's legal writings was only beginning to be published towards the end of Goldziher's life. But Schacht, working in the tradition of Goldziher, made a hypercritical study of Shafi'ite law and the Hadiths it was supposed to be based on. In *The Origins of Muhammadan Jurisprudence* (1950), he demonstrated that the end of the eighth century was a watershed in the development of Islamic law. As Patricia Crone put it, in *Roman, Provincial and Islamic Law* (1987), Schacht's book 'is a work of fundamental importance. It showed that the beginnings of Islamic law cannot be traced further back in the Islamic tradition than to about a century after the Prophet's death, and this strengthened the a priori case in favour of the view that foreign elements entered the Shar'ia.'[19] As it happens, Crone does not agree with all Schacht's conclusions and, in her own book, she argued that he had grossly underestimated the importance of pre-existing provincial law. But that is how Orientalism advances – through disagreement and criticism rather than comfortable consensus. Schacht also did important work on Isma'ili studies. The austerely brilliant Schacht was revered by those who came after him. Albert Hourani referred to him as 'that great and much regretted master of his studies'. Wansbrough similarly thought of him as the master. But Schacht's good friend, the scholarly Richard Walzer, observed of him that 'he had only principles. He had no humanity and no common sense whatsoever'. As mentioned, Schacht taught at Columbia University, which is where Edward Said was also a professor. But Said never even mentions the great scholar in *Orientalism*.

Marshall Hodgson was one of the first major contributors to Islamic studies to have been born in the United States.[20] He was also one of the first to try to break free from a vision of Islamic history that was conditioned by the philological and classicizing preoccupations of the German tradition. He queried the contention of Grunebaum and others that around the ninth or tenth century the Islamic world had experienced its classical moment and thereafter went into a steep decline. By contrast with Grunebaum, Hodgson, who also taught at Chicago and who died aged only forty-seven in 1968, has inspired quite a few historians with his vision of the central role of Islam in world history. This was set out in the three-volume *The Venture of Islam: Conscience and History in a World Civilization* (posthumously published in 1974), a pioneering work of synthesis that aimed at rethinking the way Islamic history had been written about. In part, this was done by giving full weight to the shaping role of the physical environment of the torrid zone of the Eurasian landmass. In part, it was done by paying more attention to the political and cultural contributions of the Persians, Turks and Indians (with correspondingly less emphasis on the overweening role of the Arabs). This in turn led him to dismiss the notion that Islamic civilization had peaked in the eighth or ninth century. Rather he suggested that Islamic civilization was at its height in what he called the 'Middle Period' extending from the late tenth century to the beginning of the sixteenth century. He also drew attention to the considerable cultural achievements of the 'gunpowder empires' of the sixteenth and seventeenth centuries.

In order to foster new ways of thinking about the subject, he created a new (and rather unattractive) vocabulary: 'Islamdom' designated the territories within which the Muslims and their religion were predominant; 'Islamicate' referred to the culture of those territories; the 'Oikumene' was the settled world of high culture that spread over Europe, Asia and Africa. Hodgson argued that Islam's wide territorial sway from the eighth century onwards served to break down previously existing cultural barriers in the three continents. His was a highly sympathetic portrait of Islamic culture and the *Venture* was emphatically not a history of the 'Triumph of the West'. He also gave full weight to the Chinese contribution to the Oikumene and more specifically to what the neighbouring Islamicate civilization derived from it. He argued that the Oikumene should be considered as a single unit of study. His grand vision of history, like so many grand visions of history, was heavily influenced by Ibn Khaldun. But Hodgson was also a Christian who had embraced Massignon's notion of history as the 'science of compassion'.

Hodgson took frequent issue with his predecessors in his entertainingly aggressive footnotes. In the main text, his presentation of his arguments, though occasionally eloquent, was often turgid and difficult. Even so, he has turned out to be one of the most influential writers on Islamic culture in modern times. Quite a few of today's professors would describe themselves as Hodgsonians. According to the novelist Saul Bellow, who knew him, 'Marshall was a vegetarian, a pacifist, and a Quaker – most odd, most unhappy, a quirky charmer.' Bellow, a passionately blinkered Zionist, could not understand how any scholar could interest himself in the barbarous Arabs: 'Why should a pacifist fall in love with militant Islam?'[21] The question is rhetorical. If Bellow, an intellectual who seems extraordinarily ignorant about Islam, had wanted that question answered, he could have attended Hodgson's lectures or, later, read *The Venture of Islam*.

ALBERT HOURANI

One of the longest and most thoughtful reviews of *The Venture of Islam* appeared in the *Journal of Near Eastern Studies*. This was by Albert Hourani (1915–93).[22] Hourani was born in Manchester, the son of a Protestant Lebanese businessman. He read PPE (philosophy, politics and economics) at Oxford – not classics. The farouche Margoliouth supervised his unfinished D. Phil. thesis. He then worked for Chatham House and the Foreign Office before becoming a Fellow of Magdalen College and subsequently director of the Middle East Centre at St Antony's College, Oxford. Before turning to academic life, he had been an eloquent advocate of the Palestinian cause and, more generally, he had been optimistic about the future of Arab nationalism. He was then bitterly disappointed by the British betrayal of the Arabs of Palestine and thereafter he seems to have found a refuge from the setbacks of contemporary politics in the study of the nineteenth- and early twentieth-century Arab world.

He was a master of intellectual biography and his best book, *Arabic Thought in the Liberal Age* (1962), is, like Edmund Wilson's classic study of the ideological origins of Soviet Communism, *To the Finland Station*, a mixture of character study and intellectual history. Hourani emphasized and perhaps overemphasized the role of British and French liberal ideas in shaping modern Arab thought. Before the achievement of independence by Arab nations and the bitter realities of post-colonialism, the days of hope were to be found in the 'Liberal age'. An essay entitled 'Ottoman Reform and the Politics of the Notables' has proved hardly less influential. In it he sought to show how local Arab notables, especially in Syria, used to operate as mediators between the Ottoman central government and local interests. However, in the colonial era, the notable go-betweens were more or less forced to become leaders of their local communities with consequences that were often deleterious. His interest in urban elites and informal power structures closely reflected his own position and personality. He was an urbane, liberal patrician Oxford don, who invariably preferred courteous negotiation and debate to confrontation. His elegant cadenced prose added force to his arguments.

Late in life he produced a bestseller. This was *A History of the Arab Peoples* (1991), which came out at the time of the Gulf War and which was described by another Middle Eastern historian, Malcolm Yapp, as 'a book which evoked like no other the sights, the smells and the rhythms of Arab life, and which integrated these insights into a flowing narrative of the course of Arab history'. Hourani's overview of Arab history, which competed with earlier works by Philip Hitti and Bernard Lewis, was strongly influenced by Ibn Khaldun's model of the cyclical rise and decline of Muslim regimes. (It is noteworthy that the historical visions of Kremer, Gibb and Marshall Hodgson were similarly shaped by their reading of the fourteenth-century North African.) The other great influence was that of Goldziher. 'Our view of Islam and Islamic culture is very largely that which Goldziher laid down.'[23] In the 1950s Hourani had converted to Catholicism. Though a Christian, like many Christian Arabs in modern times he identified with the achievements of the Muslims. 'Islam was what the Arabs had done in history.' His fascination with the life and thought of Massignon may have been one of the factors behind his conversion. For Hourani, as for Massignon, the practice of history was a series of exercises in empathy. A gentle and civilized man himself, he tended to play down the importance of confrontation, schism, warfare, persecution, poverty and plague in Arab history. He produced a sunlit, almost cloudless, version of that history.

Hourani also wrote a series of essays on the formation of Orientalism in which he argued that it was not an independent discourse, but took ideas from German philosophers of history such as Herder and Hegel, as well as from Darwin, Marx and others working in widely differing fields. His interest in German thought was fostered by his association in Oxford with distinguished Orientalists such as Richard Walzer and Samuel Stern, who had been trained in Germany. Richard Walzer (1900–1975), Schacht's close friend, was an expert on Arab philosophy, and had fled Nazi Germany and ended up in Oxford. Walzer also taught Hourani about 'the importance of scholarly traditions: the way in which scholarship was passed from one generation to another by a kind of apostolic succession, a chain of witnesses (a *silsila* to give it its Arabic name). He also told me much about the central tradition of Islamic scholarship in Europe, that expressed in German.'[24] By contrast, Hourani was aware how weakly established British Orientalism was and how the small number of teaching posts in the field tended to force academic specialists to be generalists. (It is pretty easy to find a publisher for a general book on Islamic culture or Arab history. But if one is trying to publish on Fatimid coinage or on the ideology of the Almoravids, things are not so easy and a publishing house may require a subsidy before it can consider publishing such recondite stuff.) Although he was a friend of Edward Said, Hourani lamented that Said's book had made Orientalism a dirty word. Hourani deplored the ammunition it gave to those Muslims who argued that Islam can only properly be studied by Muslims. He also wondered why those Orientalists who wrote in German, especially Goldziher, had been omitted from consideration.[25]

MARXISTS AND OTHERS IN FRANCE

Attempts to present Orientalism as a monolithic discourse necessarily ignore or downplay the importance of the contributions made by Marxists to the field. Russian Marxist Orientalism has already been discussed. The contribution of French Marxists was no less important. Claude Cahen (1909–91) has been described by an American historian of the Arab world, Ira Lapidus, as the greatest historian of the Middle East in the twentieth century.[26] The break away from the focus on the anecdotal and heroic was largely pioneered by this historian. When Cahen was six years old, his mother made him cry by relating to him the misfortunes of Louis IX in Egypt. By the time he was ready to produce his first great work, *La Syrie du Nord à l'époque des Croisades* (1940), he was prepared to take a much sterner and more detached view of the respective fortunes of Christians and Muslims in the Near East in the twelfth and thirteenth centuries. Cahen was a Marxist, and in *La Syrie du Nord* he struggled to present the region as a territory in its own right, rather than as a temporary imperial extension of medieval Europe. He paid particularly careful attention to the topography and economy of northern Syria. He wanted to get away from history as the story of the doings of great men. At the 1954 Orientalist Congress at Cambridge, he denounced what he saw as the amateur historiography produced by imperialists, colonialists and missionaries, and their excessive preoccupation with the affairs of sultans, scholars and great artists. (He was very surprised when at the end of his speech, Gibb came up and shook him warmly by the hand. But as we have already seen, Gibb was similarly keen to break down the old boundaries of conventional Orientalism.)

Cahen was also hostile to assigning religion or philosophy a central role in the history of the medieval Near East. He disliked using Islam as the explanatory or structuring force in that history. He was not keen on using poetry and belles-lettres as historical sources either. He was an unrivalled expert on the historical sources as more narrowly defined, whether printed or in manuscript. No one did more to identify, edit and translate Arabic texts bearing on the history of twelfth- and thirteenth-century Egypt or Syria – or ever will, I guess. His Marxism was also evidenced in his interest in the role of those urban groups in medieval Cairo and Baghdad who might be seen as fore-runners of a modern *Lumpenproletariat*. But, despite his Marxism, he was suspicious of many of the applications of 'feudal' and 'bour-geois' to the Near East. He was similarly suspicious of the idea of the 'Asiatic mode of production', argued by some Marxists to be the precursor of the ancient, feudal and capitalist modes of production.

He taught at the Sorbonne. His stress on economic and socio-logical factors was obviously a world away from Massignon's eccen-tric spiritualized version of Islam's past. However, Cahen was, like Massignon, anti-imperialist and anti-Zionist, and he campaigned for Palestinian rights. He belonged to the French Communist party and loyally accepted the Soviet invasions of Hungary and Czechoslovakia. (He did break ranks over the scientific basis to Lysenko's work on evolution and crop modification, however. It is clear he thought that the Soviet scientist was a fraud.) Cahen only let his party membership lapse sometime around 1960. He was by no means unique as a French Marxist anti-colonialist Orientalist.

Maxime Rodinson (1915–2004) came, like Cahen, from a Jewish family.[27] His parents were working-class communists in Paris. As a boy, he took part in demonstrations in favour of the Moroccan Rif uprising of the 1920s against the French colonial administration. He began working life as a messenger boy delivering croissants to typists, but in his spare time he set to work in libraries teaching himself the elements of scholarship. A reading of Renan got him interested in the comparative philology of the Semitic languages. Eventually he was taken on to study various Semitic languages, as well as Amharic, at the Ecole spéciale des langues orientales vivantes. He spent the war mostly in Beirut where he had many contacts with Arab communists.

In 1955 he became Professor of Old Ethiopic at the Ecole pratique des hautes études. He belonged to the Communist party from 1937 to 1958. As a loyal communist, he was obliged to argue against all the evidence that Russian Jews did not want to go to Israel. 'Through Zionism, treason penetrated the socialist world,' according to Rodinson. While Jewish doctors and other Jews were falling victim to Stalin's purges, Rodinson was maintaining that there was no such thing as Soviet anti-Semitism. He hoped that Marxism would provide the necessary ideology for the modernization of the Arab world.

Rodinson, who had studied with Massignon, did not share Said's enthusiasm for the man and, reacting against Massignon's flamboyant spirituality, he decided to concentrate on an aspect of material culture. So he published a series of articles on medieval Arab cookery. After all, he argued, not all Muslims were mystics, but, mystical or not, they did all have to eat. Since childhood, Rodinson had sensed an affinity between Islam and communism. In 1961, he produced a biography of Muhammad, of which he later wrote as follows: 'Probably in an unconscious fashion I compared him to Stalin.'[28] Rodinson produced an atheistic, positivist life of Muhammad, that placed him within the changing mercantile economy of the Quraysh tribe in Mecca. Islam was presented as resembling a political party more than it did a spiritual movement. The later Shi'ite Isma'ili movement was presented as a kind of early precursor of the Communist International. In 1966 Rodinson published *Islam and Capitalism* (1966), in which he argued that Islam did not hinder the growth of capitalism, but on the other hand, neither did it help it. His *Israel and the Arabs* (1968) argued that in essence the struggle of the Arabs against Israel was an anti-colonialist war, rooted 'in the struggle of an indigenous population against the occupation of part of its territory by foreigners'.

Rodinson's *La Fascination de l'Islam* (1980, translated as *Europe and the Mystique of Islam*) is a short and astringent account of the development of Arabic and Islamic studies. He was especially critical of religious polemic and philological bias. His book tends to overemphasize the importance of French Orientalists at the expense of those of other nations. Although Rodinson welcomed the challenge to what he judged to be the smug self-satisfaction of so many Orientalists, he thought that Said's earlier critique was overstated, based on limited reading, and unreasonably limited to French and British Orientalists. He considered the linkage made by Said between colonialism and Orientalism was too naive. Said's book was too exclusively focused on Arabs, whereas Rodinson pointed out that four out of five Muslims are not Arabs. Moreover, unlike Said, he did not believe that the bad faith or polemical intent of a scholar necessarily and intrinsically vitiated everything that that scholar wrote. He made a speech at the Leiden Conference of Orientalists where, among other things, he pointed out that the fact that Champollion had racist ideas about the degeneracy of modern Egyptians did not affect the correctness of his decipherment of ancient Egyptian hieroglyphics.

Although French Orientalism was not monopolized by Marxists, it does seem to have been dominated by the left wing. Jacques Berque (1910–95) was born in Algeria and served in colonial administration in Morocco.[29] But slowly he came to detach himself from the colonial viewpoint, to adopt socialist positions and to identify with the oppressed. He held the chair of social history of contemporary Islam at the Collège de France and produced books on the modern history of the Arab world. His most ambitious work was a fanatically francophone-biased history of modern Egypt. As a *pied-noir*, he was understandably slow to accept that the colonial experiment in Algeria was doomed. He never entirely emancipated himself from chauvinism and he maintained that the Arab countries of the Maghreb (Morocco, Algeria and Tunisia) 'are still for us the place of our pride and our tears' and that the French language 'still remains – I dare to proclaim it today – the Hellenism of the Arab peoples'. Having early on maintained that the future of the Arab world would be democratic, socialist and secular, he was disconcerted by the Islamic revival in Egypt, Iran and elsewhere. His was a highly literary sociology of the Arab world, embellished with sensuous evocations of the colours and smells of everyday life in that world. At a more theoretical level he struggled to trace the passage from 'the sacral to the historic' and discussed the problems of alienation and identity in rather ponderous, allusive, even flatulently vacuous essays about the characteristics of Mediterranean societies and of Islamic culture.

By contrast with these committed left-wing Orientalists, the Arabist André Miquel (b. 1929) chose Arabic on aesthetic grounds.[30] As a schoolboy, he decided that he wanted to work in a field that was obscure and marginal, in which he could peacefully do research and publish. So he taught himself Arabic. Since there were few university teaching posts in his chosen field, he initially worked as a representative of French culture in Ethiopia and Egypt (and during the latter stint, he spent five months in prison as a suspected spy). On release he secured a university post in Aix-en-Provence and it was in part at least under the influence of his friend, the famous Annales historian Fernand Braudel, that he produced important work on medieval Arab geography. He is chiefly important as a translator and popularizer of medieval Arab literature. From 1968 he taught in Paris and it was there that he assembled a team of scholars which produced a series of specialized studies on *The Thousand and One Nights*. He is also the author of a charming autobiography, *L'Orient d'une vie* (1990).

THE BRITISH PATRICIANS

British Orientalism was less radicalized than the French. Middle Eastern studies, particularly in London, were dominated by a rather grand patriciate of scholars who espoused what can loosely be described as right-wing positions. These scholars (among them Bernard Lewis, Elie Kedourie, P. J. Vatikiotis (Taki) and Ann Lambton) tended to be sceptical about the declared aims of Arab socialism and nationalism, defensive about Britain's role in the Middle East and sympathetic towards Israel. However, they were (or in some cases still are) scholars and, even if one has detected a right-wing strain in their writings, that in itself does not absolve one from carefully considering their researches and the conclusions to be drawn from them (and, of course, the same sort of consideration applies to the writings of the French Marxists discussed above). Professors at the School of Oriental and African Studies in the 1960s had more power than they do today. Malcolm Yapp, then a junior lecturer at the School, described it as follows: 'At that time the School constituted a loose framework intended to facilitate the personal academic initiatives of its academic staff rather than a scheme of neat and purposive pigeonholes in which individual scholars laboured to achieve a greater good.'[31] Moreover, the influence of the senior figures in Middle Eastern studies was not restricted to academic circles. In the eighteenth and nineteenth centuries, Orientalists wrote for one another, but in the twentieth century and particularly after the Second World War this changed as experts on the Arabs and Islam were invited to write general books for a lay public as well as to contribute to newspapers, literary journals and programmes on radio and television.

Bernard Lewis is a Fellow of the British Academy, Fellow of the Royal Historical Society, Member of the American Philosophical Society, Emeritus Professor of Princeton University and the possessor of various honorary degrees and a member of the Athenaeum, yet he also features as one of the darkest of the demons that stalk the pages of Said's phantasmagorical *Orientalism*.[32] Lewis, born in 1916, learned Hebrew as a schoolboy (he is Jewish). He read history at London University and studied with Gibb, before doing a diploma in Semitic studies in Paris in 1937, where he studied with Massignon. After receiving a London University doctorate in 1939, he taught briefly at the School of Oriental Studies, but, having been called up, he served in the Royal Armoured Corps and the Intelligence Corps before being seconded to a department of the Foreign Office. During the war, the book of his thesis, *The Origin of Isma'ilism* (1940), was published. This short book presented the medieval Shi'a movement as one of class-based social protest. (Though Lewis considered the possibility that the Isma'ili movement might have been some kind of precursor of communism, he came to the conclusion that it was not.) His war work in the Foreign Office led on to his next book, *A Handbook of Diplomatic and Political Arabic* (1947). Throughout his career he has maintained a constant, philological preoccupation with terminology, particularly the Arabic vocabulary of politics, diplomacy and warfare.

In 1950 he published *The Arabs in History*, a classic work of compressed synthesis, in which he put the golden age of the Arabs firmly back in the Abbasid era. In early editions of this book (for it has gone through many editions), he presented the semi-covert Isma'ili Shi'a movement of the ninth and tenth centuries as a kind of revolution *manqué*, which, had it succeeded, might have heralded a humanist Renaissance and freed Muslims from too literal an interpretation of the Qur'an. As for the future of the Arab world, he maintained that the Arabs had the choice of coming to terms with the West and participating as equal partners in the political, social and scientific benefits or of retreating into some kind of medievalist, theocratic shell. He surely exaggerated the freedom of choice available to the Arabs, since he wrote as if America, Europe and Israel exercised no kind of military, diplomatic and economic sway in the Middle East. Still, it is an interesting book in that its first draft was written before the full impact of the existence of vast oil reserves in the Middle East had been felt and, of course, before the rise of fundamentalism and the revival of Shi'ism. Although the future political importance of Shi'ism was far from clear in the 1940s, nevertheless Lewis, presumably fired up by his original research topic, did in fact devote quite a lot of attention to various Shi'a and other oppositional movements. In the decades to come, he was increasingly inclined to find parallels between such movements and both communism and Arab terrorist organizations.

In 1949, aged only thirty-three, he became Professor of the History of the Near and Middle East at the School of Oriental and African Studies. He was a fluent and popular lecturer. In 1961 he published what is almost certainly his most substantial book, *The Emergence of Modern Turkey*. Anybody who wishes to determine Lewis's merits as an Orientalist has to engage with this book and other works of the 1960s. It is not sufficient to pillory him only on the basis of later essays and *pièces d'occasion*. In *The Emergence of Modern Turkey*, Lewis praised the Turks for having shed their decayed imperial past and moved towards nationhood and democracy, thanks in large part to the quality shown by the Turks – 'a quality of calm self-reliance, of responsibility, above all of civic courage'. What was unusual at the time it was published was that Lewis had made more use of Turkish sources than of those produced by Western observers.

His next book, *The Assassins* (1967), presented this medieval off-shoot of the Isma'ilis, with their penchant for political murder, as a precursor of modern terrorist organizations. (The PLO had been founded in 1964. In 1966 Israelis in the vicinity of Hebron were killed by a landmine planted by Palestinians, a harbinger of things to come.) *Race and Color in Islam* (1970) attacked the pious myth that there has been no such thing as racial prejudice in Islamic culture. *Race and Slavery in the Middle East: An Historical Enquiry* (1990) similarly explored the notion that the slave trade and the enslavement of black Africans was peculiarly the historical crime of the Christian West. One of the questions tackled in *The Muslim Discovery of Europe* (1982) was why, until the nineteenth century at least, were Muslims so uninterested in Europe? On the other hand, thanks to his erudition and wide reading, he was able to produce more evidence for a limited interest in Europe on the part of Muslims than anyone had hitherto guessed. In *The Jews of Islam* (1984) Lewis repeatedly stressed that the Jews had been fairly well treated and tolerated in the pre-modern Muslim world. But he also drew attention to the limits of that tolerance and to the occasional anti-Jewish pogroms.

In general, it must be clear that he has a knack of looking at awkward subjects – subjects that Muslim apologists and starry-eyed believers in an unalloyed golden age of the Arabs would rather not see discussed. Although his selection of topics might suggest an agenda, the identification of Bernard Lewis as both a friend of Israel and a supporter of American policies in the Middle East and the consequent polemics directed against his past scholarly achievements have obscured just how positive his portrayal of Arab and Islamic culture has been and how profound his knowledge of that culture is.

In 1974, Lewis left SOAS for the United States. One factor behind his move was rumoured to be his growing disillusionment with the radicalization of the student body at SOAS. He became Cleveland E. Dodge Professor of Near Eastern Studies at Princeton. Although he retired in 1986, he has continued to lecture and publish. Among other things, he has published some fine translations of poetry from Arabic, Persian, Turkish and Hebrew. As for his prose, it is always elegant and cadenced. One never has any doubt about exactly what it is that he is trying to say (and that is something that is not always the case with most of his opponents). Among the later works, *The Middle East: 2000 Years of History from the Rise of Christianity to the Present Day* (1995) summarized his views at some length. In its conclusion, he observed that 'the larger problem that had been exercising Muslim minds for centuries [was] the problem of

Western wealth and power contrasted with the relative poverty and powerlessness of the Muslim states and peoples.' This echoes in a blunter form the conclusion of *The Arabs in History*, written so many decades earlier. The Arabs had their day in the Middle Ages. For Lewis, history in the longer term has been the story of the Triumph of the West. Islam just has to come to terms with a modernity shaped by the West. It is not the kind of message that most Muslims want to hear. On the other hand, it is hard to say that it is obviously wrong.

Since his retirement, Lewis has tended to recycle ideas and evidence from other works in a series of general books and survey articles and it is these that his critics have tended to engage with. Inevitably, his broad surveys have relied to some extent on generalizations. One particularly controversial article, 'The Roots of Muslim Rage', was published in *Atlantic Monthly* (September 1990) and it was in this article that the phrase 'the clash of civilizations' was first used – a phrase that was later picked up by Samuel Huntington and used as the title of a controversial book. Although most right-thinking liberals and believers in multiculturalism would reject the notion of a clash, it is clear that some Muslims believe in exactly that and it is a clash that they hope to win. On the other hand, Arabs with secular backgrounds have accused Lewis of having exaggerated both the centrality of Islam in Middle Eastern history and its role as a brake on the acceptance of science, democracy and women's rights.

Lewis was one of the main targets of *Orientalism* and later publications by Said, though Said tended to concentrate on Lewis's later essays of popularization and failed to engage with the early major works. In some ways Said's criticisms are surprisingly obtuse. He failed to notice how much Lewis in his early works owed to Massignon (whom Said admired) and how he sympathized with the revolutionary and the underdog. On the other hand, Said and Lewis share quite a lot of common ground and Said may have taken more from Lewis than he realized. Lewis has placed great stress on the French expedition to Egypt as a pivotal moment in the history of the Arab world and as the harbinger of the Triumph of the West. Lewis, like Said, stresses the lamentable lack of a civil society in the Islamic world. Lewis, like Said, regards Orientalism as important. Lewis was not really attacked by Said for being a bad scholar (which he is not), but for being a supporter of Zionism (which he is).

Elie Kedourie (1926–92) was born to a wealthy Jewish family in Baghdad.[33] (Until the 1950s at least there was a thriving Jewish community in Iraq that was then more or less wiped out by successive purges.) Though he was to write superbly in English, it was his third language after Arabic and French. He went to study at the London School of Economics and then to do historical research at St Antony's College, Oxford. Hamilton Gibb, who was one of Kedourie's thesis examiners, disliked Kedourie's fierce criticisms both of British policy in Iraq and of Arab nationalism. The two men clashed bitterly and Kedourie withdrew his thesis. Despite this setback, the famous conservative philosopher Michael Oakeshott saved Kedourie's academic career by securing him a teaching post at the London School of Economics.

Kedourie went on to produce a series of important books and articles, most of them based on detailed research in archives and all of them argued with incisive eloquence. In an essay entitled 'The Chatham House Version', he dissected the kind of well-meaning but misconceived Arabism represented by Gibb. Martin Kramer (on whom see below) has characterized the essay as follows: 'It was an exacting refutation of an entire school of error, one rested on a nihilistic philosophy of Western guilt, articulated by a self-appointed priesthood of expertise.'[34] Kedourie lamented the destruction of the Ottoman empire and the collapse after it of the British empire. He was cynical about the projects and boasts of contemporary Arab politicians. He described the Middle East as 'a wilderness of tigers'. Like Massignon, he was influenced by that extraordinary political thinker, Joseph de Maistre, though his reading of de Maistre's grim teachings was quite different from that of Massignon.

Chatham House was a particular target of Kedourie's, as he was contemptuous of those who were attached to that institute of international studies and their penchant for apologizing for the evils of British colonialism and their readiness to fudge unpleasant realities about modern Arab history. In Chatham House he discovered 'the shrill and clamant voice of English radicalism, thirsting with self-accusatory and joyful lamentation'. Kedourie did not subscribe to

Hourani's vision of an Arabic liberal age and he wrote debunking studies of some of the key figures associated with that supposed phenomenon. He took a consistently hard-nosed approach to political and economic issues and he maintained that 'the possession of political and military power determines who will enjoy the fruits of labour'. Kedourie's hostility to Arab nationalism made him favoured reading among supporters of Israel and, for example, the following passage from Kedourie's *Nationalism in Asia and Africa* on the accursed export of Western political theory, especially nationalism, to other continents was quoted in Saul Bellow's *To Jerusalem and Back*: 'A rash, a malady, an infection spreading from Western Europe through the Balkans, the Ottoman Empire, India, the Far East, and Africa, eating up the fabric of settled society to leave it weakened and defenceless before ignorant and unscrupulous adventurers for further horror and atrocity: such are the terms to describe what the West has done to the rest of the world, not wilfully or knowingly, but mostly out of excellent intentions and by example of its prestige and prosperity.'[35]

Like Kedourie, Panayiotis J. Vatikiotis (1928–97) grew up in a multiracial, multi-confessional Levantine environment that has now all but vanished.[36] He was born in Jerusalem and grew up in Haifa to a Palestinian Greek family and later taught in Egypt and the United States before moving to London. From 1965 onwards he taught Middle Eastern politics at SOAS where he was a friend and ally of Bernard Lewis. He fiercely criticized the despotisms of the Arab world. He was sceptical about the aims and capacity of the Palestine Liberation Organization and cynical about Nasser. *The Egyptian Army in Politics* (1961) was one of Vatikiotis's most important books.

It was inevitable that he should be selected as a leading target by Said in *Orientalism*. Said chose to focus on an essay Vatikiotis had written as an introduction to a volume of collected studies on revolutions in the Middle East. In that introduction, he had argued that though there were frequent coups in the Middle East, the region lacked the political categories that are essential to a revolution in the full sense of the word. Said read the introduction as 'saying nothing less than that revolution is a bad kind of sexuality'.[37] It is most unlikely that this eroticized reading of Vatikiotis would have occurred to anyone other than Said. But it is fair to criticize Vatikiotis's writings for their occasional tendency to slip into an opaque sociological jargon. Unlike Hourani, Lewis and Kedourie, he was not an elegant writer. Towards the end of his career at SOAS, he became increasingly depressed by the cuts in the college's funding imposed by the Conservative government: 'Beginning with ad hoc rationalization policies, as new funding schemes for higher education were being brought in, we suddenly lost most of our star quality colleagues, either through early or premature retirement, resignation, or relocation across the Atlantic. Their departure impoverished the academic, scholarly standard of the institution as well as its intellectual quality . . .' He thought that SOAS's reputation thereafter rested on nothing more than past achievements.

From the 1960s onwards and for the first time ever, English-speaking Arabists had a decent dictionary of modern Arabic, though it was one based in the first instance on German scholarship. Milton Cowan's *A Dictionary of Modern Written Arabic* (1961) was an expanded English version of Hans Wehr's *Arabisches Wörterbuch für die Schriftsprache der Gegenwart* (1952), which was actually the result of a collaborative effort by German Orientalists during the early 1940s. It was chiefly based on combing modern works of Arabic literature for lexical items, rather than culling them from medieval Arab dictionaries, which was what Lane had done in the nineteenth century.

The publication of the Hayter Report in 1961 gave only a brief fillip to Arab studies and Orientalism more generally.[38] As we have seen, the Scarborough Report had recommended that significant sums be allocated to the teaching of exotic subjects, but, after only a few years, the funding that had been promised was whittled away. The Hayter Commission was set up by the University Grants Commission as a follow-up to Scarborough and to remedy the failure to implement the previous report's recommendations in a sustained way. Sir William Hayter, the chairman of the new commission, recommended the extension of social studies and modern studies relating to Africa and Asia. The kind of expansion his report had recommended was funded for a while, but in the 1970s almost all departments in all British universities began to suffer from the sort of retrenchment that had so dismayed Vatikiotis. Exotic subjects were especially badly hit.

What, after all, was the point in lavishly funding Arabic studies? During the 1950s and 1960s Britain's position in the Middle East was eroded with surprising speed. Besides, in the post-war period, the Arabs with whom the British were dealing almost all spoke English or French anyway. Occasionally one might surprise and delight an Arab host by addressing him in his language, but this was a limited gain for such heavy expenditure on teaching facilities in London and elsewhere. As far as the study of Islam was concerned, Western academics and associated pundits had tended to regard the religion as a post-medieval survival, doomed to wither away in the face of Western-style secularism. It took the Iranian revolution of 1978–9 to change perceptions.

Outside London, the study and teaching of Arabic was less tied to contemporary agendas. Alfred Felix Landon Beeston (1911–95), long-haired, pot-bellied, chain-smoking and convivial, was one of Oxford's great eccentrics.[39] When I was a student in Oxford in the 1960s I remember hearing how on a previous evening Beeston had cycled naked through Oxford pursued by the police, but successfully eluded his pursuers by abandoning his bicycle and swimming across the Cherwell. Beeston had originally done research under Margoliouth. His great passion was the study of ancient South Arabian inscriptions. When Gibb left for America, Beeston replaced him as the Laudian Professor. Besides publishing copiously on the old Arabian scripts and on medieval Arabic poetry, he also wrote an incisive handbook on the contemporary Arabic language and it was he who got modern Arabic on to the Oxford syllabus. Making heavy weather at conversation with him at a college dinner table, I asked him if he had read anything good in Arabic recently. Yes, he replied. He had found a copy of an Arabic translation of Ian Fleming's *Diamonds Are Forever* in his hotel room in Cairo and thought the novel terribly good.

In Cambridge, Malcolm Lyons, who held the Thomas Adams Chair from 1985 to 1996, was primarily interested in medieval literature and popular story-telling, though he co-wrote an important biography of Saladin.[40] Like his Cambridge predecessors, Lyons was steeped in Latin and Greek literature and he had been awarded a first in the Cambridge Classical Tripos before he turned his attention to Arabic.

The young Lyons decided that classical studies was far too heavily covered and that the study of classical Arabic, which offered some of the same charms as the study of ancient Greek and Latin, would offer far greater opportunities for doing pioneering work and making independent discoveries.

William Mongomery Watt's life of the Prophet Muhammad had been studied by Maxime Rodinson, who then decided that it was not sufficiently Marxist and proceeded to write his own version. However, for several decades Watt's two-volume biography was effectively the authorized version for non-Muslims. William Montgomery Watt (b. 1909) had studied at Oxford and Jena.[41] He taught moral philosophy at Edinburgh before being ordained an Anglican minister. He became interested in Islam while working for the Bishop of Jerusalem in the 1940s. From 1947 onwards he taught Arabic at Edinburgh University and in 1964 became Professor of Arabic and Islamic Studies there, a post that he held until his retirement in 1979. Although he published copiously on Islamic matters, his most important books were his life of Muhammad, published as *Muhammad at Mecca* (1953) and *Muhammad at Medina* (1956). Watt placed a great deal of stress upon what he supposed was the economic background to the Prophet's preaching. He presented Mecca as the centre of a trading empire in which the Quraysh tribe (to which Muhammad belonged) grew wealthy on the profits of the transit trade in spices, as well as their custodianship of a pagan shrine crowded with idols. (Later this pseudo-historical construct was efficiently demolished by Patricia Crone.[42]) According to Watt, the transition in the seventh century to a mercantile economy in Mecca produced social tensions. Islam was in a sense a product of those tensions and a solution to them.

In his introduction to the first volume, Watt wrote that 'I have endeavoured, while remaining faithful to the standards of Western historical scholarship, to say nothing that would entail rejection of any of the fundamental doctrines of Islam.' Although his portrayal of the Prophet was extremely sympathetic, it still failed to satisfy many Muslims as it did not accept the Prophet as the 'seal of prophecy'. A. L Tibawi (on whom see the final chapter) denounced Watt for writing that the Prophet 'was aware of Jewish teaching' and that the Qur'an showed dependence on 'biblical tradition'. For Tibawi and many other Muslims, any account of the Qur'an that suggested that it was anything else than the revealed word of God was deeply offensive. Watt, on the other hand, though he was at pains not to present Muhammad as an impostor, believed that the Qur'an was 'the product of creative inspiration', something that arose from the unconscious. It was inevitable that Watt should be attacked as a missionary Orientalist. But he was also criticized by other Western scholars in the field, particularly from the 1970s onwards, for accepting uncritically what the sources told him, except when they told him about something miraculous – for example the angels who fought for Muhammad at the Battle of Badr. Evidently this dot-and-pick approach to the source materials is not entirely satisfactory. John Wansbrough, who pioneered an approach to the history of the first centuries of Islam that was the polar opposite of Watt's, presented the Battle of Badr as a literary fiction – an account of something that never happened that had been constructed from familiar literary and religious clichés, 'clientship and loyalty, plunder and pursuit, challenges and instances of single combat'.[43]

DECONSTRUCTING THE BEGINNINGS

John Wansbrough (1928–2002) was born in Illinois, studied at Harvard, served in the US Marines in South East Asia and worked as a mining engineer in Sweden before arriving at SOAS in 1957.[44] I have heard that in his youth he was a friend of William Faulkner and of Ludwig Wittgenstein. His doctorate on Mamluk–Venetian commercial relations, based on Italian archive materials, was supervised by Lewis, but Wansbrough seems to have been more strongly influenced by seminars conducted by the Ottomanist Paul Wittek, and by the latter's philological methodology. Study of language was the key to the underlying truths of history. In 1960 Wansbrough joined the history department and started to learn Arabic. In 1967 he switched to teaching Arabic in the Department of the Near and Middle East.

A decade later he published two devastatingly original and controversial books, *Quranic Studies: Sources and Methods of Scriptural Interpretation* (1977) and *The Sectarian Milieu: Content and Compo-*

sition of Islamic Salvation History (1978). Noting that none of the Arabic sources for the life of Muhammad are contemporary ones, Wansbrough argued that the final text of the Qur'an was put together some two hundred years after its supposed revelation. Moreover, much of that text was generated by two centuries of confessional polemic against Christians and Jews. Even so, there was a strong Jewish rabbinic influence on the Qur'an. As for the details of the life of the Prophet, these were not the product of documentary reporting, but were rather topoi (stock literary or rhetorical themes) that had been used to construct a salvation history, that is to say 'the history of God's plan for mankind'. The deeds and sayings of the Prophet were modelled on Old Testament prototypes. Rather than being suddenly revealed in Arabia, Islam evolved elsewhere in the Middle East, especially in Iraq. The Qur'an, Qur'an commentaries and the earliest lives of the Prophet are not straightforward historical sources and were never intended to be.

Wansbrough admired the scholarship and methodological boldness of Goldziher and Schacht, but he went much further than his masters in his sweeping scepticism. His arguments were based on close study of the key texts. Although he demolished the traditional narrative about the early history of Islam, he refrained from speculating about the real events behind the unreliable sources. In a later short publication, *Res Ipsa Loquitur: History and Mimesis* (1987), he stated that 'bereft of archaeological witness and hardly attested in pre-Islamic Arabic or external sources, the seventh-century Hijaz owes its historiographical existence almost entirely to the creative endeavour of Muslim and Orientalist scholarship'. It is worth noting that he took a similarly hypercritical view of the Old and New Testament narrative traditions and that he regarded Islam as being, like Judaism and Christianity, a valid expression of the monotheistic tradition.

Although some Muslims attacked Wansbrough's conclusions, the obscurity of his prose, which was densely and allusively argued, with frequent recourse to Hebrew, Syriac, Greek and German, presented a difficult target. Wansbrough was also criticized by many Western Orientalists who found such extreme scepticism hard to stomach and who could not seriously contemplate such a drastic revision of the historical narrative. A leading American historian of the medieval

Near East, R. Stephen Humphreys, wrote as follows: 'It is perhaps tempting to think of him as one of those scholars whose premises and conclusions are drastically wrongheaded, but whose argumentation is brilliant and filled with intriguing perspectives.'[45]

Wansbrough, despite his intimidating presence, was an inspiring teacher. He was easily bored and never one to suffer fools gladly. I remember his telling me back in the 1970s that he believed in changing subjects completely every seven years. Having delivered his two bombshells, he did not bother to defend and elaborate upon his controversial conclusions, but instead moved on to research in Hebrew and Ugaritic. He became Professor of Semitic Studies in 1984 and left SOAS in 1992. He retired to a chateau in south-western France where he took to writing (unpublished) novels. However, one Kafkaesque short story, 'Let Not the Lord Speak', had previously been published in *Encounter* in 1980.

Other scholars have taken a deconstructive approach to the history of Islam that is broadly similar to that espoused by Wansbrough, though almost none of them has followed him in his extreme agnosticism. In *Hagarism* (1977), Michael Cook and Patricia Crone used non-Arabic sources to present a history of the first century, in which the initial Arab conquest of the Middle East was a purely military one and in which the leading features of Islam were slowly elaborated outside the Arabian peninsula. They also stressed the influence of Samaritan Jewish doctrines and practices on early Islam. In *Meccan Trade and the Rise of Islam* (1987), Patricia Crone raised great doubts about the reliability of the earliest Arabic sources on Islam. In Germany, Albrecht Noth (1938–99) who started off working on medieval European history, brought source-critical techniques to the study of early Arabic sources and published *Quellenkritische Studien zu Themen, Formen und Tendenzen frühislamischer Geschichtsüberlieferung* (1973). In this book, he demolished Wellhausen's theory regarding the regional and thematic compilation of history. Noth's book was a guide on how to work with the difficult early sources. It took an extremely sceptical approach to those sources and showed how the same topoi cropped up again and again in various guises. However, the deconstructive approaches of Noth, Wansbrough, Cook, Crone and others remain extremely controversial and continue to be opposed by large numbers of Orientalists working in the same field. Because of the possible offence to Muslim susceptibilities, Western scholars who specialize in the early history of Islam have to be extremely careful what they say and some of them have developed subtle forms of double-speak when discussing contentious matters.

ISRAEL, A LEADING CENTRE OF ARABIC STUDIES

The deconstructive work done on early Arabic sources has been echoed by work done by archaeologists in Israel. There J. Koren and Y. D. Nevo have deduced that there was never one great Arab conquest of the Byzantine province of Syria.[46] Rather the Arabs entered Syria as raiders and settlers over a long period of time and by the late sixth century the Byzantines had already withdrawn their defence forces from almost all of Syria south of Antioch. More generally, Israeli academics have made an enormous contribution to Orientalist scholarship in the twentieth century.[47] In Jerusalem, Tel Aviv, Haifa and elsewhere the standards of research and teaching of Arabic and Islamic studies are remarkable. For obvious reasons, Israel has a use for trained Arabists and some of them do important work for the army and Mossad while on national service. Many of Israel's leading Orientalists came to Israel as refugees from the rise of Nazism and thus the old German tradition of Orientalist scholarship has been perpetuated in modern Israel. Israeli Arabists have combined the Germanic tradition of philological exactitude with the rabbinic tradition of discriminating exegesis and interpretation.

The Hebrew University of Jerusalem was founded in 1925 and Leo Ary Mayer (1895–1959), who arrived in Palestine in 1921 from Austrian Poland, went on to become Director of the School of Oriental Studies in Jerusalem and a great specialist on Islamic art and artefacts. David Ayalon (who died in 1998) was born in Haifa in 1914 and, after compiling the standard Arabic–Hebrew dictionary, moved on to become one of the world's greatest experts on the history of medieval Egypt and Syria.[48] Eliyahu Ashtor, who left Austria in 1938, was similarly a great expert on medieval Egypt and Syria, though he chose to concentrate on economic and social issues.[49] Gabriel Baer fled Germany in 1933 and in Israel became an authority on the economic history of the Ottomans.

Unlike Arab academics working in the same area, Israeli Orientalists were and are comparatively well funded and had access to good library resources. The Israelis also tended to publish in English. Israeli Arabists mostly worked on such neutral topics as pre-Islamic poetry, the novels of Naguib Mahfouz and Sufi texts. But in some cases, one can detect a latent polemical intent. Emmanuel Sivan, Professor of History at the Hebrew University of Jerusalem, who had started out by doing brilliant work on the Muslim response to the Crusades (published as *L'Islam et la Croisade* in 1968), later produced (well-researched) articles on such topics as propagandistic and inaccurate histories of the Crusades produced by Arab historians, the medieval roots of Islamic terrorism and Arab critics of Edward Said.[50]

Martin Kramer, a former student of Bernard Lewis, who is based at the Moshe Dayan Centre in Tel Aviv, published *Ivory Towers on Sand* in 2001.[51] In this short polemic against the corruption of American Orientalism, he scored some palpable hits. Among other things, he denounced the fashion in recent decades for 'Area Studies', as opposed to more traditional ways of studying the Orient and Africa. He mounted a particularly damaging attack on John L. Esposito, an academic based at Georgetown University, who has produced a string of books presenting an apologetic, even Polyannaish version of Islam that belittles the prospect of any threat from Islamic fundamentalism or Arab terrorism. Yet Kramer's depiction of a craven, politically correct, tacitly anti-Semitic, Orientalist academic establishment in the United States is overdrawn. More Americans read Lewis than Esposito.

A couple of quite exceptional Jewish scholars who worked outside Israel must be mentioned. Paul Kraus (1904–44) grew up in Prague and then studied at the University of Berlin, but fled Germany in 1933.[52] He spent time in Paris, where he impressed many with his brilliance, though he was a melancholy eccentric and his genius was close to madness. The prominent Parisian intellectual and expert on Hegel, Alexandre Kojève, commented: 'I see a lot of Kraus and thanks to him I know nothing of Islam. That's progress.' Then Massignon (whose anti-Semitism was not absolutely consistent and who had been asked by Becker to look after leading Jewish scholars on the run) found Kraus a job in Cairo. His great work, *Jabir ibn Hayyan: Contribution à l'histoire des idées scientifiques dans l'Islam*, published in Cairo, is an esoteric work in respect of both content and presentation, but is a wonderful, amazing thing to read, as it ranges widely and eruditely over early Islamic occultism. Kraus argued (and surely rightly) that the suspiciously prolific Jabir was not an individual alchemist who lived in the eighth century, but rather the name concealed an esoteric movement in the ninth or tenth century. The Jabirian corpus related to Qarmatian and Isma'ili propaganda. Unfortunately, he moved on from the study of alchemy to develop a daft theory of Semitic metrics. In October 1944 Albert Hourani and his brother found Kraus's body hanging in the bathroom of his Cairo flat. Though there were rumours that this was a political murder, it was probably suicide.

Samuel Stern inherited his interest in Isma'ilis from his friendship with Kraus. Stern was born in 1920 and grew up in Budapest.[53] He went to Israel in 1939 and studied in the Hebrew University of Jerusalem, before going on to work in Oxford under Gibb. He became a research fellow at All Souls in 1958. His most important work was on the relationship of Arabic and Christian European poetry in Andalusia and he made major discoveries in this field, but he was also an expert on diplomatics. He died in 1969.

GERMANY AFTER THE DIASPORA

It must be obvious that American, Israeli and, to a lesser extent, British Orientalism owed an enormous amount to scholars who had trained in Germany or Austria. From the 1930s onwards German Orientalism went into a marked decline. Brockelmann and Schaeder were among the few major figures to continue to teach and research during the Nazi period. Schaeder's star pupil, Annemarie Schimmel (1922–2003), was a fabulously prolific author and translator.[54] She learnt Arabic at the age of fifteen and became comfortable not only in Arabic, but also in Persian, Turkish, Urdu and Sindhi, as well as most of the useful

European languages. (In an idle moment she also translated one of my novels into German.) Schaeder taught her to love Goethe and Goethe's pastiches of the medieval Persian poet, Hafiz of Shiraz. Early on in her academic career, she also came under the influence of Massignon. She wrote widely on Islamic matters, but it was on Sufism that she concentrated. Though she was a devout Lutheran, there seems to have been a decidedly Sufic flavour to her Christianity. Apart from Sufism, she made herself an expert on the Persian and Urdu poetry of the Indian poet and thinker, Muhammad Iqbal (1873?–1938). Her work in these fields made her an intellectual heroine to many Turks, Pakistanis and Indian Muslims. She was a professor in Bonn and Harvard. She had an amazing memory and, since she needed no notes, she usually lectured with her eyes shut.

Schimmel was exceptional in Germany for the numerous popularizing accounts of Islamic matters that she published. Traditionally German scholars have been experts in editing texts. But philology is now out of fashion and the public is hungry for big ideas. German readers have usually gone to translations of books by more accessible Orientalists such as Bernard Lewis for more general accounts of Islam. Of course much important work has been done and continues to be done in Germany. Noth's deconstructive work on the early history of Islam has already been mentioned. Hans Wehr's dictionary of modern written Arabic, the *Arabisches Wörterbuch* (1952), has also been mentioned. Another great German lexicographer, Manfred Ullmann at Tübingen, was also an expert on the history of science and medicine. Josef van Ess, an expert on early Islamic theology, and Heinz Halm, a historian of Fatimid Egypt, are also at Tübingen. Hans Robert Roemer (Fribourg) researched and wrote on medieval Egyptian history. His brilliant student Ulrich Haarmann (1942–99) became professor at Kiel and before his untimely death made himself one of the foremost historians of medieval Egypt, inspiring a whole generation of historians in this field.[55] Stefan Wild has written important studies of medieval and modern Arabic literature. Ulrich Marzolph at Göttingen studies Arab folk literature and humour. Fribourg and Bonn are leading centres for the study of the modern Middle East.[56] The German contribution to recent Islamic studies has certainly been respectable, but the big battalions are now in the United States (where indeed several of the above-mentioned scholars spent part of their careers). These days in the United States thousands of Islamicists and Arabists attend the annual MESA conferences. Even so, recent events in the Middle East suggest that the United States does not possess nearly enough experts on Arab matters.

ENDING UP

I have not attempted to cover in any sustained fashion developments in the last three decades or so. That would involve the risk of offending even more people than I already have. Besides, it is difficult to get recent developments into perspective. The amateur Orientalists who used to dominate such bodies as the Royal Asiatic Society are disappearing. That Society's meetings used to be attended by colonial administrators, Indian army officers and managers of rubber plantations, some of whom took up the study of, say, pre-Islamic poetry or Indonesian shadow theatre, but of course that generation is all but extinct now and the Society's meetings are dominated by a dwindling band of academics. As for universities, the pressure to publish has been pushed to absurd lengths. This is especially true of British scholars who, at regular intervals, come up for judgement by the Research Assessment Exercise. In many ways the field, or rather fields, are better organized and better supplied with resources. MESA in the United States and the British Society for Middle Eastern Studies (BRISMES) in the United Kingdom bring Middle East experts together and act as lobbying organizations. But one reason Arabists come together is that their field is under threat, especially in Britain where posts are frequently left unfilled and one department after another is closed down. (Just recently Durham abandoned the teaching of Arabic to undergraduates and the Thomas Adams Chair in Arabic at Cambridge is currently in abeyance.) Area Studies, Development Studies and Anthropology departments flourish at the expense of more traditional fields of Orientalism.

In the 1950s and 1960s SOAS's Middle Eastern History section was a world leader, but more recently foreign scholars have told me that in that field and related ones SOAS is living on its past reputation.

As we have already noted, many of the best British brains in the discipline have been lured to the United States. Arabic and Middle Eastern history suffer from budgetary constraints and cuts in resources like almost all departments in all universities, but other factors count against the Arabists. One is the current government's extremely narrow view of the economic value of university education. Another factor is the malign influence of Said's *Orientalism*, which has been surprisingly effective in discrediting and demoralizing an entire tradition of scholarship. Another dismal consequence of polemics like *Orientalism* is that some university departments of Arabic or Middle Eastern history appear to have an unavowed policy of excluding Jews from serious consideration as candidates for jobs in those departments.

9

An Enquiry into the Nature of a Certain Twentieth-Century Polemic

A possible riposte could be that one neutralizes Pooh's *ideological effect in the very act of exposing and denouncing it. That's one up on the empire, true enough, and I shall be doing a spot of such neutralizing myself in just a twinkling. Yet the mode of indignant alarm wears precious thin after a while. If, instead, we make full use of* postmodern *postcolonial conceptions – among others, "aporia, ambivalence, indeterminacy, the question of discursive closure, the threat to agency, the status of intentionality, the challenge to 'totalizing concepts'" – our critique can be immeasurably more efficacious, even revolutionary.*

Das Nuffa Dat, 'Resident Aliens' in
Frederick Crews, *Postmodern Pooh* (2001)

THE MAN OF THE BOOK

Edward Said, who died on 25 September 2003, had many friends and even more admirers. He was handsome and always sharp-suited. He was also stylish, sensitive, witty, learned and cultured. He played the piano and was exceptionally knowledgeable about classical music. He was a subtle and well-respected literary critic. An intellectual himself, he had always taken the duties of the intellectual extremely seriously. He was also a tireless campaigner for Palestinian rights and was appropriately sceptical about the Oslo agreement and the later 'road map' for peace in the Middle East. He opposed the corrupt and oppressive regime of Yasser Arafat and his coterie of favoured friends on the West Bank. When not actually engaged in furious debate with those whom he had identified as Zionist and imperialist enemies (and he took no hostages in debate), he was by all accounts a gentle and soft-spoken man. He was widely honoured in his lifetime, being, among other things, a member of the American Academy of Arts and Sciences, the Royal Society of Literature, the American Philosophical Society, and the American Academy of Arts and Letters.

Said was born in Jerusalem in 1935. This seems to have been because his parents preferred Jerusalem's hospitals to those of Cairo. However, his parents, who were Christian Protestants, came from the Lebanon and Said, who was mostly educated in Egypt and then in the United States, had Egyptian and American citizenship. His family usually summered in Lebanon. In his memoir, *Out of Place*, Said wrote about his childhood and his life in Egypt with an overbearing father and an indulgent mother.[1] He spent only a few months in a school in Jerusalem. So his self-presentation as a Palestinian is questionable. But perhaps the matter is not important. He certainly thought of himself as a Palestinian and passionately identified with their sufferings. He grew up in a wealthy household in which Arabic was used only to speak to the servants. (He only mastered literary Arabic much later in life after taking lessons.) Most of his schooling was at the smart Victoria College in Cairo, 'a school designed to be the Eton of the Middle East'. The school houses were named after the heroes of British exploration and imperialism: Kitchener, Cromer, Frobisher and Drake. It was forbidden to speak Arabic within the grounds. Said was a rebel and an outsider in the school. The head prefect, Omar Sharif (the actor; original name Michael Shalhoub), was one of those who beat him. In *Out of Place*, Said describes his response to another flogging, this time by a master: 'a ruthless fury took over as I vowed to make "their" lives miserable, without getting caught, without allowing myself ever to get close to any of them, taking from them what they had to offer entirely in my own way'.[2]

His further education took place in the United States from 1951 onwards. As he himself presented it, his youth was gilded yet unhappy. He was a driven young man, struggling to live up to his parents' expectations and always looking for new goals to achieve, forever unwilling or unable to relax. All his life he suffered from insomnia. He was an undergraduate at Princeton and then did a doctorate on Joseph Conrad at Harvard. From 1962 to 1967 he was unhappily married. In 1970 he married again. In 1967 (the year of the Six Day War) he started teaching in the English department of Columbia University in New York and he continued to teach there for the rest of his life. Though he became an acclaimed and comfortably-off author and academic, who taught at an elite university and jet-setted all over the world, he chose to see himself as an outsider all his life.

The literary critic Erich Auerbach (1892–1957) was one of Said's role models. Auerbach was a leading practitioner of romance philology and his great book, *Mimesis* (1946), was an exercise in comparative literature and, more specifically, a study of men's changing perceptions of reality as reflected in literature. The range of texts was impressive, as he began with the Bible and Homer and ended with Proust. Auerbach used to work from the *Ansatzpunkt* (starting point) of the study of a particular text, or part of a text, in order to understand history and the world as a whole. One incidental factor behind Said's adulation of Auerbach was the fact that the latter had written his masterpiece in exile in Istanbul. Said, who considered himself to be an exile from Palestine, used to quote Auerbach's citation of Hugh of St Victor: 'The man who finds his homeland sweet is still a tender beginner; he to whom every soil is as his native one is already strong; but he is perfect to whom the entire world is as a foreign land.'

Auerbach particularly revered the historian and professor of rhetoric, Giambattista Vico (1668–1744), and Said also followed him in this. Vico's *Principi di una scienza nuova* (1725) attempted to study the cultures of past times on their own terms and argued that it was pointless to judge men according to the ethos of later times. Vico argued that cultures were very largely shaped by their own perception of their past. In every society, laws and codes of behaviour were based on a '*senso commune*', a consensus based on common structures of thought and feeling. Said praised the 'oppositional quality to Vico's work – his being anti-Cartesian, anti-rationalistic and anti-Catholic'.[3] Additionally Vico's use of philological evidence to make broad historical points fascinated Said. But the adulation of Vico was a little odd, given Vico's ferocious racialism. For example,

Vico's derisive and patronizing comments about Chinese philosophy and painting would strike most modern readers as really rather shocking.

In 1966 Said published *Joseph Conrad and the Fiction of Autobiography*. Conrad was an appropriate choice, for not only was he an exile, but he was a specialist in fictions set in exotic locales and his *Heart of Darkness* must be read as a dark parable about colonialism. Said used Conrad's letters to study the ease with which Conrad presented his past life in order, as it were, to invent himself. Said's next book, *Beginnings: Intention and Method* (1975), was strongly influenced by Vico and by Michel Foucault (on whom see below). The notion of individual literary works being shaped by the discursive formation of the age rather than by the individual author is distinctively Foucaldian. In *Beginnings*, Said promoted the literary critic to the same status or even higher than the creative artist. He also fired off some early salvoes at the adventurer and literary fantasist, T. E. Lawrence. (Lawrence's self-invention in *The Seven Pillars of Wisdom* was even more flagrant than that of Conrad.) *Beginnings*, which was produced before Said had thought of reinventing himself as the defender of Islam against stereotypes and generalizations, contains some remarkable instances of just that sort of thing, for example: 'It is significant that the desire to create an alternative world, to modify, or augment the real world through the act of writing . . . is inimical to the Islamic world-view.'[4] While on the subject of stereotypes, it is worth considering whether it is possible or even desirable to dispense with them altogether. As a leading mathematician has pointed out: 'many stereotypes permit the economy of expression necessary for rapid communication and effective functioning. *Chair* is a stereotype, but one never hears complaints from bar stools, recliners, bean bags, art deco pieces, high-back dining-room varieties, precious antiques, chaises longues, or kitchen instances of the notion.'[5]

THE POLITICIZATION OF A
LITERARY CRITIC

The young Edward Said was not particularly political. But 1967 saw the Six Day War and the consequent Israeli occupation of the West Bank and Gaza Strip. The catastrophe of 1967 was not just a military defeat for the Arabs, it was also a challenge to their self-image and it drove Arab intellectuals to consider what was wrong within the Arab world, as well as the obvious injustices of an American and Israeli hegemony in the Middle East. Increasingly, Said identified with Arab causes and he started taking lessons in Arabic in the 1970s. However, it seems to me that, though he was to become an enthusiastic partisan for a handful of contemporary Arab novelists, he never acquired a profound knowledge of the Arab literary heritage.

In March 1973 Palestinian terrorists seized the Saudi embassy in Khartoum and three American diplomats were killed. Later that year, in October, Egyptian troops crossed the Suez Canal and attempted to take back the Sinai Desert and Gaza Strip from Israel. Egypt's war was supported by the Soviet Union. But American support of Israel was more whole-hearted and more effective. In a series of bold manoeuvres Israeli troops encircled a large part of the Egyptian army. Arab regimes cut back oil production in protest at American intervention in the region. Arabs, whether wealthy shaykhs or Palestinian freedom fighters, were the victims of an outrageously bad press in American newspapers as well as on television (a phenomenon that has persisted to the present day). It was the Middle East crisis of 1973 that provoked Said to research and write *Orientalism*, which was published in 1978. Despite early highly critical reviews, the book went on to become a cult classic and has been translated into thirty-five languages. Although the English language version has been reprinted again and again, Said made no attempt to correct any of the factual errors that were pointed out when it first appeared. Indeed, Said subsequently added a smug 'Afterword' in which he refused to concede any points and roundly abused critics of the book.

Orientalism is not a history of Oriental studies, but rather a highly selective polemic on certain aspects of the relation of knowledge and power. Its style and content strongly suggest that it is addressed exclusively to a Western readership. Said's targets included academic Orientalists, but they also included proconsuls, explorers and novelists, as he believed that all these groups participated in a common Orientalist discourse. Said restricted his argument to the Arab heartland and offered no substantial discussion of Persian or Turkish studies and he even neglected the Arab lands in North Africa (which meant that French Orientalists get off relatively lightly). In his introduction he set out his aims and methodology. Vico, Foucault, Antonio Gramsci and Raymond Schwab (the author of the muddled but interesting study of European interest in India, *La Renaissance orientale*, 1950) are invoked as the presiding *maîtres à penser* for the exercise. The first chapter, 'The Scope of Orientalism', swoops backwards and forwards through the centuries, as it indicts Arthur Balfour, Aeschylus, Dante, Gibb and many others for racist and colonialist attitudes. The next chapter, 'Orientalist Structures and Restructures', contains a more sustained criticism of certain leading nineteenth-century figures, such as Lane and Renan. 'Orientalism Now' is the most polemical chapter. Jewish academics and journalists are the particular objects of Said's denunciations here. It is obvious that bitterness about what had been happening to the Palestinians since the 1940s fuelled the writing of this book. But rather than blame British, American and Soviet politicians, Zionist lobbyists, the Israeli army and, for that matter, poor Palestinian leadership, in a weird kind of displacement Arabist scholars of past centuries, such as Pococke and Silvestre de Sacy, were presented as largely responsible for the disasters of Said's own time.

SOME PROBLEMS WITH *ORIENTALISM*

Orientalism has the look of a book written in a hurry. It is repetitious and contains lots of factual mistakes. Said refers to 'Peter the Venerable and other Cluniac Orientalists'.[6] Which other Cluniac Orientalists? It would be interesting to know their names. (But, of course, the idea that there was a whole school of Cluniac Orientalists is absurd. Peter the Venerable was on his own.) As Bernard Lewis pointed out,

Said has Muslim armies conquering Turkey before they conquered North Africa. That really does suggest a breathtaking ignorance of Middle Eastern history, as does his belief that Britain and France dominated the eastern Mediterranean from about the end of the seventeenth century.[7] Said says many of Bonaparte's Orientalist translators were students of Silvestre de Sacy, but he does not trouble to produce any evidence for this and, as has been noted in an earlier chapter, de Sacy began teaching only in 1796. Bonaparte's chief interpreter was a dragoman, rather than an academic product, and, since de Sacy did not know colloquial Egyptian, his tuition would in any case have been of limited assistance. Said has the Swiss historian Jacob Burckhardt (famous for his *Civilization of the Renaissance in Italy*) working on Egyptian proverbs.[8] That is absurd. Said claims that Edward William Lane's *Manners and Customs of the Modern Egyptians* was addressed to an academic public, but, as we have seen, the book was published by an organization dedicated to educating a broad reading public. Said claimed that Muir's nineteenth-century *Life of Mahomet* and his book on the Caliphate were still treated as authoritative in the 1970s (as if the later books on the same subjects and articles by Wellhausen, Nöldeke, Goldziher, Lammens, Brockelmann, Watt and Rodinson had never been written). Said claimed that Gibb insisted on the title *Mohammedanism* for his little monograph on Islam, when in fact, if Said had bothered to read the introduction to that book, he would have learnt that the title was imposed on Gibb by the publisher, because that was the title of the previous guide by Margoliouth.

One could go on and on listing the mistakes. Some are small ones, but others are large indeed. Sophisticated allies of Said have suggested that facts, or factual errors, are not the point. Indeed, recourse to 'facts' and 'evidence' are, it is hinted, a time-honoured recourse of reactionary Orientalists. It is suggested that such is the essential truth of Said's indictment of Orientalism that the sweep of his argument is not undermined by the lack of a detailed factual basis. The 'tensions and contradictions' that so obsess his critics (including me) are 'fundamental to his transnational framework'.[9] Said himself, in a later essay 'Orientalism Reconsidered', appeared to have (obscure) doubts about the value of consistency, suggesting that 'the claim made by some that

I am ahistorical and inconsistent would have more interest if the virtues of consistency, whatever may be intended by the term, were subjected to rigorous analysis'.[10] One may feel tempted by this sort of argument, though, of course, if Said and his allies do not feel bound to respect facts, there is no reason why their critics should do so either, for if it is permissible to misrepresent Orientalism, Christianity and British imperialism, it would not be so obviously wrong similarly to misrepresent Islam, Arab history or the Palestinian predicament. As Sir Thomas More observed in Robert Bolt's play, *A Man for All Seasons*, 'This country's planted thick with laws from coast to coast – Man's laws, not God's – and if you cut them down – and you're just the man to do it – d'you really think you could stand upright in the winds that would blow then? (*Quietly.*) Yes, I'd give the Devil the benefit of the law, for my own safety's sake.'[11] Others have suggested that, though *Orientalism* is full of mistakes, the book is still of enormous value because it stimulated discussion and debate about major problems. However, the value of a debate that is based on a fantasy version of past history and scholarship is not obvious.

Though there may indeed be a problem with the unanalysed 'virtues of consistency', that is as nothing compared with the problems that arise from an argument that is frequently and flagrantly inconsistent, as it then becomes difficult even to discover what the argument is. To take one example, Said cannot make up his mind about when Orientalism began. A lot of the time he wishes to link its origins to Bonaparte's invasion of Egypt in 1798. Orientalism is repeatedly presented as a secular Enlightenment phenomenon. (This would loosely parallel Foucault's argument in *The Order of Things* that before the late eighteenth century Man did not exist and that it was only then that God was displaced from the centre of the universe and Man became both the object and subject of knowledge.) But at other times, Said seems to regard d'Herbelot's *Bibliothèque orientale* (1697) as the founding charter of Orientalism. But then again, maybe Postel was the first Orientalist? Another possible date offered by Said is 1312 when the Council of Vienne set up chairs in Hebrew, Arabic and other languages (though Said seems unaware that the Council's decrees regarding the teaching of Arabic were a dead letter).

We have already encountered the legendary Cluniac Orientalists of the twelfth century. But one can go further back to discover typical Western and sinister anti-Oriental attitudes in the dramas of Aeschylus and Euripides. Their plays distilled distinctions between Europe and the Orient which 'will remain essential motifs of European emotional geography'. Sadik Jalal al-'Azm (one of Said's many Arab critics) describes the ensuing muddle rather well: 'In other words, Orientalism is not really a thoroughly modern phenomenon, as we thought earlier, but is the natural product of an ancient and irresistible European bent of mind to misrepresent the realities of other cultures, peoples and their languages, in favour of Occidental self-affirmation, domination and ascendancy.'[12]

In part, Said's wish to include Homer, Aeschylus and Dante in his gallery of Orientalist rogues stemmed from his humanist engagement with a canon of great books, somewhat on the pattern of Auerbach, though, of course, Said's engagement was an adversarial one. The chronological issue is of some importance, for if Aeschylus, Dante and Postel are to be indicted for Orientalism, it follows that the necessary linkage between Orientalism and imperialism that Said posits elsewhere cannot be true. Until the late seventeenth century at least, Europe was threatened by Ottoman imperialism and it is hard to date Western economic dominance of the Middle East to earlier than the late eighteenth century. Britain acquired effective political and military control of Egypt in the 1880s. Britain and France secured mandates over other Arab territories in the wake of the First World War.

At one point in *Orientalism*, Said argues that there was no essential difference between twelfth- and thirteenth-century views of Islam on the one hand and those held in the twentieth century on the other hand.[13] From this, one would have to deduce that the invention and development of Orientalism from the eighteenth century onwards has had no impact whatsoever, for good or ill, on the way Europeans have thought and felt about Islam in modern times. Elsewhere, Said suggested that the schematization of the Orient, which began in antiquity, continued in the Middle Ages.[14] He cited Dante's treatment of Muslims in *The Divine Comedy* to make his point. According to Said, Dante was, like the eighteenth-century enyclopedist d'Herbelot, guilty of incorporating and schematizing the Orient.[15] However, it must be evident from my chapter on medieval writers that Dante had no schematized view of Islam. He seems to have been almost wholly ignorant about it and he was not very interested in Arab culture.

Said's presentation of the history of Orientalism as a canon of great but wicked books, almost all by dead white males, was that of a literary critic who wildly overvalued the importance of high literature in intellectual history. One of his favourite modes of procedure was to subject key texts to deconstructive readings – not just Lane's *Manners and Customs of the Modern Egyptians* and *The Cambridge History of Islam*, but also such hardy staples of the literature department as Walter Scott's *The Talisman*, George Eliot's *Daniel Deronda* and Flaubert's diary and his letters from Egypt. Said, who also overvalued the contestatory role of the intellectual, seems to have held the view that the political problems of the Middle East were ultimately textual ones that could be solved by critical reading skills. As he saw it, it was discourse and textual strategies that drove the imperial project and set up the rubber plantations, dug out the Suez Canal and established garrisons of legionnaires in the Sahara. Since Orientalism is by its nature a Western sickness, the same must be true of imperialism. The Persians, who under Cyrus, Darius and Xerxes built up a mighty empire and sought to add Greece to that empire, were not denounced by Said for imperialism. On the contrary, they were presented as the tragic and innocent victims of misrepresentation by Greek playwrights. Later the Umayyads, Abbasids, Fatimids and Ottomans presided over great empires, but those dynasties escaped censure. Indeed, they were considered to be the victims of Western misrepresentation.

WHAT WAS THE LANGUAGE OF ORIENTALISM?

To Said's way of thinking, since Britain was the leading imperial power in modern times, it follows that it must have been the leading centre for Oriental studies and, since Germany had no empire in the Arab lands, it followed that Germany's contribution to Oriental studies must have been of secondary importance.[16] But, as we have seen, the claim that Germans elaborated only on British and French Orientalism is simply not sustainable. Consider the cases of Hammer-Purgstall, Fleischer, Wellhausen, Goldziher (Hungarian, but writing and teaching in German), Nöldeke and Becker. It is impossible to find British forerunners for these figures. The reverse is much easier to demonstrate. We have seen how much Nicholson's *Literary History of the Arabs*, Wright's *Arabic Grammar*, Lyall's translations of Arabic poetry and Cowan's *Arabic–English Dictionary* explicitly owed to German scholarship. These works are not marginal, but central to Arabic studies in Britain. Is it really possible that British scholars were mistaken in their belief that they needed to follow German scholars of Arabic and Islam? And why did Renan, whom Said believes to have been a major French Orientalist, believe that Germans dominated the field? And what about the overwhelming pre-eminence of German scholars in Sanskrit studies? In 'Orientalism Reconsidered', Said declared that objections that he had excluded German Orientalists from the argument 'frankly struck me as superficial or trivial, and there seems no point in even responding to them'. The importance or unimportance of German Orientalism is hardly trivial as Said has tried to suggest, for if German scholarship was important, then Said's argument that imperialism was dependent on the discourse of Orientalism collapses. (If one did want to argue for the near identity of imperialism and scholarly Orientalism, then surely Russia with its great empire over territories inhabited by Muslims is the place to start? But Said did not seem to have heard of Russian Orientalism.)

His neglect of Orientalist literature written in Latin was even more damaging than his neglect of German material. His failure to consider works written in Latin by Erpenius, Golius, Pococke, Marracci and many others may have contributed to his erroneous contention that Orientalism's origins lay in the last decades of the eighteenth century, which was when it became fairly common to publish works of scholarship in the various vernaculars. But almost all the important work in the seventeenth and eighteenth centuries was published in Latin. Even in the nineteenth century and beyond scholars still published in Latin (see, for example, Flügel's *Concordantiae Corani Arabicae*, first published in 1834, and de Goeje's *Bibliotheca Geographorum Arabicorum*, which was published in eight volumes from

1879 to 1939). Moreover, it was not just a matter of what language the scholars published in. It is also the case that, even in the early twentieth century, most scholars had received a classical formation and were likely to be better informed about the constitution of the Roman empire than that of the British empire. It is further arguable that when one considers the great British imperial proconsuls, such as Lord Curzon or Lord Cromer, their mindset and the ways in which they thought about the native peoples they governed owed more to their reading of Caesar, Tacitus and Suetonius than it did to any substantial familiarity with Orientalist texts. At several points in his book, Said contends that the Orient had no objective existence. In other places he seems to imply that it did exist, but that the Orientalists systematically misrepresented it. If either proposition were true, what use would the writings of Orientalists be to the men who went out to govern the British and French empires?

If all that Said was arguing was that Orientalists have not always been objective, then the argument would be merely banal. Orientalists themselves would be the first to assent to such a proposition. Bernard Lewis is only one of many scholars who were ahead of Said in drawing attention to the ways in which those who wrote about Islam and Arabs in past centuries tended to write according to the prejudices of their age and culture. In particular, Lewis drew attention to the way in which Jewish Orientalists of the nineteenth century played a large part in creating a myth of a golden age of Muslim culture and tolerance in medieval times. Said's vision of Orientalism owed more to Lewis's writings than Said would have been happy to acknowledge.

Said veered wildly between praise and denunciation, between maximalist and minimalist positions, so that at times all Orientalists are racists and imperialists, whereas at other times Said asserts that he is not attacking Orientalists, for he would not dream of disputing their genuine achievements. As Alan Sokal and Jean Bricmont have pointed out in *Impostures intellectuelles* (translated as *Intellectual Impostures*), a book dedicated to exposing certain kinds of fraudulent postmodernist writing about science, the fraudsters frequently resort to ambiguities as their subterfuge, both advancing and denying their theses: 'Indeed they offer a great advantage in intellectual battles: the radical interpretation can serve to attract relatively inexperienced listeners or readers; and if the absurdity of this version is exposed, the author can always defend himself by claiming to have been misunderstood, and retreat to the innocuous interpretation.'[17]

MASTERS TO THINK WITH

As Sokal and Bricmont also observe, 'Not all that is obscure is profound.'[18] Much of the obscurity in *Orientalism* arises from Said's frequent references to Gramsci and Foucault. Said has sought to yoke these two *maîtres à penser* in the service of Orientalist bashing. This is difficult, as Foucault and Gramsci have different and contrasting notions of discourse. Foucault's notion of discourse, unlike that of Gramsci, is something that cannot be resisted. Although at times Said finds it convenient to work with this idea and to present Orientalism as a discursive formation that cannot be escaped, at other times he wants to blame Orientalists for embracing the evil discourse, or even for actively engaging in fabricating that discourse. They are both victims and villains. Early in the introduction to *Orientalism* he declares that 'unlike Michel Foucault, to whose work I am greatly indebted, I do believe in the determining imprint of individual authors upon the otherwise anonymous collective body of texts constituting a discursive formation like Orientalism'.[19] But in the very next chapter he seems to be supporting and relying on 'what Foucault calls a discourse, whose material presence or weight, not the originality of a given author, is really responsible for the texts produced out of it'.[20] The slipperiness of the argument(s) is typical. Foucault's notion of discourse is also incompatible with that of the canonical tradition that Said seems to have acquired from his reading of Auerbach, as Foucault rejected the notion of a tradition that could survive the great disjunction of the nineteenth century.[21]

Said's dot-and-pick approach to Foucault is combined with a similar approach to Antonio Gramsci (1891–1937). Foucault and Gramsci had rather different ideas about the relationship between power and knowledge. The first believed that 'Power is everywhere', whereas the second thought in terms of hegemony. 'Hegemony' was the term used by Gramsci to describe the imposition of a system of beliefs on the ruled. Despite his allegiance to communism, he, like Said after him, was inclined to believe in the primacy of ideology in history (rather than that of economic factors). Intellectuals have a central role both in maintaining the status quo and in undermining it. They are experts in the legitimization of power; they are crucial figures in society. Gramsci disliked 'common sense', which he deemed to be hegemonic, a device for the upper class to secure the assent of the lower class to their rule. Although he had nothing to say about Orientalists as such, in his *Prison Notebooks* he did touch upon the arbitrariness of the concept of an Orient: 'Obviously East and West are arbitrary and conventional, that is historical constructions, since outside of real history every point on earth is East and West at the same time. This can be seen more clearly from the fact that these terms have crystallized not from the point of view of a hypothetical melancholic man in general, but from the point of view of the European cultural classes who, as a result of their world-wide hegemony, have caused them to be accepted everywhere.'[22]

Said, having read Foucault and Gramsci, was unable to decide whether the discourse of Orientalism constrains Orientalists and makes them the victims of an archive from which they are powerless to escape, or whether, on the other hand, the Orientalists are the willing and conscious collaborators in the fabrication of a hegemonic discourse which they employ to subjugate others. When Said found it convenient to be a Foucaldian, he produced passages such as the following: 'It is therefore correct that every European, in what he could say about the Orient, was consequently a racist, an imperialist, and almost totally ethnocentric.'[23] Earlier, as we have noted, he professed his belief in 'the determining imprint of individual authors'. But the whole point about Foucault's use of the term 'discursive formation' is that discursive formations do not have individual authors. Moreover, an archive in the Foucaldian sense is the law governing what can or cannot be said in certain situations. It is not a grab-bag of loaded terminology that individual authors can have recourse to when it suits them. Said, however, denounced Dante, Renan, Lewis and the rest as if they were evil geniuses who actively fashioned a racist and imperialist discourse. At the same time, there seems to be no option for the Orientalist other than to be constrained by the discursive formation of Orientalism.

Said presented Orientalism as a unified, self-confirmatory discourse, but in so doing he ignored Reiske's outsider status, Goldziher's quarrels with Vámbéry and Renan, Kedourie's hostility towards Gibb, Rodinson's suspicions of Massignon and Hodgson's criticisms of most of his predecessors. Moreover, he is of course guilty of racially stereotyping Orientalists and Orientalism. Orientalism has become a reified 'Other'. The 'Other' is a key concept in post-colonial theory. In his book, which was a major influence on post-colonial theory, Said suggests that Orientalists through the ages have consistently sought to present Islam and Arabs as the 'Other', something alien, threatening and, in a sense, dehumanized. The West confirmed its own identity by conjuring up a fictitious entity that was not Western. At first sight, this might seem plausible, but if one considers, for example, how medieval churchmen misrepresented Islam, they tended to portray it as a Christian heresy (usually Arianism), rather than as something exotic and alien. In the seventeenth century, many Orientalists thought of Islam as a kind of Unitarianism. Then again, in the late nineteenth and early twentieth centuries, quite a few German Orientalists argued that Islam was, together with Western Christendom and Byzantium, the joint heir of classical antiquity. In the twentieth century, Orientalists who studied Sufism, such as Massignon and Arberry, tended to Christianize what they studied. Moreover, if people in past centuries needed the notion of an 'Other' to shore up their own identity, Islam was not necessarily the obvious candidate. For most seventeenth-century Protestant Englishmen, the territories of Islam were remote and they knew little about them. A French or Catholic 'Other' was much closer at hand.

The postmodern sociologist Jean Baudrillard once notoriously declared that the first Gulf War never took place. Said's insistence that the Orient does not exist, but is merely a figment of the Western imagination and a construction of the Orientalists, seems hardly less improbable. If indeed the Orient did not exist, it should not be possible to misrepresent it. But he was not consistent and at times he lapsed into writing about a real Orient and, for example, he wrote about Orientalism in the second half of the twentieth century facing 'a challenging and politically armed Orient'.[24]

DOES THE SUBALTERN HAVE PERMISSION TO SPEAK?

Said also argued that Orientalism denied Orientals the possibility of representing themselves. I have tended in this chapter to concentrate on his attitude to Western historians of the Middle East, but it is worth noting that he was no less hostile to Arab scholarship. In many cases, the contributions of Arab academics are simply ignored: among the many are the modern political historian Philip Khoury, the economic historian Charles Issawi, the Lebanese historian Kamal Salibi, the papyrologist Nabia Abbott, the political scientist Ibrahim Abu-Lughod, the expert on religion Mohammed Arkoun, the in tellectual historians George Makdisi, Muhsin Mahdi and Aziz Al-Azmeh and the literary historians Pierre Cachia and Mustafa Badawi, the expert on pre-modern Cairo, Afaf Lutfi al-Sayyid Marsot, the architectural historian Nasser Rabat, the maritime historian George Hourani, the expert on the Arabic language Yasser Suleiman, the expert on Arabic and Persian literature Ihsan Abbas, and the political scientist Majid Khadduri. The above is only a selection of well-known Arab scholars who have published in English. (As we have noted in a previous chapter, American Orientalism was created by recruiting scholars from both Europe and the Arab world.) If one added well-known Arab scholars writing in Arabic, the list would fill the rest of this book. But Said did not want the Arabs to represent themselves and it is he who wishes to deny them permission to speak. Yet, if one reads the anti-Orientalist essays of the Arab writers, Anouar Abdel-Malek, A. L. Tibawi and Abdallah Laroui (on all of whom see the final chapter), it becomes evident that Said could not have written *Orientalism* without drawing on these precursors.

Other Arabs, however, have been actively attacked by Said in *Orientalism* and later publications. 'The Arab world today is an intellectual, political and cultural satellite of the United States.' According to Said, Fouad Ajami is 'a disgrace. Not just because of his viciousness and hatred of his own people, but because what he says is so trivial and so ignorant.' Ajami's crime was to have written in a downbeat way in

The Arab Predicament (1981) and *The Dream Palace of the Arabs* (1998) about the betrayal of Arab hopes and ambitions in the second half of the twentieth century. Said never attempted to show exactly how Ajami's criticisms of modern Arab regimes were 'trivial and ignorant'.[25] Shabbier yet was his attack on Kanan Makiya (who wrote under the pen name Samir al-Khalil) as the 'epigone of Bernard Lewis' and an 'Iraqi publicist'.[26] Said made no attempt to show what sort of connection, if any, there was between Lewis and Makiya. In *Republic of Fear* (1989), published some years before Saddam Hussein's invasion of Kuwait and his falling out with the Western powers, the Iraqi architect and writer Makiya, at considerable risk to his own life, denounced the Iraqi Ba'ath party's use of mass executions and torture to stay in power. Makiya's crime was to have written in a critical way about an Arab regime. To return to the broader issue, the notion that the Orient is incapable of representing itself must be nonsense. In modern times Chinese scholars have overwhelmingly dominated Sinology and Indian scholars have dominated Indian studies. (Said himself cited K. M. Panikkar's *Asia and Western Dominance* as a classic analysis of Western hegemony in the Orient.)

FURTHER PROBLEMS WITH *ORIENTALISM*

Sir William Jones and then the German Sanskritists established the undoubted relationship between Sanskrit and various Indo-European languages. Today no serious linguist doubts that Sanskrit, Latin, German and Greek all derive ultimately from a common ancestor. But, as we have seen, Said refused to acknowledge that there is such a thing as an Indo-Aryan family of languages and the German Romantic writer Friedrich Schlegel was denounced by him for persisting in his belief 'that Sanskrit and Persian on the one hand and Greek and German on the other had more affinities with each other than with the Semitic, Chinese, American or African languages'.[27] Said seemed to regard the establishment of the Indo-Aryan family of languages as a kind of club that had set up arbitrary rules in order to exclude the 'wog' tongue, Arabic. More generally, Said appeared to hate any kind of taxonomy, regarding attempts to classify languages, cultures or anything else as tools for the conquest and enslavement of the Third World. Taxonomy is one of the besetting sins of the West. On the other hand, one of his own favourite devices was to list strings of vastly disparate figures and, in so doing, briskly and cursorily tar the listed line-up with the same brush.

Said was proud to be a secular humanist. Although he took it upon himself to defend Islam in *Orientalism, Covering Islam* (1981) and other writings, he does not seem to have liked the religion very much. In *After the Last Sky: Palestinian Lives* (1986) Said wrote as follows: 'Lift off the veneer of religious cant – which speaks of the "best and noblest in the Judaic, Christian, or Muslim tradition," in perfectly interchangeable phrases – and a seething cauldron of outrageous fables is revealed, seething with several bestiaries, streams of blood and innumerable corpses.'[28] Since he hated religion in all its forms, he was unable to accept that Islam has really been important in determining the shape of Arab culture, in the same way that Christianity has been important in the shaping of Europe and America. Said seemed to believe that when people were talking about religion, they were really talking about something else. Of course, as we have seen, certain Orientalists did go too far in talking about the Islamic city, the Islamic mind and so forth. In the nineteenth century, religion played such a large part in shaping Western culture (think of Matthew Arnold, Ernest Renan, Fyodor Dostoevsky and so many others) that some Orientalists may have overstressed the importance of religion in Middle Eastern culture and society. But Islam has been and remains a dominant feature in Middle Eastern life, affecting or at times even determining law, the educational curriculum, the rhythm of the working week, women's dress and other matters in the region. Again, because of his anti-religious prejudice, Said failed properly to engage with the Christian motivations of the majority of pre-twentieth-century Orientalists, among them Ricoldo da Monte Croce, Postel, Pococke and Muir.

Though he detested all Orientalism, some of it was less detestable than the rest. Said claimed that the English tradition was more scientific and impersonal while the French was more aesthetic. He could be seen as guilty of racial stereotyping here, but, in any case, it does not strike me as particularly true. It was after all the French who produced the *Bibliothèque orientale* and the *Description de l'Egypte*. According to Said, the 'official genealogy of Orientalism would certainly include Gobineau, Renan, Humboldt'.[29] But why then did he not actually discuss the works of Gobineau and Humboldt? Said noted that Renan and Gobineau shared a common Orientalist and philological perspective and that Renan took ideas from Gobineau for his *Histoire générale*, but he does not say what these ideas were. The conviction grows that he had never actually read Gobineau or Humboldt. And his acquaintance with Renan was of the slightest. The names of Renan and Gobineau come up many times in the book, but their ideas are not analysed or criticized in any detail. Their importance is something that is taken as a given, rather than as something that badly needs to be proved. As we have seen, the status of both Renan and Gobineau as Orientalists is somewhat marginal.

Said libelled generations of scholars who were for the most part good and honourable men and he was not prepared to acknowledge that some of them at least might have written in good faith. He accused de Sacy of doctoring texts.[30] But he provided no evidence for this nor did he suggest why he should have done so. Lane was denounced for all sorts of things, including denying himself the sensual enjoyments of domestic life in order to preserve his superiority as a Western observer, but in fact, in his third period of residence in Egypt, he did marry a freed slave of Greek origin.[31]

Karl Marx was not an academic Orientalist, nor a desert adventurer, nor an imperialist proconsul. Although there was no compelling reason to include him in a book on Orientalism, Marx did feature and his writings were travestied. A passage from Marx was quoted (selectively) in which he argued that the Indian villagers would suffer as a result of the transformation of their society by British colonialism, but that, though their sufferings might arouse compassion in Western breasts, these sufferings were necessary if economic and social progress was to be achieved in India. Typically, Said first conceded that Marx did feel some compassion for the Oriental peasant and then denied that he did. The numbing of Marx's capacity to feel compassion was then attributed to the grip Goethe's *West–östlicher Divan* held over his imagination, and to a racialist essentialism similar to that found in Renan's writings. Thus, in the end, 'the Romantic Orientalist vision' won out over Marx's humanity.[32] Surely only the most literary-minded academic will find this sort of interpretation satisfactory? Why do we not find here some discussion of the Asiatic mode of production, Oriental despotism and Marx's belief that there was no private property in land in the East? For it was these elements – they could be termed *idées reçues* – that came to form Marx's vision of the Orient. It is of course true that Marx was the victim of Western generalizations about the Orient, but these were generalizations about types of government and land tenure, not born out of a romantic sentiment that the dark-skinned do not feel as much pain as the white-skinned. Sadik Jalal al-'Azm has summarized Marx's approach to the Raj as follows: 'Like the European capitalist class, British rule in India was its own grave-digger. There is nothing particularly "Orientalistic" about this explanation.'[33]

Writing about individualist adventurers and Middle Eastern experts, Said observed: 'they substituted a sort of elaboration of latent Orientalism, which was easily available to them in the imperial culture of their epoch. Their scholarly frame of reference, such as it was, was fashioned by people like William Muir, Anthony Bevan, D. S. Margoliouth, Charles Lyall, E. G. Browne, R. A. Nicholson, Guy le Strange, E. D. Ross and Thomas Arnold, who also followed directly in the line of descent from Lane.'[34] This is the only reference to Edward Granville Browne in the whole book. As we have seen, Browne campaigned tirelessly for Persian independence and democracy. He was a bane of the British Parliament and Foreign Office. What on earth is he doing in this sneery list? And in what sense is he in the direct line of descent from Lane? Browne's *A Year Among the Persians* is, like Lane's *Manners and Customs of the Modern Egyptians*, set in the Middle East, but in other respects it is hard to imagine two more different books.

'None of the Orientalists I write about seems ever to have intended an Oriental as a reader,' wrote Said in a later article.[35] So why on earth did Hamilton Gibb write articles in Arabic? Why does Said not discuss Gibb's 'Khawatir fi-Adab al-Arabi' ('Reflections on Arabic Literature')? What about all the Western contributors to *Muslim World* and *Islamic Culture*, both periodicals with a largely Muslim

Indian readership? And what about Lewis's evident pride in his being translated into Arabic, Persian and Turkish? Said's treatment of Gibb was particularly harsh. He was presented by Said as a typical British Orientalist. In contrast to Massignon, who was 'irremediably the outsider', Gibb was presented as an institutional figure. Lucky old Massignon, not only 'irremediably an outsider figure', but also counsellor of Marshal Lyautey, head of the Near East section of the Ministry of Information during the Second World War, Director of the elite Ecole pratique des hautes études, member of the Académie arabe du Caire, President of the Institut d'études iraniennes, founder of the Comité Chrétien d'entente France Islam, founder of the Comité France Maghreb and member of the Commission des Musées Nationaux.

Of course Said, the professor at Columbia and one-time president of the MLA (Modern Language Association), was also an outsider figure. Gibb, by contrast, was racially stereotyped by him as a typical British Orientalist and the product of 'an academic-research consensus or paradigm'.[36] But when Gibb was a young man there were so few Arabists in Britain that it is hard to imagine how they could have generated any sort of academic consensus or paradigm. Come to that, what would the consensus have been about? Muslim invasions of Central Asia? Saladin? Sunni Islam? Modern Arabic literature? Ibn Battuta (the fourteenth-century Moroccan traveller)? One would not guess from Said's presentation of Gibb as an establishment hack that Gibb repeatedly denounced Zionism and the British betrayal of undertakings made to the Arabs and that he was also an enthusiastic supporter of Arab nationalism and of Sunni Islam. (Most of these things had made Gibb a target of Kedourie's writings.)

It may be that in Said's fantasy world Gibb stood in for the headmaster of Victoria College, Cairo. Said much preferred the charismatic, cranky, mystical, chauvinist Frenchman Louis Massignon. Massignon was more spiritual than Gibb and also more aesthetic. Not only did Said fail to note Massignon's anti-Semitism, he also failed to remark on his decidedly patronizing attitude towards Arabs as well as his debt to Renan in that respect. Said argued that Massignon's empathy for the Arabs was the result of his genius. (So one gets the impression that one had to be very clever indeed to like Arabs.) The

Syrian critic Sadik Jalal al-'Azm remarked on Said's near deification of Massignon: 'Now the question to which I have no ready answer is, how can the most acute and versatile critic of Orientalism praise so highly an Orientalist who obviously subscribed to the entire apparatus of Orientalism's discredited dogmas?'[37] Just as Gibb was presented as representative of British Orientalism (but surely not a representative of his fiercest critic, Kedourie), so Massignon was presented as representative of French Orientalism. But it is hard to understand how Massignon represented the kind of Orientalism practised by the atheist Marxists, Rodinson and Cahen – or, for that matter, by André Raymond (a leading historian of pre-modern Cairo) and Jacques Berque.

Even so, it must be conceded that Said has perhaps as much as half a point, for it is evident from the foregoing chapters that not all Orientalists did write in good faith. However, once one has identified an intellectual agenda on the part of a scholar, this does not absolve one from the task of evaluating that scholar's evidence and conclusions. To take one example among many, Lammens certainly had a militantly Catholic agenda and the intensity with which he scrutinized the sources for the early history of Islam was in large degree motivated by his hostility towards that religion, but that does not in itself invalidate all his findings about those sources.

I have confined my discussion of *Orientalism* mostly to its (mis)-treatment of academic Orientalists, as I think it is muddling and misleading to jumble them up together with poets, proconsuls and explorers as if they had very much in common.

In *Orientalism* Clifford Geertz had been highly praised as an excellent example of an anthropologist who had dispensed with the *idées reçues* of Orientalism and 'whose interest in Islam is discrete and concrete enough to be animated by the specific societies and problems he studies and not by the rituals, preconceptions, and doctrines of Orientalism'.[38] But five years later, in 'Orientalism Reconsidered', Said wrote of the 'standard disciplinary rationalizations and self-congratulatory clichés about hermeneutic circles offered by Clifford Geertz'.[39] Had Geertz's methodology changed in those five years? Not really. What had changed was that Geertz had written critically of Said's *Covering Islam* in the *New York Review of Books* in 1982, where he had referred to Said's 'easy way with the evidence' and his 'tone of high moral panic' and concluded that the book left 'a bad taste in the mind'.[40]

THE RECEPTION OF *ORIENTALISM*

Early reviews of *Orientalism* were mostly hostile. Even those praised by Said, such as Hourani, Watt, Berque and Rodinson, were highly critical.[41] But slowly the book acquired a cult status, particularly among people who were not Orientalists and who had no special knowledge of the field. Though specialists in the field listed its errors and misrepresentations, subsequent editions of the book were published with no corrections or retractions whatsoever. Criticisms of the book by Western Orientalists such as Bernard Lewis or Donald Little may be dismissed as the defensive posturing of the Orientalists' 'guild'. But some of the book's hardest critics were Arabs. Sadik Jalal al-'Azm's bafflement regarding Said's adulation of Massignon, as well as his doubts about the chronology of Orientalism offered by Said, have already been mentioned. More generally, al-'Azm in his brilliant article 'Orientalism in Reverse' agreed with Said on the self-righteousness of Orientalists and their tendency to create 'an ontological rift' between East and West, but he attacked Said for stereotyping Orientalism and for grotesquely misrepresenting Islam. Said was wrong to trace Orientalism's origins back to Homer and Dante, as that disguised the fact that it was essentially a modern phenomenon. Al-'Azm suggested that for Said representation seemed more real than reality and that his hostility to the schematization and codification of knowledge was irrational. Nadim al-Bitar, a Lebanese Muslim, denounced Said for wildly over-generalizing about the nature of Orientalism, as well as grotesquely exaggerating the prevalence of racism in Western intellectual circles.[42] Arab critics were particularly offended by Said's dismissal of Arab cultural critiques as 'second-order' analyses and contemporary Arab thought as a shallow reflection of Western thinking.

In 'Between Orientalism and Historicism', Aijaz Ahmad, an Indian Marxist teacher of English, was scathing about Said's old-fashioned,

Western-style humanism, as well as his muddled use of Derrida's ideas about identity and difference. He accused Said of trying 'to exploit three quite different definitions of Orientalism', but it was Said's allegiance to Foucault that got him into the worst muddles, as Said accused Orientalists of wilfully misrepresenting objective reality, whereas Foucault denied the possibility of an objective reality.[43] The British Muslim Ziauddin Sardar criticized Said for his location in a Western academy and for narrowness of scope. As Sardar pointed out, Islam is not confined to the Middle East and indeed most Muslims are found outside that region. He also criticized Said for not acknowledging his predecessors' work in the field. Sardar shared the Marxists' hostility towards Said's 'humanism', which, he claimed, came from the same culture that produced Orientalism, imperialism and racism. Sardar had also noticed that a later book by Said, *The Question of Palestine*, revealed a strong dislike of Islam.[44]

Others, however, took a much more favourable view of *Orientalism* and in the long run the book set a trend for books that proposed to 'negotiate the other', 'reinvent alterity' and suchlike enterprises. Said was canonized by the Western intelligentsia and acclaimed as a leading proponent of post-colonial studies; there was a tendency to associate him with such figures as Homi Bhaba, the post-colonial theorist, and Gayatri Spivak, the Bengali cultural-literary critic. This school of writing has developed its own distinctive prose style. Consider, for example, this gem from Spivak: 'The rememoration of the "present" as space is the possibility of the utopian imperative of no-(particular)-place, the metropolitan project that can supplement the post-colonial attempt at the impossible cathexis of place-bound history as the lost time of the spectator.'[45]

Orientalism fostered a plethora of narratives of oppression, and its arguments fed into subaltern studies. (In subaltern studies the voices of the colonized are given preference over those of the colonialists.) In *Orientalism* and the later *Culture and Imperialism* Said presented himself as engaged in a contestatory enterprise: this particular literary critic was on the front line in the struggle against post-colonial Western hegemony. But what had he achieved? Have Orientalists changed their working practices? They have not, as Said made no positive suggestions as to how they should change those practices and, indeed, at several points he seemed to be suggesting that it was impossible to change. Were imperialists disturbed by Said's book? It seems not. Sheldon Pollock put his finger on the problem here: 'Why, in other words, should central apparatuses of empire so hospitably embrace those who seek to contest it, and why is it that the empire should all the while be so thoroughly unconcerned? It may be a tired and tiresome issue (a reprise of the 1960s hit "Repressive Desublimation"), but late capitalism's blithe insouciance towards its unmaskers, its apparently successful domestication of anti-imperialist scholarship and its commodification of oppositional theory are hard to ignore and certainly give pause to those who seriously envision some role for critique in the project of progressive change.'[46]

LEWIS AND GELLNER VERSUS SAID

Unsurprisingly the most magisterial of the responses to *Orientalism* came from Bernard Lewis. 'The Question of Orientalism' was belatedly published in the *New York Review of Books* (24 June 1982). Lewis eloquently defended old-fashioned scholarship and concluded his defence as follows:

The most important question – least mentioned by the current wave of critics – is that of the scholarly merits, indeed scholarly validity, of Orientalist findings. Prudently, the anti-Orientalists hardly touch on this question and indeed give very little attention to the scholarly writings of the scholars whose putative attitudes, motives, and purposes form the theme of their campaign. Scholarly criticism of Orientalist scholarship is a legitimate and indeed a necessary, inherent part of the process. Fortunately, it is going on all the time – not a criticism of Orientalism, which would be meaningless, but a criticism of the research and results of individual scholars or schools of scholars. The most rigorous and penetrating critique of Orientalist, as of any other scholarship has always been and will remain that of their fellow-scholars, especially, though not exclusively, those working in the same field.

Lewis's defence of Orientalism as pure scholarship, or at least as a discipline that strives for objectivity, will strike many as absurd. But if one actually sits down and reads Pococke's edition of *Hayy ibn*

Yaqzan, or Cresswell on the chronology of Egyptian mosques, or Cahen on the topography of Syria in the Middle Ages, or de Slane on the classification of manuscripts in the Bibliothèque Nationale, or Charles Burnett on the transmission of Arabic learning in medieval England, it is extremely difficult to detect a political agenda in such scholarship – even an unconscious one. There are such things as pure scholars. I have even had tea with a few of them.

In 1986 the American Middle East Studies Association tried to mount a debate between Lewis and Said, but though Lewis appeared on the same platform as Said, he scarcely debated with him, but coolly delivered what was in effect a prepared position paper. He did not deny that there were stereotypes, particularly with respect to Oriental despotism and to sexual licence in the harem. He asked for civility and cool debate rather than polemic.[47] Said, in response, was not particularly civil. He argued that knowledge is never abstract, but always reflects power. He concentrated his attack on the American media and its coverage of Arabs and Islam (and that was of course a pretty soft target as American coverage of the Middle East and especially of Palestinian matters has mostly been disgraceful – biased, ignorant and abusive). He went on to suggest that media distortion of Middle Eastern realities had worked 'because of the active collaboration of a whole cadre of scholars, experts and abettors drawn from the ranks of the Orientalists and special-interest lobbies'. Orientalists were malevolent plotters who knew better, or, at best, they were guilty of having failed to combat press stereotypes. Among the guilty experts he listed Lewis, Kedourie and Ernest Gellner. They were guilty, that is, of being hostile to the religion and culture of Islam. (But I suspect that their real crime was that they had all criticized Said.) Lewis was denounced for attempting to supply a medieval religious ancestry for modern hijackings. Gellner was alleged to maintain that 'Muslims are a nuisance and viscerally anti-Semitic'. Why, Said wanted to know, had some Orientalists participated in a symposium on terrorism? He claimed that the only things Orientalists chose to study were Arab ignorance of Europe and Arab anti-Semitism and that they wholly neglected Arab literature. Lewis in his concluding response said that 'it is hardly honest or fair to try to refute someone else's point of view not in terms of what he says, but of motives which you choose to attribute to him in order to make your refutation easier. It is hardly an example of truth or fairness to use the smear tactics that became well known in this country at an earlier stage, by lumping together writers, scholars and journalists of very disparate characters and origins, thereby conveying rather than asserting that they are all the same, that they constitute one homogenous, centrally directed, conspiratorial whole.'[48]

Gellner, another of Said's supervillains, had a remarkable intellectual career. He started as a professional philosopher and in 1959 published *Words and Things*. In this controversial book, Gellner vigorously attacked Professor Gilbert Ryle for the latter's contention that there are no such things as minds, but only physical objects and physical happenings. The philosophical journal *Mind* (edited by Ryle) refused to review Gellner's book and the ensuing academic scandal ensured the book's author a great deal of publicity. Ved Mehta, the Indian author of a book on philosophers and historians, *Fly and Fly-Bottle*, visited Gellner just a few years later and described the thirty-four-year-old man as 'dark, of medium height, and casually dressed. His hair was uncombed, and he had the air of an offbeat intellectual.' (The talented writer Mehta was blind from birth.)[49] When I first met Gellner in the 1970s, I was struck by the sense of intellectual power that seemed to radiate from the man. Subsequently, Gellner transformed himself into a sociologist and did anthropological fieldwork on Berber saints in the highlands of Morocco. A growing interest in Islam more generally led to the publication of a volume of essays, *Muslim Society*, in 1981. By then he was Professor of Social Anthropology in Cambridge. In 1992 he published *Postmodernism, Reason and Religion*. As the blurb on the back of the paperback put it: 'Do we live in a postmodern world? If so, how can we explain the extraordinary resurgence of Islamic fundamentalism?'

In 1993 he turned his baleful attention to Edward Said and in a lengthy review in the *Times Literary Supplement* of the latter's *Culture and Imperialism* tore the book to pieces.[50] The book and the review are chiefly concerned with cultural interaction as reflected in Western literature, but Gellner did touch on the question of Orientalism, remarking that 'Said is left with an objectivism which hangs in thin air, without support, but allows him to explain and put down the

"Orientalists" and reduce their vision to the allegedly important role it played in world domination.' Gellner wondered how, while the Orientalists were the prisoners of a discursive formation, Said felt confident enough of the objectivity of his own moral judgements? Gellner went on to denounce Said's misreadings of Gide, Camus, Fanon and others, before ending his review with these words: 'Truth is not linked to political virtue (either directly or inversely). To insinuate the opposite is to be guilty of that sin which Said wishes to denounce. Like the rain, truth falls on both the just and the unjust. The problems of power and culture, and their turbulent relations during the great metamorphosis of our social world, is too important to be left to lit crit.'

Said's friends rallied to his defence and they did succeed in pointing out that Gellner's review contained a number of factual errors. Said himself, in a letter to the *Times Literary Supplement*, unconvincingly tried to present Gellner as anti-Muslim. Gellner, in the course of his reply to this letter, referred to *Orientalism* as 'quite entertaining but intellectually insignificant' and pointed out that Said's book recommended 'cognitive discrimination': 'The ex-officio disqualification of "Orientalists" goes hand in hand with an endorsement or preferential treatment of those privileged and enlightened who see the problem "from within his subject" . . . Such a privileged insider status seems to be acquired primarily by origin, or sometimes by political stance.' Said, in a further letter, denounced Gellner for making generalizations about Muslims without knowing any of the Islamic languages and for belittling the high status of literary criticism. He claimed that on page 322 he explicitly denied that 'only an insider, a Muslim, a woman, a Black can write meaningfully about Islamic, women's or Black experience'. But in only answering half of Gellner's accusation, Said had failed to answer it at all, as it is evident that in *Orientalism* 'political stance' could also privilege certain kinds of commentator on, for example, Islam. He further claimed that making fun of lit crit, as Gellner had done, was to exhibit 'bad faith and complicity with imperial power'.[51] Elsewhere, Gellner referred to Said as 'a dandy and a Manhattan bon viveur'. It was one of the finest intellectual dog-fights of recent decades. I believe that Gellner was working on a book-length attack on *Orientalism* when he died in 1995.

THE REST OF THE SAIDIAN CANON

Edward Said's other books can be discussed more briefly. In *The Question of Palestine* (1980) he protested at the denial by the Israelis and their allies of a Palestinian identity. It is interesting that in order to bolster that identity, he found himself obliged to call on the support of the infernal Orientalists: 'Read through any eighteenth- or nine-teenth-century account of travels in the Orient – Chateaubriand, Mark Twain, Lamartine, Nerval, Disraeli – and you will find chronicled there accounts of the Arab inhabitants of Palestine.'[52] Although Christian Arabs have from the first played a leading role in the Palestine Liberation Organization, Said's attitude towards Arab Christians was militantly hostile: 'I think it must also be said that militant minorities in the Middle East have almost always been aggressors against what Hourani called the universality, self-confidence, and sense of responsibility of Sunni – that is, majority Islam.' On the same page that this quotation occurs, Said managed to conflate the Christian Arab polemicist al-Kindi with the later and much more famous Muslim polymath of the same name.[53] Presumably Said had not bothered to read either of the two writers in question. (For a directly contrasting view of the fate of the Christian communities in the Middle East, see William Dalrymple's *From the Holy Mountain*.) In *The Question of Palestine*, Said confidently declared that the fortunes of Islamic fundamentalism were in steep decline after 1967.[54] For the rest of his life he would find it difficult to acknowledge the continuing vitality of Islamic fundamentalist movements.

He went on to write several more books on the Palestine issue, including *After the Last Sky: Palestinian Lives* (1986) and *The End of the Peace Process: Oslo and After* (2000), as well as articles too numerous to list. He rightly suspected that the Oslo agreement would be used as a device further to oppress and despoil the Palestinians. When writing about contemporary Palestine and the sufferings of its people, he had a straightforward case to make and he was clear and articulate. From 1977 onwards, he sat on the Palestinian National Council, but he became increasingly unhappy with the way it was being run by Arafat and resigned in 1991. As Said continued to denounce the corruption of the Palestinian administration, Arafat banned the sale of his books in the West Bank and Gaza Strip. He was also under attack by Zionists and right-wingers in the United States. His office was fire-bombed and he received death threats. Yet, despite being called 'a professor of terror' by the right-wing journal, *Commentary*, Said consistently rejected terrorism or the policy of armed struggle as the way forward. In 2001, after he was photographed throwing a stone at an Israeli guardhouse on the Lebanese border, there were determined though unsuccessful attempts to get him expelled from his post at Columbia University.

In 1981 *Covering Islam: How the media and the experts determine how we see the rest of the world* appeared. In this book Said returned to the attack on Orientalists, but he paid more (hostile) attention to the press and television, especially to their coverage of the American hostage crisis in Iran and the execution of a princess in Saudi Arabia. It was typical of his style of thought that he seemed to find Western coverage of the execution more reprehensible than the execution itself. The general drift of the book was to argue that Western society did not face a significant threat from terrorists of an Islamic fundamentalist persuasion. The real danger in the encounter between East and West arose from Western misrepresentations of Islam. Malcolm Yapp, an expert on the history of Afghanistan and British India, reviewed the book in the *Times Literary Supplement* (9 October 1981) and found much to disagree with, especially Said's cavalier way with quotations. He drew attention to Said's misrepresentation of an article that Edmund Bosworth, a historian of medieval Islam, had written in the *Los Angeles Times*. Said claimed that Bosworth had written that all political activity in the Muslim lands for almost twelve hundred years 'can be understood as emanating from the Muslim call for *jihad*'. But Bosworth had written no such thing and Said must have known that. Said's letter of response to the review was incandescent and incoherent, but Yapp returned to the charge in a further letter that began as follows: 'One may understand Edward W. Said's wounded feelings ... A man charged with responsibility for guiding the studies of others must be uncomfortable when his methods are shown to be unscholarly. And that demonstration is unaffected by the bluster, the abuse, and the misrepresentation with which he endeavours to confuse the issue in his letter.'[55]

Culture and Imperialism, which appeared in 1993, opened with a weasel-worded statement of the case for Iraq's invasion and occupation of Kuwait: 'As construed by the Iraqi Ba'ath Party, modern Arab history shows the unrealized, unfulfilled promise of Arab independence, a promise traduced by the "West" and Zionism. Iraq's bloody occupation of Kuwait was, therefore, justified on Bismarckian grounds but also because it was believed that the Arabs had to right the wrongs done against them and wrest from imperialism one of its greatest prizes.'[56] But of course, Said was in no way condoning what Saddam Hussein had done. *Culture and Imperialism* was primarily a work of literary criticism. Gellner was not the only critic to be unhappy with the particular way that this book had politicized and pilloried certain literary works. In particular, Said's contention that colonial plantations must be significant in Jane Austen's *Mansfield Park* because they are barely mentioned attracted widespread ridicule. Said's general argument in this book was that literature, in representing or reporting on colonialism, made it seem more part of the natural order of things and thus more acceptable.

Until 1999 most of Said's readers were under the impression that he was a Palestinian exile, having grown up in Jerusalem until, at the age of twelve, he and his family had to flee to Cairo and the state of Israel was established. However, in 1999 the Jewish scholar Justus Reid Weiner published an article in *Commentary* entitled '"My Beautiful Old House" and Other Fabrications by Edward Said', in which, among other things, he queried Said's credentials as a Palestinian.[57] Weiner had spent several years researching Said's youth and his article was based on eighty-five interviews. Said's own account of his youth, the memoir entitled *Out of Place*, appeared only a month or so after Weiner's article. It gave an account of his life up to 1962. It was an honest, self-searching, melancholy work. Said presented himself as an exile from happiness and his story makes depressing reading.

Throughout his life Said was a consistent critic of whatever the United States was doing in the Middle East. As already noted, he also savagely attacked those Arabs in the West, such as Kanan Makiya and Fuad Ajami, who dared to be critical of Saddam Hussein. After the atrocity of the Twin Towers occurred on September 11, 2001, he wrote a long article for the *Observer* in which, while in no way condoning what the terrorists did (for he never did that), he explained why they did it (for he always did that). He put the terrorists' case for them, just as he had put the case for Saddam Hussein. He never ever condoned the violence, terror or torture. He merely praised those things with faint damns.

He was not fond of Arab music and he wrote (in *Out of Place*) about his dislike of the Egyptian Um Kulthum's singing which he 'found horrendously monotonous in its interminable unison melancholy and desperate mournfulness, like the unending moans and wailing of someone enduring an extremely long bout of colic'. On the other hand, he loved Western classical music and, late in life, he formed a friendship with the Israeli pianist Daniel Barenboim. Together they produced a book, *Parallels and Paradoxes: Explorations in Music and Society* (2002), in which they mostly debated musical issues in a civilized and amiable fashion. Said's last book, *Freud and the Non-European* (2003), an extended essay based on a lecture delivered in the London house where Freud spent his last years as an exile, concentrated on *Moses and Monotheism*. In this essay, Said drew attention to Freud's Eurocentric view of culture, before continuing with unwonted tolerance: 'But why should it not be? His world had not yet been touched by the globalization, or rapid travel, or decolonization, that were to make many formerly unknown or repressed cultures available to Europe.'[58] (That is well said, but why was Said not prepared to extend the same charity to Dante, who must have been far less well informed about Asia and Africa?) Nevertheless, the main point of the essay was to emphasize Freud's readiness to acknowledge 'Judaism's non-Jewish antecedents and contemporaries', as in the case of 'Moses the Egyptian'. The essay was in large part a tract for the times, as Said used Freud's writings as a pretext for meditations on the fluidity of both Jewish and Palestinian identity and the consequent possibility of a single state solution in Israel/Palestine. Said's advocacy of coexistence and tolerance in a single state may be applauded and admired. But currently it seems to have the same degree of political practicality as plans to establish the Kingdom of

Shangri-La. Still, it would be a fine thing if his vision did one day become a reality.

In 1991 Said had been diagnosed as having leukaemia. In his final platform appearances he seemed tired and drawn. He died, aged sixty-seven, on 24 September 2003. He received many respectful and affectionate obituaries.[59]

But it is a scandal and damning comment on the quality of intellectual life in Britain in recent decades that Said's argument about Orientalism could ever have been taken seriously. Obviously I find it impossible to believe that his book was written in good faith. If Said's book is as bad as I think it is, why has it attracted so much attention and praise in certain quarters? I am uncertain of what the correct answer might be. Perhaps part of it may be a resentment of the long-established 'guild of Orientalists' on the part of some adherents of younger disciplines such as cultural studies and sociology. Some writers have joined the fray on Said's side, not because they care two hoots about the real history of Orientalism, but because they are anti-Zionist or anti-American. In such cases, sneering at Orientalists must serve as a soothing displacement activity. Said's fashionable brandishing of Gramsci and Foucault must have attracted some students. His obscurely voiced and facile doubts about the possibility of objectivity also fitted in with recent intellectual fashions. The book's general thesis fed upon the West's hand-wringing and guilt about its imperialist past. There are, of course, some grains of truth in the charges that Said raised and, for example, a few Orientalists, including Snouck Hurgronje, Massignon and Berque did work for colonial authorities. On the whole, though, the good qualities of *Orientalism* are those of a good novel. It is exciting, it is packed with lots of sinister villains, as well as an outnumbered band of goodies, and the picture that it presents of the world is richly imagined, but essentially fictional.

10

Enemies of Orientalism

> *If these writings of the Greeks agree with the book of God,*
> *they are useless and need not be preserved; if they disagree,*
> *they are pernicious and ought to be destroyed.*

> Edward Gibbon's account in *The Decline and Fall of*
> *the Roman Empire* of how the Caliph Umar allegedly
> had the library of Alexandria burnt in 641, but both
> remark and fire are entirely apocryphal. The library
> had been destroyed long before the coming of Islam.

KURD ʿALI

The refusal of most Orientalists to take Islam at its own valuation as
a revelation from the Divine has caused offence to many Muslims.
The sheer degree of hatred with which Western culture in general and
Orientalism in particular have been regarded in some Muslim circles
is not widely understood. Mullahs and *'ulamá* (Muslim religious
scholars) have become accustomed over the centuries to engaging in
polemic with Christian and Jewish religious scholars, and it is perhaps
because of this that they often find it difficult to accept that Orientalist
reinterpretations of such matters as the career of the Prophet or the
revelation of the Qur'an are not always motivated by Christian or
Jewish confessional rivalry with Islam.

Kurd ʿAli (1876–1953), a historian and journalist, twice became
Minister of Education in Syria.[1] He was also one of the first to challenge the intellectual hegemony of the Orientalists. In 1931 he had

attended an international conference of Orientalists held at Leiden and was horrified by what he saw as an outrageous misrepresentation of Islam on the part of Western scholars. His *al-Islam wa al-Hadara al-'Arabiyya* ('Islam and Arabic Civilization') (2 volumes, 1934–6) sought to explain and correct the misconceptions of the Orientalists. According to Kurd 'Ali, the main reason that the Orientalists fell into error was their belief that Christianity was superior to Islam. Moreover, the West's belittlement of Arab achievements was essentially a form of *Shu'ubiyya*. That is to say that it was a modern European revival of the cultural and literary movement that had flourished in the ninth and tenth centuries in which Persians, Nabataeans and others disparaged the language and culture of the Arabs, while vaunting their own histories and achievements. Kurd 'Ali denounced the triumphalism of the West and declared the European conquest of America to be a great crime. Like the nineteenth-century Islamic philosopher and political activist al-Afghani, he tried to rebut Ernest Renan's thesis that the Arabs, because of their Semitic mindset, were innately anti-scientific. Kurd 'Ali suggested that the only Arabs that Renan had ever met were Syrian fishermen and, on that basis, he had decided that Arabs were innately anti-science. Even so, Kurd 'Ali decided that Renan was by no means all bad, as he had once expressed the wish to be a Muslim praying in a mosque.

Kurd 'Ali polemicized against Christian missionaries and Jesuit scholars such as Père Lammens, whom he characterized as the 'Peter the Hermit of Orientalism'. As we have seen, Kurd 'Ali's hostility was entirely understandable, as most of what Lammens wrote was indeed driven by a ferocious and religiously motivated hostility towards Islam. Though Kurd 'Ali resented most of what the Orientalists had written about his culture, he tended to defend that culture and to refute hostile portrayals of the Qur'an, polygamy, Arab cultural achievements and so on by quoting more positive judgements by other Westerners. He was especially fond of quoting from Gustave Le Bon's favourable portrait of Islam in the popularizing history, *La Civilisation des Arabes* (1884). In this book, the Arab mind was presented as having been shaped by its cultural achievements. Le Bon was an unscholarly hack writer who knew no Arabic, but Kurd 'Ali thought that this was of less importance than Le Bon's positive attitude towards

Islam and Arabs.[2] Though Le Bon was a racist, he seemed to be a pro-Arab racist, but what Kurd 'Ali and other Muslim enthusiasts for Le Bon's work failed to spot was that, though he had written enthusiastically about the achievements of Arab civilization, those achievements were all in the past, and Le Bon believed that Arab culture was incapable of any further development. (This line of reasoning was to have a great impact on nineteenth- and twentieth-century Arab historians of Islamic civilization, who tended to present that civilization as a glory that was past.) Unlike many who came after him, Kurd 'Ali was also impressed by the *Encyclopaedia of Islam*, as well as by Western scholarly editions of the medieval biographical dictionaries of Ibn Hajar and al-Safadi.

A GENIUS CAUGHT BETWEEN TWO WORLDS

A more conspiratorial view of Orientalism was put forward by a leading Iranian intellectual, Jalal Al-i Ahmad (1923–69).[3] Al-i Ahmad was a stylish, witty, vigorous novelist, short-story writer and essayist. He was also a friend of the great Iranian writer, Sadeq Hedayat, and a brilliant commentator on Hedayat's extraordinary novel, *The Blind Owl*. Though Al-i Ahmad flirted with communism, he became disillusioned with it and with life in general. His most curious work, *Gharbzadegi* (later translated as *Occidentosis: A Plague from the West*, 1984), circulated as an underground publication from 1962. *Gharbzadegi* can be (awkwardly) translated as 'Occidentosis', 'Euromania', 'West-toxification' or 'West-struckness'. 'I speak of "Occidentosis" as of tuberculosis. But perhaps it more closely resembles an infestation of weevils. Have you seen how they attack wheat? From the inside. The bran remains intact, but it is just a shell, like a cocoon left behind on a tree.'[4] Al-i Ahmad's angry polemic could never have been published in the Shah's Iran, for, though he attacked the West, his denunciation of the Shah's regime was no less fervent, as he regarded both the modernization policies and the extravagant imports of the imperial Pahlavi family as major factors behind the pernicious Westernization of Iran. *Gharbzadegi* presented history as a millennial conflict between the West on the one hand and Iran and the rest of the world on the other. Everything of importance that happened in Iran and in the world at large was masterminded by the West: 'One must see what would-be corporate colonists and what supportive governments are secretly plotting, under cover of every riot, coup d'état, or uprising in Zanzibar, Syria or Uruguay.'[5] In Iran's case it was oil that attracted the predatory interest of Britain and other powers.

Politics apart, Al-i Ahmad was disturbed by what he saw happening to Iranian culture. Occidentosis, an undiscriminating enthusiasm for all things Western, had reduced the Iranians to a people who had lost their tradition and historical continuity, 'but having only what the machine brings them'. He denounced the Orientalists' treatment of Asians as if they were raw material for a laboratory: 'This explains why foremost among all the encyclopaedias written in the West is the *Encyclopaedia of Islam*. We remain asleep, but the Westerner has carried us off to the laboratory in this encyclopaedia.'[6] Elsewhere in *Gharbzadegi*, he lamented that his fellow citizens had become 'the playthings of orientalists'.[7] The practice of citing books by Westerners as if they were absolutely authoritative seemed to him pretty stupid: 'Even when he [the Oriental] wants to learn about the East, he resorts to Western sources. It is for this reason that orientalism (almost certainly a parasite growing on the root of imperialism) dominates thought and opinion in the occidentotic nations.'[8] The West had become a repository of plundered relics and manuscripts from the East. The Orientalist conspiracy ran in tandem with the triumph of Western technology, for 'the Orientalist hums a pretty Iranian tune, while his colleague sells machine parts'. Even Western intellectuals were disturbed by the mechanization of the spirit and Al-i Ahmad, cultured polyglot that he was, cited Camus's *The Plague*, Ionesco's *Rhinoceros*, and Ingmar Bergman's *Seventh Seal* in support of this contention.

Gharbzadegi is an original and passionate piece of writing and as such an appealing read. Al-i Ahmad was incapable of being dull. He asked far more questions than he could answer and there were painful ambiguities in his anti-Western polemic, for even in *Gharbzadegi* he had used Western sources to support his arguments. While he gave

Islam credit for being that element in Iranian culture that was least infected by Occidentosis, he still attacked the mullahs for their rigidity, hypocrisy and superstition. While he loathed machines and conferred an apocalyptic significance on mechanization, he still feared that the triumph of mechanization might be inevitable.

Al-i Ahmad was a bon viveur who was steeped in Western culture. He drank plenty and rarely said his prayers. When he went on the haj pilgrimage, he raged against his fellow pilgrims and against the Saudi authorities. At first sight he seems an unlikely figure to be a harbinger of the Islamic revolution in Iran. Yet it is so, for his treatise against West-toxification was read by and crucially influenced 'Ali Shariati and Ayatollah Khomeini, as well as other key spiritual authorities in the holy city of Qum. Later Khomeini would denounce Orientalists in terms similar to Al-i Ahmad's: 'They sent missionaries into Muslim cities, and there found accomplices within the universities and various information or publication centres, mobilized their Orientalist scholars in the service of imperialism – all of that only so as to distort Islamic truths.'[9] As far as Khomeini and his followers were concerned, the West was only gathering knowledge about Iran in order to control it.

MUSLIM CONVERTS CRITICIZE ORIENTALISM

The influence of Al-i Ahmad's critique of Orientalism was felt only in Iran. A separate tradition of anti-Orientalism developed in the Arab-speaking world and non-Arab converts to Islam played a significant part in its development. Muhammad Asad (1900–1992) was chiefly famous in his lifetime for his books *Islam at the Crossroads* (1934) and *The Road to Mecca* (1954), as well as for his translation of the Qur'an into English.[10] He was born Leopold Weiss, a Polish Jew. He travelled widely and had an adventurous life, about which he wrote unreliably. He converted to Islam in 1926. *Islam at the Crossroads*, in its Arabic version *Al-Islam 'ala muftariq al-turuq*, had a great deal of influence on Sayyid Qutb (on whom see below). In this book, Asad championed Islam against the West. In his eyes, modern

Europe, with its monstrous racism, imperialism and Orientalism, was born out of the spirit of the Crusades. 'With very few exceptions, even the most eminent of European Orientalists are guilty of an unscientific partiality in their writings on Islam.' Asad traced the Orientalists' hostility back to the Crusades. (In general, Muslim historians and cultural commentators have tended to over-exaggerate the importance of the Crusades and they often attempt to make a rather dubious link between the Crusades and modern imperialism.)

Another convert to Islam, René Guénon (1886–1951), was raised a Catholic and dabbled with various occult and Masonic groups, but soon became disillusioned. He embarked on a quest for a primordial tradition that would be free of the contamination of the modern age.[11] (Guénon hated democracy, science, feminism and anything else that was not part of an ancient elitist tradition.) Guénon believed that in the Hindu Vedanta he had found the primordial tradition but, somewhat curiously, he decided to convert to Islam and become a Sufi, as this was more 'convenient'. There was enough of an authentic primordial tradition in Islam for it to be acceptable to him. He converted in 1912 and settled in Egypt where he produced a steady stream of treatises on the Vedanta, Sufism, occultism and the horrors of mass culture.

His elitist views meant that his books were sought out by fascists and neo-Nazis. Since Guénon despised both academic research and common sense, it was inevitable that he would denounce both the methods and findings of Orientalists. In *Orient et Occident* (1924) he condemned what he saw as the fantasies and errors of the Orientalists. English translators of Oriental texts took no real effort to understand the texts they were translating. Orientalists suffered from intellectual myopia. Their failure to take the advice of the authorized representatives of the civilizations they studied was disgraceful. German Orientalists were worse than the English, and German Orientalists had a near monopoly in the interpretation of Oriental doctrines. They invariably reduced those doctrines to something systematic that they could understand. Guénon thought the Germans grossly exaggerated the importance of Buddhism in the history of Indian culture and he thought that the notion of an Indo-Aryan group of languages was absurd. German Orientalism was 'an instrument in the service of

German national ambition'. According to Guénon, the West was interested in Oriental philosophies 'not to learn from them . . . but to strive, by brutal or insidious means, to convert them to her own way of thinking and to preach to them'.[12] The irony is that his ideas about the primordial nature of the Vedanta derived ultimately from the theories of German Orientalists.

OTHER MUSLIM CRITIQUES

There is some overlap between the thinking of René Guénon and that of the Iranian academic and Sufi, Hossein Nasr (b. 1933).[13] Nasr, who studied at Harvard and MIT, nevertheless sneers at the trappings of modernity and abhors the secular premises of academic thinking. Thus, for example, he rejects orthodox scientific theories about the evolution of life on earth. He supports polygamy because four wives symbolize stability. Nasr writes as a member of a moral and intellectual elite who are certain that they know the great truth behind all exoteric religions. Nasr acknowledges that Orientalists have found certain aspects of the Qur'an problematic, but he maintains that the problems 'arise not from scholarship but from a certain theological and philosophical position that is usually hidden under the guise of rationality and objective scholarship. For Muslims, there has never been the need to address these "problems" because Muslims accept the revealed nature of the Qur'an, in the light of which these problems simply cease to exist.'[14] The use of source-critical techniques by Orientalists to date and test the authenticity of Hadiths has also been denounced by Nasr as 'one of the most diabolical attacks made against the whole structure of Islam'.

Nasr's version of Islam is a Gnostic one, in which the exoteric religion is a vehicle for an inner truth that is revealed only to initiates. Not all Muslims are happy with Nasr's particular interpretation of Islam. One finds a more orthodox strain of Muslim religious criticism of Orientalism in the writings of Sayyid Qutb, an Egyptian writer and religious activist (1906–66).[15] In the 1930s and 1940s Qutb worked for the Egyptian Ministry of Education and led a second life as a literary man about town. However, everything changed when in 1948 he was sent to the United States to study education there. He was disgusted by the loose morals and anti-Arab racism he encountered: 'During my years in America, some of my fellow Muslims would have recourse to apologetics as though they were defendants on trial. Contrariwise, I took an offensive position, excoriating the Western *jahiliyya* [paganism], be it in its much-acclaimed religious beliefs or in its depraved and dissolute socio-economic and moral conditions: this Christian idolatry of the Trinity and its notion of sin and redemption which make no sense at all; this Capitalism, predicated as it is on monopoly and interest-taking, money-grubbing, and exploitation; this Individualism which lacks any sense of solidarity and social responsibility other than that laid down by the law; that crass and vacuous materialistic perception of life, that animal freedom which is called permissiveness, that slave-market dubbed "women's liberation".'[16] Among other things, he denounced the churches as 'entertainment centres and sexual playgrounds'.

On his return to Egypt, Qutb joined the Muslim Brotherhood and became a religious activist. In 1954 he and other members of the Brotherhood were rounded up by Nasser's regime and Qutb was to spend ten years in prison. He was released in 1964 and then rearrested in 1965 for his alleged part in a plot to assassinate Nasser. He was hanged in 1966. Qutb was a prolific writer, particularly on the need for a new jihad against all forms of infidelity. His main work was a multi-volume commentary on the Qur'an, *Fi Zilal al-Qur'an* ('In the Shade of the Qur'an'). In that commentary, he returned again and again to the argument that modern Muslims were living in an age of *jahiliyya*, that is to say that they were to all intents and purposes pagans and that their nominal profession of Islam did not absolve them of the charge of infidelity. As noted above, Qutb had read Muhammad Asad and he shared Asad's hostile view of Orientalists: 'Hundreds and thousands have infiltrated the Muslim world, and they still do in the guise of Orientalists.' Qutb also maintained that 'it would be extremely short-sighted of us to fall into the illusion that when the Jews and Christians discuss Islamic beliefs or Islamic history, or when they make proposals concerning Muslim society or Muslim politics or economics, they will be doing it with good intentions'.[17] In another clear echo of Asad, Qutb wrote: 'Thus the orientalist prejudice against Islam is an inherited instinct and a natural characteristic based upon the effects created by the Crusades with all their sequels on the minds of the early Europeans.' More generally, Qutb's writings have had a vast influence on Muslim fundamentalist activism in recent decades.

The absolute authenticity of the divine revelation of the Qur'an and the categorical truth of the Prophet's mission are so evident to some Muslims that they have found it impossible to accept that such matters can ever be criticized in good faith. Historically or philologically based criticisms made by Orientalists of the traditional Muslim account of the origins of Islam have been dismissed as being an expression of something sinister – perhaps a Zionist conspiracy, or a recrudescence of the spirit of the Crusades. The Pakistani Maryam Jameelah, in *Islam Versus the West* (1962), picked on Wilfred Cantwell Smith, who had taught in Lahore before moving to McGill University in Montreal, and denounced his *Islam in Modern History* for its alleged hostility to Palestine (though I can find no such hostility anywhere in the book). More reasonably, she attacked him for expressing the wish that Muslims would make their religion more compatible with Western ideas.[18] That kind of thing was very common among Western pundits on Islam writing in the 1950s and 1960s. Cantwell Smith thought that the Arabs' failure to produce a Paine or a Voltaire meant that there was no principled secular alternative to Islam in Arab society, whereas Jameelah did not believe that there should be a secular alternative to Islam. She also targeted the Egyptian intellectual Taha Husayn, who, she claimed, had forgotten that the Christians had lost the true gospel: 'All that the Christians possess are four of the apocryphal biographies of Jesus which were not canonized until centuries after his death.' In another book, *Islam and Orientalism*, Jameelah described Orientalism as 'an organized conspiracy ... based on social Darwinism to incite our youth to revolt against their faith and scorn the entire legacy of Islamic history and culture as obsolete'.[19]

In an article entitled 'The Problems of Orientalists', published in 1971, Hamid Algar, the Professor of Persian and Islamic Studies at Berkeley, California, denounced the unfavourable picture of Islam that Grunebaum presented in *Medieval Islam*. He quite reasonably criticized Arberry for spreading himself too widely. He thought that it was extraordinary that some Muslims regarded the unbelieving Schacht as a great expert on Hadith with almost as much authority as the great medieval Muslim experts, al-Bukhari and Muslim ibn al-Hajjaj. More generally Algar noted that Orientalists were curiously obsessed with issues to do with alien influences on Islam and forgeries. Most sweepingly of all, he questioned the special status of Western-style rationality.[20]

A. L. TIBAWI

A. L. Tibawi's ferocious polemics, 'English-Speaking Orientalists: a Critique of Their Approach to Islam and Arab Nationalism', 'A Second Critique of English-Speaking Orientalists and Their Approach to Islam and the Arabs', and 'On the Orientalists Again', published in 1964, 1979 and 1980 respectively, provide striking examples of an embittered Muslim's response to Orientalism.[21] Tibawi, a Muslim of Palestinian origin who taught at London University's Institute of Education, resented the way Islamic topics were being taught at the School of Oriental and African Studies next door. He had also read and been influenced by Kurd 'Ali and in the 'Second Critique' he cited Kurd 'Ali's view that most Orientalists had 'political aims, inimical to our interests, that some of them are priests, missionaries or spies using Orientalism as a means towards an end'.

He prefaced his onslaught in 'English-Speaking Orientalists' by declaring that his remarks were 'not conceived in any spirit of contro-versy. It must not be mistaken for an apology for any creed, religious or national.' But what followed was fierce (and the two articles that followed 'English-Speaking Orientalists' were even more vehement and the attacks increasingly *ad hominem*). Taken together, the three articles constitute a thesaurus of academic abuse: 'speculation and guesswork', 'offensive', 'speculative', 'very little respect for the intelli-gence of the reader', 'audacious and extreme', 'chose to join the ranks of those who denigrate Islam and Arab nationalism', 'arrogant assurance', 'subjective prejudice', 'reckless writer and presumptuous pupil', 'an undercurrent of fanaticism', 'famous for nothing in particu-lar, except in adapting or adopting well-known ideas', 'prolific in an area where little effort is required', 'blatant factual mistakes', 'fantastic theory', 'disjoint, digressive and rambling', 'insidious campaign to adulterate Islamic history', 'howling anachronisms', 'tendentious statements', 'untenable assertions', 'partisan and unscientific', 'political Zionist bias', 'jumpy and shallow patchwork', 'affected rhetoric and absurd hyperbole', 'pseudo-historians', 'blind bias', 'drivel', 'useless journalese', 'rash irony', 'streak of vanity', 'immoderate vehemence', 'biased citation of witnesses', 'discourteous writer', 'plagiarism', 'colossal failures', 'hackneyed dictum', 'arrogant assurance', 'excessive use of polysyllabic vocabulary', 'shackled by a legacy of medieval prejudices', 'the purveyors of "amity of hate"', and so on and on in a torrent of bile. The proposition that the misconceptions of Orientalists are so absurd that they are not worth refuting in detail recurs as a favourite leitmotiv throughout Tibawi's three articles.

As a devout Muslim, Tibawi believed that only Muslims were competent to interpret their religion and at several points he suggested that non-Muslim scholars should steer clear of discussing what were matters of faith, for, as far as he was concerned, 'scientific detachment' could only be achieved by submitting to Islam. It is not surprising that few Orientalists in Britain agreed. Though Tibawi perceived that Christians were doomed to misunderstand Islam, he could not imagine that the converse might be possible. The Christian refusal to accept Muhammad as the last and most important of God's prophets was offensive to him: it never seems to have occurred to him that any Christians might take offence at his refusal to accept the Gospels and their message that Jesus was the Son of God.

Besides being a Muslim, Tibawi was also an Arab of Palestinian origin who believed fervently in Arab nationalism, as well as identifying strongly with the sufferings of the Palestinian Arabs. He believed that Orientalism had a political as well as a religious agenda and that much of what the Orientalists wrote was intended to damage the Arab cause or to conceal the past crimes of the colonialists. Furthermore he tended to identify Arab nationalism with Islam, so that whoever attacked the one attacked the other. Given his anti-Zionism, it was inevitable that he should particularly single out Jewish scholars as Orientalist villains: 'There is an abundance of evidence that the old spirit of hatred still animates a great deal of the works that pass under the academic label.' The 'Jewish writer' Bernard Lewis, in *The Arabs in History* (1950), refused to accept the Qur'an as the Word of God and suggested that the Prophet's teachings had been influenced by Jewish and Christian doctrines. Lewis's failure to accept the divine origin of Islam was offensive to Tibawi, who judged him to be 'audacious and extreme'. Lewis was also attacked for an article he wrote in *The Cambridge History of Islam*, in which he cited some medieval Arab historians who had described Saladin as an 'ambitious military adventurer'. It is easy to guess that Lewis's frequently declared support for the state of Israel provoked Tibawi's attacks on his scholarship.

Tibawi tastelessly accused Elie Kedourie (another Jew) of having written an Orientalist equivalent to the Nazi textbook, *Der Weg zum Reich*. Tibawi does not actually name the book in question, but he seems to be referring to the volume of scholarly essays by Elie Kedourie entitled *The Chatham House Version and Other Middle Eastern Essays* (1970). Kedourie was also accused of not being 'courteous to predecessors he did not agree with'. (It would be pleasant to think that Tibawi was making a joke at his own expense here.) One of Kedourie's many sins was to have produced evidence that two of the leading intellectuals and social agitators in the nineteenth-century Middle East, Jamal al-Din al-Afghani and Muhammad 'Abduh, were not believing Muslims. Tibawi did not dispute the evidence but claimed that they had subsequently been 'rehabilitated and became recognized as leaders of modern Islamic thought'.

Tibawi claimed that Jews and Christians had played too large a part in contributing to the *Bulletin of the School of Oriental and African Studies*, as well as to the *Encyclopaedia of Islam*. Since this was the case, the *Encyclopaedia* should be submitted to censorship by Muslims. As for the *Bulletin of the School of Oriental and African Studies*, Tibawi quoted a friend's quip that it had been nicknamed the '*Bulletin of the Hebrew University*'. Two volumes of essays, *The Legacy of Islam* (1974) and *The World of Islam* (1976), were similarly denounced for having mostly Christian and Jewish contributors. Oxford Arabists were also attacked. R. B. Serjeant, treated favourably in the first piece, was subsequently denounced for writing to *The Times* about the torture of a Yemeni by Egyptian intelligence officers.

Serjeant's interest in colloquial Arabic was mysteriously deemed to be a disgrace. Patricia Crone was dismissed as 'a female art specialist'. (Well, the 'female' bit is correct.) Hourani was guilty of getting Crone appointed to a job in Oxford. Tibawi considered Arabs and Muslims working within the Orientalist mode to be 'alienated individuals, denationalized and deculturalized, who try to live in two worlds at the same time, but who are at peace in neither'. Apart from their sins of commission, the Orientalists were corporately guilty of not denouncing what had been happening to the Palestinian people. I know several Orientalists who treasure offprints of Tibawi's articles as masterpieces of unintentional comedy. Even so, of course he did sometimes hit the mark, though more by luck than design. I never met the man, but I guess that it must have been difficult for him to harbour so much resentment and still feel that life was worth living.

SECULAR ARAB CRITIQUES

Tibawi, who criticized the Orientalists from a traditional Islamic stance, still retained a certain respect for Hamilton Gibb. But for the Moroccan historian and novelist Abdallah Laroui (b. 1933) and other secular-minded Marxist critics, Gibb was the enemy par excellence. Laroui, writing in *L'Idéologie arabe contemporaine* (1967), declared that Gibb's Orientalism was the worst sort, as it had broken with the Germano-French school of erudition and presented itself as empiricism, which was a cover for generalized pontificating.[22] Even so, Laroui does not really seem to have had any more respect for the older style of erudite Orientalism, as he attacked Ignaz Goldziher and those who came after him for dissecting and analysing events like the Battle of Badr (624) so intensively that they turned them into non-events. Goldziher's kind of history was too negative, as was Joseph Schacht's approach. Laroui was strongly influenced by the writings of Antonio Gramsci and, in particular, by Gramsci's ideas about the manufacture by intellectuals of consent to the hegemony of the ruling class. As Laroui saw it, the Orientalist's production and administration of a specialized kind of knowledge made him an accomplice of the colonialist.

In *The Crisis of the Arab Intellectual. Traditionalism or Historicism?* (first published in French in 1974), Laroui returned to the attack on Gibb, accusing him of being too sympathetic to traditional Islam and, on the other hand, neglecting progressive and modernizing forces in the Middle East. (Cantwell Smith was similarly guilty.)[23] According to Laroui, Gibb was downright hostile to contemporary Islamic reformism. There was a strange kind of collusion between Orientalists like Gibb and Islamic fundamentalists, as both parties could agree on propositions like 'Islam and democracy are incompatible'. Tibawi, in his 'On the Orientalists Again', had observed that he 'knew Von Grunebaum fairly well and was always amused by observing his arrogant assurance'. Laroui took the ideological threat posed by Grunebaum more seriously and in a chapter entitled 'The Arabs and Cultural Anthropology: Notes on the Method of Gustave von Grunebaum' he attacked the scholar, whom he described as a philologist and specialist in classical poetry who had turned himself into an anthropologist of Islam. Von Grunebaum had repeatedly laid stress on Arab atomism in poetry, natural philosophy and political science – that is to say that entities such as Islamic towns or Islamic poems tended to be composed of discrete elements and to lack an overarching unity. For Grunebaum, Islam's culture was a mysteriously postulated timeless essence. He imposed his own pattern rather than accepting any self-description by the Muslims of their culture. He also tended to describe Islamic culture in terms of what it lacked, such as the genres of theatre and drama. He judged Islam to be inimical to humanism 'in that it is not interested in the richest possible unfolding and evolving of man's potentialities'. He also argued that its cultural development had been arrested in the eleventh century (something echoed by Bernard Lewis in his *The Arabs in History*). Islamic science was bound to peter out because it was founded upon an inadequate theory of knowledge. Von Grunebaum had infuriated Laroui by insisting that Islam will have to modernize in the Western way, for Islam 'cannot undergo modernization unless it reinterprets itself from the Western point of view and accepts the Western idea of man and the Western definition of truth'.[24]

A less impressive critique of Orientalism from a Marxist perspective had previously been published by an Egyptian of Coptic Christian origin, Anouar Abdel-Malek. In 'Orientalism in Crisis', published in 1963, he had accused Orientalists of positing 'an essence which constitutes the inalienable and common basis of all Eastern beings considered'.[25] Islam was viewed by them as a passive object. Abdel-Malek, who taught at the Paris Centre Nationale de la Recherche Scientifique, demanded that Orientalists adopt Oriental methodologies. His views about Western scholars positing an Oriental 'Other' were to be picked up later by Said, but Abdel-Malek's knowledge of the history of Orientalism was shaky. For example, he believed that traditional Orientalism was established by a decision of the Council of Vienna (*sic*) in 1245 (*sic*). Like Said after him, Abdel-Malek argued that Orientalism was a child of the age of European hegemony, but his argument lacked supporting detail. He argued that traditional Orientalism was doomed by the rise of national liberation movements and the end of the age of colonialism. The Orientalists faced a crisis as their compatriots no longer controlled the territories that the scholars studied. Orientals were destined then to take over the interpretation of their own culture. One is not surprised to find no reference to the Soviet overlordship of Muslim territories in Central Asia and no reference either to Soviet Orientalism. Unlike Said, Abdel-Malek regarded Massignon as a misguided racist who had argued that the Arabs were inferior Semites compared to the Jews. Nevertheless, like Said, Abdel-Malek preferred French to British Orientalism.

In 'Apology for Orientalism', published in *Diogenes* in 1965, a leading Italian Orientalist, Francesco Gabrieli, replied to Abdel-Malek. Gabrieli had supervised a complete translation of *The Thousand and One Nights* into Italian. He later published an anthology of Arabic primary sources on the history of the Crusades as well as various general introductions to aspects of Arab culture and politics. Gabrieli viewed Orientalism as essentially a benign Enlightenment phenomenon. He denied that Orientalists were invariably the accomplices of colonialism, citing the counter-examples of Browne, Massignon and 'Caetani who was scoffed at in Italy as the "Turk" for having opposed the conquest of Libya'. Gabrieli's response was quite aggressive. He regarded the East as a methodological desert: 'Because so far as *modern* conceptions, master-ideas, interpretations of history or of life that have been developed in the East are concerned, we confess that we are still waiting to hear of them.' Orientals had no choice but to work with the methods and materials of the Orientalist. In adopting a Marxist perspective, Abdel-Malek was in no sense emancipating himself from the Western style of thought.[26]

Hitherto this chapter has considered Said's Islamist and Marxist precursors. Said, in his book, seems to have drawn quite heavily on Abdel-Malek, Laroui and Tibawi without fully acknowledging his debt. The publication of *Orientalism* in 1978 also provided more fuel for further Islamist attacks on Orientalism – this despite Said's hostility to Islamism and religion in general. Only a few of these will be mentioned here in order to suggest the flavour of the polemic.

MUSLIMS WRITING AFTER SAID

Writing in 1984 in a volume entitled *Orientalism, Islam and Islamists*, Professor Ziya-ul-Hasan Faruqi, an Indian writer and editor, indicted Hamilton Gibb for the crime of writing about Islam even though he was not a Muslim: 'It seems to have been beyond his comprehension to see in Muhammad a divinely inspired Prophet ordained to give mankind a message of hope and happiness in all walks of life.'[27] Gibb had given an economic and political slant to the early history of Islam, when that history could only really be understood in religious terms. Gibb was also guilty of doubting the reliability of Hadiths as source material. In the same volume, Suleyman Nyang and Samir Abed-Rabbo attempted to defend Islam against all the slurs that they had detected in the writings of Bernard Lewis. Not all the pleas for the defence were wholly convincing. Lewis had produced clear documentary evidence that Muslims traded in slaves in the Mediterranean (and on quite a considerable scale), but, according to Abed-Rabbo, the ignorant Lewis had failed to realize that 'a person who acts contrary to the teachings of Islam by acting as a slave trader cannot be called a Muslim'.[28]

This kind of devotional approach to the history of Islam taken by Faruqi and Abed-Rabbo is never likely to be adopted by Western Orientalists. It reminds me of a Muslim friend of mine who, in Oxford back in the 1960s, was set an essay by Professor Beeston in which he was asked to explain the victory of Muhammad and the Medinans over the polytheistic Quraysh tribe. He produced an essay in which he argued that Muhammad had won because, according to earliest sources, a thousand angels fought on his side. The eighth Sura of the Qur'an referred to this incident. My friend's essay received no marks.

Dr Ahmad Ghorab, a Saudi religious scholar, has expressed a remarkable hostility towards Orientalism. In a pamphlet published in 1995, he wrote as follows: 'Whoever knows its long history will recognize in it the influence of the mentality of the Crusades and the rancour of the Jews against Islam. It soon becomes clear that the Orientalists are networks of Christians and Jews, who, behind the façade of academic institutions and the pretence of scholarly curiosity and objectivity, have been engaged in an unrelenting effort to distort Islam in all its aspects.'[29] Collaboration with Orientalists was forbidden in the Qur'an. In the Old and New Testaments the Jews and Christians had received flawed and corrupted revelations. It is because of this that Orientalist textual critics are encouraging Muslims to experience the same kind of intellectual doubts that Christians and Jews are bound to experience about the Bible. The most striking thing about Ghorab's polemical pamphlet is the sheer amount of hatred he evinces for Christians and Jews, as well as for scholarship.

Ziauddin Sardar is also a believing Muslim, but he has attacked Orientalism from a more sophisticated point of view. He is a science journalist and columnist for the *New Statesman* who has published numerous books on modernism and Islam.[30] His short book, *Orientalism*, was published in 1999.[31] The influence of Said's earlier book is pervasive, though Sardar has added some digressions on cultural studies, as well some factual errors that are entirely original to him. His treatment of what he chooses to regard as medieval Orientalism is peculiarly unsatisfactory. He claims that the 'foundation of Orientalism was laid by John of Damascus' and adds that his book became 'the classical source of all Christian writings on Islam'. But John wrote in Greek and most of those Christians who wrote about Islam in the following centuries knew no Greek. Sardar has Pope Urban preach the First Crusade at Clermont in 1096. The correct date is 1095. Writing about the Crusades, he claims that 'Jerusalem itself did not fall back into Muslim hands until 1244'. Actually Saladin occupied it in 1187. He cites Norman Daniels on the Crusaders' hostility to Islam, but he must be thinking of Norman Daniel.

Sardar claims that the *Chanson de Roland* was written by Cretien de Troyes *circa* 1130. Actually the name of the author of this work is not known and Chrétien de Troyes, who flourished *c.* 1166–85, wrote nothing about Roland. Sardar claims that the *Chanson* shows the Muslims worshipping 'Mohomme', as well as a trinity of gods, Tergavent, Apolin and Jupiter. But the *Chanson* does not mention 'Mohomme' and it calls the trinity of idols Termagant, Mahound and Apollyon. The matter is not important, except perhaps that it indicates that Sardar has not troubled to read the work of literature that he wishes to attack.

A page later he tells his readers that Europeans borrowed the concept of the university from 'the *madrasas* as they had developed from the eighth century in the Muslim world'. But there were no madrasas in the Muslim world in the eighth century. The institution spread slowly from the East in later centuries. The first Egyptian madrasas were founded in the late twelfth century and the first Moroccan ones were founded in the fourteenth century. Further down the same page he claims that St Thomas Aquinas decreed that Muslims and Jews were 'invincibly ignorant'. This is not correct. In the *Summa Theologica*, Aquinas specifically allows for the conversion of Muslims to Christianity. Only he argued that they should not be compelled to convert. The chief aim of another of his books, the *Summa contra Gentiles*, was precisely to provide theological ammunition for debates with Muslims, Jews and heterodox Christians.[32]

Occasionally Sardar gets his facts right, particularly when he follows Richard Southern's fine book, *Western Views of Islam in the Middle Ages* (1962). At times he follows Southern rather closely. For example Southern, writing about John of Segovia's fifteenth-century translation of the Qur'an, wrote this: 'But the only really important question was this: Is the Koran the word of God or not? If, by a simple examination of the text, it can be shown to contain contradictions, confusions, errors, traces of composite authorship, these should – so he thought – convince anyone that it was not what it claimed to be.' Sardar agrees: 'The basic question was, is the Qur'an the word of God or not? If by examination of the text it could be shown to contain contradictions, confusions, errors, traces of composite authorship these should convince anyone that it was not what it claimed to be.'[33] At times he follows Southern less closely. So that whereas, for instance, Southern refers to the Council of Vienne (1312), Sardar decides to move this great church council from the South of France to Vienna. He then states that this Council decided that, since it was impossible to convert Muslims who all rejected rational argument, academics trained in Arabic should launch assaults on Islam. But he must have known when he wrote this that it was a straightforward misrepresentation of the truth. In fact, the Council decided to set up chairs in Oriental languages in order to propagate the faith among unbelievers, including Muslims and Jews. On the next page Sardar claims that Ricoldo da Monte Croce, who went to Baghdad in 1291, 'was totally blind to Muslim learning and intellectual achievements, which at that time represented the zenith of civilization'. This is a libel on the dead. Presumably Sardar read Ricoldo before writing about him. Why then suppress the fact that Ricoldo specifically praised the 'Saracens' for their 'attention to study'? Ricoldo added that 'They have in Baghdad many places devoted to study and contemplation alone, in the manner of our great monasteries . . .'[34] And so the book blunders on from error to misspelling, to misquotation to misdating. Did Sardar think that no one would check up on him? His book was published by the Open University Press.

Said and his allies in cultural studies popularized the idea that it is more important to destroy Orientalism than to represent its history accurately. However, despite his debt to Said, Sardar is no fan of his predecessor in this field, since, as a pious Muslim, he rejects Said's secular humanist perspective. Said's 'location in the metropolitan academy of the West and the fashionable genre of literary criticism' meant that he was not properly equipped to defend Islam against the real or imagined slurs of the Orientalists.[35] As we have seen in the previous chapter, as far as Sardar is concerned, Said's humanism derives from the same culture that produced Orientalism and racism.

Naturally there have been better researched and more reasoned Muslim critiques of Orientalism. Fazlur Rahman (1911–88), a professor at the University of Chicago and author of numerous books on

Islam, protested at Western reductionist approaches to his religion, such as 'the attempt to "explain" Islam's genesis and even its nature with reference to Jewish, Christian, or other "influences"'. This was an aspect of the West's cultural arrogance.[36] He also suggested that in order for a statement about a religion to be valid it had to be acceptable to at least some members of that religion, though he did not spell out his reasons for thinking this. He took particular offence at John Wansbrough's strategy of treating the story of early Islam not as a piece of documentary history but as a narrative compiled from literary clichés. He also questioned the stress Wansbrough had placed on Jewish themes (such as covenant and exile) in the Qur'an. Rahman asked why, if those themes really were so important, had Muslims who studied the Qur'an not found them to be important?

Muhsin Mahdi's article 'Orientalism and the Study of Islamic Philosophy' was also written from within the 'academy of the West' as he was at the time Professor of Arabic at Harvard.[37] Mahdi has written numerous studies on Islamic philosophy, as well as producing a fine critical edition of *The Thousand and One Nights*. His strictures on Orientalism were harsh, but not unjust: 'Oriental studies have for long suffered from a stodgy self-satisfaction and the belief that hard work and rhetorical flourish are sufficient to make one a celebrity in a field where it is not common for others to have access to one's sources and to be in a position to judge one's work apart from the impression it makes.' He criticized Grunebaum for writing and teaching in such a way that made his thinking about Islam inaccessible to ordinary students and set out his reservations about Gibb's approach to Ibn Khaldun and to Islam more generally. Mahdi notes the resentment widely felt by Muslims at the arrogance of the West in producing a vast reference work, the *Encyclopaedia of Islam*, that was neither by nor for Muslims and the notion that it should be written by Westerners or those who conformed to Western standards of scholarship. 'It made no difference what Muslims thought of such an encyclopedia, whether they liked it or not, whether it agreed with their views of Islam or not, whether they saw themselves reflected in it or not.' Mahdi also has interesting things to say about the role of German Romanticism in shaping German Orientalism and about those German Orientalists, like Schaeder, who argued that there was no such thing as Islamic philosophy, as philosophers in the Muslim world were all really unbelievers.

Mahdi at least was thoroughly familiar with what he was writing about – something that is not true of most of those discussed in this chapter. The shrillness and defensiveness of most of the attacks on Orientalists are both depressing and unnecessary. The past and present achievements of Arab culture are so considerable that they do not need to be exaggerated or to be defended from all and every single possible kind of criticism. As for Islam, a religion that embodies essential truths about the nature of the universe and man's relation to God has nothing to fear from the most advanced techniques of Western textual criticism.

Notes

1 The Clash of Ancient Civilizations

1. Aziz S. Atiya, *Crusade, Commerce and Culture* (Bloomington, Ind., 1962), pp. 19, 23.

2. Edward Said, *Orientalism* (London, 1978), p. 56.

3. Robert Drews, *The Greek Accounts of Eastern History* (Cambridge, Mass., 1973), pp. 5–6.

4. Roberto Calasso, *The Marriage of Cadmus and Harmony* (London, 1993), p. 240.

5. Bernard Lewis, *The Middle East: 2000 Years of History from the Rise of Christianity to the Present Day* (London, 1995), p. 32.

6. Said, *Orientalism*, pp. 56–7.

7. Aeschylus, *Prometheus Bound, The Suppliants, Seven Against Thebes, The Persians*, translated by Philip Vellacott (London, 1961). My interpretation of *The Persians* is based on my reading of this translation in the Penguin Classics series. However, it should be noted that some classicists have provided a very different (and I think somewhat strained) reading of this play. See Edith Hall, *Inventing the Barbarian: Greek Self-Definition through Tragedy* (Oxford, 1989), especially pp. 76–86; Thomas Harrison, *The Emptiness of Asia: Aeschylus's Persians and the History of the Fifth Century* (London, 2000); Neal Ascherson, *Black Sea: The Birthplace of Civilization and Barbarism* (London, 1996), pp. 61–2.

8. Herodotus, *Histories*, translated by Aubrey de Sélincourt (Harmondsworth, 1954), pp. 69–70. On this historian, see also John Gould, *Herodotus* (London, 1989). Again for a different reading of the text from mine, see Hall, *Inventing the Barbarian*, as well as François Hartog, *The Mirror of Herodotus: The Representation of the Other in the Writing of History* (Berkeley, Los Angeles and London, 1998); Ascherson, *Black Sea*, pp. 51–5, 77–9.

9. Said, *Orientalism*, p. 58.

10. Euripides, *The Bacchae and Other Plays*, translated by Philip Vellacott (London, 1954).

11. Said, *Orientalism*, pp. 56–7.

12. E. R. Dodds, *The Greeks and the Irrational* (Berkeley and Los Angeles, 1951), p. 273.

13. Said, *Orientalism*, p. 57.

14. E. H. Gombrich, *Aby Warburg: An Intellectual Biography* (London, 1970), p. 243.

15. Drews, *Greek Accounts*, pp. 119–21.

16. Italo Calvino, *Why Read the Classics?* (London, 1999), p. 23.

17. Aristotle, *The Politics*, translated by T. A. Sinclair (Harmondsworth, 1962), p. 225.

18. Ibid., p. 136.

19. Ibid., p. 269.

20. Franco Cardini, *Europe and Islam* (London, 1999), p. 2.

21. On Roman attitudes to the Arabs and Persians and on Arabs settled within the Roman empire, see Irfan Shahid, *Roma and the Arabs: A Prolegomena to the Study of Byzantium and the Arabs* (Washington, 1984); Kevin Butcher, *Roman Syria and the Near East* (London, 2003). In 'Il Petrarca e gli Arabi', *Rivista di Cultura Classica e Medioevale*, 7 (1965), pp. 331–6, Enrico Cerulli provides a revealing account of the stereotypical Arab as he appeared in Virgil, Catullus and other Roman authors.

2 An Ancient Heresy or a New Paganism

1. Patricia Crone, 'The Rise of Islam in the World', in Francis Robinson (ed.), *The Cambridge Illustrated History of the Islamic World* (Cambridge, 1996), p. 2.

2. Richard Southern, *The Making of the Middle Ages* (London, 1953), p. 40.

3. Armand Abel, 'Bahira' in *Encyclopaedia of Islam*, 2nd edn (Leiden, 1960–2002); Norman Daniel, *Islam and the West: The Making of an Image* (Edinburgh, 1960), pp. 4–5, 88–9, 93, 235–7, 241, 281, 286, 290, 344, 345, 347.

4. For examples of anti-Christian polemic, see *The Sea of Precious Virtues (Bahr al-Fava'id): A Medieval Islamic Mirror for Princes*, translated and edited by Julie Scott Meisami (Salt Lake City, 1991), pp. 232–4; Richard Gottheil, 'An Answer to the Dhimmis', *Journal of the American Oriental Society*, vol. 41 (1921), pp. 383–457; Aziz al-Azmeh, 'Mortal Enemies, Invisible Neighbours: Northerners in Andalusi Eyes', in Salma Khadra Jayyusi (ed.), *The Legacy of Muslim Spain* (Leiden, 1992), pp. 259–72.

5. For stimulating and scholarly surveys of medieval Christian attacks on Islam, see Dana Carlton Munro, 'The Western Attitude towards Islam during the

Period of the Crusades', *Speculum*, vol. 6 (1931), pp. 329–43; Richard Southern, *Western Views of Islam in the Middle Ages* (Cambridge, Mass., 1962); Daniel, *Islam and the West*; Daniel, *The Arabs and Medieval Europe*, 2nd edn (London, 1979); John V. Tolan, *Saracens: Islam in the Medieval European Imagination* (New York, 2002).

6. Daniel 7: 7.

7. 'The Travels of Bishop Arculf in the Holy Land, towards A.D. 700' in Thomas Wright (ed. and tr.), *Early Travels in Palestine* (London, 1848), pp. 1–2.

8. *The Koran Interpreted*, translated by A. J. Arberry, 2 vols (London, 1955), vol. 2, pp. 125–6 (Sura 33, verses 36–9).

9. On John of Damascus, see Daniel J. Sahas, *John of Damascus on Islam: The 'Heresy of the Ishmaelites'* (Leiden, 1972); Sahas, 'John of Damascus on Islam Revisited', *Abr Nahrain*, vol. 23 (1984–5), pp. 104–18; Tolan, *Saracens*, pp. 50–55, 58–9; Peter Brown, *The Rise of Western Christendom*, 2nd edn (Oxford, 2003), pp. 307–8, 397–9.

10. On 'Abd al-Masih al-Kindi, see Daniel, *Islam and the West*, pp. 239, 235; Tolan, *Saracens*, pp. 60–64.

11. Southern, *Western Views of Islam*, p. 21; Robert Hillenbrand, '"The Ornament of the World": Medieval Córdoba as a Cultural Centre', in Salma Khadra Jayyusi (ed.), *The Legacy of Muslim Spain* (Leiden, 1992), p. 115; Tolan, *Saracens*, pp. 86–97.

12. Jessica A. Coope, *The Martyrs of Córdoba: Community and Family Conflict in an Age of Mass Conversion* (Lincoln, Nebr., 1995); Benjamin Z. Kedar, *Crusade and Mission: European Approaches towards the Muslims* (Princeton, 1984), pp. 15–18; Tolan, *Saracens*, pp. 85–98, 100–102.

13. On toleration in Muslim Spain and its limits, see Anwar G. Chejne, *Muslim Spain: Its History and Culture* (Minneapolis, 1974), pp. 115–20; Richard Fletcher, *Moorish Spain* (London, 1992), especially chapter 7; Mikel de Epalza, 'Mozarabs: An Emblematic Christian Minority in Islamic Andalus', in Jayyusi (ed.), *The Legacy of Muslim Spain*, pp. 148–70; Bernard Lewis, 'An Ode Against the Jews', in *Islam in History: Ideas, People and Events in the Middle East*, 2nd edn (Chicago and La Salle, Ill., 1993), pp. 167–74.

14. Bernard Lewis, *The Jews of Islam* (London, 1984), pp. 45, 54, 197; Fletcher, *Moorish Spain*, pp. 96–7; Raymond P. Scheindlin, 'The Jews in Muslim Spain', in Jayyusi (ed.), *The Legacy of Muslim Spain*, pp. 195–6, 199.

15. E. Lévi-Provençal, *Séville musulmane au début du XIIe siècle: Traité d'Ibn 'Abdun sur la vie urbaine et les corps de métiers* (Paris, 1947), p. 128.

16. Charles Burnett, 'The Translating Activity in Mediaeval Spain', in Jayyusi (ed.), *The Legacy of Muslim Spain*, pp. 1036–58.

17. James Kritzek, *Peter the Venerable and Islam* (Princeton, 1964), p. 30.

18. M. T. d'Alverny, 'Deux traductions latines du Coran au Moyen Age', *Archives d'histoire doctrinale et littéraire du moyen-âge*, vols 22–23 (1947–8),

NOTES

pp. 69–131; Kritzek, *Peter the Venerable and Islam, passim*; Thomas E. Burman, 'Tafsir and Translation: Traditional Arabic Qur'an in Exegesis and the Latin Qur'ans of Robert of Ketton and Robert of Toledo', *Speculum*, vol. 73 (1998), pp. 703–32.

19. Kritzek, *Peter the Venerable*, pp. 45–6.

20. Ibid., pp. 155–99, 220–91.

21. D'Alverny, 'Deux traductions', pp. 113–19; D'Alverny and G. Vajda, 'Marc de Tolède, traducteur d'Ibn Tumart', *Al-Andalus*, vol. 16 (1951), pp. 99–140, 259–308; vol. 17, pp. 1–56.

22. On medieval translations from Arabic of scientific, mathematical and philosophical works in general, see Burnett, 'The Translating Activity'; Burnett, *Adelard of Bath: An English Scientist and Arabist of the Early Twelfth Century*, Warburg Institute Surveys and Texts, vol. 14 (London, 1987); Burnett, *The Introduction of Arabic Learning into England* (London, 1996); W. Montgomery Watt, *The Influence of Islam on Medieval Europe* (Edinburgh, 1972), pp. 58–71; Donald R. Hill, *Islamic Science and Engineering* (Edinburgh, 1993), pp. 220–35.

23. On the impact of Arabic mathematics in Europe, see George Gheverghese Joseph, *The Crest of the Peacock: Non-European Roots of Mathematics* (London, 1991), pp. 301–47; Alexander Murray, *Reason and Society in the Middle Ages* (Oxford, 1978), pp. 167–75.

24. Bertrand Russell, *A History of Western Philosophy* (London, 1961), p. 417.

25. On the philosophy of Avicenna and its transmission to the West, see Salvador Gómez Nogales, 'Ibn Sina', in M. L. J. Young, J. D. Latham and R. B. Serjeant (eds), *The Cambridge History of Arabic Literature: Religion, Learning and Science during the 'Abbasid Period* (Cambridge, 1990), pp. 398–404; Gordon Leff, *Medieval Thought: St Augustine to Ockham* (Harmondsworth, 1958), pp. 148–55.

26. Burnett, 'Translating Activity', pp. 1038–9.

27. Paul Kraus, *Jabir ibn Hayyan: Contribution à l'histoire des idées scientifiques dans l'Islam*, 2 vols (Cairo, 1942–3).

28. [Pseudo-]al-Majriti, *Ghayat al-Hakim*, edited by H. Ritter (Leipzig and Berlin, 1933); David Pingree (ed.), *Picatrix: The Latin Version of the Ghayat al-Hakim* (London, 1986); David Pingree, 'Some of the Sources of the Ghayat al-Hakim', *Journal of the Warburg and Courtauld Institutes*, vol. 43 (1980), pp. 1–15; Vittore Perrone Compagni, 'Picatrix Latinus: concezioni filosofico-religiose e prassi magica', *Medioévo, Rivista di storia della filosofia medievale*, 1 (1975), pp. 237–337.

29. G. N. Atiyeh, *Al-Kindi: The Philosopher of the Arabs* (Rawalpindi, 1966); M. T. d'Alverny and F. Hudry, 'De Radiis', *Archives d'histoire doctrinale et littéraire du moyen-âge*, 41 (1975), pp. 139–60, reprinted in Sylvie Matton

(ed.), *La Magie arabe traditionelle* (Paris, 1977), pp. 77–128; Fritz W. Zimmerman, 'Al-Kindi', in Young, Latham and Serjeant (eds), *The Cambridge History of Arabic Literature: Religion, Learning and Science in the 'Abbasid Period*, pp. 364–9.

30. On the pseudepigrapha of Aristotle, see Lynn Thorndike, *A History of Magic and Experimental Science During the First Thirteen Centuries of Our Era* (New York, 1923), vol. 2, pp. 246–78; A. F. L. Beeston, 'An Arabic Hermetic Manuscript', *Bodleian Library Record*, 7 (1962), pp. 11–23; Dorothy Metzlitzki, *The Matter of Araby in Medieval England* (New Haven and London, 1977), pp. 86–92, 106–11; Norman Penzer, *Poison Damsels and Other Essays in Folklore and Anthropology* (London, 1952), pp. 113–71; J. Kraye, W. F. Ryan and C. B. Schmidt (eds), *Pseudo-Aristotle in the Middle Ages*, Warburg Institute Surveys and Texts vol. 11 (London, 1987).

31. Dag Nikolaus Hasse, *Avicenna's De Anima in the Latin West: The Formation of a Peripatetic Philosophy of the Soul 1160–1300* (London and Turin, 2000), pp. 168–9, 172.

32. Charles Homer Haskins, *Studies in the History of Medieval Science*, 2nd edn (Cambridge, Mass., 1927), p. 19.

33. Oswei Temkin, *Galenism: The Rise and Decline of Medical Philosophy* (Ithaca, NY, 1973); Manfred Ullman, *Islamic Medicine* (Edinburgh, 1978), pp. 33–8; Franz Rosenthal, *The Classical Heritage in Islam* (London, 1975), pp. 182–3, 192–4; Michael Dols, *Majnun: The madman in medieval Islamic society* (Oxford, 1992), pp. 17–47.

34. Ullman, *Islamic Medicine*, pp. 45–6; Haskell D. Isaacs, 'Arabic Medical Literature', in Young, Latham and Serjeant (eds), *The Cambridge History of Arabic Literature: Religion, Learning and Science in the 'Abbasid Period*, pp. 356–8; Ursula Weiser, 'Ibn Sina und die Medzin des arabisch-islamischen Mittelalters-Alte und Neue Urteile und Vorurteile', *Medizinhistorisches Journal*, 18 (1983), pp. 283–305; Nancy G. Siraisi, *Avicenna in Renaissance Italy: The Canon and Medical Teaching in Italian Universities after 1500* (Princeton, NJ, 1987); Dols, *Majnun*, pp. 73–103.

35. On Ptolemaic astronomy and astrology in the Arab lands and their transmission to the West, see Thorndike, *A History of Magic and Experimental Science*, vol. 1, pp. 697–719; vol. 2, pp. 66–98; David King, 'Astronomy', in Young, Latham and Serjeant (eds), *The Cambridge History of Arabic Literature: Religion, Learning and Science during the 'Abbasid Period*, pp. 274–89; David Pingree, 'Astrology', in ibid., pp. 290–300; F. J. Carmody, *Arabic Astronomical and Astrological Sciences in Translation* (Berkeley and Los Angeles, 1956); Hill, *Islamic Science and Engineering*, pp. 42–6; Joseph F. O'Callaghan, *The Learned King: The Reign of Alfonso X of Castile* (Philadelphia, 1993), pp. 141–3.

36. Ernest Renan's unreliable and outdated *Averroès et l'Averroïsme* (Paris,

1861) is discussed and criticized in chapter six. More reliable accounts of Averroes's thinking can be found in Oliver Leaman, *Averroes and His Philosophy*, revised edn (Richmond, Surrey, 1998); Majid Fakhry, *Averroes (Ibn Rushd), His Life, Works and Influence* (Oxford, 2001). For his impact on the West, see Leff, *Medieval Thought*, pp. 155–62; Paul Oscar Kristeller, 'Paduan Averroism and Alexandrism in the Light of Recent Studies', in Kristeller, *Renaissance Thought II, Papers on Humanism and the Arts* (New York, 1965), pp. 111–18; Kristeller, 'Petrarch's "Averroists": A note on the history of Averroism in Venice, Padua and Bologna', *Bibliothèque d'Humanisme et Renaissance*, 14 (1952), pp. 59–65.

37. Leff, *Medieval Thought*, p. 218; Daniel, *The Arabs and Medieval Europe*, pp. 250, 281–3.

38. Southern, *Western Views of Islam*, pp. 30–31; Daniel, *The Arabs and Medieval Europe*, pp. 236, 238; John France, 'The First Crusade and Islam', *Muslim World*, vol. 67 (1977), pp. 247–57; Tolan, *Saracens*, pp. 135–47.

39. Jacques de Vitry, *Lettres de la Cinquième Croisade: 1160/1170–1240, évêque de Saint-Jean d'Acre*, edited by R. B. C. Huygens (Leiden, 1960); Kedar, *Crusade and Mission*, pp. 112–31.

40. Southern, *Western Views of Islam*, pp. 62–3; Kedar, *Crusade and Mission*, pp. 180–82; Daniel, *The Arabs and Medieval Europe*, pp. 211–12, 243; Tolan, *Saracens*, pp. 203–9.

41. Ricoldo de Monte Croce, *Pérégrination en Terre Sainte et au proche Orient. Texte latin et traduction. Lettres sur la chute de Saint-Jean d'Acre*, edited and translated by René Kappler (Paris, 1997); Southern, *Western Views of Islam*, pp. 69–70; Daniel, *The Arabs and Medieval Europe*, pp. 201–2, 218–20, 247–9; Tolan, *Saracens*, pp. 245–54.

42. *Encyclopaedia of Islam*, 2nd edn (Leiden, 1954–2002), s.v. 'Ibn Hazm' [Arnaldez]; Anwar G. Chejne, *Muslim Spain: Its History and Culture* (Minneapolis, 1974), pp. 306–7; William Montgomery Watt, *Muslim–Christian Encounters, Perceptions and Misperceptions* (London, 1991), pp. 33, 65–7; Jacques Waardenburg, 'Muslim Studies of Other Religions: The Medieval Period', in Geert van Gelder and Ed de Moor, *Orientations. The Middle East and Europe: Encounters and Exchanges* (Amsterdam, 1992), pp. 21–4.

43. Nancy N. Roberts, 'Reopening the Muslim–Christian Dialogue of the 13th–14th Centuries: Critical Reflections on Ibn Taymiyyah's Response to Christianity in *al-Jawab al-Sahih li-man Baddala Din al-Masih*', *Muslim World*, 86 (1996), pp. 432–66; S. M. Stern, 'The Oxford Manuscript of Ibn Taymiyya's Anti-Christian Polemics', *Bulletin of the School of Oriental and African Studies*, 22 (1959), pp. 124–8.

44. Aziz al-Azmeh, 'Mortal Enemies, Invisible Neighbours: Northerners in Andalusi Eyes', in Jayyusi (ed.), *The Legacy of Muslim Spain*, pp. 267–8.

45. Meisami, *The Sea of Precious Virtues*, pp. 231–2.

46. Lévi-Provençal, *Séville Musulmane*, pp. 108–9.

47. On Arab popular epics, see Wolfdietrich Fischer, 'Die Nachwirkung der Kreuzzüge in der arabischen Volksliteratur', in Wolfdietrich Fischer and Jürgen Schneider (eds), *Das Heilige Land im Mittelalter: Begegungsraum zwischen Orient und Okzident* (Neustadt an der Aisch, 1982), pp. 145–54; M. C. Lyons, *The Arabian Epic: Heroic and oral story-telling*, 3 vols (Cambridge, 1995).

48. *The Song of Roland*, tranlated by Dorothy L. Sayers (Harmondsworth, 1957), p. 87; cf. p. 21.

49. Norman Daniel, *Heroes and Saracens: A Re-interpretation of the Chansons de Geste* (Edinburgh, 1984).

50. Dante, *Inferno*, Canto XXVIII.

51. Dante, *Purgatorio*, Canto IV.

52. On Dante and Islam, see Miguel Asin Palacios's still highly controversial *Islam and the Divine Comedy* (London, 1926). See also Southern, *Western Views of Islam*, pp. 55–6; Southern, 'Dante and Islam', in Derek Baker (ed.), *Relations between East and West in the Middle Ages* (Edinburgh, 1973), pp. 133–45; Philip F. Kennedy, 'Muslim Sources of Dante', in Dionysius A. Agius and Richard Hitchcock (eds), *The Arab Influence in Medieval Europe; Folia Scholastica Mediterranea* (Reading, 1994), pp. 63–82.

53. A. C. Lee, *The Decameron: Its Sources and Analogues* (London, 1909), p. 171; cf. p. 312; Robert Irwin, *The Arabian Nights: A Companion* (London, 1994), pp. 64, 96–7.

54. Ramon Lull, *Selected Works of Ramon Lull*, edited by A. Bonner (Princeton, 1985); E. Allison Peers, *Ramon Lull: A Bibliography* (London, 1929); J. N. Hillgarth, *Lull and Lullism in Fourteenth-Century France* (Oxford, 1972); Frances Yates, *Lull and Bruno: Collected Essays* (London, 1982). On Lull and Islam, see Aziz Suriyal Atiya, *The Crusade in the Later Middle Ages* (London, 1938), pp. 74–94; Southern, *Western Views of Islam*, pp. 68, 72n; Kedar, *Crusade and Mission*, pp. 188–99; Tolan, *Saracens*, pp. 256–74.

55. Lull, *Blanquerna*, translated by E. A. Peers (London, 1925).

56. Southern, *Western Views of Islam*, p. 72n; Louis Massignon, *Opera Minora*, edited by Y. Moubarac (Beirut, 1963), vol. 1, p. 12.

57. Edward Said, *Orientalism* (London, 1978), pp. 49–50.

58. Southern, *Western Views of Islam*, pp. 72–3, 88; Roberto Weiss, 'England and the Decree of the Council of Vienne on the Teaching of Greek, Arabic, Hebrew and Syriac', *Bibliothèque d'Humanisme et Renaissance*, 14 (1952), pp. 1–9.

59. Southern, *Western Views of Islam*, p. 78.

60. Ibid., pp. 86–93; Robert Schwoebel, *The Shadow of the Crescent: The Renaissance Image of the Turk (1453–1517)* (Nieuwkoop, 1967), pp. 223–5; John Robert Jones, *Learning Arabic in Renaissance Europe (1505–1624)*,

Ph.D. thesis (School of Oriental and African Studies, London University, July 1988), pp. 20–21.

61. Southern, *Western Views of Islam*, pp. 77–83.

62. Metzlitzki, *The Matter of Araby in Medieval England*, pp. 197–203, 205–7.

63. Robert Bartlett, *England under the Norman and Angevin Kings* (Oxford, 2000), pp. 660–61.

64. On Mandeville, see Malcolm Letts, *Sir John Mandeville: The Man and His Book* (London, 1949); Robert Fazy, 'Jehan de Mandeville. Ses voyages et son séjour discuté en Egypte', *Etudes Asiatiques*, 3 (1949), pp. 30–54; Donald R. Howard, *Writers and Pilgrims: Medieval Pilgrimage Narratives and Their Posterity* (Berkeley and Los Angeles, 1980); Metzlitzki, *The Matter of Araby in Medieval England*, pp. 220–39; Mary B. Campbell, *The Witness and the Other World: Exotic European Travel Writing 400–1600* (Ithaca, 1988), pp. 122–61.

65. *The Travels of Sir John Mandeville*, edited and translated by C. W. R. D. Mosley (Harmondsworth, 1983), p. 107.

66. Letts, *Sir John Mandeville*, p. 50–51.

67. Ibid., p. 49.

68. Ziauddin Sardar, *Orientalism* (Buckingham, 1999), p 25.

69. Campbell, *The Witness and the Other World*, p. 122.

3   Renaissance Orientalism

1. Charles Burnett, 'The Second Revelation of Arabic Philosophy and Science: 1492–1562', in Charles Burnett and Anna Contadini (eds), *Islam and the Italian Renaissance* (Warburg Institute Colloquia, 5), pp. 185–98.

2. Ibid., p. 186.

3. 'Petrarca's Aversion to Arab Science' (a letter to Giovanni de Dondi) in Ernst Cassirer, Paul Otto Kristeller and John Herman Randall, Jr (eds and trs), *The Renaissance Philosophy of Man* (Chicago and London, 1948), p. 142. On Petrarch and the Arabs more generally, see H. A. R. Gibb, 'Literature', in Sir Thomas Arnold and Alfred Guillaume (eds), *The Legacy of Islam*, 1st edn (Oxford, 1931), p. 192; Enrico Cerulli, 'Petrarca e gli Arabi', *Rivista di Cultura Classica e Medioevale*, 7 (1965), pp. 331–6; Francesco Gabrieli, 'Il Petrarca e gli Arabi', *Rivista di Cultura Classica e Medioevale*, 7 (1965), pp. 487–94; Paul Otto Kristeller, 'Petrarch's "Averroists": A Note on the History of Averroism in Venice, Padua and Bologna', *Bibliothèque d'Humanisme et Renaissance*, 14 (1952), pp. 59–65; Charles Burnett, 'Learned Knowledge of Arabic Poetry, Rhymed Prose, and Didactic Verse from Petrus Alfonsi to Petrarch', in John Marenbon (ed.), *Poetry and Philosophy in the Middle Ages: A Festschrift*

for Peter Dronke (Leiden, 2001), pp. 29–62; Charles Burnett, 'Petrarch and Averroes: An Episode in the History of Poetics', in Ian Macpherson and Ralph Penny (eds), *The Medieval Mind: Hispanic Studies in Honour of Alan Deyermond* (Woodbridge, 1997), pp. 49–56.

4. 'An Averroist Visits Petrarca', in Cassirer et al., *Renaissance Philosophy of Man*, p. 140.

5. 'A Request to Take Up the Fight Against Averroes', in Cassirer et al., *Renaissance Philosophy of Man*, p. 144.

6. 'Petrarca on his own Ignorance', in Cassirer et al., *Renaissance Philosophy of Man*, p. 77.

7. Lynn Thorndike, *A History of Magic and Experimental Science*, vol. 2 (New York, 1923), p. 633.

8. John Edwin Sandys, *A History of Classical Scholarship*, 3 vols (Cambridge, 1908), vol. 2, p. 67.

9. F. Pall, 'Ciriaco d'Ancona e la crociata contro i Turchi', *Bulletin de la section historique de l'Académie roumaine*, 20 (1938), pp. 9–68; Franz Babinger, 'Notes on Cyriac of Ancona and Some of his Friends', *Journal of the Warburg and Courtauld Institutes*, 25 (1962), pp. 321–3; E. W. Bodnar, *Cyriacus of Ancona and Athens* (Brussels, 1960).

10. E. Borsook, 'The Travels of Bernardo Michelozzi and Bonsignore Bonsignori in the Levant (1497–8)', *Journal of the Warburg and Courtauld Institutes*, 36 (1973), pp. 145–97.

11. George Gheverghese Joseph, *The Crest of the Peacock: Non-European Roots of Mathematics* (London, 1991), pp. 17, 308, 331; Richard Mankiewicz, *The Story of Mathematics* (London, 2000), p. 49; G. J. Toomer, *Eastern Wisedome and Learning: The Study of Arabic in Seventeenth-Century England* (Oxford, 1996), pp. 233–42; George Molland, 'The Limited Lure of Arabic Mathematics', in G. A. Russell (ed.), *The 'Arabick' Interest of the Natural Philosophers in Seventeenth-Century England* (Leiden, 1994), pp. 218–21.

12. On Nicholas of Cusa, see E. F. Jacob, 'Cusanus the Theologian', in *Essays in the Conciliar Epoch*, 2nd edn (Manchester, 1953), pp. 154–69; Norman Daniel, *Islam and the West: The Making of an Image* (Edinburgh, 1960), pp. 276–8; R. W. Southern, *Western Views of Islam in the Middle Ages* (Cambridge, Mass., 1962), pp. 92–4.

13. On Pico della Mirandola, see E. Garin, *Giovanni Pico della Mirandola: Vita e dottrina* (Florence, 1937); P. Kibre, *The Library of Pico della Mirandola* (New York, 1936); Cassirer et al., *Renaissance Philosophy of Man*, pp. 215–54; Joseph L. Blau, *The Christian Interpretation of the Cabala in the Renaissance* (New York, 1944); K. H. Dannenfeldt, 'Renaissance Humanists and the Knowledge of Arabic', *Studies in the Renaissance*, 2 (1955), p. 101.

14. M. Bernal, *Black Athena: The Afroasiatic Roots of Classical Civilization* (London, 1987).

15. Erik Iversen, *The Myth of Egypt and its Hieroglyphs in European Tradition* (Princeton, 1993), pp. 59–74; Umberto Eco, *The Search for the Perfect Language* (London, 1997), pp. 146–54.

16. On Renaissance esotericism, see, amongst much else, Paul Otto Kristeller, *The Philosophy of Marsilio Ficino* (New York, 1943); Wayne Shumaker, *The Occult Sciences in the Renaissance: A Study in Intellectual Patterns* (Berkeley and Los Angeles, 1972); D. P. Walker, *Spiritual and Demonic Magic from Ficino to Campanella* (London, 1958); Blau, *The Christian Interpretation of the Cabala*; François Secret, *Les Kabbalistes Chrétiens de la Renaissance* (Paris, 1964); Frances Yates, *Giordano Bruno and the Hermetic Tradition* (London, 1964).

17. On Christian captives in the Islamic lands, particularly in North Africa, see Samuel C. Chew, *The Crescent and the Rose: Islam and England during the Renaissance* (New York, 1937), pp. 340–46, 373–85; Nabil Matar, *Islam in Britain 1558–1685* (Cambridge, 1998), *passim*; Nabil Matar, *Turks, Moors and Englishmen in the Age of Discovery* (New York, 1998), pp. 71–82; Linda Colley, *Captives: Britain, Empire and the World, 1600–1850* (London, 2002), pp. 23–134; Bartolomé Bennassar and Lucile Bennassar, *Les Chrétiens d'Allah: L'histoire extraordinaire des renégats, XVIe–XVIIe siècles* (Paris, 1989); Robert C. Davis, *Christian Slaves, Muslim Masters: White Slavery in the Mediterranean, the Barbary Coast and Italy, 1500–1800* (London, 2004).

18. Aziz S. Atiya, *The Crusade in the Later Middle Ages* (New York, 1938), pp. 258–9; cf. Norman Housley (ed. and tr.), *Documents on the Later Crusades, 1274–1580* (Basingstoke, 1986), pp. 169–73.

19. B. Rekers, *Benito Arias Montano (1527–1598)* (London, 1972); Alastair Hamilton, *Arab Culture and Ottoman Magnificence in Antwerp's Golden Age* (Oxford, 2001), p. 65.

20. Busbecq, *The Turkish Letters of Ogier Ghiselin de Busbecq, Imperial Ambassador at Constantinople 1554–1562*, translated by Edward Seymour Forster (Oxford, 1927), p. 40.

21. Bernard Lewis, *The Emergence of Modern Turkey* (Oxford, 1961), p. 27.

22. Matar, *Turks, Moors and Englishmen*, pp. 100–127.

23. On travel writing in this period, see, among much else, Margaret T. Hodges, *Early Anthropology in the Sixteenth and Seventeenth Centuries* (Philadelphia, 1964); Hamilton, *Arab Culture and Ottoman Magnificence*, pp. 26–39; Ulrich Haarmann, 'The Mamluk System of Rule in the Eyes of Western Travellers', *Mamluk Studies Review*, 5 (2001), pp. 1–24; Anne Wolf, *How Many Miles to Babylon? Travels to Egypt and Beyond from 1300 to 1640* (Liverpool, 2003).

24. Jean Thenaud, *Le Voyage d'Outremer*, edited by Charles Schefer (Paris, 1884).

25. Hamilton, *Arab Culture and Ottoman Magnificence*, pp. 40–41.

26. *The Turkish Letters of Ogier Ghiselin de Busbecq*; cf. Hamilton, *Arab Culture and Ottoman Magnificence*, pp. 41–5.

27. Nicolas de Nicolay, *Les Navigations et Voyages, faicts en la Turquie* (Antwerp, 1576); cf. Julian Raby, *Venice, Dürer and the Oriental Mode* (London, 1982), p. 95n; Yvelie Bernard, *L'Orient du XVIe siècle: Une société musulmane florissante* (Paris, 1988), *passim*; Alastair Hamilton, *Europe and the Arab World: Five Centuries of books by European scholars and travellers from the libraries of the Arcadian Group* (Oxford, 1994), pp. 9–10.

28. Peter Burke, *A Social History of Knowledge* (London, 2002), p. 109.

29. Jean Léon l'Africain, *Description de l'Afrique*, translated by Alexis Epaulard, 2 vols (Paris, 1956). On Leo, see Louis Massignon, *Le Maroc dans les premières années du XVIe siècle* (Algiers, 1906); Toomer, *Eastern Wisdome and Learning*, pp. 21–2; John Robert Jones, *Learning Arabic in Renaissance Europe (1505–1624)*, Ph.D. thesis (School of Oriental and African Studies, London University, July 1988), pp. 65–72, 144–5.

30. On the Maronites in Italy and on Western interest in Eastern Christians more generally, see the next chapter.

31. On Postel, see William Bousma, *Concordia Mundi, The career and thought of Guillaume Postel (1510–1580)*, (Cambridge, Mass., 1957); Bousma, 'Postel and the Significance of Renaissance Cabalism', in Paul O. Kristeller and Philip P. Wiener (eds), *Renaissance Essays* (New York, 1968), pp. 252–66; Johann Fück, *Die Arabischen Studien in Europa bis in den Anfang des 20. Jahrhunderts* (Leipzig, 1955), pp. 36–44; Secret, *Les Kabbalistes Chrétiens de la Renaissance*; F. Secret, 'Guillaume Postel et les Etudes Arabes à la Renaissance', *Arabica*, vol. 9 (1962), pp. 21–36; Hamilton, *Europe and the Arab World*, pp. 44–9; Hamilton, *Arab Culture and Ottoman Magnificence*, pp. 48–54; Marjorie Reeves, *The Influence of Prophecy in the Later Middle Ages* (Oxford, 1969), pp. 382–5, 479–81; Umberto Eco, *The Search for the Perfect Language* (London, 1995), pp. 75–80; Francine de Nave (ed.), *Philologia Arabica: Arabische studiën en drukken Nederlanden in 16de en 17de eeuw* (Antwerp, 1986), pp. 81–7; Georges Weill and François Secret, *Vie et caractère de Guillaume Postel* (Milan, 1987); Lucien Febvre, *Le Problème de l'incroyance au 16e siècle) La religion de Rabelais*, 2nd edn (Paris, 1968), pp. 107–19; Jones, *Learning Arabic*, pp. 149–58; Josée Balagna, *L'Imprimerie arabe en occident (XVIe, XVIIe et XVIIIe siècles)* (Paris, 1984), pp. 23–7.

32. On the Qur'an printed by Bibliander, see Fück, *Die Arabischen Studien in Europa*, pp. 6–8; James Kritzek, *Peter the Venerable and Islam* (Princeton, NJ, 1964), pp. vii–ix; Hamilton, *Europe and the Arab World*, pp. 38–41; De Nave (ed.), *Philologia Arabica*, pp. 92–4.

33. Chew, *The Crescent and the Rose*, pp. 101–2.

34. Southern, *Western Views of Islam*, pp. 104–7.

35. Errol F. Rhodes, 'Polyglot Bibles', in Bruce M. Metzger and Michael D.

Coogan (eds), *The Oxford Companion to the Bible* (New York and Oxford, 1993), pp. 601–3.

36. Rhodes, 'Polyglot Bibles', pp. 601–2; Hamilton, *Arab Culture and Ottoman Magnificence*, pp. 61–6.

37. Hamilton, *Arab Culture and Ottoman Magnificence*, pp. 65–6.

38. Fück, *Die Arabischen Studien*, pp. 57, 63–4; Hamilton, *Arab Culture and Ottoman Magnificence*, pp. 71–6, 79–87; De Nave, *Philologia Arabica*, pp. 124–36; Toomer, *Eastern Wisdome*, pp. 41–2; Jones, *Learning Arabic*, pp. 185–6; Balagna, *L'Imprimerie arabe*, pp. 41–3.

39. On the Medici Press, see Jones, *Learning Arabic*, pp. 85–90, 167, 169–83; John Robert Jones, *The Medici Oriental Press (Rome 1584–1614) and Renaissance Arabic Studies*, Exhibition Leaflet at SOAS, London, 1983; Jones, 'The Medici Oriental Press (Rome 1584–1614) and the Impact of its Arabic Publications on Europe', in Russell (ed.), *The 'Arabick' Interest*, pp. 88–108; Balagna, *L'Imprimerie arabe*, pp. 34–41, 51; Hamilton, *Europe and the Arab World*, pp. 58–63; Toomer, *Eastern Wisdome*, pp. 22–4; De Nave, *Philologia Arabica*, pp. 73–5.

40. Jonathan M. Bloom, *Paper Before Print: The History and Impact of Paper in the Islamic World* (New Haven and London, 2001), pp. 214–26.

41. On the life and works of Scaliger, see Fück, *Die Arabischen Studien*, pp. 47–53; Dannenfeldt, 'Renaissance Humanists', p. 112; Jones, *Learning Arabic*, pp. 184–5; Anthony Grafton, *Joseph Scaliger: A Study in the History of Classical Scholarship*, 2 vols (Oxford, 1983 and 1993); De Nave, *Philologia arabica*, pp. 116–22; Toomer, *Eastern Wisedome*, pp. 42–3; Alastair Hamilton, *William Bedwell, the Arabist, 1563–1632* (Leiden, 1985), pp. 83–5; Sandys, *History of Classical Scholarship*, vol. 2, p. 199.

42. Hamilton, *William Bedwell*, p. 84.

43. On the life and works of Casaubon, *Oxford Dictionary of National Biography*, edited by H. C. G. Matthew and Brian Harrison (Oxford, 2004), s.v.; Fück, *Die Arabischen Studien*, pp. 60–61; Dannenfeldt, 'Renaissance Humanists', p. 112; Mark Pattison, *Isaac Casaubon* (Oxford, 1892); Hamilton, *William Bedwell*, passim.

4 The Holiness of Oriental Studies

1. On the pervasiveness of a Latinate culture in the early modern period, see H. von Wilamowitz-Mollendorff, *History of Classical Scholarship*, translated by Alan Harris (London, 1982); John Edwyn Sandys, *A History of Classical Scholarship*, vol. 2 (Cambridge, 1908); Rudolf Pfeiffer, *History of Classical Scholarship from 1300 to 1850* (Oxford, 1976); Françoise Waquet, *Latin or the Empire of a Sign from the Sixteenth to the Twentieth Century*

(London, 2001); Bill Bryson, *Mother Tongue* (London, 1990), pp. 58, 128–9.

2. David C. Douglas, *English Scholars* (London, 1939), p. 352.

3. Alastair Hamilton, *William Bedwell, the Arabist, 1563–1632* (Leiden, 1985), p. 79.

4. Nabil Matar, *Islam in Britain 1558–1685* (Cambridge, 1988), p. 76.

5. For the life and works of Bedwell, see Alastair Hamilton's exemplary study, *William Bedwell*; cf. *Oxford Dictionary of National Biography* [ODNB], edited by H. C. G. Matthew and Brian Harrison (Oxford, 2004) s.v.; G. J. Toomer, *Eastern Wisedome and Learning: The Study of Arabic in Seventeenth-Century England* (Oxford, 1996), pp. 56–64.

6. On the life and works of Andrewes, see John Aubrey, *Brief Lives*, edited by John Buchanan-Brown (London, 2000), pp. 6–8; T. S. Eliot, *Essays Ancient and Modern* (London, 1936), pp. 11–29; Robert L. Otley, *Lancelot Andrewes* (London, 1894); *ODNB*, s.v.; G. Lloyd Jones, *The Discovery of Hebrew in Tudor England: A Third Language* (Manchester, 1983), p. 147.

7. Toomer, *Eastern Wisedome*, pp. 55–6.

8. On Laud's career and his Oriental interests, see H. R. Trevor-Roper, *Archbishop Laud 1573–1645* (London, 1940); *ODNB*, s.v.; Mordechai Feingold, 'Patrons and Professors: The Origins and Motives for the Endowment of University Chairs – in Particular the Laudian Chair of Arabic', in G. A. Russell (ed.), *The 'Arabick' Interest of the Natural Philosophers in Seventeenth-Century England* (Leiden, 1994), pp. 109–27. On the Laudian Chair, see also Mordechai Feingold, 'Oriental Studies', in Nicholas Tyacke (ed.), *The History of the University of Oxford*, vol. 4, *The Seventeenth Century* (Oxford, 1997), pp. 449–503, esp. pp. 487–8.

9. Alastair Hamilton, 'An Egyptian Traveller in the Republic of Letters: Joseph Barbatus or Abudacnus the Copt', *Journal of the Warburg and Courtauld Institutes*, 57 (1994), pp. 123–50.

10. On Pasor, see Toomer, *Eastern Wisedome*, pp. 98–101; Feingold, 'Patrons and Professors', in Russell (ed.), *The 'Arabick' Interest*, pp. 120–21.

11. Mordechai Feingold, 'Decline and Fall: Arabic Science in Seventeenth-Century England', in *Tradition, Transmission, Transformation: Proceedings of Two Conferences on Pre-Modern Science Held at the University of Oklahoma*, edited by F. Jamil Ragep and Sally Ragep with Steven Livesey (Leiden, 1996), pp. 442–3; cf. Matar, *Islam in Britain*, p. 87.

12. John Aubrey, *Brief Lives*, pp. 280–82; *ODNB*, s.v.; G. H. Martin and J. R. L. Highfield, *A History of Merton College* (Oxford, 1997), pp. 159–98; Feingold, 'Patrons and Professors', in Russell (ed.), *The 'Arabick' Interest*, pp. 110–17.

13. On John Greaves, see *ODNB*, s.v.; Martin and Highfield, *A History of Merton College*, pp. 204–7; Geoffrey Roper, 'Arabic Printing and Publishing

in England before 1820', *British Society for Middle Eastern Studies Bulletin*, 12 (1985), pp. 15–16.

14. On the life and works of Pococke, *ODNB*, s.v.; Johann Fück, *Die Arabischen Studien in Europa bis in den Anfang des 20. Jahrhunderts* (Leipzig, 1955), pp. 85–90; Peter Holt, 'An Oxford Arabist: Edward Pococke', in Holt, *Studies in the History of the Near East*, (London, 1973), pp. 1–26; Holt, 'The Study of Arabic Historians in Seventeenth-Century England', in *Studies in the History of the Near East*, pp. 27–49; Feingold, 'Patrons and Professors', pp. 123–5; Toomer, *Eastern Wisedome*, pp. 116–26, 131–6, 155–67, 212–26; G. A. Russell, 'The Impact of Philosophus Autodidactus: Pococke, John Locke and the Society of Friends', in Russell (ed.), *The 'Arabick' Interest*, pp. 224–66; John B. Pearson, *A Biographical Sketch of the Chaplains to the Levant Company Maintained at Constantinople, Aleppo and Smyrna 1611–76* (Cambridge, 1883), pp. 19–21.

15. Errol Rogers, 'Polyglot Bibles', in Bruce M. Metzger and Michael D. Coogan (eds), *The Oxford Companion to the Bible* (New York and Oxford, 1993), pp. 602–3; Henry John Todd, *Memoirs of the Life and Writings of the Right Rev. Brian Walton*, vol. 1 (London, 1821); Holt, 'An Oxford Arabist', pp. 14–16; Toomer, *Eastern Wisedome*, pp. 202–10.

16. H. T. Norris, 'Edmund Castell (1606–86) and his Lexicon Heptaglotton' (1669)', in Russell (ed.), *The 'Arabick' Interest*, pp. 70–71.

17. On coffee, see Matar, *Islam in Britain*, pp. 110–17; Samuel C. Chew, *The Crescent and the Rose: Islam and England during the Renaissance* (New York, 1937), pp. 183–6, 407; Alexandrine N. St Clair, *The Image of the Turk in Europe* (New York, 1973), pp. 16–17.

18. Norris, 'Edmund Castell', p. 78.

19. Toomer, *Eastern Wisedome*, p. 89. On the life and works of Wheelocke in general, see Toomer, *Eastern Wisedome*, pp. 86–93; *ODNB*, s.v.

20. On Castell's sad career, see *ODNB*, s.v.; Norris, 'Edmund Castell', pp. 70–87; Toomer, *Eastern Wisedome*, pp. 255–65; Roper, 'Arabic Printing', p. 19.

21. Feingold, 'Oriental Studies', p. 495. On the life of Hyde more generally, see *ODNB*, s.v.; P. J. Marshall, 'Oriental Studies', in L. S. Sutherland and L. G. Mitchell (eds), *The History of the University of Oxford*, vol. 5, *The Eighteenth Century* (Oxford, 1986), pp. 556–8; Toomer, *Eastern Wisedome*, pp. 248–50, 295–8; Roper, 'Arabic Printing', p. 17; P. J. Marshall and Glyndwr Williams, *The Great Map of Mankind: British Perceptions of the World in the Age of the Enlightenment* (London, 1982), pp. 11–12, 17, 102–3. See also Dominic Parviz Brookshaw, 'The Study of Persian in Oxford in the Seventeenth Century', forthcoming in Ada Adamova, Bert Fragner and Michael Rogers (eds), *The Study of Persian Culture in the West: Sixteenth to Early Twentieth Century* (London, 2006).

22. On the life and works of Prideaux, see *ODNB*, s.v.; Peter Holt, 'The

Treatment of Arab History by Prideaux, Ockley and Sale', in Holt, *Studies in the History of the Near East*, pp. 50–54; Toomer, *Eastern Wisedome*, pp. 289–92.

23. Prideaux quoted in Holt, 'The Treatment of Arab History', p. 51.

24. On the life and works of Raphelengius, see Alastair Hamilton, '"Nam Tirones Sumus": Franciscus Raphelengius' *Lexicon Arabico–Latinum* (Leiden, 1613)', in Marcus de Schepper and Francine de Nave (eds), *Ex Officina Plantiniana. Studia in memoriam Christophori Plantini (ca. 1520–1589)* (Antwerp, 1989), pp. 557–89; Alastair Hamilton, 'Arabic Studies in the Netherlands in the Sixteenth and Seventeenth Centuries', in Francine de Nave (ed.), *Philologia Arabica: Arabische Studiën en drukken Nederlanden in 16de en 17de eeuw* (Antwerp, 1986), pp. xcvii–xcviii and De Nave, *Philologia Arabica*, pp. 124–35; Alastair Hamilton, *Arab Culture and Ottoman Magnificence in Antwerp's Golden Age* (Oxford, 2001); Josée Balagna, *L'Imprimerie arabe en occident (XVIe, XVIIe et XVIIIe siècles)* (Paris, 1984), pp. 41–3; J. Brugman and F. Schröder, *Arabic Studies in the Netherlands* (Leiden, 1979), p. 4.

25. On Erpenius, see Fück, *Die Arabischen Studien*, pp. 59–73; John Robert Jones, *Learning Arabic in Renaissance Europe (1505–1624)*, Ph.D. thesis (School of Oriental and African Studies, London University, July 1988), pp. 13–14, 187–212; Brugman and Schröder, *Arabic Studies in the Netherlands*, pp. 4–10, 12–13, 16; Balagna, *L'Imprimerie arabe en occident*, pp. 53–4, 58; Hamilton, 'Arabic Studies in the Netherlands', pp. xcix–ciii; De Nave, *Philologia Arabica*, pp. 139–69; Hamilton, *Arab Culture and Ottoman Magnificence*, pp. 87, 94.

26. On Golius, see Fück, *Die Arabischen Studien*, pp. 79–84; Brugman and Schröder, *Arabic Studies in the Netherlands*, pp. 10, 13–14, 17–20; Hamilton, 'Arabic Studies in the Netherlands', pp. ciii–cv; De Nave, *Philologia Arabica*, pp. 169–80; Hamilton, *Arab Culture and Ottoman Magnificence*, pp. 91, 94.

27. On Maronite scholarship in Italy, see Toomer, *Eastern Wisedome*, pp. 15, 30–31, 76; Balagna, *L'Imprimerie arabe en occident*, pp. 33, 34. On Western interest in Eastern Christians more generally, see Alastair Hamilton, 'The English Interest in Arabic-Speaking Christians', in Russell (ed.), *The 'Arabick' Interest*, pp. 30–53.

28. Alastair Hamilton and Francis Richard, *André du Ryer and Oriental Studies in Seventeenth-Century France* (Oxford, 2004).

29. On Marracci, see E. Dennison Ross, 'Ludovico Marracci', *Bulletin of the School of Oriental Studies*, 2 (1921), pp. 117–23; Hamilton, *Europe and the Arab World*, pp. 104–5; Hamilton and Richard, *André du Ryer*, pp. 97–103, 105–6.

30. On Kircher, see Joscelyn Godwin, *Athanasius Kircher: A Renaissance Man and the Quest for Lost Knowledge* (London, 1979); Daniel Stolzenberg, *The*

Great Art of Knowing: The Baroque Encyclopedia of Athanasius Kircher (Fiesole, 2001); Brian L. Merrill (ed.), *Athanasius Kircher (1602–1680) Jesuit Scholar. An Exhibition of His Works in the Harold B. Lee Library Collections at Brigham Young University* (Provo, Utah, 1989); Erik Iversen, *The Myth of Egypt and Its Hieroglyphs* (Princeton, NJ, 1961), pp. 92–102; Umberto Eco, *The Search for the Perfect Language* (London, 1997), pp. 83–5, 154–65; David Kahn, *The Codebreakers: The Story of Secret Writing* (London, 1966), pp. 864, 904–5; Enrichetta Leospo, 'Athanasius Kircher und das Museo Kircheriano', in Gereon Sieverich and Hendrik Budde (eds), *Europa und der Orient 800–1900* (Berlin, 1989), pp. 56–71; Paula Findlen (ed.), *Athanasius Kircher: The Last Man Who Knew Everything* (London, 2004). For Kircher's lost Arabic translation, see Stolzenberg, *The Great Art of Knowing*, p. 20.

31. On seventeenth-century Egyptology, see Iversen, *The Myth of Egypt*, pp. 88–102; Alberto Silotti, *Egypt Lost and Found: Explorers and Travellers on the Nile* (London, 1998), pp. 26–35.

32. Martin Bernal, *Black Athena: The Afroasiatic Roots of Classical Civilization* (London, 1987); for (mostly hostile) responses to Bernal's thesis, see Mary Lefkowitz, *Not Out of Africa: How Afrocentrism Became an Excuse to Teach Myth as History* (New York, 1996); Lefkowitz and Guy Maclean Rogers (eds), *Black Athena Revisited* (Chapel Hill, NC, 1996); Matar, *Islam in Britain*, p. 88.

5 Enlightenment of a Sort

1. Knolles quoted in Bernard Lewis, *From Babel to Dragomans: Interpreting the Middle East* (London, 2004), p. 115. More generally, on the Turkish threat to Vienna and Europe as a whole, see Richard Schwoebel, *The Shadow of the Crescent (1453–1517)* (Nieuwkoop, 1967); Dorothy M. Vaughan, *Europe and the Turk: A Pattern of Alliances 1350–1700* (Liverpool, 1954); Paul Coles, *The Ottoman Impact on Europe* (London, 1968); Halil Inalcik, 'Ottoman Methods of Conquest', *Studia Islamica*, 3 (1954), pp. 103–29.

2. Busbecq, *The Turkish Letters of Ogier Ghiselin de Busbecq, Imperial Ambassador at Constantinople 1554–1562*, translated by Edward Seymour Forster (Oxford, 1927), p. 112; cf. p. 40.

3. Thévenot quoted in Alastair Hamilton, *Europe and the Arab World* (Oxford, 1994), p. 82.

4. Harold Bowen, *British Contributions to Turkish Studies* (London, 1945).

5. Bernard Lewis, 'From Babel to Dragomans', *Proceedings of the British Academy*, 101 (1998), pp. 37–54; reprinted in Lewis, *From Babel to Dragomans*, pp. 18–32.

6. On the Levant Company, see A. C. Wood, *A History of the Levant Company*

(London, 1964); John B. Pearson, *A Biographical Sketch of the Chaplains to the Levant Company* (London, 1964); Ralph Davis, *Aleppo and Devonshire Square: English Traders in the Levant in the Eighteenth Century* (London, 1967).

7. B. B. Misra, *The Central Administration of the East India Company 1773–1834* (Manchester, 1959), pp. 387–400.

8. On d'Herbelot and the *Bibliothèque orientale*, see Henri Laurens, *Aux Sources de l'orientalisme: La Bibliothèque orientale de Barthélémi d'Herbelot* (Paris, 1978); Ahmad Gunny, *Images of Islam in Eighteenth-Century Writings* (London, 1996), pp. 45–54. On Gibbon's aversion to alphabetical order, Edward Gibbon, *The History of the Decline and Fall of the Roman Empire*, 3 vols, edited by David Womersley (London, 1994), vol. 3, p. 238n; cf. Peter Burke, *A Social History of Knowledge* (London, 2000), p. 185.

9. Gibbon, *Decline and Fall*, vol. 3, p. 238n.

10. Hajji Khalifa, *Bibliographicum et Encyclopaedicum = Kashf al-zunun 'an asami al-kutub wa-al-funun*, edited and translated by Gustav Flugel, 7 vols (London and Leipzig, 1853–8); cf. *Encyclopaedia of Islam*, 2nd edn, s.v. 'Katib Celebi'; Mohamed Abdel-Halim, *Antoine Galland: sa vie et son oeuvre* (Paris, 1964), pp. 76, 163–5; Gunny, *Images of Islam in Eighteenth-Century Writings*, pp. 44, 47.

11. On Galland's life and work, see, above all, Abdel-Halim, *Antoine Galland*. See also Georges May, *Les Mille et une nuits d'Antoine Galland* (Paris, 1986); Raymond Schwab, *L'Auteur des Mille et Une Nuits. Vie d' Antoine Galland* (Paris, 1964); Robert Irwin, *The Arabian Nights: A Companion* (Harmondsworth, 1994), pp. 14–19; Gunny, *Images of Islam in Eighteenth-Century Writings*, pp. 37–47; Ulrich Marzolph and Richard Van Leeuwen (eds), *Encyclopaedia of the Arabian Nights* (Santa Barbara, Calif., 2004), vol. 2, pp. 556–60.

12. Byron Porter Smith, *Islam in English Literature*, 2nd edn (New York, 1975), pp. 79–81; Ahmad Gunny, *Perceptions of Islam in European Writings* (Markfield, Leicestershire, 2004), pp. 62–7.

13. Smith, *Islam in English Literature*, pp. 102–4; Gunny, *Images of Islam*, pp. 132–62.

14. On the soporific tenor of scholarship in Oxford, see G. J. Toomer, *Eastern Wisedome and Learning: The Study of Arabic in Seventeenth-Century England* (Oxford, 1996), pp. 306, 313. For the study of Arabic and Islam there, see P. J. Marshall, 'Oriental Studies', in L. S. Sutherland and L. G. Mitchell (eds), *The History of the University of Oxford*, vol. 5, *The Eighteenth Century* (Oxford, 1986), pp. 551–63.

15. Edward Gibbon, *Autobiography*, edited by Lord Sheffield (London, 1907), pp. 36–42. For Gibbon's enthusiasm for Oriental matters, see Smith, *Islam in English Literature*, pp. 114–18; Bernard Lewis, 'Gibbon on Muhammad', in

Islam and the West (New York and Oxford), pp. 85–98; D. O. Morgan, 'Edward Gibbon and the East', *Iran*, 33 (1995), pp. 85–92.

16. John Sparrow, *Mark Pattison and the Idea of a University* (Cambridge, 1967), p. 67.

17. *Oxford Dictionary of National Biography* [*ODNB*], edited by H. C. G. Matthew and Brian Harrison (Oxford, 2004), s.v.; Alastair Hamilton, 'Western Attitudes to Islam in the Enlightenment', *Middle Eastern Lectures*, 3 (1999), p. 81; Gunny, *Images of Islam*, pp. 81–2, 145–7; Marshall, 'Oriental Studies', pp. 553, 560.

18. For the life and works of Ockley, see A. J. Arberry, *Oriental Essays: Portraits of Seven Scholars* (London, 1960), pp. 13–47; P. M. Holt, 'The Treatment of Arabic History by Prideaux, Ockley and Sale', in Peter Holt, *Studies in the History of the Near East* (London, 1973), pp. 54–7; *ODNB*, s.v.; Paul Hazard, *The European Mind* (London, 1953), p. 32–3; Smith, *Islam in English Literature*, pp. 37, 64–8; P. J. Marshall and Glyndwr Williams, *The Great Map of Mankind* (London, 1982), pp. 71–2; Gunny, *Images of Islam*, pp. 57–63; Isaac Disraeli, *The Curiosities of Literature* (London, 1867), pp. 12–13.

19. Gibbon, *Decline and Fall*, vol. 3, p. 248n.

20. Ibid., p. 173n. On Sale more generally, *ODNB*, s.v.; Johann Fück, *Die Arabischen Studien in Europa bis in den Anfang des 20 Jahrhunderts* (Leipzig, 1955), pp. 104–5; Smith, *Islam in English Literature*, pp. 68–71; Holt, 'The Treatment of Arabic History', pp. 57–60; Gunny, *Images of Islam*, pp. 134–5; Alastair Hamilton, *Europe and the Arab World: Five Centuries of books by European scholars and travellers from the libraries of the Arcadian Group* (Oxford, 1994), pp. 9–10, 106–7.

21. On the Russells, see Smith, *Islam in English Literature*, pp. 108–10; Hamilton, *Europe and the Arab World*, p. 132.

22. Edward William Lane, *Manners and Customs of the Modern Egyptians*, 3rd edn (London, 1842), p. x.

23. On the life and works of Jones, see Fück, *Die Arabischen Studien*, pp. 129–35; Arberry, *Oriental Essays*, pp. 48–86; Garland Cannon, *The Life and Mind of Oriental Jones*, 2nd edn (Cambridge, 1990); R. K. Kaul, *Studies in William Jones: An Interpreter of Oriental Literature* (Simla, 1995); Fatma Moussa Mahmoud, *Sir William Jones and the Romantics* (Cairo, 1962); Alexander Murray (ed.), *Sir William Jones, 1746–1794* (Oxford, 1998); Nigel Leask, *British Romantic Writers and the East: Anxieties of Empire* (Cambridge, 1992); Hans Arsleff, *The Study of Language in England, 1780–1860* (Minneapolis, 1983), pp. 115–61; Marzieh Gail, *Persia and the Victorians* (London, 1952), pp. 13–34; O. P. Kejariwal, *The Asiatic Society of Bengal and the Discovery of India's Past, 1784–1838* (New Delhi, 1988), pp. 27–75; Charles Allen, *The Buddha and the Sahibs: The men who discovered India's lost religion* (London, 2002), *passim*.

24. William Jones, 'An Essay on the Poetry of the Eastern Nations', *The Works of Sir William Jones*, edited by Lord Teignmouth (London, 1807), vol. 10, pp. 329–38.

25. William Jones, *A Grammar of the Persian Language*, 4th edn (London, 1797), p. 126.

26. Edward Said, *Orientalism* (London, 1978), p. 127; cf. p. 98. But see also Raymond Schwab, *The Oriental Renaissance: Europe's Rediscovery of India and the East, 1680–1880*, translated by Gene Patterson Black and Viktor Reinking (New York, 1984), p. 41; Marshall and Williams, *The Great Map of Mankind*, p. 136; Allen, *The Buddha and the Sahibs*, p. 63. Jones's announcement of the Indo-Aryan hypothesis appeared in his 'Third Discourse': see *Works*, vol. 2, pp. 34–6.

27. Kejariwal, *The Asiatic Society of Bengal*; Leili Anvar, 'L'Asiatick Society of Bengal', *Qantara*, no. 44 (Summer 2002), pp. 39–42.

28. Schwab, *The Oriental Renaissance, passim.*

29. Francesco Venturi, 'Despotismo Orientale', *Rivista di Studia Islamica*, 72 (1960), pp. 121–4; Schwab, *The Oriental Renaissance, passim.*

30. Johnson quoted by James Boswell in *Journal of a Tour of the Hebrides with Samuel Johnson, LLD. 1773*, edited by Frederick E. Pottle and Charles H. Bennett (London, 1963), p. 168.

31. On Leiden's decline after Golius, see Toomer, *Eastern Wisedome*, pp. 52, 301; J. Brugmann and F. Schröder, *Arabic Studies in the Netherlands* (Leiden, 1979), pp. 20–21.

32. Fück, *Die Arabischen Studien*, pp. 102–3; Brugman and Schröder, *Arabic Studies*, pp. 23–5; Hamilton, 'Western Attitudes to Islam in the Enlightenment', pp. 75–7.

33. Fück, *Die Arabischen Studien*, pp. 124–5; Brugman and Schröder, *Arabic Studies*, pp. 26–7; Toomer, *Eastern Wisedome*, p. 313.

34. Fück, *Die Arabischen Studien*, pp. 108–24; Toomer, *Eastern Wisedome*, p. 113. On Reiske as a classicist, see Rudolf Pfeiffer, *History of Classical Scholarship from 1300 to 1850* (Oxford, 1976), p. 172.

35. Reiske quoted in I. Y. Kratchkovsky, *Among Arabic Manuscripts: Memories of Libraries and Men* (Leiden, 1953), p. 166.

36. On the craze for Chinese culture, see Paul Hazard, *The European Mind 1680–1715*, translated by J. Lewis May (Harmondsworth, 1964), pp. 36–40; Charles MacKerras, *Western Images of China* (Hong Kong, 1989), pp. 28–45; Marshall and Williams, *The Great Map*, pp. 20–23, 80–87, 107–10. But on the lack of British scholarly interest in China, see T. H. Barrett, *Singular Listlessness: A Short History of Chinese Books and Scholars* (London, 1989).

37. On Peter the Great's Cabinet of Curiosities, see Robert K. Massie, *Peter the Great: His Life and World* (London, 1981), pp. 814–15. On cabinets of curiosity more generally see Peter Burke, *A Social History of Knowledge: From*

Gutenberg to Diderot (Cambridge, 2000), p. 106; Alvar González-Palacios, *Objects for a Wunder Kammer* (London, 1981); Oliver Impey and Arthur MacGregor, *The Origins of Museums: the cabinet of curiosities in sixteenth- and seventeenth-century Europe* (Oxford, 1985); Patrick Mauriès, *Cabinets of Curiosities* (London, 2002). On Peter's interest in Oriental studies, I. J. Kratschkowski [= I. Y. Kratchkovsky], *Die Russische Arabistik: Umrisse ihrer Entwicklung* (Leipzig, 1955), pp. 37–43; Richard N. Frye, 'Oriental Studies in Russia', in Wayne S. Vucinich (ed.), *Russia and Asia: Essays on the Influence of Russia on the Asian Peoples* (Stanford, Calif., 1972), pp. 35–6.

38. On the expansion of Russia into Asia and Russian Orientalism, Kratsch-kowski, *Die Russische Arabistik*, pp. 37–66; Kalpan Sahni, *Crucifying the Orient: Russian Orientalism and the Colonization of the Caucasus and Central Asia* (Bangkok, 1997); Frye, 'Oriental Studies in Russia', pp. 30–51.

39. Fück, *Die Arabischen Studien*, pp. 119–20; Thorkild Hansen, *Arabia Felix: The Danish Expedition of 1761–1767*, translated by James and Kathleen McFarlane (London, 1964).

40. Stig T. Rasmussen, 'Journeys to Persia and Arabia in the 17th and 18th centuries', in *The Arabian Journey: Danish connections with the Islamic world over a thousand years* (Århus, 1996), pp. 47–54.

41. Rasmussen, 'Journeys to Persia and Arabia', pp. 55–7.

42. Hansen, *Arabia Felix*; Rasmussen, 'Journeys to Persia and Arabia', pp. 57–64; Hamilton, *Europe and the Arab World*, pp. 140–41.

43. Henry Laurens, *Les Origines intellectuelles de l'Expédition d'Egypte: l'orientalisme islamisant en France (1698–1798)* (Istanbul and Paris, 1987), pp. 108–12, 116–17.

44. Laurens, *Les Origines*, pp. 63–5; Jean Gaulmier, *Un grand témoin de la révolution et dé l'Empire: Volney* (Paris, 1959), p. 37.

45. Nora Crook and Derek Guiton, *Shelley's Venomed Melody* (Cambridge, 1986), p. 99.

46. Constantin-François de Chasseboeuf, comte de Volney, *Voyage en Egypte et en Syrie pendant les années 1783, 1784 et 1785 suivi de considérations sur la Guerre des Russes et des Turcs*, 2 vols, 5th edn (Paris, 1822); Volney, *Les Ruines, on Méditations sur les révolutions des empires* (Paris, 1791); Gaulmier, *Un grand témoin*; Laurens, *Les Origines*, pp. 67–82, 95–6, 123–9, 176–7. For Volney on ruins, see Daniel Reig, *Homo orientaliste* (Paris, 1988), esp. pp. 43–4; Gaulmier, *Un grand témoin*, pp. 112–28; Albert Hourani, 'Volney and the Ruins of Empire' in Hourani, *Europe and the Middle East* (London, 1980), pp. 81–6. On ruins more generally and their power to evoke thought, see Rose Macaulay, *The Pleasure of Ruins* (London, 1953); Christopher Woodward, *In Ruins* (London, 2001).

47. On de Sacy's limitations as an Arabist, see Gaulmier, *Un grand témoin*,

p. 279; Reig, *Homo orientaliste*, pp. 81, 102. The life and work of Silvestre de Sacy more generally form an important part of the next chapter.

48. J. Christopher Herold, *Bonaparte in Egypt* (London, 1963); Henry Laurens et al., *L'Expédition d'Egypte: 1798–1801* (Paris, 1989); Laure Murat and Nicola Weill, *L'Expédition d'Egypte: Le rêve oriental de Bonaparte* (Paris, 1998); Darrell Dykstra, 'The French Occupation of Egypt, 1798–1801', in M. W. Daly (ed.), *The Cambridge History of Egypt*, vol. 2, *Modern Egypt, from 1517 to the end of the twentieth century*, pp. 113–38; Irene Bierman (ed.), *Napoleon in Egypt* (Ithaca, 2004). On the intellectual background, see Laurens, *Les Origines*.

49. Said, *Orientalism*, p. 81. But for the contrary view, see Gaulmier, *Un grand témoin*, pp. 39–40; Zachary Lockman, *Contending Visions of the Middle East: The History and Politics of Orientalism* (Cambridge, 2004), p. 71.

50. Al-Jabarti, *'Abd al-Rahman al-Jabarti's History of Egypt: Aja'ib al-Athar fi'l-Tarajim wa'l-Akhbar*, Thomas Philipp and Moshe Perlmann (eds), 4 vols (Stuttgart, 1994), vol. 3, pp. 4–8; cf. Herold, *Bonaparte in Egypt*, pp. 69–70.

51. On Venture de Paradis, see Jean Gaulmier, 'Introduction' to Venture de Paradis's translation, *La Zubda Kachf al-Mamalik de Khalil az-Zahiri* (Beirut, 1950), pp. vii–li; Laurens, *Les Origines*, pp. 181–2; Reig, *Homo orientaliste*, pp. 72–7.

52. Yves Lassius, *L'Egypte, une aventure savante, 1798–1801* (Paris, 1998), *passim*; Reig, *Homo orientaliste*, pp. 97–8, 155.

53. Lassius, *L'Egypte*, p. 30.

54. Herold, *Bonaparte in Egypt*, p. 171.

55. On Jones's 1784 manifesto 'A Discourse on the Institution of a Society for Inquiry into the History, Civil and Natural, the Antiquities, Arts, Sciences and Literature of Asia', Jones, *Works*, 10 vols (London, 1807), vol. 3, pp. 1–9; see also Cannon, *The Life and Mind of Oriental Jones*, pp. 203–4.

56. Gast Mannes, *Le grand ouvrage. Description de l'Egypte* (Luxembourg, 2003); Lassius, *L'Egypte*; Patrice Bret (ed.), *L'Expédition d'Egypte, une entreprise des Lumières, 1798–1801. Actes du colloque international* (Paris, 1997).

6 Oriental Studies in the Age of Steam and Cant

1. On the life and works of Silvestre de Sacy, see J. Reinaud, 'Notice historique et littéraire sur M. le baron Silvestre de Sacy', *Journal Asiatique*, 3rd series, vol. 6 (1838), pp. 113–95; Pierre Claude-François Daunou, 'Notice historique sur la vie et les ouvrages de M. le Baron Silvestre de Sacy', *Mémoires de l'Académie des Inscriptions et Belles-Lettres*, vol. 12, pt. 1 (1839), pp. 507–31; Hartwig

NOTES

Derenbourg, *Silvestre de Sacy (1758–1838)* (Paris, 1895); Henri Dehérain, *Silvestre de Sacy: ses contemporains et ses disciples* (Paris, 1938); Johann Fück, *Die Arabischen Studien in Europa bis in den Anfang des 20. Jahrhunderts* (Leipzig, 1955), pp. 140–52; Raymond Schwab, *The Oriental Renaissance: Europe's Rediscovery of India and the East, 1680–1880*, translated by Gene Patterson-Black and Viktor Reinking (New York, 1984), *passim*, but especially pp. 295–8; Robert Irwin, 'Oriental Discourses in Orientalism', *Middle Eastern Lectures*, 3 (1999), pp. 92–6; Farhad Daftary, *The Assassin Legends: Myths of the Isma'ilis* (London, 1994), pp. 6, 122, 131–5.

2. On medieval Arabic grammar, see the excellent article by M. G. Carter, 'Arabic Grammar', in M. J. L. Young, J. D. Latham and R. B. Serjeant (eds), *The Cambridge History of Arabic Literature. Religion, Learning and Science in the 'Abbasid Period* (Cambridge, 1990), pp. 118–38.

3. Silvestre de Sacy, 'Traité des monnoies musulmanes traduit de l'Arabe du Makrizi', reprinted in *Bibliothèque des Arabisants Français*, IFAO (Cairo, 1905), p. 9; cf. p. 37n.

4. Daniel Reig, *Homo orientaliste* (Paris, 1988), p. 12.

5. Maxime Rodinson, *Europe and the Mystique of Islam*, translated by Roger Veinus (Seattle and London, 1987), pp. 56–7; Baber Johansen, 'Politics, Paradigms and the Progress of Oriental Studies. The German Oriental Society (Deutsche Morgenländische Gesellschaft) 1845–1989', *MARS. Le Monde Arabe dans la Recherche Scientifique*, 4 (Winter 1994), pp. 79–94; Zachary Lockman, *Contending Visions of the Middle East: The History and Politics of Orientalism* (Cambridge, 2004), pp. 68–9.

6. On the aristocratic complexion of the RAS, see C. F. Beckingham, 'A History of the Royal Asiatic Society, 1823–1973', in Stuart Simmonds and Simon Digby (eds), *The Royal Asiatic Society: Its History and Treasures* (Leiden, 1979), pp. 1–12.

7. On Muir, see below.

8. Schwab, *The Oriental Renaissance*, *passim*; J. J. Clarke, *Oriental Enlightenment: The Encounter Between Asia and Western Thought* (London, 1997), esp. pp. 61–70; Sheldon Pollock, 'Deep Orientalism? Notes on Sanskrit and Power Beyond the Raj', in Carol A. Buckeridge and Peter Van der Veer, *Orientalism and the Postcolonial Predicament* (Philadelphia, 1993), pp. 76–133.

9. O. P. Kejariwal, *The Asiatic Society of Bengal and the Discovery of India's Past, 1784–1838* (New Delhi, 1988); David Kopf, *British Orientalism and the Bengal Renaissance. The Dynamics of Modernization, 1773–1835* (Berkeley and Los Angeles, 1969).

10. On the life and works of Quatremère, see Gignault, 'Quatremère', in *Memoires de l'Académie des Inscriptions et Belles-Lettres* (Paris, 1877), pp. 195–218; *Biographie Universelle*, 45 vols (Paris, 1854–7), vol. 34, pp. 604–8; Fück, *Die Arabischen Studien*, pp. 152–3. Robert Irwin, 'Orientalism and

the Early Development of Crusader Studies', in Peter Edbury and Jonathan Phillips (eds), *The Experience of Crusading*, vol. 2, *Defining the Crusader Kingdom* (Cambridge, 2003), pp. 224–5.

11. Franz Rosenthal, 'Translator's Introduction', in Ibn Khaldun, *The Muqaddimah: An Introduction to History*, translated by Franz Rosenthal, vol. 1, 2nd edn (London, 1967), p. cii.

12. Ibid., p. c.

13. The literature on Ibn Khaldun is vast. For a bibliography which deserves to be updated, see Aziz al-Azmeh, *Ibn Khaldun in Modern Scholarship: A Study in Orientalism* (London, 1981), pp. 231–318. (Al-Azmeh's bibliography lists more than 850 items.)

14. Ernest Gellner, *Muslim Society* (Cambridge, 1981), especially pp. 16–98. See also below in chapter 8, for a discussion of Gellner's role as a defender of Orientalism.

15. On the life and works of von Hammer-Purgstall, see Fück, *Die Arabischen Studien*, pp. 158–66; Sepp Reichl, *Hammer-Purgstall: Auf den romantischen Pfaden eines österreichischen Orientforschers* (Graz, 1973); Irwin, 'Orientalism and the Early Development of Crusader Studies', pp. 223–4.

16. R. A. Nicholson, *Studies in Islamic Mysticism* (London, 1929), p. 189.

17. Joseph Freiherr von Hammer-Purgstall, 'Mysterium Baphometis Revelatum seu fraters militiae templi, qua Gnostici et quidem Ophiani apostasie et impuritatis convicti per ipsa eorum monumenta', *Fundgruben des Orients*, 6 (1818), pp. 1–120, 455–99; Hammer-Purgstall, 'Die Schuld der Templer', *Denkschriften der kaiserlichen Akademie der Wissenschaften, Philosophische-historische Classe*, 6 (1835). See also Norman Cohn, *Europe's Inner Demons: An Enquiry Inspired by the Great Witch Hunt* (London, 1975), pp. 87–8; Peter Partner, *The Murdered Magicians: The Templars and Their Myth* (London, 1981), pp. 138–45, 156–7.

18. Von Hammer-Purgstall, *The History of the Assassins*, English translation (London, 1835), pp. 36–7. See also von Hammer-Purgstall, 'Sur le paradis du Vieux de la Montagne', *Fundgruben des Orients*, 3 (1813), pp. 201–6; cf. Bernard Lewis, *The Assassins, A Radical Sect in Islam* (London, 1967), pp. 12–13; Farhad Daftary, *The Assassin Legends: Myths of the Isma'ilis* (London, 1994), pp. 118–20.

19. Fück, *Die Arabischen Studien*, pp. 167–8; Herbert Prang, *Friedrich Rückert: Geist und Form der Sprache* (Wiesbaden, 1963).

20. Gustave Dugat, *Histoire des orientalistes de l'Europe du XIIe au XIXe siècles*, 2 vols (Paris, 1868), vol. 2, pp. 74–90; Fück, *Die Arabischen Studien*, pp. 170–73.

21. On Göttingen and on German Orientalism, more generally, see Ulrich Haarmann, 'L'Orientalisme allemand', *MARS.: Le Monde Arabe dans la Recherche Scientifique*, 4 (Winter 1994), pp. 69–78; Rudi Paret, *The Study of*

Arabic and Islam at German Universities: German Orientalists since Theodor Nöldecke (Wiesbaden, 1968).

22. Fück, *Die Arabischen Studien*, p. 160; John Rogerson, *Old Testament Criticism in the Nineteenth Century: England and Germany* (London, 1984), pp. 15–17.

23. Christopher Stray, *Classics Transformed. Schools, Universities and Society in England, 1830–1960* (Oxford, 1988), p. 26.

24. Fück, *Die Arabischen Studien*, pp. 174–5; Jacob Lassner, 'Abraham Geiger: A Nineteenth-Century Jewish Reformer on the Origins of Islam', in Martin Kramer (ed.), *The Jewish Discovery of Islam: Studies in Honour of Bernard Lewis* (Tel Aviv, 1999), pp. 103–35.

25. On Weil, see Dugat, *Histoire des orientalistes*, vol. 1, pp. 42–8; Fück, *Die Arabischen Studien*, pp. 175–6; D. M. Dunlop, 'Some Remarks on Weil's History of the Caliphs', in Bernard Lewis and P. M. Holt (eds), *Historians of the Middle East* (London, 1962), pp. 315–29; Bernard Lewis, 'The Pro-Islamic Jews', in Lewis, *Islam in History: Ideas, People, and Events in the Middle East*, 2nd edn (Chicago and La Salle, 1993), p. 142.

26. Fück, 'Islam as an Historical Problem in European Historiography since 1800', in Lewis and Holt, *Historians of the Middle East*, p. 307; Baber Johansen, 'Politics and Scholarship: The Development of Islamic Scholarship in the Federal Republic of Germany', in Tareq Y. Ismael (ed.), *Middle East Studies. International Perspectives on the State of the Art* (New York, 1990), pp. 79–83.

27. Dugat, *Histoire des orientalistes*, vol. 2, pp. 91–100; Fück, *Die Arabischen Studien*, p. 157.

28. Schlegel quoted in Schwab, *The Oriental Renaissance*, p. 71.

29. Schwab, *Oriental Renaissance*, *passim*, but especially pp. 177–80.

30. T. H. Barrett, *Singular Listlessness. A Short History of Chinese Books and Scholars* (London, 1989), p. 78.

31. Ibid., pp. 98–9.

32. On Russian Orientalism in general see I. J. Kratschkowski, *Die Russische Arabistik, Umrisse ihrer Entwicklung* (Leipzig, 1959); Wayne S. Vucinich (ed.), *Russia and Asia: essays on the influence of Russia on the Asian peoples* (Stanford, Calif., 1972); Kalpana Sahni, *Crucifying the Orient: Russian Orientalism and the Colonization of the Caucasus and Central Asia* (Bangkok, 1997); Susan Layton, *Russian Literature and Empire* (Cambridge, 1994). On Silvestre de Sacy's role as intellectual patron of Russian Orientalism, see the index to Kratschkowski, *Die Russische Arabistik*. On Dorn, see Kratschkowski, *Die Russische Arabistik*, pp. 71–2, 118–20.

33. On Frähn, see Kratschkowski, *Die Russische Arabistik*, pp. 72–104.

34. On Tantawi, see ibid., pp. 110–12; I. Y. Kratchkovsky, *Among Arabic Manuscripts* (Leiden, 1953), pp. 115–23.

35. On Rosen, see Kratschkowski, *Die Russische Arabistik*, pp. 134–43; *The Great Soviet Encyclopedia*, 32 vols, translated from the third Moscow edition (New York and London, 1973–83), vol. 22, p. 307.

36. Richard Jenkyns, *The Victorians and Ancient Greece* (Oxford, 1980), p. 16.

37. William Dalrymple, *White Mughals: Love and Betrayal in Eighteenth-Century India* (London, 2002), pp. xl–xli.

38. On the Indian 'Orientalists' and their Evangelical and Utilitarian critics, see David Kopf, *British Orientalism and the Bengal Renaissance: The Dynamics of Indian Modernization 1773–1835* (Berkeley and Los Angeles, 1969); cf. Schwab, *Oriental Renaissance*, pp. 192–4.

39. Fück, *Die Arabischen Studien*, pp. 135–40; Sisir Kumar Das, *Sahibs and Muslims. An Account of the College of Fort William* (New Delhi, 1978); Kopf, *British Orientalism*, pp. 45–126.

40. *Oxford Dictionary of National Biography* [*ODNB*], edited by H. C. G. Matthew and Brian Harrison (Oxford, 2004) s.v.; Ulrich Marzolph and Richard Van Leeuwen (eds), *Encyclopedia of the Arabian Nights* (Santa Barbara, Calif., 2004), vol. 2, p. 629.

41. James Mill, *The History of British India* (London, 1820); cf. Kopf, *British Orientalism*, p. 236.

42. On Macaulay's contempt for Indian culture, see David Kopf, 'The Historiography of British Orientalism, 1772–1992', in Garland Cannon and Kevin R. Brine (eds), *Objects of Enquiry. The Life, Contributions, and Influences of Sir William Jones (1746–1794)* (New York, 1995), pp. 146–9; Kopf, *British Orientalism*, p. 244; Schwab, *Oriental Renaissance*, p. 194.

43. Macaulay quoted in Stray, *Classics Transformed*, p. 53.

44. George Cowell, *Life and Letters of Edward Byles Cowell* (London, 1904), p. 83; cf. Marzieh Gail, *Persia and the Victorians* (London, 1951), pp. 35–7, 133–6.

45. Cowell, *Life and Letters*; *ODNB*, s.v.

46. Obituary in *The Times*, 12 July 1905; Charles Lyall's obituary of Muir in the *Journal of the Royal Asiatic Society* (1905), pp. 875–9; *ODNB*, s.v.; D. M. Dunlop, 'Some Remarks on Weil's History of the Caliphs', in *Historians of the Middle East*, edited by Bernard Lewis and P. M. Holt (London, 1962), pp. 327–9; Jabal Muhammad Buaben, *Image of the Prophet Muhammad in the West: A Study of Muir, Margoliouth and Watt* (Leicester, 1996), pp. 21–47.

47. Edward William Lane, *Description of Egypt*, edited by Jason Thompson (Cairo, 2000), p. 3. For the life and works of Lane, see Jason Thompson's introduction to the *Description* (pp. i–xxxii) and Thompson, 'Edward William Lane's "Description of Egypt"', *International Journal of Middle Eastern Studies*, 28 (1996), pp. 545–83. See also Fück, *Die Arabischen Studien*, pp. 168–70; A. J. Arberry, *Oriental Essays: Portraits of Seven Scholars* (London, 1960), pp. 87–121; Leila Ahmed, *Edward W. Lane: A Study of his*

life and works and of British ideas of the Middle East in the nineteenth century
(London, 1978); John Rodenbeck, 'Edward Said and Edward William Lane', in Paul and Janet Starkey (eds), *Travellers in Egypt* (London, 1998), pp. 233–43; Geoffrey Roper, 'Texts from Nineteenth-Century Egypt: The Role of E. W. Lane', in Starkey and Starkey (eds), *Travellers in Egypt*, pp. 244–54.

48. Robert Irwin, *The Arabian Nights: A Companion* (Harmondsworth, 1994), pp. 23–5; Marzolph and Van Leeuwen, *Encyclopedia of the Arabian Nights*, vol. 2, pp. 618–20.

49. J. Heyworth-Dunne, 'Printing and translations under Muhammad 'Ali of Egypt: the foundation of modern Arabic', *Journal of the Royal Asiatic Society* (1940), pp. 325–49; Peter Colvin, 'Muhammad Ali Pasha, the Great Exhibition of 1851 and the School of Oriental and African Studies', *Library Culture*, 33 (1998), pp. 249–59.

50. E. W. Lane, *An Arabic–English Lexicon, Derived from the Best and Most Copious Eastern Sources* (London, 1863), reprinted in 2 vols (Cambridge, 1984); cf. Robert Irwin, 'The Garden of the Forking Paths', *Times Literary Supplement*, 26 April 1985, p. 474.

51. On the life and works of Renan, see J. M. Robertson, *Ernest Renan* (London, 1924); Jean Pommier, *La Pensée religieuse de Renan* (Paris, 1925); David C. J. Lee, *Ernest Renan: In the Shadow of Faith* (London, 1966); Charles Chauvin, *Renan* (Paris, 2000); Schwab, *The Oriental Renaissance passim*. On Renan's modest achievements as an Arabist, see Renan, *Souvenirs d'enfance et de jeunesse* (Paris, 1881), p. 288; cf. Fück, *Die Arabischen Studien*, pp. 201–2.

52. On Renan's misapprehensions with respect to Averroes, see Paul Otto Kristeller, 'Petrarch's "Averroists": A Note on the History of Averroism in Venice, Padua and Bologna', *Bibliothèque d'Humanisme et Renaissance*, 14 (1952), pp. 59–65; Jean-Paul Charnay, 'Le dernier surgeon de l'averroïsme en Occident: Averroès et l'Averroïsme de Renan', in J. Jolivet (ed.), *Multiple Averroès* (Paris, 1978), pp. 333–48.

53. The Goncourts are quoted in Lee, *Ernest Renan*, p. 3.

54. Ernest Renan, 'Mahomet and the Origins of Islam' in *Studies of Religious History and Criticism*, translated by O. B. Fotheringham (New York, 1864), p. 247.

55. Albert Hourani, *Arabic Thought in the Liberal Age 1798–1939* (London, 1962), pp. 110–12, 120–23, 135; Edward Said, *The World, the Text and the Critic* (London, 1983), pp. 279–81; Zachary Lockman, *Contending Visions of the Middle East: The History and Politics of Orientalism* (Cambridge, 2004), pp. 78–83.

56. Lawrence I. Conrad, 'The Pilgrim from Pest: Goldziher's Study Tour to the Near East (1873–4)', in Ian Richard Netton (ed.), *Golden Roads: Migration, Pilgrimage and Travel in Mediaeval and Modern Islam* (London, 1993), pp. 143–5; Lawrence I. Conrad, 'Ignaz Goldziher on Ernest Renan: From

Orientalist Philology to the Study of Islam', in Kramer (ed.), *The Jewish Discovery of Islam*, pp. 137–80; cf. Maurice Olender, *The Languages of Paradise: Race, Religion and Philology in the Nineteenth Century* (Cambridge, Mass., 1992), p. 121.

57. Quoted in Chauvin, *Renan*, p. 24; Edmond and Jules Goncourt, *Pages from the Goncourt Journal*, edited and translated by Robert Baldick (London, 1962), p. 170. See also Robertson, *Ernest Renan*, p. 23.

58. On the life and works of Gobineau, see, above all, Jean Gaulmier's introduction to volume 2 of the Pléiade edition of Gobineau's works (Paris, 1983). See also Robert Dreyfus, *La Vie et prophéties du comte de Gobineau* (Paris, 1909), pp. ix–lx; Maurice Lange, *Le Comte Arthur de Gobineau. Etude biographique et critique* (Strasbourg, 1924); Pierre Louis Rey, *L'Univers romanesque de Gobineau* (Paris, 1981); Gail, *Persia and the Victorians*, pp. 56–8; Michael D. Biddis, *Father of Racist Ideology: The social and political thought of Count Gobineau* (London, 1970). Ahmad Gunny, 'Gobineau's Perspective on the World of Islam', *International Journal of Islamic and Arabic Studies*, 9 (1992), pp. 17–30; Ahmad Gunny, *Perceptions of Islam in European Writings* (Markfield, Leicestershire, 2004), pp. 262–77; J. Calmard, 'Gobineau', in *Encyclopaedia Iranica*, edited by Ehsan Yarshater (London, 1985–), vol. 11, pp. 20–24.

59. Gobineau's key works on Persia and Central Asia are *Trois ans en Asie* (Paris, 1859), *Les Religions et les philosophies dans l'Asie Centrale* (Paris, 1865) and *Histoire des Perses*, 2 vols (Paris, 1869). See also Robert Irwin, 'Gobineau Versus the Orientalists', forthcoming in Adel Adamova, Bert Fragner and Michael Rogers (eds), *The Study of Persian Culture in the West* (London, 2006).

60. Gobineau's main works on cuneiform are *Lectures des textes cunéiformes* and *Traité des écritures cunéiformes*, 2 vols (Paris, 1864). See also Irwin, 'Gobineau Versus the Orientalists'.

61. For different aspects of nineteenth-century racism, see Léon Poliakov, *Le Mythe aryen: Essai sur les sources du racisme et des nationalismes* (Paris, 1971); Olender, *The Languages of Paradise*; Tzvetan Todorov, *On Human Diversity: Nationalism, Racism and Exoticism in French Thought* (Cambridge, Mass., 1993).

62. On the life and works of Dozy, see Dugat, *Histoire des orientalistes*, vol. 2, pp. 44–65; Fück, *Die Arabischen Studien*, pp. 181–5; M. J. de Goeje, *Biographie de Reinhardt Dozy*, translated by V. Chauvin (Leiden, 1883); J. Brugman and F. Schröder, *Arabic Studies in the Netherlands* (Leiden, 1979), pp. 36–9; J. Brugman, 'Dozy. A Scholarly Life According to Plan', in Willem Otterspeer (ed.), *Leiden Oriental Connections, 1850–1940* (Leiden, 1989), pp. 62–81.

63. G. M. Young, *Victorian England: Portrait of an Age* (Oxford, 1960), p. 14.

64. Ibid., p. 74.

65. Richard Burton, *A Plain and Literal Translation of the Arabian Nights Entertainments, Now Entitled the Book of a Thousand Nights and a Night*, 10 vols (Benares and Stoke Newington, London, 1885), vol.1, p. xxiii; cf. Gail, *Persia and the Victorians*, pp. 36–7.

66. On Burton's early attempts to learn Arabic, see Fawn M. Brodie, *The Devil Drives: A Life of Sir Richard Burton* (New York, 1967), pp. 43–4; Edward Rice, *Captain Sir Richard Francis Burton* (New York, 1990), pp. 21–2.

67. John Sparrow, *Mark Pattison and the Idea of University Reform* (Cambridge, 1967), pp. 110–12.

68. On the life and works of William Wright, see Fück, *Die Arabischen Studien*, pp. 206–9; *ODNB*, s.v.

69. William Wright, *A Grammar of the Arabic Language*, 2nd edn (Cambridge, 1874), p. vi.

70. On the life and works of Palmer, see Walter Besant, *The Life and Achievements of Edward Henry Palmer* (London, 1883); A. J. Arberry, *Oriental Essays: Portraits of Seven Scholars* (London, 1960), pp. 122–59; *ODNB*, s.v.

71. On the life and works of Robertson Smith, see John Sutherland Black and George Chrystal, *The Life of William Robertson Smith* (London, 1912); Fück, *Die Arabischen Studien*, pp. 210–11; Rogerson, *Old Testament Criticism*, pp. 275–80; T. O. Beidelman, *W. Robertson Smith and the Sociological Study of Religion* (Chicago, 1974); *ODNB*, s.v.

72. On Wellhausen, see Fück, *Die Arabischen Studien*, pp. 223–6; R. C. Ostle, foreword to Julius Wellhausen, *The Religio-Political Factions in Early Islam*, edited by R. C. Ostle (Amsterdam, 1975), pp. ix–xi ('Introduction'); G. R. Hawting, *The First Dynasty of Islam; The Umayyad Caliphate AD 661–750* (Beckenham, Kent, 1986), pp. 123–5; Josef Van Ess, 'From Wellhausen to Becker: The Emergence of *Kulturgeschichte* in Islamic Studies', in Malcolm Kerr (ed.), *Islamic Studies: A Tradition and Its Problems* (Cambridge, 1980), pp. 42–4; Robert Morgan and John Barton, *Biblical Interpretation* (Oxford, 1988), pp. 76–88, 92–7, 334; Rogerson, *Old Testament Criticism*, pp. 2, 257–74.

73. Albert Hourani, *Europe and the Middle East* (London, 1980), p. 14.

74. Wellhausen cited by Kurt Rudolph, 'Wellhausen as an Arabist', *Semeia*, 23 (1983), pp. 111–12.

75. Fück, *Die Arabischen Studien*, pp. 176–9.

76. Ibid., pp. 187–9.

7 A House Divided Against Itself

1. *The Encyclopaedia of Islam*, 2nd edn, edited by H. A R. Gibb, E. Lévi-Provençal and J. Schacht, 11 vols (Leiden, 1960–2002).

2. R. Stephen Humphreys, *Islamic History: A Framework for Inquiry*, 2nd edn (London, 1991), p. 4.

3. Johann Fück, *Die Arabischen Studien in Europa bis in den Anfang des 20. Jahrhunderts* (Leipzig, 1955), pp. 211–16; J. Brugman and F. Schröder, *Arabic Studies in the Netherlands* (Leiden, 1979), pp. 39–41.

4. Arminius Vámbéry, 'The Future of Continental Turkey', *The Nineteenth Century and After* (March 1901), pp. 361–2 (cited in Martin Kramer, 'Introduction' in Kramer (ed.), *The Jewish Discovery of Islam: Studies in Honor of Bernard Lewis* (Tel Aviv, 1999), p. 9).

5. On Vámbéry generally, see L. Adler and R. Dalby, *The Dervish of Windsor Castle* (London, 1979). On the antagonism between Vámbéry and Goldziher, see Lawrence I. Conrad, 'The Dervish's Disciple: On the Personality and Intellectual Milieu of the Young Ignaz Goldziher', *Journal of the Royal Asiatic Society* (1990), pp. 225–66.

6. Lawrence I. Conrad, 'Ignaz Goldziher on Ernest Renan: From Orientalist Philology to the Study of Islam', in Kramer, *The Jewish Discovery*, p. 147.

7. Fück, *Die Arabischen Studien*, pp. 187–9.

8. On the life and works of Goldziher, see Fück, *Die Arabischen Studien*, pp. 226–31; Jean-Jacques Waardenburg, *L'Islam dans le miroir de l'Occident* (Paris, 1963), pp. 11–18, 71–5, 97–104, 111–15, 125–7, 239–45, 265–70, 291–2, 304–6; Raphael Patai, *Ignaz Goldziher, and His Oriental Diary: A Translation and Psychological Portrait* (Detroit, 1987); Conrad, 'The Dervish's Disciple'; Conrad, 'The Near East Study Tour Diary of Ignaz Goldziher', *Journal of the Royal Asiatic Society* (1990), pp. 105–26 (this article and the foregoing one by Conrad make numerous connections to Patai's work on Goldziher's *Oriental Diary*); Conrad, 'The Pilgrim from Pest: Goldziher's Study Tour to the Near East (1873–1874)', in Ian Richard Netton (ed.), *Golden Roads: Migration, Pilgrimage and Travel in Mediaeval and Modern Islam* (London, 1993), pp. 110–59; Conrad, 'Ignaz Goldziher on Ernest Renan', in Kramer (ed.), *The Jewish Discovery*, pp. 137–80; Robert Simon, *Ignaz Goldziher. His Life and Scholarship as Reflected in His Works and Correspondence* (Leiden, 1986); Shalom Goldman, 'Ignaz Goldziher (1850–1921), Nestor of Islamic Studies in the West', *Al-'Usur al-Wusta*, 10 (1998), pp. 49–51.

9. Conrad, 'The Dervish's Disciple', p. 6.

10. Albert Hourani interviewed in Nancy Elizabeth Gallagher (ed.), *Approaches to the History of the Middle East: Interviews with Leading Middle East Historians* (Reading, 1994), p. 42.

11. Louis Massignon, 'Ignaz Goldziher (1850–1921)', in *Opera Minora*, 3 vols (Beirut, 1963), pp. 391–9.

12. Bernard Lewis, 'The Pro-Islamic Jews' in *Islam in History: Ideas, People, and Events in the Middle East*, 2nd edn (Chicago and La Salle, Illinois, 1993), p. 144.

13. I. Y. Kratchkowsky, *Among Arabic Manuscripts: Memories of Libraries and Men*, translated by Tatiana Minorsky (Leiden, 1953), p. 134; cf. p. 124.

14. Waardenburg, *L'Islam dans le miroir de l'Occident*, p. 244.

15. Nöldeke quoted in Simon, *Ignaz Goldziher*, p. 30. For his life and work more generally, see Fück, *Die Arabischen Studien*, pp. 217–20; Jaroslav Stetkevych, 'Arabic Poetry and Assorted Poetics', edited by Malcolm H. Kerr, *Islamic Studies: A Tradition and its Problems* (Malibu, 1980), pp. 111, 113–14; Ulrich Haarmann, 'L'Orientalisme allemand', *MARS. Le Monde Arabe dans la Recherché Scientifique*, 4 (Winter, 1994), pp. 75–6.

16. Nöldecke quoted in Baber Johansen, 'Politics, Paradigms and the Progress of Oriental Studies. The German Oriental Society (Deutschen Morgenländischen Gesellschaft) 1845–1989', *MARS. Le Monde Arabe dans la Recherche Scientifique*, 4 (Winter, 1994), p. 82.

17. Becker quoted in Albert Hourani, 'Islam and the Philosophers of History' in Hourani, *Europe and the Middle East* (London, 1980), p. 60. On the career of Becker, see Fück, *Die Arabischen Studien*, pp. 318–19; Haarmann, 'L'Orientalisme allemand', pp. 70–73; Josef van Ess, 'The Emergence of *Kulturgeschichte* in Islamic Studies', in Kerr (ed.), *Islamic Studies*, pp. 27–51; Johansen, 'Politics, Paradigms and the Progress of Oriental Studies', pp. 84–6; Johansen, 'Politics and Scholarship: The Development of Islamic Studies in the Federal Republic of Germany', in Tareq Y. Ismael (ed.), *Middle East Studies: International Perspectives on the State of the Art* (New York, 1990), pp. 84–6, 88–9.

18. On Snouck Hurgronje, see Fück, *Die Arabischen Studien*, pp. 231–3; Brugman and Schröder, *Arabic Studies*, pp. 44–7; Brugman, 'Snouck Hurgronje's Study of Islamic Law', in Willem Otterspeer (ed.), *Leiden Oriental Connections, 1850–1940* (Leiden, 1989), pp. 82–93.

19. Kurd 'Ali, *Memoirs of Kurd 'Ali: A Selection*, translated by Khalil Totah (Washington, 1954), p. 70.

20. On the life and works of Lammens, see Fück, *Die Arabischen Studien*, pp. 292–4; K. S. Salibi, 'Islam and Syria in the Writings of Henri Lammens', in Bernard Lewis and P. M. Holt (eds), *Historians of the Middle East* (London, 1962), pp. 330–42.

21. Patricia Crone, *Meccan Trade and the Rise of Islam* (Oxford, 1987), p. 3.

22. Fück, *Die Arabischen Studien*, pp. 297–99; Fück, 'Islam as a Historical Problem', in Lewis and Holt (eds), *Historians of the Middle East*, pp. 310–11; Hourani, 'Islam and the Philosophers of History', p. 59; Humphreys, *Islamic*

History: A Framework for Inquiry, pp. 71–2. Kurd 'Ali wrote admiringly of him in his *Memoirs*, pp. 68–9.

23. On the life and works of Browne, see Fück, *Die Arabischen Studien*, pp. 280–81; Marzieh Gail, *Persia and the Victorians* (London, 1951), pp. 97–104; Edward Denison Ross, 'A Memoir', a preface to Edward Granville Browne, *A Year Among the Persians*, 3rd edn (London, 1950), pp. vii–xxii; A. J. Arberry, *Oriental Essays: Portraits of Seven Scholars* (London, 1960), pp. 160–96; C. Edmund Bosworth, 'E. G. Browne and His *A Year Among the Persians*', *Iran, Journal of the British Institute of Persian Studies*, 33 (1995), pp. 115–22; Bosworth, 'Edward Granville Browne', in Bosworth (ed.), *A Century of British Orientalists 1902–2001* (Oxford, 2001), pp. 74–86. A full-length biography by John Gurney is in progress.

24. Browne, *A Year Among the Persians*, pp. 3–4.

25. Ibid., pp. 16–17.

26. Laurence Graffety-Smith, *Bright Levant* (London, 1970), pp. 6–7.

27. Reader Bullard, *The Camels Must Go* (London, 1961), pp. 47–8.

28. Edward Denison Ross, *Both Ends of the Candle* (London, 1943), p. 55.

29. Andrew Ryan, *The Last of the Dragomans* (London, 1951), p. 23.

30. Edward Granville Browne, *A Literary History of Persia*, vol. 2, *From Firdawsí to Sa'dí* (London, 1906), p. x.

31. A. K. S. Lambton, *Persian Grammar*, revised edn (Cambridge, 1974), p. 181.

32. Fück, *Die Arabischen Studien*, pp. 281–3; *Oxford Dictionary of National Biography* [*ODNB*], edited by H. C. G. Matthew and Brian Harrison (Oxford, 2004), s.v.; Arberry, *Oriental Essays*, pp. 198–232; Franklin D. Lewis, *Rumi: Past and Present, East and West: The Life, Teachings and Poetry of Jalal al-Din Rumi* (Oxford, 2000), *passim*, but especially pp. 531–3, 578–9.

33. R. A. Nicholson, *A Literary History of the Arabs* (London, 1907), p. x.

34. Ibid., p. 161.

35. Lewis, *Rumi: Past and Present, East and West*, p. 578.

36. On the life and works of Margoliouth, see the obituary in *The Times*, 23 March 1940, p. 8; obituary by Arthur Jeffrey in *Muslim World*, 30 (1940), pp. 295–8; obituary by Gilbert Murray in *Proceedings of the British Academy*, 26 (1940), pp. 389–97; *ODNB*, s.v.; Jabal Muhammad Buaben, *Image of the Prophet in the West: A Study of Muir, Margoliouth and Watt* (Leicester, 1996), pp. 49–128; Fück, *Die Arabischen Studien*, pp. 273–8.

37. Gertrude Bell, *The Letters of Gertrude Bell*, 2 vols (London, 1927), vol. 2, p. 453; H. V. F. Winstone, *Gertrude Bell* (London, 1978), p. 205.

38. Hamilton Gibb in his obituary of Margoliouth in *Journal of the Royal Asiatic Society* (1940), p. 393.

39. Lyall quoted by R. A. Nicholson in his obituary of Lyall in *Proceedings of the British Academy*, 9 (1919–20), p. 495.

40. On the life and works of Lyall, see the anonymous obituary in *Bulletin of the School of Oriental Studies*, 2 (1921), pp. 175–6; Fück, *Die Arabischen Studien*, pp. 279–80; obituary by Nicholson in *Proceedings of the British Academy*, 9 (1919–20), pp. 492–6; *ODNB*, s.v.

41. On the life and works of Stanley Lane-Poole, *ODNB*, s.v.; M. Mansoor, *The Story of Irish Orientalism* (Dublin, 1944), pp. 44–6.

42. On Salisbury, see Benjamin R. Foster, 'Edward R. Foster: America's First Arabist', *Al-'Usur al-Wusta*, 9 (1997), pp. 15–17.

43. On Torrey, see Benjamin R. Foster, 'Charles Cutler Torrey (1863–1956), Nobody's Pet Chicken: Theodor Noeldeke and Charles Cutler Torrey', *Al-'Usur al-Wusta*, 11 (1999), pp. 12–15.

44. On Duncan Black MacDonald, see William Douglas Mackenzie, 'Duncan Black MacDonald, scholar, teacher and author', in W. G. Shellbear et al. (eds), *The MacDonald Presentation Volume* (Princeton, London and Oxford, 1933), pp. 3–10; Fück, *Die Arabischen Studien*, pp. 285–6; Waardenburg, *L'Islam dans le miroir*, *passim*; Gordon E. Pruett, 'Duncan Black MacDonald: Christian Islamist', in Asaf Hussain, Robert Olson and Jamil Qureishi (eds), *Orientalism, Islam and Islamists* (Vermont, 1984), pp. 125–76; Robert Irwin, *The Arabian Nights: A Companion* (Harmondsworth, 1994), pp. 51–2, 113.

45. Tolkien, quoted in T. A. Shippey, *The Road to Middle-Earth* (London, 1982), p. 7.

46. Fück, *Die Arabischen Studien*, pp. 290–92; Michael Rogers, *The Spread of Islam* (London, 1976), pp. 16–17; Robert Hillenbrand, 'Cresswell and Contemporary European Scholarship', *Muqarnas*, 8 (1991), pp. 23–35; Stephen Vernoit, 'The Rise of Islamic Archaeology', *Muqarnas*, 14 (1997), pp. 3–6; Vernoit, 'Islamic Art and Architecture: An Overview of Scholarship and Collecting, c. 1850–1950', in Vernoit (ed.), *Discovering Islamic Art: Scholars, Collectors and Collections* (London, 2000), pp. 32–5, 37.

47. *Islamic Urban Studies, Historical Reviews and Perspectives*, edited by Masashi Haneda and Toru Miura (London, 1994), is a comprehensive bibliographical survey of scholarly studies on the Islamic city. See also Ira M. Lapidus (ed.), *Middle Eastern Cities: A Symposium on Ancient, Medieval and Modern Middle Eastern Urbanism* (Berkeley and Los Angeles, 1969); A. H. Hourani and S. M. Stern (eds), *The Islamic City: A Colloqium* (Oxford, 1970); Humphreys, *Islamic History*, pp. 228–30.

48. *Muqarnas*, 8 (1991) is devoted to the life and legacy of Cresswell.

49. Haneda and Miura (eds), *Islamic Urban Studies*, *passim*; Humphreys, *Islamic History*, pp. 234–8, 243, 245–6.

50. On the early history of the School of Oriental Studies, see C. H. Philips, *The School of Oriental and African Studies, University of London, 1917–1967: An Introduction* (London, 1967); Philips, *Beyond the Ivory Tower: The Autobiography of Sir Cyril Philips* (London, 1995).

51. Ross, *Both Ends of the Candle*; see also Fück, *Die Arabischen Studien*, p. 284; obituary by Ralph Turner in *Bulletin of the School of Oriental and African Studies*, vol. 10 (1940–42), pp. 831–6; *ODNB*, s.v.

52. On Thomas Arnold, see Aurel Stein's obituary of him in *Proceedings of the British Academy*, 16 (1930), pp. 439–74; Fück, *Die Arabischen Studien*, pp. 284–5; Vernoit, 'Islamic Art and Architecture', pp. 44–5.

53. For Bailey's lack of small talk, Philips, *Beyond the Ivory Tower*, p. 42. On Bailey's scholarship, see Roland Eric Emmerick in Bosworth, *A Century of British Orientalists*, pp. 10–48.

54. Philips, *Beyond the Ivory Tower*, p. 41.

55. Philips, *The School of Oriental and African Studies*, p. 18.

56. There is a huge literature on Massignon, much of it tending towards hagiography. See J. Morillon, *Massignon* (Paris, 1964); *Cahiers de l'Herne (Massignon)*, 12 (1970); Herbert Mason, *Memoir of a Friend, Louis Massignon* (Notre Dame, Indiana, 1981); Christian Destremau and Jean Moncelon, *Massignon* (Paris, 1994); Mary Louise Gude, *Louis Massignon. The Crucible of Compassion* (Notre Dame, Indiana, 1996); Jacques Keryell (ed.), *Louis Massignon au coeur de notre temps* (Paris, 1999). For a comprehensive bibliography of Massignon's works, see Youakim Moubarak, *L'Oeuvre de Louis Massignon* (Beirut, 1986). Jean-Jacques Waardenburg provides the best guide to Massignon's academic achievements in *L'Islam dans le miroir de l'Occident*, and see also Waardenburg's article, 'Massignon: Notes for Further Research', *Muslim World*, 56 (1996), pp. 157–62. See also Pierre Rocalve, *Louis Massignon et l'Islam* (Damascus, 1993); Albert Hourani, 'Islam in European Thought' and 'T. E. Lawrence and Louis Massignon' in Hourani, *Islam and European Thought* (Cambridge, 1991), pp. 43–8 and 116–28; Robert Irwin, 'Louis Massignon and the Esoteric Interpretation of Islamic Art', in Vernoit (ed.), *Discovering Islamic Art*, pp. 163–70.

57. De Maistre quoted and translated by Isaiah Berlin in his introduction to Joseph de Maistre, *Considerations on France*, edited and translated by Richard A. Lebrun (Cambridge, 1994), pp. xvii–xviii.

58. Gude, *Louis Massignon*, p. 65.

59. On Massignon's wartime service in the Near East, see, in particular, Hourani, 'T. E. Lawrence and Louis Massignon'.

60. Humphreys, *Islamic History: A Framework for Inquiry*, p. 194.

61. Julian Baldick, 'The Substitute as Saint', *Times Literary Supplement*, 23 September 1983, p. 1023.

62. Destremau and Moncelon, *Massignon*, p. 102.

63. Maxime Rodinson was not totally enchanted by Massignon's intensely spiritual approach to Islamic studies and his interview-based memoirs shed a curious light on the personality and teachings of Massignon. Rodinson, *Entre Islam et Occident: Entretiens avec Gérard D. Khoury* (Paris, 1998).

64. André Miquel, *L'Orient d'une vie* (Paris, 1990), p. 39.

65. Austin Flannery (ed.), *The Basic Sixteen Documents. Vatican Council II. Constitutions, Decrees, Declarations* (New York, 1996), pp. 570–71.

66. Edward W. Said, 'Islam, Philology and French Culture', in Said, *The World, the Text and the Critic* (London, 1984), p. 285.

67. On Bartold, see *The Great Soviet Encyclopedia* (a translation of the third edition), 32 vols (New York and London, 1973–83), vol. 3, pp. 39–40; I. M. Smilyanskaya, *History and Economy of the Arab Countries* (Moscow, 1986), pp. 8–9; E. A. Belyaev, *Arabs, Islam and the Arab Caliphate in the Early Middle Ages* (New York, 1969), *passim*; Kalpana Sahni, *Crucifying the Orient: Russian Orientalism and the Colonization of the Caucasus and Central Asia* (Bangkok, 1977), pp. 233–4.

68. Bernard Lewis, 'The Mongols, the Turks and the Muslim Polity' in Lewis, *Islam in History: Ideas, People, and Events in the Middle East*, 2nd edn (Chicago and La Salle, Illinois, 1993), pp. 190–91.

69. I. Y. Kratchkovsky, translated by Minorsky as *Among Arabic Manuscripts: Memories of Libraries and Men*. He also gave an account of some of his teachers in I. J. Kratschkowski [*sic*], *Die Russische Arabistik: Umrisse ihrer Entwicklung* (Leipzig, 1957). On him, see also Belyaev, *Arabs, Islam and the Arab Caliphate*, *passim*.

70. Kratchkovsky, *Among Arabic Manuscripts*, p. 123.

71. Ibid., p. 185.

72. I. Y. Kratchkovsky, *Istoria Arabskoi Geograficheskoi Literatury* (Moscow and Leningrad, 1957), translated into Arabic by Salah al-Din Uthman Hashim as *Tarikh al-Adab al-jughrafi al-'Arabi* (Cairo, 1965).

73. On Russian oppression of Muslims and on Soviet Orientalism in general, see 'Arabic Studies', *The Great Soviet Encyclopedia*, vol. 2, pp. 221–2; N. A. Smirnov, *Islam and Russia: A Detailed Analysis of an Outline of the History of Islamic Studies in the USSR*, with an introduction by Ann K. S. Lambton (Oxford, 1956); R. N. Frye, 'Soviet Historiography on the Islamic Orient', in Lewis and Holt (eds), *Historians of the Middle East*, pp. 367–74; G. E. Wheeler, 'Soviet Writing on Persia from 1906 to 1946', in Lewis and Holt (eds), *Historians of the Middle East*, pp. 375–87; Wayne S. Vucinich (ed.), *Russia and Asia: essays on the Influence of Russia on the Asian peoples* (Stanford, Calif., 1972), *passim*; Sahni, *Crucifying the Orient, passim*.

74. Belyaev, *Arabs, Islam and the Arab Caliphate, passim*.

75. Ibid., p. 86; Ibn Warraq, *The Quest for the Historical Muhammad* (New York, 2000), p. 49; Smirnov, *Islam and Russia*, pp. 43, 48; Dimitri Mikoulski, 'The Study of Islam in Russia and the Former Soviet Union: An Overview', in Azim Nanji (ed.), *Mapping Islamic Studies: Genealogy, Continuity and Change* (Berlin, 1997), p. 102.

76. Belyaev, *Arabs, Islam and the Arab Caliphate*, p. 86; Ibn Warraq, *The

Quest for the Historical Muhammad, p. 49; Smirnov, *Islam and Russia*, p. 48.

77. On the Nazi obsession with India, Tibet and Central Asia, see Sven Hedin, *German Diary* (Dublin, 1951); Karl Meyer and Shareen Brysac, *Tournament of Shadows: The Great Game and the Race for Empire in Asia* (London, 2001), pp. 509–28; J. J. Clarke, *Oriental Enlightenment: The Encounter Between Asia and Western Thought* (London, 1997), p. 196; Christopher Hale, *Himmler's Crusade: The True Story of the 1938 Nazi Expedition into Tibet* (London, 2003).

78. Adolf Hitler, *Mein Kampf*, anon. translator and abridgement (London, 1933), pp. 258–9.

79. Haarmann, 'L'Orientalisme allemand', p. 71.

80. On the life and works of Brockelmann, see Carl Brockelmann, 'Autobiographische Aufzeichnungen und Erinnerung von Carl Brockelmann, als Manuskript herausgeben von H. H. Biesterfeld', *Oriens*, 27–8 (1986), pp. 1–101; Van Ess, 'The Emergence of *Kulturgeschichte*', pp. 28–9.

81. On the life and works of Schaeder, see O. Pritsak, 'Hans Heinrich Schaeder', *Zeitschrift der Deutschen Morgenländischen Gesellschaft*, 33 (1958), pp. 24–5; Martin Kramer, 'Introduction' to Kramer (ed.), *The Jewish Discovery of Islam*, pp. 20–21; Annemarie Schimmel, *Morgenland und Abendland: mein west-östliches Leben* (Munich, 2002), pp. 46–50; Johansen, 'Politics and Scholarship', pp. 84–6, 88–9.

82. Schimmel, *Morgenland und Abendland*, p. 47.

8   The All Too Brief Heyday of Orientalism

1. On SOAS in wartime, see Cyril Philips, *The School of Oriental and African Studies, University of London, 1917–1967* (London, 1967), pp. 33–9; Lesley McLoughlin, *In a Sea of Knowledge: British Arabists in the Twentieth Century* (Reading, 2002), pp. 99–101, 105–6. On the history of MECAS, see Lesley McLoughlin, *A Nest of Spies . . . ?* (London, 1994); McLoughlin, *In a Sea of Knowledge*, pp. 120–22, 134–44, 151–63, 212–15, 242–9; James Craig, *Shemlan: A History of the Middle East Centre for Arab Studies* (Basingstoke, 1998).

2. A. J. Arberry, *Oriental Essays: Portraits of Seven Scholars* (London, 1960), p. 241. On the Scarborough Report, see Philips, *The School of Oriental and African Studies*, pp. 38–51; McLoughlin, *In a Sea of Knowledge*, pp. 128–9.

3. Craig, *Shemlan*, pp. 52, 82–3.

4. Stephan Conermann reviewing N. Mahmud Mustafa, *Al-ʿAsr al-Mamluki* in *Mamluk Studies Review*, 4 (2000), p. 259.

5. Albert Hourani, 'Patterns of the Past', in Thomas Naff (ed.), *Paths to the Middle East: Ten Scholars Look Back* (New York, 1993), p. 54.

6. On SOAS after the war, see Philips, *The School of Oriental and African Studies*, pp. 43–8. On MECAS, see note 1 above.

7. On the life and works of Hamilton Gibb, see Albert Hourani, 'H. A. R. Gibb: The Vocation of an Orientalist' in Hourani, *Europe and the Middle East* (London, 1980), pp. 104–34; Muhsin Mahdi, 'Orientalism and the Study of Islamic Philosophy', *Journal of Islamic Studies*, 1 (1990), pp. 84–90; William R. Polk, 'Islam and the West, I. Sir Hamilton Gibb between Orientalism and History', *International Journal of Middle Eastern Studies*, 6 (1975), pp. 131–9; Robert Irwin, 'Saladin and the Third Crusade: A Case Study in Historiography and the Historical Novel', in Michael Bentley (ed.), *Companion to Historiography* (London, 1997), pp. 144–5; McLoughlin, *In a Sea of Knowledge*, pp. 99–101; Zachary Lockman, *Contending Visions of the Middle East: The History and Politics of Orientalism* (Cambridge, 2004), pp. 105–10; *Oxford Dictionary of National Biography* [*ODNB*], edited by H. C. G. Matthew and Brian Harrison (Oxford, 2004), s.v. Gibb is attacked in Said's *Orientalism*, *passim*. There is also a denunciation of Gibb's work from a hardline Muslim point of view: Ziya-ul-Hasan al-Faruqi, 'Sir Hamilton Alexander Roskeen Gibb', in Asaf Hussain, Robert Olson and Jamil Qureishi (eds), *Orientalism, Islam and Islamists* (Vermont, 1984), pp. 177–89.

8. Obituary of Gibb by Anne Lambton, *Bulletin of the School of Oriental and African Studies*, 35 (1972), p. 341.

9. Arberry, 'The Disciple' in *Oriental Essays*, p. 234. On the life and works of Arberry more generally, see 'The Disciple', which is an autobiographical essay. See also Susan Skilliter's obituary in *Bulletin of the School of Oriental and African Studies*, 33 (1970), pp. 364–7; *ODNB*, s.v.

10. Obituary of Arberry by G. M. Wickens, *Proceedings of the British Academy*, 58 (1972), pp. 355–66.

11. On American Orientalism in the second half of the twentieth century, see Martin Kramer, *Ivory Towers on Sand: The Failure of Middle Eastern Studies in America* (Washington, 2001), and Lockman, *Contending Visions*, present strongly contrasting perspectives.

12. On Gustave von Grunebaum, see Brian S. Turner, 'Gustave E. von Grunebaum and the Mimesis of Islam', in Asaf et al. (eds), *Orientalism, Islam and Islamists*, pp. 193–201; Muhsin Mahdi, 'Orientalism and the Study of Islamic Philosophy', pp. 83–4; Amin Banami, 'Islam and the West. G. E. von Grunebaum: Towards Relating Islamic Studies to Universal Cultural History', *International Journal for Middle Eastern History*, 6 (1975), pp. 140–47.

13. On Richard Ettinghausen, see Robert Hillenbrand, 'Richard Ettinghausen and the Iconography of Islamic Art', in Stephen Vernoit (ed.), *Discovering Islamic Art: Scholars, Collectors and Collections* (London, 2000), pp. 171–81.

14. On Oleg Grabar, see *Muqarnas*, 10 (1993) [= *Essays in Honor of Oleg*

Grabar], pp. vii–xiii. Sheila S. Blair and Jonathan M. Bloom, 'The Mirage of Islamic Art: Reflections on the Study of an Unwieldy Field', *Art Bulletin*, 85 (March 2003), pp. 172–3.

15. On S. D. Goitein, see R. Stephen Humphreys, *Islamic History: A Framework for Inquiry* (London, 1991), pp. 262–3, 268–73; Martin Kramer, 'Introduction' in Kramer (ed.), *The Jewish Discovery of Islam: Studies in Honor of Bernard Lewis* (Tel Aviv, 1999), pp. 30–32; Hava Lazarus-Yafeh, 'The Transplantation of Islamic Studies from Europe to the Yishuv and Israel', in Kramer (ed.), *The Jewish Discovery of Islam*, pp. 254–6.

16. Rosenthal's most important works include *Das Fortleben der Antike in Islam* (Zurich, 1965); *A History of Muslim Historiography*, 2nd edn (Leiden, 1968); *The Herb: Hashish Versus Medieval Muslim Society* (Leiden, 1971), and above all his annotated translation of Ibn Khaldun, *The Muqaddimah: An Introduction to History*, 3 vols, 2nd edn (London, 1967).

17. Quoted in Robert Hillenbrand, 'Richard Ettinghausen', p. 175.

18. On Schacht, see Bernard Lewis's obituary of him in *Bulletin of the School of Oriental and African Studies*, 33 (1970), pp. 378–81; Humphreys, *Islamic History*, esp. pp. 212–18; Ibn Warraq, *The Quest for the Historical Muhammad* (New York, 2000), pp. 49–51.

19. Patricia Crone, *Roman, Provincial and Islamic Law: The Origins of the Islamic Patronate* (Cambridge, 1987), p. 7.

20. Edmund Burke III, 'Introduction' and 'Islamic History as World History', in Marshall G. S. Hodgson, *Rethinking World History: Essays on Europe, Islam and World History* (Cambridge, 1993), pp. ix–xxi and 301–28.

21. Saul Bellow, *To Jerusalem and Back* (Harmondsworth, 1976), p. 118.

22. Albert Hourani, 'Marshall Hodgson and the Venture of Islam', *Journal of Near Eastern Studies*, 37 (1978), pp. 53–62. Hourani gave two lengthy interviews on his career and writings in Naff (ed.), *Paths to the Middle East*, pp. 27–56 and in Nancy Elizabeth Gallagher (ed.), *Approaches to the History of the Middle East: Interviews with Leading Middle East Historians* (Reading, 1994), pp. 19–45. There is also an intellectual biography, Abdulaziz A. Sudairi, *A Vision of the Middle East: An Intellectual Biography of Albert Hourani* (London, 1999). See further reviews of this book by Malcolm Yapp in the *Times Literary Supplement*, 11 March 2000, and by Robert Irwin in the *London Review of Books*, 25 January 2001, pp. 30–31. See also Donald M. Reid, '*Arabic Thought in the Liberal Age* Twenty Years After', *International Journal of Middle Eastern Studies*, 14 (1982), pp. 541–57; Malcolm Yapp, 'Two Great British Historians of the Modern Middle East', *Bulletin of the School of Oriental and African Studies*, 58 (1995), pp. 41–5.

23. Hourani in Gallagher (ed.), *Approaches to the History of the Middle East*, p. 42.

24. Hourani in Naff (ed.), *Paths to the Middle East*, p. 38.

25. Hourani reviewed Said's *Orientalism* in the *New York Review of Books*, 8 March 1979, pp. 27–30.

26. On the life and works of Claude Cahen, see *Arabica*, 43 (1996) (which is devoted to the works of Cahen); Raoul Curiel and Rike Gyselen, *Itinéraires d'Orient: Hommages à Claude Cahen* (Bares-sur-Yvette, 1994), as well as Ira Lapidus's review of this book in *Journal of the Social and Economic History of the Orient*, 39 (1996), pp. 189–90; Thierry Bianquis, 'Claude Cahen, historien d'Orient médiévale, analyse et perspective', *Journal Asiatique*, 281 (1993), pp. 1–18.

27. Rodinson produced an interview-based autobiography in *Entre Islam et Occident: Entretiens avec Gérard D. Khoury* (Paris, 1998). He was also interviewed in Gallagher (ed.), *Approaches to the History of the Middle East*, pp. 109–27. See Adam Schatz, 'The Interpreters of Maladies', *The Nation*, 13 December 2004, pp. 55–9.

28. Rodinson in Gallagher (ed.), *Approaches to the History of the Middle East*, p. 119.

29. On Jacques Berque, see his autobiography *Mémoires de deux rives* (Paris, 1989); Berque, *Andalousies* (Paris, 1981); Albert Hourani, *The Arab Cultural Scene. The Literary Review Supplement* (1982), pp. 7–11.

30. André Miquel, *L'Orient d'une vie* (Paris, 1990).

31. Malcom Yapp in the preface to the Wansbrough *Festschrift* issue, *Bulletin of the School of Oriental and African Studies*, 57 (1994), p. 1.

32. Bernard Lewis provided a very brief account of his career as the 'Introduction' to his volume of essays, *From Babel to Dragomans: Interpreting the Middle East* (London, 2004), pp. 1–11. A bibliography of his works prefaces C. E. Bosworth et al., *Essays in Honor of Bernard Lewis: The Islamic World from Classical to Modern Times* (Princeton, NJ, 1989), pp. xii–xxv. See further on Lewis in Lockman, *Contending Visions*, pp. 130–32, 173–6, 190–92, 216–18.

33. On Elie Kedourie, see Sylvia Kedourie (ed.), *Elie Kedourie CBE, FBA 1926–1992* (London, 1998); Moshe Gammer (ed.), *Political Thought and Political History: Studies in Memory of Elie Kedourie* (London, 2003); Nissim Rejwan, *Elie Kedourie and His Work: An Interim Appraisal* (Jerusalem, 1997); Yapp, 'Two Great British Historians', pp. 45–9.

34. On the clash between Kedourie and Gibb and Kedourie's subsequent attack on the values of Chatham House, see Kedourie, *The Chatham House Version and Other Middle Eastern Studies*, 3rd edition with an Introduction by David Pryce-Jones (London, 2004).

35. Bellow, *To Jerusalem and Back*, p. 142.

36. P. J. Vatikiotis, *Among Arabs and Jews: A Personal Experience (1936–1990)* (London, 1991).

37. P. J. Vatikiotis (ed.), *Revolution in the Middle East, and Other Case*

Studies; Proceedings of a Seminar (London, 1972), pp. 8–9; cf. Edward Said, *Orientalism* (London, 1978), p. 313.

38. On the Hayter Report, see Philips, *The School of Oriental and African Studies*, pp. 57–8; McLoughlin, *In a Sea of Knowledge*, pp. 147–9.

39. Edward Ullendorff, 'Alfred Felix Landon Beeston', in C. E. Bosworth (ed.), *A Century of British Orientalists 1902–2001* (Oxford, 2001), pp. 50–71; Michael Gilsenan, 'A Personal Introduction', in Alan Jones (ed.), *Arabicus Felix: Luminosus Britannicus: Essays in Honour of A. F. L. Beeston* (Reading, 1991), pp. xv–xx.

40. Personal knowledge.

41. On Montgomery Watt, see Jabal Muhammad Buaben, *Image of the Prophet Muhammad in the West. A Study of Muir, Margoliouth and Watt* (Leicester, 1996).

42. Patricia Crone, *Meccan Trade and the Rise of Islam* (Oxford, 1987).

43. J. Wansbrough, *The Sectarian Milieu: Content and Composition of Islamic Salvation History* (Oxford, 1978), p. 25.

44. On the life and works of Wansbrough, see *Bulletin of the School of Oriental and African Studies*, 57, pt. 1 (1994) (*In Honour of J. E. Wansbrough*); Andrew Rippin, 'Literary Analysis of *Qur'an*, *Tafsir* and *Sira*: The Methodologies of John Wansbrough', in Richard C. Martin (ed.), *Approaches to Islam in Religious Studies* (Tucson, 1985), pp. 151–63; Herbert Berg, 'The Implications of, and Opposition to, the Methods and Theories of John Wansbrough', *Method and Theory in the Study of Religion*, 9 (1997), pp. 3–22; G. R. Hawting, 'John Wansbrough, Islam, and Monotheism', *Method and Theory in the Study of Religion*, 9 (1997), pp. 23–38. See also the second edition of Wansbrough's *Quranic Studies* (New York, 2004), which has a foreword, annotations and a decidedly necessary glossary by Andrew Rippin. The short story 'Let Not the Lord Speak' was published in *Encounter*, 54, pt. 5 (1980), pp. 3–7.

45. Humphreys, *Islamic History*, p. 84.

46. Yehuda D. Nevo and Judith Koren, *Crossroads to Islam: The Origins of the Arab Religion and the Arab State* (New York, 2004). See also the review of this book by Chase Robinson in the *Times Literary Supplement*, 28 January 2005, p. 7.

47. On Israeli scholarship in general, see articles by Kramer and Lazarus Yafeh in Kramer (ed.), *The Jewish Discovery of Islam*.

48. On Ayalon, see Reuven Amitai, 'David Ayalon, 1914–1998', *Mamluk Studies Review*, 3 (1999), pp. 1–10; Robert Irwin, 'Under Western Eyes: A History of Mamluk Studies', *Mamluk Studies Review*, 4 (2000), pp. 37–9; Humphreys, *Islamic History*, pp. 181, 207.

49. On Ashtor, see Irwin, 'Under Western Eyes', pp. 35–7; Humphreys, *Islamic History*, pp. 269, 303–4; Kramer, *The Jewish Discovery of Islam*, p. 31;

Masashi Haneda and Toru Miura, *Islamic Urban Studies: Historical Review and Perspectives* (New York, 1994).

50. Some of Emmanuel Sivan's articles are included in Sivan, *Interpretations of Islam, Past and Present* (Princeton, NJ, 1985). See also Sivan, *Radical Islam: Medieval Theology and Modern Politics* (New Haven, 1985) and Sivan, 'Islamic Radicalism: Sunni and Shi'ite', in Sivan and Menachem Friedman (eds), *Religious Radicalism and Politics in the Middle East* (New York, 1990), pp. 39–75.

51. See note 11.

52. On Paul Kraus, see Joel L. Kraemer, 'The Death of an Orientalist: Paul Kraus from Prague to Cairo', in Kramer (ed.), *The Jewish Discovery*, pp. 181–223; Rodinson, *Entre Islam et Occident*, pp. 148–51.

53. On Stern, see John Wansbrough's obituary of him in *Bulletin of the School of Oriental and African Studies*, 33 (1970), pp. 599–602 and that by Walzer in *Israel Oriental Studies*, 2 (1972), pp. 1–14; Shulamit Sela, 'The Interaction of Judaic and Islamic Studies in the Scholarship of S. M. Stern', in Kramer (ed.), *The Jewish Discovery*, pp. 261–71; Hourani, in Gallagher (ed.), *Approaches to the History of the Middle East*, p. 35.

54. Annemarie Schimmel, *Morgenland und Abendland: Mein west–östliches Leben* (Munich, 2002); Shusha Guppy's obituary of Schimmel appeared in the *Independent*, 30 January 2003. The anonymous *Times* obituary appeared on 6 February 2003. See also the obituary by Burzine Waghmar in *Journal of the Royal Asiatic Society*, 3rd series, vol. 13 (2003), pp. 377–9.

55. Stephan Conermann, 'Ulrich Haarmann, 1942–1999', *Mamluk Studies Review*, 4 (2000), pp. 1–25 (including bibliography); Irwin, 'Under Western Eyes', p. 41.

56. On post-war developments in German Orientalism, see Ulrich Haarmann, 'L'Orientalisme allemand', in *MARS Le Monde Arabe dans la Recherche Scientifique*, no. 4 (1994), pp. 69–78; Baber Johansen, 'Politics, Paradigms and the Progress of Oriental Studies: The German Oriental Society (Deutsche Morgenländische Gesellschaft) 1845–1989' in MARS, no. 4 (1994), pp. 79–94.

9   An Enquiry into the Nature of a Certain
    Twentieth-Century Polemic

1. Edward Said, *Out of Place* (London, 1999). He also features as a naughty boy in his sister's autobiography: see Jean Said Makdisi, *Teta, Mother and Me* (London, 1994), pp. 49–51. Said's 'Between Two Worlds', which appeared in the *London Review of Books*, 7 May 1998, pp. 3–7 and 'On Writing a Memoir' in the *London Review of Books*, 29 April 1999, pp. 8–11, both deal with thoughts arising from writing his autobiography. Gary Lockman provides a

brief account of Said's life and works in *Contending Visions of the Middle East: The History and Politics of Orientalism* (Cambridge, 2004), pp. 182–214. See also the discussion of Said's *Orientalism* and the responses it provoked in A. L. MacFie, *Orientalism* (London, 2002).

2. Said, *Out of Place*, p. 187.

3. Edward Said, 'Literary Theory at the Crossroads of Public Life' in Said, *Power, Politics and Culture: Interviews with Edward Said*, edited by Gaury Viswanathan (New York, 2001), p. 79. See also Said, 'Vico on the Discipline of Bodies and Texts', in Said, *Reflections on Exile and Other Essays* (Cambridge, Mass., 2002), pp. 83–92.

4. Edward Said, *Beginnings: Intention and Method* (London, 1975), p. 81.

5. John Allen Paulos, *Once Upon a Number: The Wider Mathematical Logic of Number* (New York, c. 1998), p. 28.

6. Edward Said, *Orientalism* (London, 1978), p. 71.

7. Bernard Lewis, 'The Question of Orientalism', *New York Review of Books*, 24 June 1982, p. 53. 'The Question of Orientalism' was reprinted in Lewis, *Islam and the West* (London, 1993), pp. 99–118. Said replied to Lewis's review and Lewis dealt with Said's attempted rebuttal in the *New York Review of Books* on 12 August 1982. In addition, 'The Question of Orientalism' and various other documents relating to the controversy between Said and Lewis are reprinted in A. L. Macfie, *Orientalism: A Reader* (Edinburgh, 2000).

8. Said, *Orientalism*, p. 160 and cf. pp. 95 and 208 where it becomes clear that Said has created an imaginary composite Orientalist from the Swiss historian Jacob Burkhardt (1818–97) with John Lewis Burkhardt (1784–1817), the explorer of the Middle East. The latter's *Arabic Proverbs* was published in 1837.

9. Shelley Walia, *Edward Said and the Writing of History* (Cambridge, 2001), p. 8.

10. Edward Said, 'Orientalism Reconsidered', in Said, *Reflections on Exile*, p. 199. 'Orientalism Reconsidered' was first previously published in Francis Barker et al. (eds), *Europe and Its Others*, vol. 1 (Colchester, Essex, 1985), pp. 14–27. It is also included in Macfie, *Orientalism: A Reader*.

11. Robert Bolt, *Three Plays* (London, 1967), p. 147.

12. Sadik Jalal al-'Azm, 'Orientalism and Orientalism in Reverse', *Khamsin*, 8 (1981), p. 6.

13. Said, *Orientalism*, pp. 62–3.

14. Ibid., p. 68.

15. Ibid., p. 210.

16. Ibid., p. 19.

17. Alan Sokal and Jean Bricmont, *Intellectual Impostures* (London, 2003), p. 179. (The book was first published in Paris in 1997 as *Impostures intellectuelles*.)

18. Ibid., p. 176.

19. Said, *Orientalism*, p. 23.

20. Ibid., p. 94.

21. The key works of Michel Foucault include *Folie et déraison. Historie de la folie à l'âge classique* (Paris, 1961); *Les Mots et les choses* (Paris, 1966); *L'Archéologie du savoir* (Paris, 1969); *L'Ordre du discours* (Paris, 1971); *Histoire de la sexualité*, 3 vols (Paris, 1976–84). All have been translated into English.

22. Antonio Gramsci, *Selections from the Prison Notebooks* (London, 1971), p. 447.

23. Said, *Orientalism*, p. 204.

24. Ibid., p. 104.

25. Said, *Power, Politics and Culture*, p. 381.

26. Said, *Orientalism*, 'Afterword', pp. 346–7; cf. Said, 'Diary', *London Review of Books*, 17 April 2002, p. 39.

27. Said, *Orientalism*, p. 98.

28. Edward Said, *After the Last Sky: Palestinian Lives* (New York, 1986), p. 152.

29. Said, *Orientalism*, p. 99.

30. Ibid., p. 127.

31. Ibid., p. 63. For the various ways Said traduced Lane, see John Rodenbeck, 'Edward Said and Edward William Lane', in Paul and Janet Starkey (eds), *Travellers in Egypt* (London, 1998), pp. 233–43.

32. Said's main discussion of Marx is in pp. 153–6 of *Orientalism*. For attacks on Said's misrepresentation of Marx, see in particular Al-'Azm, 'Orientalism and Orientalism in Reverse', pp. 5–26, and Aijaz Ahmad, 'Between Orientalism and Historicism', *Studies in History*, 7 (1991), pp. 135–63. Both are reproduced in Macfie, *An Orientalist Reader*. See also Aijaz Ahmad's '*Orientalism* and After: Ambivalence and Metropolitan Location in the Work of Edward Said', in Ahmad, *In Theory: Classes, Nations, Literatures* (London, 1992), in which Ahmad suggests, among other things, that Marx's position on rural Indians was not significantly different from his position on rural Germans.

33. Al-'Azm, 'Orientalism and Orientalism in Reverse', p. 15.

34. Said, *Orientalism*, p. 224.

35. Said, 'Orientalism, an Afterword', *Raritan*, 14 (1995), p. 40. This article was subsequently appended to later editions of *Orientalism*.

36. Said, *Orientalism*, p. 275.

37. Al-'Azm, 'Orientalism and Orientalism in Reverse', p. 15.

38. Said, *Orientalism*, p. 326.

39. Said, 'Orientalism Reconsidered', in *Reflections on Exile*, p. 203.

40. Geertz's criticisms of *Covering Islam* appeared in the *New York Review of Books*, 27 May 1982, p. 28.

41. Albert Hourani, 'The Road to Morocco', *New York Times Review*, 8 March 1979, pp. 27–9. Jacques Berque, 'Au-delà de *l'Orientalisme*: Entretien avec Jacques Berque', *Qantara*, 13 (1994), pp. 27–8; Maxime Rodinson, *Europe and the Mystique of Islam*, translated by Roger Veinus (Seattle, 1987), pp. 130–31n. See also Hourani interviewed in Nancy Elizabeth Gallagher (ed.), *Approaches to the History of the Middle East* (Reading, 1994), pp. 40–41.

42. The views of Nadim al-Bitar and other Arab reviewers are summarized in Emmanuel Sivan, 'Edward Said and his Arab Reviewers' in Sivan, *Interpretations of Islam, Past and Present* (Princeton, NJ, 1985), pp. 133–54. See also Donald P. Little, 'Three Arab Critiques of *Orientalism*', *Muslim World*, 69 (1979), pp. 110–31.

43. See note 32 above.

44. Ziauddin Sardar, *Orientalism* (Buckingham, 1999), pp. 65–76.

45. Gayatri Chakravorty Spivak, 'Psychoanalysis in Left Field and Fieldworking: Examples to Fit the Title', in Sonu Shamdasani and Michael Münchow (eds), *Speculations after Freud: Psychoanalysis, Philosophy and Culture* (London, 1994), p. 63. *Postmodern Pooh* (London, 2003) by Frederick Crews places Spivak's thinking in an appropriate context.

46. Sheldon Pollock, 'Deep Orientalism? Notes on Sanskrit and Power Beyond the Raj', in Carol A. Breckenridge and Peter van den Veer (eds), *Orientalism and the Postcolonial Predicament* (Philadelphia, 1993), p. 113.

47. The text of this debate appeared in 'Scholars, Media and the Middle East' in Edward Said, *Power, Politics and Culture*, pp. 291–312.

48. Ibid.

49. On Ernest Gellner, see Ved Mehta, *Fly and the Fly-Bottle* (London, 1963), pp. 11–21, 35–40; Michael Lessnoff, *Ernest Gellner and Modernity* (Cardiff, 2002).

50. Ernest Gellner, 'The Mightier Pen? Edward Said and the Double Standards of Inside-out Colonialism', *Times Literary Supplement*, 19 February 1993, pp. 3–4.

51. Edward Said's letter attacking Gellner's review of his book appeared in the *Times Literary Supplement* on 19 March 1993. Gellner's reply to this was published on 9 April. Said returned to the fray on 4 June. Further letters for or against Gellner appeared on the letters pages of the *Times Literary Supplement* on 10 February, 17 February and 2 April 1993.

52. Edward Said, *The Question of Palestine* (London, 1980), p. 9.

53. Ibid., p. 146.

54. Ibid., p. 218.

55. M. E. Yapp reviewed *Covering Islam* in the *Times Literary Supplement* of 9 October 1981. Said's letter attacking the review appeared on 27 November and Yapp replied on 4 December.

56. Said, *Culture and Imperialism* (London, 1993), p. 3.

57. Justus Reid Weiner, '"My Beautiful Old House" and Other Fabrications by Edward Said', *Commentary*, September 1999. The text of Weiner's article can be read online at <http//ngng.co.il/CommentarySaid.html>.

58. Edward Said, *Freud and the Non-European* (London, 2003), p. 16.

59. The British obituaries and posthumous appraisals (overwhelmingly adulatory) included anonymous in *The Times*, 26 September 2003; anonymous in the *Daily Telegraph*, 26 September; Robert Fisk in the *Independent*, 26 September; Malise Ruthven in the *Guardian*, 26 September; Gabriel Pieterberg in the *Independent*, 27 September; Christopher Hitchens in the *Observer*, 28 September; Joan Smith in the *Independent on Sunday*, 28 September.

10   Enemies of Orientalism

1. On Kurd 'Ali's quarrel with the Orientalists, see above all, Joseph Escovitz, 'Orientalists and Orientalism in the Writings of Kurd 'Ali', *International Journal of Middle Eastern Studies*, 15 (1983), pp. 95–109. On Kurd 'Ali more generally, see Albert Hourani, *Arabic Thought in the Liberal Age, 1798–1939*, revised edn (London, 1967), pp. 223–4; Hourani, 'Islam and the Philosophers of History' in Hourani, *Europe and the Middle East* (London, 1980), pp. 65–6; *Memoirs of Kurd 'Ali: A Selection*, translated by Khalil Totah (Washington, 1954).

2. J. W. Fück, 'Islam as an Historical Problem in European Historiography since 1800', in Bernard Lewis and P. M. Holt (eds), *Historians of the Middle East* (London, 1962), pp. 308–9; Hourani, *Arabic Thought*, p. 173; Hourani, 'Islam and the Philosophers of History', pp. 65–6.

3. On Jalal Al-i Ahmad, see Hamid Algar's introduction to Jalal Al-i Ahmad, *Occidentosis: A Plague from the West*, translated by R. Campbell (Berkeley, Calif., 1984). See also Michael C. Hillman's introduction to Al-i Ahmad, *Lost in the Crowd*, translated by John Green (Washington, 1985); Michael C. Hillman, *Iranian Culture: A Persianist View* (Lanham, Md., 1990), pp. 119–44; Homa Katouzian, *Sadeq Hedayat: The Life and Legend of an Iranian Writer* (London, 1991), *passim*; Roy Mottahedeh, *The Mantle of the Prophet: Religion and Politics in Iran* (London, 1986), pp. 287, seq., *passim*.

4. Ahmad, *Occidentosis*, p. 27.

5. Ibid., p. 29.

6. Ibid., p. 33.

7. Ibid., p. 75.

8. Ibid., p. 98.

9. Khomeini, *Sayings of the Ayatollah Khomeini: Political, Philosophical, Social and Religious*, translated by Harold J. Salemson (New York, 1980), p. 9.

10. On the life and works of Muhammad Asad, see Martin Kramer, 'The Road

from Mecca: Muhammad Asad (born Leopold Weiss)', in Kramer (ed.), *The Jewish Discovery of Islam* (Tel Aviv, 1999), pp. 225–47.

11. On René Guénon, *Cahiers de l'Herne*, 49 (1985), contains appraisals of the man and his work by various hands. See also Robin Waterfield, *René Guénon and the Future of the West* (n.p., 1987); Mircea Eliade, *Occultism, Witchcraft and Cultural Fashions* (Chicago, 1976), pp. 65–7; D. Gril, 'Espace sacré et spiritualité, trois approches: Massignon, Corbin, Guénon', in *D'un Orient à l'autre*, 2 vols (Paris, 1991), vol. 2, pp. 56–63.

12. René Guénon, *Orient et Occident* (Paris, 1924), pp. 147–54.

13. On Hossein Nasr, see June I. Smith, 'Sayyed Hossein Nasr: Defender of the Sacred and Islamic Traditionalism', in Y. Z. Haddad (ed.), *The Muslims of America* (New York, 1991).

14. Hossein Nasr, *Islamic Spirituality* (London, 1991), vol. 1, p. 9, n.1.

15. On Sayyid Qutb, see Emmanuel Sivan, *Radical Islam: Medieval Theology and Modern Politics* (New Haven and London, 1985); Sivan, 'Ibn Taymiyya: Father of the Islamic Revolution', *Encounter*, 60, no. 5 (May 1983), pp. 41–50; Gilles Kepel, *The Prophet and Pharaoh: Muslim Extremism in Egypt* (London, 1985).

16. Sivan, *Radical Islam*, p. 68.

17. Qutb quoted in Daniel Pipes, *The Hidden Hand: Middle East Fears of Conspiracy* (Basingstoke, 1996), p. 174.

18. Maryam Jameelah, *Islam Versus the West* (Lahore, 1962).

19. Jameelah quoted in Ziauddin Sardar, *Orientalism* (Buckingham, 1999), p. 51.

20. Hamid Algar, 'The Problems of Orientalists', *Islamic Literature*, 17 (1971), pp. 31–42.

21. A. L. Tibawi, 'English-Speaking Orientalists: a Critique of Their Approach to Islam and Arab Nationalism', *Islamic Quarterly*, 8 (1964), pp. 25–45 and 73–88; 'A Second Critique of English-Speaking Orientalists and Their Approach to Islam and the Arabs', *Islamic Quarterly*, 23 (1979), pp. 3–43, and 'On the Orientalists Again', *Muslim World*, 70 (1980), pp. 56–61. These essays have been reprinted in A. L. Macfie, *Orientalism: A Reader* (Edinburgh, 2000).

22. Abdallah Laroui, *L'Idéologie arabe contemporaine* (Paris, 1967), p. 119.

23. Abdallah Laroui, *The Crisis of the Arab Intellectual. Traditionalism or Historicism?* (Berkeley and Los Angeles, 1976). The French original was published in Paris in 1974.

24. Ibid., p. 61.

25. Anouar Abdel-Malek, 'Orientalism in Crisis', *Diogenes*, no. 44 (1963), pp. 104–12. This essay has been reprinted in Macfie, *Orientalism: A Reader*.

26. Francesco Gabrieli, 'Apology for Orientalism', *Diogenes*, no. 50 (1965), pp. 128–36.

27. Ziya-ul-Hasan Faruqi, 'Sir Hamilton Alexander Roskeen Gibb', in Asaf Hussain, Robert Olson and Jamil Qureishi (eds), *Orientalism, Islam and Islamists* (Vermont, 1984), pp. 177–91.

28. Suleyman Nyang and Abed-Rabbo, 'Bernard Lewis and Islamic Studies: An Assessment', in Hussain, et. al. (eds), *Orientalism, Islam and Islamists*, pp. 259–84.

29. Ahmad Ghorab, *Subverting Islam: The Role of Orientalist Centres* (London, 1995).

30. For Sardar's life and writings, see *Ziauddin Sardar: A Reader* (London, 2004) and Sardar, *Desperately Seeking Paradise: Journeys of a Sceptical Muslim* (London, 2004).

31. Sardar, *Orientalism*.

32. Ibid., pp. 17–26.

33. Ibid., p. 23; cf. the corresponding page in R. W. Southern, *Western Views of Islam in the Middle Ages* (Harvard, Mass., 1962), p. 89.

34. Sardar, *Orientalism*, pp. 23–4.

35. Ibid., pp. 65–76.

36. Some of Fazlur Rahman's criticisms of Orientalism can be found in Rahman, 'Islamic Studies and the Future of Islam', in Malcolm H. Kerr (ed.), *Islamic Studies: A Tradition and Its Problems* (Malibu, Calif., 1980), pp. 125–33 and in Rahman, 'Approaches to Islam in Religious Studies: Review Essay', in Richard C. Martin (ed.), *Approaches to Islam in Religious Studies* (Tucson, Arizona, 1985), pp. 189–202.

37. Muhsin Mahdi, 'Orientalism and the Study of Islamic Philosophy', *Journal of Islamic Studies*, 1 (1990), pp. 73–98.

Index